HONDA CIVIC

1973-1983 STANDARD & CVCC SHOP MANUAL

By
RON WRIGHT

ALAN AHLSTRAND
Editor

JEFF ROBINSON
Publisher

CLYMER PUBLICATIONS

World's largest publisher of books devoted exclusively to automobiles and motorcycles

12860 MUSCATINE STREET • P.O. BOX 4520 • ARLETA, CALIFORNIA 91333-4520

FIRST EDITION
Published April, 1975

SECOND EDITION
Revised to include 1975-1976 models
Published July, 1976

THIRD EDITION
Revised by Jim Combs to include 1977 models
Published April, 1978

FOURTH EDITION
Revised by Jim Combs to include 1978-1979 models
Published September, 1979

FIFTH EDITION
Revised by Jim Combs to include 1980 models
Published June, 1981

SIXTH EDITION
Revised to include 1981 models
Published March, 1983

SEVENTH EDITION
Revised by Alan Ahlstrand to include 1982-1983 models
First Printing January, 1984
Second Printing November, 1984
Third Printing May, 1985
Fourth Printing December, 1985
Fifth Printing April, 1986
Sixth Printing November, 1986

Printed in U.S.A.

ISBN: 0-89287-216-0

Production Coordinator, Linda I. Glover

Technical assistance by Joe Hennessey, Hennessey Jaguar, Costa Mesa, California, and Bill Penley. Technical drawings by Steve Amos and Richard S. Dodson.

COVER: Photographed by Michael Brown Photographic Productions, Los Angeles, California. Assisted by Dennis Gilmore. Car courtesy of American Honda Motor Corporation, Gardena, California.

CONTENTS

HONDA CIVIC

1973-1983 STANDARD & CVCC

SHOP MANUAL

QUICK REFERENCE DATA

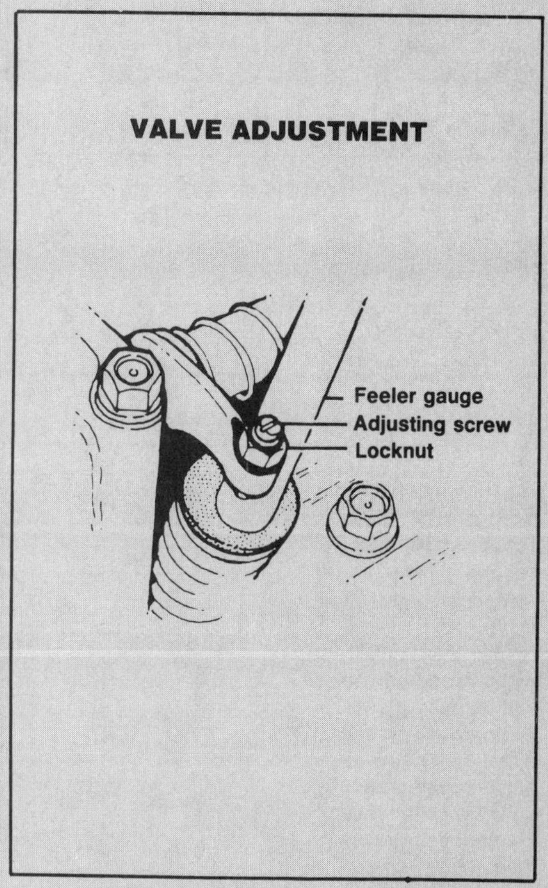

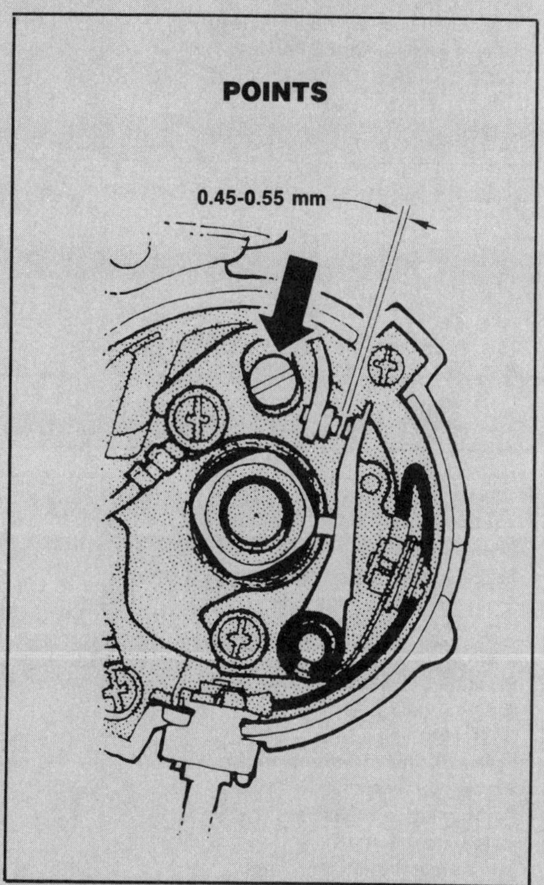

APPROXIMATE REFILL CAPACITIES

Engine oil (with filter change)	3.2 qt.
Manual transaxle oil	
1973-1979 non-CVCC	*
1975 CVCC	2.6 qt.
1976-1980 CVCC	
4-speed	2.6 qt.
5-speed	2.8 qt.
1981-on CVCC	2.6 qt.
Automatic transaxle fluid	
1973-1979 non-CVCC	2.2 qt.
1975-on CVCC	2.6 qt.
Cooling system	
1973-1978	4.2 qt.
1979	4.8 qt.
1980-1981	
1300	4.9 qt.
1500	6 qt.
1982-on	
1300	3.6 qt.
1500	4.4 qt.

* Use dipstick to determine oil level.

CYLINDER HEAD BOLT TORQUE

	mkg	ft.-lb.
Non-CVCC		
Up to engine No. EB1-1019949	4.2-4.8	30-35
From engine No. EB1-1019950	5.1-5.9	37-42
CVCC		
1975-1979	5.5-6.5	40-47
1980-on	6.0	43

RECOMMENDED LUBRICANTS

Transaxle	
Manual	SAE 10W-30, 10W-40 or 20W-40 engine oil
Automatic	DEXRON ATF
Brake fluid	DOT 3 or DOT 4
Brake caliper piston seal and dust boot	Silicone grease
Front wheel bearings	Multipurpose grease
Rear wheel bearings	Multipurpose grease
Drive shaft joints	Texaco Molytex Grease 2
Steering ball-joint	Multipurpose grease
Steering gear box	Multipurpose grease
Shift lever ball	Multipurpose grease
Brake master cylinder pushrod	Multipurpose grease
Battery terminals	Multipurpose grease
Parking brake equalizer	Multipurpose grease
Hatch side strikers	Multipurpose grease
Engine hood latch and hinge	Multipurpose grease
Pedal linkage and door hinge	Multipurpose grease

FUEL PUMP SPECIFICATIONS

	PRESSURE kg/cm^2 (psi)	DISPLACEMENT cc/(cu. in.)/min.
1975-1979 non-CVCC	0.18 (2.56)	450 (27.45) @ 300 rpm 700 (42.71) @ 700 rpm 750 (45.76) @ 3,000 rpm
1975-1979 CVCC	0.13-0.18 (1.849-2.560)	450 (27.45)
1980-on CVCC	0.15-0.20 (2.1-2.8)	500 (31)

ENGINE OIL VISCOSITY

Temperature range	Grade*
Below 20° F	SAE 5W-20 SAE 5W-30
0 to 60° F	SAE 10W-30 SAE 10W-40
20° F and above	SAE 10W-40 SAE 20W-40 SAE 20W-50

* Use only those oils certified to meet or exceed U.S. car manufacturer's requirements for API service SF. For the 1983 1300 5-speed, the factory recommends a low-friction formulation designed to improve fuel economy. These are identified by labels such as "energy conserving oil."

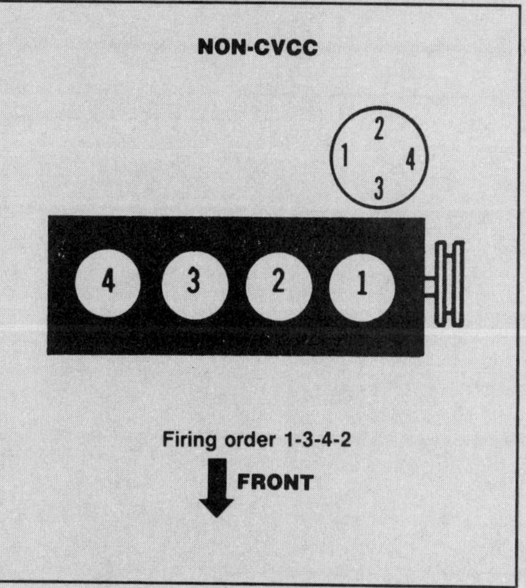

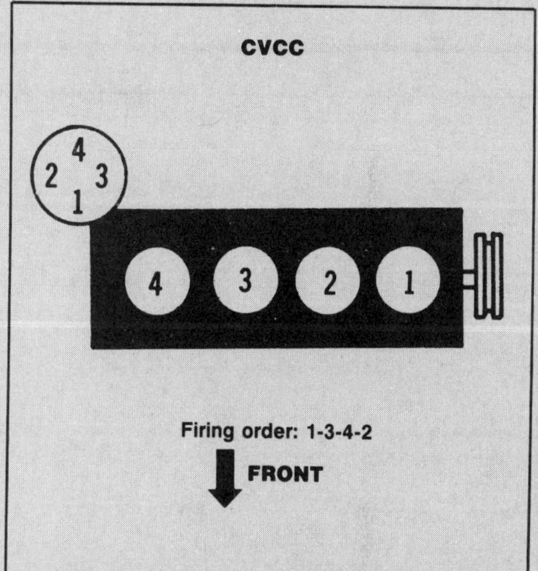

CYLINDER HEAD TORQUE SEQUENCE

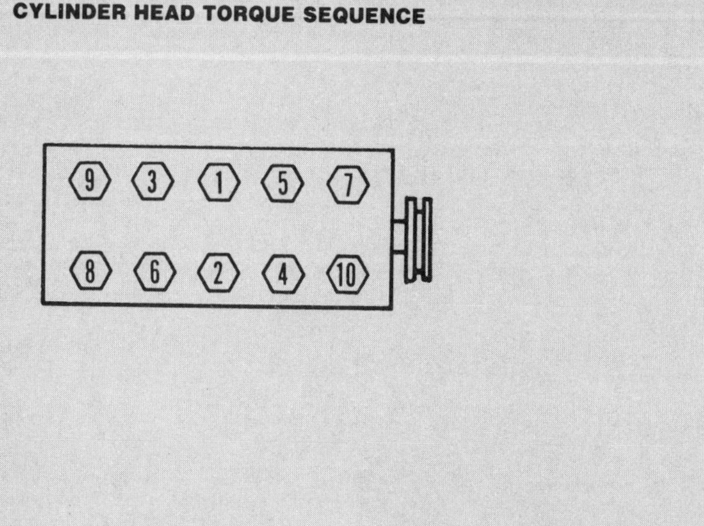

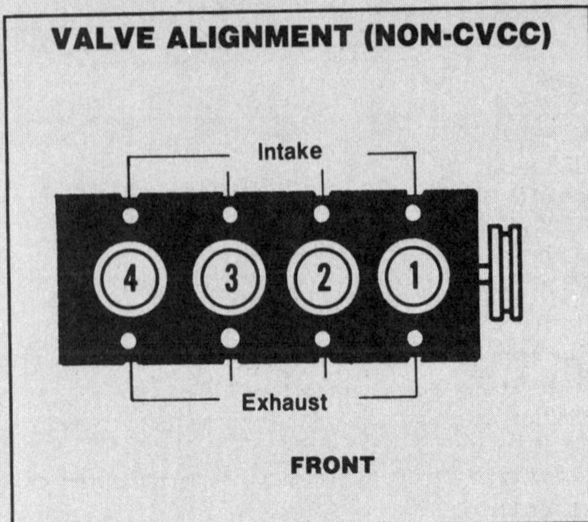
VALVE ALIGNMENT (NON-CVCC)
Intake
4
3
2
1
Exhaust
FRONT

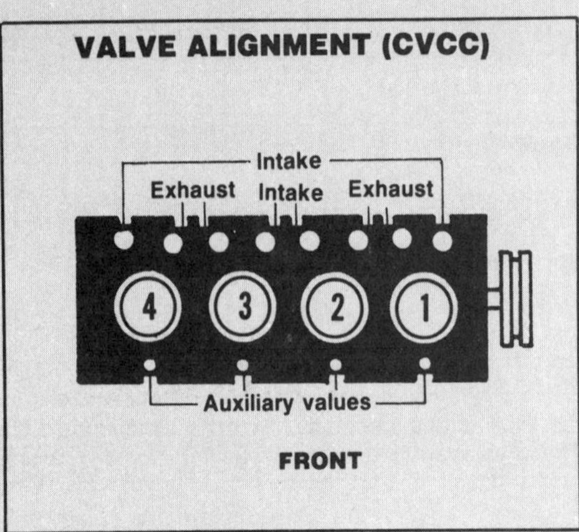
VALVE ALIGNMENT (CVCC)
Intake
Exhaust
Intake
Exhaust
4
3
2
1
Auxiliary values
FRONT

NOTES

INTRODUCTION

This detailed, comprehensive manual covers all 1973-1983 Honda Civics. The expert text gives complete information on maintenance, repair and overhaul. Hundreds of photos and drawings guide you through every step. The book includes all you need to know to keep your car running right.

Specific information for 1973-1981 models is contained in Chapters One through Twelve. The supplement at the end of the book contains information on 1982 and later models which differs from that in the main body of the book.

Throughout this book you will find references to "CVCC" and "non-CVCC" models. This relates to the type of engine used in the particular vehicle you are servicing. The "non-CVCC" is the crossflow-head design (1170 or 1237 cc displacement) available from 1973 through 1979. The "CVCC" is the stratified-charge engine available from 1975 on.

Where repairs are practical for the owner/mechanic, complete procedures are given. Equally important, difficult jobs are pointed out. Such operations are usually more economically performed by a dealer or independent garage.

A shop manual is a reference. You want to be able to find information fast. As in all Clymer books, this one is designed with this in mind. All chapters are thumb tabbed. Important items are indexed at the rear of the book. All the most frequently used specifications and capacities are summarized on the *Quick Reference* pages at the front of the book.

Keep the book handy. Carry it in your glove box. It will help you to better understand your Civic, lower repair and maintenance costs and generally improve your satisfaction with your vehicle.

CHAPTER ONE

GENERAL INFORMATION

The troubleshooting, tune-up, maintenance, and step-by-step repair procedures in this book are written for the owner and home mechanic. The text is accompanied by useful photos and diagrams to make the job as clear and correct as possible.

Troubleshooting, tune-up, maintenance, and repair are not difficult if you know what tools and equipment to use and what to do. Anyone not afraid to get their hands dirty, of average intelligence, and with some mechanical ability can perform most of the procedures in this book.

In some cases, a repair job may require tools or skills not reasonably expected of the home mechanic. These procedures are noted in each chapter and it is recommended that you take the job to your dealer, a competent mechanic, or machine shop.

MANUAL ORGANIZATION

This chapter provides general information and safety and service hints. Also included are lists of recommended shop and emergency tools as well as a brief description of troubleshooting and tune-up equipment.

Chapter Two provides methods and suggestions for quick and accurate diagnosis and repair of problems. Troubleshooting procedures discuss typical symptoms and logical methods to pinpoint the trouble.

Chapter Three explains all periodic lubrication and routine maintenance necessary to keep your vehicle running well. Chapter Three also includes recommended tune-up procedures, eliminating the need to constantly consult chapters on the various subassemblies.

Subsequent chapters cover specific systems such as the engine, transmission, and electrical systems. Each of these chapters provides disassembly, repair, and assembly procedures in a simple step-by-step format. If a repair requires special skills or tools, or is otherwise impractical for the home mechanic, it is so indicated. In these cases it is usually faster and less expensive to have the repairs made by a dealer or competent repair shop. Necessary specifications concerning a particular system are included at the end of the appropriate chapter.

When special tools are required to perform a procedure included in this manual, the tool is illustrated either in actual use or alone. It may be possible to rent or borrow these tools. The inventive mechanic may also be able to find a suitable substitute in his tool box, or to fabricate one.

The terms NOTE, CAUTION, and WARNING have specific meanings in this manual. A NOTE provides additional or explanatory information. A CAUTION is used to emphasize areas where equipment damage could result if proper precautions are not taken. A WARNING is used to stress those areas where personal injury or death could result from negligence, in addition to possible mechanical damage.

SERVICE HINTS

Observing the following practices will save time, effort, and frustration, as well as prevent possible injury.

Throughout this manual keep in mind two conventions. "Front" refers to the front of the vehicle. The front of any component, such as the transmission, is that end which faces toward the front of the vehicle. The "left" and "right" sides of the vehicle refer to the orientation of a person sitting in the vehicle facing forward. For example, the steering wheel is on the left side. These rules are simple, but even experienced mechanics occasionally become disoriented.

Most of the service procedures covered are straightforward and can be performed by anyone reasonably handy with tools. It is suggested, however, that you consider your own capabilities carefully before attempting any operation involving major disassembly of the engine.

Some operations, for example, require the use of a press. It would be wiser to have these performed by a shop equipped for such work, rather than to try to do the job yourself with makeshift equipment. Other procedures require precision measurements. Unless you have the skills and equipment required, it would be better to have a qualified repair shop make the measurements for you.

Repairs go much faster and easier if the parts that will be worked on are clean before you begin. There are special cleaners for washing the engine and related parts. Brush or spray on the cleaning solution, let it stand, then rinse it away with a garden hose. Clean all oily or greasy parts with cleaning solvent as you remove them.

WARNING

Never use gasoline as a cleaning agent. It presents an extreme fire hazard. Be sure to work in a well-ventilated area when using cleaning solvent. Keep a fire extinguisher, rated for gasoline fires, handy in any case.

Much of the labor charge for repairs made by dealers is for the removal and disassembly of other parts to reach the defective unit. It is frequently possible to perform the preliminary operations yourself and then take the defective unit in to the dealer for repair, at considerable savings.

Once you have decided to tackle the job yourself, make sure you locate the appropriate section in this manual, and read it entirely. Study the illustrations and text until you have a good idea of what is involved in completing the job satisfactorily. If special tools are required, make arrangements to get them before you start. Also, purchase any known defective parts prior to starting on the procedure. It is frustrating and time-consuming to get partially into a job and then be unable to complete it.

Simple wiring checks can be easily made at home, but knowledge of electronics is almost a necessity for performing tests with complicated electronic testing gear.

During disassembly of parts keep a few general cautions in mind. Force is rarely needed to get things apart. If parts are a tight fit, like a bearing in a case, there is usually a tool designed to separate them. Never use a screwdriver to pry apart parts with machined surfaces such as cylinder head and valve cover. You will mar the surfaces and end up with leaks.

Make diagrams wherever similar-appearing parts are found. You may think you can remember where everything came from — but mistakes are costly. There is also the possibility you may get sidetracked and not return to work for days or even weeks — in which interval, carefully laid out parts may have become disturbed.

Tag all similar internal parts for location, and mark all mating parts for position. Record number and thickness of any shims as they are removed. Small parts such as bolts can be identified by placing them in plastic sandwich bags that are sealed and labeled with masking tape.

Wiring should be tagged with masking tape and marked as each wire is removed. Again, do not rely on memory alone.

When working under the vehicle, do not trust a hydraulic or mechanical jack to hold the vehicle up by itself. Always use jackstands. See **Figure 1**.

Disconnect battery ground cable before working near electrical connections and before disconnecting wires. Never run the engine with the battery disconnected; the alternator could be seriously damaged.

Protect finished surfaces from physical damage or corrosion. Keep gasoline and brake fluid off painted surfaces.

Frozen or very tight bolts and screws can often be loosened by soaking with penetrating oil like Liquid Wrench or WD-40, then sharply striking the bolt head a few times with a hammer and punch (or screwdriver for screws). Avoid heat unless absolutely necessary, since it may melt, warp, or remove the temper from many parts.

Avoid flames or sparks when working near a charging battery or flammable liquids, such as brake fluid or gasoline.

No parts, except those assembled with a press fit, require unusual force during assembly. If a part is hard to remove or install, find out why before proceeding.

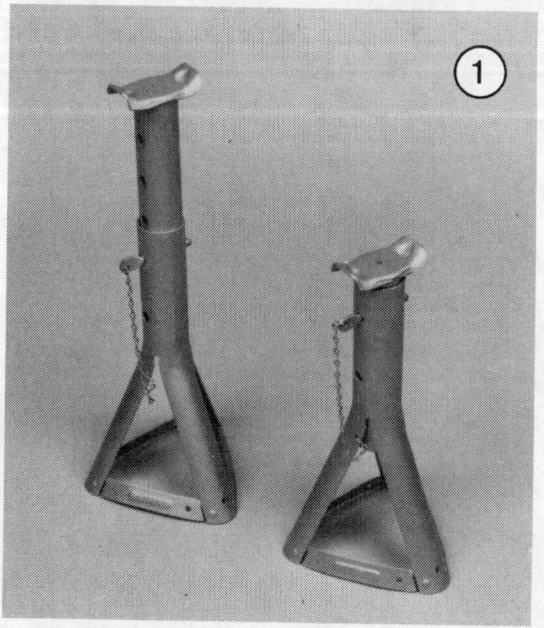

Cover all openings after removing parts to keep dirt, small tools, etc., from falling in.

When assembling two parts, start all fasteners, then tighten evenly.

The clutch plate, wiring connections, brake shoes, drums, pads, and discs should be kept clean and free of grease and oil.

When assembling parts, be sure all shims and washers are replaced exactly as they came out.

Whenever a rotating part butts against a stationary part, look for a shim or washer. Use new gaskets if there is any doubt about the condition of old ones. Generally, you should apply gasket cement to one mating surface only, so the parts may be easily disassembled in the future. A thin coat of oil on gaskets helps them seal effectively.

Heavy grease can be used to hold small parts in place if they tend to fall out during assembly. However, keep grease and oil away from electrical, clutch, and brake components.

High spots may be sanded off a piston with sandpaper, but emery cloth and oil do a much more professional job.

Carburetors are best cleaned by disassembling them and soaking the parts in a commercial carburetor cleaner. Never soak gaskets and rubber parts in these cleaners. Never use wire to clean out jets and air passages; they are easily damaged. Use compressed air to blow out the carburetor, but only if the float has been removed first.

Take your time and do the job right. Do not forget that a newly rebuilt engine must be broken in the same as a new one. Refer to your owner's manual for the proper break-in procedures.

SAFETY FIRST

Professional mechanics can work for years and never sustain a serious injury. If you observe a few rules of common sense and safety, you can enjoy many safe hours servicing your vehicle. You could hurt yourself or damage the vehicle if you ignore these rules.

1. Never use gasoline as a cleaning solvent.

2. Never smoke or use a torch in the vicinity of flammable liquids such as cleaning solvent in open containers.

3. Never smoke or use a torch in an area where batteries are being charged. Highly explosive hydrogen gas is formed during the charging process.

4. Use the proper sized wrenches to avoid damage to nuts and injury to yourself.

5. When loosening a tight or stuck nut, be guided by what would happen if the wrench should slip. Protect yourself accordingly.

6. Keep your work area clean and uncluttered.

7. Wear safety goggles during all operations involving drilling, grinding, or use of a cold chisel.

8. Never use worn tools.

9. Keep a fire extinguisher handy and be sure it is rated for gasoline (Class B) and electrical (Class C) fires.

EXPENDABLE SUPPLIES

Certain expendable supplies are necessary. These include grease, oil, gasket cement, wiping rags, cleaning solvent, and distilled water. Also, special locking compounds, silicone lubricants, and engine cleaners may be useful. Cleaning solvent is available at most service stations and distilled water for the battery is available at most supermarkets.

SHOP TOOLS

For proper servicing, you will need an assortment of ordinary hand tools (**Figure 2**).

As a minimum, these include:

a. Combination wrenches
b. Sockets
c. Plastic mallet
d. Small hammer
e. Snap ring pliers
f. Gas pliers
g. Phillips screwdrivers
h. Slot (common) screwdrivers
i. Feeler gauges
j. Spark plug gauge
k. Spark plug wrench

Special tools necessary are shown in the chapters covering the particular repair in which they are used.

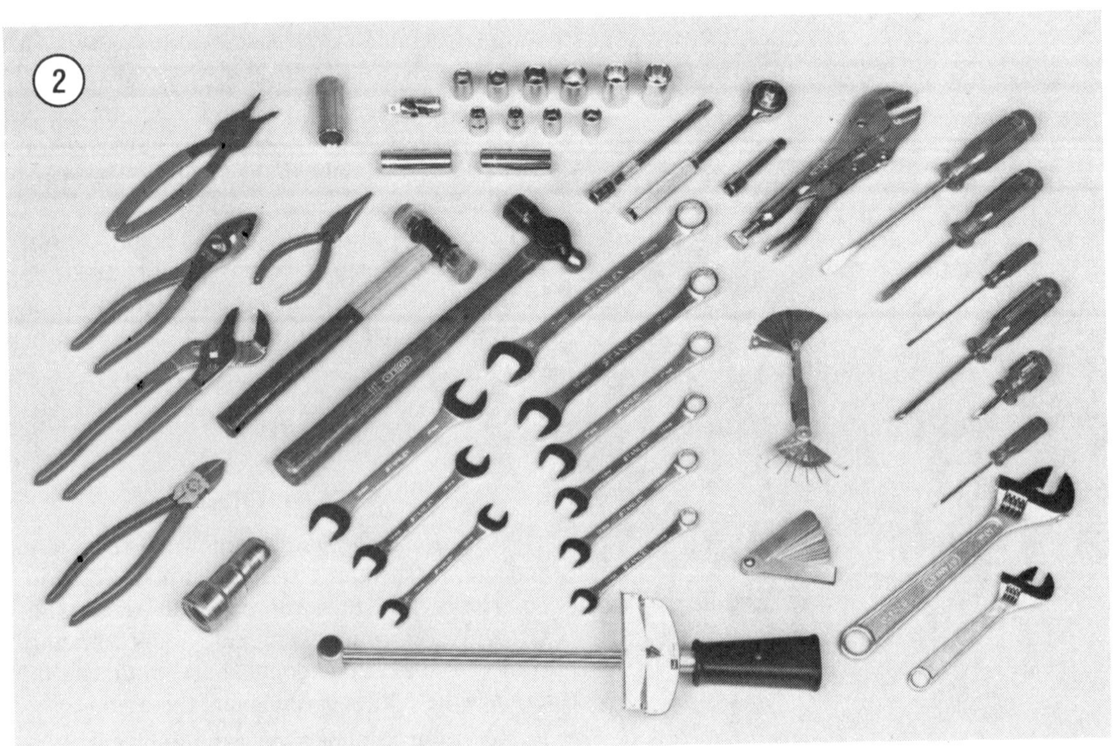

Engine tune-up and troubleshooting procedures require other special tools and equipment. These are described in detail in the following sections.

EMERGENCY TOOL KIT

A small emergency tool kit kept in the trunk is handy for road emergencies which otherwise could leave you stranded. The tools listed below and shown in **Figure 3** will let you handle most roadside repairs.

a. Combination wrenches
b. Crescent (adjustable) wrench
c. Screwdrivers — common and Phillips
d. Pliers — conventional (gas) and needle nose
e. Vise Grips
f. Hammer — plastic and metal
g. Small container of waterless hand cleaner
h. Rags for clean up
i. Silver waterproof sealing tape (duct tape)
j. Flashlight
k. Emergency road flares — at least four
l. Spare drive belts (water pump, alternator, etc.)

TROUBLESHOOTING AND TUNE-UP EQUIPMENT

Voltmeter, Ohmmeter, and Ammeter

For testing the ignition or electrical system, a good voltmeter is required. For automotive use, an instrument covering 0-20 volts is satisfac-

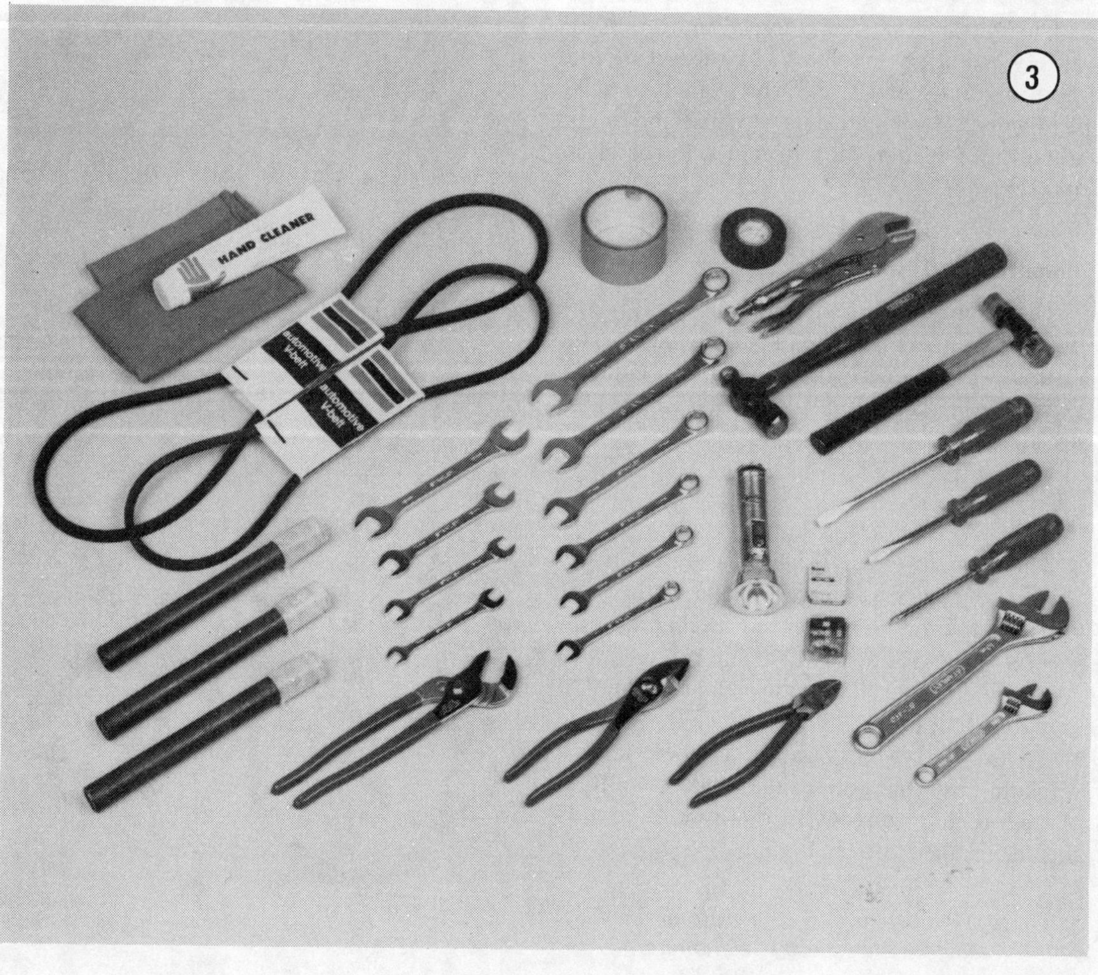

tory. One which also has a 0-2 volt scale is necessary for testing relays, points, or individual contacts where voltage drops are much smaller. Accuracy should be ± ½ volt.

An ohmmeter measures electrical resistance. This instrument is useful for checking continuity (open and short circuits), and testing fuses and lights.

The ammeter measures electrical current. Ammeters for automotive use should cover 0-50 amperes and 0-250 amperes. These are useful for checking battery charging and starting current.

Several inexpensive VOM's (volt-ohm-milliammeter) combine all three instruments into one which fits easily in any tool box. See **Figure 4**. However, the ammeter ranges are usually too small for automotive work.

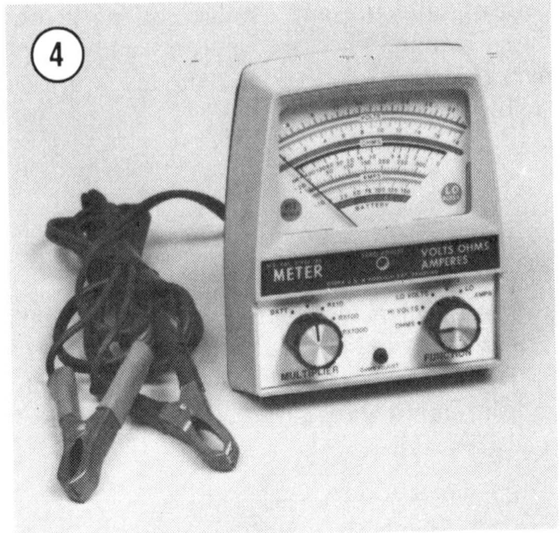

Hydrometer

The hydrometer gives a useful indication of battery condition and charge by measuring the specific gravity of the electrolyte in each cell. See **Figure 5**. Complete details on use and interpretation of readings are provided in the electrical chapter.

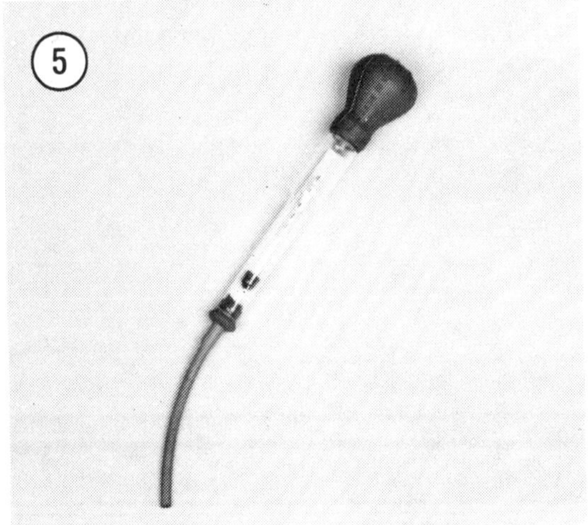

Compression Tester

The compression tester measures the compression pressure built up in each cylinder. The results, when properly interpreted, can indicate general cylinder and valve condition. See **Figure 6**.

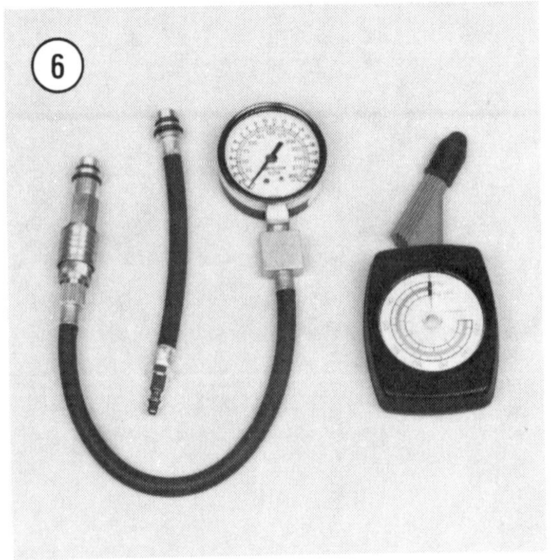

Vacuum Gauge

The vacuum gauge (**Figure 7**) is one of the easiest instruments to use, but one of the most difficult for the inexperienced mechanic to interpret. The results, when interpreted with other findings, can provide valuable clues to possible trouble.

To use the vacuum gauge, connect it to a vacuum hose that goes to the intake manifold. Attach it either directly to the hose or to a T-fitting installed into the hose.

NOTE: *Subtract one inch from the reading for every 1,000 ft. elevation.*

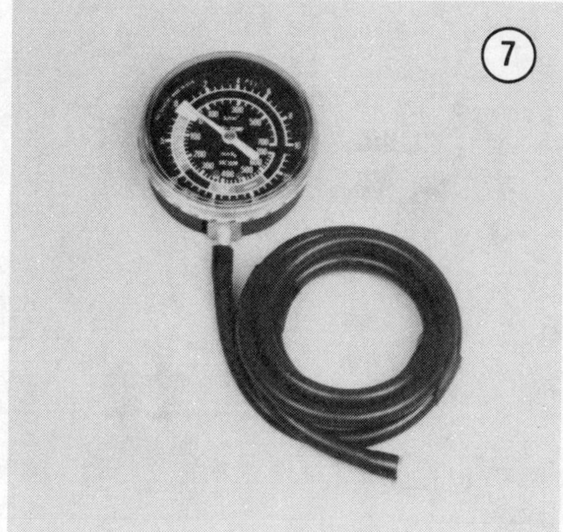

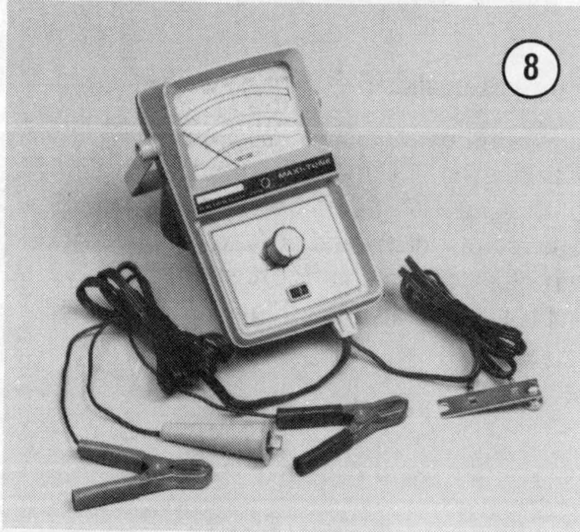

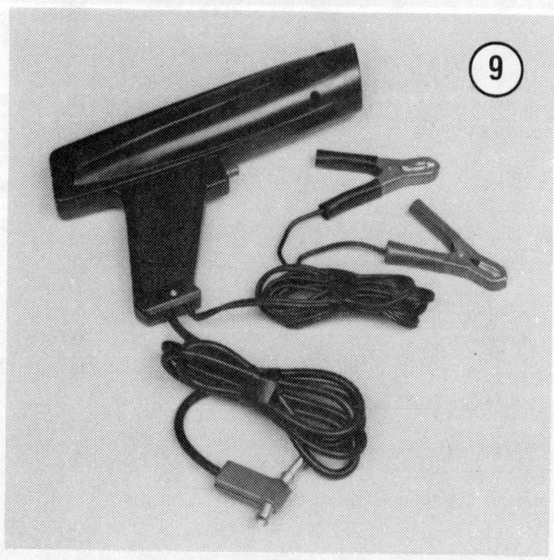

Fuel Pressure Gauge

This instrument is invaluable for evaluating fuel pump performance. Fuel system troubleshooting procedures in this manual use a fuel pressure gauge. Usually a vacuum gauge and fuel pressure gauge are combined.

Dwell Meter (Contact Breaker Point Ignition Only)

A dwell meter measures the distance in degrees of cam rotation that the breaker points remain closed while the engine is running. Since this angle is determined by breaker point gap, dwell angle is an accurate indication of breaker point gap.

Many tachometers intended for tuning and testing incorporate a dwell meter as well. See **Figure 8**. Follow the manufacturer's instructions to measure dwell.

Tachometer

A tachometer is necessary for tuning. See **Figure 8**. Ignition timing and carburetor adjustments must be performed at the specified idle speed. The best instrument for this purpose is one with a low range of 0-1,000 or 0-2,000 rpm for setting idle, and a high range of 0-4,000 or more for setting ignition timing at 3,000 rpm. Extended range (0-6,000 or 0-8,000 rpm) instruments lack accuracy at lower speeds. The instrument should be capable of detecting changes of 25 rpm on the low range.

Strobe Timing Light

This instrument is necessary for tuning, as it permits very accurate ignition timing. The light flashes at precisely the same instant that No. 1 cylinder fires, at which time the timing marks on the engine should align. Refer to Chapter Three for exact location of the timing marks for your engine.

Suitable lights range from inexpensive neon bulb types ($2-3) to powerful xenon strobe lights ($20-40). See **Figure 9**. Neon timing lights are difficult to see and must be used in dimly lit areas. Xenon strobe timing lights can be used outside in bright sunlight. Both types work on this vehicle; use according to the manufacturer's instructions.

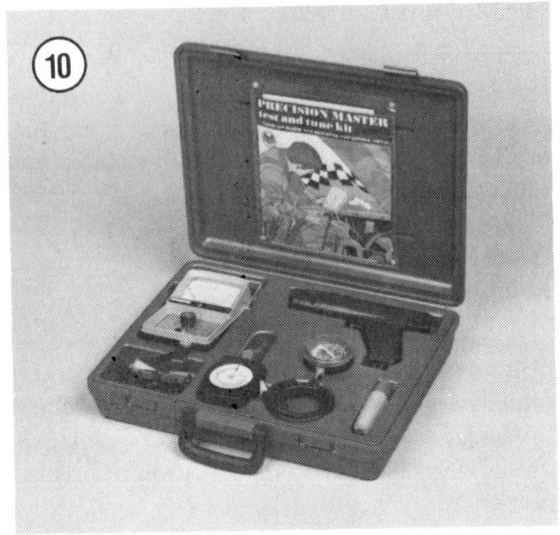

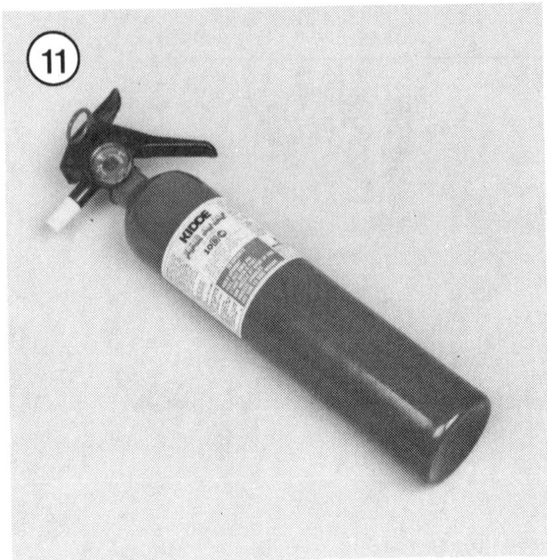

Tune-up Kits

Many manufacturer's offer kits that combine several useful instruments. Some come in a convenient carry case and are usally less expensive than purchasing one instrument at a time. **Figure 10** shows one of the kits that is available. The prices vary with the number of instruments included in the kit.

Fire Extinguisher

A fire extinguisher is a necessity when working on a vehicle. It should be rated for both *Class B* (flammable liquids—gasoline, oil, paint, etc.) and *Class C* (electrical—wiring, etc.) type fires. It should always be kept within reach. See **Figure 11**.

CHAPTER TWO

2

TROUBLESHOOTING

Troubleshooting can be a relatively simple matter if it is done logically. The first step in any troubleshooting procedure must be defining the symptoms as closely as possible. Subsequent steps involve testing and analyzing areas which could cause the symptoms. A haphazard approach may eventually find the trouble, but in terms of wasted time and unnecessary parts replacement, it can be very costly.

The troubleshooting procedures in this chapter analyze typical symptoms and show logical methods of isolation. These are not the only methods. There may be several approaches to a problem, but all methods must have one thing in common — a logical, systematic approach.

STARTING SYSTEM

The starting system consists of the starter motor and the starter solenoid. The ignition key controls the starter solenoid, which mechanically engages the starter with the engine flywheel, and supplies electrical current to turn the starter motor.

Starting system troubles are relatively easy to find. In most cases, the trouble is a loose or dirty electrical connection. **Figures 1 and 2** provide routines for finding the trouble.

CHARGING SYSTEM

The charging system consists of the alternator (or generator on older vehicles), voltage regulator, and battery. A drive belt driven by the engine crankshaft turns the alternator which produces electrical energy to charge the battery. As engine speed varies, the voltage from the alternator varies. A voltage regulator controls the charging current to the battery and maintains the voltage to the vehicle's electrical system at safe levels. A warning light or gauge on the instrument panel signals the driver when charging is not taking place. Refer to **Figure 3** for a typical charging system.

Complete troubleshooting of the charging system requires test equipment and skills which the average home mechanic does not possess. However, there are a few tests which can be done to pinpoint most troubles.

Charging system trouble may stem from a defective alternator (or generator), voltage regulator, battery, or drive belt. It may also be caused by something as simple as incorrect drive belt tension. The following are symptoms of typical problems you may encounter.

1. ***Battery dies frequently, even though the warning lamp indicates no discharge*** — This can be caused by a drive belt that is slightly too

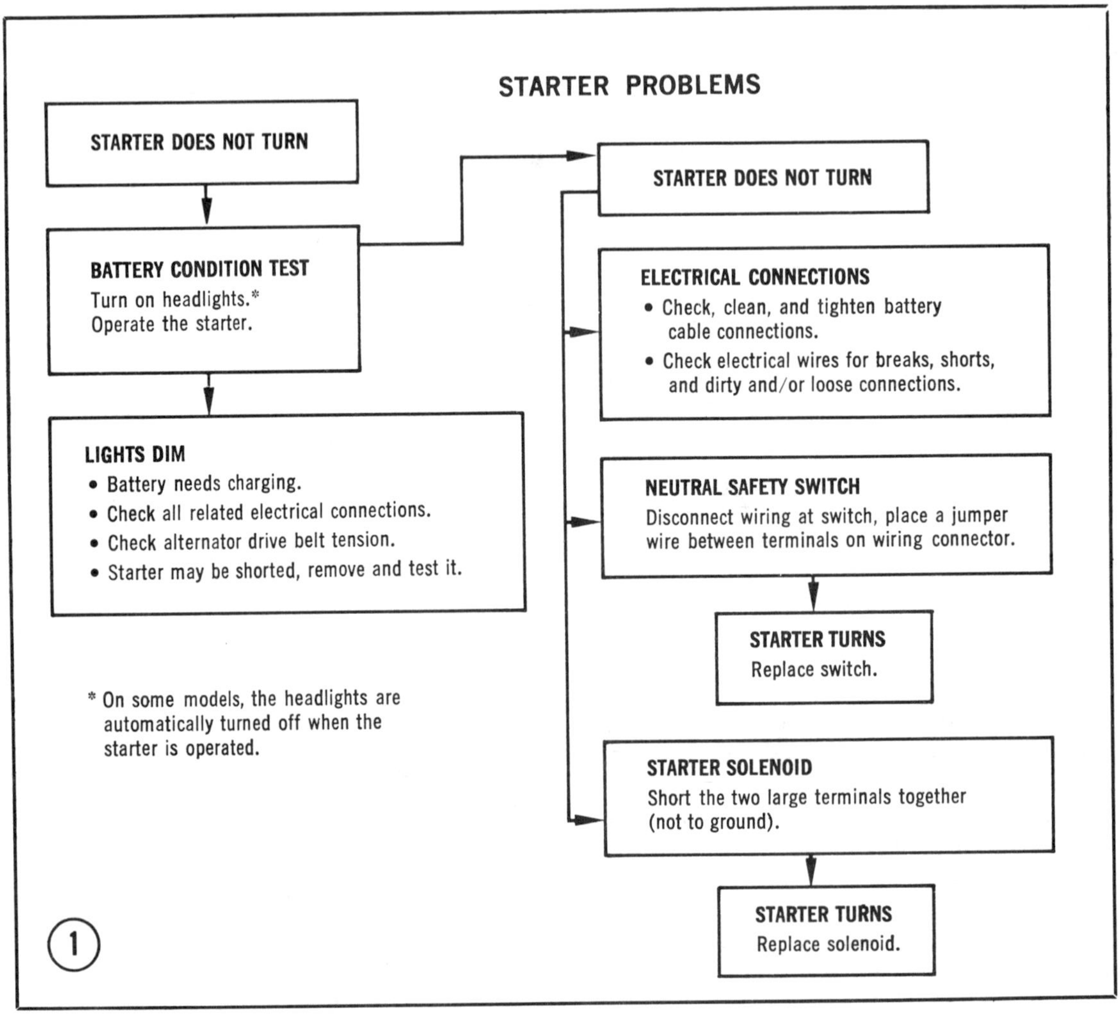

STARTER PROBLEMS
STARTER DOES NOT TURN
BATTERY CONDITION TEST
Turn on headlights.*
Operate the starter.
LIGHTS DIM
• Battery needs charging.
• Check all related electrical connections.
• Check alternator drive belt tension.
• Starter may be shorted, remove and test it.
* On some models, the headlights are automatically turned off when the starter is operated.
STARTER DOES NOT TURN
ELECTRICAL CONNECTIONS
• Check, clean, and tighten battery cable connections.
• Check electrical wires for breaks, shorts, and dirty and/or loose connections.
NEUTRAL SAFETY SWITCH
Disconnect wiring at switch, place a jumper wire between terminals on wiring connector.
STARTER TURNS
Replace switch.
STARTER SOLENOID
Short the two large terminals together (not to ground).
STARTER TURNS
Replace solenoid.
1

STARTER PROBLEMS
STARTER TURNS
DOES NOT ENGAGE WITH ENGINE
Check pinion or solenoid shifting fork and teeth on flywheel gear.
ENGAGES WITH ENGINE — WILL NOT RELEASE
Check for sticking solenoid or jammed pinion onto flywheel.
LOUD GRINDING NOISE
Check flywheel to pinion alignment. The overrunning clutch may be broken.
Remove the starter and examine the gear teeth; replace if necessary.
2

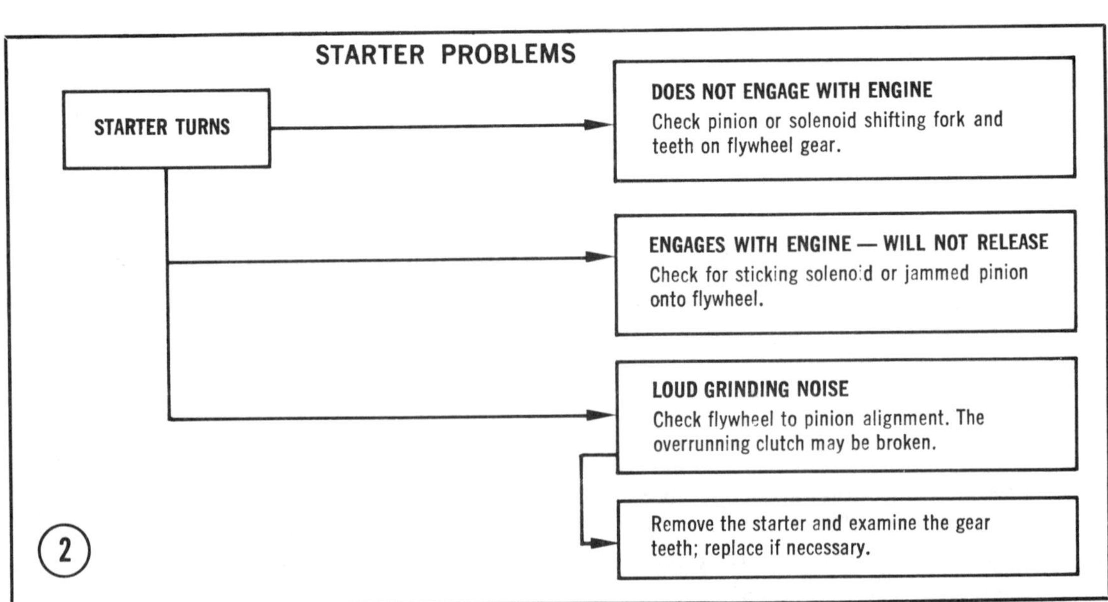

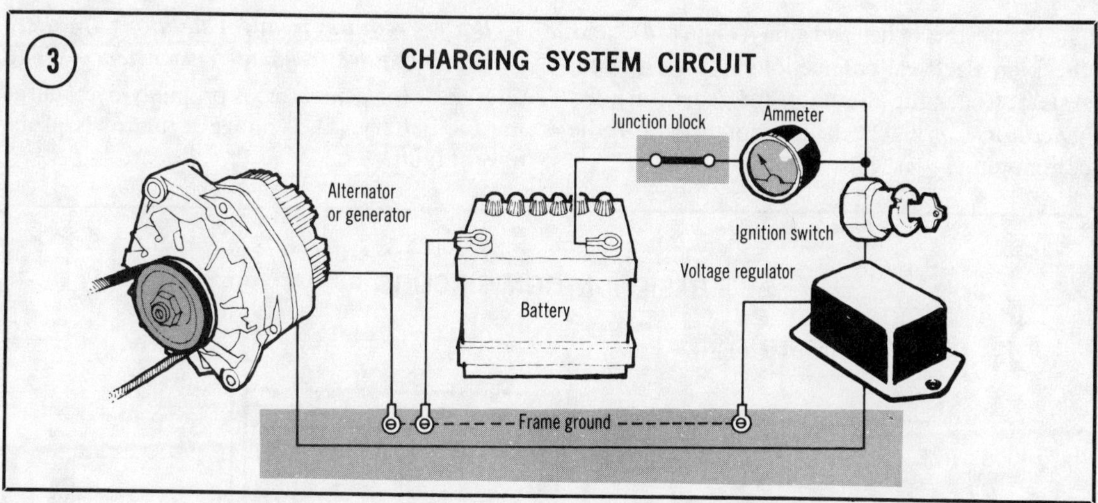

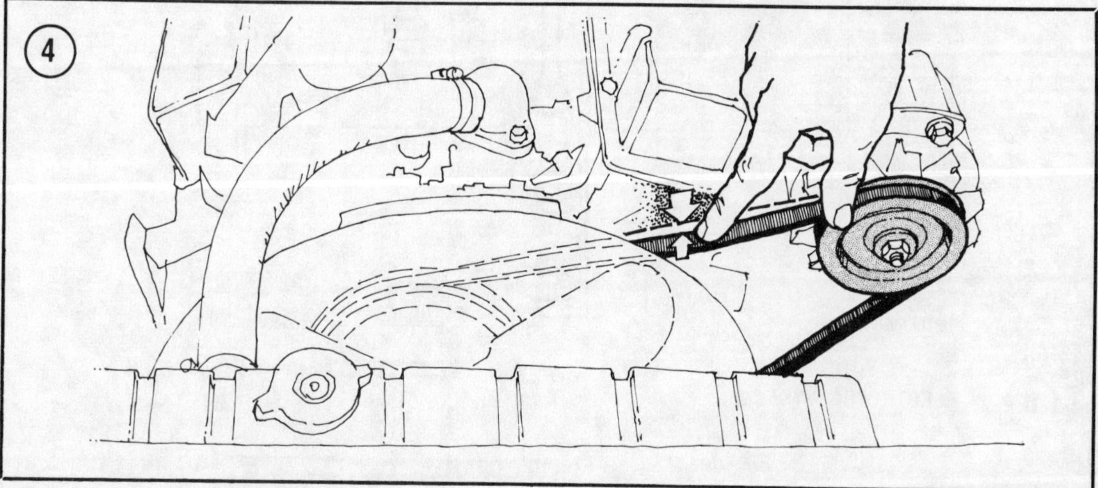

loose. Grasp the alternator (or generator) pulley and try to turn it. If the pulley can be turned without moving the belt, the drive belt is too loose. As a rule, keep the belt tight enough that it can be deflected about ½ in. under moderate thumb pressure between the pulleys (**Figure 4**). The battery may also be at fault; test the battery condition.

2. ***Charging system warning lamp does not come on when ignition switch is turned on*** — This may indicate a defective ignition switch, battery, voltage regulator, or lamp. First try to start the vehicle. If it doesn't start, check the ignition switch and battery. If the car starts, remove the warning lamp; test it for continuity with an ohmmeter or substitute a new lamp. If the lamp is good, locate the voltage regulator and make sure it is properly grounded (try tightening the mounting screws). Also the alternator (or generator) brushes may not be making contact. Test the alternator (or generator) and voltage regulator.

3. ***Alternator (or generator) warning lamp comes on and stays on*** — This usually indicates that no charging is taking place. First check drive belt tension (**Figure 4**). Then check battery condition, and check all wiring connections in the charging system. If this does not locate the trouble, check the alternator (or generator) and voltage regulator.

4. ***Charging system warning lamp flashes on and off intermittently*** — This usually indicates the charging system is working intermittently.

Check the drive belt tension (**Figure 4**), and check all electrical connections in the charging system. Check the alternator (or generator). *On generators only*, check the condition of the commutator.

5. ***Battery requires frequent additions of water, or lamps require frequent replacement*** — The alternator (or generator) is probably overcharging the battery. The voltage regulator is probably at fault.

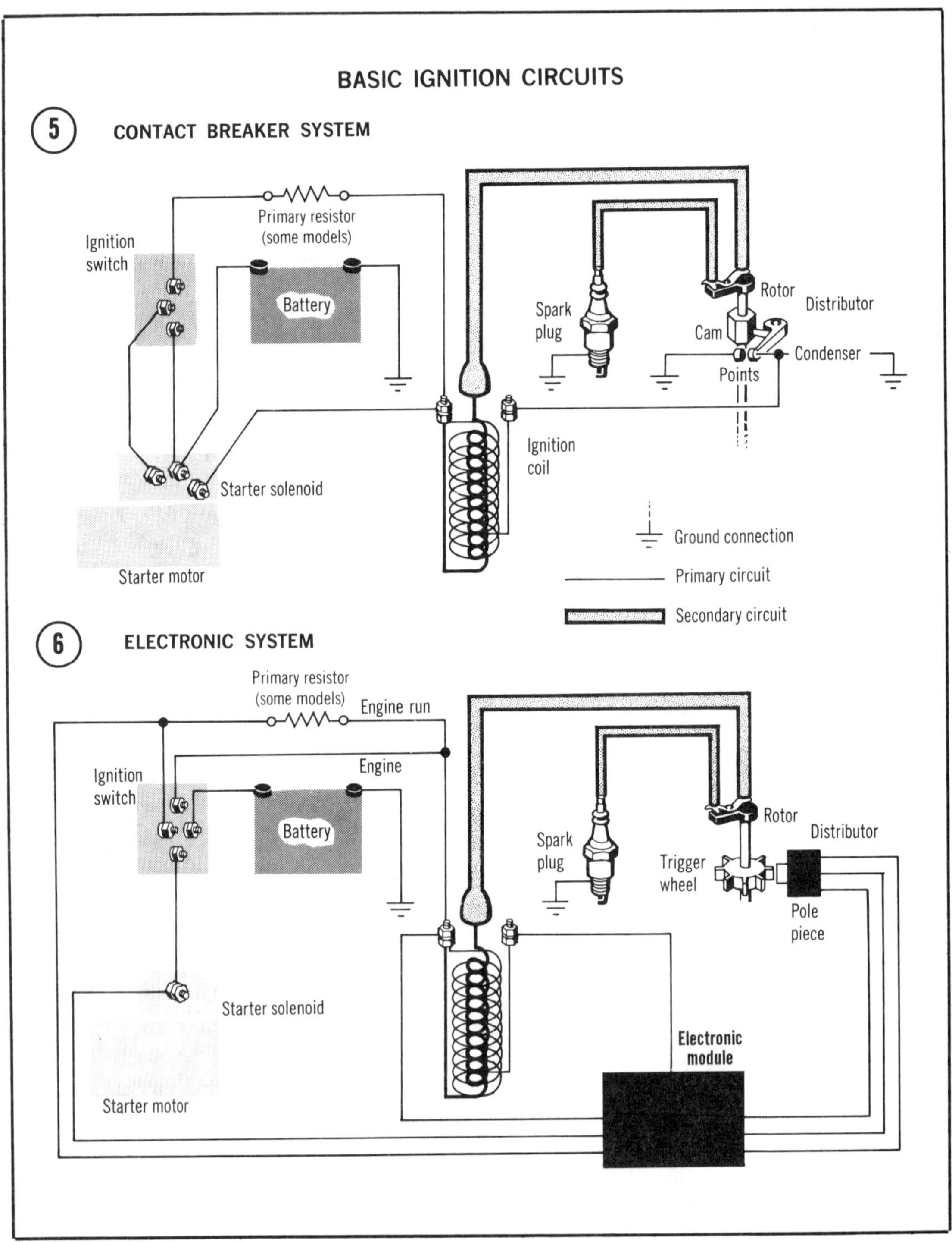

6. ***Excessive noise from the alternator (or generator)*** — Check for loose mounting brackets and bolts. The problem may also be worn bearings or the need of lubrication in some cases. If an alternator whines, a shorted diode may be indicated.

IGNITION SYSTEM

The ignition system may be either a conventional contact breaker type or an electronic ignition. See electrical chapter to determine which type you have. **Figures 5 and 6** show simplified diagrams of each type.

Most problems involving failure to start, poor performance, or rough running stem from trouble in the ignition system, particularly in contact breaker systems. Many novice troubleshooters get into trouble when they assume that these symptoms point to the fuel system instead of the ignition system.

Ignition system troubles may be roughly divided between those affecting only one cylinder and those affecting all cylinders. If the trouble affects only one cylinder, it can only be in the spark plug, spark plug wire, or portion of the distributor associated with that cylinder. If the trouble affects all cylinders (weak spark or no spark), then the trouble is in the ignition coil, rotor, distributor, or associated wiring.

The troubleshooting procedures outlined in **Figure 7** (breaker point ignition) or **Figure 8**

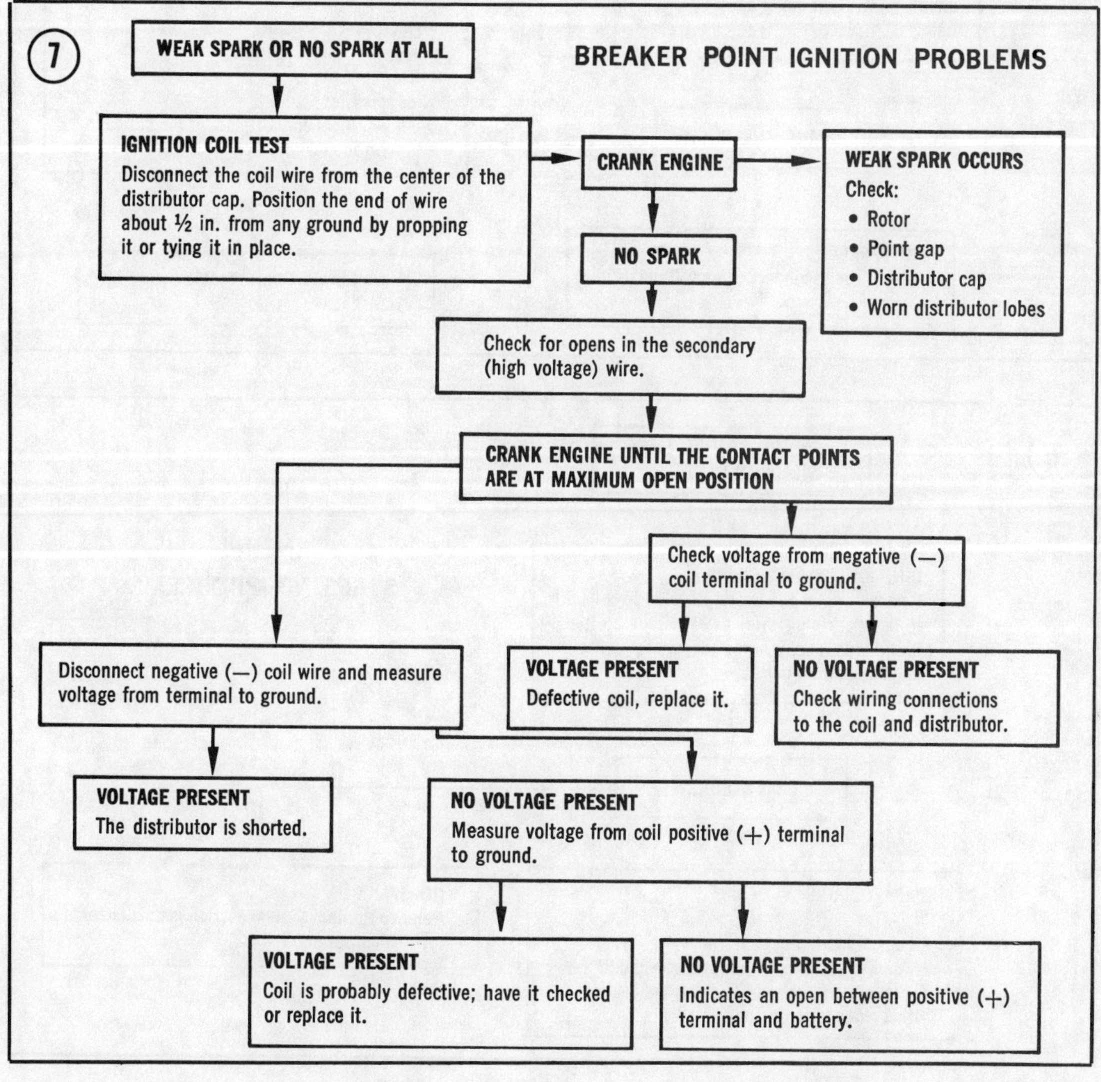

(electronic ignition) will help you isolate ignition problems fast. Of course, they assume that the battery is in good enough condition to crank the engine over at its normal rate.

ENGINE PERFORMANCE

A number of factors can make the engine difficult or impossible to start, or cause rough running, poor performance and so on. The majority of novice troubleshooters immediately suspect the carburetor or fuel injection system. In the majority of cases, though, the trouble exists in the ignition system.

The troubleshooting procedures outlined in **Figures 9 through 14** will help you solve the majority of engine starting troubles in a systematic manner.

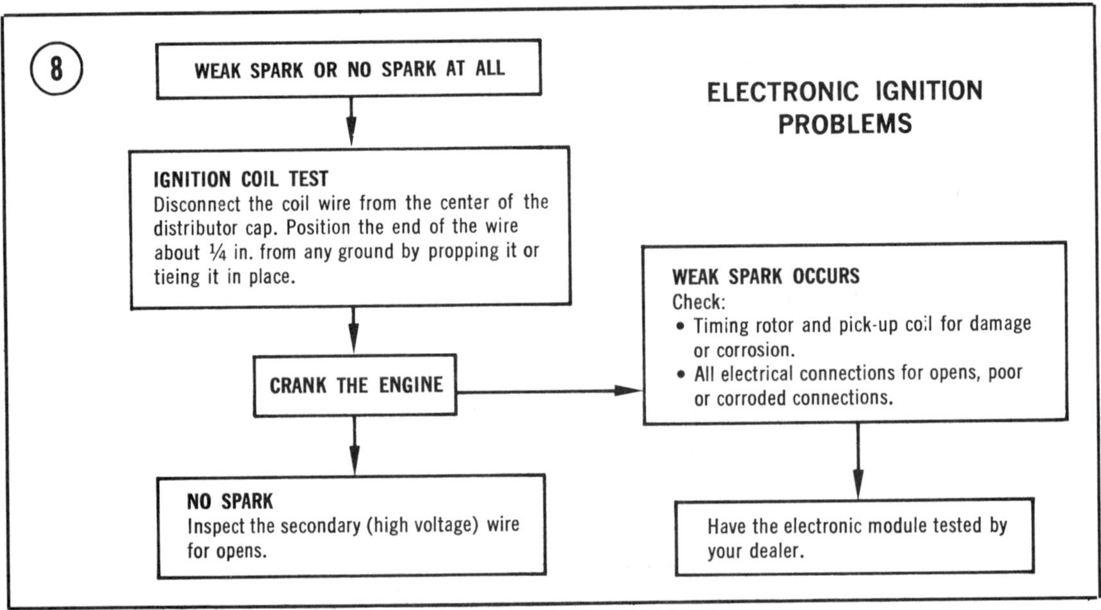

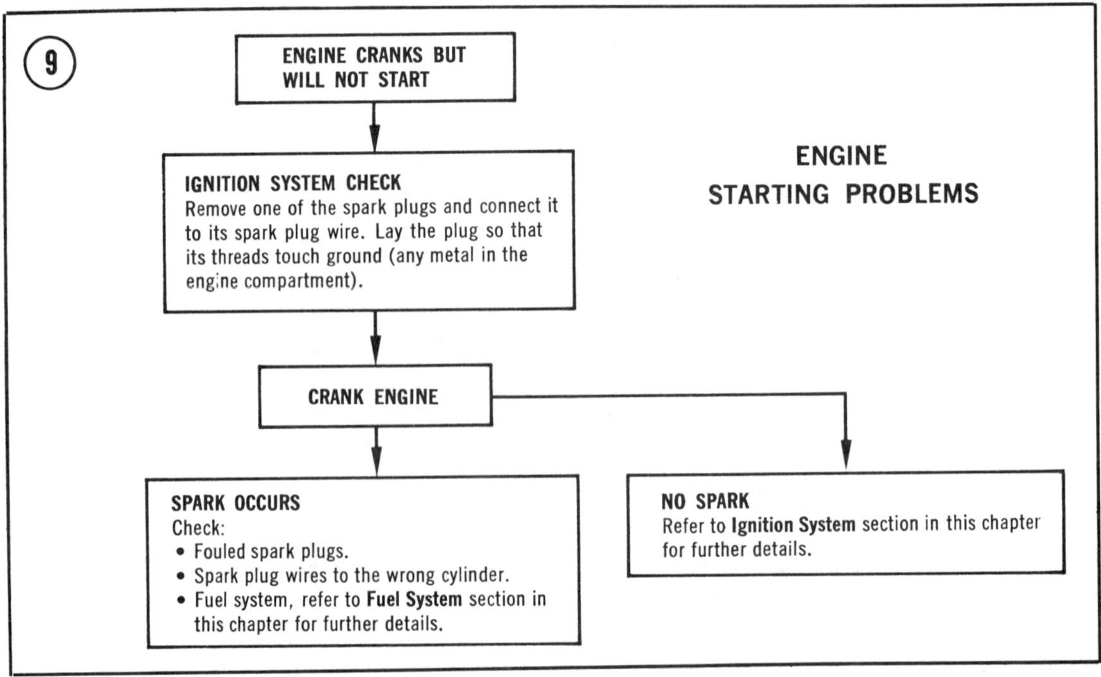

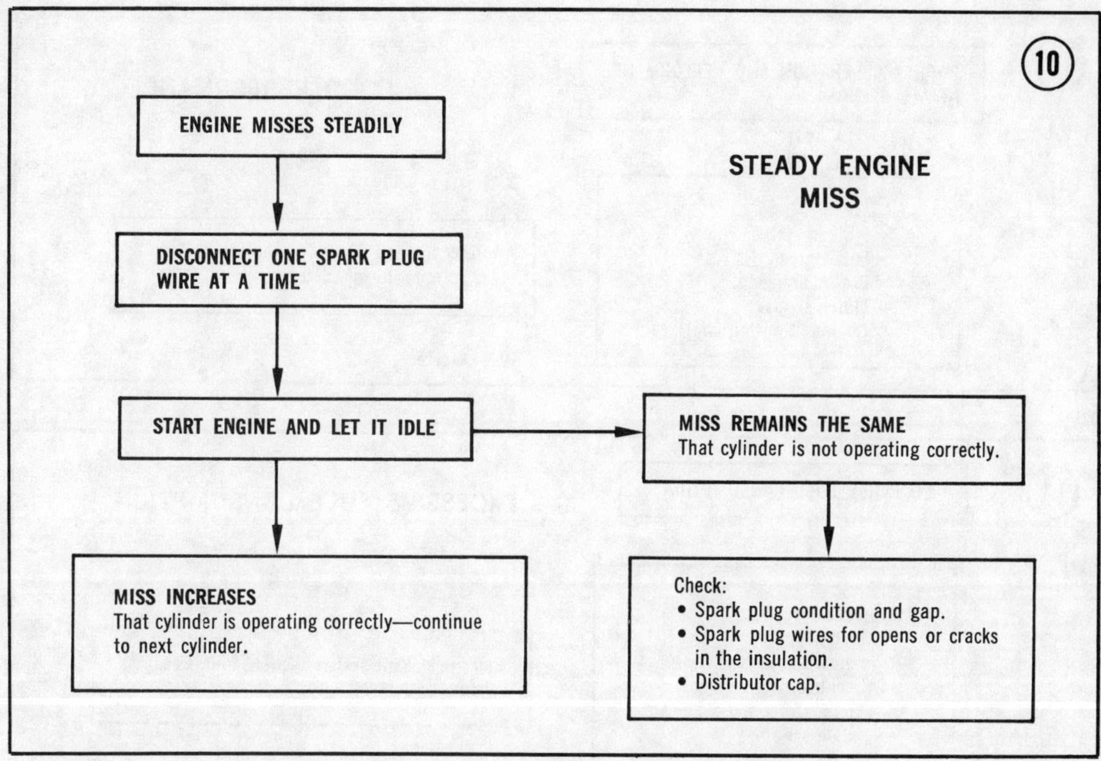

STEADY ENGINE MISS

(10)

ENGINE MISSES STEADILY

↓

DISCONNECT ONE SPARK PLUG WIRE AT A TIME

↓

START ENGINE AND LET IT IDLE

↓

MISS INCREASES
That cylinder is operating correctly—continue to next cylinder.

→

MISS REMAINS THE SAME
That cylinder is not operating correctly.

↓

Check:
- Spark plug condition and gap.
- Spark plug wires for opens or cracks in the insulation.
- Distributor cap.

ENGINE MISS AT IDLE

(11)

ENGINE MISSES — IDLE ONLY

↓

Check ignition system, refer to **Ignition System** section in this chapter for further details.

↓

Check:
- Carburetor idle adjustment.
- Vacuum lines and intake manifold for leaks. Run a compression test; one cylinder may have a defective valve or broken ring(s).

ENGINE MISS AT HIGH SPEED

(12)

ENGINE MISSES — HIGH SPEED ONLY

↓

Check the ignition system; refer to **Ignition System** section in this chapter for further details.

↓

Check:
- All vacuum lines and intake manifold for leaks.
- Fuel system, refer to **Fuel System** section in this chapter for further details.

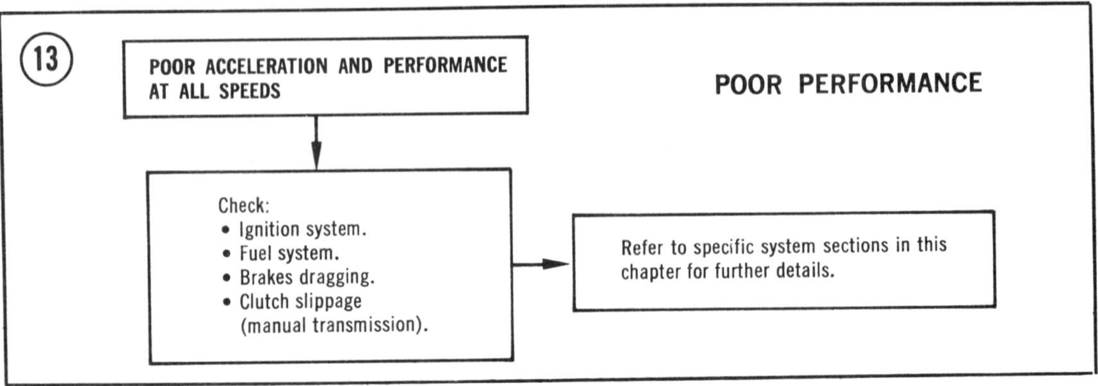

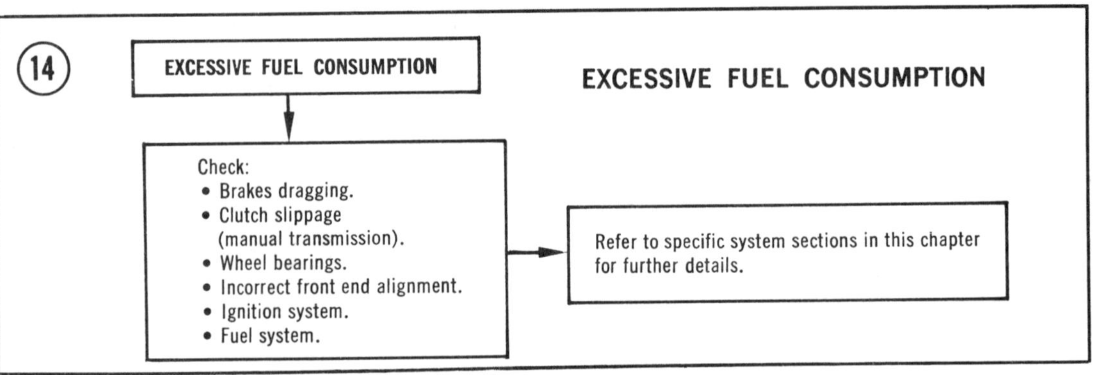

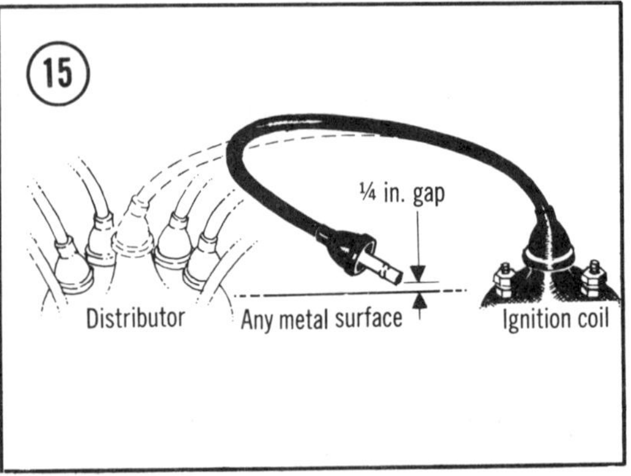

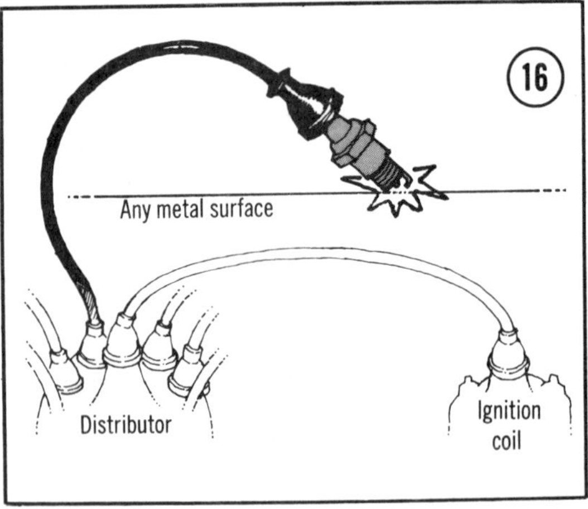

Some tests of the ignition system require running the engine with a spark plug or ignition coil wire disconnected. The safest way to do this is to disconnect the wire with the engine stopped, then prop the end of the wire next to a metal surface as shown in **Figures 15 and 16**.

WARNING

Never disconnect a spark plug or ignition coil wire while the engine is running. The high voltage in an ignition system, particularly the newer high-energy electronic ignition systems could cause serious injury or even death.

Spark plug condition is an important indication of engine performance. Spark plugs in a properly operating engine will have slightly pitted electrodes, and a light tan insulator tip. **Figure 17** shows a normal plug, and a number of others which indicate trouble in their respective cylinders.

• Appearance—Firing tip has deposits of light gray to light tan.
• Can be cleaned, regapped and reused.

• Appearance—Dull, dry black with fluffy carbon deposits on the insulator tip, electrode and exposed shell.
• Caused by—Fuel/air mixture too rich, plug heat range too cold, weak ignition system, dirty air cleaner, faulty automatic choke or excessive idling.
• Can be cleaned, regapped and reused.

• Appearance—Wet black deposits on insulator and exposed shell.
• Caused by—Excessive oil entering the combustion chamber through worn rings, pistons, valve guides or bearings.
• Replace with new plugs (use a hotter plug if engine is not repaired).

• Appearance — Yellow insulator deposits (may sometimes be dark gray, black or tan in color) on the insulator tip.
• Caused by—Highly leaded gasoline.
• Replace with new plugs.

• Appearance—Yellow glazed deposits indicating melted lead deposits due to hard acceleration.
• Caused by—Highly leaded gasoline.
• Replace with new plugs.

• Appearance—Glazed yellow deposits with a slight brownish tint on the insulator tip and ground electrode.
• Replace with new plugs.

• Appearance — Brown colored hardened ash deposits on the insulator tip and ground electrode.
• Caused by—Fuel and/or oil additives.
• Replace with new plugs.

• Appearance — Severely worn or eroded electrodes.
• Caused by—Normal wear or unusual oil and/or fuel additives.
• Replace with new plugs.

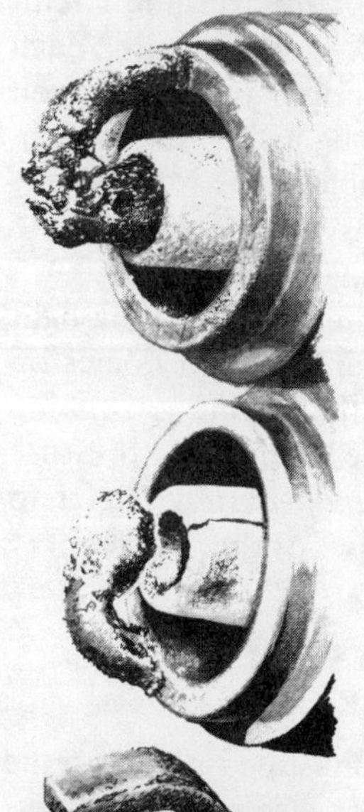

• Appearance — Melted ground electrode.
• Caused by—Overadvanced ignition timing, inoperative ignition advance mechanism, too low of a fuel octane rating, lean fuel/air mixture or carbon deposits in combustion chamber.

• Appearance—Melted center electrode.
• Caused by—Abnormal combustion due to overadvanced ignition timing or incorrect advance, too low of a fuel octane rating, lean fuel/air mixture, or carbon deposits in combustion chamber.
• Correct engine problem and replace with new plugs.

• Appearance—Melted center electrode and white blistered insulator tip.
• Caused by—Incorrect plug heat range selection.
• Replace with new plugs.

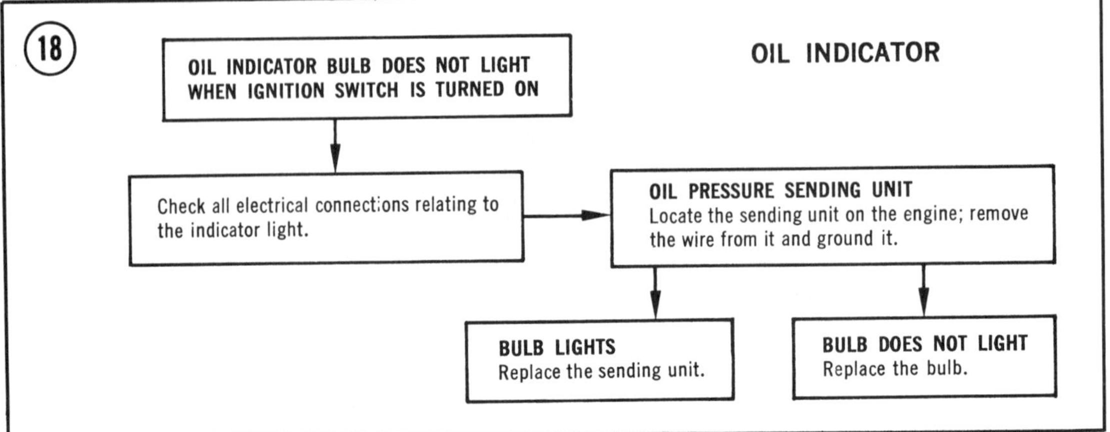

ENGINE OIL PRESSURE LIGHT

Proper oil pressure to the engine is vital. If oil pressure is insufficient, the engine can destroy itself in a comparatively short time.

The oil pressure warning circuit monitors oil pressure constantly. If pressure drops below a predetermined level, the light comes on.

Obviously, it is vital for the warning circuit to be working to signal low oil pressure. Each time you turn on the ignition, but before you start the car, the warning light should come on. If it doesn't, there is trouble in the warning circuit, not the oil pressure system. See **Figure 18** to troubleshoot the warning circuit.

Once the engine is running, the warning light should stay off. If the warning light comes on or acts erratically while the engine is running there is trouble with the engine oil pressure system. *Stop the engine immediately*. Refer to **Figure 19** for possible causes of the problem.

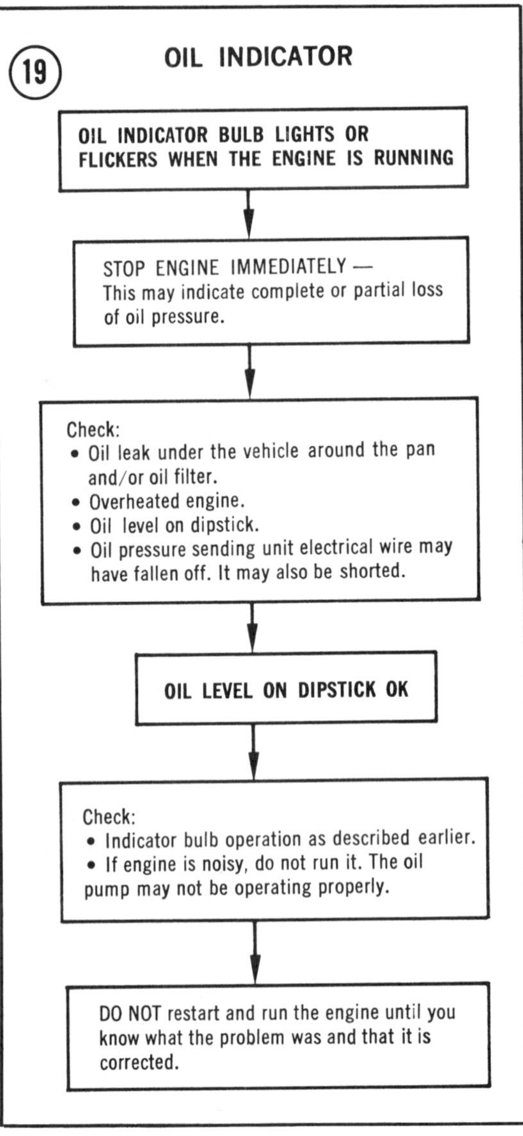

FUEL SYSTEM (CARBURETTED)

Fuel system problems must be isolated to the fuel pump (mechanical or electric), fuel lines, fuel filter, or carburetor. These procedures assume the ignition system is working properly and is correctly adjusted.

1. ***Engine will not start*** — First make sure that fuel is being delivered to the carburetor. Remove the air cleaner, look into the carburetor throat, and operate the accelerator

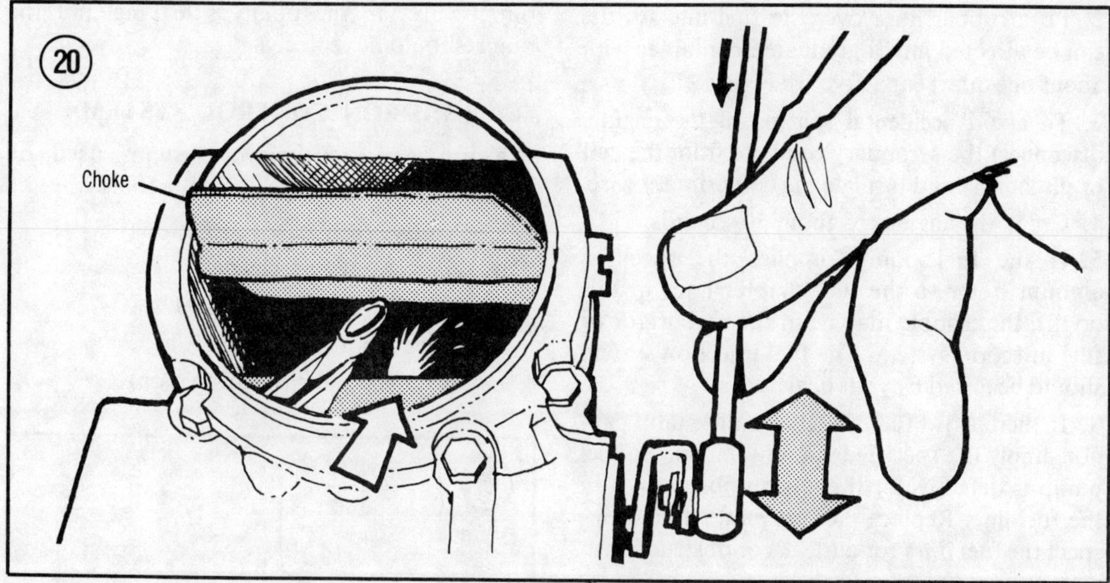

linkage several times. There should be a stream of fuel from the accelerator pump discharge tube each time the accelerator linkage is depressed (**Figure 20**). If not, check fuel pump delivery (described later), float valve, and float adjustment. If the engine will not start, check the automatic choke parts for sticking or damage. If necessary, rebuild or replace the carburetor.

2. ***Engine runs at fast idle*** — Check the choke setting. Check the idle speed, idle mixture, and decel valve (if equipped) adjustment.

3. ***Rough idle or engine miss with frequent stalling*** — Check idle mixture and idle speed adjustments.

4. ***Engine "diesels" (continues to run) when ignition is switched off*** — Check idle mixture (probably too rich), ignition timing, and idle speed (probably too fast). Check the throttle solenoid (if equipped) for proper operation. Check for overheated engine.

5. ***Stumbling when accelerating from idle*** — Check the idle speed and mixture adjustments. Check the accelerator pump.

6. ***Engine misses at high speed or lacks power*** — This indicates possible fuel starvation. Check fuel pump pressure and capacity as described in this chapter. Check float needle valves. Check for a clogged fuel filter or air cleaner.

7. ***Black exhaust smoke*** — This indicates a badly overrich mixture. Check idle mixture and idle speed adjustment. Check choke setting. Check for excessive fuel pump pressure, leaky floats, or worn needle valves.

8. ***Excessive fuel consumption*** — Check for overrich mixture. Make sure choke mechanism works properly. Check idle mixture and idle speed. Check for excessive fuel pump pressure, leaky floats, or worn float needle valves.

FUEL SYSTEM (FUEL INJECTED)

Troubleshooting a fuel injection system requires more thought, experience, and know-how than any other part of the vehicle. A logical approach and proper test equipment are essential in order to successfully find and fix these troubles.

It is best to leave fuel injection troubles to your dealer. In order to isolate a problem to the injection system make sure that the fuel pump is operating properly. Check its performance as described later in this section. Also make sure that fuel filter and air cleaner are not clogged.

FUEL PUMP TEST (MECHANICAL AND ELECTRIC)

1. Disconnect the fuel inlet line where it enters the carburetor or fuel injection system.

2. Fit a rubber hose over the fuel line so fuel can be directed into a graduated container with about one quart capacity. See **Figure 21**.

3. To avoid accidental starting of the engine, disconnect the secondary coil wire from the coil or disconnect and insulate the coil primary wire.

4. Crank the engine for about 30 seconds.

5. If the fuel pump supplies the specified amount (refer to the fuel chapter later in this book), the trouble may be in the carburetor or fuel injection system. The fuel injection system should be tested by your dealer.

6. If there is no fuel present or the pump cannot supply the specified amount, either the fuel pump is defective or there is an obstruction in the fuel line. Replace the fuel pump and/or inspect the fuel lines for air leaks or obstructions.

7. Also pressure test the fuel pump by installing a T-fitting in the fuel line between the fuel pump and the carburetor. Connect a fuel pressure gauge to the fitting with a short tube (**Figure 22**).

8. Reconnect the coil wire, start the engine, and record the pressure. Refer to the fuel chapter later in this book for the correct pressure. If the pressure varies from that specified, the pump should be replaced.

9. Stop the engine. The pressure should drop off very slowly. If it drops off rapidly, the outlet valve in the pump is leaking and the pump should be replaced.

EMISSION CONTROL SYSTEMS

Major emission control systems used on nearly all U.S. models include the following:

a. Positive crankcase ventilation (PCV)
b. Thermostatic air cleaner
c. Air injection reaction (AIR)
d. Fuel evaporation control
e. Exhaust gas recirculation (EGR)

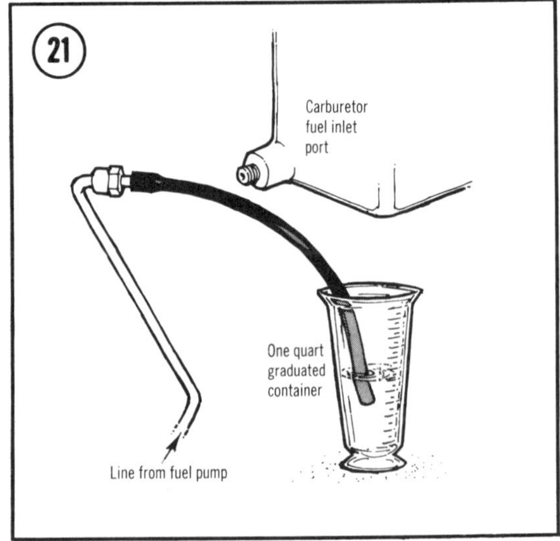

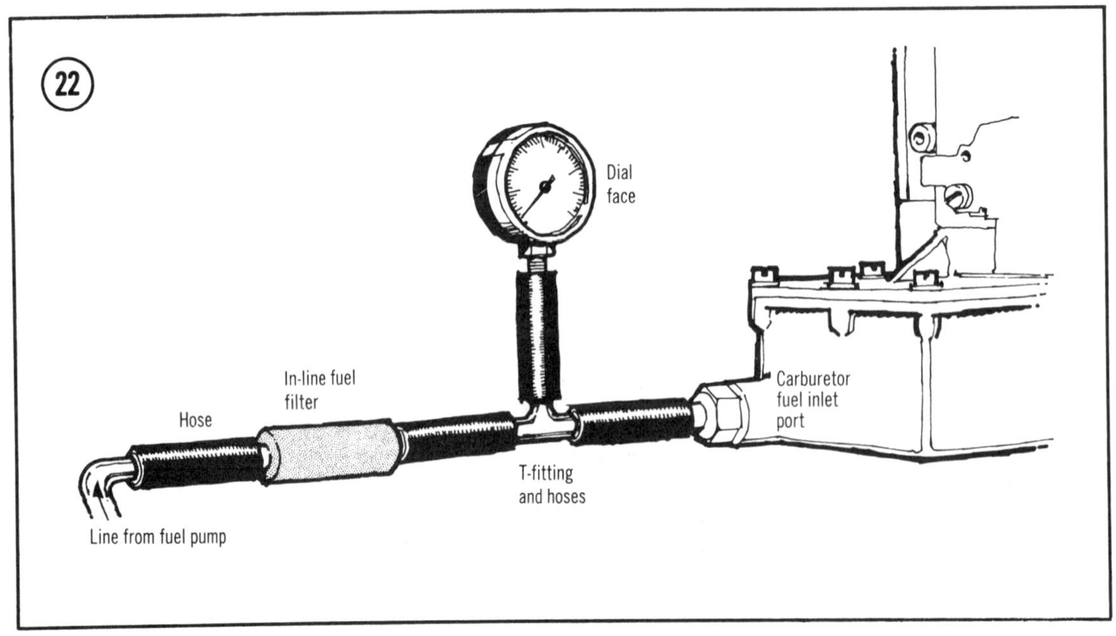

Emission control systems vary considerably from model to model. Individual models contain variations of the four systems described here. In addition, they may include other special systems. Use the index to find specific emission control components in other chapters.

Many of the systems and components are factory set and sealed. Without special expensive test equipment, it is impossible to adjust the systems to meet state and federal requirements.

Troubleshooting can also be difficult without special equipment. The procedures described below will help you find emission control parts which have failed, but repairs may have to be entrusted to a dealer or other properly equipped repair shop.

With the proper equipment, you can test the carbon monoxide and hydrocarbon levels. **Figure 23** provides some sources of trouble if the readings are not correct.

Positive Crankcase Ventilation

Fresh air drawn from the air cleaner housing scavenges emissions (e.g., piston blow-by) from the crankcase, then the intake manifold vacuum draws emissions into the intake manifold. They can then be reburned in the normal combustion process. **Figure 24** shows a typical system. **Figure 25** provides a testing procedure.

Thermostatic Air Cleaner

The thermostatically controlled air cleaner maintains incoming air to the engine at a predetermined level, usually about 100°F or higher. It mixes cold air with heated air from the exhaust manifold region. The air cleaner in-

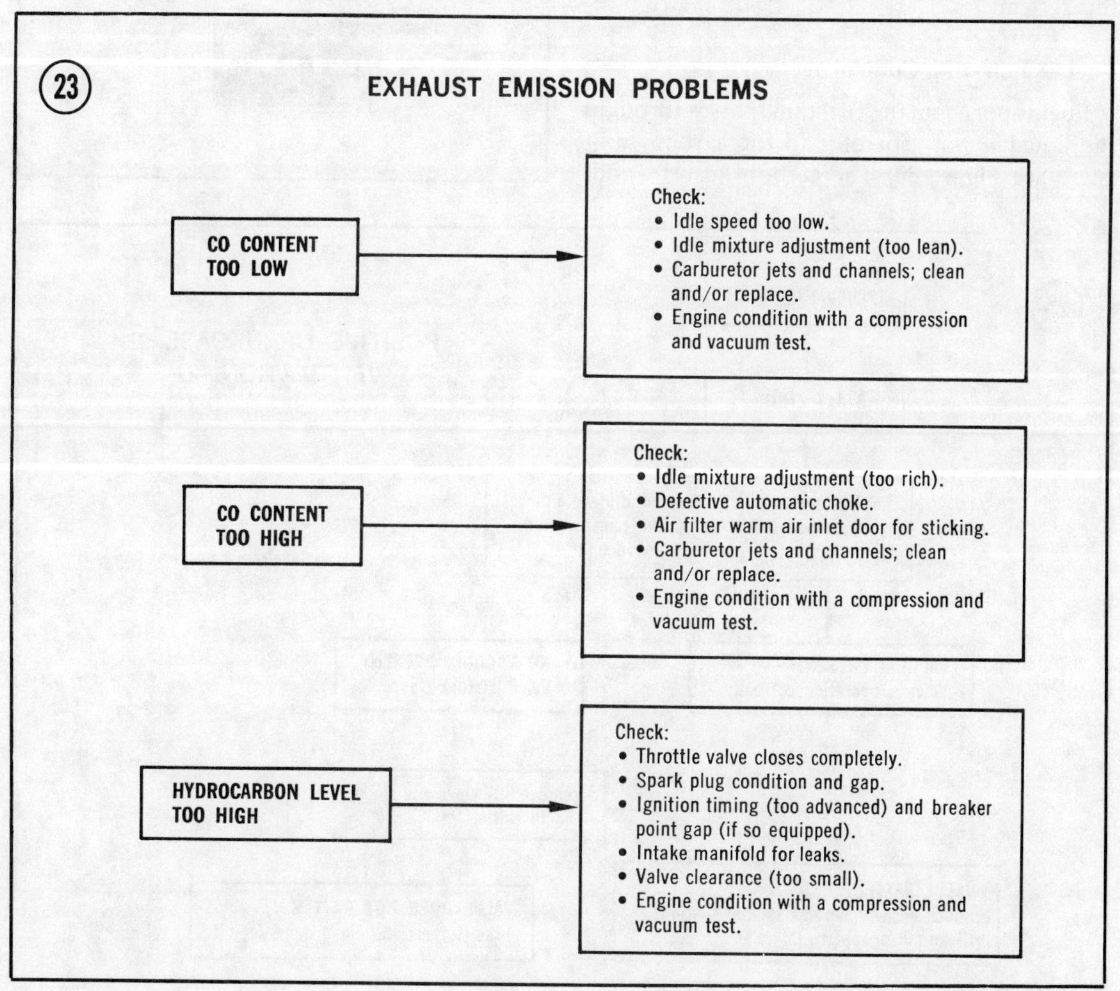

cludes a temperature sensor, vacuum motor, and a hinged door. See **Figure 26**.

The system is comparatively easy to test. See **Figure 27** for the procedure.

Air Injection Reaction System

The air injection reaction system reduces air pollution by oxidizing hydrocarbons and carbon monoxide as they leave the combustion chamber. See **Figure 28**.

The air injection pump, driven by the engine, compresses filtered air and injects it at the exhaust port of each cylinder. The fresh air mixes with the unburned gases in the exhaust and promotes further burning. A check valve prevents exhaust gases from entering and damaging the air pump if the pump becomes inoperative, e.g., from a fan belt failure.

Figure 29 explains the testing procedure for this system.

Fuel Evaporation Control

Fuel vapor from the fuel tank passes through the liquid/vapor separator to the carbon canister. See **Figure 30**. The carbon absorbs and

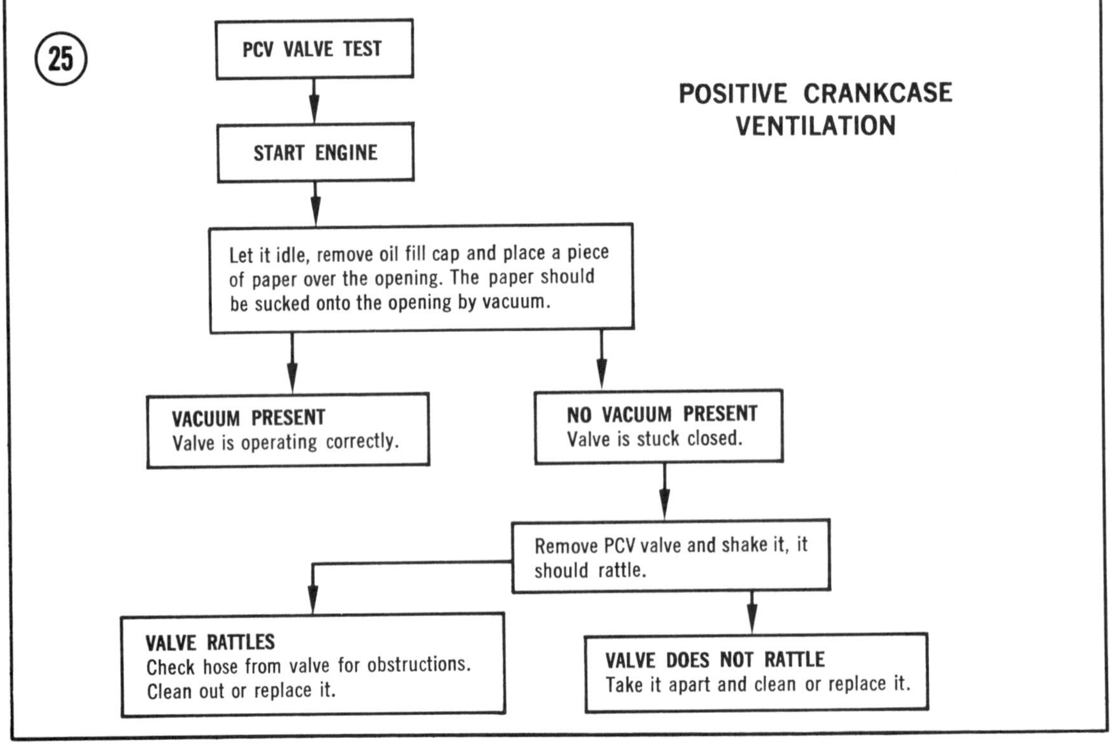

24
Air
Filtered air
PCV valve
Carburetor
Fuel-air mixture
Piston
Blow-by gases
Filtered air
Crankcase oil

25
PCV VALVE TEST
START ENGINE
Let it idle, remove oil fill cap and place a piece of paper over the opening. The paper should be sucked onto the opening by vacuum.
VACUUM PRESENT
Valve is operating correctly.
NO VACUUM PRESENT
Valve is stuck closed.
Remove PCV valve and shake it, it should rattle.
VALVE RATTLES
Check hose from valve for obstructions. Clean out or replace it.
VALVE DOES NOT RATTLE
Take it apart and clean or replace it.

POSITIVE CRANKCASE VENTILATION

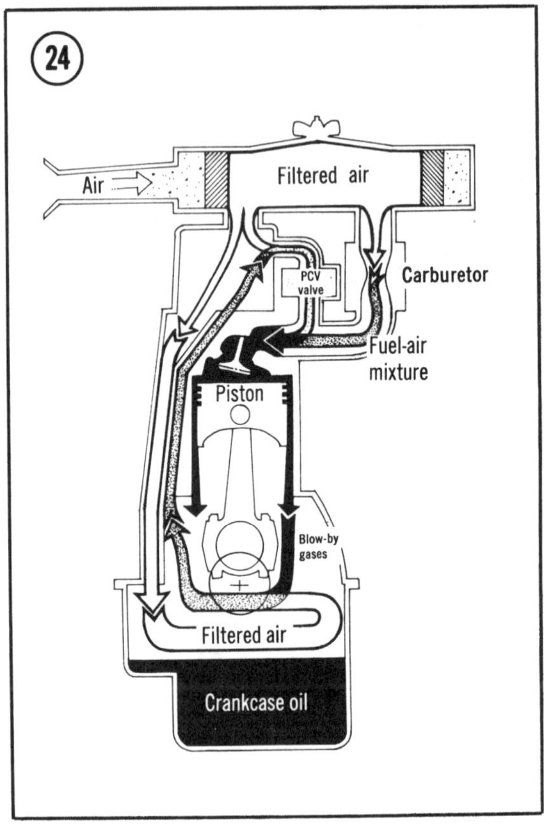

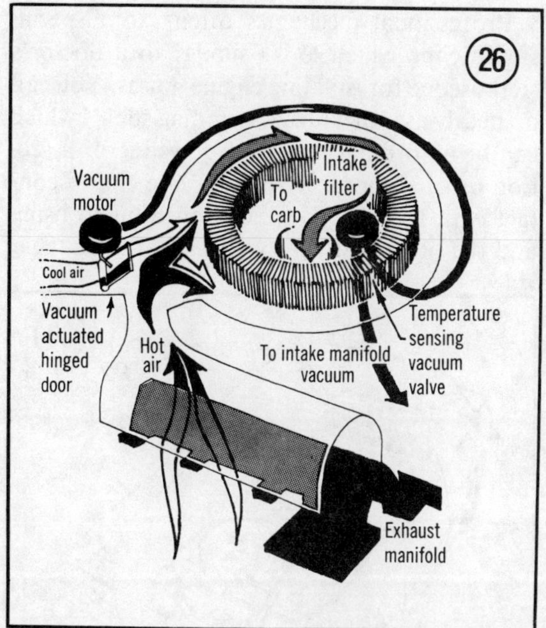
26
Vacuum motor
Intake filter
To carb
Cool air
Vacuum actuated hinged door
Hot air
To intake manifold vacuum
Temperature sensing vacuum valve
Exhaust manifold

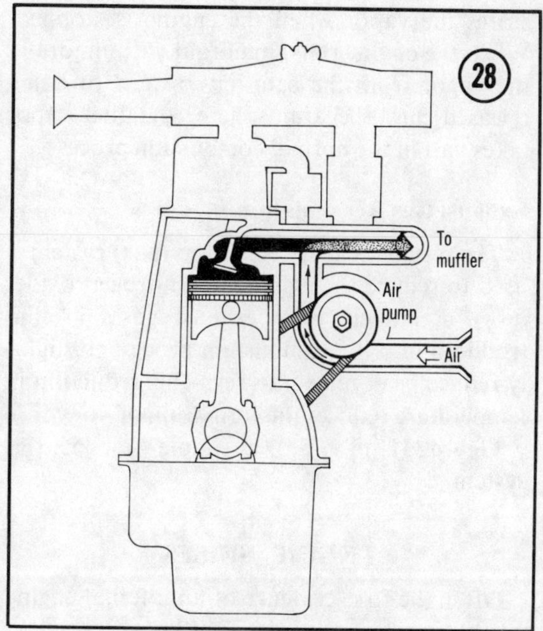
28
To muffler
Air pump
Air

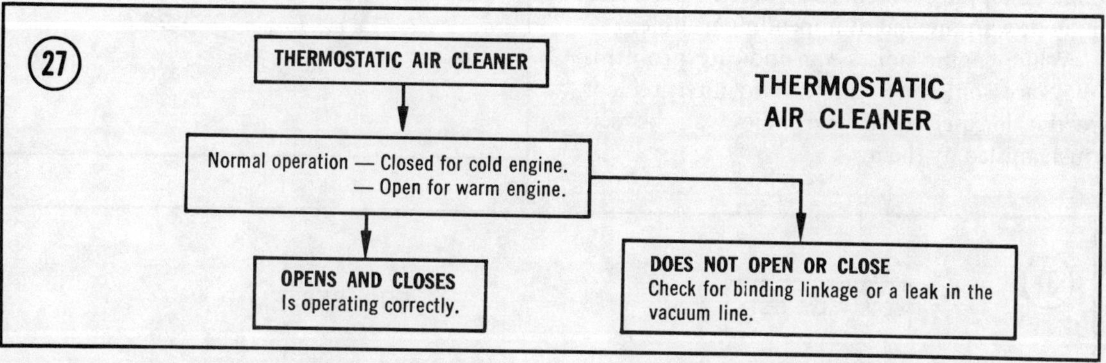
27
THERMOSTATIC AIR CLEANER
THERMOSTATIC AIR CLEANER
Normal operation — Closed for cold engine.
— Open for warm engine.
OPENS AND CLOSES
Is operating correctly.
DOES NOT OPEN OR CLOSE
Check for binding linkage or a leak in the vacuum line.

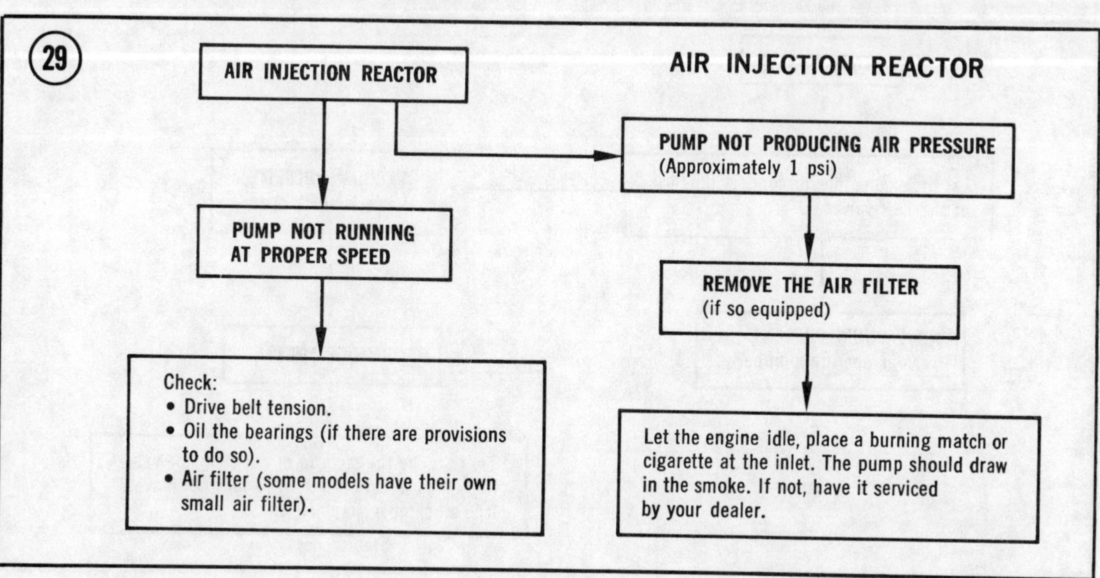
29
AIR INJECTION REACTOR
AIR INJECTION REACTOR
PUMP NOT RUNNING AT PROPER SPEED
Check:
• Drive belt tension.
• Oil the bearings (if there are provisions to do so).
• Air filter (some models have their own small air filter).
PUMP NOT PRODUCING AIR PRESSURE
(Approximately 1 psi)
REMOVE THE AIR FILTER
(if so equipped)
Let the engine idle, place a burning match or cigarette at the inlet. The pump should draw in the smoke. If not, have it serviced by your dealer.

stores the vapor when the engine is stopped. When the engine runs, manifold vacuum draws the vapor from the canister. Instead of being released into the atmosphere, the fuel vapor takes part in the normal combustion process.

Exhaust Gas Recirculation

The exhaust gas recirculation (EGR) system is used to reduce the emission of nitrogen oxides (NOx). Relatively inert exhaust gases are introduced into the combustion process to slightly reduce peak temperatures. This reduction in temperature reduces the formation of NOx.

Figure 31 provides a simple test of this system.

ENGINE NOISES

Often the first evidence of an internal engine trouble is a strange noise. That knocking, clicking, or tapping which you never heard before may be warning you of impending trouble.

While engine noises can indicate problems, they are sometimes difficult to interpret correctly; inexperienced mechanics can be seriously misled by them.

Professional mechanics often use a special stethoscope which looks similar to a doctor's stethoscope for isolating engine noises. You can do nearly as well with a "sounding stick" which can be an ordinary piece of doweling or a section of small hose. By placing one end in contact with the area to which you want to listen and the other end near your ear, you can hear

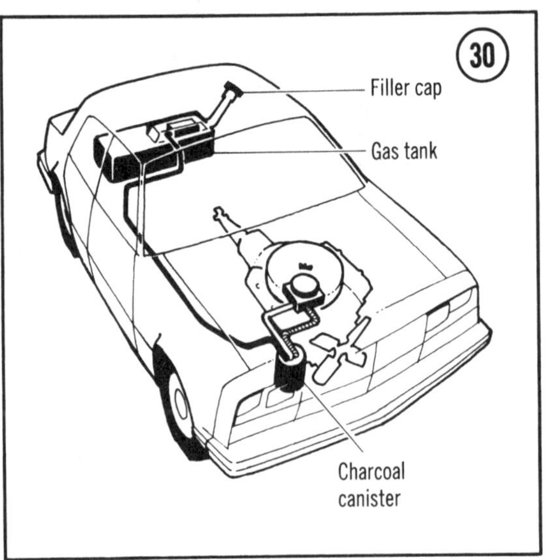

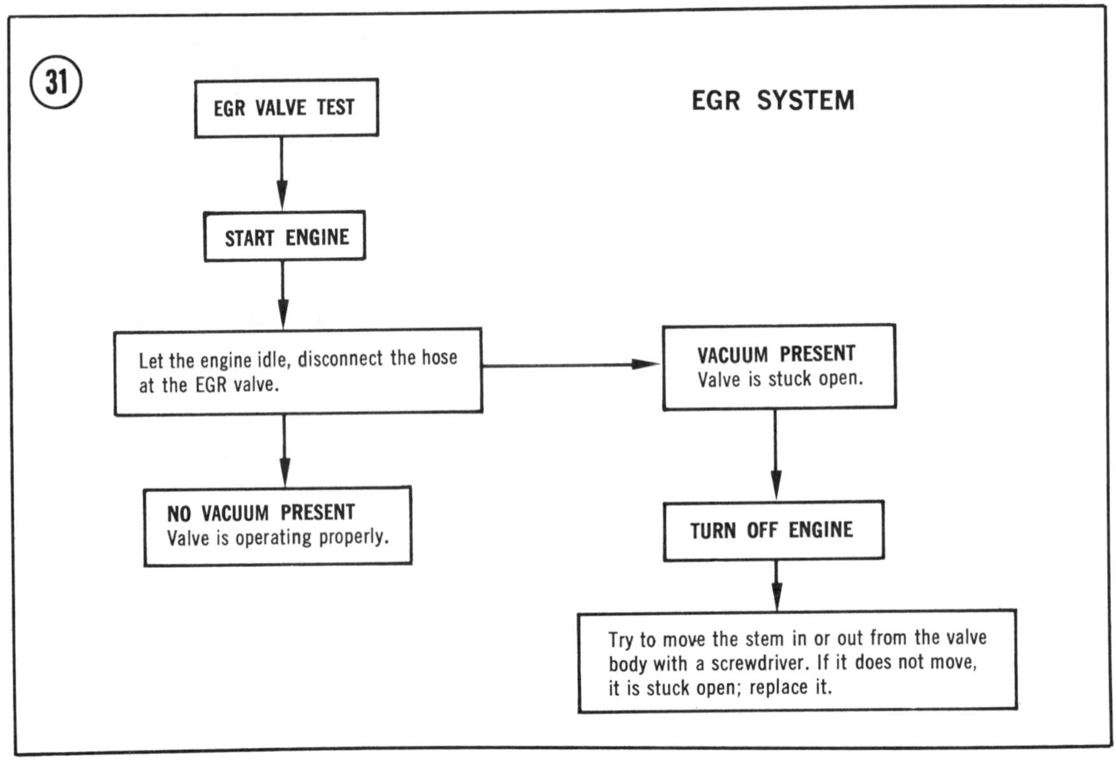

sounds emanating from that area. The first time you do this, you may be horrified at the strange noises coming from even a normal engine. If you can, have an experienced friend or mechanic help you sort the noises out.

Clicking or Tapping Noises

Clicking or tapping noises usually come from the valve train, and indicate excessive valve clearance.

If your vehicle has adjustable valves, the procedure for adjusting the valve clearance is explained in Chapter Three. If your vehicle has hydraulic lifters, the clearance may not be adjustable. The noise may be coming from a collapsed lifter. These may be cleaned or replaced as described in the engine chapter.

A sticking valve may also sound like a valve with excessive clearance. In addition, excessive wear in valve train components can cause similar engine noises.

Knocking Noises

A heavy, dull knocking is usually caused by a worn main bearing. The noise is loudest when the engine is working hard, i.e., accelerating hard at low speed. You may be able to isolate the trouble to a single bearing by disconnecting

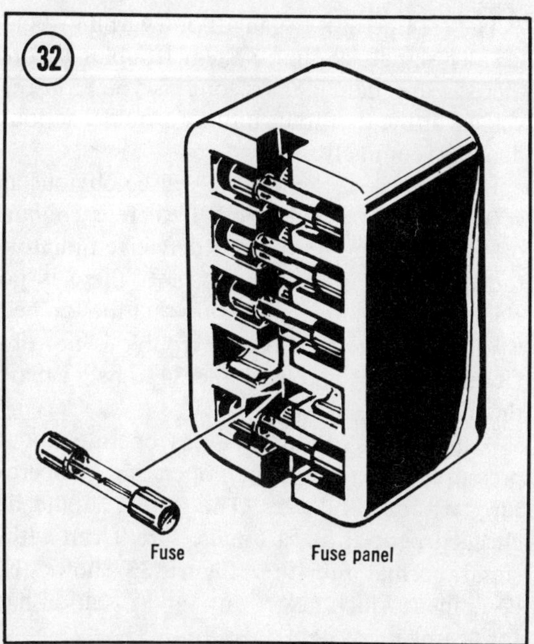

the spark plugs one at a time. When you reach the spark plug nearest the bearing, the knock will be reduced or disappear.

Worn connecting rod bearings may also produce a knock, but the sound is usually more "metallic." As with a main bearing, the noise is worse when accelerating. It may even increase further just as you go from accelerating to coasting. Disconnecting spark plugs will help isolate this knock as well.

A double knock or clicking usually indicates a worn piston pin. Disconnecting spark plugs will isolate this to a particular piston, however, the noise will *increase* when you reach the affected piston.

A loose flywheel and excessive crankshaft end play also produce knocking noises. While similar to main bearing noises, these are usually intermittent, not constant, and they do not change when spark plugs are disconnected.

Some mechanics confuse piston pin noise with piston slap. The double knock will distinguish the piston pin noise. Piston slap is identified by the fact that it is always louder when the engine is cold.

ELECTRICAL ACCESSORIES

Lights and Switches (Interior and Exterior)

1. ***Bulb does not light*** — Remove the bulb and check for a broken element. Also check the inside of the socket; make sure the contacts are clean and free of corrosion. If the bulb and socket are OK, check to see if a fuse has blown or a circuit breaker has tripped. The fuse panel (**Figure 32**) is usually located under the instrument panel. Replace the blown fuse or reset the circuit breaker. If the fuse blows or the breaker trips again, there is a short in that circuit. Check that circuit all the way to the battery. Look for worn wire insulation or burned wires.

If all the above are all right, check the switch controlling the bulb for continuity with an ohmmeter at the switch terminals. Check the switch contact terminals for loose or dirty electrical connections.

2. ***Headlights work but will not switch from either high or low beam*** — Check the beam selector switch for continuity with an ohmmeter

at the switch terminals. Check the switch contact terminals for loose or dirty electrical connections.

3. ***Brake light switch inoperative*** — On mechanically operated switches, usually mounted near the brake pedal arm, adjust the switch to achieve correct mechanical operation. Check the switch for continuity with an ohmmeter at the switch terminals. Check the switch contact terminals for loose or dirty electrical connections.

4. ***Back-up lights do not operate*** — Check light bulb as described earlier. Locate the switch, normally located near the shift lever. Adjust switch to achieve correct mechanical operation. Check the switch for continuity with an ohmmeter at the switch terminals. Bypass the switch with a jumper wire; if the lights work, replace the switch.

Directional Signals

1. ***Directional signals do not operate*** — If the indicator light on the instrument panel burns steadily instead of flashing, this usually indicates that one of the exterior lights is burned out. Check all lamps that normally flash. If all are all right, the flasher unit may be defective. Replace it with a good one.

2. ***Directional signal indicator light on instrument panel does not light up*** — Check the light bulbs as described earlier. Check all electrical connections and check the flasher unit.

3. ***Directional signals will not self-cancel*** — Check the self-cancelling mechanism located inside the steering column.

4. ***Directional signals flash slowly*** — Check the condition of the battery and the alternator (or generator) drive belt tension (**Figure 4**). Check the flasher unit and all related electrical connections.

Windshield Wipers

1. ***Wipers do not operate*** — Check for a blown fuse or circuit breaker that has tripped; replace or reset. Check all related terminals for loose or dirty electrical connections. Check continuity of the control switch with an ohmmeter at the switch terminals. Check the linkage and arms for loose, broken, or binding parts. Straighten out or replace where necessary.

2. ***Wiper motor hums but will not operate*** — The motor may be shorted out internally; check and/or replace the motor. Also check for broken or binding linkage and arms.

3. ***Wiper arms will not return to the stowed position when turned off*** — The motor has a special internal switch for this purpose. Have it inspected by your dealer. Do not attempt this yourself.

Interior Heater

1. ***Heater fan does not operate*** — Check for a blown fuse or circuit breaker that has tripped. Check the switch for continuity with an ohmmeter at the switch terminals. Check the switch contact terminals for loose or dirty electrical connections.

2. ***Heat output is insufficient*** — Check the heater hose/engine coolant control valve usually located in the engine compartment; make sure it is in the open position. Ensure that the heater door(s) and cable(s) are operating correctly and are in the open position. Inspect the heat ducts; make sure that they are not crimped or blocked.

COOLING SYSTEM

The temperature gauge or warning light usually signals cooling system troubles before there is any damage. As long as you stop the vehicle at the first indication of trouble, serious damage is unlikely.

In most cases, the trouble will be obvious as soon as you open the hood. If there is coolant or steam leaking, look for a defective radiator, radiator hose, or heater hose. If there is no evidence of leakage, make sure that the fan belt is in good condition. If the trouble is not obvious, refer to **Figures 33 and 34** to help isolate the trouble.

Automotive cooling systems operate under pressure to permit higher operating temperatures without boil-over. The system should be checked periodically to make sure it can withstand normal pressure. **Figure 35** shows the equipment which nearly any service station has for testing the system pressure.

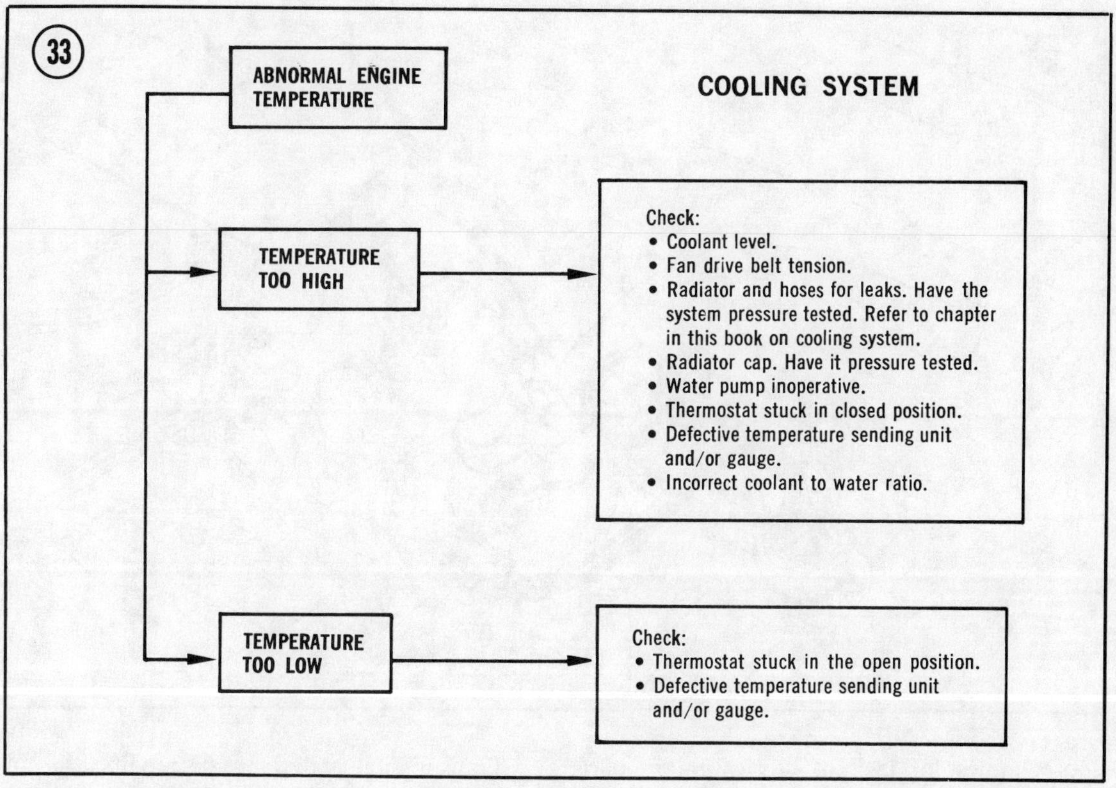

33
ABNORMAL ENGINE TEMPERATURE
COOLING SYSTEM
TEMPERATURE TOO HIGH
Check:
• Coolant level.
• Fan drive belt tension.
• Radiator and hoses for leaks. Have the system pressure tested. Refer to chapter in this book on cooling system.
• Radiator cap. Have it pressure tested.
• Water pump inoperative.
• Thermostat stuck in closed position.
• Defective temperature sending unit and/or gauge.
• Incorrect coolant to water ratio.
TEMPERATURE TOO LOW
Check:
• Thermostat stuck in the open position.
• Defective temperature sending unit and/or gauge.

34
COOLING SYSTEM
CONTINUED LOSS OF COOLANT
Check:
• Radiator and hoses for leaks. Have the system pressure tested.
• Radiator cap. Have it pressure tested.
• Water pump for leaks.

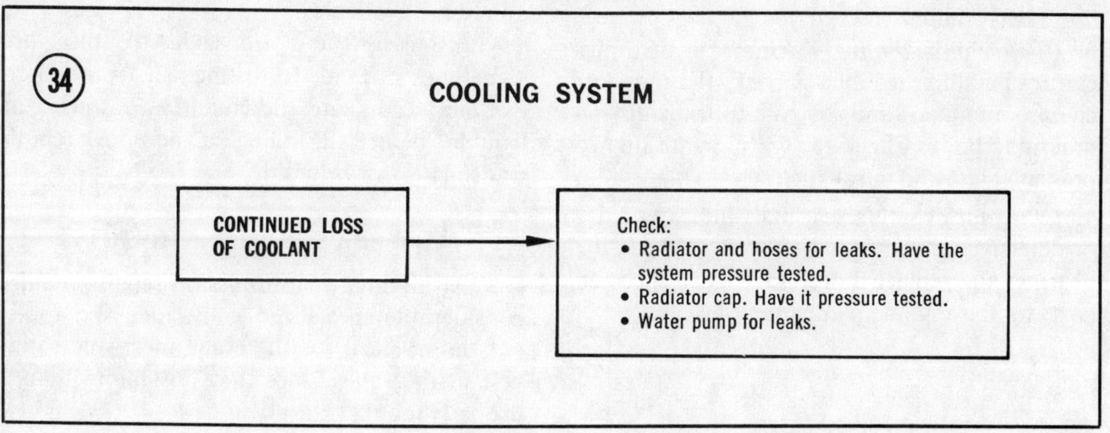

CLUTCH

All clutch troubles except adjustments require transmission removal to identify and cure the problem.

1. *Slippage* — This is most noticeable when accelerating in a high gear at relatively low speed. To check slippage, park the vehicle on a level surface with the handbrake set. Shift to 2nd gear and release the clutch as if driving off. If the clutch is good, the engine will slow and stall. If the clutch slips, continued engine speed will give it away.

Slippage results from insufficient clutch pedal free play, oil or grease on the clutch disc, worn pressure plate, or weak springs.

2. *Drag or failure to release* — This trouble usually causes difficult shifting and gear clash, especially when downshifting. The cause may be excessive clutch pedal free play, warped or bent pressure plate or clutch disc, broken or

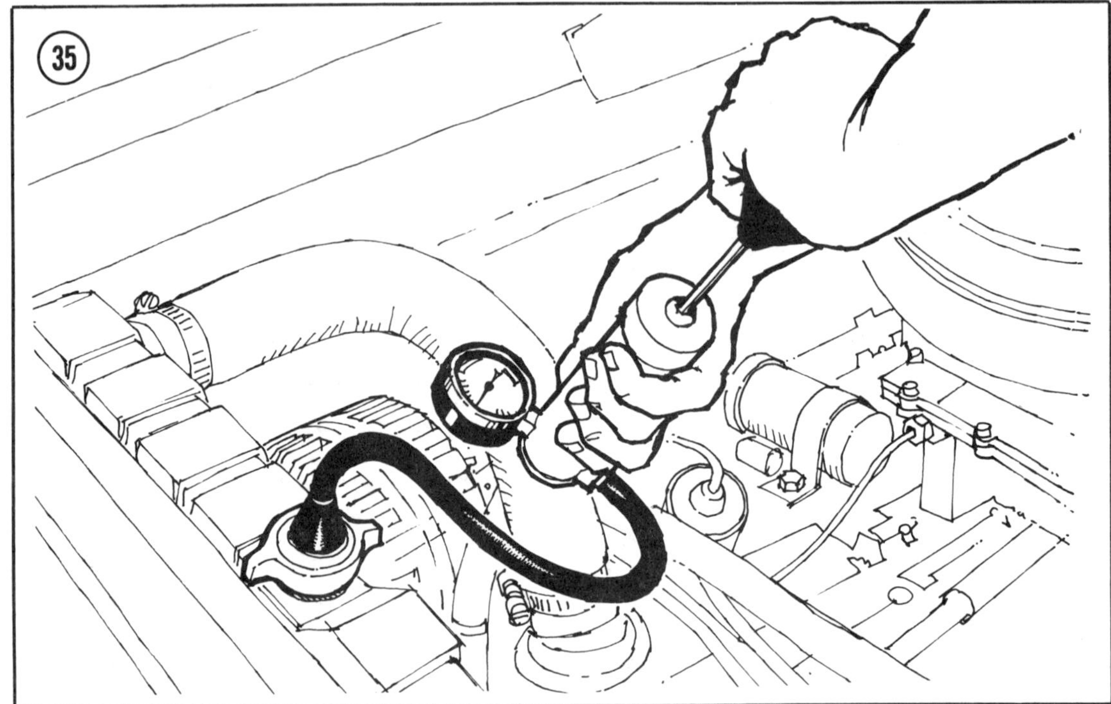

loose linings, or lack of lubrication in pilot bearing. Also check condition of transmission main shaft splines.

3. ***Chatter or grabbing*** — A number of things can cause this trouble. Check tightness of engine mounts and engine-to-transmission mounting bolts. Check for worn or misaligned pressure plate and misaligned release plate.

4. ***Other noises*** — Noise usually indicates a dry or defective release or pilot bearing. Check the bearings and replace if necessary. Also check all parts for misalignment and uneven wear.

MANUAL TRANSMISSION/TRANSAXLE

Transmission and transaxle troubles are evident when one or more of the following symptoms appear:

a. Difficulty changing gears
b. Gears clash when downshifting
c. Slipping out of gear
d. Excessive noise in NEUTRAL
e. Excessive noise in gear
f. Oil leaks

Transmission and transaxle repairs are not recommended unless the many special tools required are available.

Transmission and transaxle troubles are sometimes difficult to distinguish from clutch troubles. Eliminate the clutch as a source of trouble before installing a new or rebuilt transmission or transaxle.

AUTOMATIC TRANSMISSION

Most automatic transmission repairs require considerable specialized knowledge and tools. It is impractical for the home mechanic to invest in the tools, since they cost more than a properly rebuilt transmission.

Check fluid level and condition frequently to help prevent future problems. If the fluid is orange or black in color or smells like varnish, it is an indication of some type of damage or failure within the transmission. Have the transmission serviced by your dealer or competent automatic transmission service facility.

BRAKES

Good brakes are vital to the safe operation of the vehicle. Performing the maintenance speci-

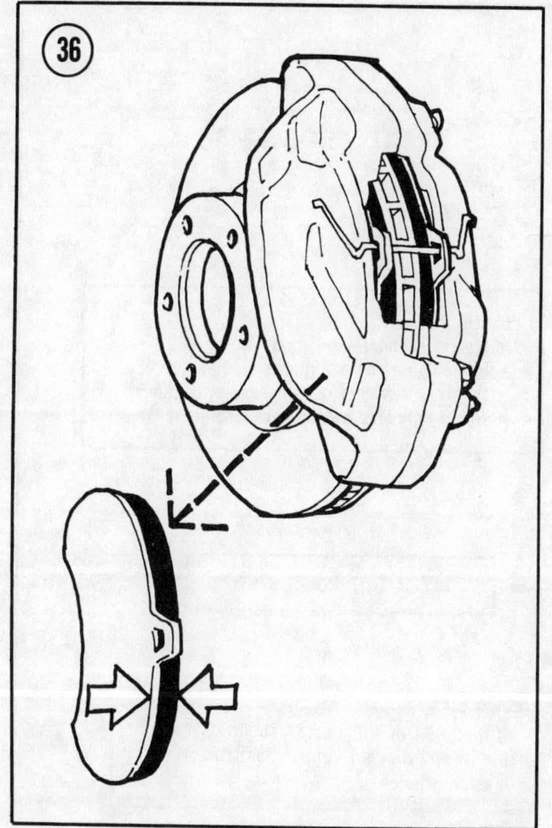

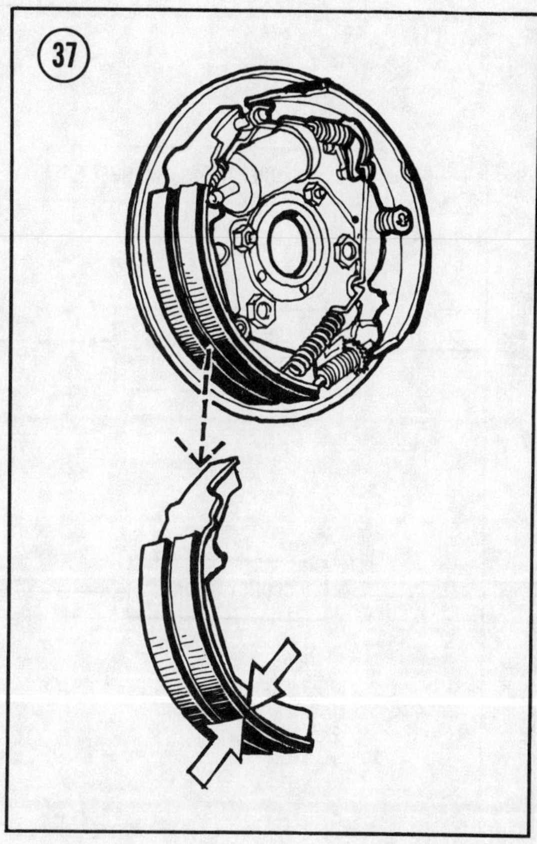

fied in Chapter Three will minimize problems with the brakes. Most importantly, check and maintain the level of fluid in the master cylinder, and check the thickness of the linings on the disc brake pads (**Figure 36**) or drum brake shoes (**Figure 37**).

If trouble develops, **Figures 38 through 40** will help you locate the problem. Refer to the brake chapter for actual repair procedures.

STEERING AND SUSPENSION

Trouble in the suspension or steering is evident when the following occur:

a. Steering is hard
b. Car pulls to one side
c. Car wanders or front wheels wobble
d. Steering has excessive play
e. Tire wear is abnormal

Unusual steering, pulling, or wandering is usually caused by bent or otherwise misaligned suspension parts. This is difficult to check without proper alignment equipment. Refer to the suspension chapter in this book for repairs that you can perform and those that must be left to a dealer or suspension specialist.

If your trouble seems to be excessive play, check wheel bearing adjustment first. This is the most frequent cause. Then check ball-joints (refer to Suspension chapter). Finally, check tie rod end ball-joints by shaking each tie rod. Also check steering gear, or rack-and-pinion assembly to see that it is securely bolted down.

TIRE WEAR ANALYSIS

Abnormal tire wear should be analyzed to determine its causes. The most common causes are the following:

a. Incorrect tire pressure
b. Improper driving
c. Overloading
d. Bad road surfaces
e. Incorrect wheel alignment

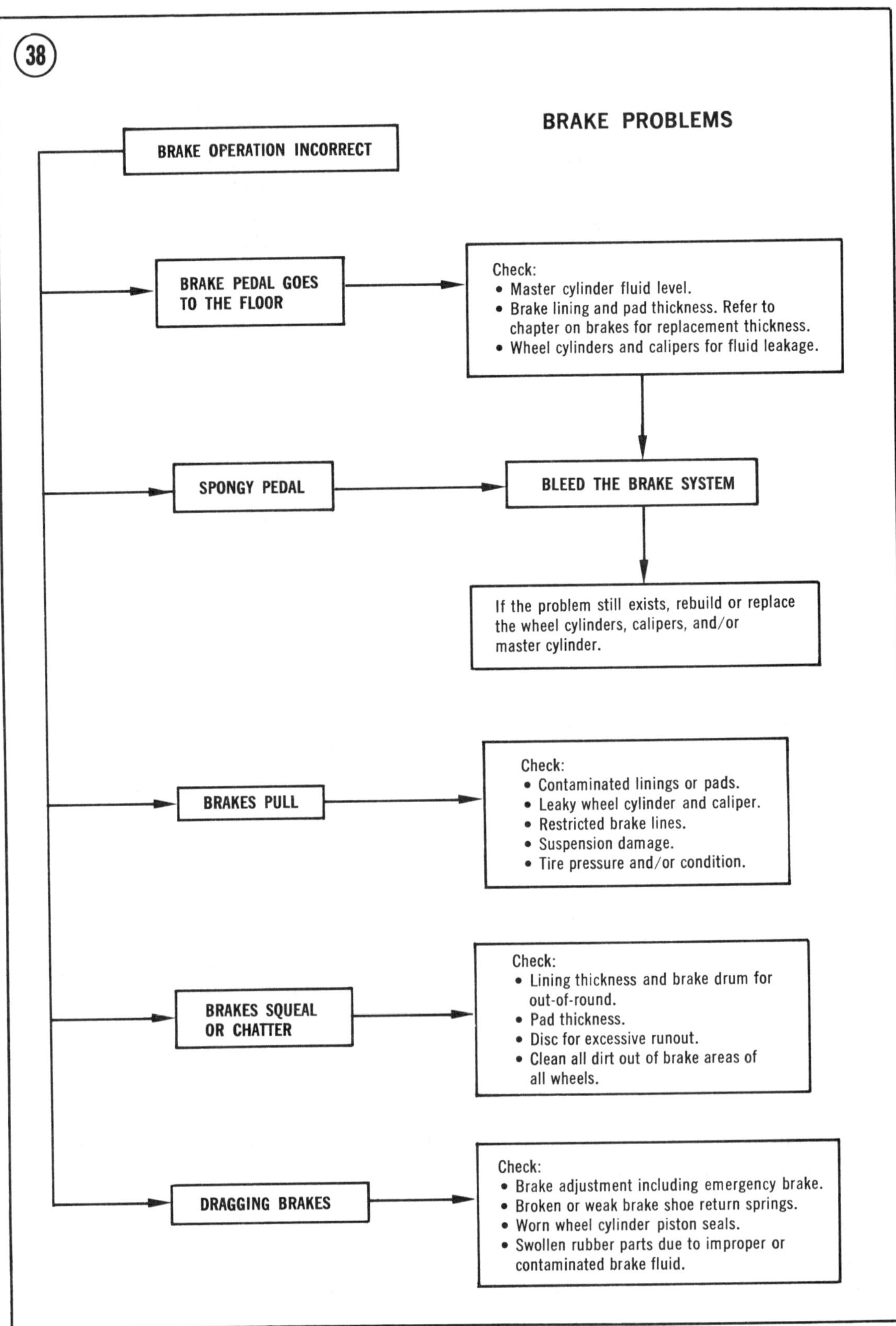
38
BRAKE PROBLEMS
BRAKE OPERATION INCORRECT
BRAKE PEDAL GOES TO THE FLOOR
Check:
• Master cylinder fluid level.
• Brake lining and pad thickness. Refer to chapter on brakes for replacement thickness.
• Wheel cylinders and calipers for fluid leakage.
SPONGY PEDAL
BLEED THE BRAKE SYSTEM
If the problem still exists, rebuild or replace the wheel cylinders, calipers, and/or master cylinder.
BRAKES PULL
Check:
• Contaminated linings or pads.
• Leaky wheel cylinder and caliper.
• Restricted brake lines.
• Suspension damage.
• Tire pressure and/or condition.
BRAKES SQUEAL OR CHATTER
Check:
• Lining thickness and brake drum for out-of-round.
• Pad thickness.
• Disc for excessive runout.
• Clean all dirt out of brake areas of all wheels.
DRAGGING BRAKES
Check:
• Brake adjustment including emergency brake.
• Broken or weak brake shoe return springs.
• Worn wheel cylinder piston seals.
• Swollen rubber parts due to improper or contaminated brake fluid.

39

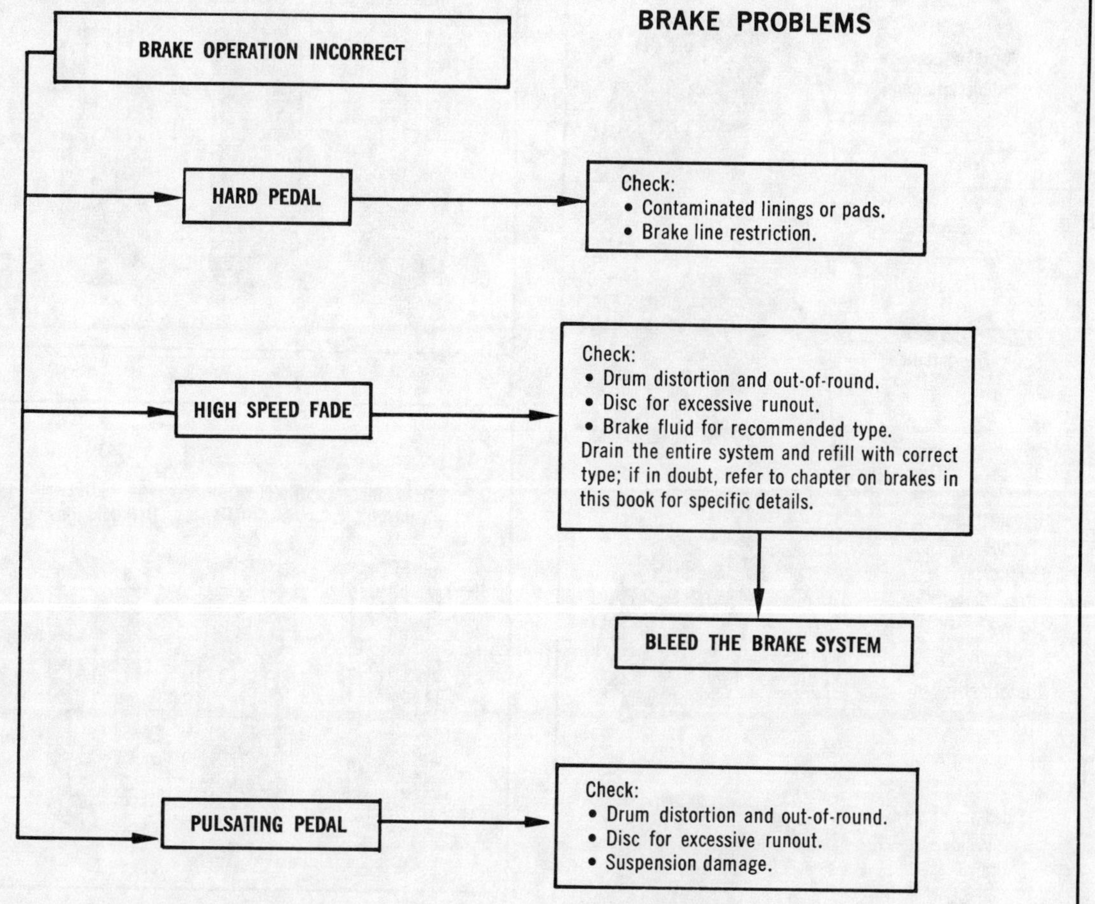

BRAKE PROBLEMS
BRAKE OPERATION INCORRECT
HARD PEDAL
Check:
• Contaminated linings or pads.
• Brake line restriction.
HIGH SPEED FADE
Check:
• Drum distortion and out-of-round.
• Disc for excessive runout.
• Brake fluid for recommended type.
Drain the entire system and refill with correct type; if in doubt, refer to chapter on brakes in this book for specific details.
BLEED THE BRAKE SYSTEM
PULSATING PEDAL
Check:
• Drum distortion and out-of-round.
• Disc for excessive runout.
• Suspension damage.

40

BRAKE PROBLEMS
BRAKE LIGHT ON INSTRUMENT PANEL COMES ON AND STAYS ON (1968 and later models)
PARTIAL OR COMPLETE BRAKE SYSTEM FAILURE
Check the entire brake system for signs of brake fluid leakage and/or damage. Thoroughly inspect the master cylinder, wheel cylinders, calipers, brake lines, and flexible hoses.
DO NOT drive the vehicle until you know what the problem was and that it is corrected.

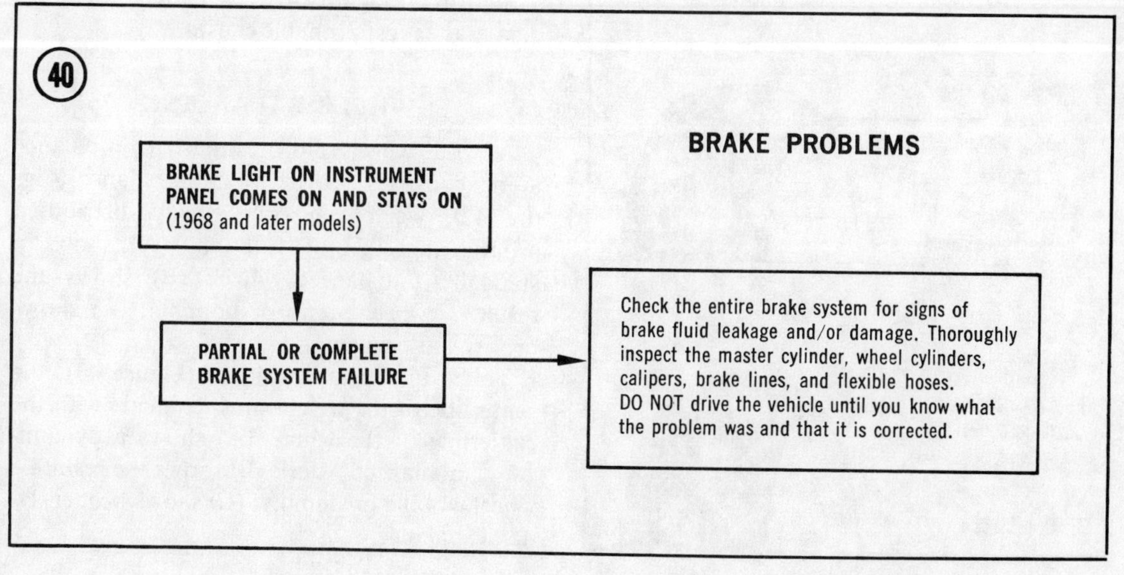

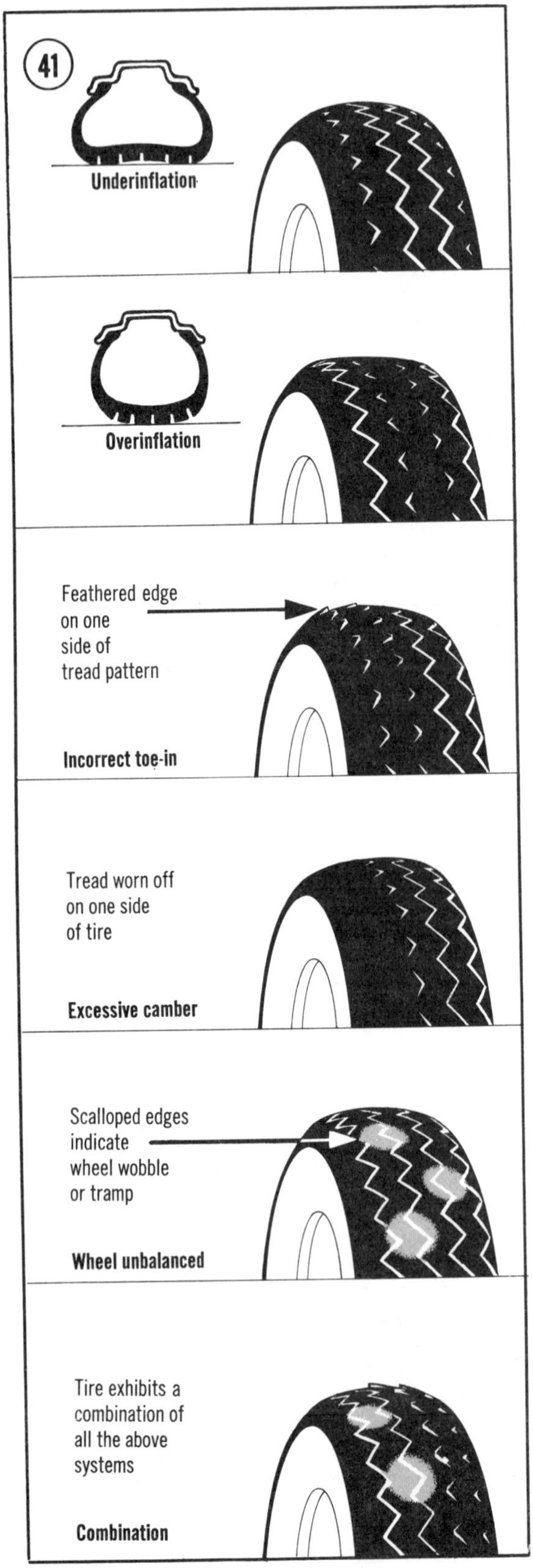

41

Underinflation

Overinflation

Feathered edge on one side of tread pattern

Incorrect toe-in

Tread worn off on one side of tire

Excessive camber

Scalloped edges indicate wheel wobble or tramp

Wheel unbalanced

Tire exhibits a combination of all the above systems

Combination

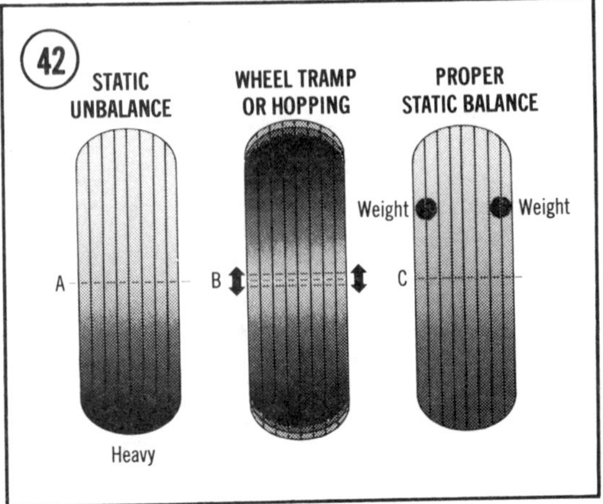

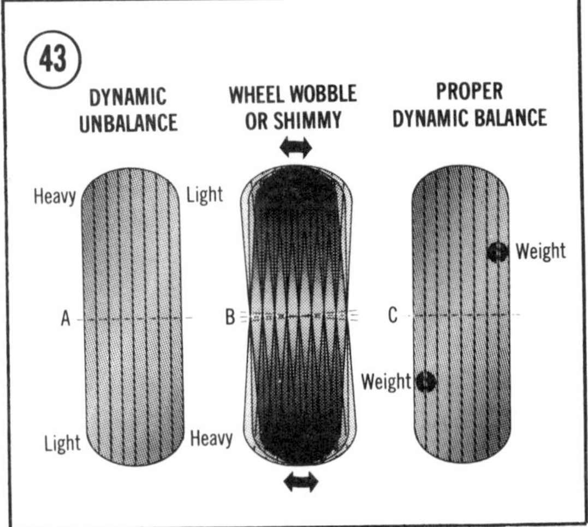

Figure 41 identifies wear patterns and indicates the most probable causes.

WHEEL BALANCING

All four wheels and tires must be in balance along two axes. To be in static balance (**Figure 42**), weight must be evenly distributed around the axis of rotation. (A) shows a statically unbalanced wheel; (B) shows the result — wheel tramp or hopping; (C) shows proper static balance.

To be in dynamic balance (**Figure 43**), the centerline of the weight must coincide with the centerline of the wheel. (A) shows a dynamically unbalanced wheel; (B) shows the result — wheel wobble or shimmy; (C) shows proper dynamic balance.

NOTE: If you own a 1982 or later model, first check the Supplement at the back of the book for any new service information.

CHAPTER THREE

3

LUBRICATION, MAINTENANCE, AND TUNE-UP

To ensure good performance, dependability and safety, regular preventive maintenance is necessary. This chapter outlines periodic lubrication and maintenance for a car driven by an average owner. A car driven more than average may require more frequent attention, but even without use, rust, dirt and corrosion may cause unnecessary damage. Whether performed by the owner or dealer, regular routine attention helps to avoid expensive repairs.

The recommended schedule in this chapter includes routine checks which are easily performed at each fuel stop and periodic maintenance to prevent future trouble. Also included is a systematic engine tune-up procedure which simplifies this important task. **Tables 1-3** summarize all periodic maintenance required in an easy-to-use format. Recommended lubricants for your Honda are listed in **Table 4**. **Table 5** lists engine oil viscosities for various driving conditions. **Tables 1-9** are at the end of the chapter.

NOTE

Honda's warranty requirements state that the vehicle must be maintained and serviced in accordance with Honda specifications. See ***Tables 1-3*** *and your Honda Owner's Manual. When performing maintenance procedures, make sure to keep accurate records, as well as dated bills for parts (and service performed by independent garages) to serve as proof that the services were performed when required.*

ROUTINE CHECKS

The following simple checks should be performed at each fueling stop.

1. *Check engine oil*—Shut off the engine and allow a few moments for the oil to return to the crankcase. Remove the dipstick, wipe it off and insert, making sure it is seated in the tube. See **Figure 1**. Remove it again and inspect; add oil

only when the level is below the "ADD" mark. One quart will raise the level from "ADD" to "FULL". See **Table 5** for recommended oil grades.

2. *Check battery condition*–Observe the level of the battery fluid on the side of the battery. See **Figure 2**. Level should be maintained between the "UPPER" and "LOWER" marks. Top up level with distilled water only; do not add electrolyte to a battery that is in service. Do not overfill.

3. *Check drive belt condition and tension*–Correct tension depends on the distance between the pulleys. See **Figure 3**. The alternator drive belt should deflect about 12-17 mm (1/2-5/8 in.) under moderate thumb pressure. If necessary, adjust tension as described in this chapter.

4. *Check tire pressure*–This should be done when tires are cold. Maximum pressure is imprinted on each tire.

5. *Check windshield washer container level*–It should be kept full. See **Figure 4**.

6. *Check coolant level in reservoir*—Note markings indicating correct level for hot and cold engine. See **Figure 5**. Use an ethylene glycol-based antifreeze compounded for use in aluminum engines.

SCHEDULED MAINTENANCE

All of the following procedures are done at specified intervals of mileage or time. See

6

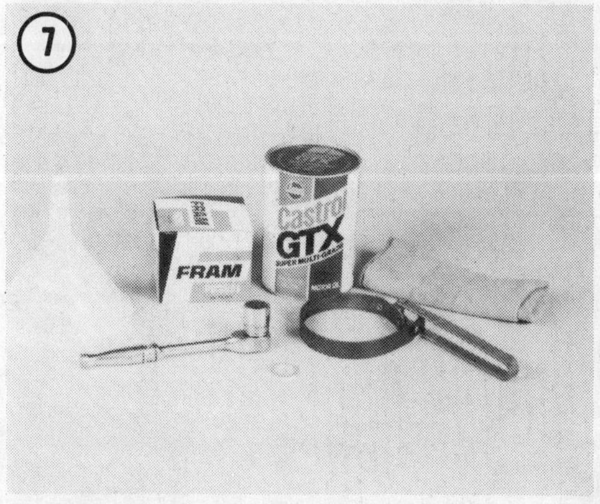

7

Table 1 (1973-1974), **Table 2** (1975-1979) or **Table 3** (1980-on).

Engine Oil and Filter Change

The oil and filter change interval varies depending on the type of driving that you do. For normal driving, including some city traffic, change oil and filter at the intervals specified in **Tables 1-3**. If driving is primarily stop-and-go traffic, includes trailer hauling or involves short trips in cold climates, change oil and filter every 3,000 miles or 3 months. Change oil and filter at least twice a year if the car is driven only a few hundred miles a month.

Any oil used must be rated "SE" or "SF." See **Figure 6**. Non-detergent oils are not recommended. See **Table 5** for recommended oil grades.

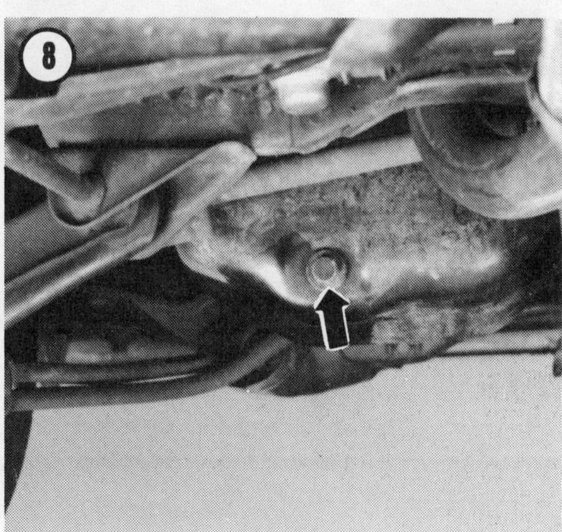

8

NOTE
Engine oil with the rating "SF" is designed for use in all 1980 and later models and its use is required to meet all manufacturer warranty standards. At the time of their introduction, all 1973-1979 models were required to use oil rated "SE." However, to benefit from the added protection that "SF" oil offers against engine deposits, rust and corrosion, its use is recommended in all models covered in this manual.

To drain the oil and change the filter, you will need the following tools (**Figure 7**):

a. Drain pan
b. Funnel
c. Can opener or pour spout
d. Filter wrench
e. Adjustable wrench
f. Engine oil (see **Table 6** for oil capacity)
g. Oil filter
h. New drain plug washer

There are a number of ways of discarding the old oil safely. The easiest way is to pour it from the drain pan into a gallon bleach bottle. Tighten the cap and throw it in your household trash, if local regulations permit. Many service stations accept oil for recycling.

1. Warm engine to operating temperature, then shut it off.
2. Put drain pan under oil drain plug and remove plug with wrench (**Figure 8**). Discard the drain plug gasket.
3. Let oil drain for at least 10 minutes.

4. Unscrew oil filter counterclockwise by hand or use a filter wrench. See **Figure 9**.
5. Wipe the gasket surface of the engine block with a clean, lint-free cloth.
6. Coat the neoprene gasket on the new filter with clean oil.
7. Screw the filter onto the engine *by hand* until the filter gasket just touches the base, i.e., until you feel the slightest resistance when turning the filter. Then tighten the filter *by hand* 2/3 turn more.

CAUTION
Do not overtighten and do not use a filter wrench or the filter will leak.

8. Install oil drain plug with a new gasket and tighten securely.
9. Remove the oil filler cap. See **Figure 10**.
10. Pour the correct amount of oil into the engine (**Table 6**).
11. Start the engine and let it idle. The oil pressure light on the instrument panel will remain on for a short time (15-30 seconds), then it will go out.

CAUTION
Do not rev engine to make oil light go out. It takes time for the oil to reach all areas of the engine—excessive engine speed could damage dry parts.

12. While the engine is running, make sure that the drain plug and oil filter are not leaking.
13. Turn the engine off and check the oil level with the dipstick. See **Figure 1**. Add oil if necessary to bring oil up to the "FULL" mark, but *do not overfill.*

Manual Transaxle Oil Check

At the specified intervals, check the fluid level in manual transaxle as follows:

a. *1973-1979 4-speed*: With the oil at operating temperature and the car sitting level, remove the dipstick and wipe off the gauge end. Place the dipstick back into the transaxle, but do not screw it in. Remove the dipstick and check the level. See **Figure 11**. It should be between the 2 marks. If necessary, add oil through the dipstick hole (**Table 4**) to correct the level. The difference between the 2 marks

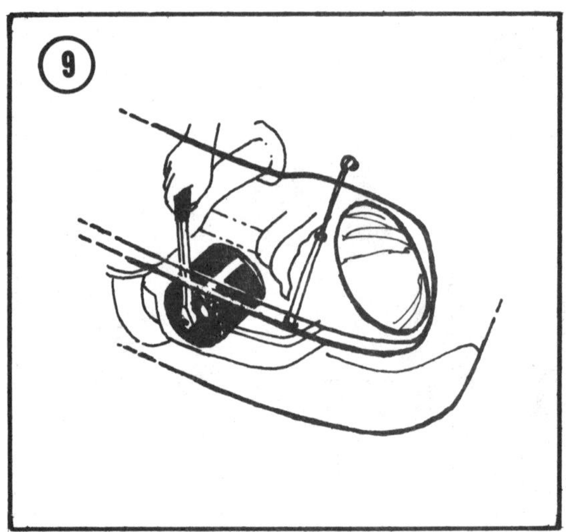
9

10

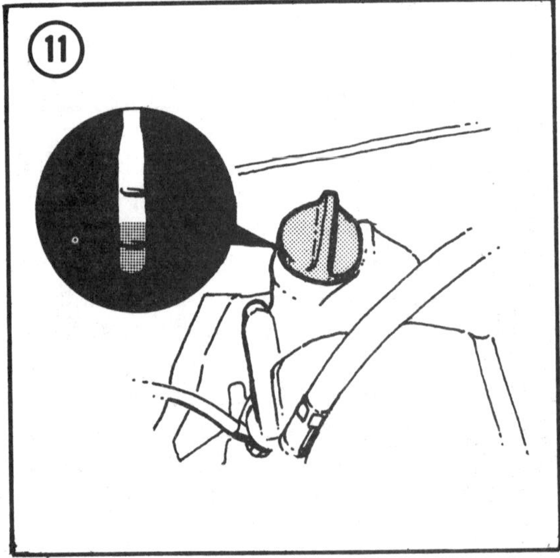
11

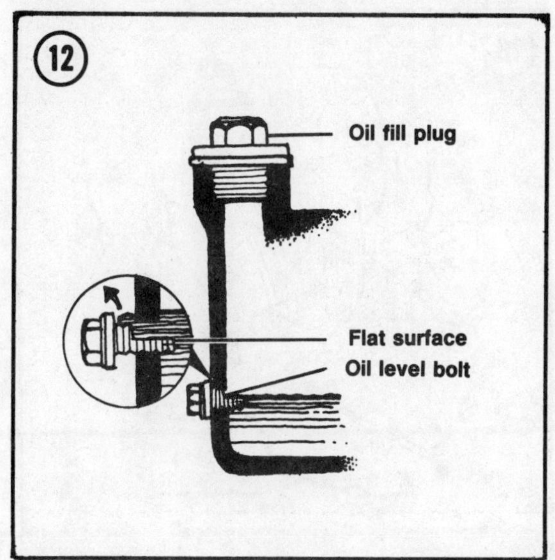

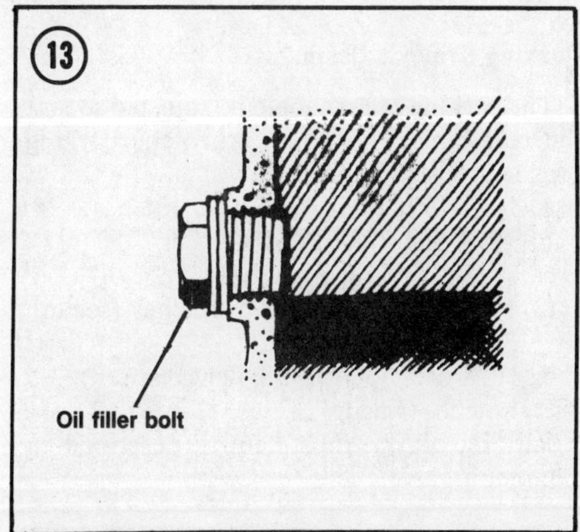

represents about 2 quarts. Reinstall the dipstick and hand-tighten.

b. *1973-1979 5-speed*: With the oil at operating temperature and the car sitting level, unscrew the level bolt until oil begins to run out of the transaxle. If it does not, turn the bolt so that the flat side faces up (**Figure 12**). Then remove the oil fill plug (underneath the battery) and add oil (**Table 4**) until it begins to seep past the bolt (**Figure 12**). Tighten the level bolt and install the filler plug and tighten. Wipe any oil from the outside of the transaxle.

c. *1980-on models*: With the oil at operating temperature and the car sitting level, remove the transaxle oil filler bolt and check the oil level with your finger. It should be level with the bottom of the filler bolt hole (**Figure 13**). If it is not, add oil (**Table 4**) until it just begins to run out. Reinstall the plug and tighten to 4.5 mkg (33 ft.-lb.).

Manual Transaxle Oil Change

The oil in the manual transaxle should be replaced at the intervals specified in **Tables 1-3**. Use only a quality oil recommended in **Table 4**.

Prior to draining the transaxle, drive the car for several miles to warm the oil so that it will flow freely. Remove the fill/level plug. See **Figure 11**, **Figure 12** or **Figure 13**. Discard the fill/level plug gasket. Place a drain pan beneath the transaxle and unscrew the drain plug (**Figure 14**). Allow the oil to drain for several minutes and then install a new gasket on the drain plug. Install the plug and tighten securely, but not tight enough to strip the threads in the transaxle. Refer to **Table 4** and refill the transaxle. Check transaxle oil level as described in this chapter.

Automatic Transaxle Fluid Level

At every engine oil change, check the automatic transaxle fluid level. The transaxle must be thoroughly warmed up and the car level. Unscrew the dipstick (**Figure 15**), wipe it with a clean cloth and reinsert it. *Do not* screw it back in. Pull the dipstick out again and check

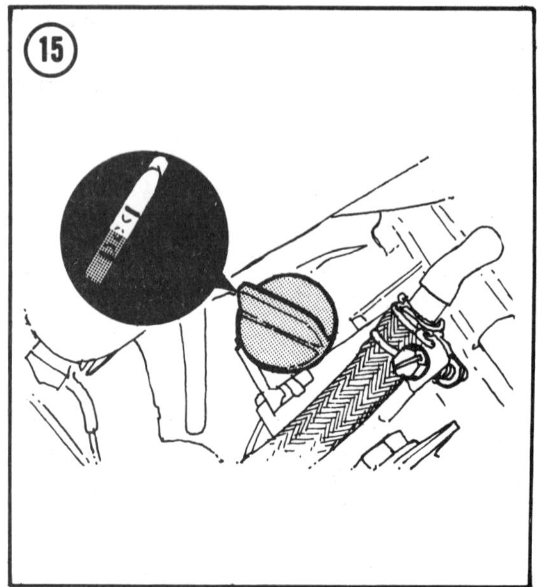

15

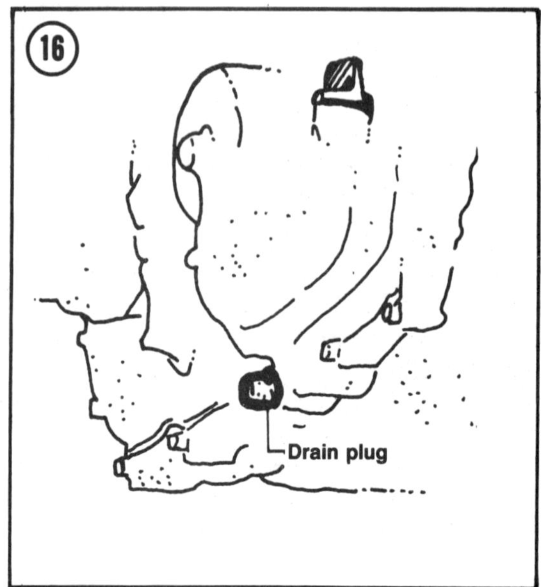

16

the level (**Figure 15**). Fluid must be maintained between the "FULL" and "LOW" marks.

If necessary, add fluid but do not overfill. See **Table 4** for automatic transaxle fluid for your car. If level is above the top mark, fluid must be drained to restore proper level or seals may be damaged.

Automatic Transaxle Fluid Change

Prior to draining the oil, drive the car for several miles to allow the oil to reach normal operating temperature. Place a drain pan beneath the transaxle. Remove the drain plug (**Figure 16**) and discard the gasket. Allow several minutes for the oil to drain. Install the drain plug with a new washer.

Refer to the instructions for checking the automatic transaxle level and fill the transaxle with the fluid specified in **Table 4**. Automatic transaxle capacity is specified in **Table 6**, but because residual fluid will remain in the transaxle when it is drained, pour in less than the capacity and carefully check the level with the dipstick until the correct level is obtained. Too much fluid in the transaxle will damage it.

Rear Brake Adjustment

The rear brake should be adjusted at the intervals specified in **Tables 1-3**. Refer to Chapter Twelve.

Parking Brake Adjustment

The parking brake should be adjusted so that the rear brakes fully lock when the parking brake lever is pulled as follows:

a. 1973-1978 non-CVCC: 1-5 notches
b. 1979 non-CVCC: 3-7 notches
c. 1975 CVCC: 1-5 notches
d. 1976-1977 CVCC: 1-3 notches (sedan); 3-5 notches (wagon)
e. 1978-on CVCC: 2-3 notches (sedan); 2-5 notches (wagon)

Parking brake adjustment is described in Chapter Twelve.

Front Brake Pad Inspection

The thickness of the disc brake pads and the condition of the brake rotor should be checked at the intervals specified in **Tables 1-3**. These procedures are described in Chapter Twelve.

Brake Fluid

Brake fluid level should be checked at the intervals specified in **Tables 1-3**, as well as any time the pedal can be pushed within a couple of inches of the floor. The level should be maintained between the upper and lower reservoir marks. The fluid should be replaced at the specified intervals.

NOTE
Some Civic models use master cylinders with dual reservoirs. Thus, when checking and maintaining brake fluid on these models, the level should be maintained between the upper and lower reservoir marks in both reservoirs.

If the level is below the lower mark, clean the area around the master cylinder cover and remove it. Add type DOT 3 or DOT 4 brake fluid to bring the level up to the top reservoir mark. Install the cap and check the movement of the pedal. To replace brake fluid, remove the master cylinder cover and use a suction tool to remove as much of the fluid as possible. Then bleed the brake system as described in *Bleeding the Brake System,* Chapter Twelve.

Brake Lines and Hoses

Brake lines and hoses should be routinely checked for signs of deterioration, chafing and kinks each time the brake pad and lining condition is checked. Any line or hose that is less than perfect should be replaced immediately.

Check all connections for tightness and look for signs of leakage which may indicate a cracked or otherwise unserviceable fitting. As with lines and hoses, any connections or fittings that are less than perfect should be replaced immediately. When a line has been replaced or in any situation where a brake line or hose has been disconnected, refer to Chapter Twelve and fill and bleed the system before operating the vehicle.

Clutch Adjustment

The clutch release arm adjustment and the clutch pedal free play should be checked at the specified intervals. These services are discussed in Chapter Eight.

Engine Compartment Check

Every 3,000 to 7,500 miles, check entire engine compartment for leaking or deteriorated oil and fuel lines. Check electrical wiring for breaks in insulation caused by deterioration or chafing. Check the radiator and hose connections for coolant residue rust. Check for loose or missing bolts, nuts and screws. On vehicles with automatic transaxles, check oil cooler lines at radiator and transaxle for leakage.

Rear Wheel Bearing Grease

The bearings in the rear brake hub should be removed, inspected and repacked with new grease. See Chapter Eleven.

3

Exhaust System

Examine mufflers, tailpipes, exhaust header and system fasteners for rust, holes and other damage. Replace any damaged parts. See Chapter Five.

CAUTION
The replacement of damaged exhaust system components is important to prevent the entry of exhaust fumes into the driving compartment. In addition, damaged fasteners which are not replaced can eventually allow exhaust components to fall off the car and become a driving hazard to other drivers.

Fuel Filter

The fuel filter should be replaced at the intervals specified in **Tables 1-3**.

NOTE
If the vehicle is operated for long periods of time in dusty or sandy areas, it may be necessary to change the filter more often. If the engine loses power or "stumbles" at high speed or when accelerating or climbing long hills, the problem may be caused by a clogged fuel filter.

Before removing the filter, first remove the gas tank filler cap to release any pressure in the system.

1973-1979 Non-CVCC models

The fuel filter is located in the engine compartment. To replace the filter, disconnect the filter from the fuel lines (**Figure 17**) and discard. Reverse to install.

1975-1979 CVCC sedan models

The fuel filter is located underneath the rear seat.

1. Remove the rear seat center attaching bolt at the bottom of the seat. Lift the back of the seat up and move aside.
2. Remove the access cover attaching screws and remove the cover.
3. Loosen the filter clamps and remove the filter. See **Figure 18**. Reverse to install.

1976-on CVCC wagon models

Refer to **Figure 19** for this procedure.

1. Raise the vehicle rear end and secure with jackstands.
2. The fuel filter is located near the fuel pump at the rear of the car. Loosen the fuel filter attaching clamps and remove the filter from the fuel line.
3. Installation is the reverse of these steps.

1980-on CVCC sedan models

Refer to **Figure 20** for this procedure.

1. Raise the vehicle rear end and secure with jackstands. Remove the left rear wheel.
2. The fuel filter is located near the fuel pump. Loosen the fuel filter attaching clamps and remove the filter from the fuel line.
3. Installation is the reverse of these steps.

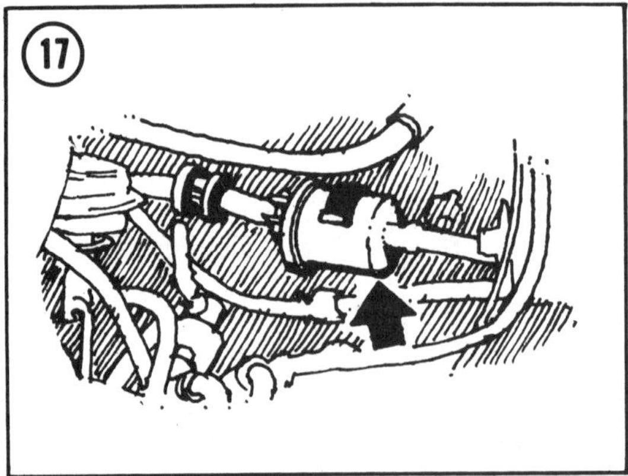

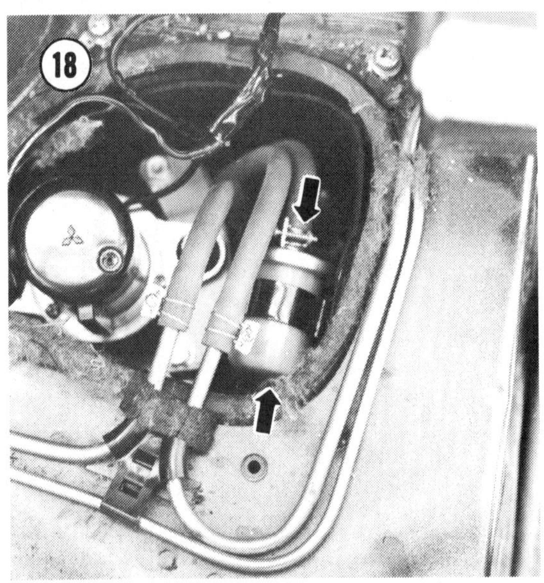

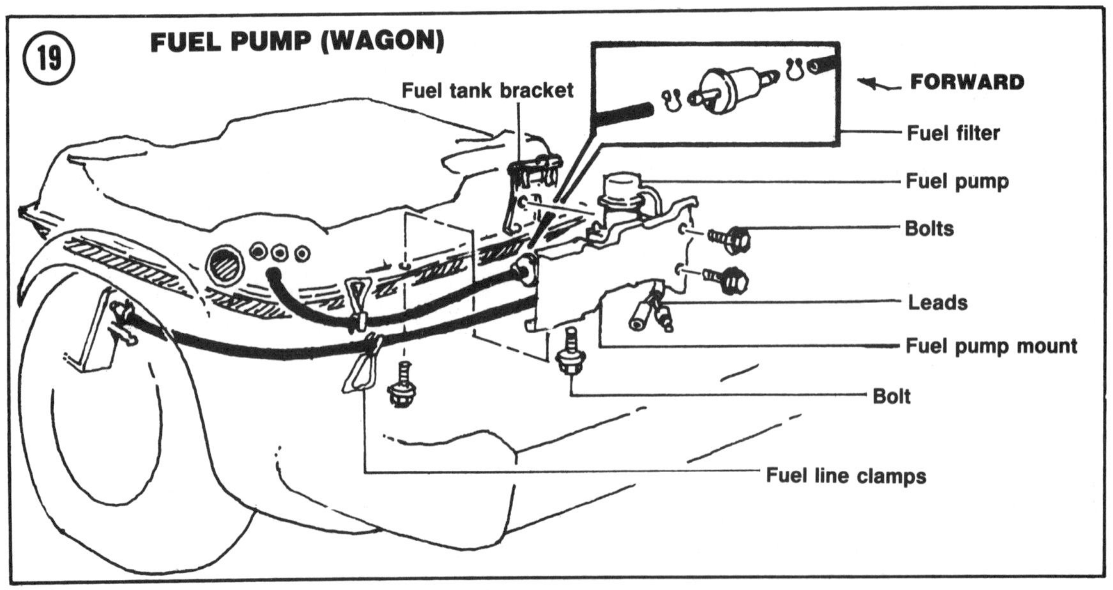

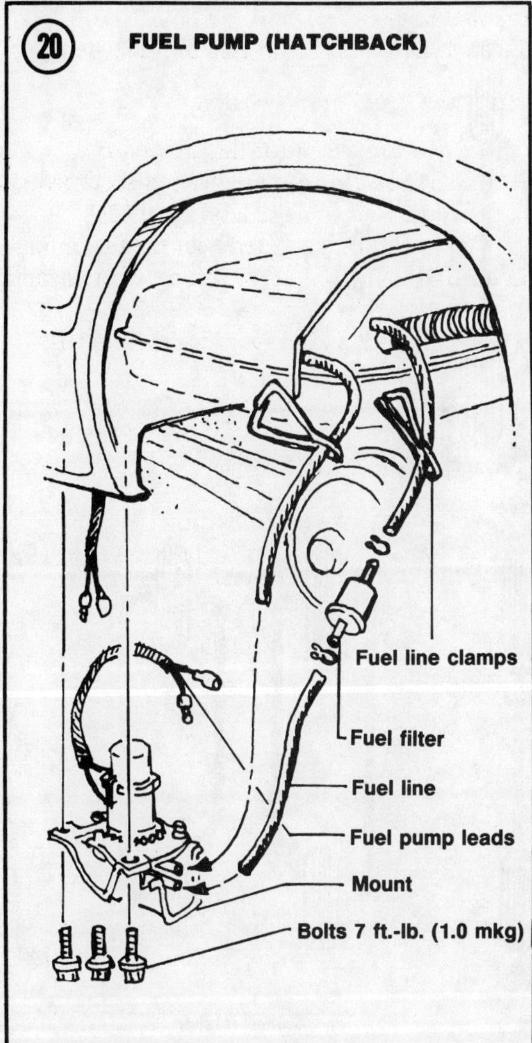

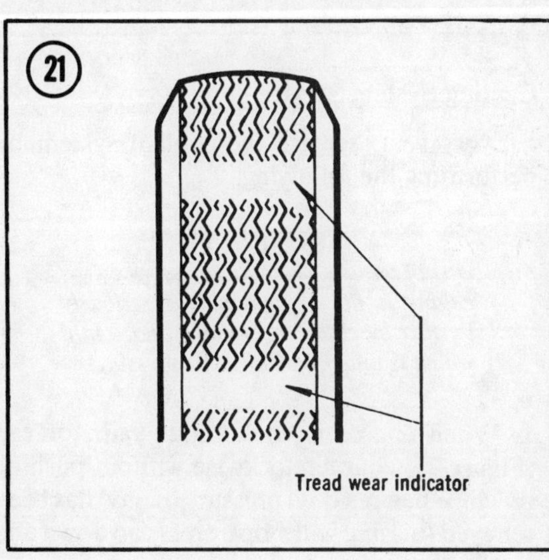

Steering Box and Tie Rods

The steering gear linkage should be checked for proper adjustment. This is described in Chapter Ten.

Tire and Wheel Inspection

Routinely check the condition of all tires. Check local traffic regulations concerning minimum tread depth. Most recommend replacing tires when tread depth is less than 1/32 inch. Original equipment tires have tread wear indicators molded into the bottom of the tread grooves. Tread wear indicators appear as 1/2 inch bands (see **Figure 21**) when tread depth becomes 1/16 inch. Tires should be replaced at this point.

Honda recommends rotating tires initially at 6,000 miles. **Figure 22** shows how this should be done. Inspect front disc brakes as described in Chapter Twelve while the front tires are off for rotation.

Windshield Wiper Blades

Long exposure to weather and road film hardens the rubber wiper blades and destroys their effectiveness. When blades smear or otherwise fail to clean the windshield, they should be replaced.

CAUTION

Whenever it is necessary to test the wiper motor, always wet the windshield first to prevent damage to blades or glass surface.

Drive Belts

The drive belts drive the water pump, alternator and air conditioner compressor. A belt in poor condition or improperly tensioned can cause serious engine cooling and battery charging problems.

At the specified time or mileage, check the belts for wear, fraying or cracking. If any of these conditions exist, replace the belt.

NOTE

Steps 1-4 described replacement of the alternator/water pump drive belt. Replacement of the air conditioning drive belt should be left to a Honda

3

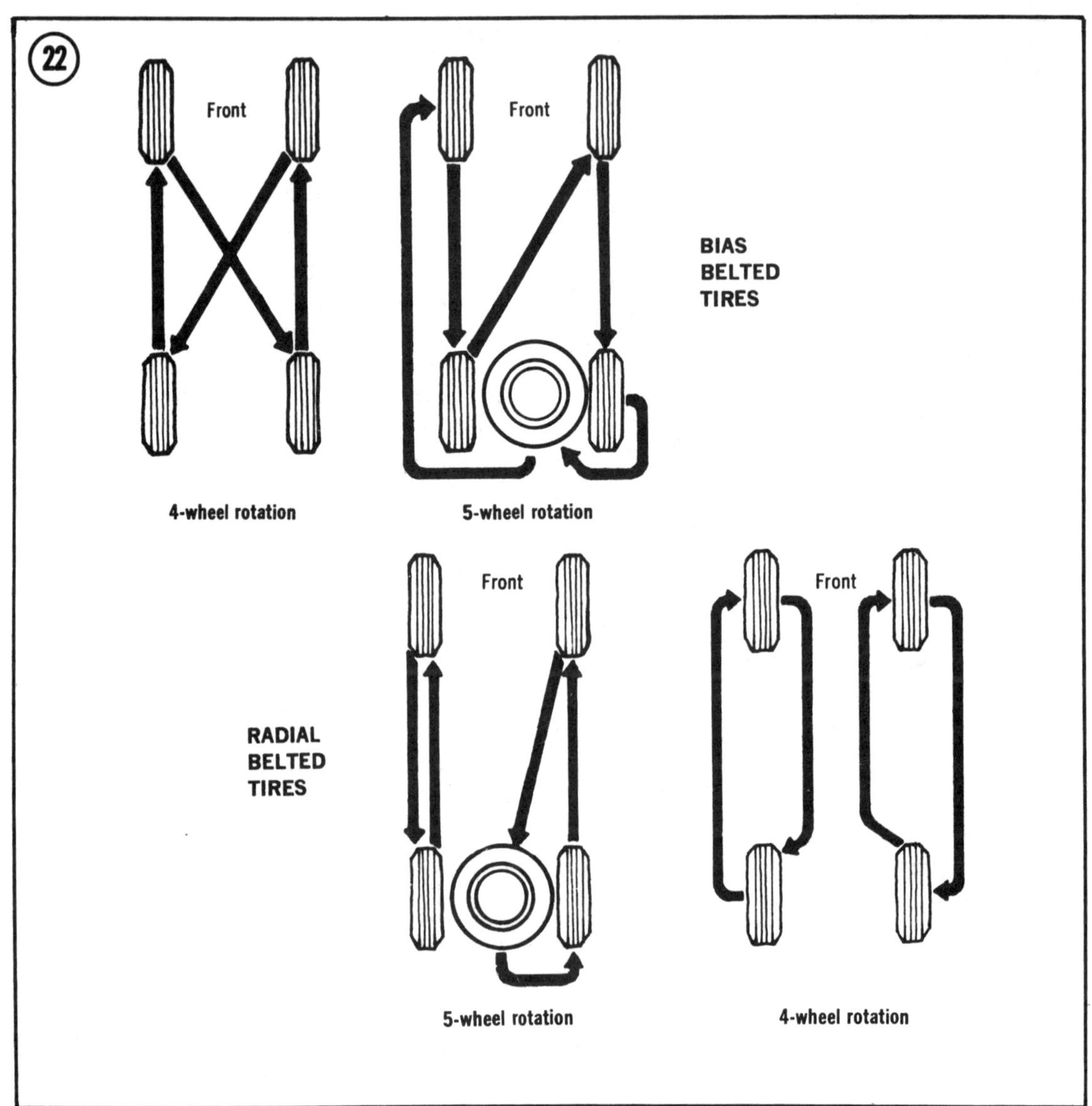

dealer because replacement requires removal of the compressor, its mounting bracket and the top engine mount. Adjustment of the air conditioning drive belt is described in Chapter Six.

1. Loosen the alternator arm and lower mounting bolts (**Figure 23**) and move the alternator as required to loosen the belt.
2. Remove the belt.
3. Install the new belt around the pulleys.
4. Pull up on the alternator to tension the belt. Tighten the adjuster bolts when the belt deflects 12-17 mm (1/2-5/8 in.) under moderate thumb pressure. See **Figure 24**.

Cooling System Service

Every year, service the coolant system by performing the following:

WARNING
Do not remove the radiator cap when the engine is hot. You could be seriously burned by escaping coolant and steam which is under considerable pressure.

1. When engine is cool, rotate radiator cap (**Figure 25**) counterclockwise without pushing down. When residual pressure (if any) has been relieved (hissing will stop), press cap down and

rotate counterclockwise until cap can be removed.
2. Wash radiator cap and filler neck with clean water.

NOTE
Steps 3 and 4 require special equipment available at most service stations or at your dealer.

3. Test freeze protection with an antifreeze hydrometer. System must be protected to at least -34° F (-37° C) to provide corrosion protection, but protection must exceed lowest anticipated temperature in your area.
4. Test system and radiator cap pressure capacity with appropriate testing device. Both must be able to maintain 15 psi.
5. Check condition of hoses. If there are signs of swelling, cracking or other deterioration, replace them. See Chapter Six.
6. Check tightness of hose clamps. Replace questionable clamps with adjustable stainless steel clamps.
7. Clean bugs and dirt from front of radiator core and air conditioner condenser. Direct compressed air from the back of the radiator.

Coolant Change

Initial coolant change should be performed at the intervals specified in **Tables 1-3**.

A mixture of ethylene glycol-based antifreeze and water compounded for aluminum engines protects the cooling system.
1. Remove the radiator cap. See **Figure 25**.

WARNING
Do not remove the radiator cap while the engine and radiator are hot. Scalding fluid and steam may be blown out under pressure and cause serious injury.

2. Drain the cooling system by opening the radiator drain tap.
3. *1981 models*: Remove the coolant drain bolt from the front side of the engine cylinder block and allow heater and engine to drain. See **Figure 26**.
4. Remove the coolant recovery tank from its bracket (**Figure 27**) and pour out the coolant. Reinstall the tank in its bracket.

3

5. Once system is drained, reinstall the radiator drain plug. Reinstall the engine block coolant drain bolt (using a new gasket) on all 1981 models.
6. *1975-1979 CVCC models*: Remove the thermostat as described in Chapter Six. Insert the end of a garden hose into the thermostat opening in the cylinder head. Turn on the water to backflush the engine, heater and radiator. Turn off the water and remove the hose when the water coming out of the upper radiator hose is clean. Install the thermostat and cover, making sure to use a new gasket. See Chapter Six. Remove the radiator cap and radiator drain bolt and drain the system again. Reinstall the radiator drain plug.
7. Be sure all hoses are connected and the radiator and recovery tank caps are removed.
8. Loosen the cooling system bleed valve (**Figure 28A**, non-CVCC; **Figure 28B**, CVCC).
9. Fill the cooling system with a 50/50 mixture of ethylene glycol-based antifreeze and water to the base of the radiator fill neck and add sufficient coolant to the recovery tank to raise fluid level to the "FULL" mark. Continue to add coolant and water until the coolant running out of the bleed valve (**Figure 28**) is free of air bubbles. Close the bleed valve. Install the recovery tank cap.
10. Set the heater temperature control on HIGH and start the engine. Allow it to run until it is thoroughly warmed up, open the bleed valve (**Figure 28**) and bleed the system again. When air bubbles are no longer present in the coolant running out of the bleed valve, close the valve and fill the radiator to the bottom of the filler neck. Install the radiator cap and inspect all cooling system connections for leaks.

NOTE

Even if you live in a climate that does not require this degree of freeze protection, the 50/50 mixture of antifreeze and water will provide a good corrosion inhibitor.

11. Drive vehicle for several miles and recheck coolant level. It takes some time for all the air to be removed from the system. Maintain fluid level between "COLD FULL"

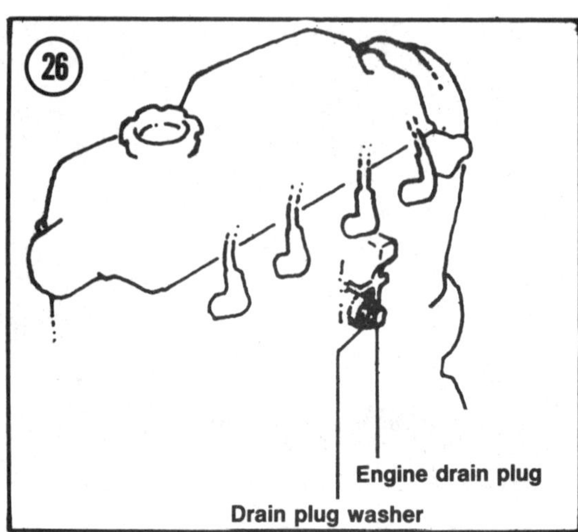

and "HOT FULL" marks on the coolant reservoir (**Figure 27**).

Air Cleaner

Replace the air cleaner element at the specified intervals. If you live in a very dusty area, you may have to change it more often. Check with a local dealer for recommendations.

1. Remove the side clips (if present) and center wing nut securing the air cleaner cover to the housing (**Figure 29** or **Figure 30**).
2. Remove the air cleaner cover from the housing and discard air cleaner element (**Figure 31**). Inspect cover gasket and wipe inside of housing with damp cloth. Replace housing if damaged or cracked.
3. Install new air cleaner element. Install cover and secure with side clips and/or wing nut.

NOTE
*On some models, arrows have been stamped on the air cleaner cover and on the intake tunnel (**Figure 32**). On models so equipped, the arrows should be aligned before the cover clips are secured.*

Vacuum Fittings and Hoses

Check the vacuum fittings and connections to make sure they are tight and inspect the hoses for cracking, kinking or deterioration. Any unsatisfactory hoses should be replaced.

Controlled Spark Advance

The various transmission-controlled and temperature-controlled spark advance systems used in different years affect the performance of the emission control system and should be serviced only by a Honda dealer or an emission specialist.

Crankcase Emission Control

The crankcase emission control system should be inspected and cleaned every 15,000 miles on 1973-1979 models and every 60,000 miles on 1980 and later models.

Fixed orifice service

On all 1973-1977 non-CVCC and 1975-1976 CVCC models, service the fixed orifice as follows:

1. Disconnect the drain tube from the condensation chamber under the air cleaner housing (**Figure 33**).
2. If the tube has a slit end (**Figure 34**), squeeze the end of the tube to open and drain it. If not, remove and invert the tube to drain it.
3. Disconnect the outside hose from the joint at the intake manifold and clean the joint end with the shank end of a 0.035 in. (1973-1977 non-CVCC) or 0.041 in. (1975-1976 CVCC) diameter drill bit. See **Figure 35**.
4. Inspect all hoses for deterioration and replace as necessary. Reconnect all hoses previously disconnected.

On all 1978-1979 non-CVCC and 1977-on CVCC models, service the fixed orifice as follows:

1. Disconnect the condensation chamber-to-joint breather hose. **Figure 36** shows the hose leading to the intake manifold at the joint for 1977-1979 CVCC models; other models are similar. Clean the joint end with the shank end of a drill bit as follows:
   a. 1978-1979 non-CVCC: No. 65 (0.035 in.) drill
   b. 1977-1979 CVCC: No. 59 (0.41 in.) drill
   c. 1980-on CVCC: No. 57 (0.43 in.) drill
2. Inspect all hoses for deterioration and replace as necessary. Reconnect all hoses.

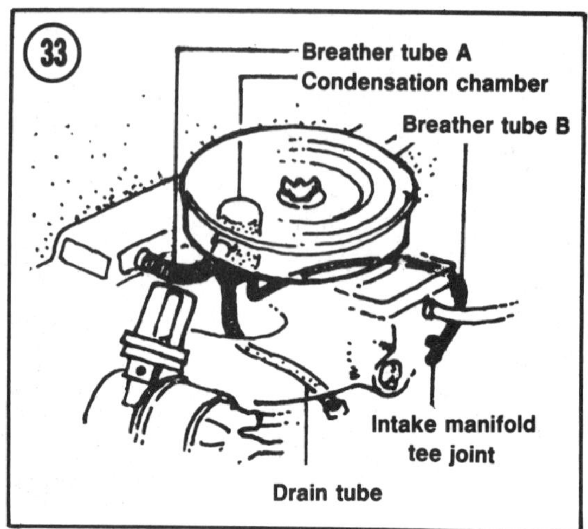

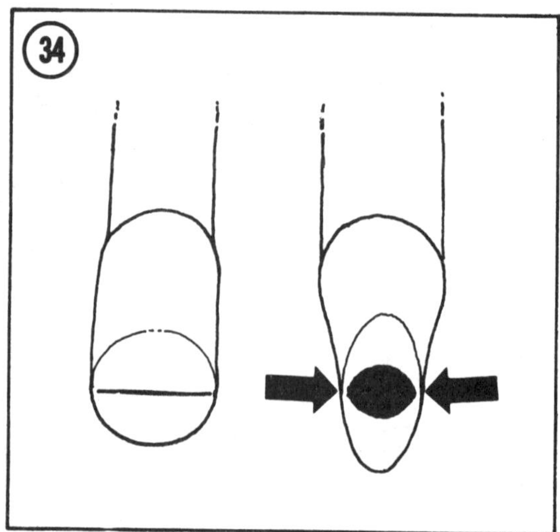

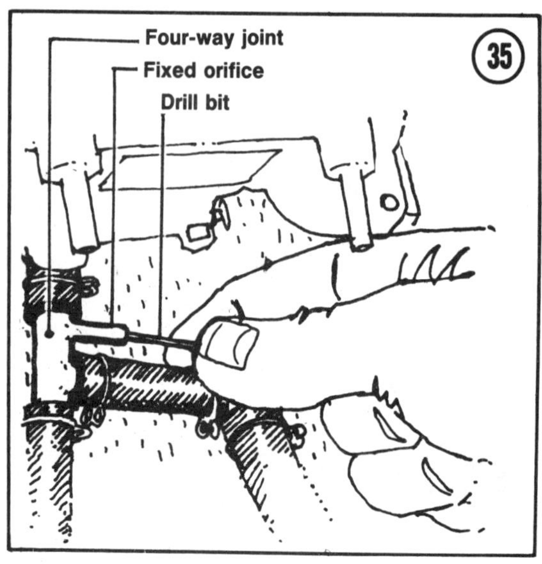

36

Condensation chamber inspection

On all models, the condensation chamber (**Figure 37**) should be inspected and cleaned of all sludge and varnish buildup. To do so, remove the air cleaner. Remove the top rubber gasket and clean the inside of the chamber with contact cleaner (**Figure 38**). Reverse to install, making sure to install the rubber gasket as removed to prevent breather restriction.

Emission Controls

Emission control systems and components which can be inspected by the owner/mechanic are described in Chapter Five. Periodic inspection intervals for emission control components are found in **Tables 1-3**.

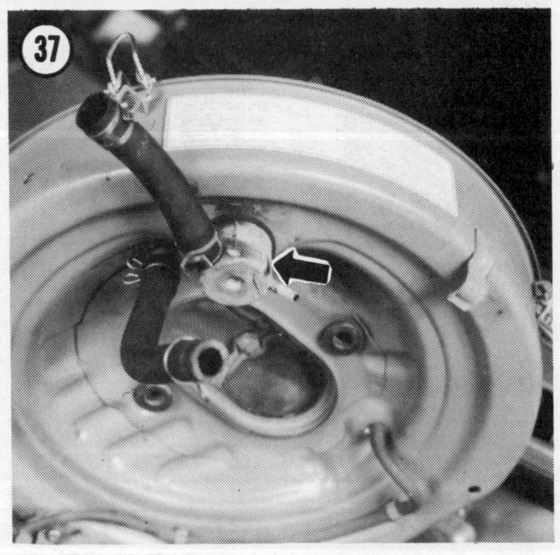

37

ENGINE TUNE-UP

In order to maintain a car in perfect running condition, the engine must receive periodic tune-ups. The procedures presented in this section consist of a series of visual and mechanical checks, using the test equipment described in Chapter One. The procedures outlined here are performed at the intervals specified in **Tables 1-3**. Tune-up specifications applying to your specific car are given on the Vehicle Emission Control Information sticker located on the underside of the hood (**Figure 39**). If the sticker is missing or defaced, use the specifications contained in **Table 7**. Since

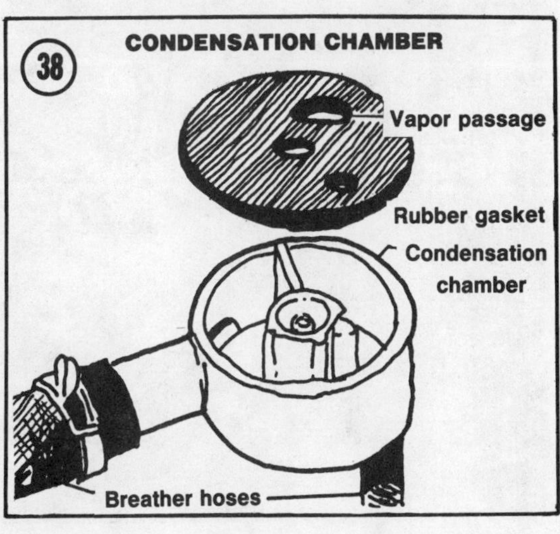

38 CONDENSATION CHAMBER

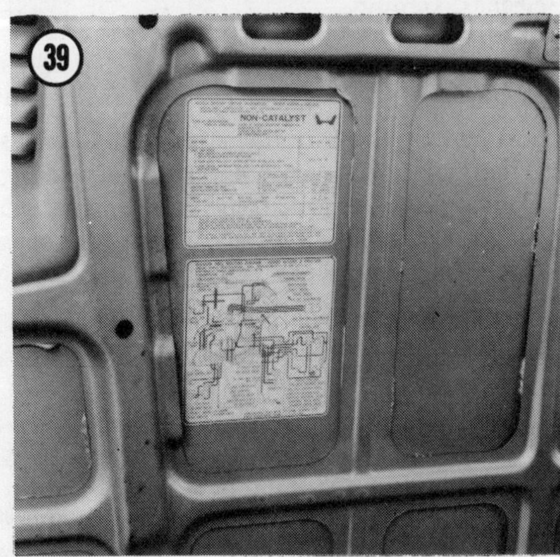

39

different systems in an engine interact to affect overall performance, a tune-up must be accomplished in the following order:

a. Cylinder head bolt torque
b. Compression test
c. Valve adjustment
d. Spark plug replacement
e. Distributor inspection
f. Ignition timing
g. Carburetor adjustment

To perform a tune-up on your vehicle, you will need the following tools and parts:

a. Spark plug wrench
b. Universal joint for socket wrench
c. Socket wrench
d. 12-inch extension for socket
e. Common screwdriver
f. Spark plug gapper tool
g. Compression gauge
h. Ignition timing light
i. Phillips screwdriver
j. Torque wrench

Firing Order

The cylinder firing order for all engines is 1-3-4-2. See **Figure 40** (non-CVCC) or **Figure 41** (CVCC).

CYLINDER HEAD BOLT TORQUE

1. Refer to Chapter Five and remove the air cleaner assembly.

2. Disconnect the breather hose at the valve cover (**Figure 42**).

3. Identify each of the spark plug cables (**Figure 43**) with masking tape, numbering from the left (timing belt) end of the engine. See **Figure 40** or **Figure 41**. Carefully pull the caps off the plugs and route them out of the way.

4. Remove the throttle cable bracket and ground wire from the valve cover (**Figure 44**).

5. Remove the valve cover attaching bolts and remove the valve cover.

6. Tighten the cylinder head bolts in the pattern shown in **Figure 45**. Cylinder head bolt torque specifications are found in **Table 8**.

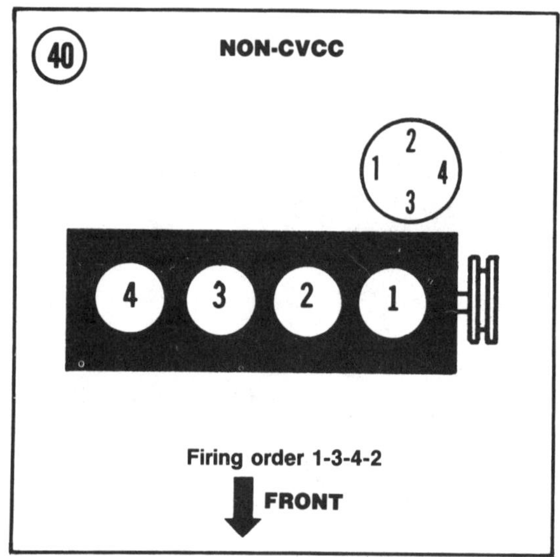

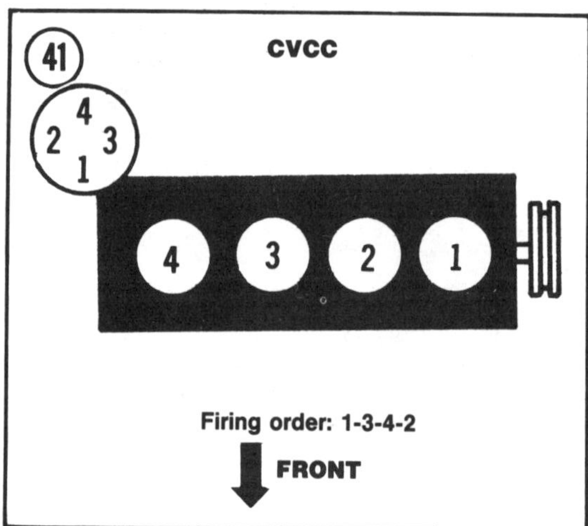

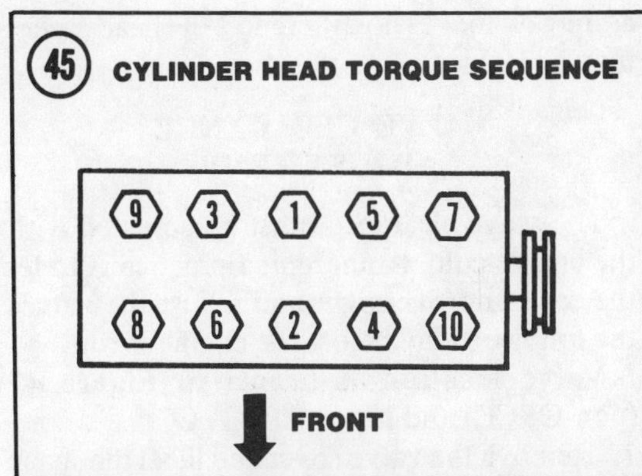

COMPRESSION TEST

A "dry" compression test and a "wet" compression test must be interpreted together to isolate problems in cylinders or valves.

Dry Compression Test

1. Warm the engine to normal operating temperature. Ensure that the choke valve and throttle valve are completely open.
2. Remove the spark plugs as described in this chapter.
3. Connect the compression tester to one cylinder following the tester manufacturer's instructions. See **Figure 46**.
4. Have an assistant crank the engine over until there is no further rise in pressure.
5. Remove the tester and record the reading.
6. Repeat Steps 3 through 5 for each cylinder.

When interpreting the results, actual readings are not as important as the difference between readings. All readings should be between the maximum and minimum readings indicated in **Table 7**. Readings below minimum indicate than an engine overhaul is due. A maximum difference of 28 psi between any 2 cylinders is acceptable. Greater differences indicate worn or broken rings, leaky or sticky valves or a combination of all. Compare with vacuum gauge reading to isolate the trouble more closely.

Wet Compression Test

Add one tablespoon of heavy oil (at least SAE 30) through the spark plug hole of any cylinder which checks low. Repeat the procedure above. If compression increases noticeably, the rings are probably worn. If adding oil produces no change, the low reading may be caused by a broken ring or valve trouble. If 2 adjacent cylinders test low and adding oil makes no difference, the head gasket may be leaking.

VALVE CLEARANCE ADJUSTMENT

The valve clearance must be adjusted with the engine cold. An accepted practice is to let the car stand overnight and adjust the valves the following day before the engine is run.

Valve location is shown in **Figure 47** (non-CVCC) and **Figure 48** (CVCC).

1. Remove the valve cover and label the spark plug wires as described under *Cylinder Head Bolt Torque*, this chapter.
2. Remove the spark plugs as described in this chapter.
3. Refer to the appropriate valve adjustment procedure for your vehicle. Valve adjustment is made by inserting a flat feeler gauge between the stem of the valve being adjusted and the adjusting screw. See **Figure 49**. If clearance is incorrect, loosen the adjuster locknut and turn the adjuster screw in or out (**Figure 50**) until a slight resistance can be felt when the feeler gauge is pulled between the adjuster and the stem. When the clearance is correct (**Table 7**), hold the adjuster screw to keep it from turning further and tighten the locknut. Then recheck the clearance with the feeler gauge to make sure the adjuster hasn't moved.

NOTE
*When turning the crankshaft to align valves in the following procedures, always turn the crankshaft **counter-clockwise**. Use a socket wrench with extension through the access hole in the left fender well.*

Non-CVCC Models (1973-1978)

1. Using a wrench to turn the crankshaft pulley bolt, align the top dead center (TDC) timing mark on the crankshaft pulley with the index mark on the timing belt cover. See **Figure 51**.

NOTE
*Check the position of the valves on the No. 1 cylinder (**Figure 47**). If all valves are closed, the No. 1 piston is at TDC on the compression stroke and you are ready to begin. If not, rotate the crankshaft 360° (one revolution).*

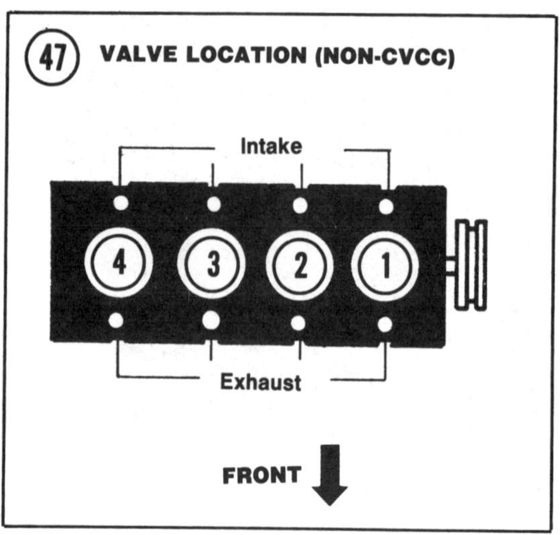

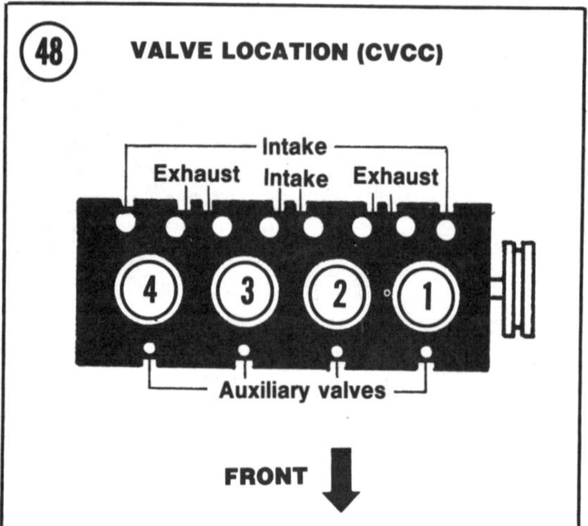

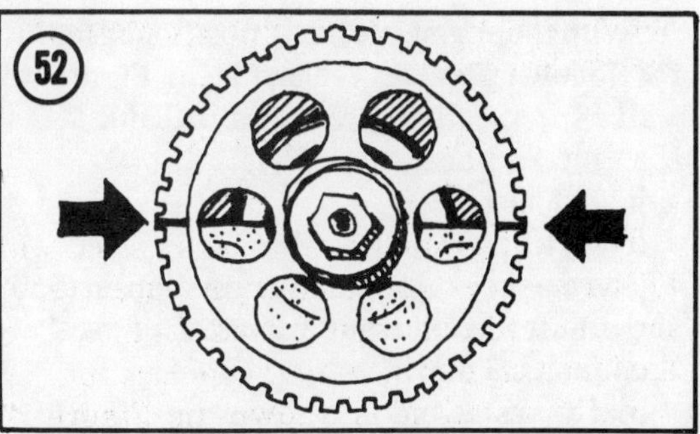

3

2. With the engine correctly positioned, adjust the following valves, referring to **Figure 47**:
   a. Intake 1 and 2
   b. Exhaust 1 and 3

3. Rotate the crankshaft one revolution (360°) and adjust the following valves:
   a. Intake 3 and 4
   b. Exhaust 2 and 4

Non-CVCC Models (1979)

1. Using a wrench to turn the crankshaft pulley bolt, align index marks on the camshaft sprocket with the gasket surface as shown in **Figure 52**.

NOTE

*Check the position of the valves on the No. 1 cylinder (**Figure 47**). If all valves are closed, the No. 1 piston is at TDC on the compression stroke and you are ready to begin. If not, rotate the crankshaft 360° (one revolution).*

2. Referring to **Figure 47**, check the valves as follows:
   a. Check all No. 1 cylinder valves, then rotate crankshaft 180°.
   b. Check all No. 3 cylinder valves, then rotate crankshaft 180°.
   c. Check all No. 4 cylinder valves, then rotate crankshaft 180°.
   d. Check all No. 2 cylinder valves.

CVCC Models (1975-1978)

1. Remove the top timing belt cover screws and remove the cover (**Figure 53**).
2. Using a wrench to turn the crankshaft pulley bolt, align the camshaft sprocket as shown in **Figure 52** (1975) or **Figure 54** (1976-1978). This positions the No. 1 cylinder at TDC.

CAUTION

*Check the position of the valves on the No. 1 cylinder (**Figure 48**). If all valves are closed, the No. 1 piston is at TDC on the compression stroke and you are ready to begin. If not, rotate the crankshaft 360° (one revolution).*

3. With the engine correctly positioned, adjust the following valves, referring to **Figure 48**. Valve specifications are found in **Table 7**.
   a. Intake 1 and 2
   b. Exhaust 1 and 3
   c. Auxiliary 1 and 2
4. Rotate the crankshaft one revolution (360°) and adjust the following valves:
   a. Intake 3 and 4
   b. Exhaust 2 and 4
   c. Auxiliary 3 and 4
5. Install the top timing belt cover. Tighten the screws to 1.0 mkg (7 ft.-lb.).

CVCC Models (1979-on)

Valve position is shown in **Figure 48**.

1. Using a wrench to turn the crankshaft pulley bolt, align mark on camshaft sprocket with mark on upper cover to bring the No. 1 cylinder to TDC. See **Figure 55** for all 1979 models; 1980-on camshaft sprocket alignment is shown in **Figure 56** (1300cc) and **Figure 57** (1500cc).

CAUTION
*Check the position of the valves on the No. 1 cylinder (**Figure 48**). If all valves are closed, the No. 1 piston is at TDC on the compression stroke and you are ready to begin. If not, rotate the crankshaft counterclockwise 360° (one revolution).*

2. With the engine correctly positioned, adjust all No. 1 cylinder valves. Proper clearance is indicated in **Table 7**.
3. Rotate the crankshaft 180° counterclockwise (camshaft will rotate 90°) to bring the No. 3 cylinder to TDC. See **Figure 55**, **Figure 56** or **Figure 57** for correct camshaft sprocket alignment. Adjust all No. 3 cylinder valves.
4. Rotate the crankshaft 180° counterclockwise to bring the No. 4 cylinder to TDC. See **Figure 55**, **Figure 56** or **Figure 57** for correct camshaft sprocket alignment. Adjust all No. 4 cylinder valves.
5. Rotate the crankshaft 180° counterclockwise to bring the No. 2 cylinder to TDC. See **Figure 55**, **Figure 56** or **Figure 57** for correct camshaft sprocket alignment. Adjust all No. 2 cylinder valves.

54

SPARK PLUGS

Removal

1. Blow out any foreign matter from around spark plugs with compressed air.

CAUTION
When spark plugs are removed, dirt around the plug can fall into the spark plug hole. This could cause expensive engine damage.

NOTE
Small cans of compressed, inert gas used to blow off photographic equipment are available at photo supply stores.

2. Mark spark plug wires with cylinder number so that you can reconnect them properly. A small strip of masking tape numbered in sequence works well. See **Figure 40** (non-CVCC) or **Figure 41** (CVCC).
3. Disconnect the spark plug wires. Pull off by grasping the connector, *not* the spark plug wire. If you pull on the wire, it could break.

CAUTION
If the boots seem to be stuck, twist them a half turn by hand to break the seal. Do not pull boots off with pliers. The pliers could cut through the wire material and permit the spark to arc to ground.

4. Remove the spark plugs. Keep plugs in order so that you know which cylinder they came from.

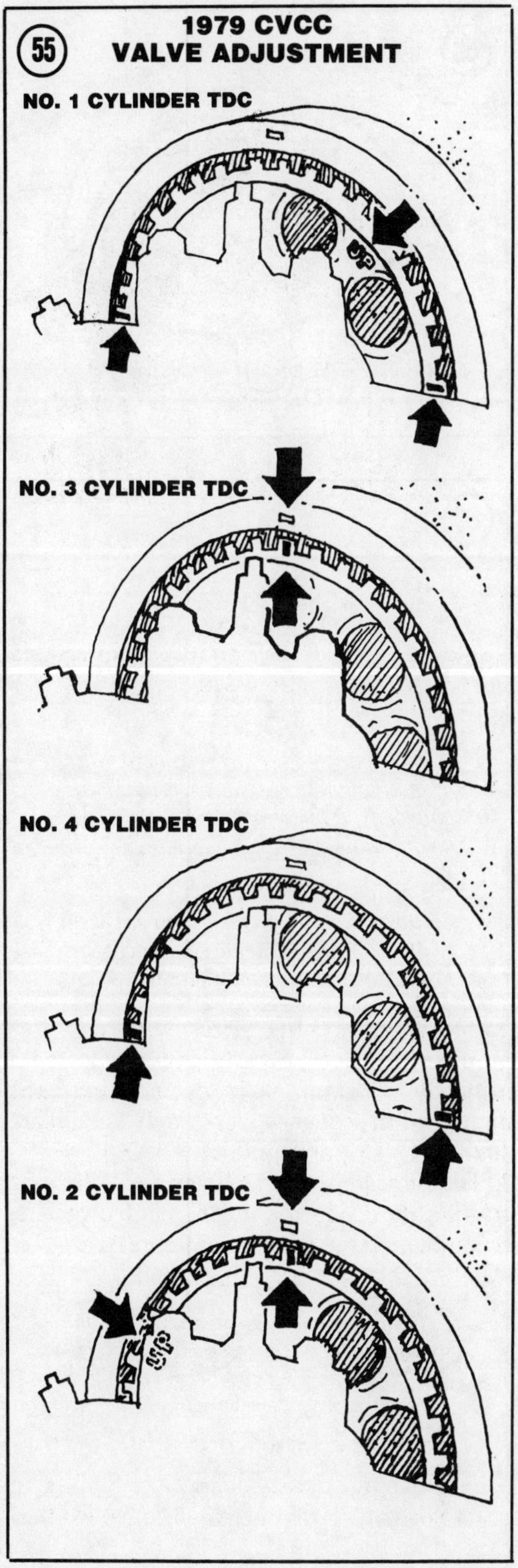

55

1979 CVCC VALVE ADJUSTMENT

NO. 1 CYLINDER TDC

NO. 3 CYLINDER TDC

NO. 4 CYLINDER TDC

NO. 2 CYLINDER TDC

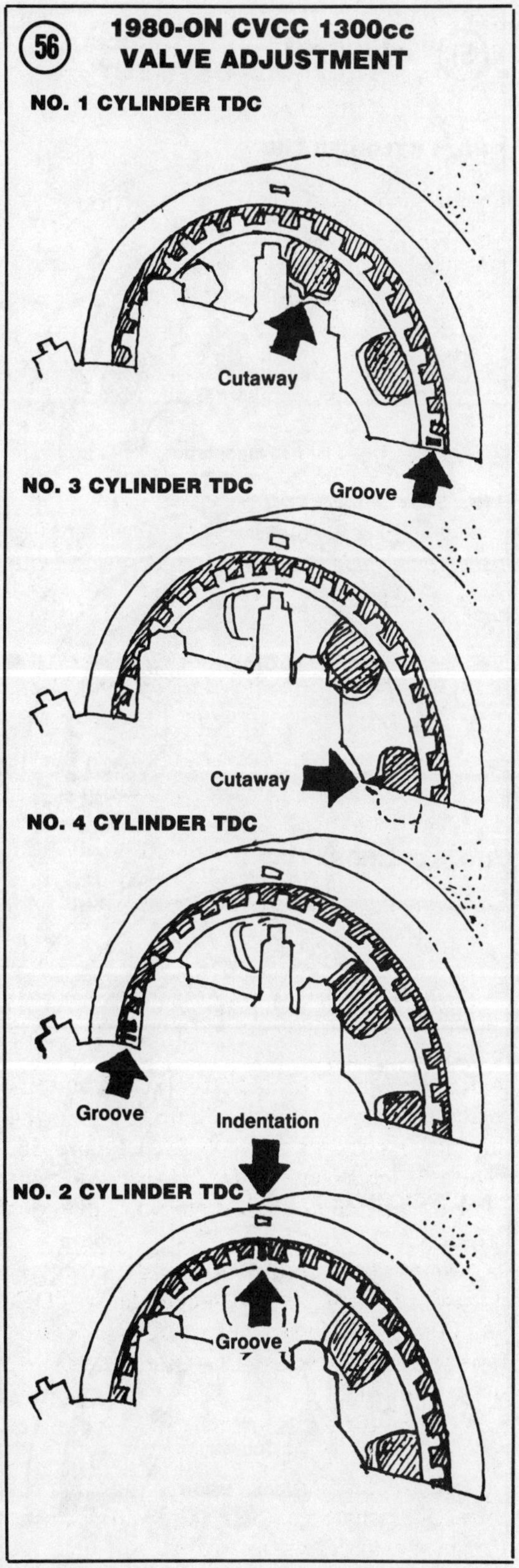

56

1980-ON CVCC 1300cc VALVE ADJUSTMENT

NO. 1 CYLINDER TDC

Cutaway

Groove

NO. 3 CYLINDER TDC

Cutaway

NO. 4 CYLINDER TDC

Groove

Indentation

NO. 2 CYLINDER TDC

Groove

57

1980-ON CVCC 1500cc VALVE ADJUSTMENT

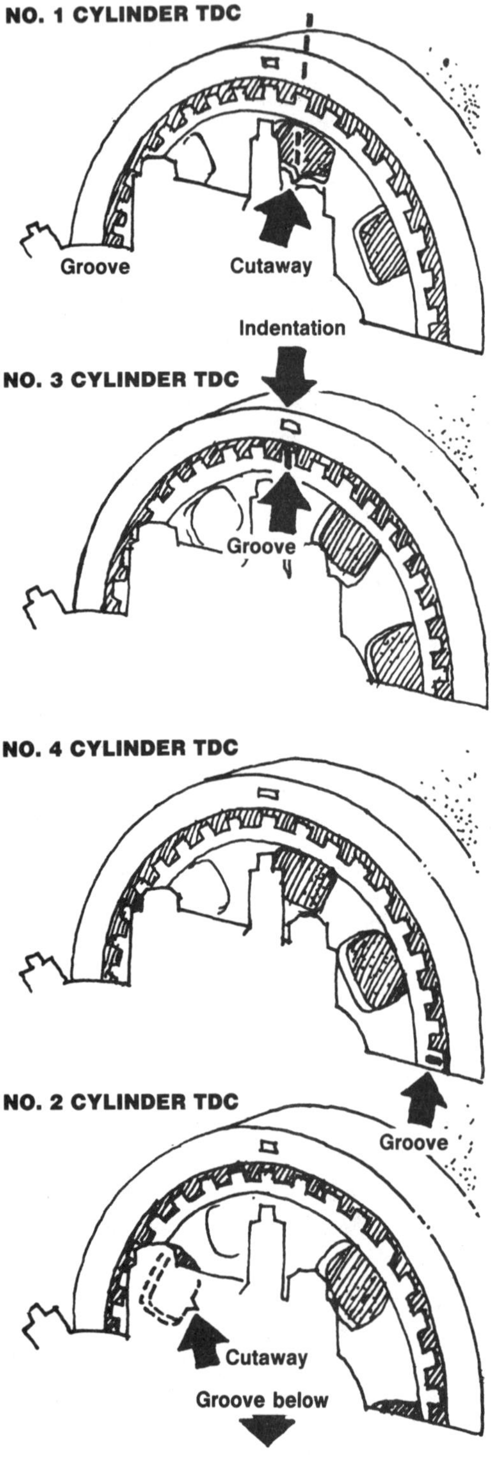

NO. 1 CYLINDER TDC
Groove
Cutaway
Indentation
NO. 3 CYLINDER TDC
Groove
NO. 4 CYLINDER TDC
Groove
NO. 2 CYLINDER TDC
Cutaway
Groove below

58

59

60

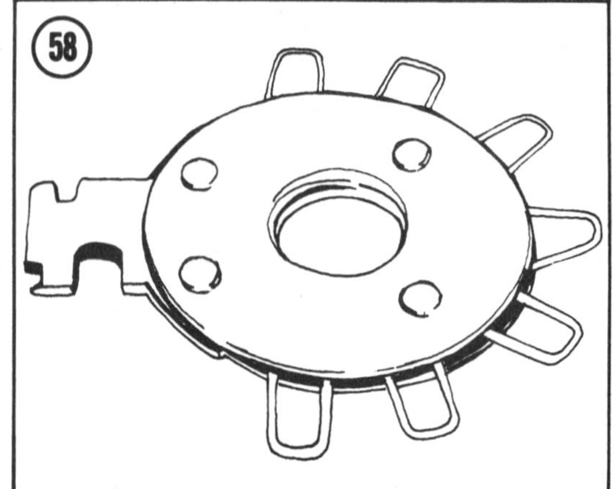

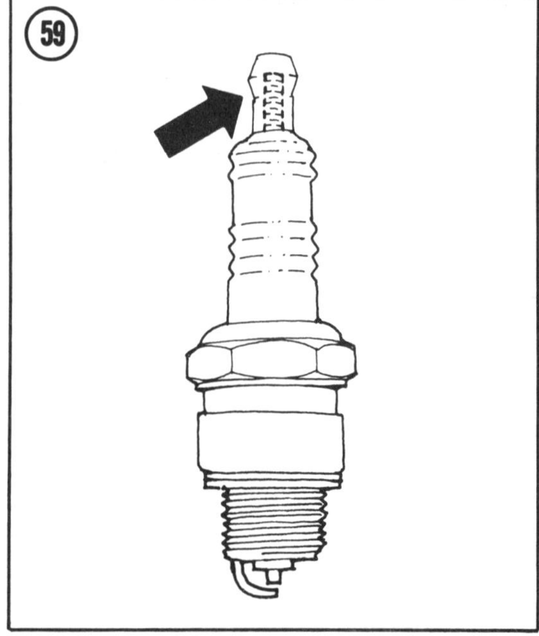

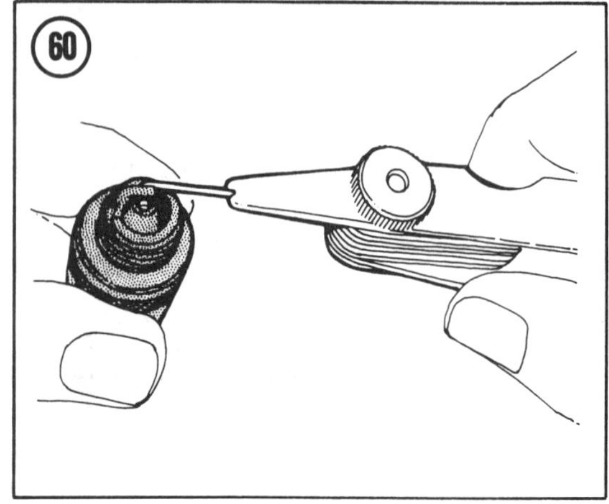

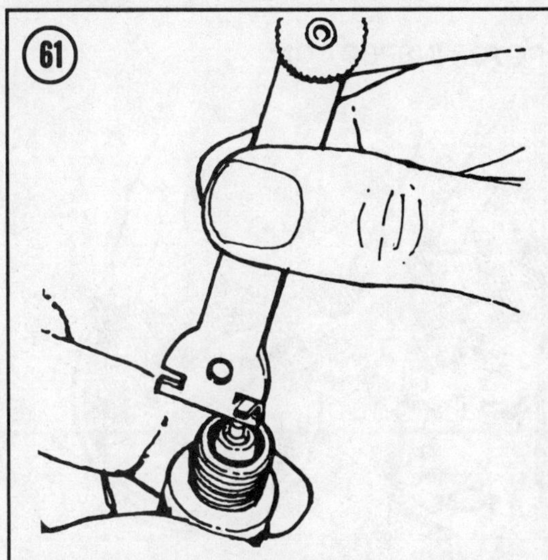

5. Examine each spark plug and compare its condition to the illustrations in Chapter Two. Condition of spark plugs is an indication of engine condition and can warn of developing trouble.
6. Discard the plugs. Although they could be cleaned, gapped, and reused if in good condition, they rarely last very long; new plugs are not very expensive and will be far more reliable.

Gapping and Installing the Plugs

New plugs should be carefully gapped to ensure a reliable, consistent spark. You must use a special spark plug gapping tool with a wire gauge. See **Figure 58**.

1. Remove new plugs from box and screw on the small end pieces that are loose in each box. See **Figure 59**.
2. Refer to **Table 7** and insert the proper size gauge wire between the center and side electrode of each spark plug. See **Figure 60**. If the gap is correct, you will feel a slight drag as you pull the wire through. If there is no drag, or the gauge won't pass through, bend the side electrode *with the gapping tool* (see **Figure 61**) to set the proper gap.
3. Put a *small* drop of oil or aluminum anti-seize compound on the threads of each spark plug.
4. Crank starter for about 5 seconds to blow out any debris around spark plug holes.
5. Screw each spark plug in by hand until it seats. Very little effort is required. If force is necessary, you have the plug cross-threaded; unscrew it and try again.
6. Tighten the spark plugs. If you have a torque wrench, tighten them to 23 N•m (17 ft.-lb.). If you don't have a torque wrench, an additional 1/4 to 1/2 turn after finger-tight is sufficient.

NOTE

Do not overtighten. This prevents the plug from sealing.

7. Install the spark plug wires. Make sure each is connected to the proper spark plug. Refer to **Figure 40** or **Figure 41** for spark plug wire routing.

DISTRIBUTOR

On 1973-1979 models, several different breaker point distributors were used. On all 1980 and later models, a transistorized distributor is used.

Inspection (1973-1979)

Refer to **Figure 62** for this procedure.

1. Spring clamps secure the distributor cap to the distributor housing. To remove the cap, pry back the spring clamps with a screwdriver (**Figure 63**). Do not apply pressure directly to the cap when removing the clamps as the cap may be damaged. Clean the cap carefully to remove grease and dirt.
2. Examine the inside of the cap for dirt and wear. Look for signs of carbon tracks (arcing) from contact to contact inside the distributor cap. If any are found, replace the cap and rotor as a set.
3. Remove rotor and inspect for excessive wear or burning around the top metal contact surface. If defective, replace the rotor and cap as a set. As a matter of good practice, replace the rotor whenever the contact points are replaced.
4. Gently open the contact points with a screwdriver and check their condition. If the points are only slightly pitted or irregular, they are acceptable; if they are badly pitted they must be replaced. If they show wear or pitting, remove the contact point assembly and clean or replace the points. Use a point file to clean

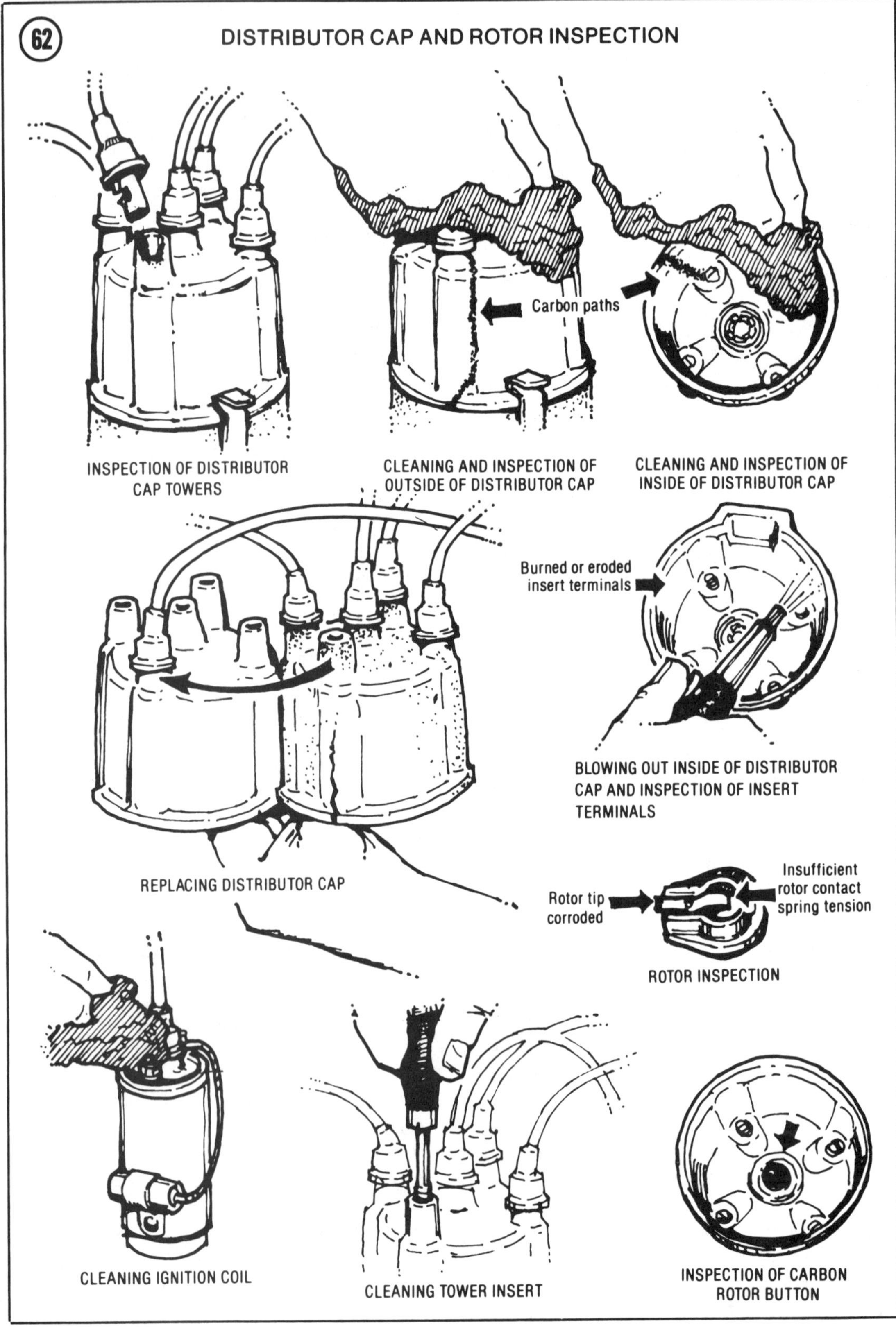
62
DISTRIBUTOR CAP AND ROTOR INSPECTION
Carbon paths
INSPECTION OF DISTRIBUTOR CAP TOWERS
CLEANING AND INSPECTION OF OUTSIDE OF DISTRIBUTOR CAP
CLEANING AND INSPECTION OF INSIDE OF DISTRIBUTOR CAP
Burned or eroded insert terminals
BLOWING OUT INSIDE OF DISTRIBUTOR CAP AND INSPECTION OF INSERT TERMINALS
REPLACING DISTRIBUTOR CAP
Rotor tip corroded
Insufficient rotor contact spring tension
ROTOR INSPECTION
CLEANING IGNITION COIL
CLEANING TOWER INSERT
INSPECTION OF CARBON ROTOR BUTTON

contacts. Do not attempt to remove all roughness. See **Figure 64**.

5. To remove the points, note the position of the ground lead connector and unscrew the contact breaker mounting screws (**Figure 65**). Remove the contact breaker assembly (and internal condenser, if so equipped) and disconnect the lead from the moveable contact.

6. On distributors with external condensers, loosen the screw in the condenser contact block and disconnect the condenser lead. Unscrew the condenser mounting screw and remove the condenser (**Figure 66**).

7. Check the movement of the centrifugal advance mechanism by carefully turning the contact breaker cam by hand and releasing it. It should snap back against spring tension. If it does not, have the distributor serviced by a Honda dealership or competent automotive electrical repair shop.

8. Wipe the cam and breaker plate clean. Lightly coat the contact breaker cam with special distributor cam grease. Never use oil or common grease; they will break down under high temperatures and frictional loads and are likely to find their way onto the contacts.

9. Install the new contact breaker assembly and condenser by reversing the removal steps. Make certain the ground wire and condenser-to-contact wire are installed exactly as they were before and double check the connections and screws to ensure that they are tight.

10. Rotate the crankshaft using a wrench on the pulley nut until the contacts are at their maximum opening. Check the gap with a feeler gauge and compare to the specifications in **Table 7**. See **Figure 67**. To adjust the contact gap, loosen the retaining screws. Then loosen the adjuster screw and turn to increase or decrease the gap as necessary (**Figure 67**). Tighten the retaining screws.

11. If a dwell meter is available, connect it in accordance with the manufacturer's instructions. Ground the ignition coil secondary wire (**Figure 68**) and turn the engine over with the starter. Check the point dwell angle. It should be 52 +/-3°. Correct dwell setting can be obtained by turning the adjustment screw shown in **Figure 67**.

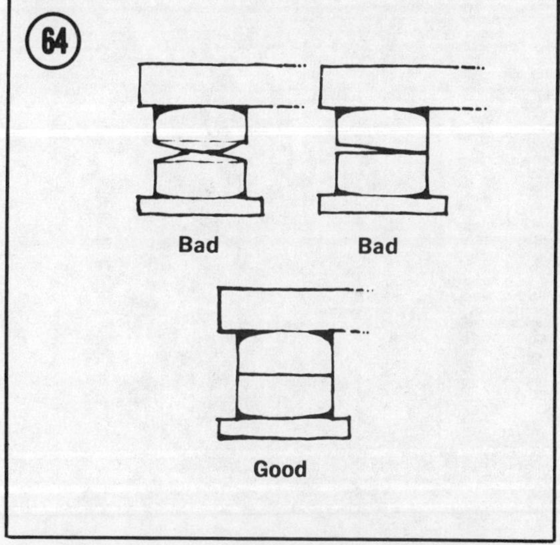

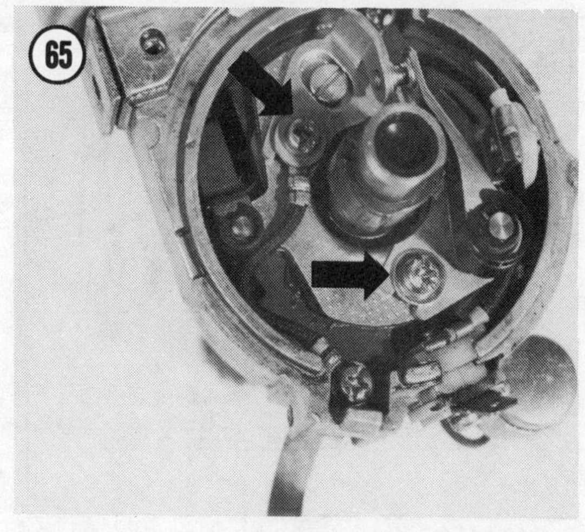

3

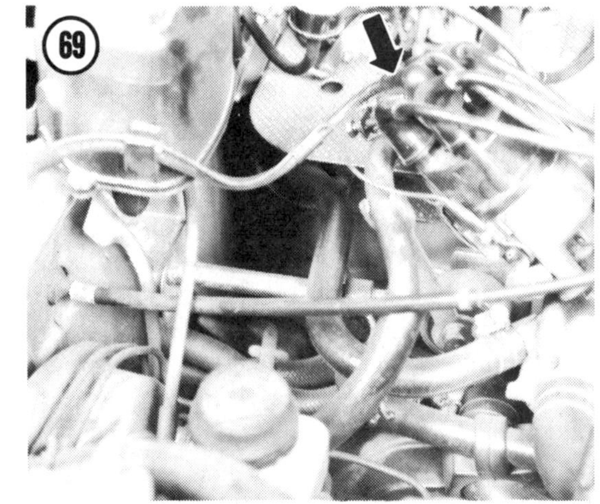

NON-CATALYST

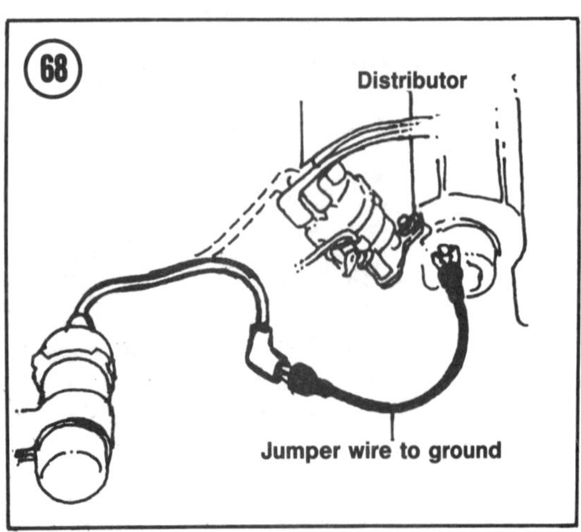
Distributor
Jumper wire to ground

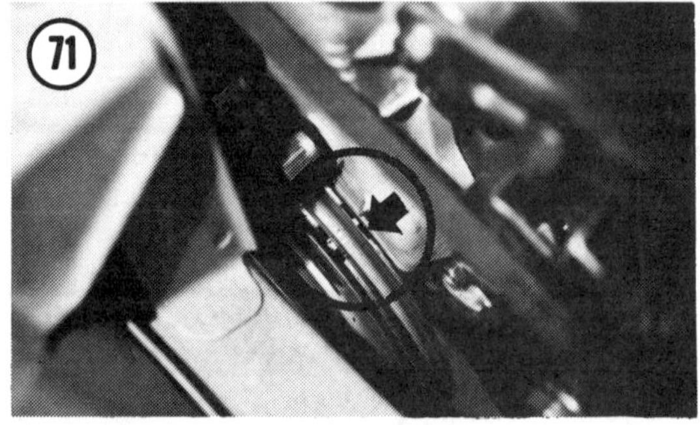

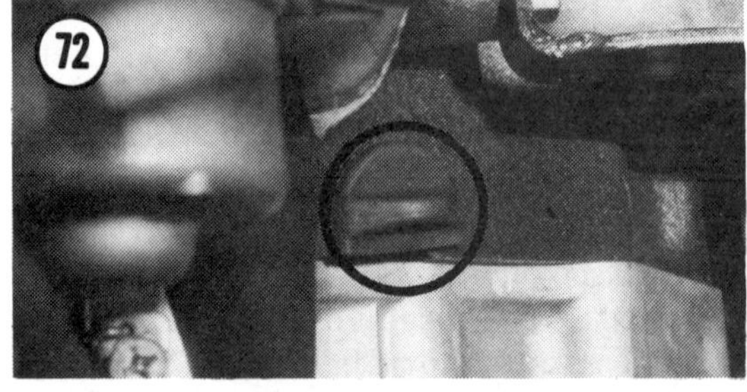

73

74

NOTE
Dwell adjustment automatically sets point gap.

12. Inspect the insulation on all wires leading to or within the distributor. Replace wires if defective.
13. Install the rotor and distributor cap. Connect the secondary wire between the distributor and the ignition coil (**Figure 69**). Connect the spark plug and coil high-tension leads at the distributor.

Inspection (1980-on)

Inspection procedures for transistorized distributors are the same as for 1973-1979 models. Ignore all references to contact breaker points.

IGNITION TIMING

The distributor must be aligned to fire each plug at precisely the right moment. The emission control sticker under the hood specifies this time for different combinations of engine and optional equipment and for different original point of sale. See **Figure 70**. Due to varying state and Federal regulations, your sticker may differ from the one shown. Always use the specifications on the sticker on your own car. If the emission sticker is defaced or unreadable, use the tune-up specifications in **Table 7**.

Ignition timing marks for non-CVCC engines are located on the crankshaft pulley, with a pointer fixed to the lower front cover. These are visible from the left side of the engine (**Figure 71**). On all CVCC engines, ignition timing marks are visible through an inspection cover on the flywheel housing at the front of the engine. To view the marks on the CVCC engine, remove the rubber plug (**Figure 72**); timing marks are found on either the flywheel (manual) or on the drive plate (automatic). The pointer is fixed to the rear of the engine block.

1. On all 1973-1974 non-CVCC engines, disconnect and plug the 2 vacuum lines at the distributor (**Figure 73** shows one of the 2 vacuum lines). On all 1975 and later non-CVCC engines, turn on the headlights when adjusting the ignition timing. On all CVCC engines, leave the distributor vacuum lines connected during timing adjustment (**Figure 74**).
2. Connect timing light according to the manufacturer's instructions.

NOTE
***Figure 75** shows typical connections if you have no instructions. Refer to **Figure 76** or **Figure 77** for the No. 1 cylinder spark plug location.*

3. On non-CVCC engines, clean the timing marks (**Figure 71**) to make the marks clearly visible. On CVCC engines, remove the rubber timing mark plug from the engine (**Figure 72**).
4. Make sure the timing light wires are out of the way of the drive belts, then start the engine.
5. Refer to the emission control sticker (**Figure 70** or **Table 7**) and set the idle speed to the correct speed for ignition timing as described in this chapter.
6. Pull the trigger on the timing light and point it at the timing scale. The timing mark will

75
Spark plug No. 1
(in firing order)
+

76
NON-CVCC
2
1
4
3
4
3
2
1
Firing order 1-3-4-2
FRONT

77
CVCC
4
2
3
1
4
3
2
1
Firing order 1-3-4-2
FRONT

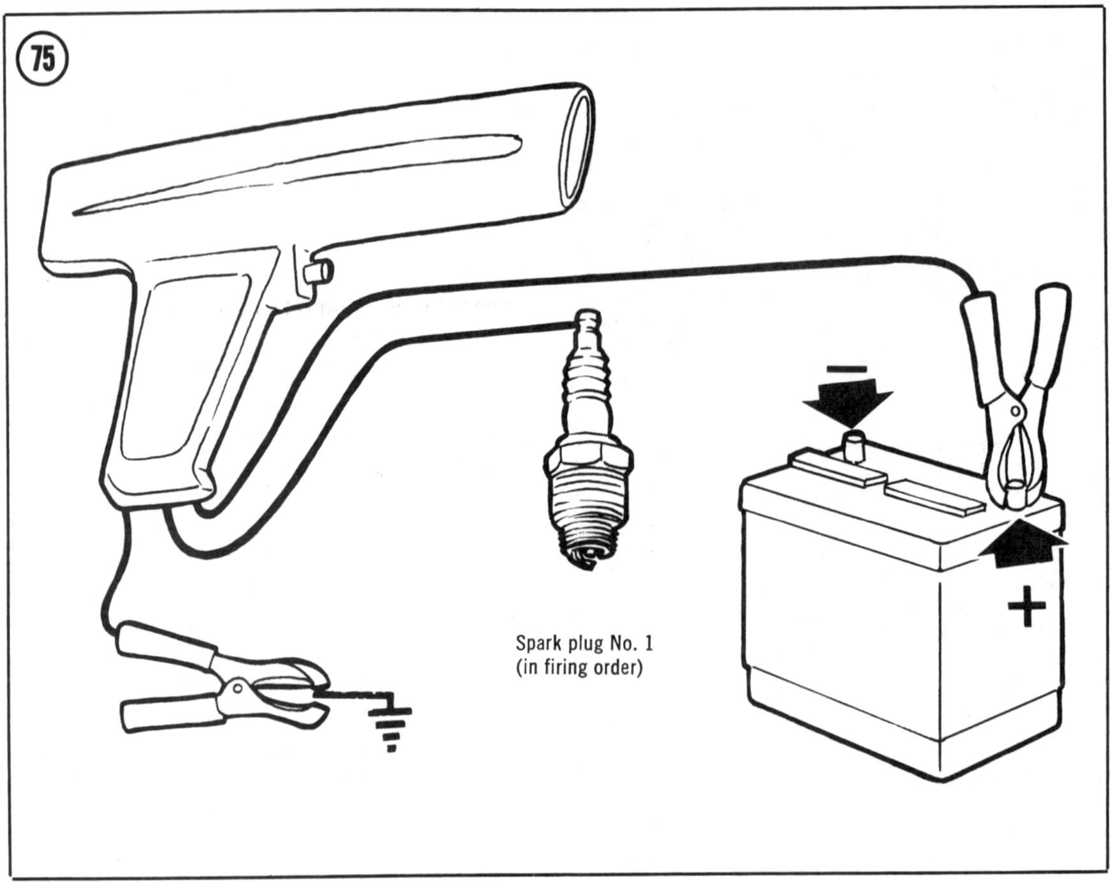

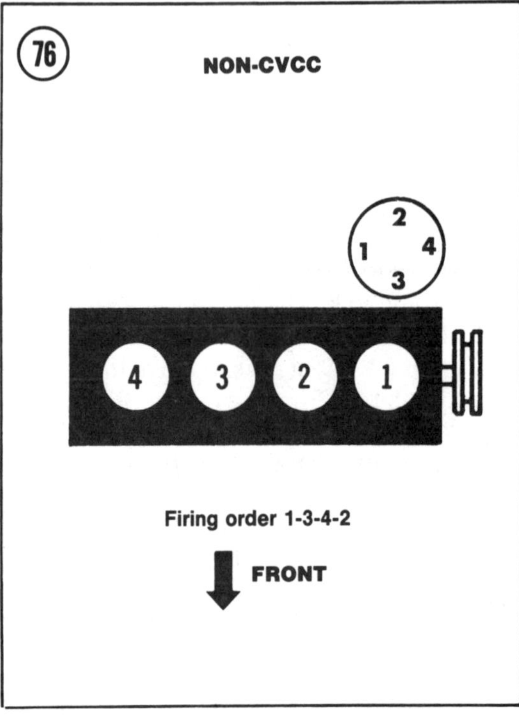

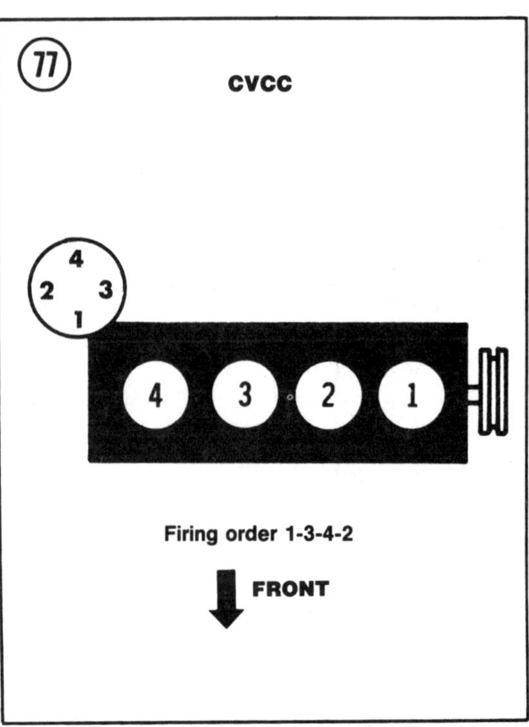

appear to stand still (it may waver occasionally) opposite the pointer. See **Figure 78** (non-CVCC), **Figure 79** (1975-1979 CVCC), **Figure 80** (1980 CVCC), or **Figure 81** (1981 CVCC) for timing marks. If it aligns with the timing mark indicated on your emission control sticker, the timing is correct—no adjustment is necessary. If not, adjust as described in the next step.

78 NON-CVCC TIMING MARKS

FRONT
TDC
Timing mark

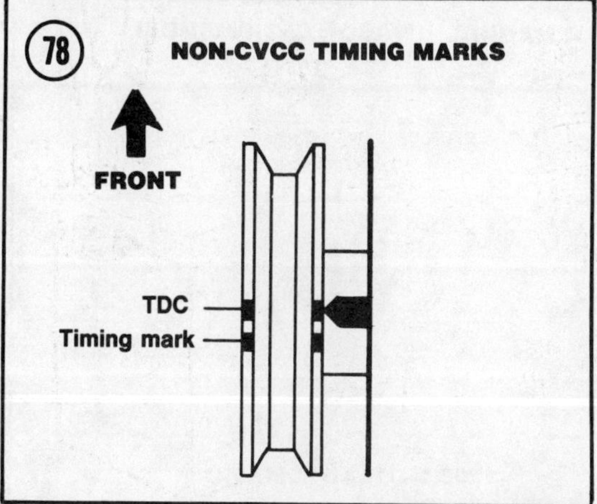

7. If adjustment is required, turn off the engine and loosen the distributor hold-down clamp (A, **Figure 82**). Start the engine, point the timing light at the scale and slowly rotate the distributor body until the notch aligns with the proper timing mark. Turn the distributor clockwise to advance the timing or counterclockwise to retard the timing. Stop the engine and tighten the distributor locknut. Repeat Steps 5 and 6 to make sure adjustment has not changed.

NOTE
If the ignition timing cannot be adjusted to the correct specification by loosening the top distributor clamp bolt (A, ***Figure 82****) loosen the bottom distributor clamp bolt (B,* ***Figure 82****) for additional adjustment.*

8. Turn engine off.
9. Disconnect the timing light and tachometer. On 1973-1974 non-CVCC models, reconnect the distributor vacuum lines. On 1975 and later non-CVCC models,

3

79 1975-1979 CVCC TIMING MARKS

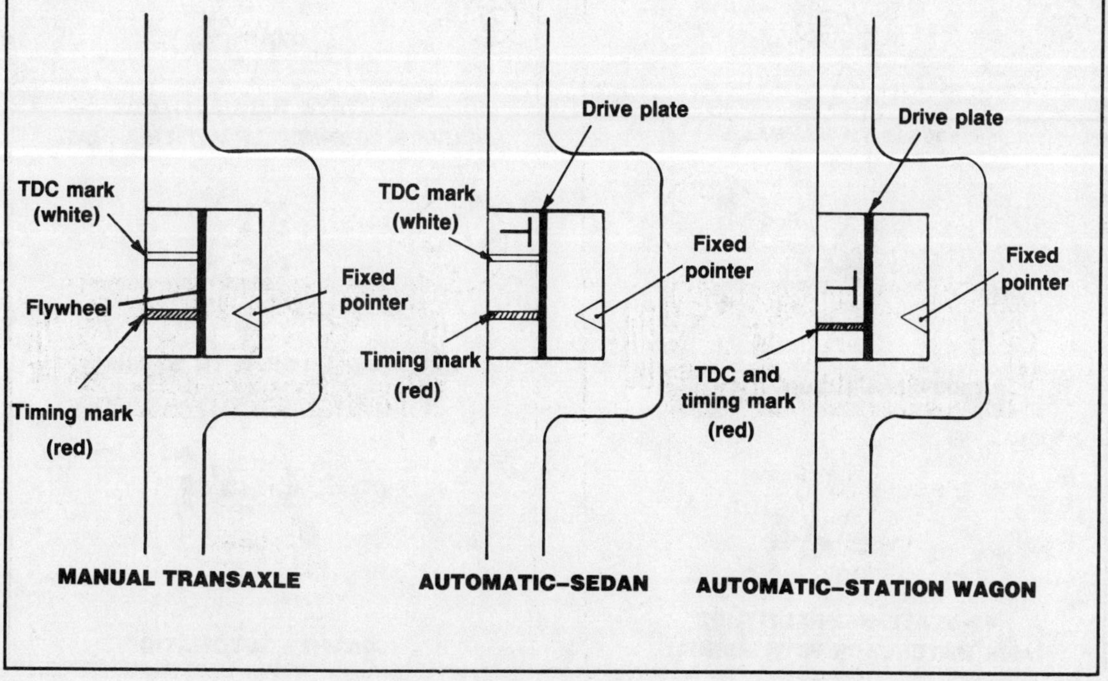

TDC mark (white)
Flywheel
Timing mark (red)
Fixed pointer
MANUAL TRANSAXLE
Drive plate
TDC mark (white)
Timing mark (red)
Fixed pointer
AUTOMATIC–SEDAN
Drive plate
Fixed pointer
TDC and timing mark (red)
AUTOMATIC–STATION WAGON

80

1980 CVCC TIMING MARKS

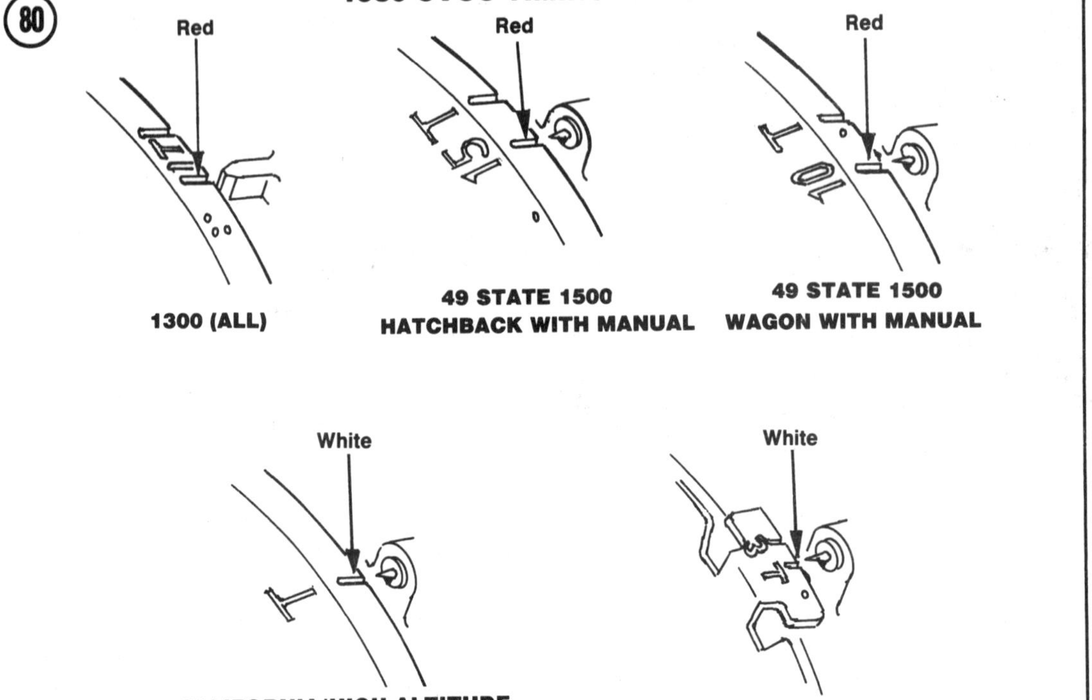

Red

1300 (ALL)

Red

49 STATE 1500
HATCHBACK WITH MANUAL

Red

49 STATE 1500
WAGON WITH MANUAL

White

CALIFORNIA/HIGH-ALTITUDE
1500 WITH MANUAL

White

1500 WITH AUTOMATIC

81

1981 CVCC TIMING MARKS

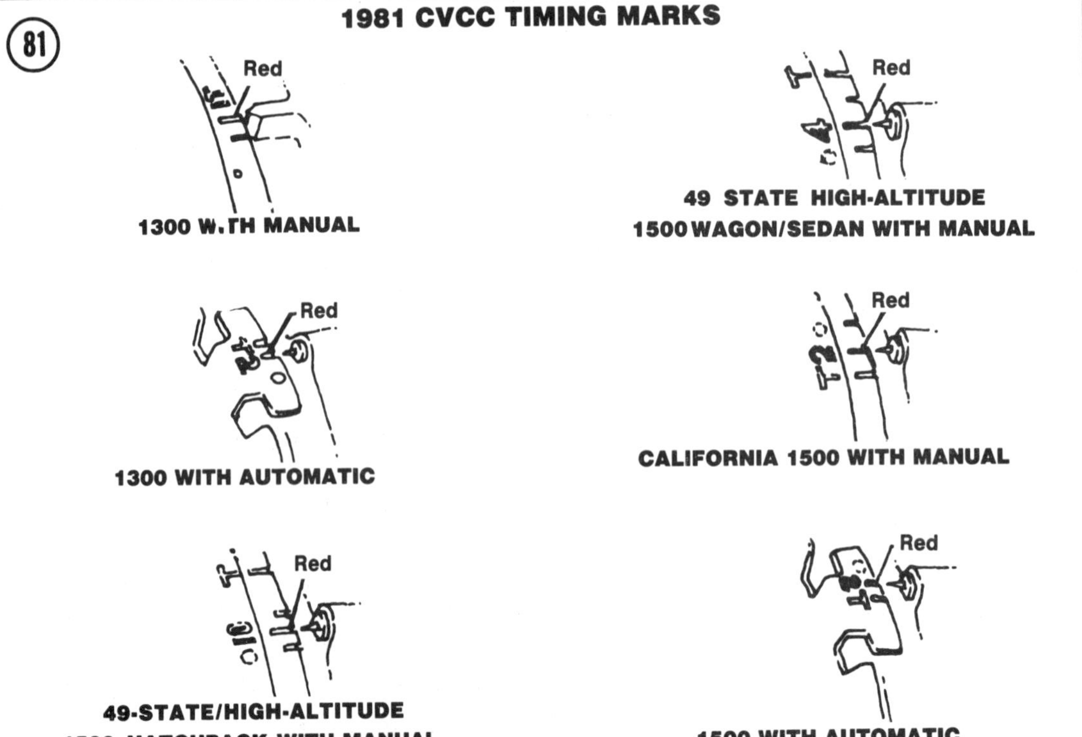

Red

1300 WITH MANUAL

Red

49 STATE HIGH-ALTITUDE
1500 WAGON/SEDAN WITH MANUAL

Red

1300 WITH AUTOMATIC

Red

CALIFORNIA 1500 WITH MANUAL

Red

49-STATE/HIGH-ALTITUDE
1500 HATCHBACK WITH MANUAL

Red

1500 WITH AUTOMATIC

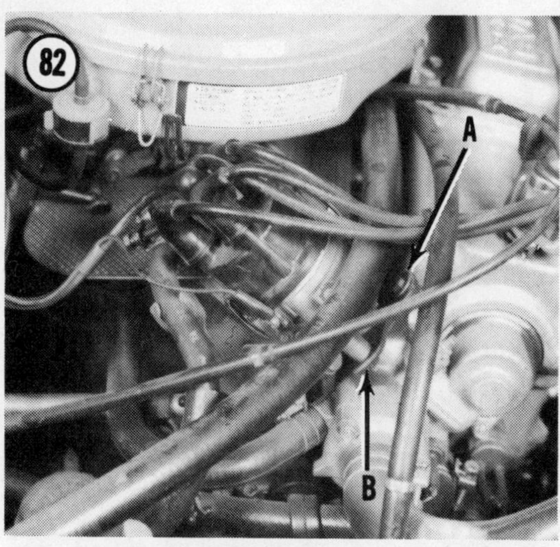

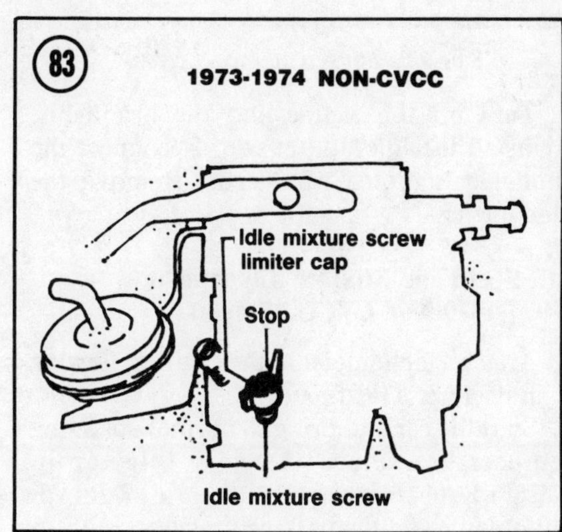

turn off the headlights. On CVCC models, install the timing mark plug (**Figure 72**).

CARBURETOR ADJUSTMENTS

Carburetor adjustments are limited to setting the idle speed and the idle mixture to the values stated on the emission control sticker (**Figure 70** or **Table 7**).

Idle Speed and Mixture Adjustment (1973-1976 Non-CVCC Models)

The engine must be at normal operating temperature before starting this procedure.

1. Attach a tachometer to the engine following manufacturer's instructions.
2. Start the car and bring to normal operating temperature. Disconnect the cooling fan motor wire leads at the fan motor. Place the gear selector in NEUTRAL (manual) or in DRIVE (automatic). Set the parking brake.

WARNING
On automatic transaxle cars, make sure to block the wheels to prevent the car from creeping forward during this procedure.

3. Turn on the headlights.

NOTE
Steps 4-6 pertain to 1973 models. Adjustment procedures for 1974-1976 models are described in Steps 7 and 8.

4. Turn the idle speed screw to obtain the best idle at 800 rpm (manual) or 750 rpm (automatic).
5. Referring to **Figure 83**, remove the idle mixture limiter cap. Then turn the mixture screw counterclockwise until the engine speed drops.
6. Turn the idle mixture screw clockwise until the engine reaches its highest speed.

NOTE
If the speed exceeds 800 rpm (manual) or 750 rpm (automatic) while turning the mixture screw, repeat Steps 4 and 5.

Continue to turn the idle mixture screw clockwise until the engine idle speed drops by 40 rpm (manual) or 20 rpm (automatic).

NOTE
Steps 7 and 8 describe 1974-1976 adjustment procedures.

7. Referring to **Figure 84**, remove the idle mixture limiting cap, turn the idle speed screw and the idle mixture adjusting screw counterclockwise to obtain the best idle at 870 rpm (manual) or 770 rpm (automatic).
8. Turn the idle mixture screw clockwise until the idle drops to 800 rpm (manual) or 750 rpm (automatic).

NOTE
Step 9 pertains to all model years.

9. Turn off the engine and the headlights. Reinstall the idle limiter cap. Reconnect the cooling fan motor wire leads. Remove the tachometer.

Idle Speed and Mixture Adjustment (1977-1979 Non-CVCC Models)

1. Attach a tachometer to the engine following manufacturer's instructions.
2. Start the car and bring to normal operating temperature. Place the gear selector in NEUTRAL (manual) or in DRIVE (automatic). Set the parking brake.

WARNING
On automatic transaxle cars, make sure to block the wheels to prevent the car from creeping forward during this procedure.

3. Turn on the headlights. Then, make sure the cooling fan is on. If not, turn the heater fan to HIGH.

NOTE
If the cooling fan comes on while performing this adjustment, turn off the heater fan.

4. Remove the idle limiter cap (**Figure 85**).
5. Turn the idle speed screw and the idle mixture adjusting screw counterclockwise to obtain the best idle at the following specifications:
   a. 1977 models: 850 rpm (manual) or 800 rpm (automatic)
   b. 1978 and 1979 models: 800 rpm (manual) or 750 rpm (automatic)
6. Turn the idle mixture screw clockwise until the idle drops to 750 rpm (1977) or 700 rpm (1978-1979).
7. Turn off the engine and headlights. Reinstall the idle limiter cap. Remove the tachometer.

Idle Speed and Mixture Adjustment (1975-1979 CVCC Models)

1. Block the vehicle's front and rear wheels and set the parking brake. Start the engine and

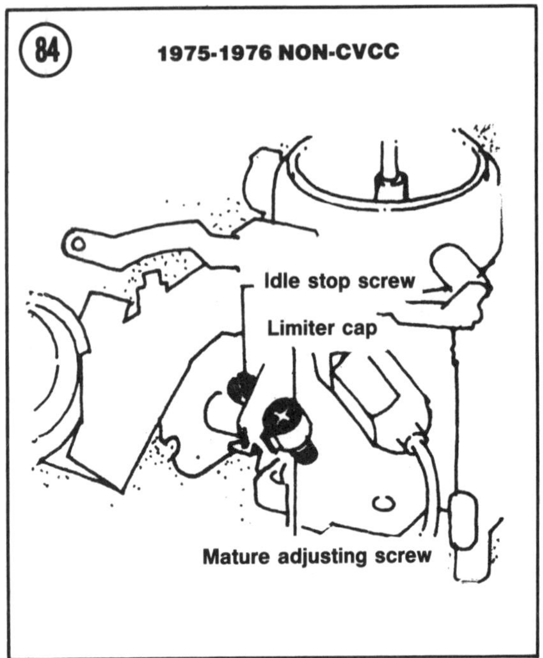

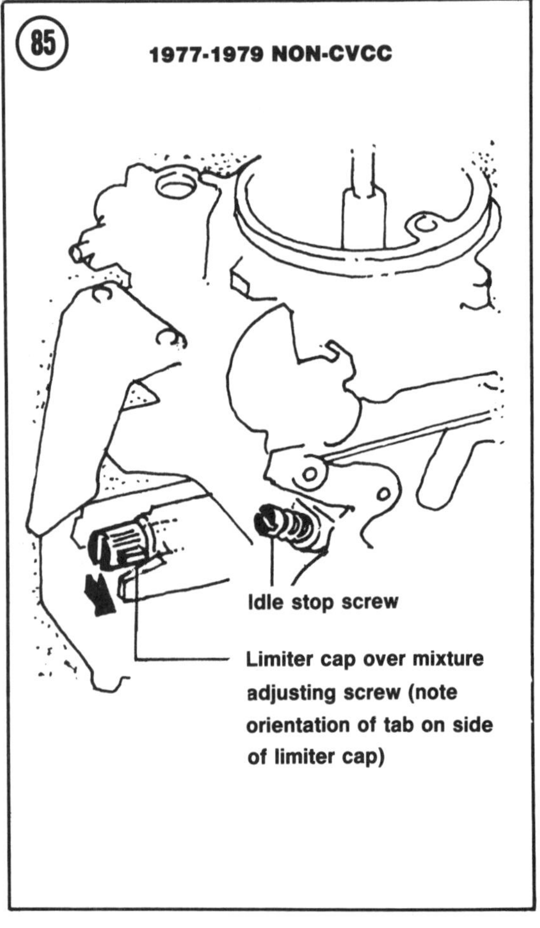

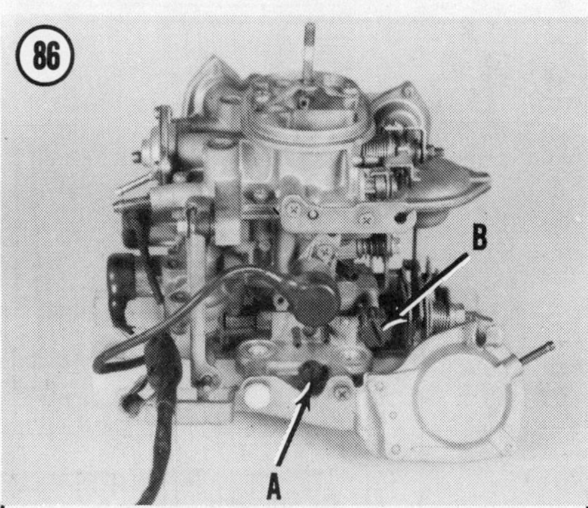

A. Mixture adjusting screw (limiter cap in place)
B. Throttle stop screw

warm to normal operating temperature (cooling fan will turn on).

2. Connect a tachometer to the engine following the manufacturer's instructions.

3. Turn the headlights on. In addition, either the cooling fan or high speed heater fan must be on, but not both.

4. Remove the idle limiter cap (**Figure 86**).

5. Turn the mixture screw counterclockwise until the highest rpm is obtained.

NOTE

When turning the mixture screw, it will reach a point of highest rpm; then if screw is turned past this point, the rpm will drop because of an excessively rich mixture. It will probably be necessary to try the adjustment procedure (Step 5) more than once to obtain the best high idle rpm.

6. Turn the idle speed screw to obtain the first step idle speed specified in **Table 9**.

7. Turn the mixture screw clockwise to obtain the final idle speed specified in **Table 7**.

8. Turn off the engine. Reinstall the idle limiter cap. On 1976 and later models, install cap with pointer positioned 180° away from carburetor boss.

Idle Speed and Mixture Adjustment (1980 and Later CVCC Models)

A propane enrichment kit is required for this procedure. In addition, a special mixture adjustment tool is required on all 1980 California models. As this adjustment is normally required every 60,000 miles, it may be more economical to have the adjustment done by your Honda dealer or a competent automotive specialist.

1. Block the vehicle's front and rear wheels and set the parking brake.

2. Start the engine and bring to normal operating temperature (cooling fan will come on). Turn the engine off. Disconnect the vacuum hose from the air control diaphragm at the air cleaner housing (**Figure 87**) and close the end of the hose.

3. Connect a tachometer to the engine following the manufacturer's instructions.

4. Start the engine. Make sure the headlights, cooling fan and air conditioner are off and check the engine idle speed. See **Table 7** for idle speed specifications for your car. If necessary, adjust the idle speed by turning the idle speed screw (**Figure 88**).

5. Remove the air cleaner intake tube from the duct on the radiator bulkhead and insert the tube of the propane enrichment kit about 4 inches into the intake tube.

6. Verify that the propane bottle has adequate gas and then, with the engine idling, slowly turn on the propane until maximum idle speed is obtained.

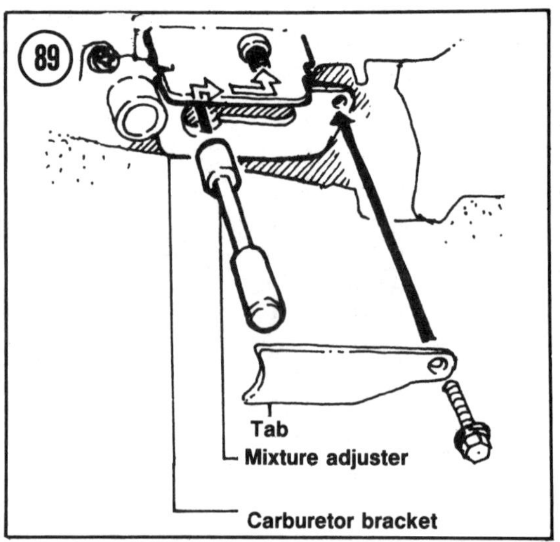

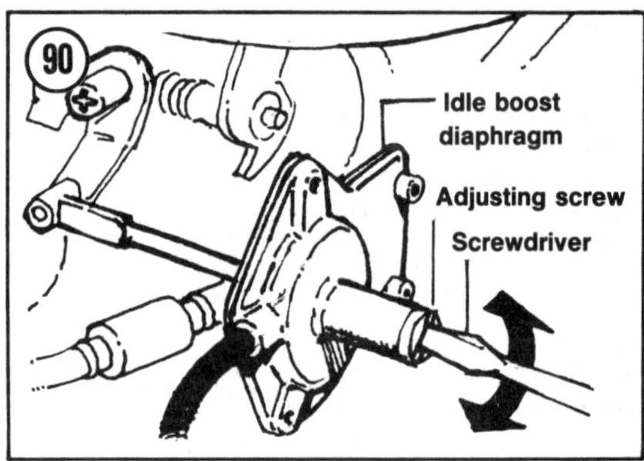

7. If engine speed does not increase, lean out the mixture (with propane on) until the idle speed increases. To gain access to mixture screws, perform the following:

a. 1980 49-state models: Remove the idle mixture screw limiter cap.
b. 1980 California models: Remove the screw on the right side of the carburetor bracket and swing the tab out of the way. Insert the special tool through the large hole in the bracket, then slide it to the right and engage the mixture screw. See **Figure 89**.
c. All 1981 models: Remove the mixture adjusting hole cap.

NOTE
Specified propane enriched maximum rpm increase for 1300cc engines is 120. For 1500cc engines, the maximum increase is 100 rpm for manual transaxle and 50 rpm for Hondamatics (in DRIVE).

8. If necessary, adjust idle speed to the specified increase by turning the idle mixture screw (clockwise to increase, counterclockwise to decrease).
9. Shut off the propane, open throttle briefly to 2,500 rpm and recheck idle speed. Readjust to specifications, if necessary, using the idle speed screw (**Figure 88**). If readjustment is necessary, repeat the propane enriched mixture adjustment (Steps 6-8).
10. Remove the propane enrichment kit and install the air cleaner intake tube on the radiator bulkhead.
11. On 1980 49-state models, reinstall the limiter cap on the mixture screw with the pointer 180° away from the boss on the carburetor body. On 1980 California models, remove the mixture adjuster tool and reinstall the tab on the carburetor bracket. On all 1981 models, reinstall the mixture adjusting hole cap.
12. Turn on the air conditioner, if so equipped, and verify that the idle speed remains within specifications. If it does not, turn the adjusting screw on the idle boost diaphragm as required to bring idle speed back into specifications. See **Figure 90**.

EXHAUST EMISSION CONTROL CHECK

After every engine tune-up, have a Honda dealer check carbon monoxide (CO) content of exhaust gas.

Table 1 MAINTENANCE SCHEDULE (1973-1974)

		Mileage Interval × 1,000 Miles (KM)								
		3 (5)	6 (10)	12 (20)	18 (30)	24 (40)	30 (50)	36 (60)	42 (70)	48 (80)
Engine	Valve clearance	A		A		A		A		A
	Alternator drive belt	A		I		I		I		I
	Vacuum fittings, hoses, and connections			I		I		I		I
	Engine oil	R	R	R	R	R	R	R	R	R
	Engine oil filter	R	R	R	R	R	R	R	R	R
	Coolant					R				R
	Cooling system, hoses, and connections			I		I		I		I
	Exterior of radiator core			C		C		C		C
	Intake and exhaust manifold tighteness check	A								
Fuel system	Idle speed and idle CO	A		A		A		A		A
	Choke mechanism	I		I		I		I		I
	Throttle opener and control valve	I		I		I		I		I
	Air cleaner element			R		R		R		R
	Fuel filter					R				R
	Intake air temperature control system			I		I		I		I
	Tank, fuel lines, and connections	I				I				I
Evaporative emission system	Carbon canister and idle cut-off valve			I		R		I		R
	One way valve			I		I		I		I
	Fuel filler cap			I		I		I		I
Ignition components	Ignition timing			A		A		A		A
	Contact breaker points			R		R		R		R
	Spark plugs			R		R		R		R
	Distributor cap and rotor			I		R		I		R
	Ignition wiring					I				I
	Idle retarder (spark control)			I		I		I		I
	Advance mechanism in distributor					I				I
	Crankcase emission system			I		I		I		I
4-Speed	Transmission controlled spark advance					I				I
Hondamatic	Temperature controlled spark advance					I				I
Rear brake		A	A	A	A	A	A	A	A	A
Parking brake		A								
Brake hoses, lines, master cylinder fluid level			I	I	I	I	I	I	I	I
Brake fluid *2						R				R
Front brake pads, yoke performance			I	I	I	I	I	I	I	I
Rear brake linings				I		I		I		I
Air filter of vacuum booster *1				C		C		C		C
Front wheel alignment				I		I		I		I
Clutch pedal travel			I	I	I	I	I	I	I	I
Transmission oil		R				R				R
Radiator fan			I	I	I	I	I	I	I	I
Engine exhaust silencer, suspension mounting bolts			I	I	I	I	I	I	I	I
Steering operation, tie rod ends, rack guide, grease steering gear box		I		I		I		I		I

A. Adjust R: Replace C: Clean I: Inspect, adjust or replace if necessary

*1. Every 12,000 miles (20,000 km) or 12 months, whichever comes first.

*2. Every 24,000 miles (40,000 km) or 24 months, whichever comes first.

Table 2 MAINTENANCE SCHEDULE 1975-1979

Every 5,000 miles	•Change the engine oil and filter. •Inspect condition of radiator fan. •Inspect the exhaust pipe and muffler condition and check tightness of all bolts. •Check the ignition timing and adjust if necessary. •Check the idle speed and idle mixture and adjust if necessary. •Check the clutch pedal travel distance and adjust if necessary. •Adjust the rear brakes. •Inspect the front brake pads, rotor and yoke. •Check the condition of the brake hoses and lines and repair damage if necessary. •Check the level of the brake master cylinder fluid level. •Check the tightness of all suspension mounting bolts and retighten if necessary.
Every 10,000 miles (1975-1976 only)	•Clean the vacuum booster air filter on 1975-1976 models. •Check the front wheel alignment.
Every 15,000 miles	•Replace the air filter element on 1975-1976 models. •Inspect the alternator belt and adjust if necessary. •Adjust the air pump drive belt on •1977-1979 non-CVCC models. •Change coolant on 1975-1976 models at first 15,000 miles, then every 30,000 miles thereafter. Inspect coolant every 15,000 miles. •Clean the radiator core tubes and inspect all cooling system hoses and connections. •Replace spark plugs. •Replace contact points. •Inspect distributor cap and rotor and replace if necessary. •Check choke cable adjustment and adjust if necessary. •Check carburetor butterfly valve clearance and adjust if necessary. •Check choke opener operation. •Check choke fast idle speed and adjust if necessary. •Clean the crankcase control fixed orifice. •Inspect the crankcase control condensation chamber and clear if necessary. •Inspect all emission control hoses and vacuum tubes; replace hoses and tubes if necessary. •Replace the charcoal canister. •Inspect the idle cutoff valve. •Inspect the 2-way valve. •Inspect the start control system. •Inspect the air intake control system. •Inspect the air pump and air control devices on 1977-1979 non-CVCC models. •Inspect the ignition timing control system.

(continued)

Table 2 MAINTENANCE SCHEDULE 1975-1979 (continued)

Interval	Service
Every 15,000 miles (continued)	•Inspect the rear brake linings. •Inspect the front brake pad and rotor wear. •Check the tightness of all suspension mounting bolts and retighten if necessary. •Check the front wheel alignment on 1977-1979 models.
At first 15,000 miles and every 30,000 miles thereafter	•Replace the air filter element on 1977-1979 models. •Replace the engine coolant on 1977-1979 models. Inspect coolant at first 30,000 miles and every 15,000 miles thereafter. •Replace the fuel filter. •Replace the transaxle oil (manual and automatic). •Replace the brake fluid on 1977-1979 models.
Every 20,000 miles (1976-1979 only)	•Change the brake fluid.
Every 30,000 miles (1977-1979 only)	•Clean the vacuum booster air filter on 1977-1979 models.

Table 3 MAINTENANCE SCHEDULE 1980-ON

Interval	Service
At first 7,500 miles	•Replace engine oil and filter. •Inspect parking brake when parking brake lever is applied. •Check the tightness of all suspension mounting bolts and tighten if necessary. •Check the condition of the exhaust system. Tighten fasteners or replace parts as necessary. •Check the brake lines and hoses for condition. Repair as necessary. •Check the brake master cylinder fluid level and top up if necessary. •Check the steering box for sufficient grease. Relubricate if necessary. •Check the steering linkage adjustment and adjust if necessary. •Check the clutch release arm end play and adjust if necessary.
Every 7,500 miles	•Replace engine oil and filter. •Check the clutch release arm end play and adjust if necessary.
Every 15,000 miles	•Check the valve clearances and adjust if necessary. •Inspect the front brake pad and rotor. Replace parts as necessary. •Check the tightness of all suspension mounting bolts and tighten if necessary. •Check the condition of the exhaust system. Tighten fasteners or replace parts as required. •Check the brake lines and hoses for condition. Repair as necessary. •Check the brake master cylinder fluid level and top up if necessary. •Check the front wheel alignment.

(continued)

Table 3 MAINTENANCE SCHEDULE 1980-ON (continued)

Interval	Maintenance
At first 15,000 miles, then every 30,000 miles	•Change the automatic transaxle fluid.
Every 30,000 miles	•Change the manual transaxle fluid. •Check the thickness of the rear brake shoes. Replace all 4 brake shoes if necessary. •Replace the brake fluid. •Inspect the cooling system hoses and connections. •Change the engine coolant on 1980 models. •Check the alternator belt tension and adjust if necessary. •Replace the spark plugs. •Replace the air cleaner element. •Clean the choke coil tension and linkage.
At first 45,000 miles, then every 2 years or 30,000 miles	•Replace the engine coolant on 1981 models.
Every 60,000 miles	•Check the ignition timing and adjust if necessary. •Check the idle speed and idle mixture and adjust if necessary. •Check the idle control system on air-conditioned models and adjust if necessary. •Replace the fuel filter. •Replace the rear wheel bearing grease. •Replace the fuel hose. •Inspect condensation chamber, hoses and connections. •Inspect the distributor cap and rotor. •Inspect the ignition wiring. •Inspect the choke opener operation. •Inspect the intake air control system. •Inspect the ignition control system (1980 1300 models and 1981 1300 California models). •Inspect the fast idle unloader system. •Check the choke coil tension and heater system. •Check the fast idle and adjust if necessary. •Inspect the throttle controller diaphragm, dashpot, control valve and speed sensor (also revolution detector on 1981 1500 49-state/ high-altitude manual transaxle, hatchback models). •Inspect the anti-afterburn valve on 1980 1300 models. •Check the purge control/unloader solenoid valve. •Inspect the air vent cutoff diaphragms. •Inspect the vacuum holding solenoid valve on 1981 models. •Inspect the 2-way valve. •Inspect the EGR system (1980 1500 models and all 1981 models). •Inspect the power valve control solenoid on 1981 California models. •Check the condition and tightness of the catalytic converter heat shield (1980 1500 models and all 1981 models).

Table 4 RECOMMENDED LUBRICANTS

Lubrication point	Lubricant
Transaxle	
Manual	SAE 10W-30 or 10W-40 SE engine oil
Automatic	DEXRON ATF
Brake fluid	DOT 3 or DOT 4
Brake caliper	
Piston seal and dust boot	Silicone grease
Front wheel bearing	Multipurpose grease
Rear wheel bearing	Multipurpose grease
Drive shaft joint	Texaco Molytex Grease 2
Steering ball-joint Steering gearbox Shift lever ball Brake master cylinder pushrod Battery terminals Parking brake equalizer Hatch side strikers Engine hood latch and hinge Pedal linkage & door hinge	Multipurpose grease

Table 5 ENGINE OIL VISCOSITY

Temperature Range	Grade
Below 20° F	SAE 5W/20 SAE 5W/30
0 to 60° F	SAE 10W/30; SAE 10W/40
20° F and above	SAE 10W/40 SAE 20W/40 SAE 20W/50
Use only those oils certified to meet or exceed U.S. car manufacturer's requirements for Service SE or SF.	

Table 6 APPROXIMATE REFILL CAPACITIES

Engine oil	
With filter change	3.2 quarts
Manual transaxle	
1973-1979 non-CVCC	*
1975 CVCC	2.6 quarts
1976-1980 CVCC	
4-speed	2.6 quarts
5-speed	2.8 quarts
1981 CVCC	2.6 quarts

(continued)

Table 6 APPROXIMATE REFILL CAPACITIES (continued)

Automatic transaxle	
1973-1979 non-CVCC	2.2 quarts
1975-on CVCC	2.6 quarts
Cooling system	
1973-1978	4.2 quarts
1979	4.8 quarts
1980-on	
1300 models	4.9 quarts
1500 models	6 quarts

* Use dipstick to determine oil level.

Table 7 TUNE-UP SPECIFICATIONS

1973-1976 Non-CVCC Models	
Ignition timing/1973-1974(1)	
Manual transaxle	5° BTDC @ idle
Automatic transaxle	5° BTDC @ idle
Ignition timing/1975-1976(2)	
Manual transaxle	7° BTDC @ idle
Automatic transaxle	7° BTDC @ idle
Idle speed	
Manual transaxle	750-850 rpm (1) (2)
Automatic transaxle	700-800 rpm (1) (2)
Distributor	
Point gap	0.45-0.55 mm (0.018-0.022 in.)
Dwell angle	49-55°
Spark plug type	
1973-1974 (standard)	NGK B-6ES & Nippondenso W-22EP
1975-1976	
Standard	NGK BP-6ES, Nippondenso W-20EP
Colder	NGK BP-7ES, Nippondenso W-22EP
Spark plug gap	0.7-0.8 mm (0.028-0.032 in.)
Valve clearance	0.10-0.16 mm (0.004-0.006 in.)
Compression	
Standard	142-199 psi
Maximum variation	28 psi
1977-1979 Non-CVCC Models	
Ignition timing	
1977	0° BTDC @ idle
1978-1979	2° BTDC @ idle
Idle speed	
1977	700-800 rpm (2)
1978-1979	650-750 rpm (2)
Idle mixture CO%	1.5%
Distributor	
Point gap	0.45-0.55 mm (0.018-0.022 in.)

(continued)

Table 7 TUNE-UP SPECIFICATIONS (continued)

1977-1979 Non-CVCC models (continued)	
Dwell angle	52° ±3°
Spark plug type	
Standard	NGK B-6E2 & Nippondenso W20EP
Cold type	NGK B-7EB & Nippondenso W22EP
Spark plug gap	0.7-0.8 mm (0.028-0.032 in.)
Valve clearance	
Intake & exhaust	0.10-0.16 mm (0.004-0.016 in.)
Compression	
Standard	142-199 psi
Maximum variation	20 psi
1975 CVCC	
Ignition timing (3)	
Manual transaxle	0° TDC @ idle
Automatic transaxle (4)	3° ATDC @ idle
Idle speed (3)	
Manual transaxle	800-900 rpm
Automatic transaxle (4)	700-800 rpm
Distributor	
Point gap	0.45-0.55 mm (0.018-0.022 in.)
Dwell	49-55°
Idle mixture CO%	0.1-0.4%
Spark plug type	
Standard	NGK B-6ES; Nippondenso W-20ES
Hot type	NGK B-5ES; Nippondenso W-16ES
Spark plug gap	0.7-0.8 mm (0.028-0.032 in.)
Valve clearance	
All	0.12-0.18 mm (0.005-0.007 in.)
Compression	
Normal	150-178 psi
Maximum variation	20 psi
1976-1977 CVCC	
Ignition timing/1976 (3)	
Manual transaxle	
Sedan	2° BTDC @ idle
Wagon	6° BTDC @ idle
Automatic transaxle	
Sedan	2° BTDC @ idle
Wagon	0° BTDC @ idle
Ignition timing/1977 (3)	
Manual transaxle	
49-state	6° BTDC @ idle
California	2° BTDC @ idle

(continued)

Table 7 TUNE-UP SPECIFICATIONS (continued)

1976-1977 CVCC (continued)	
Automatic transaxle	
Sedan (49-state)	6° BTDC @ idle
Sedan (California)	6° BTDC @ idle
Wagon (49-state)	6° BTDC @ idle
Wagon (California)	0° BTDC. @ idle
Idle speed (3)	
Manual transaxle	800-900 rpm
Automatic transaxle (4)	700-800 rpm
Distributor	
Point gap	0.45-0.55 mm (0.018-0.022 in.)
Dwell	49-55°
Idle mixture CO%	0.1-0.4%
Spark plug type/1976	
Standard	NGK B-6ES; Nippondenso W-20ES
Hot type	NGK B-5ES; Nippondenso W-16ES
Spark plug type/1977	
Standard	NGK B-6EB; Nippondenso W-20ES-L
Hot type	NGK B-5EB; Nippondenso W-16ES-L
Spark plug gap	0.7-0.8 mm (0.028-0.032 in.)
Valve clearance	
All	0.12-0.18 mm (0.005-0.007 in.)
Compression/1976	
Normal	150-178 psi
Maximum variation	20 psi
Compression/1977	
Normal	136-192 psi
Maximum variation	20 psi
1978-1979 CVCC	
Ignition timing/All (3)	
49-state & low altitude	6° BTDC @ idle
Calif. & high altitude	2° BTDC @ idle
Idle speed (3)	
Manual transaxle	650-750 rpm
Automatic transaxle (4)	600-700 rpm
Distributor	
Point gap	0.45-0.55 mm (0.018-0.022 in.)
Dwell	49-55°
Idle mixture CO%	0.1-0.4%
Spark plug type	
Standard	NGK B-6EB; Nippondenso W-20ES-L
Hot type	NGK B-5EB; Nippondenso W-16ES-L
Spark plug gap	0.7-0.8 mm (0.028-0.032 in.)
Valve clearance	
Intake/auxiliary	0.12-0.18 mm (0.005-0.007 in.)
Exhaust	0.17-0.23 mm (0.007-0.009 in.)

(continued)

Table 7 TUNE-UP SPECIFICATIONS (continued)

1978-1979 CVCC (continued)	
Compression	
Normal	136-192 psi
Maximum variation	20 psi
1980 CVCC	
Ignition timing	
1300cc	2° BTDC @ idle
1500cc	
49-state hatchback	
Manual	15° BTDC @ idle
Automatic	0° BTDC @ idle
49-state wagon	
Manual	10° BTDC @ idle
Automatic	0° BTDC @ idle
Calif. & high altitude	0° BTDC @ idle
Idle speed (4)	700-800 rpm
Idle mixture CO%	
1300cc	0.4% CO maximum
1500cc	0.1% CO maximum
Spark plugs	
1300cc	ND W20ES-L11
1500cc	NGK B7EB-11
Spark plug gap	1.0-1.1 mm (0.039-0.043 in.)
Valve clearance	
Intake & auxiliary	0.12-0.17 mm (0.005-0.007 in.)
Exhaust	0.17-0.22 mm (0.007-0.008 in.)
Compression	
Normal	156 psi
Minimum	128 psi
Maximum variation	28 psi
1981 CVCC	
Ignition timing	
1300cc	2° BTDC @ idle
1500cc	
49-state hatchback	
Manual	10° BTDC @ idle
Automatic	2° ATDC @ idle
49-state wagon/sedan	
Manual	4° BTDC @ idle
Automatic	2° ATDC @ idle
Calif. & high altitude	2° ATDC @ idle

(continued)

Table 7 TUNE-UP SPECIFICATIONS (continued)

1981 CVCC (continued)	
Idle speed	
1300cc	
Manual	750-850 rpm
Automatic (4)	700-800 rpm
1500cc (4)	700-800 rpm
Idle mixture CO%	
1300cc	0.4% CO maximum
1500cc	0.1% CO maximum
Spark plugs	NGK B6EB-11; ND W20ES-L11
Spark plug gap	1.0-1.1 mm (0.039-0.043 in.)
Valve clearance	
Intake & auxiliary	0.12-0.17 mm (0.005-0.007 in.)
Exhaust	0.17-0.22 mm (0.007-0.008 in.)
Compression	
Normal	185 psi
Minimum	156 psi
Maximum variation	28 psi

(1) Idle on 1973-1974 models is set with the headlights on. On automatic transaxle models, gear selector in DRIVE.

(2) Idle on 1975-1979 non-CVCC models is set with the headlights on and the cooling fan off. On automatic transaxle models, gear selector in DRIVE.

(3) Engine at normal operating temperature, headlight on, and either the cooling fan or high speed heater fan on (but not both). Air conditioner, if so equipped, turned off.

(4) Automatic transaxle in DRIVE.

Table 8 CYLINDER HEAD BOLT TORQUE

	mkg	ft.-lb.
Non-CVCC		
Up to engine No. EB1-1019949	4.2-4.8	30-35
From engine No. EB1-1019950	5.1-5.9	37-42
CVCC		
1975-1979	5.5-6.5	40-47
1980-on	6.0	43

Table 9 IDLE SPEEDS (FIRST STEP)

Model	First Step
1975	
Manual	910
Automatic (1)	810
1976	
Manual	930
Automatic (1)	780
1977	
High altitude model	
Manual	920 (2)
Automatic (1)	780 (3)
49-state model	
Manual	
Sedan	870
Wagon	860
Automatic (1)	740
Calif. model	
Manual	
Sedan	870
Wagon	860
Automatic (1)	760
1978-1979	
High altitude model	
Manual	810 (4)
Automatic (1)	730 (5)
49-state model	
Manual	810
Automatic (1)	730
California model	
Manual	810
Automatic (1)	730

(1) Automatic transmission in DRIVE.
(2) 970 rpm at sea level.
(3) 800 rpm at sea level.
(4) 910 rpm at sea level.
(5) 780 rpm at sea level.

NOTE: If you own a 1982 or later model, first check the Supplement at the back of the book for any new service information.

CHAPTER FOUR

ENGINE

Two basic engine types have been used in the Honda Civic sold in the U.S. and Canadian markets. From 1973 through 1979, a crossflow-head engine of 1170cc and 1237cc displacements was available. The only difference between these engines is piston diameter. These will be referred to as "non-CVCC" engines. From 1975 on, the "CVCC" engine has also been used in 1355cc and 1488cc displacements. The CVCC engine has an additional (auxiliary) intake valve for each cylinder to create a stratified charge in the combustion chamber. See **Table 1** for a complete listing of the engines used in the Honda Civic.

The non-CVCC engine has a cast aluminum cylinder head and block. The CVCC engine has a cast aluminum cylinder head and a steel block. Both engines are 4-cylinder, transversely mounted, with overhead cam (OHC) valve mechanism. The camshaft is driven by the crankshaft through a toothed belt. Helical gears on the camshaft drive the distributor and the sump-mounted oil pump.

In both engine types, the crankshaft is supported by 5 main bearings. In the non-CVCC engine, a full main bearing cradle is used and in the CVCC engine the main bearing caps are individual.

Service work for all models is nearly identical. Where differences occur, they are identified by engine type.

Tables 2-4 at the end of this chapter provide complete engine service specifications.

Prior to engine service or removal, clear a large area for placement of parts after removal. In addition, it is a good idea to tag parts as removed to make sure they are installed correctly during assembly and installation. During service work, clean parts as they are removed.

ENGINE REMOVAL/INSTALLATION (NON-CVCC)

1. Disconnect the engine ground cable at the battery (**Figure 1**) and transaxle.
2. Remove the combination lights, grille and then the hood.
3. Raise the vehicle front end and secure with jackstands. Remove the front wheels.
4. Drain the engine, transaxle, and cooling system as described in Chapter Three.
5. Remove the air cleaner assembly as described in Chapter Five.
6. Disconnect the following components:
   a. Fuel vapor storage canister hose at the carburetor.

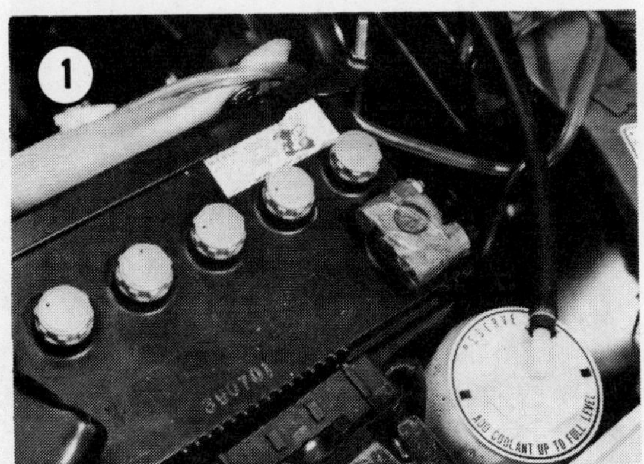

b. Upper and lower coolant hoses at the thermostat and water pump.

c. Fuel line at fuel pump (**Figure 2**).

d. Throttle cable (**Figure 3**) and choke cable (**Figure 4**) at the carburetor.

e. Clutch cable at clutch release arm.

f. Wiring at distributor, starter and alternator.

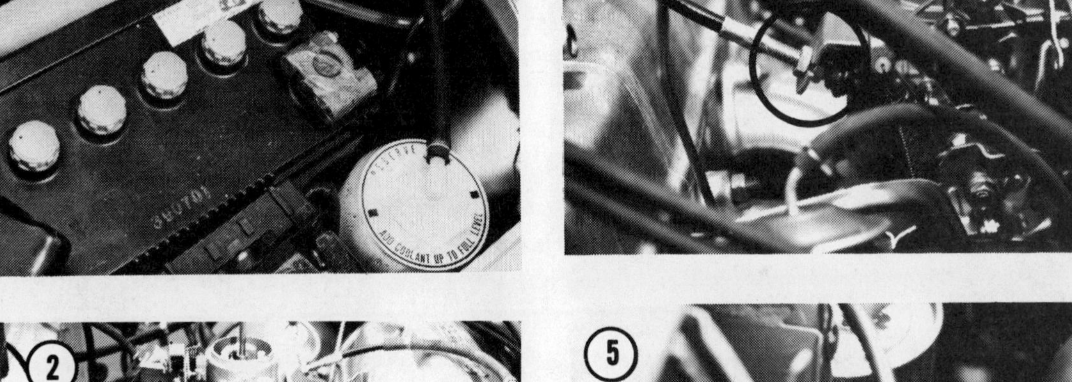

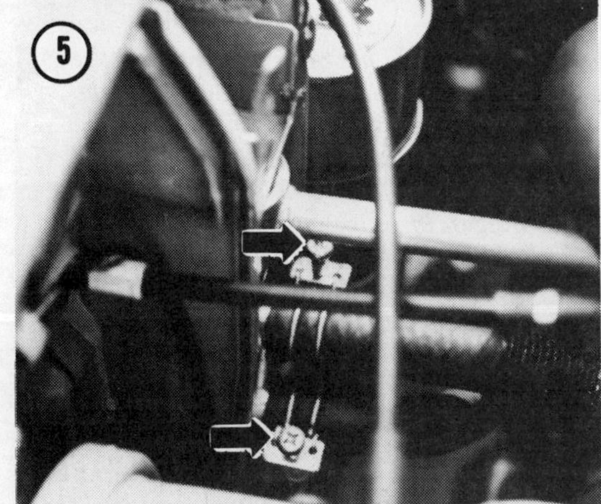

g. Wiring at the water temperature sensor and water temperature gauge unit on the intake manifold.

h. Cooling fan wire connector at the cooling fan.

i. Radiator thermo switch wires at bottom of radiator.

j. Automatic transaxle coolant hoses at the radiator.

7. Disconnect the heater hoses at engine firewall (**Figure 5**).
8. Remove the radiator (Chapter Six) and the starter (Chapter Seven).
9. Grasp the speedometer cable and slide the rubber dust boot up the cable. Then remove the wire clip from its groove in the cable holder and pull the speedometer cable up and out of the holder. *Do not* remove the speedometer securing bolt and the holder assembly.

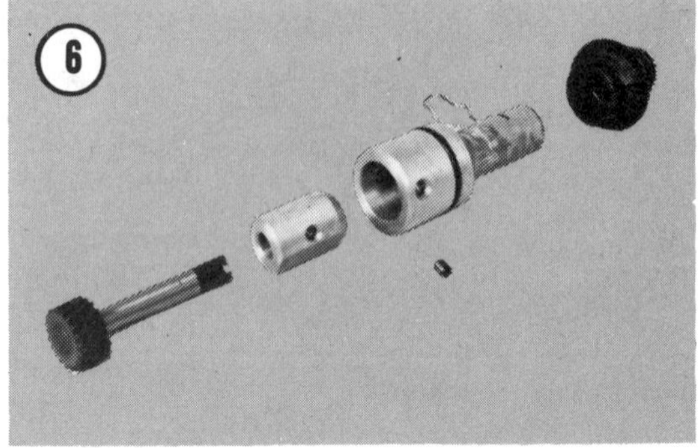

CAUTION
*When removing the speedometer cable (Step 9), do not attempt to remove the cable and holder at the same time. If the holder securing bolt is removed and the holder rotates slightly in the transaxle, it is possible for the holder-to-collar pin (**Figure 6**) to drop into the transaxle case. Transaxle disassembly would then be required to retrieve the pin.*

10. Remove the engine torque rod (**Figure 7**).
11. Disconnect the exhaust pipe at the exhaust manifold.
12. Disconnect the lower arm ball-joints by removing the locknuts. Then, using Honda tool part No. 07941-6340100, separate the joints as shown in **Figure 8**.
13. Pry the inboard drive shaft joints out of the transaxle about 1/2 in. and pull the shafts from the transaxle.
14. On vehicles equipped with manual transaxle, use a punch as indicated in **Figure 9** to drive the pin out of the shift rod and remove rod at engine. Discard the pin.

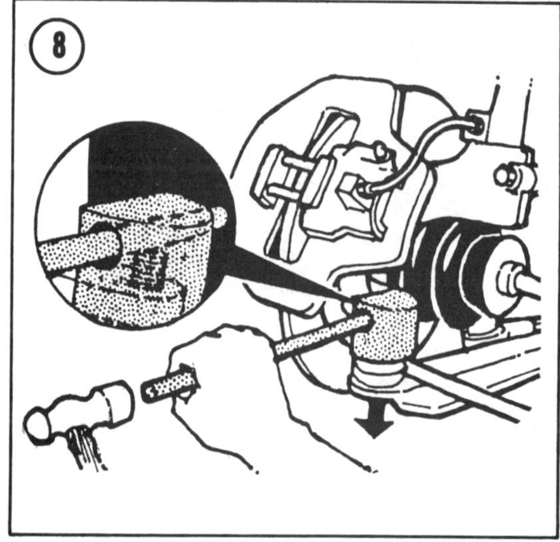

NOTE
Do not disconnect shift rod at transaxle.

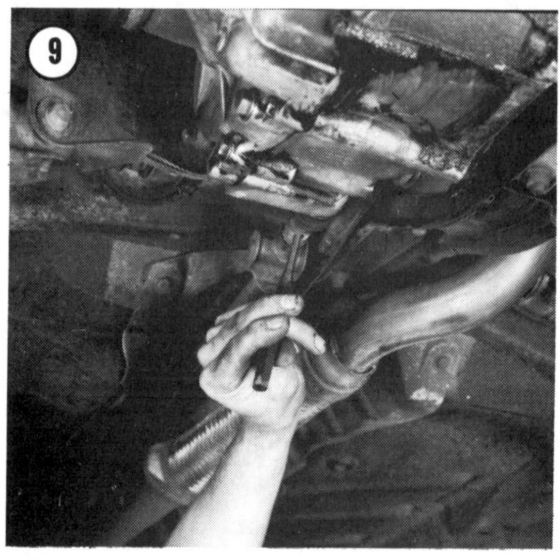

15. On vehicles equipped with automatic transaxle, disconnect the shift cable at the shift console.
16. Attach an engine lifting sling to the engine at the lifting points. Make sure the tension on both legs of the sling is approximately equal. Adjust the sling, if required. Raise the engine slightly to remove engine weight from the mounts.

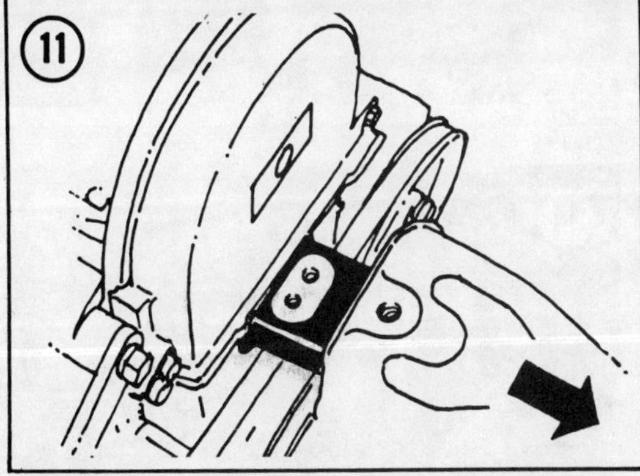

17. Remove the center engine mount bolts at the center beam. On 1973 and 1974 models, remove the center beam.
18. Unscrew the bolts from the left engine mount (**Figure 10**) and push the support into the left shock absorber bracket (**Figure 11**).
19. Check the engine again carefully for any wiring, hoses or parts which are still attached to the engine and disconnect them at this time.
20. Lift the engine slowly, taking care not to snag wiring and hoses set aside. When the engine is clear of the car, lower it onto a stand or a suitable support and disconnect the hoist.
21. Installation is the reverse of removal Steps 1-20, plus the following steps.
22. *1973-1974 models*: Install the engine center beam as follows.
   a. Lower engine into vehicle using hoist. Then secure left engine mount (**Figure 10**).
   b. Make sure the lower engine mount is installed on the bottom side of the engine. Then position the front of the center beam between the stabilizer bar and frame. Do not secure with bolts at this time.

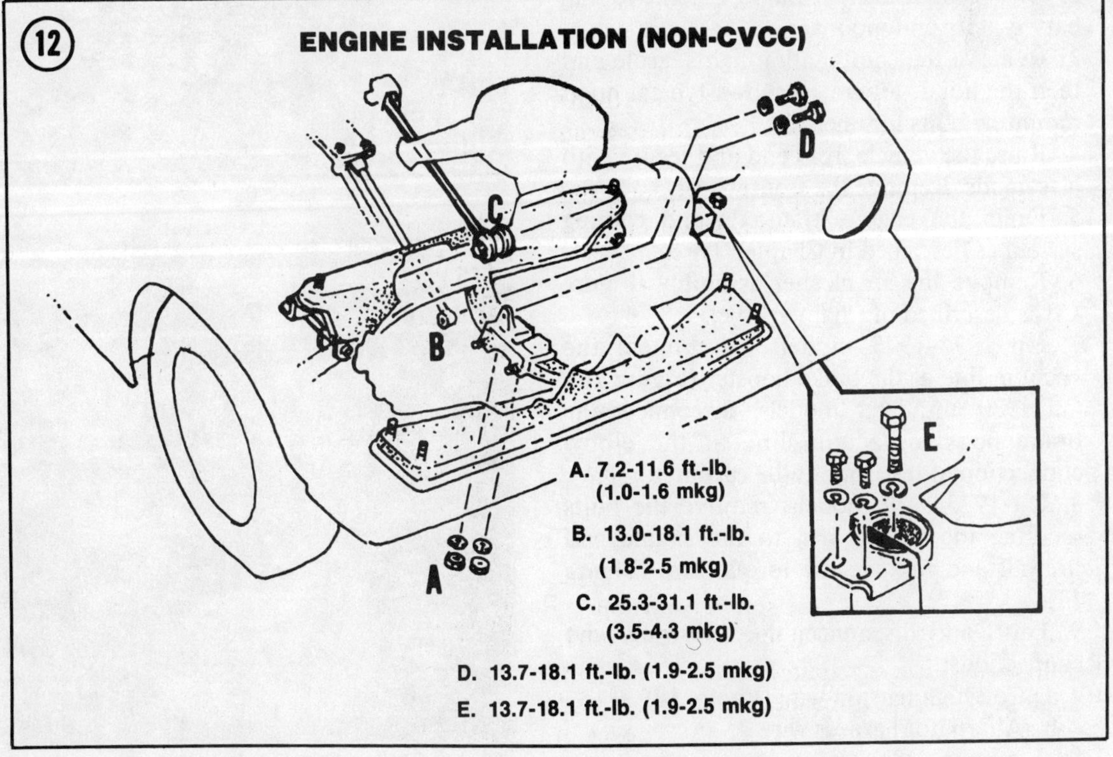

c. Align the center beam with the lower engine mount and install the nuts loosely (thread onto engine mount 2-3 turns). Attach the center beam rear end to the subframe. The center beam front end can now be attached. Torque the center beam front and rear end bolts to specifications (**Figure 12**).
d. Lower the engine so that it rests on the lower engine mount. Torque the lower engine mount to specifications (**Figure 12**).

23. Use a new shift rod pin when attaching the shift rod to the engine (**Figure 9**).
24. Refer to Chapter Three and fill the engine and transaxle with the correct oil and to the proper level. Fill the cooling system with a 50/50 mixture of antifreeze and water.
25. Perform the *Engine Tune-up* as described in Chapter Three.

ENGINE REMOVAL/INSTALLATION (CVCC)

1. Disconnect the engine ground cable at the battery (**Figure 13**) and transaxle.
2. On 1980 and later models, remove the battery, tray and mount.
3. Remove the combination lights, grille and then the hood. **Figure 14** shows typical hood mounting bolts for one side.
4. Raise the vehicle front end and secure with jackstands. Remove the front wheels.
5. Drain the engine, transaxle and cooling system as described in Chapter Three.
6. Remove the air cleaner assembly (**Figure 15**) as described in Chapter Five.
7. On 1975-1979 models, disconnect the vacuum line at the brake booster (**Figure 16**). On 1980 and later models, disconnect the brake booster vacuum line at the elbow connection at the front of the carburetor.
8. On 1975-1979 models, remove the bolts securing the torque arm to the engine and firewall and remove the torque arm (**Figure 17**).
9. Label and disconnect the following wire connections:
   a. Coil high tension wire (**Figure 18**)
   b. Alternator harness wire

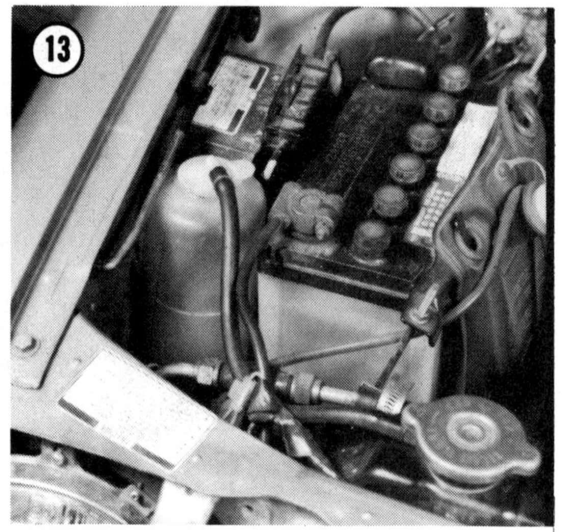

c. Starter wire and cable
d. Oil pressure sender harness wire
e. Engine compartment harness connector
f. Spark plug wires
g. Engine ground wire (**Figure 19**)

10. On 1975-1979 models, disconnect the coolant thermosensor A and thermosensor B wire connectors and the temperature gauge sending unit wire. See **Figure 20**.

11. Remove the starter and distributor as described in Chapter Seven.

12. Label and disconnect the radiator and heater hoses at the engine. On 1980 and later models, do not detach the water valve cable when disconnecting the heater hose.

13. On vehicles equipped with automatic transaxle, disconnect and plug the transaxle oil cooler hoses at the transaxle.

14A. On 1975-1979 manual transaxle-equipped vehicles, remove the clutch adjustment clip from the clutch cable as shown in **Figure 21**. At the clutch release arm, pull the clutch cable up and then push out to release from bracket. Remove clutch cable end from clutch arm.

14B. On 1980 and later manual transaxle-equipped models, loosen the clutch cable adjusting nut at the clutch cable. Then disconnect the clutch cable from the release arm.

15. On 1975 models, remove the fan and housing as one unit.

16. Disconnect the throttle and choke cables at the carburetor. See **Figure 22**.

17. Disconnect the carburetor fuel line at the carburetor (**Figure 23**).

NOTE

If a T-fitting is used to attach the fuel line at the carburetor, disconnect the fuel line at the fitting.

18. Label and disconnect all emission control hoses at the engine.
19. Disconnect and remove the emission control box at the firewall (**Figure 24**).

NOTE
On some models, it will be easier to leave the hoses attached to the emission control box, disconnect the wire coupler at the control box and then allow the box to hang down.

20. On 1980 and later models, remove either the EGR or high altitude control box from the left side of the firewall.
21. On 1980 and later models equipped with California and high altitude emission controls, disconnect the hoses to the air jet controller (**Figure 25**).
22. Disconnect the charcoal canister-to-carburetor hoses at the canister.
23. Disconnect the backup switch connectors at the transaxle (**Figure 26**).
24. On 1975-1979 models, remove the rear engine mount heat shield at the mount.
25. Remove the speedometer cable as follows:

   a. *1975-1977 models*: Remove the right side fender well cover. Then remove the bolt securing the speedometer cable holder to the transaxle case (**Figure 27**). Pull the speedometer cable and holder out of the transaxle case.

CAUTION
When removing the speedometer cable and holder, make sure that you do not

24

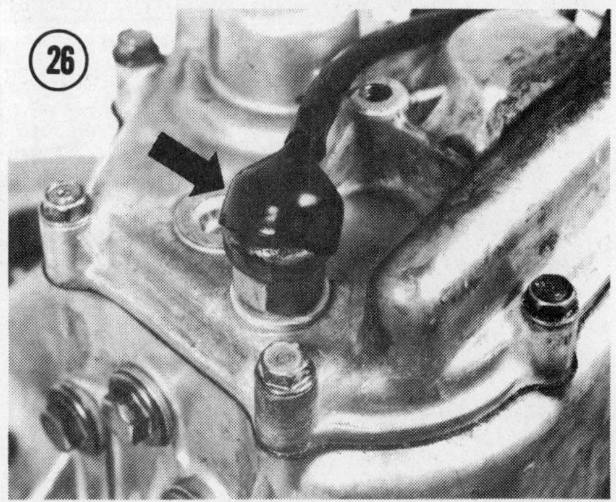

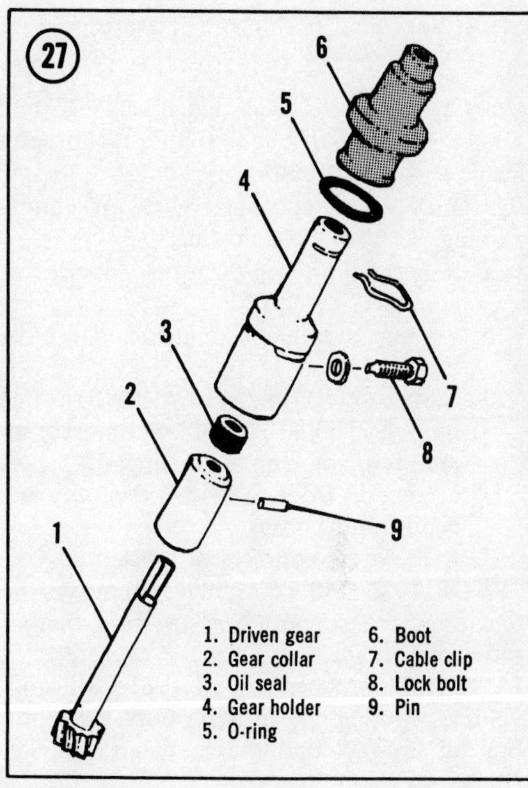

*rotate the holder in the housing but pull it straight up and out. When the holder bolt is removed and the holder is rotated slightly in the transaxle, it is possible for the holder-to-collar pin (**Figure** 27) to drop into the transaxle case. Transaxle disassembly would then be required to retrieve the pin.*

b. *1978-on models*: Grasp the speedometer cable and slide the rubber dust boot up the cable (**Figure 28**). Then remove the wire clip from its groove in the cable holder and pull the speedometer cable up and out of the holder. See **Figure 29**. *Do not* remove the speedometer securing bolt and the holder assembly.

CAUTION
*When removing the speedometer cable on 1978-on models, do not attempt to remove the cable and holder at the same time. If the holder securing bolt is removed and the holder rotates slightly in the transaxle, it is possible for the holder-to-collar pin (**Figure** 27) to drop into the transaxle case. Transaxle*

disassembly would then be required to retrieve the pin.

26. On 1980-on 1500cc hatchback GL and sedan models, disconnect the tachometer cable at the distributor.

27. On vehicles equipped with air conditioning, perform the following:
   a. Remove the compressor belt cover (if so equipped).
   b. Loosen the belt adjusting nut and remove the compressor belt.
   c. Remove compressor-to-bracket mounting bolts. Then lift compressor up and remove from vehicle with hoses attached. *Do not* disconnect any air conditioning hoses.
   d. Remove the compressor bracket.

28. On 1980 1500cc vehicles, remove the vacuum hose support bracket from behind the camshaft sprocket cover.

29. On 1980 1300cc and all 1981 California vehicles, remove the anti-afterburn valve and bracket from behind the camshaft sprocket cover.

30A. *1975-1979 models*: Disconnect the lower arm ball-joints by removing the locknuts and using Honda tool part No. 07941-6340100 to separate the joints, as shown in **Figure 30**.

30B. *1980-on models*: Remove the ball-joint securing nuts at the tie rod and lower arm. Then remove the ball-joints from the tie rod (**Figure 31**) and lower arm (**Figure 32**) using Honda tool part No. 07941-6920001 or an equivalent size puller.

31. Turn the right steering knuckle outward as far as it will go. Then pry the right side inboard drive shaft joint out of the transaxle about 1/2 in. and pull the shaft from the transaxle. Repeat for opposite side.

32. On vehicles equipped with manual transaxle, perform the following:
   a. Using a punch as shown in **Figure 33**, drive the pin out of the shift rod and remove rod at engine. Discard the pin.

NOTE

Do not disconnect shift rod at transmission.

   b. Disconnect the shift lever torque rod from the clutch housing (**Figure 34**).

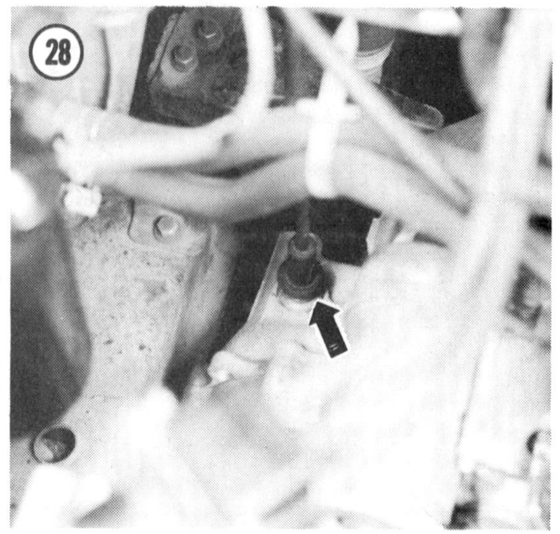

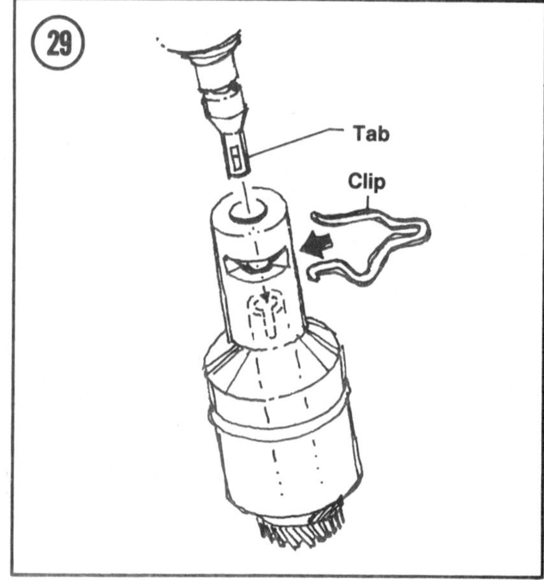

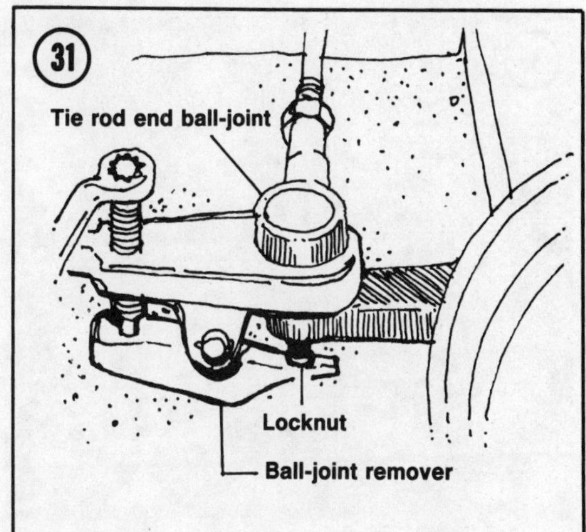

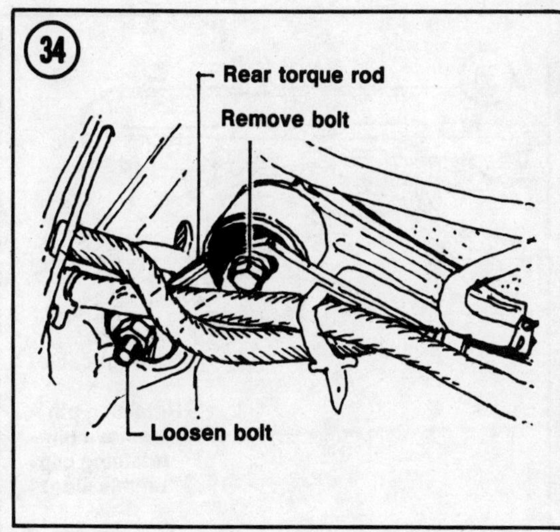

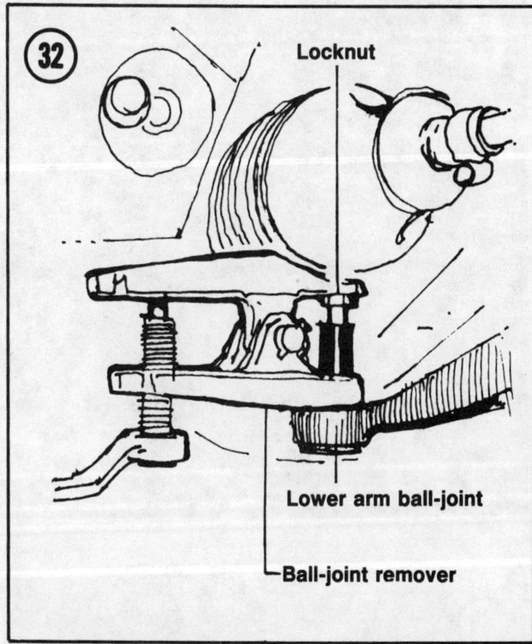

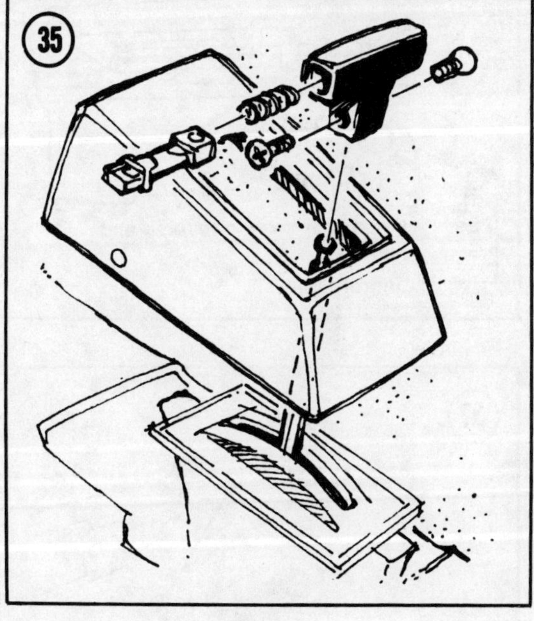

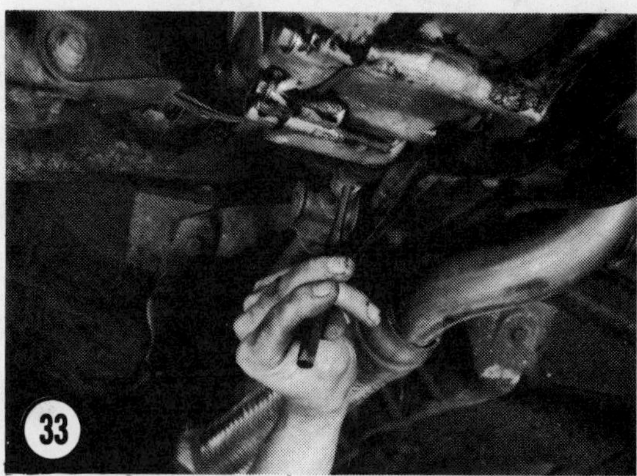

33. On vehicles equipped with automatic transaxle, perform the following:

a. From inside the driver's compartment, remove the center console attaching screws (**Figure 35**) and the console.
b. *1975-1979 models*: Remove the clip securing control pin A to the control housing (**Figure 36**). Then shift transaxle into REVERSE and remove control pin A from opposite side. Working underneath the car, remove the bolt securing the control cable stay. Then remove the 2 housing U-bolt nuts and

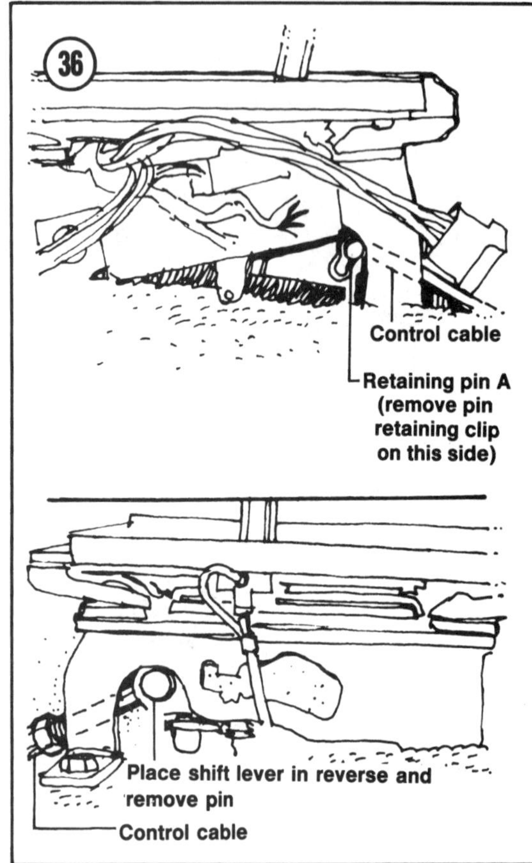
36
Control cable
Retaining pin A
(remove pin
retaining clip
on this side)
Place shift lever in reverse and
remove pin
Control cable

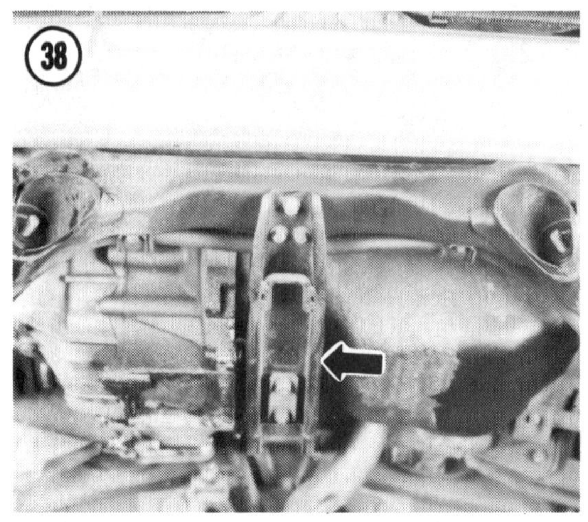
38

39

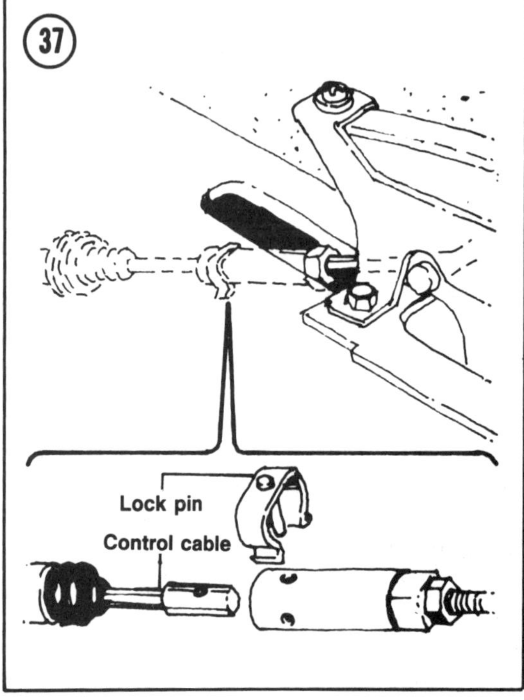
37
Lock pin
Control cable

40

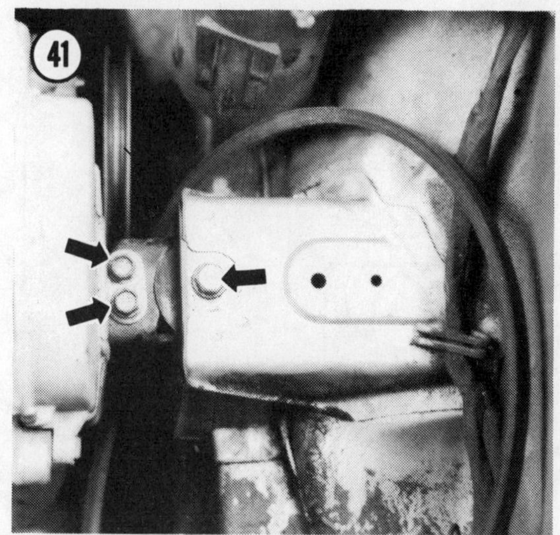

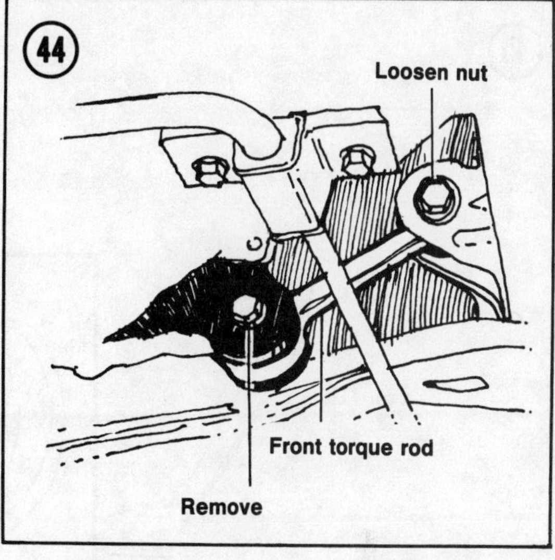

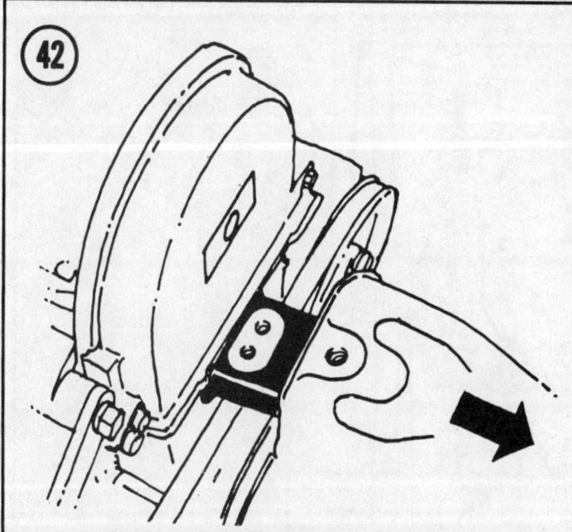

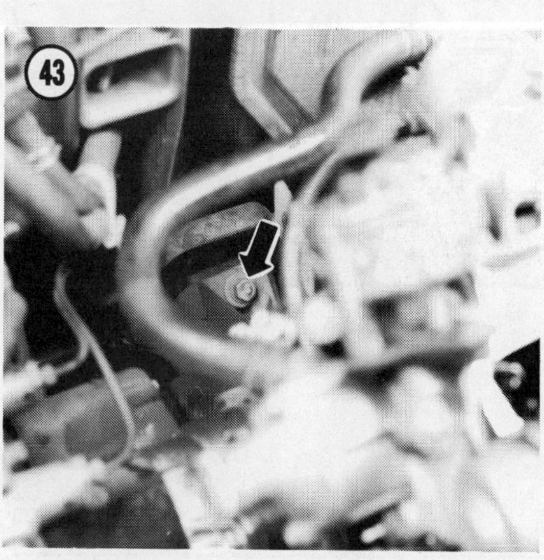

remove the control cable from the housing.

c. *1980-on models*: Shift transaxle into REVERSE. Then remove the shift cable lock pin. See **Figure 37**. Slide the cable out of the housing.

34. Disconnect the exhaust pipe from the exhaust manifold.

35. *On 1975 models*: Remove the center beam (**Figure 38**).

36. Attach an engine lifting sling to the engine at the lifting points indicated in **Figure 39**. Make sure the tension on both legs of the sling is approximately equal. Adjust the sling, if required. Raise the engine slightly to remove engine weight from the mounts.

37. Remove the front engine mount bolts at the center beam (**Figure 40**).

38. Unscrew the bolts from the left engine mount (**Figure 41**) and push the support into the left shock absorber bracket (**Figure 42**).

39. Remove the rear engine mount (**Figure 43**).

40. *On 1980-on models*: Refer to **Figure 44** and remove the bolt securing the torque rod to the engine, then loosen bolt in frame and pivot rod down and out of the way.

41. Check the engine again carefully for any wiring, hoses or parts which are still attached to the engine and disconnect them at this time.

42. Lift the engine slowly, taking care not to snag wiring and hoses set aside. When the

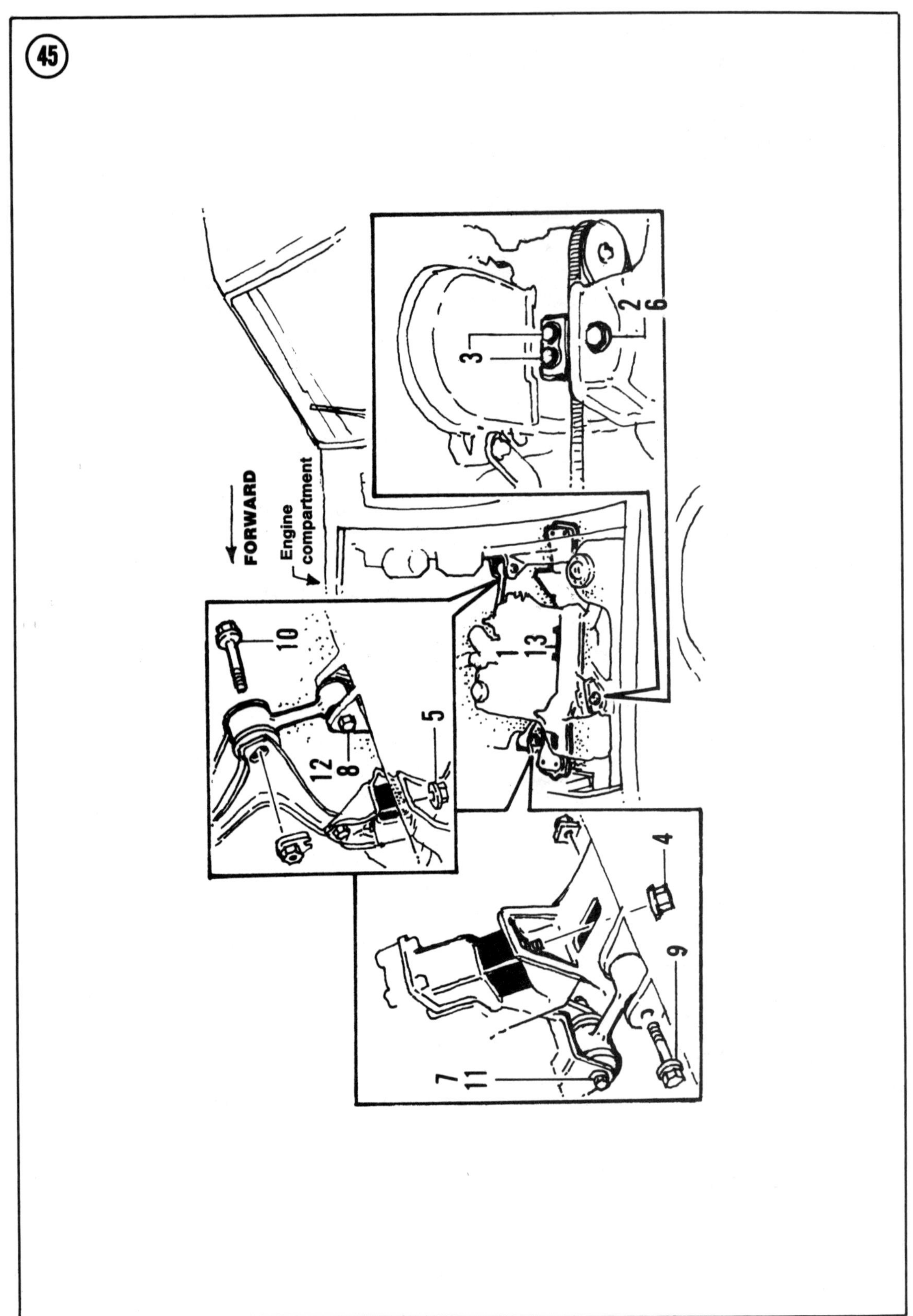
45
FORWARD
Engine compartment
1
2
3
4
5
6
7
8
9
10
11
12
13

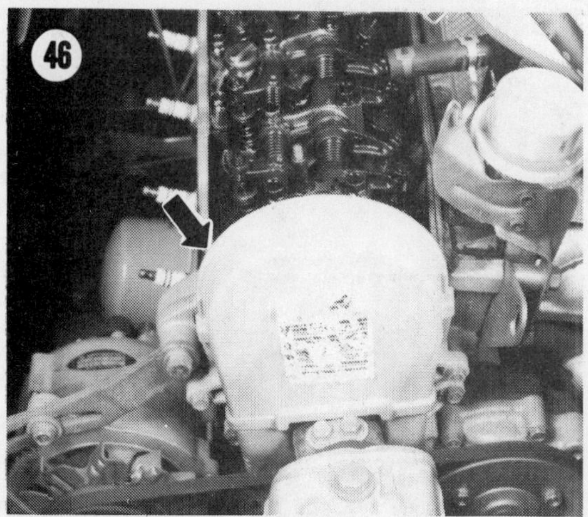

engine is clear of the car, lower it onto a stand or a suitable support and disconnect the hoist.

43. Installation is the reverse of Steps 1-43, plus the following:
   a. After engine is positioned in car, tighten all motor mount bolts to specifications in **Table 5**. For 1980-on models, tighten bolts in sequence specified in **Figure 45**.
   b. *Manual transaxle*: Check the clutch pedal free play as described in Chapter Eight.
   c. *Automatic transaxle*: Adjust the throttle cable tension as described in Chapter Nine.
   d. Make sure, when installing drive shafts, that spring clip on end of drive shafts snaps into transaxle. An audible *click* assures proper driveshaft installation.
   e. Add the correct amount and type of engine and transaxle oils specified in Chapter Three.
   f. Fill and bleed cooling system as described in Chapter Three.
   g. When installing speedometer cable on 1980-on vehicles, align tab on cable with slot in holder. Then install securing clip so that bent leg is inserted on groove side (**Figure 29**).
   h. Replace exhaust pipe-to-manifold gasket.
   i. Perform *Engine Tune-up* as described in Chapter Three.

DISASSEMBLY SEQUENCES

The following sequences are checklists that tell how much of the engine to remove and disassemble in order to do a specific type of service.

To use these sequences, remove and inspect each part mentioned. Then reverse the sequences to install the parts. Each part is covered in detail in this chapter, unless otherwise noted.

Decarbonizing or Valve Service

1. Remove the exhaust and intake manifolds (Chapter Five).
2. Remove the rocker arms and camshaft.
3. Remove the cylinder head.
4. Remove and inspect valves (this includes removal of auxiliary valves on CVCC engines). Inspect valve guides and seats, repairing or replacing as necessary.
5. Assemble by reversing Steps 1-4.

Valve and Ring Service

1. Perform Steps 1-4 for valve service.
2. Remove the oil pan.
3. Remove the pistons together with the connecting rods.
4. Remove the piston rings. It is not necessary to separate the pistons from the connecting rods unless a piston, connecting rod or piston pin needs repair or replacement.
5. Assemble by reversing Steps 1-4.

General Overhaul

1. Remove the engine.
2. Remove the alternator and the distributor (Chapter Seven).
3. Remove the fuel pump (non-CVCC), carburetor and manifolds.
4. Remove the water pump and thermostat (Chapter Six).
5. Remove the rocker arms and camshaft.
6. Remove the front covers. Remove the timing belt.
7. Remove the cylinder head.
8. Remove the flywheel.
9. Remove the oil pan and oil pump.
10. Remove the piston/connecting rod assemblies.
11. Remove the crankshaft.
12. Inspect the cylinder block.
13. Assembly is the reverse of these steps.

CAMSHAFT AND ROCKER ARMS

Rocker Arm/Camshaft Removal

1. Remove the valve cover as described under *Cylinder Head Bolt Torque*, Chapter Three.
2. Unscrew the bolts from the upper timing belt cover and remove it (**Figure 46**).
3. Rotate the crankshaft with a wrench on the crankshaft pulley bolt and bring the No. 1 piston to TDC on the compression stroke (both valves closed).

NOTE
If the engine is installed in the vehicle during this procedure, the crankshaft nut can be turned by using a socket with a ratchet and extension through the left fender well as shown in ***Figure 47****.*

4. Loosen the timing belt pivot and adjustment bolts (**Figure 48**). Then slip the timing belt off the camshaft sprocket (**Figure 49**).

CAUTION
Do not remove the timing belt pivot and adjustment bolts.

CAUTION
Do not bend or twist the belt or use sharp instruments when removing it. Also keep grease and oil out of contact with the belt as they will cause the belt to deteriorate.

5. Align the camshaft sprocket as indicated in **Figure 50**.

6A. *Non-CVCC models*: Remove the camshaft sprocket retaining bolt and washer. Then remove the camshaft sprocket.

6B. *CVCC models*: Remove the camshaft sprocket retaining bolt and washer. Then remove the camshaft sprocket (**Figure 51**).

7. Measure the camshaft axial play with a dial indicator as shown in **Figure 52**. When new, the play should be as follows:
   a. 1973-1979 non-CVCC: 0.05 mm (0.002 in.)
   b. 1975-1979 CVCC: 0.05-0.09 mm (0.002-0.0039 in.)
   c. 1980-on: 0.05-0.15 mm (0.002-0.006 in.)

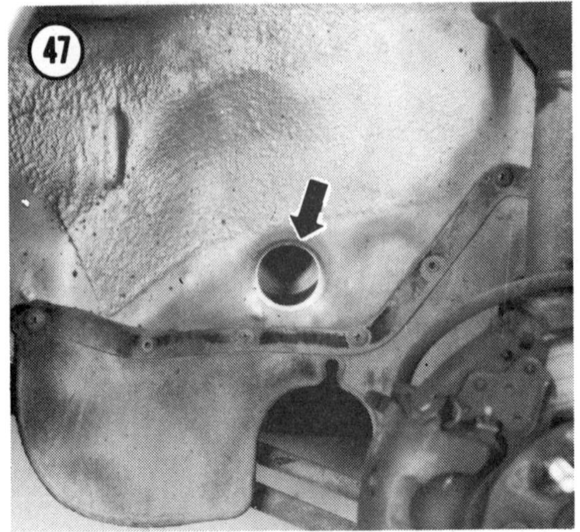
47

48

49

50 **CAMSHAFT TIMING**

1973-1979 NON-CVCC

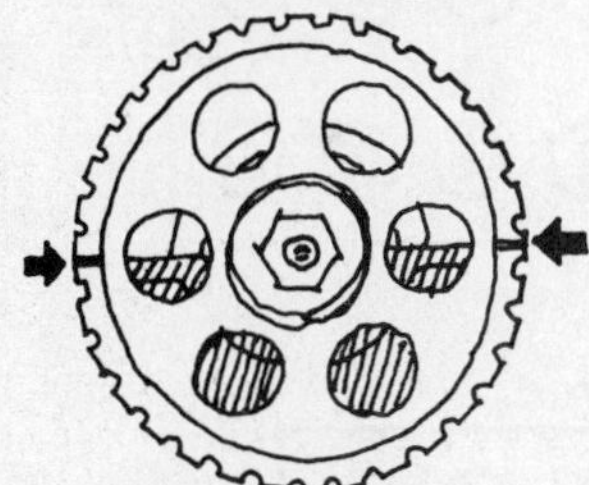

Turn pulley until both timing marks are aligned with the valve cover surface.

1975-1979 CVCC

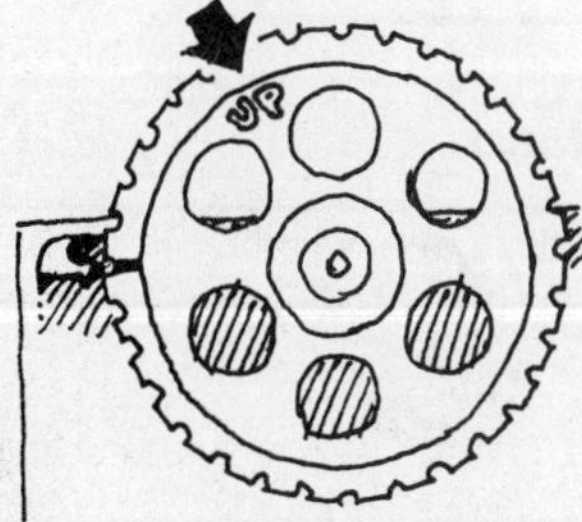

Turn pulley until "UP" mark is at top and the timing mark is aligned with arrow on cylinder head

1980-ON 1300cc CVCC

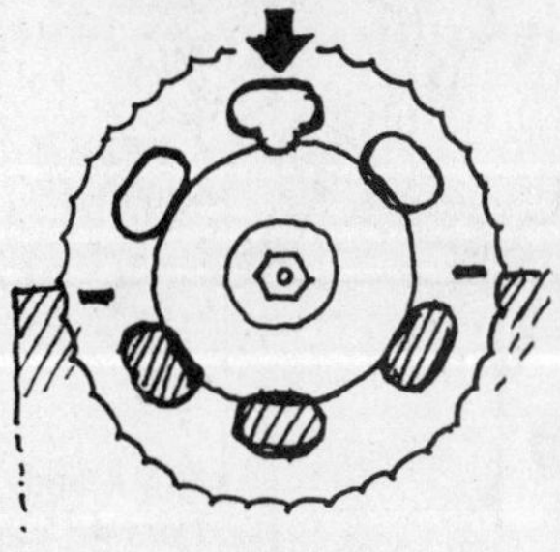

Turn pulley until cutaway faces up and both timing marks are aligned with the valve cover surface

1980-ON 1500cc CVCC

Turn pulley until cutaway faces up and the front timing mark is aligned with arrow on cylinder head

51

52

Maximum service limit is 0.5 mm (0.020 in.). If the maximum service limit is exceeded, complete rocker arm and camshaft removal. Then refer to *Camshaft Inspection*.

8. On non-CVCC engines, remove the tachometer body if so equipped.
9. Loosen the camshaft and rocker shaft holder bolts 2 turns at a time, following the sequence shown in **Figure 53**. When all bolts are loose, unscrew them completely and remove the rocker arms and holders as an assembly.
10. Lift the camshaft from the head.

Rocker Arm Disassembly

Figure 54 shows the rocker arm assembly for CVCC engines. Non-CVCC engines do not use the auxiliary valves.

1. Lay the rocker arm assembly on the workbench (**Figure 55**).

2. Remove the pin from the left-end camshaft holder as shown in **Figure 56**.
3. Disassemble the rocker arm assembly, making sure to keep all parts in order so they may be installed in the same way (**Figure 57**).

Rocker Arm Inspection

Measure the rocker arm shaft outside diameter at each rocker arm location with a micrometer (**Figure 58**). Record the measurement at each location. Then measure the inside diameter of each rocker arm with a bore gauge (**Figure 59**). Measure the bore gauge with a micrometer to determine the rocker arm bore diameter (**Figure 60**). The difference between the rocker shaft and the rocker arm measurements is the rocker arm operating clearance. Service limit is 0.08 mm (0.0032 in.). Replace the rocker arm shaft if measurements are not within specifications.

53

NON-CVCC
7 11 1 4 9 5
8 12 3 2 10 6
CVCC
7 3 2 6 10
8 4 1 5 9
FORWARD

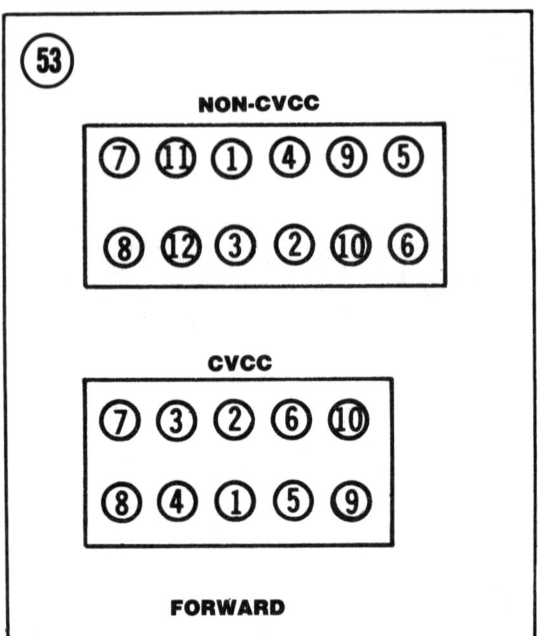

54

ROCKER ARM ASSEMBLY

Rocker arm collar (4)
Auxiliary rocker arm (4)
Auxiliary rocker arm spring (4)
Auxiliary rocker shaft
Center bearing cap
Pin
Right end bearing cap
Exhaust rocker arm (4)
Intake rocker arm (4)
Intake/exhaust rocker shaft
Intake/exhaust rocker arm spring (4)
Pin
Left end bearing cap

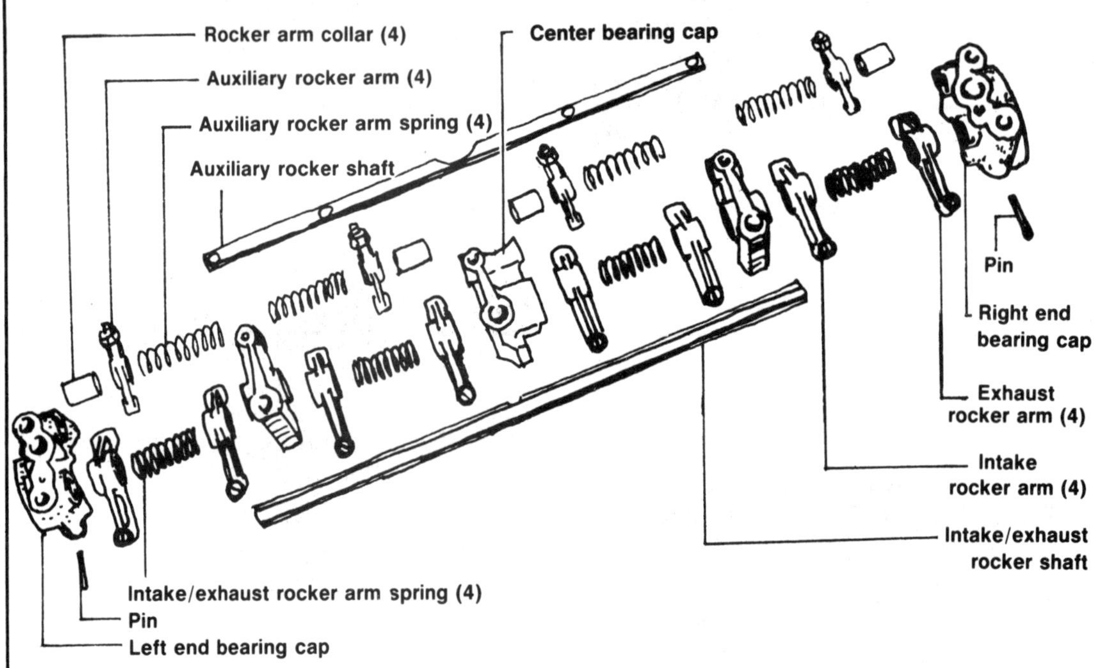

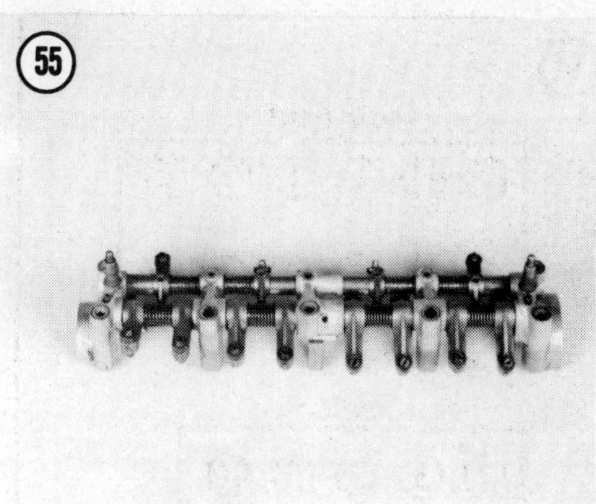

55

56

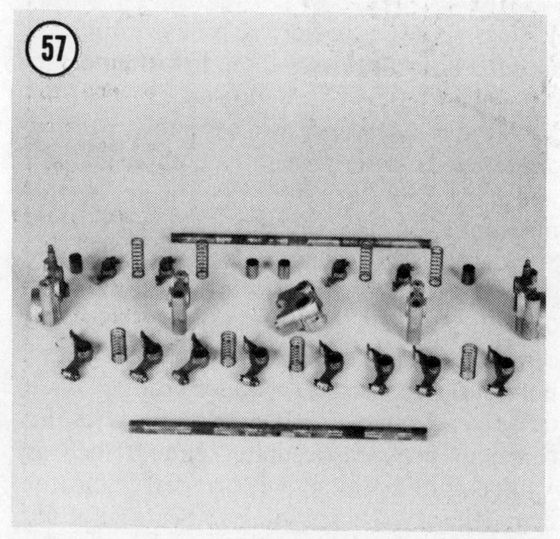

57

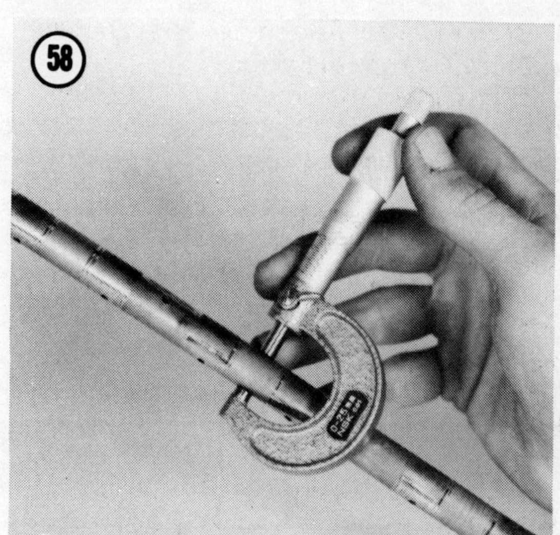

58

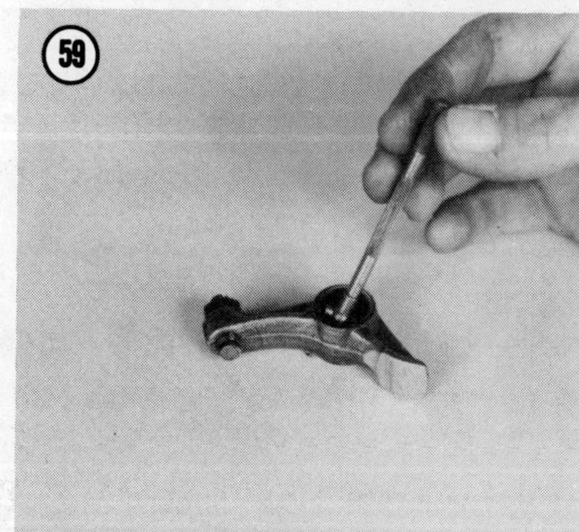

59

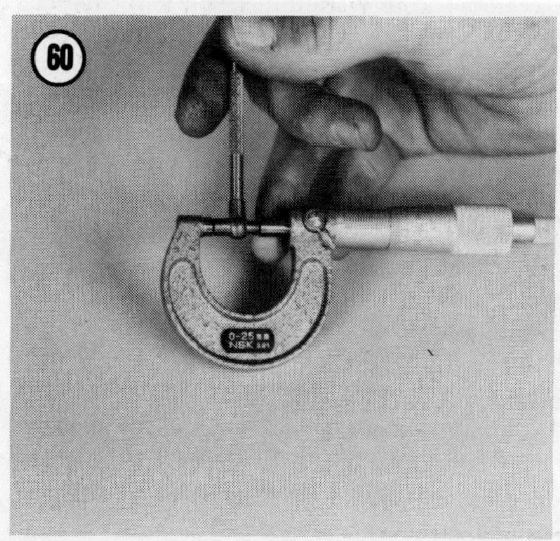

60

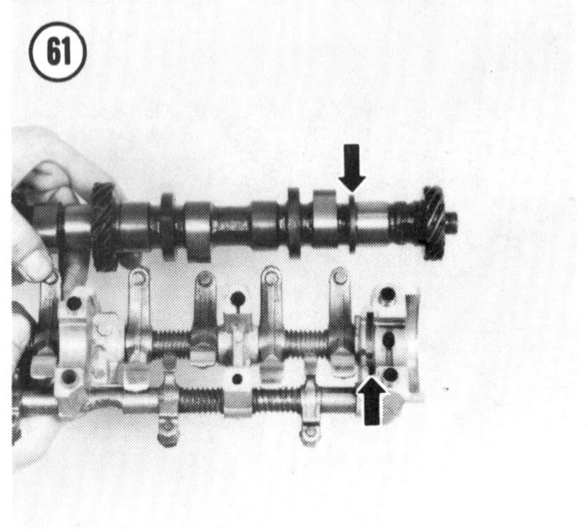

Camshaft Inspection

1A. *CVCC models*: If the camshaft axial play exceeded the service limit (see Step 7 under *Rocker Arm/Camshaft Removal*), examine the right-end bearing cap and camshaft thrust areas indicated in **Figure 61**. If the right-end bearing cap is worn in the thrust area, replace it with a new one and recheck camshaft axial play during reassembly.

1B. *Non-CVCC models*: If the camshaft axial play exceeds the service limit take the camshaft and bearing caps to a Honda dealer for further examination.

2. Place the camshaft into position on the cylinder head (**Figure 62**).

3. Cut a piece of Plastigage the width of each camshaft journal. Place the pieces of Plastigage on each camshaft journal (**Figure 63**). Then install the rocker arm assembly.

NOTE
Do not rotate the camshaft while the Plastigage is in place.

4. Tighten the rocker arm assembly to specifications (**Tables 6-7**, end of chapter) in the sequence shown in **Figure 64**.

5. Remove the rocker arm assembly. Bearing clearance is determined by comparing the width of the flattened Plastigage to the markings on the envelope (**Figure 65**). Standard bearing clearance is 0.050-0.098 mm (0.002-0.004 mm). If any bearing clearance is 0.15 mm (0.006 in.) or more, replace the camshaft. If the camshaft has been replaced previously, replace the cylinder head.

6. Measure camshaft bend. Rotate the camshaft between accurate centers (such as V-blocks or a lathe) with a dial indicator contacting the center journal. See **Figure 66.**

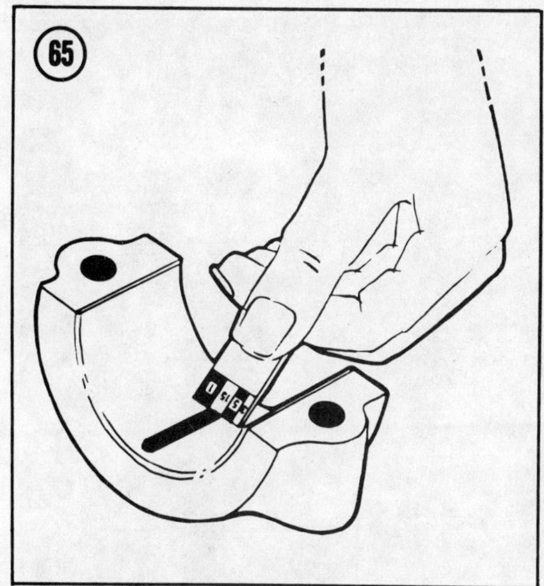

Actual bend is half the reading shown on the gauge when the camshaft is rotated one full turn. Normal bend is 0.03 mm (0.01 in.) or less. Replace the camshaft if bend exceeds 0.06 mm (0.002 in.).

7. Inspect the sprocket for wear. Replace if necessary.

Rocker Arm/Camshaft Installation

1. Coat the camshaft journals and bearing surfaces with clean engine oil. Turn camshaft in bearings until keyway seat is facing upward indicating No. 1 cylinder is at TDC. See **Figure 67**.
2. Assemble the rocker arm assembly, making sure all parts are installed in their original order. Line up the notches in the rocker shafts with their respective bolt holes (**Figure 68**). When the bolts are installed, the rocker shafts are locked in place so there is an adequate flow of lubricating oil through the system. See **Figure 54**.
3. Install a new pin into the left-end bearing cap (**Figure 69**). Then check the movement of the rocker arms to make sure there is no binding or stiffness.
4. Loosen each valve locknut and back off each valve adjusting screw.
5. Coat the left-end and right-end bearing caps with silicone rubber sealant.
6. Set the rocker assembly into place on the cylinder head. Install the bolts finger-tight.

NOTE
After tightening rocker arm bolts finger-tight, check each valve for alignment, i.e., bottom of rocker arm aligned with top of valve. In addition, check to see that each rocker arm is not binding on its respective valve. If so, the valve adjusting screw must be backed out further.

7. Tighten the rocker assembly bolts in the sequence shown in **Figure 53**.
8. Coat the inside of a new camshaft seal with engine oil. Then install seal into the left-end bearing cap with an equivalent size drift. See **Figure 70**. Make sure when installing seal that seal spring side faces in.
9. On non-CVCC engines, install the tachometer body, if so equipped.

4

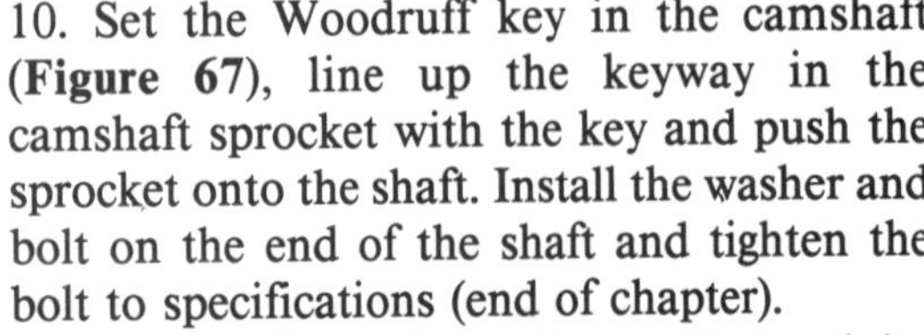

10. Set the Woodruff key in the camshaft (**Figure 67**), line up the keyway in the camshaft sprocket with the key and push the sprocket onto the shaft. Install the washer and bolt on the end of the shaft and tighten the bolt to specifications (end of chapter).

11. Line up the marks on the sprocket and the head as shown in **Figure 50**.

12A. *Non-CVCC models*: Turn the crankshaft nut counterclockwise to align the TDC mark on pulley with the front cover pointer. See **Figure 71**.

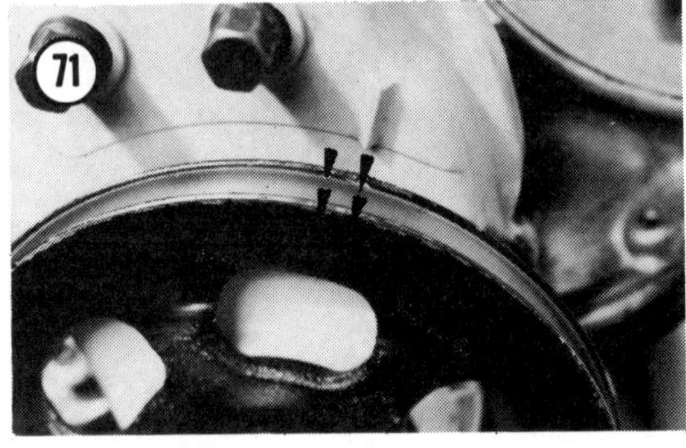

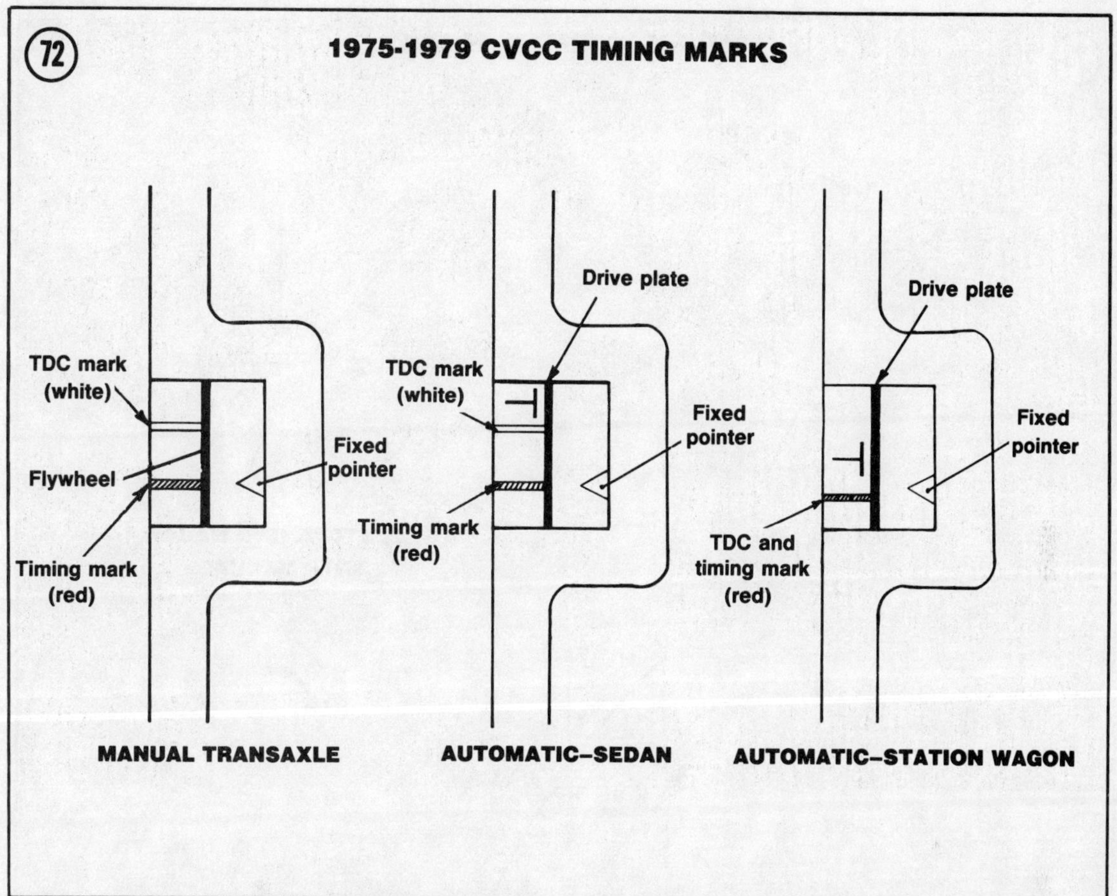

12B. *CVCC models*: Turn the crankshaft nut counterclockwise to align the TDC mark on the flywheel or drive plate with the crankcase pointer. See **Figure 72** (1975-1979), **Figure 73** (1980) or **Figure 74** (1981).

NOTE
*If the engine is installed in the vehicle during this procedure, the crankshaft nut can be turned by using a socket with a ratchet and extension through the left fender well as shown in **Figure 75**.*

13. Install the timing belt on the camshaft sprocket without changing the position of the sprocket (**Figure 76**). Do not twist the belt any more than necessary.
14. Adjust the valves as described in Chapter Three.

NOTE
Step 15 describes timing belt tension adjustment.

15. Loosen the cam tensioner pivot and adjustment bolts (**Figure 77**). Then rotate the crankshaft counterclockwise 90° (one-quarter turn). See **Figure 78**. This puts tension on the timing belt. Tighten the adjustment bolt (bottom bolt, **Figure 77**) and then the pivot bolt (top bolt, **Figure 77**) to specifications (end of chapter).

CAUTION
Do not remove the tensioner pivot and adjustment bolts.

16. Install the upper timing belt cover (**Figure 79**).
17. Start engine and check for leaks.

FRONT COVERS, TIMING BELT AND TENSIONER

Figure 80 shows the front cover/cam drive assembly for CVCC models (non-CVCC

(73)

1980 CVCC TIMING MARKS

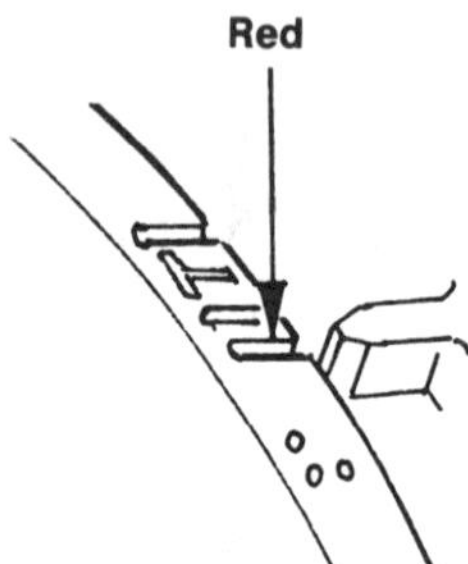

1300 (ALL)

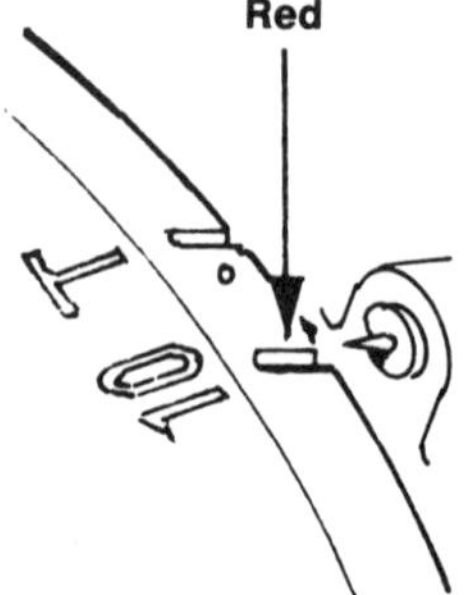

49 STATE 1500 WAGON WITH MANUAL

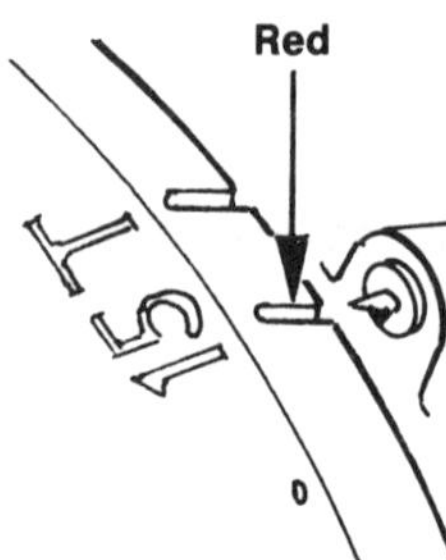

49 STATE 1500 HATCHBACK WITH MANUAL

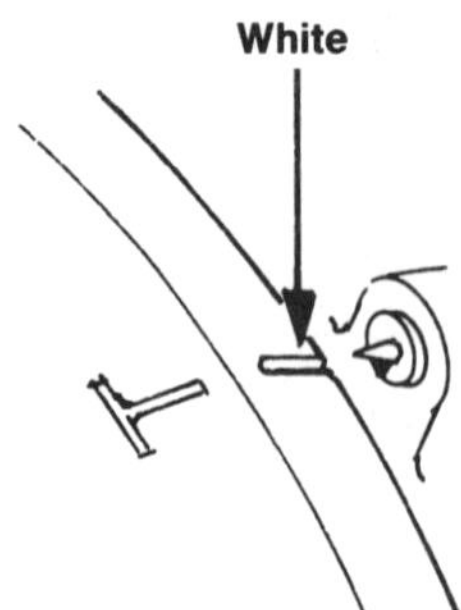

CALIFORNIA/HIGH-ALTITUDE 1500 MANUAL

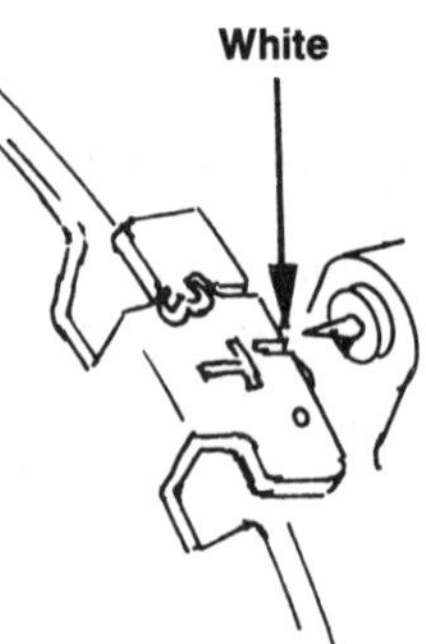

1500 WITH AUTOMATIC

1981 CVCC TIMING MARKS

1300 WITH MANUAL

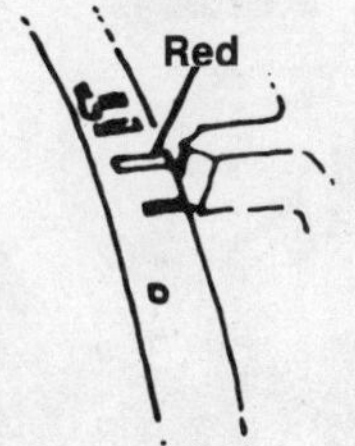

49 STATE/HIGH-ALTITUDE 1500 WAGON/SEDAN WITH MANUAL

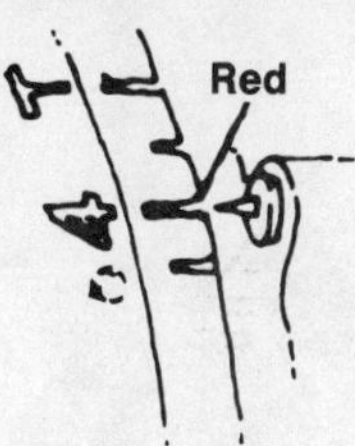

1300 WITH AUTOMATIC

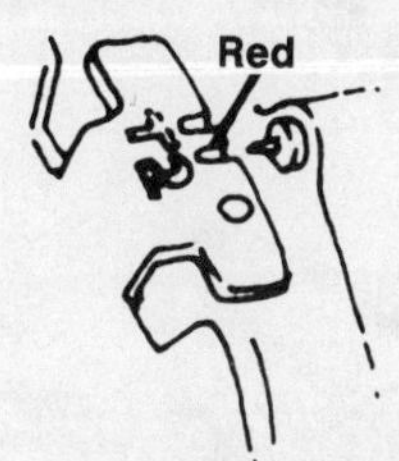

CALIFORNIA 1500 WITH MANUAL

49 STATE/HIGH-ALTITUDE 1500 HATCHBACK WITH MANUAL

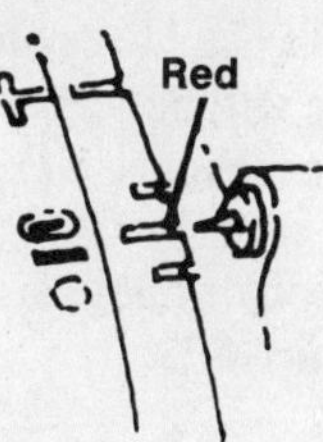

1500 WITH AUTOMATIC

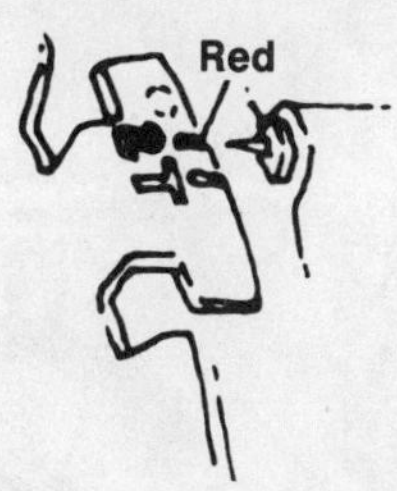

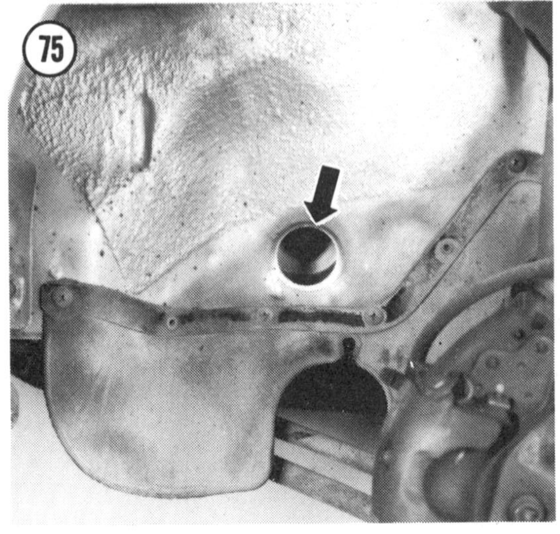

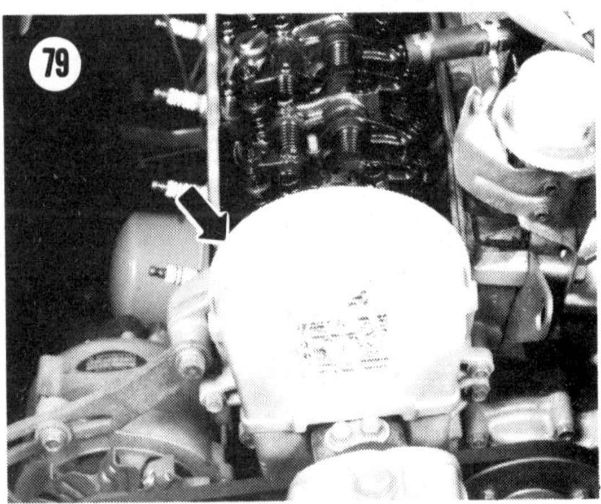

models are similar). Refer to it as necessary when performing the following procedures.

Front Covers Removal/Installation

Two covers are used to protect the cam drive assembly. These will be referred to as the upper and lower covers (**Figure 81**).

1. Remove the front left side engine motor mount. See **Figure 82**.

2. If equipped with air conditioning, remove the compressor (**Figure 83**) as described under *Engine Removal/Installation,* in this chapter.

3. Loosen the upper and lower alternator adjustment bolts and remove the drive belt. On

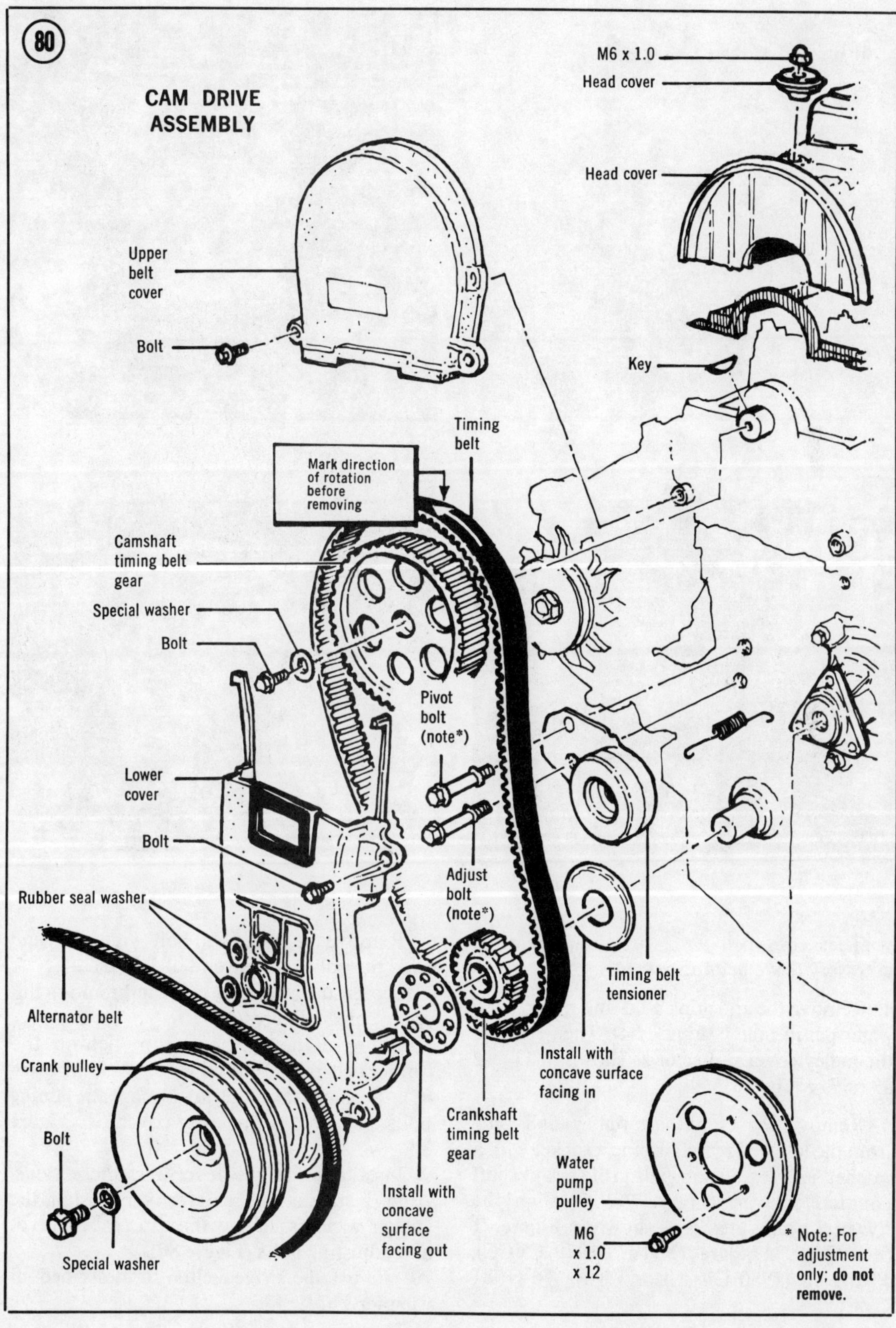
80
CAM DRIVE ASSEMBLY
M6 x 1.0
Head cover
Head cover
Upper belt cover
Bolt
Key
Timing belt
Mark direction of rotation before removing
Camshaft timing belt gear
Special washer
Bolt
Pivot bolt (note*)
Lower cover
Bolt
Adjust bolt (note*)
Rubber seal washer
Timing belt tensioner
Alternator belt
Install with concave surface facing in
Crank pulley
Crankshaft timing belt gear
Bolt
Water pump pulley
Install with concave surface facing out
M6 x 1.0 x 12
Special washer
* Note: For adjustment only; do not remove.

4

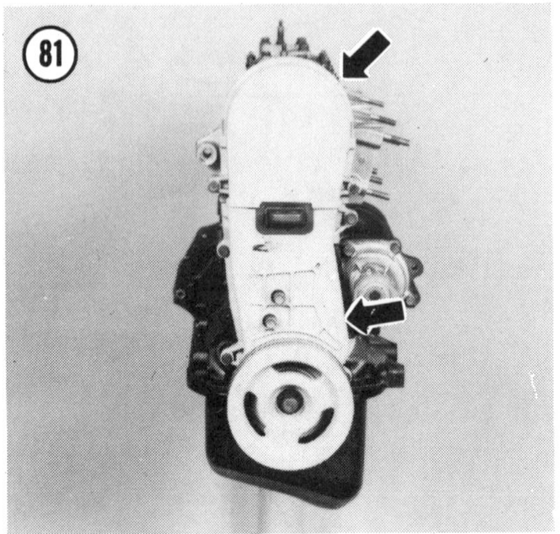

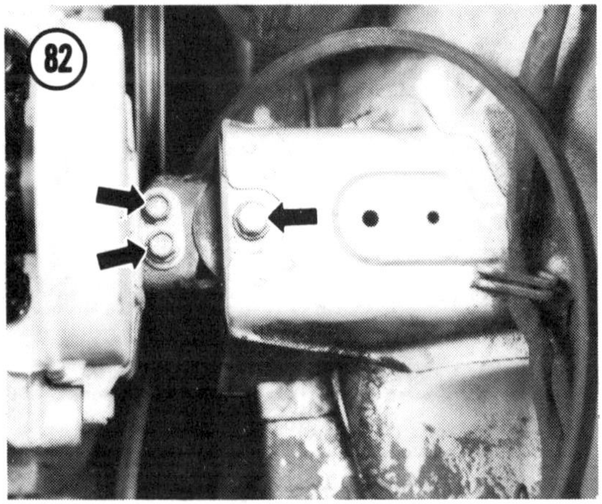

vehicles equipped with air pump, remove accessory drive belts also.

4. Remove the attaching bolts and remove the water pump pulley (**Figure 84**). Then remove the pulley cover protector as shown in **Figure 85** (if so equipped).

5. Remove the crankshaft pulley bolt plug from the left fender well. Using a socket with a ratchet and extension, turn the crankshaft counterclockwise (**Figure 78**) to align the flywheel timing marks as shown in **Figure 71** (non-CVCC), **Figure 72** (1975-1979 CVCC), **Figure 73** (1980 CVCC) or **Figure 74** (1981 CVCC).

6. Remove the crankshaft bolt (**Figure 86**) and slide the pulley off the end of crankshaft.

7. Loosen the attaching bolts and remove the upper cover (**Figure 79**).

8. Remove the washers from behind the timing belt pivot and adjusting bolts (**Figure 80**). Then remove the lower cover retaining bolts and remove the lower cover. See **Figure 80**.

9. Installation is the reverse of these steps. After installing the front cover, install the rubber washers behind the timing belt pivot and adjusting bolts (**Figure 80**).

10. Adjust the drive belt(s) as described in Chapter Three.

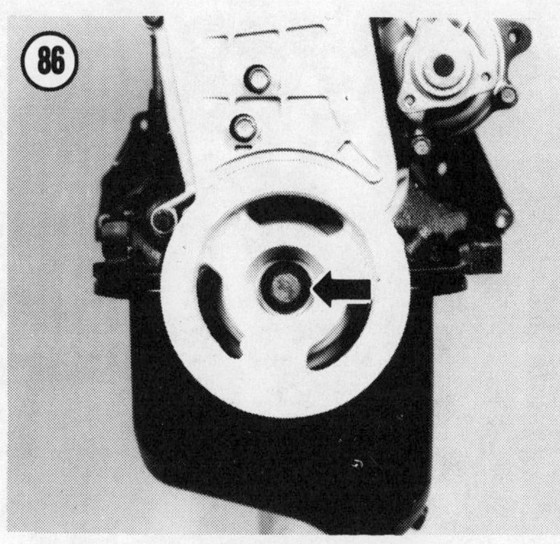

Timing Belt Replacement

The timing belt is made of fiberglass and should be handled with care. When removing the belt, do not use sharp objects to pry the belt off the sprockets; do not bend or twist the belt. Do not oil the belt for any reason.

1. Remove the upper and lower front covers as described in this chapter.

2. Remove the crankshaft pulley bolt plug from the left fender well (**Figure 75**). Using a socket with a ratchet and extension, turn the crankshaft counterclockwise to align the timing marks as shown in **Figures 71-74**.

3. Draw an arrow on the timing belt with chalk, pointing in the counterclockwise direction (**Figure 80**).

4. Slide the timing belt off the camshaft sprocket and the crankshaft gear and remove from the engine. Be careful not to twist or nick the belt.

5. Inspect the timing belt for cracks, excessive wear marks and oil which may be on the belt. Replace the belt if any of these problems are found.

6. Line up the marks on the camshaft sprocket and the head as shown in **Figure 50**.

7A. *Non-CVCC models*: Turn the crankshaft counterclockwise to align the TDC mark on pulley with the front cover pointer. See **Figure 71**.

7B. *CVCC models*: Turn the crankshaft counterclockwise to align the TDC mark on the flywheel or drive plate with the crankcase pointer. See **Figures 72-74**.

NOTE
Align the pointer with the top dead center mark, not the timing mark.

8. Position the timing belt on the crankshaft gear and then slide the belt onto the camshaft sprocket.

9. Install the upper and lower front covers as described in this chapter.

10. Loosen (do not remove) the cam tensioner pivot and adjustment bolts (**Figure 77**). Then rotate the crankshaft counterclockwise 90° (one-quarter turn). This puts tension on the timing belt. Tighten the adjustment and pivot bolts to specifications (end of chapter).

Lower Front Cover
Oil Seal Replacement

1. Remove the lower front cover as described in this chapter.

2. Carefully pry out the old oil seal using a screwdriver. Do not gouge the cover.

3. Coat the seal lip with multipurpose grease. Tap in the new seal using a suitable size drift or socket.

4. Install the lower cover as described in this chapter.

CYLINDER HEAD

Removal

The cylinder head should be removed only when the engine temperature is below 100° F to prevent warpage.

1. Disconnect the negative battery cable.
2. Drain the radiator and disconnect the top hoses from the thermostat cover and cylinder head (**Figure 87**).
3. Remove the spark plugs.
4. Refer to Chapter Five and perform the following:
   a. Remove the air cleaner assembly.
   b. Disconnect the fuel line, choke cable and throttle cable at the carburetor.
   c. Remove the carburetor (1980-on models).

5A. *Non-air conditioned vehicles*: Loosen the alternator bracket bolts. Then remove the upper alternator bracket-to-cylinder head bolt.
5B. *Air conditioned vehicles*: Remove the compressor as described under *Engine Removal/Installation* in this chapter. Then remove the upper alternator bracket and alternator. See Chapter Seven.

WARNING
Do not disconnect any hoses from the compressor.

6. Remove the distributor as described in Chapter Seven.
7. Unscrew the nuts from the exhaust pipe flange at the bottom of the manifold.
8. Disconnect the tachometer cable, if so equipped.
9. Label and disconnect or remove any emission control plugs or hoses which will interfere with cylinder head removal.
10. Unscrew the nuts on the valve cover and remove it (**Figure 88**).
11. Unscrew the bolts from the upper front cover and remove it (**Figure 79**).
12. Rotate the crankshaft with a wrench on the crankshaft pulley bolt. Bring the No. 1 piston to TDC on the compression stroke (both valves closed) and align the camshaft pulley with the cylinder head surface as shown in **Figure 89**.
13. Loosen the timing belt pivot and adjustment bolts (**Figure 77**). Then slip the timing belt off the camshaft sprocket.

CAUTION
Do not remove the timing belt pivot and adjustment bolts.

CAUTION
Do not bend or twist the belt or use sharp instruments when removing it. Also keep grease and oil out of contact with the belt as they will cause the belt to deteriorate.

14. Unscrew the bolts from the oil pump gear housing (**Figure 90**), then remove the housing, gear and shaft. See **Figure 91**.
15. Unscrew the cylinder head bolts in the pattern shown in **Figure 92**. Remove the cylinder head with the intake and exhaust

89

CAMSHAFT PULLEY TIMING

1973-1979 NON-CVCC

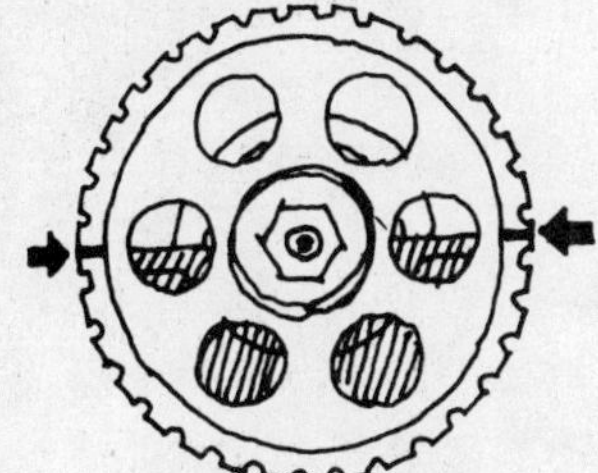

Turn pulley until both timing marks are aligned with the valve cover surface.

1975-1979 CVCC

Turn pulley until "UP" mark is at top and the timing mark is aligned with arrow on cylinder head

1980-ON 1300cc CVCC

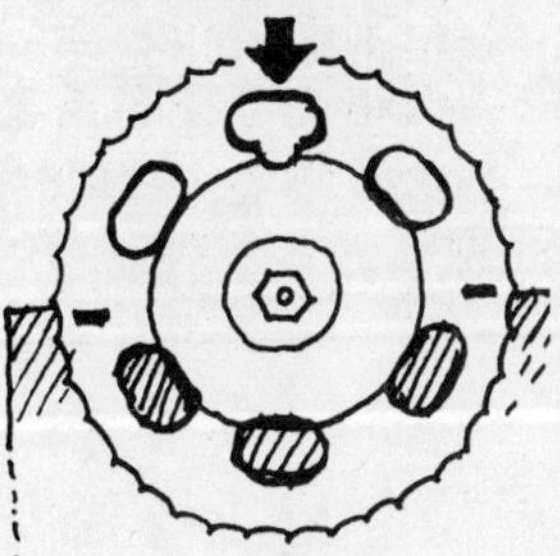

Turn pulley until cutaway faces up and both timing marks are aligned with the valve cover surface

1980-ON 1500cc CVCC

Turn pulley until cutaway faces up and the front timing mark is aligned with arrow on cylinder head

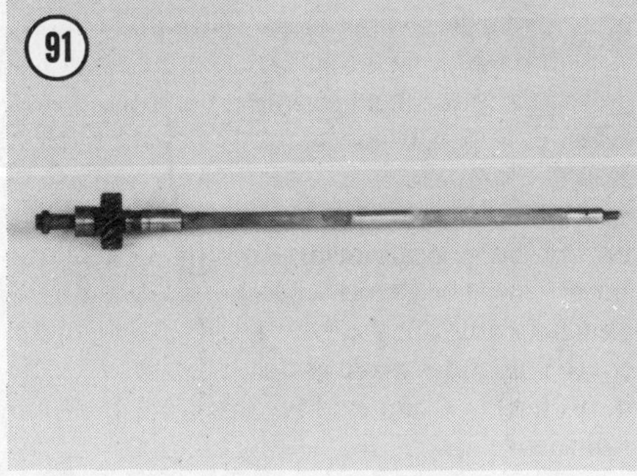

92

CYLINDER HEAD TORQUE SEQUENCE

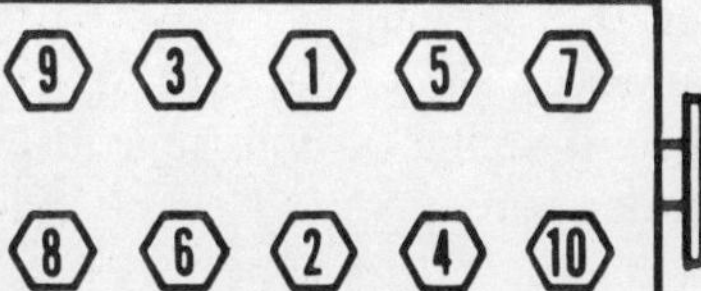

4

manifolds attached. Cover the top of the block with a clean shop cloth.

16. Remove the intake and exhaust manifolds from the cylinder head as described in Chapter Five.

Inspection

1. Check the cylinder head for water leaks before cleaning.
2. Clean the cylinder head thoroughly in solvent. While cleaning, check for cracks or other visible damage. Look for corrosion or foreign material in oil or water passages. Clean the passages with a stiff spiral wire brush, then blow them out with compressed air.
3. Check the cylinder head bottom (block mating) surface for flatness. Place an accurate straightedge along the surface. See **Figure 93**. If there is any gap between the straightedge and cylinder head surface, measure it with a feeler gauge. Compare with specifications (end of chapter). If warpage exceeds service limit, have the cylinder head resurfaced by a machine shop.
4. Check studs in the cylinder head for general condition and replace as needed.

Decarbonizing

1. Without removing valves, remove all deposits from the combustion chambers, intake ports and exhaust ports. Use a wire brush dipped in solvent or make a scraper out of hardwood. Be careful not to scratch or gouge the combustion chambers.
2. After all carbon is removed from the combustion chambers and ports, clean the entire head in solvent.
3. Clean away all carbon on the piston tops. Do not remove the carbon ridge at the top of the cylinder bore.

Installation

1. Clean the cylinder head mating surfaces and the engine block, intake manifold and valve cover surfaces to which the cylinder head mounts. Be sure that the cylinder bores are

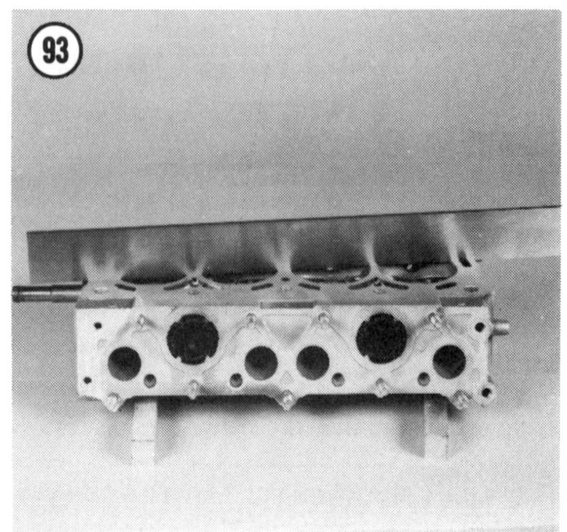

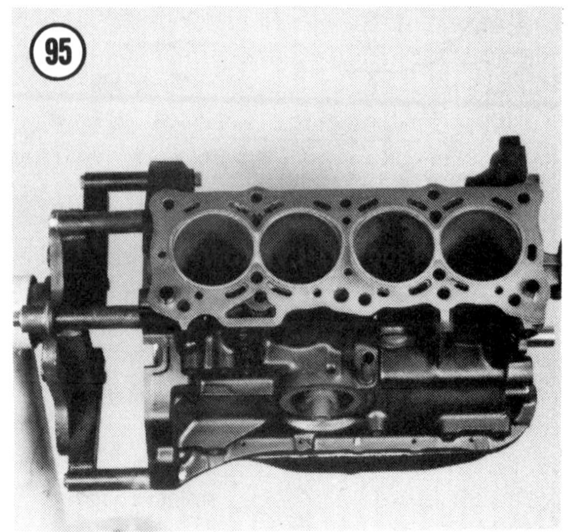

clean and check all visible oil and water passages for cleanliness.

NOTE
Make sure to clean all cylinder bolt threads in the cylinder block and the cylinder head bolt threads. Dirt present will affect bolt torque.

2. Return any dowel pins from the cylinder head back into position in the cylinder block to help in positioning the cylinder head gasket (**Figure 94**).
3. Install the camshaft and rocker arm assembly onto the cylinder head, if removed. See *Rocker Arm/Camshaft Installation*, this chapter.

NOTE
Do not install the oil pump gear and cover at this time.

4. Install the exhaust/intake manifold assemblies to the cylinder head as described in Chapter Five.

NOTE
Install a new exhaust flange gasket when attaching the exhaust pipe to the exhaust manifold.

5. Make sure the No. 1 piston is at TDC by viewing the timing marks shown in **Figures 71-74**.
6. Place a new cylinder head gasket onto the cylinder block. Make sure the gasket matches correctly with the dowel pins and cylinder bolt thread holes (**Figure 95**).
7. Position the cylinder head onto the cylinder block.
8. With the engine cool, tighten the head bolts in 2 stages, following the sequence in **Figure 92**. Tighten to specifications at the end of the chapter.
9. Insert the oil pump gear and shaft into the cylinder head. Tighten the gear cover to specifications (end of chapter).
10. Install the timing belt, camshaft sprocket and front covers as described in this chapter.
11. Adjust the valve clearances as described in Chapter Three.
12. Install the spark plugs and valve cover.

VALVES AND VALVE SEATS

Intake/Exhaust Valve Removal

Figure 96 (non-CVCC) and **Figure 97** (CVCC) show the intake and exhaust valve assemblies.

1. Remove the cylinder head as described in this chapter.
2. Install a valve spring compressor squarely over the head of the valve (**Figure 98**). Position the opposite end of the compressor over the valve retainer.
3. Compress the spring compressor until the valve spring keepers separate (**Figure 99**). Remove the valve keepers.
4. Slowly loosen the valve spring compressor and remove from the cylinder head.
5. Lift off the valve retainer.

CAUTION
Remove any burrs from valve stem grooves before removing the valves. Otherwise, the valve guides will be damaged.

6. Remove the inner and outer valve springs, then remove the valve.
7. Use needlenose pliers and remove the old valve guide oil seal. Discard seal.
8. Remove the lower valve spring seats.
9. Place the valve, spring, retainer, keepers and lower seat in a small bag. Label the bag as to cylinder number.

CAUTION
The valve assembly parts should not be intermixed, nor should they be installed in any location other than the one from which they were removed.

10. Repeat procedure for remaining valves.

4

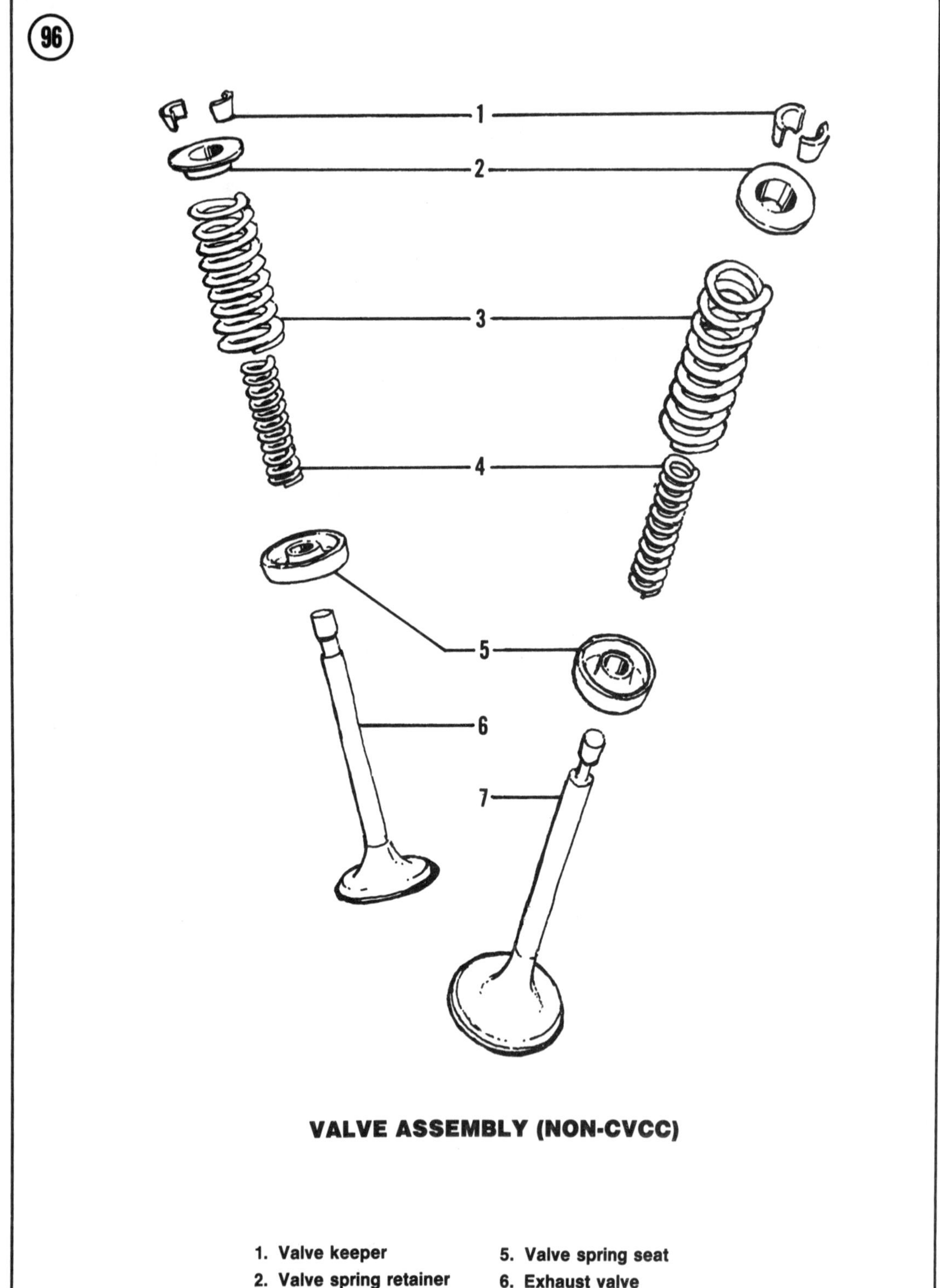

VALVE ASSEMBLY (NON-CVCC)

1. Valve keeper
2. Valve spring retainer
3. Outer valve spring
4. Inner valve spring
5. Valve spring seat
6. Exhaust valve
7. Intake valve

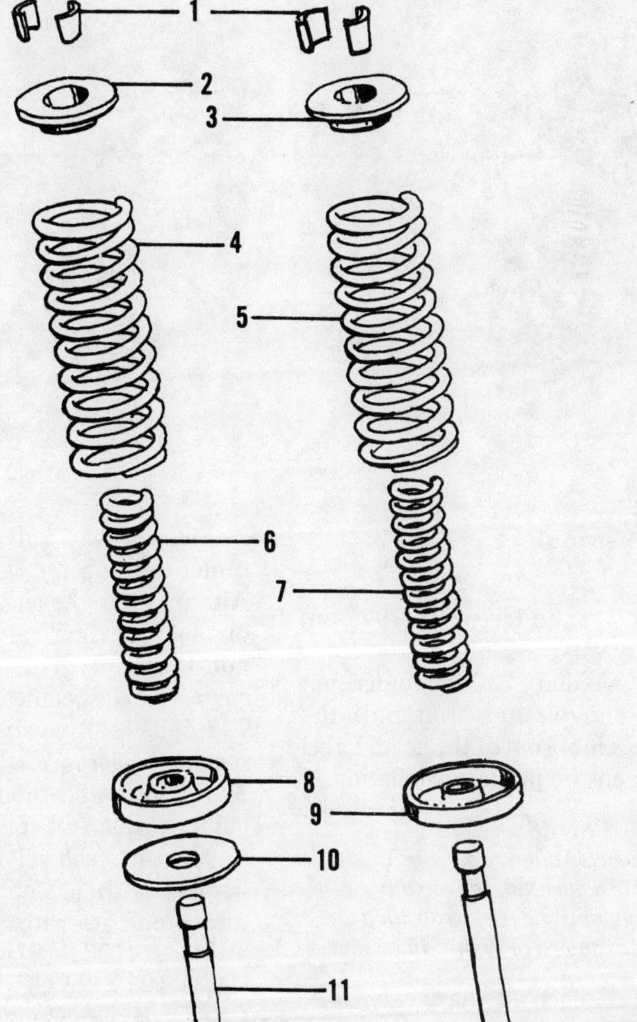

VALVE ASSEMBLY (CVCC)

1. Valve keepers
2. Exhaust valve spring retainer
3. Intake valve spring retainer
4. Exhaust valve outer spring
5. Intake valve outer spring
6. Exhaust valve inner spring
7. Intake valve inner spring
8. Exhaust valve spring seat
9. Intake valve spring seat
10. Exhaust spring seat spacer
11. Exhaust valve
12. Intake valve

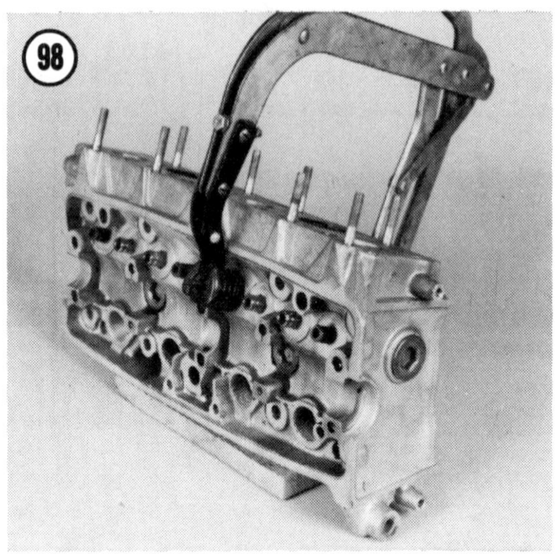

98

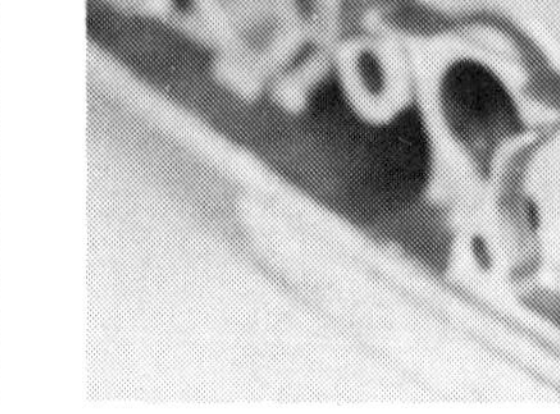

99

Auxiliary Valve Removal (CVCC Only)

Figure 100 (1975) and **Figure 101** (1976-on) show the auxiliary valve assembly.

1. Unscrew the auxiliary valve holder nut using an open-end wrench and pull the auxiliary valve assembly out of the head. Label valve position to ensure proper installation.

NOTE

*On 1981 models, after removing the auxiliary valve holder nut, the auxiliary valve assembly must be removed with a knock puller as shown in **Figure 102**.*

2. Repeat Step 1 for each auxiliary valve.
3. Place the auxiliary valve assembly into a valve spring compressor as shown in **Figure 103**. Compress the auxiliary valve and remove the valve keepers. Disassemble each auxiliary valve. Place each valve assembly in a bag and mark it for location in the cylinder head.

CAUTION

The valve assembly parts should not be intermixed, nor should they be installed in any location other than the one from which they were removed.

Intake/Exhaust Valve and Valve Guide Inspection

1. Clean the valves with a wire brush and solvent. Discard cracked, warped or burned valves.
2. Measure the valve stems at the bottom, center and top for wear, using a micrometer. Also measure the length of each valve and the diameter of each valve head. See **Table 2** for non-CVCC valve specifications. CVCC engine valve specifications are found in **Table 9**. Replace any valve which is not within specified tolerance.
3. Remove all carbon and varnish from valve guides with a stiff spiral wire brush.
4. Measure each valve guide at top, center and bottom with a small hole gauge. Compare measurements with service specifications in **Table 2** (1973-1979 non-CVCC), **Table 3** (1975-1979 CVCC) or **Table 4** (1980-on CVCC). Have a Honda dealer or machine shop replace any guide which exceeds the maximum service limit.

NOTE

The next step assumes that all valves and valve guides have been measured and are within service specifications. Replace any valves with worn stems or worn valve guides before performing Step 5.

5. Subtract the valve stem measurements made in Step 2 from the valve guide measurements made in Step 4. The difference between the measurements equals the valve guide-to-valve stem clearance. Compare difference with service specifications in **Table**

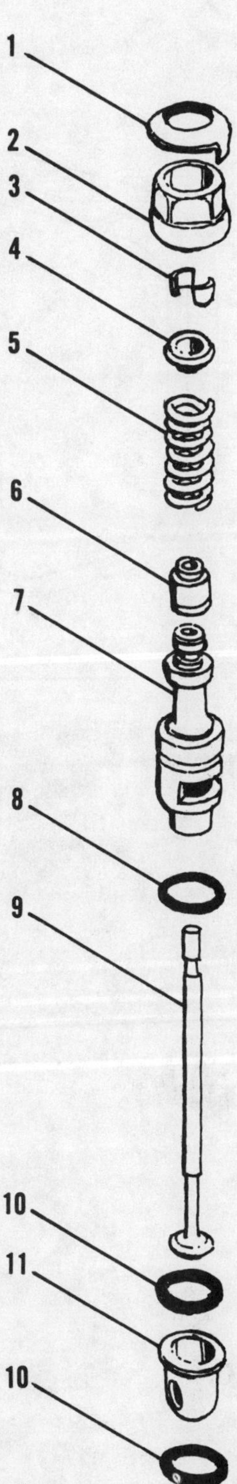

AUXILIARY VALVE (1975 CVCC)

1. Nut lock cap
2. Valve holder nut
3. Valve keeper
4. Valve spring retainer
5. Valve spring
6. Valve stem seal
7. Valve holder assembly
8. O-ring
9. Auxiliary valve
10. Valve holder gasket
11. Chamber collar

4

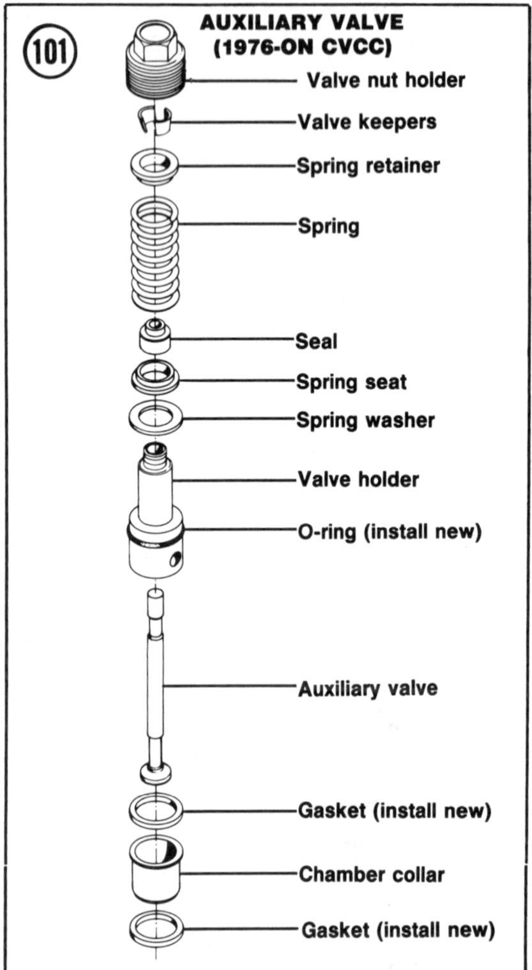
101
AUXILIARY VALVE
(1976-ON CVCC)
Valve nut holder
Valve keepers
Spring retainer
Spring
Seal
Spring seat
Spring washer
Valve holder
O-ring (install new)
Auxiliary valve
Gasket (install new)
Chamber collar
Gasket (install new)

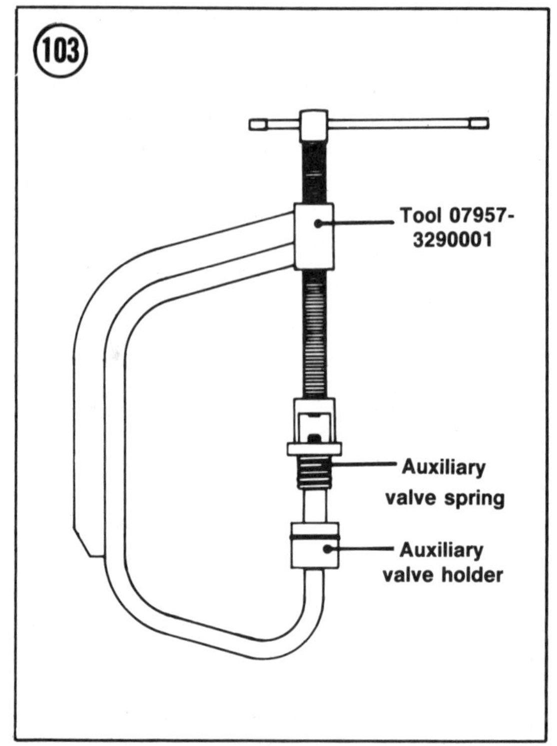
103
Tool 07957-
3290001
Auxiliary
valve spring
Auxiliary
valve holder

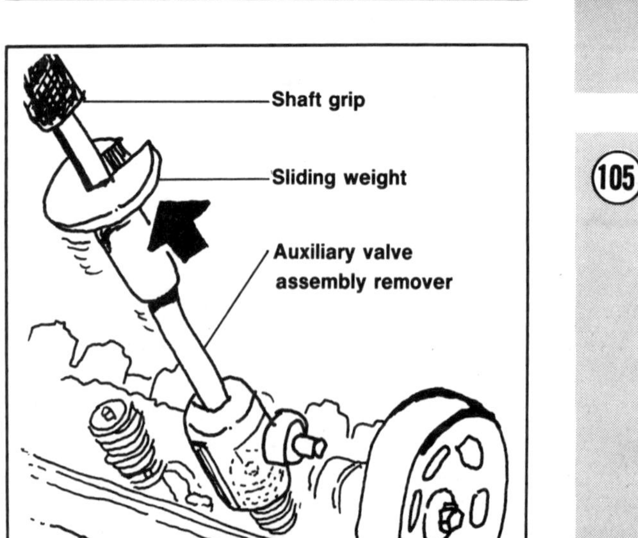
Shaft grip
Sliding weight
Auxiliary valve
assembly remover
102

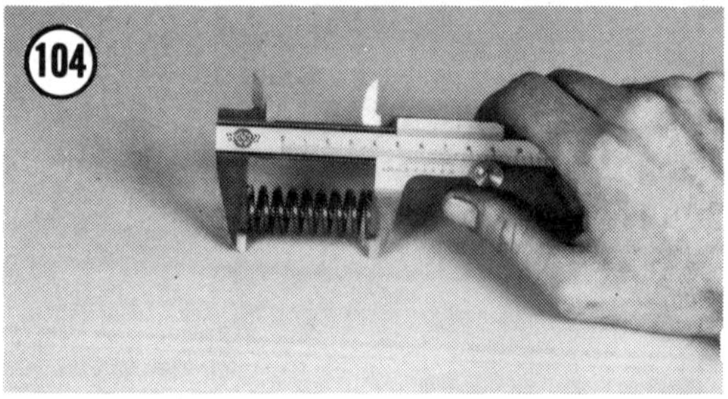

104

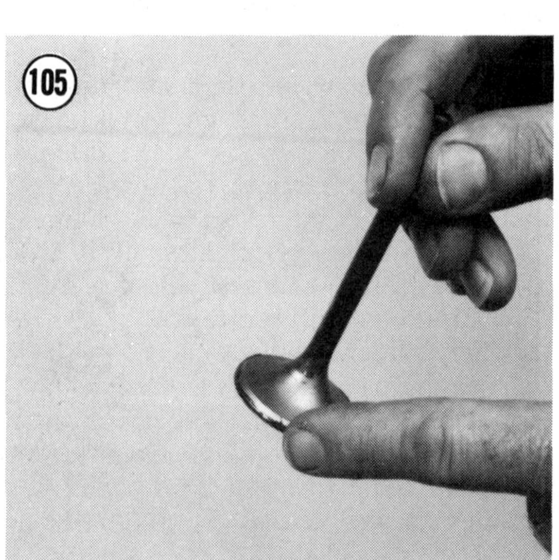
105

2, **Table 3** or **Table 4**. Replace any guide or valve as necessary.

6. Measure valve spring free length (**Figure 104**) and compare with specifications in **Table 2**, **Table 3** or **Table 4**. Replace springs that are too long or too short. Measure spring bend with a square. Replace springs that are bent more than 1.5 mm (0.06 in.).

7. Have the valve springs tested under load on a spring tester by your Honda dealer. Replace weak springs.

8. Check valve spring retainer and valve keepers. If they are in questionable condition, they must be replaced.

Auxiliary Valve Inspection (CVCC Only)

1. Clean the valves with a wire brush and solvent. Discard cracked, warped or burned valves.

2. Measure the valve stems at the bottom, center and top for wear, using a micrometer. Also measure the length of each valve and the diameter of each valve head. See **Table 9**. Replace any valve which is worn beyond service tolerances.

3. Measure the auxiliary valve holder inside diameter. Record measurement for each holder assembly.

NOTE

The next step assumes that all auxiliary valves have been measured and are within service specifications.

4. Subtract the valve stem measurements made in Step 2 from the valve holder measurements made in Step 3. The difference between the measurements equals the valve holder-to-valve stem clearance. Compare clearance with service specifications in **Table 3** (1975-1979 CVCC) or **Table 4** (1980-on CVCC). If clearance is excessive, replace the auxiliary valve assembly.

5. Measure the auxiliary valve seat width in the cylinder head. Compare with specifications in **Table 3** or **Table 4**. Replace any auxiliary valve and its valve holder if valve seat width exceeds service tolerance. Refer valve holder replacement to a Honda dealer.

6. Check the auxiliary valve retainer and valve keepers. If they are in questionable condition, they must be replaced.

Intake/Exhaust Valve Guide Replacement

This procedures requires Honda special tools. Refer all service to a Honda dealer.

Intake/Exhaust Valve Guide Reaming

Newly installed valve guides must be reamed to the proper size. Refer this procedure to your Honda dealer or a machine shop.

Valve Lapping

Valve lapping should only be performed on cylinder heads whose valves and seats are in good condition. Lapping should be considered a "touch up" operation, not a cure for burned or damaged valves and/or seats.

1. Remove and inspect the valves as described in this chapter.

2. Smear a light coating of fine grade valve lapping compound on seating surface of valve (**Figure 105**).

3. Install valve into head and use "suction cup" type lapping tool to lap valves. Spin tool between palms while lifting and moving valve around seat 1/4 turn at a time.

NOTE

An excellent homemade tool to spin valves is a length of fuel line hose. For strength, insert a screw in one end of the hose. When the valve is inserted in the cylinder head, push the hose onto the end of the valve and spin the valve by turning the hose as in Step 3 (above).

4. Wipe off valve and seat frequently to check progress of lapping. Lap only enough to achieve a precise seating ring around valve head (**Figure 106**). Measure width of seat as shown in **Figure 107**. If seat width is not within tolerance (**Tables 2-4**), the valve seat in the cylinder head must be resurfaced. See *Intake/Exhaust Valve Seat Reconditioning*.

5. Closely examine valve seat in cylinder head. It should be even with a smooth, polished seating ring.

106

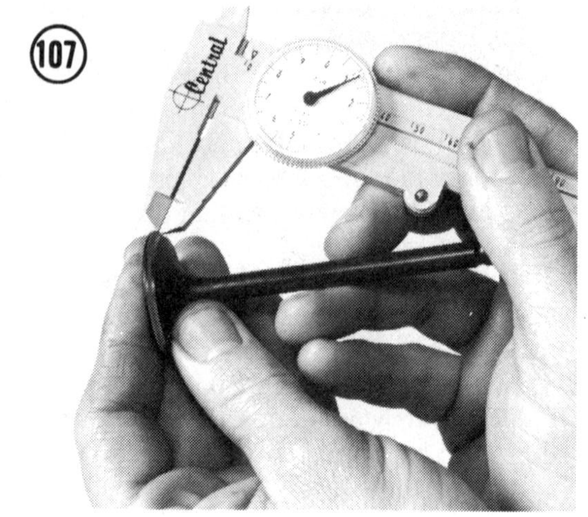
107

6. Repeat for each valve.
7. Use solvent and clean off all traces of grinding compound from valves and seats.
8. Perform *Intake/Exhaust Valve Installation.*

Intake/Exhaust Valve Seat Reconditioning

This job is best left to a Honda dealer or competent machine shop. They have the special knowledge and equipment for this precise job. You can save considerable time by removing the cylinder head and just taking the head to the dealer. The following procedure is provided in the event that you are not near a dealer or machine shop.

Valve seats are shrunk into the cylinder head. Damaged or burned seats may be reconditioned until valve exceeds a specified installed height tolerance.

1. Clean the cylinder head thoroughly. Remove all oil and grease with solvent. Carbon collected in the combustion chamber area can be removed with a wire brush.
2. Clean and check the condition of the valve guides as described in this chapter. Always replace worn valve guides before cutting valve seats.
3. Using a valve seat cutter or special stone, cut the valve seat face. Do not take off any more metal than necessary to provide a clean, concentric seat. See **Figure 108** (non-CVCC) or **Figure 109** (CVCC) for valve seat specifications.
4. With the correct valve seat cutter (see **Figure 108** or **Figure 109**), remove just enough metal from the top of seat to make it concentric. Change cutters and repeat at bottom of seat.

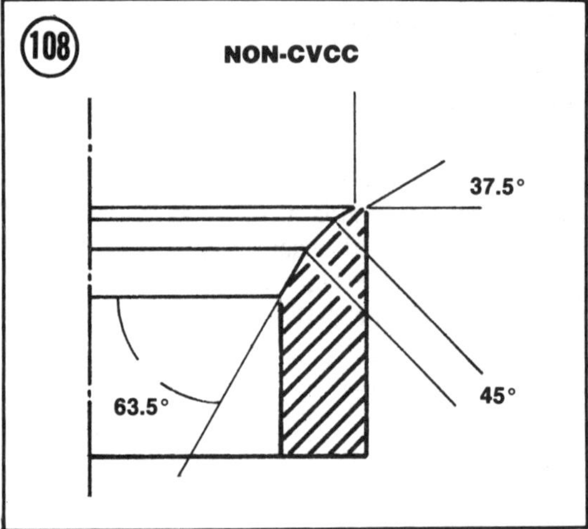

108

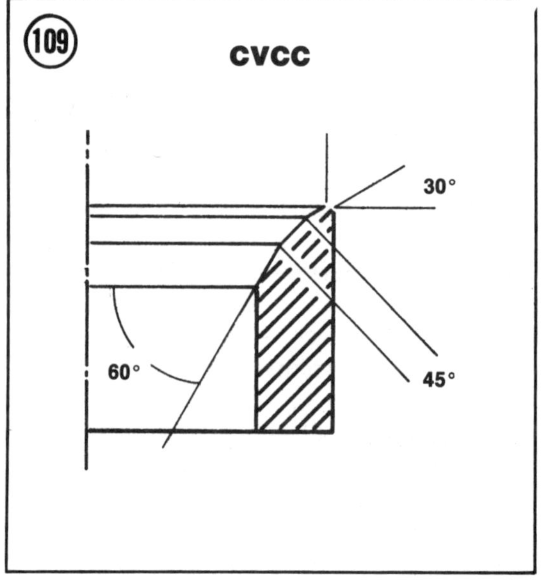

109

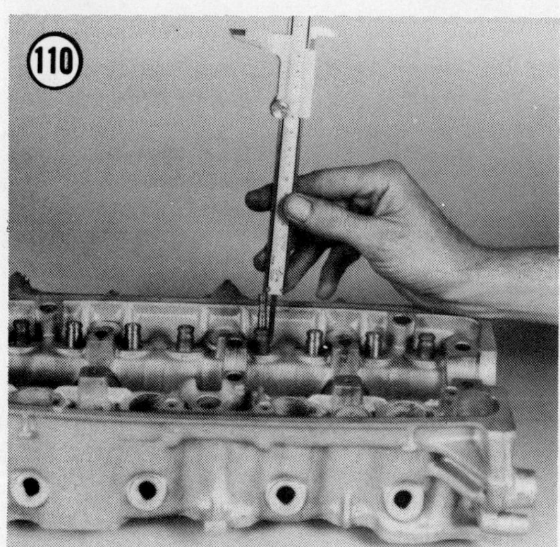

5. Measure width of valve seat and compare to specifications in **Table 2**, **Table 3** or **Table 4**. If the valve seat width is not within specification, perform the following:
   a. If the valve seat is too high, make a cut with the bottom seat cutter. This will lower the valve seat.
   b. If the valve seat is too low, make a cut with the top seat cutter. This will raise the valve seat.
6. After performing Step 5 as necessary, make one more cut with the face cutter to restore the valve seat width.

NOTE
The cylinder head must be replaced if valve seats cannot be serviced to provide correct angle and seat width.

7. *CVCC models:* Install valve into its valve guide. Press valve into its seat firmly and measure the installed height as indicated in **Figure 110**. Compare with specifications in **Table 10**. If installed height exceeds service limit, repeat check with new valve. If height is still excessive, replace the cylinder head as the valve seat in head is worn too deep.
8. Repeat Steps 1-6 (non-CVCC) or Steps 1-7 (CVCC) for each valve.

Intake/Exhaust Valve Installation

Clean the valve and cylinder head thoroughly in solvent before installing. Proper cleaning is especially critical if valve lapping compound was used; any trace of the compound left on a valve or in the cylinder head will cause excessive component wear during engine operation.

1. Coat the valves with oil and insert them in the cylinder head.
2. Install the valve spring seats, oil seals, springs, and spring retainers. Compress the valve springs and install the keepers (**Figure 99**).
3. Hit the valve end lightly with a plastic hammer to ensure correct valve and valve keeper seating.

4

Auxiliary Valve Reconditioning (CVCC Only)

Reconditioning of auxiliary valves requires a number of special tools. This job should only be performed by a Honda dealer.

Auxiliary Valve Installation (CVCC Only)

Refer to **Figure 100** (1975 CVCC) or **Figure 101** (1976-on CVCC) for this procedure.

1. Coat a new auxiliary valve O-ring with molybdenum disulfide grease and install it.
2. Install 2 new gaskets onto top and bottom of auxiliary chamber and insert chamber into cylinder head. Round hole in chamber should face toward spark plug hole. Insert a drift through spark plug hole and into hole in auxiliary chamber. This ensures that the auxiliary chamber will not turn when tightening the auxiliary valve.
3. Coat the auxiliary valve assembly with engine assembly lube.
4. Place the auxiliary valve into position in the auxiliary chamber in the cylinder head. Make sure to align the dowel pin in the side of the valve holder with the slot in the cylinder head (if so equipped).
5. Tighten the auxiliary valve locknut to specifications (**Table 7** or **Table 8**).
6. Repeat Steps 1-5 for each auxiliary valve.

OIL PAN AND PUMP

A typical oil pan assembly is shown in **Figure 111**. Refer to it when performing the following procedures.

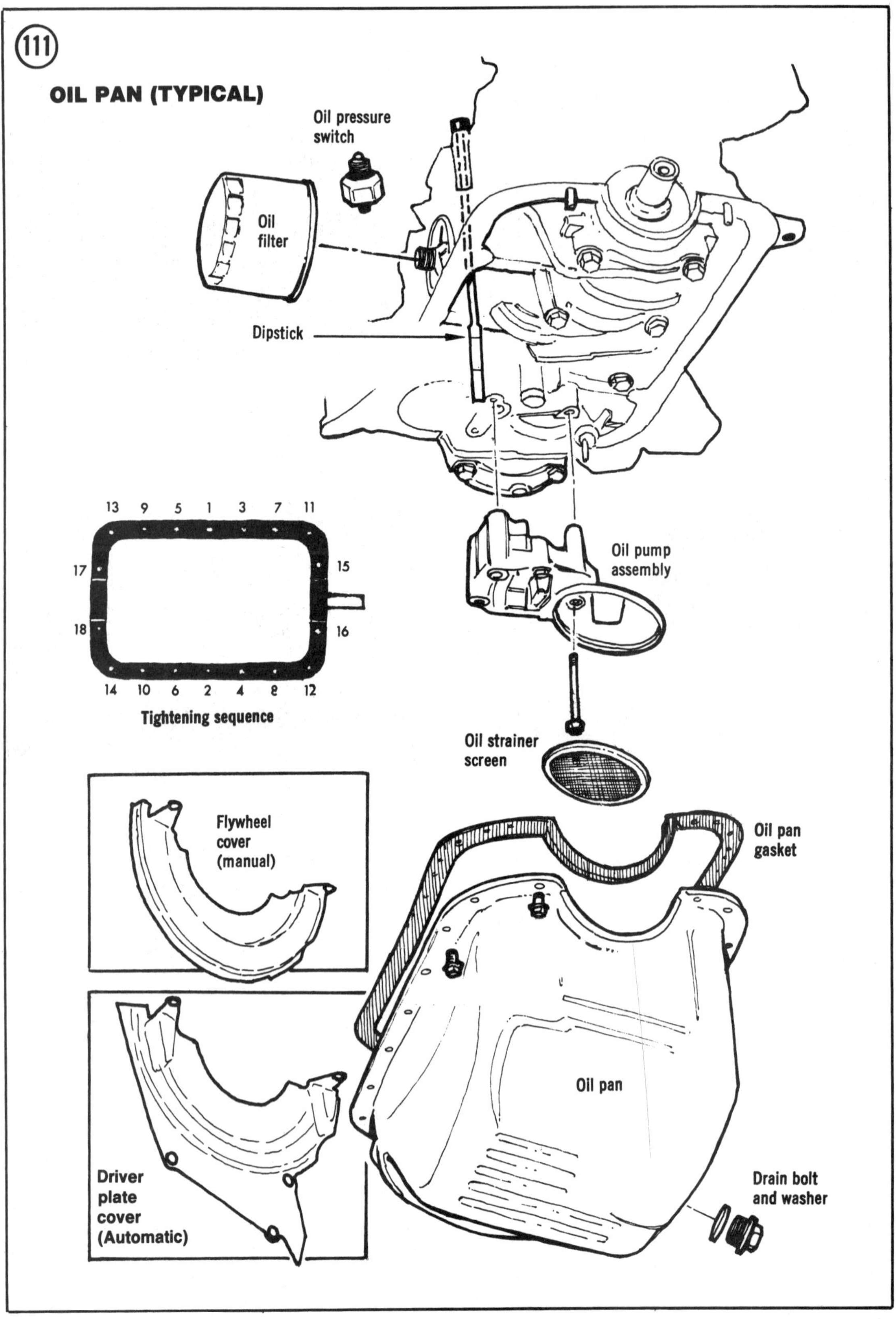
111
OIL PAN (TYPICAL)
Oil pressure switch
Oil filter
Dipstick
13 9 5 1 3 7 11
17
15
18
16
14 10 6 2 4 8 12
Tightening sequence
Oil pump assembly
Oil strainer screen
Flywheel cover (manual)
Oil pan gasket
Oil pan
Driver plate cover (Automatic)
Drain bolt and washer

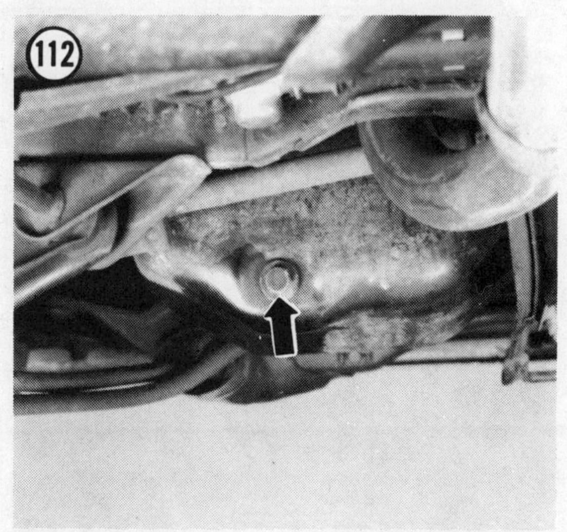

4

Oil Pan Removal/Installation

1. Jack up the front end of the vehicle and place it on jackstands.
2. Remove the engine drain plug (**Figure 112**) and drain the oil. Discard the drain plug gasket.
3. Hook a chain hoist to the clutch cable bracket and lift the engine just enough to remove engine weight from the center beam mount. Then remove the center beam and lower engine mount (if so equipped).
4. Unscrew the oil pan bolts in the pattern shown in **Figure 111** and remove the oil pan and dust shield from the bellhousing. It may be necessary to tap on the corners of the pan with a soft mallet to break it loose. If the pan gasket is in good shape, it may be left in place and reused.
5. Clean the oil pan thoroughly. If it is difficult to clean, have the pan boiled out by a machine shop. Check for cracks, dents, bent gasket surfaces and damaged drain hole threads. Replace the oil pan if damage is severe.
6. Check for a clogged oil strainer screen. See **Figure 113** (non-CVCC and 1300 CVCC) or **Figure 114** (1500 CVCC). Remove the strainer and clean it if necessary.
7. Installation is the reverse of these steps. Coat the gasket surface with sealer except where the gasket fits around the crankshaft oil seal. Tighten the oil pan bolts in the pattern shown in **Figure 111** a little at a time, to prevent warping the pan.

Oil Pump Removal/Installation

1. Remove the oil pan as described in this chapter.
2. Unscrew the oil pump attaching bolts on the outside of the pump. See **Figure 115** (non-CVCC and 1300 CVCC) or **Figure 116**

(1500 CVCC). Then remove the oil strainer screen and remove the one hidden bolt (**Figure 116**).
3. Remove the oil pump.
4. Installation is the reverse of these steps.

Oil Pump Disassembly/Assembly

Refer to **Figure 117** (non-CVCC) or **Figure 118** (CVCC) for this procedure.

1. Remove the cotter pin from the pump relief valve. See **Figure 119** (non-CVCC) or **Figure 120** (CVCC). Remove the valve seat, spring, and valve. Discard the cotter pin.

2. Place the pump so that the oil pump cover faces upward. Unscrew the bolts from the pump body and remove the oil pump cover from the pump body. Note any index markings on the outer and inner rotor parts, then disassemble the pump.

3. Clean all of the parts thoroughly with solvent and blow them dry with compressed air. Then inspect all pump parts as described in this chapter.

4. Lightly oil all parts.

5. Insert the relief valve, spring and valve seat into the oil pump cover. Secure with new cotter pin.

6. Assemble the outer rotor and inner rotor assembly into the oil pump body. Make sure the alignment marks on both rotors are lined up when assembled. Install the pump shaft and lock pin.

7. Assemble both housings, making sure the center gasket is not torn or damaged. Replace it if necessary.

8. Install the housing retaining screws and tighten securely.

Oil Pump Inspection

Oil pump specifications are found in **Table 2** (1973-1979 non-CVCC), **Table 3** (1975-1979 CVCC) and **Table 4** (1980-on CVCC).
1. Assemble the inner and outer rotors in the pump body and check their radial clearance with a flat feeler gauge (**Figure 121**).

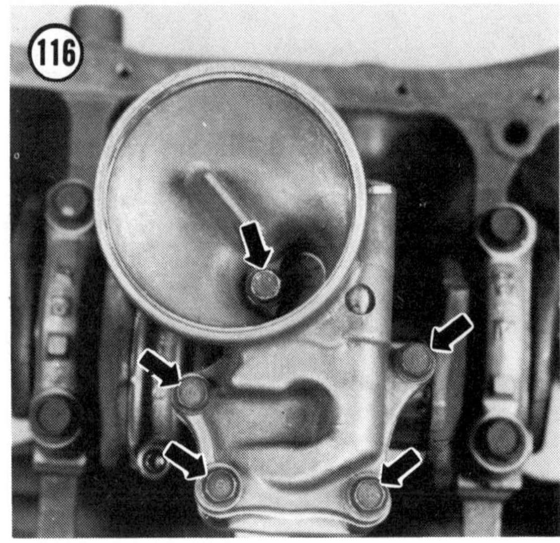
116

2. Measure the side clearance between the outer rotor and the pump body with a flat feeler gauge. See **Figure 122**.
3. Install the gasket and measure the axial clearance between the rotors and a precision flat edge with a feeler gauge as shown in **Figure 123**.
4. Install the relief valve(s) and check its fit. It should move freely in the valve bore without any wobble.
5. Any parts that are obviously worn or damaged or that exceed the service limits should be replaced.

NOTE
Steps 6-8 describe CVCC oil pump inspection procedures that are performed with the pump installed on the car.

6. Remove the valve cover as described in this chapter.
7. Remove the oil pump gear cover (**Figure 124**). Install a dial indicator as shown in **Figure 125**. Place the tip of the indicator against the gear teeth. Press down on the gear and then gently turn the gear back and forth. Backlash specification is found in **Table 3** or **Table 4**. Replace the gear and shaft if backlash is excessive.

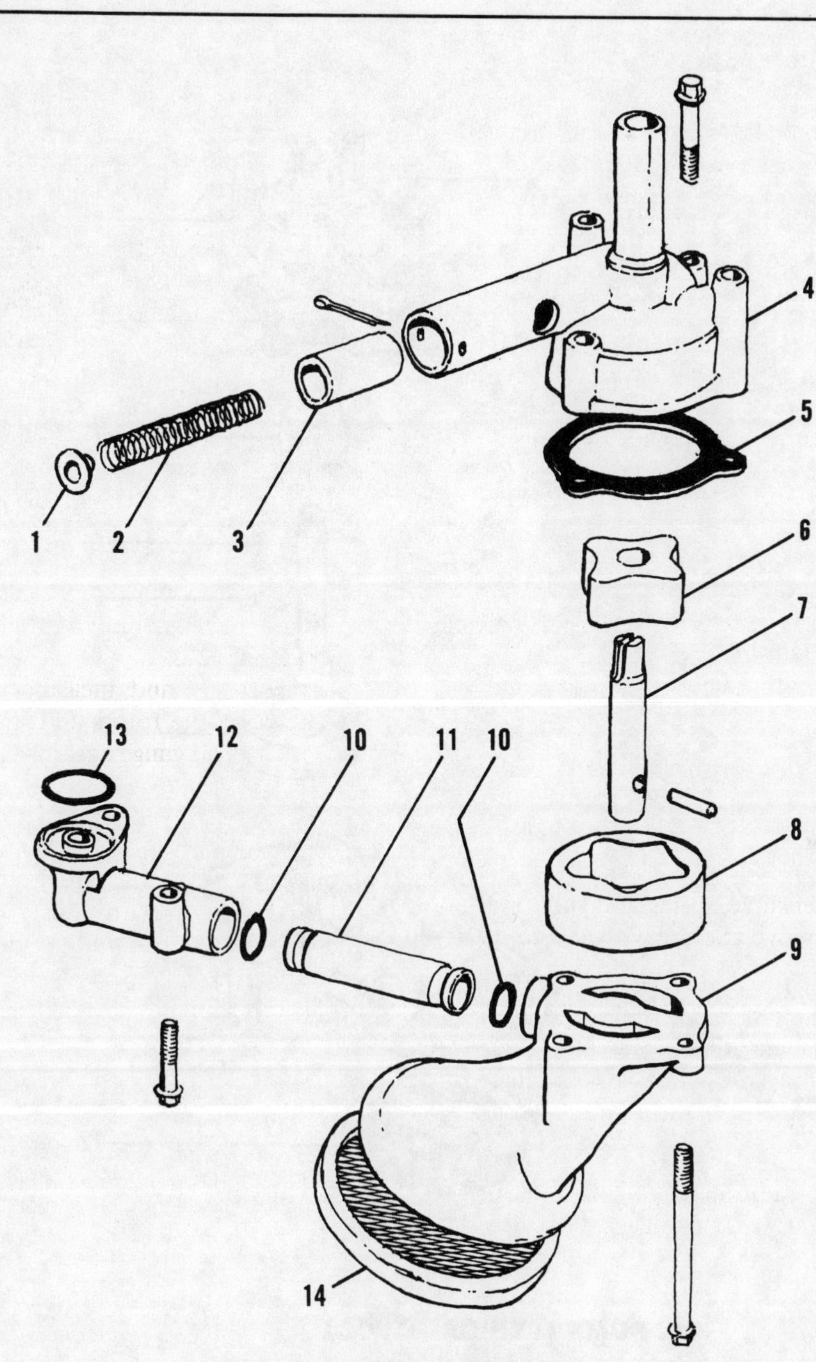

OIL PUMP (NON-CVCC)

1. Relief valve spring seat
2. Relief valve spring
3. Oil pressure relief valve
4. Oil pump body
5. Pump body gasket
6. Inner rotor
7. Oil pump shaft
8. Outer rotor
9. Strainer body
10. O-ring
11. Oil passage pipe
12. Oil passage block
13. O-ring
14. Filter screen

118

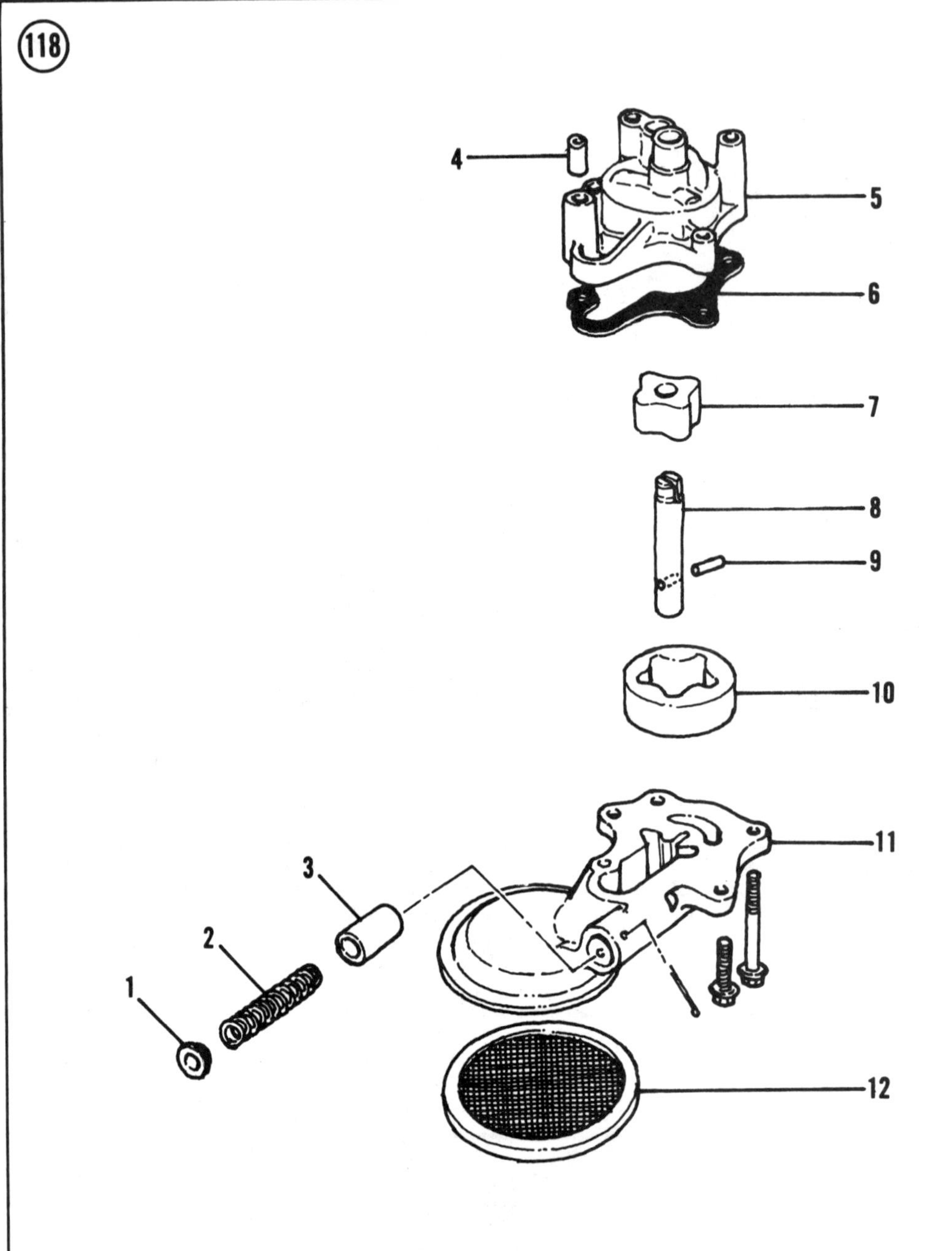

OIL PUMP (TYPICAL CVCC)

1. Relief valve spring seat
2. Relief valve spring
3. Oil pressure relief valve
4. Dowel pin
5. Oil pump body
6. Body gasket
7. Inner rotor
8. Oil pump shaft
9. Roller
10. Outer rotor
11. Oil strainer body
12. Oil strainer screen

119

123

120

124

121

125

122

8. Measure the clearance between oil pump and gear cover with a feeler gauge as indicated in **Figure 126**. It should be:
   a. 1975-1979 models: 0.1 mm (0.004 in.)
   b. 1980-on models: 0.05 mm (0.002 in.)

The maximum allowable clearance is 0.3 mm (0.012 in.). Replace the cover or gear if clearance is excessive.

PISTON AND CONNECTING ROD ASSEMBLY

CAUTION
When performing the following procedures, handle the piston assemblies with care. Do not clamp the piston in a vise or allow it to hit against another piston or object. Conditions such as these can ruin the piston.

Piston/Connecting Rod Removal

1. Remove the cylinder head as described in this chapter.
2. Remove the oil pan as described in this chapter.
3. Check the axial clearance between the crankshaft and each connecting rod as shown in **Figure 127**. Clearance when new should be 0.15-0.30 mm (0.006-0.012 in.); service limit is 0.40 mm (0.016 in.). If clearance is greater than the service limit for any connecting rod, replace the rod. If clearance is still too great, the crankshaft must be replaced.
4. Check for carbon ridges at the tops of the cylinder bores. If these are present, remove the ridge from the top of the bore with a ridge reamer (**Figure 128**). These are available from tool rental dealers.

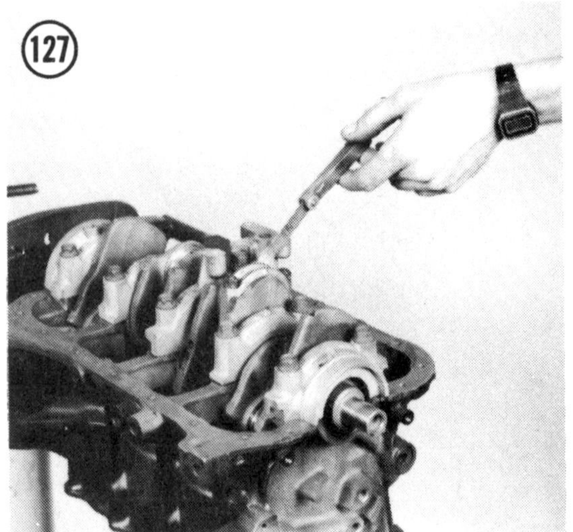

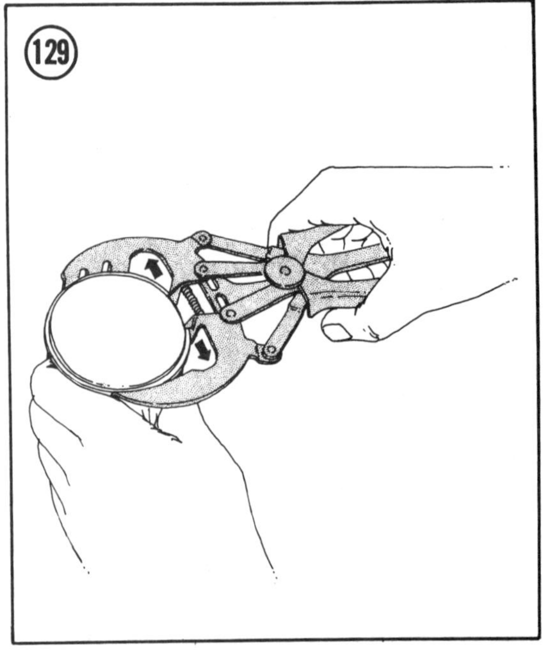

CAUTION
Do not cut more than 1/32 in. into the ring travel area when using the ridge reamer.

5. Rotate the crankshaft until the piston is at bottom dead center and the connecting rod is centered in the cylinder bore.
6. Check the rods and bearing caps for cylinder number markings. If there are no marks visible, scribe your own with a sharp tool. Make the marks on the same side of rod and cap so they can be reassembled in their original positions.
7. Unbolt the connecting rod cap and remove the rod cap and bearing from the crankshaft.

NOTE
Wrap the connecting rod studs with tape so the cylinder bores won't be damaged during removal.

8. Free the connecting rod and piston assembly from the crankshaft by tapping gently with a wooden hammer handle. Continue to push the piston/connecting rod assembly out of the cylinder.
9. Remove the rings using a ring expander tool. See **Figure 129**.

Piston Pin Removal/Installation

The pistons pins are installed with a tight press fit and a hydraulic press and a special fixture are required to remove and install them. This is a job for a Honda dealer or machine shop equipped to fit the pistons and pin, as well as align the pistons with the connecting rods. When reassembling a piston assembly, make sure to have the mark on the piston crown assembled on the same side as the oil jet in the connecting rod. See **Figure 130**. During piston installation, these marks must face toward the intake manifold.

Piston Cleaning and Inspection

1. Clean the pistons thoroughly in solvent. Scrape carbon deposits from the piston top with a flat blunt-edge scraper. The ring grooves can be cleaned with a piston ring groove cleaner or with a broken piston ring.
2. Examine the piston for cracks at the skirts, ring grooves, pin or bushing bosses and top. Any noticeable fault requires that the piston be replaced.

NOTE
The following procedures should be done at room temperature. The cylinder walls must be clean and dry.

3. Measure the cylinder bore as described under *Cylinder Block Inspection* in this chapter.
4. Measure the piston diameter with a micrometer. See **Tables 2-4** for specifications. If the piston diameter is less than the service limit, replace the piston.
5. Determine the difference between the cylinder bore and piston diameter taken in Steps 4 and 5. This gives the piston clearance. Compare this number with the specifications listed at the end of this chapter (**Tables 2-4**). If clearance is excessive, the cylinders must be rebored to the next oversize and new pistons fitted. See your Honda dealer for oversize pistons and rings.

NOTE
The new pistons should be obtained before the cylinders are bored so that the pistons can be measured; slight manufacturing tolerances must be taken into account to determine the actual bore size and working clearance.

6. Repeat this procedure for all cylinders and pistons.

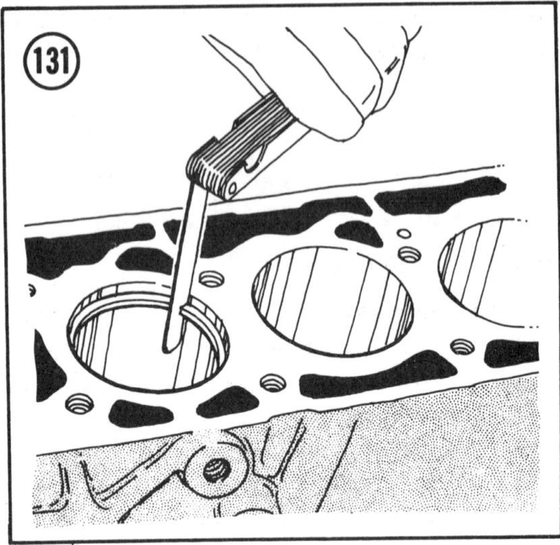
131

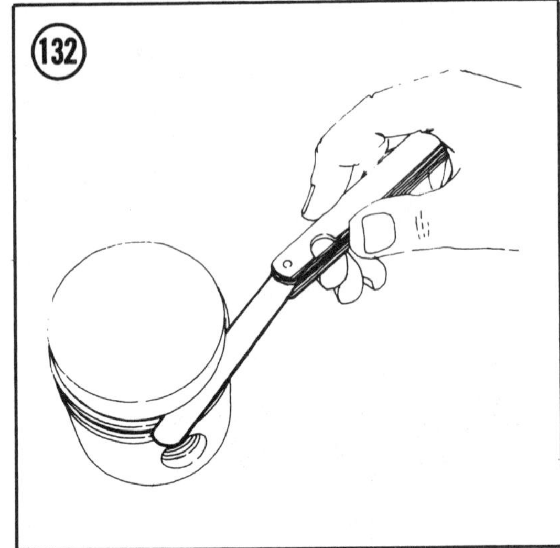
132

Piston Ring Fitting/Installation

1. Check the ring gap of each piston ring. To do this, first press the ring about one inch down the cylinder bore and square it by tapping gently with an inverted piston.

NOTE
If the cylinders have not been rebored, check the ring gap at the bottom of the ring travel, where the cylinder is least worn.

2. Measure the ring gap with a feeler gauge, as shown in **Figure 131**. Compare the ring gap with the specifications at the end of this chapter. If the ring gap is not within specification, use another set of rings.
3. Check side clearance of the rings as shown in **Figure 132**. Place the feeler gauge beneath the ring and insert all the way into the ring groove. The feeler gauge should slide all the way around the piston without binding. Any wear that occurs will form a step at the inner portion of the ring groove's lower edge. If large steps are discernible (**Figure 133**), the pistons should be replaced. Compare the inserted feeler gauge size with the specifications at the end of this chapter.
4. Using a ring expander tool, carefully install the oil control ring assembly, making sure to stagger the oil ring rails so that they are 20-30 mm (25/32-1 3/16 in.) apart (**Figure 134**). Now

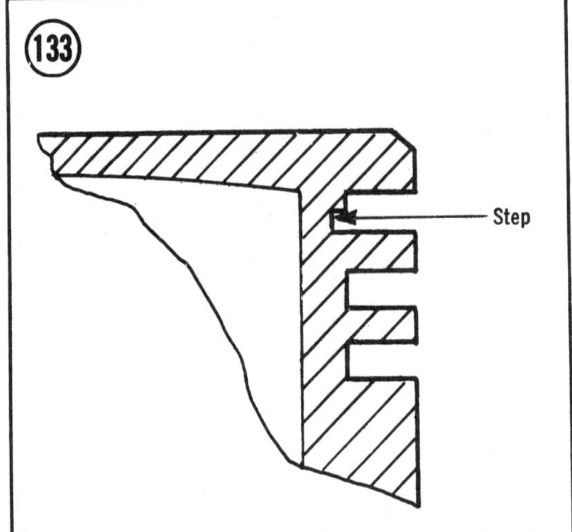

133

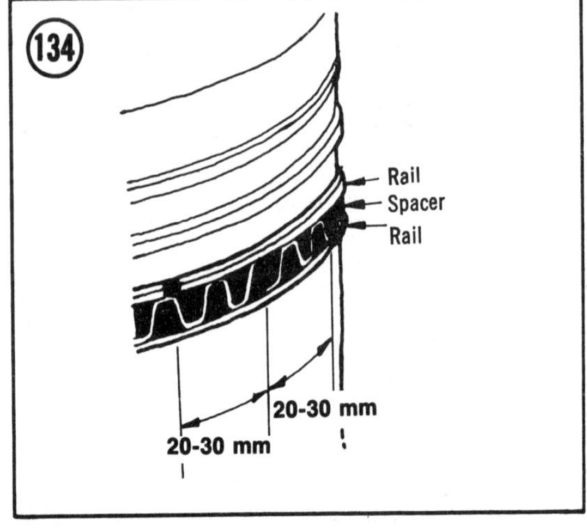

134

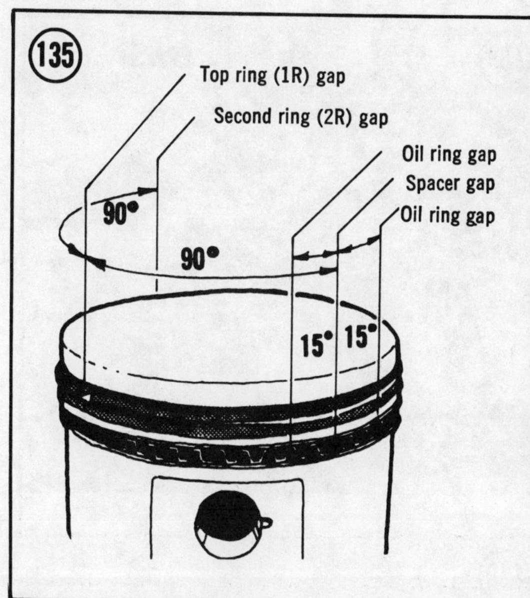

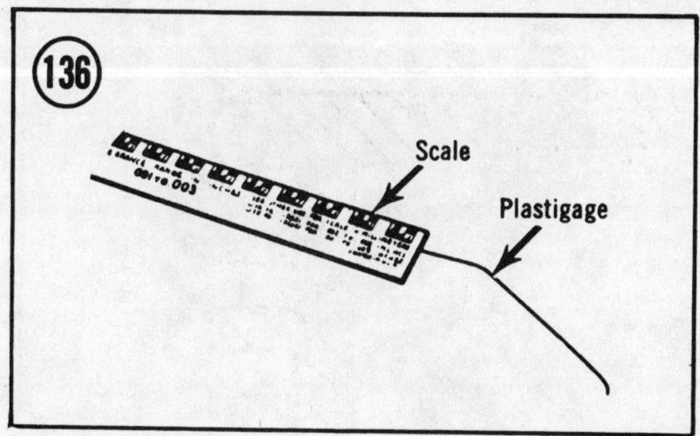

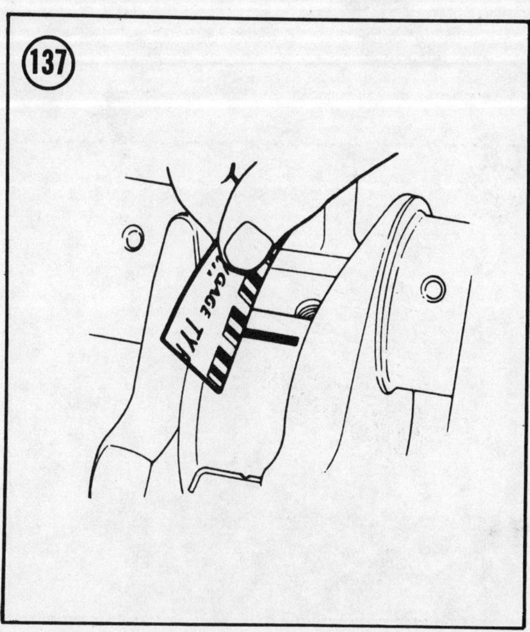

install the top compression rings. Stagger as shown in **Figure 135**.

NOTE
Piston ring manufacturing marks must be facing up when installing piston rings.

Connecting Rod Inspection

1. Check the pistons for shiny, scuffed areas above the piston pin on one side and below the piston pin on the other. This indicates a bent connecting rod.
2. Have the connecting rods checked by your Honda dealer or a competent machine shop for twisting, bends and overall straightness and alignment.

4

Connecting Rod Bearing Clearance Measurement

1. Assemble connecting rods with bearings on the proper crankshaft journal.
2. Cut a piece of Plastigage the width of the bearing (**Figure 136**). Place the Plastigage on the crankshaft journal.

NOTE
Do not place the Plastigage over the crankshaft journal oil hole.

3. Install connecting rod cap and bearing and torque nuts to specifications. See **Table 6** (1973-1979 non-CVCC), **Table 7** (1975-1979 CVCC) or **Table 8** (1980-on CVCC). Do not rotate crankshaft while Plastigage is in place.
4. Remove the connecting rod cap. Bearing clearance is determined by comparing width of flattened Plastigage with scale markings on the Plastigage envelope (**Figure 137**). Compare actual clearance with specified clearance in **Tables 2-4**.
5. If the bearing clearance is greater than specified, use the following steps for new bearing selection.
6. The connecting rods and caps are marked with numbers 1, 2, 3 or 4 that indicate the connecting rod journal dimension. The crankshaft is marked with letters A, B, C or D on the counterbalance weights (**Figure 138**) that indicate the rod bearing journal sizes.

NOTE

The crankshaft counterbalance weights are also marked with a number; however, disregard the number when checking the connecting rod bearing sizes.

7A. *Non-CVCC models:* Select new bearings by cross-referencing the crankpin journal OD letter (**Figure 138** and vertical column, **Table 11**) to the connecting rod ID number (horizontal column, **Table 11**). Where the 2 columns intersect, the new replacement bearing size and color is indicated.

7B. *CVCC models:* Select new bearings by cross referencing the crankpin journal OD letter (**Figure 138** and vertical column, **Table 12**) to the connecting rod ID number (horizontal column, **Table 12**). Where the 2 columns intersect, the new replacement color is indicated. With the correct bearing color known, refer to **Table 13** for the new connecting rod bearing tolerance.

8. After new bearings have been installed, recheck clearance as described in Steps 2-4.

9. Repeat Steps 2-8 for the other 3 cylinders.

Piston/Connecting Rod Installation

1. Remove cylinder wall glaze with a hone if new piston rings are to be installed. Follow hone manufacturer's recommendations.

2. Oil piston rings, pistons and cylinders walls with light engine oil. Be sure to install pistons in same cylinders from which they were removed or to which they were fitted.

3. Install piston rings on piston using piston ring expander tool.

4. Install piston ring compressor on No. 1 piston (**Figure 139**).

5. Rotate the crankshaft to bring the No. 1 crankpin to BDC. Set the piston assembly into the No. 1 cylinder, making sure the mark on the piston crown faces the intake side of the engine. Slowly push piston into the cylinder with a hammer handle until it is slightly below top of cylinder (**Figure 140**). Be sure to guide connecting rod onto the crankshaft to avoid damage to bearings. Install the ring compressor on the No. 4 piston and install it in

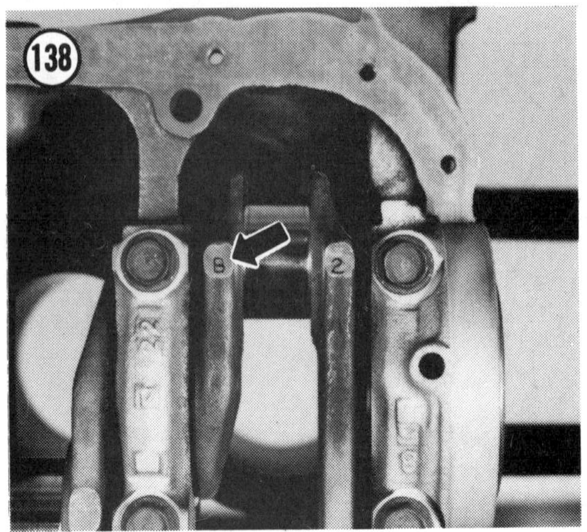

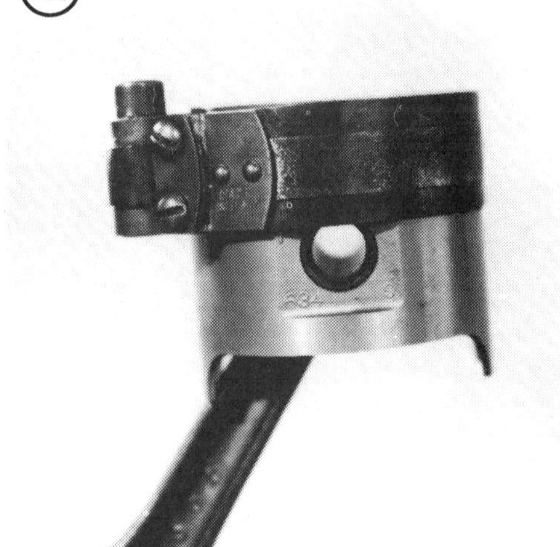

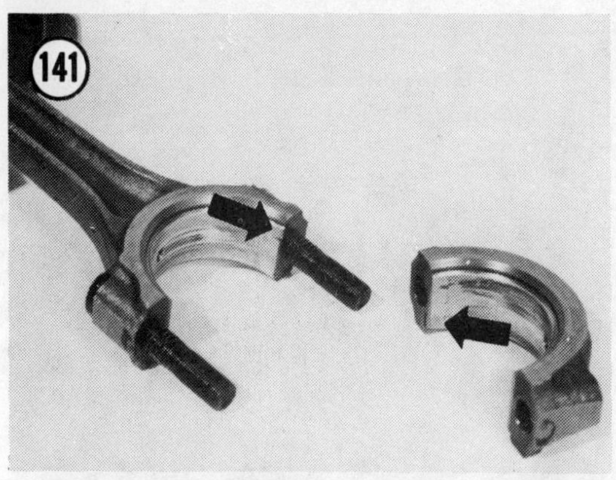
141

142

its cylinder in the same manner. When both pistons and rods are installed, install the rod end caps, making sure the bearing recess notches in the caps are on the same side as the notches in the rod (**Figure 141**). Install the washers and nuts and tighten to specification (end of chapter).

6. Rotate the crankshaft 180° to bring the No. 2 and No. 3 crankpins to BDC. Install the other pistons and rods in the manner just described. When all the pistons and rods are installed and the nuts tightened to the specified torque, rotate the crankshaft several complete revolutions to make sure it turns smoothly.
7. Recheck side clearance between connecting rods on each crankshaft journal after piston and connecting rod assemblies are installed. See *Piston/Connecting Rod Removal* in this chapter.
8. Install the cylinder head and oil pan as described in this chapter.

NOTE
If the rings, pistons, cylinders and bearings were renewed, the engine should be run in at the same speeds and mileages recommended for a new engine.

9. When the engine is first started, allow it to warm up for several minutes. Then check for coolant and oil leaks and correct them immediately. Observe the gauges and indicators and shut off the engine if any trouble is indicated. Increased friction during the early state of break-in may cause the engine to run slightly hotter than normal but this should not persist for more than a couple hundred miles.

After 3,000 miles, the cylinder head bolts should be tightened, the valves adjusted and the engine oil and filter replaced. See Chapter Three.

CRANKSHAFT, MAIN BEARINGS AND REAR OIL SEALS

Crankshaft/Main Bearing Removal

1. Remove the engine from the vehicle as described under *Engine Removal/Installation* in this chapter.
2. Remove the front covers and timing belt as described in this chapter. When removing the belt, be careful not to twist or nick the belt.
3. Remove the flywheel or drive plate as described in this chapter.
4. Remove the oil pan and oil pump assembly as described in this chapter.
5. Remove the connecting rod bearing caps as described in this chapter.

6A. *Non-CVCC and 1300 CVCC models*: Remove the bearing cradle bolts in a crisscross pattern beginning at one end

(**Figure 142**). When all bolts are loosened, unscrew them completely and lift them off the bearing cradle.

6B. *1500 CVCC models*: Remove the main bearing cap bolts, then remove the main bearing caps with bearing inserts attached. See **Figure 143**. Lay the main bearings and bearing caps in order on a clean surface.

CAUTION
Mark each of the main bearings for location and direction.

7. Push the connecting rod/piston assemblies toward the top of each cylinder to provide clearance for crankshaft removal and installation.

NOTE
If piston removal is required, make sure to remove the ridge at the top of the cylinder as described under ***Piston/ Connecting Rod Removal*** *in this chapter.*

8. Carefully remove the crankshaft from the main bearing journals in the block so that the thrust bearing surfaces are not damaged. Handle the crankshaft with care to avoid damage to the crankshaft finished surfaces.

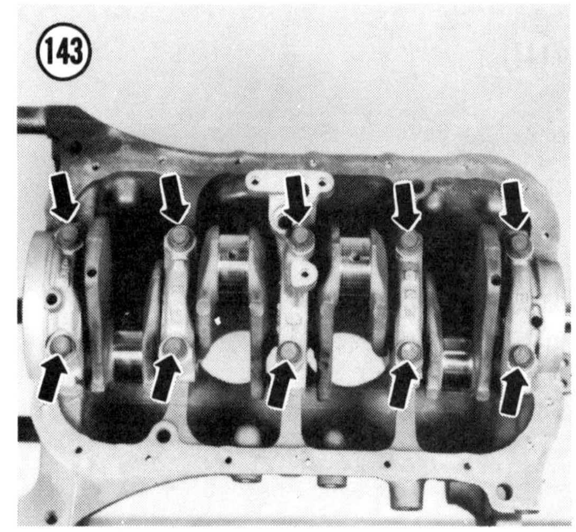
143

144

145

Inspection

1. Clean the crankshaft thoroughly in solvent. Blow out the oil passages with compressed air.
2. Examine crankpins and main bearing journals for wear, scoring and cracks. Check all journals against specifications (end of chapter) for out-of-roundness, taper and wear using a micrometer. If necessary, have the crankshaft reground.
3. Check the crankshaft for bending. Mount the crankshaft between accurate centers (such as V-blocks or a lathe) and rotate it one full turn with a dial gauge contacting the center journal (**Figure 144**). Actual bend is half the reading shown on the gauge. The crankshaft must be reground if bent beyond specifications.
4. Measure crankshaft end play. Install the crankshaft in the block. Install all bearing shells and caps and tighten bolts to specifications. Rotate crankshaft to make sure drag is not excessive.

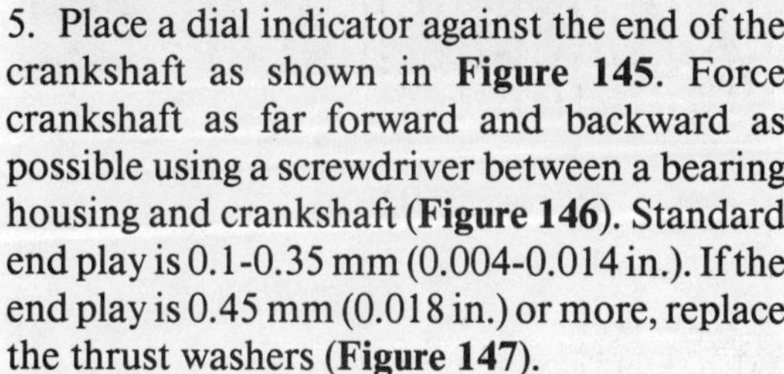

5. Place a dial indicator against the end of the crankshaft as shown in **Figure 145**. Force crankshaft as far forward and backward as possible using a screwdriver between a bearing housing and crankshaft (**Figure 146**). Standard end play is 0.1-0.35 mm (0.004-0.014 in.). If the end play is 0.45 mm (0.018 in.) or more, replace the thrust washers (**Figure 147**).

Main Bearing Clearance Measurement

1. Install the main bearings previously removed from the cylinder block in their original positions, then install the crankshaft on these bearings taking care not to damage the thrust bearing surfaces.
2. Cut a piece of Plastigage the width of the main bearing journal to be measured (**Figure 148**). Lay the Plastigage on the main bearing journal. Install the main bearing cap or cradle, complete with main bearing inserts, and tighten bolts to specifications. Tighten the cradle bolts in the sequence shown in **Figure 142**.

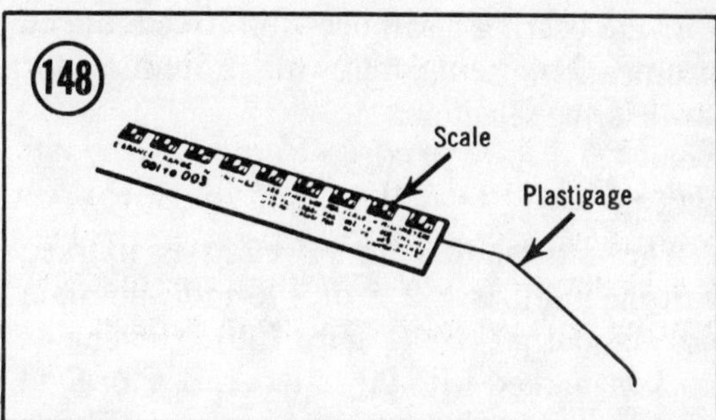

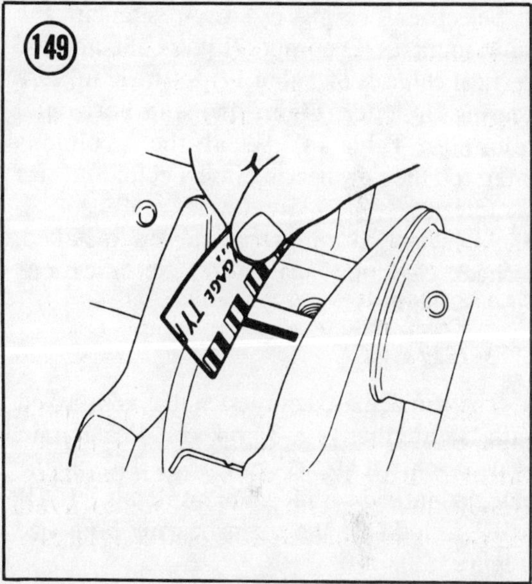

NOTE

Do not place Plastigage across crankshaft oil holes. Do not rotate the crankshaft while the Plastigage is in place.

3. Remove the bearing cradle or main bearing caps and bearing inserts. Compare the width of the flattened Plastigage to the markings on the envelope to determine main bearing clearance (**Figure 149**). Compare the narrowest point on the Plastigage with the widest point to determine journal taper. Specifications are found in **Tables 2-4**.

4. If the bearing clearance is in excess of the specification, use the following procedures for new bearing selection.

Non-CVCC

1. The crankshaft counterweight is marked with the number 1, 2, 3 or 4 to indicate main bearing journal size (**Figure 150**). The engine block is marked with the letter A, B, C or D to indicate the main bearing bore size (**Figure 151**).
2. Select new bearings by cross-referencing the main journal OD number (**Figure 150** and the vertical column of **Table 14**) to the crankcase bearing ID letter (**Figure 151** and horizontal column in **Table 14**). Where the 2 columns intersect, the new bearing insert color and size is indicated.
3. After new bearings have been installed, recheck clearance against the specifications (end of chapter).

1975-1979 CVCC

1. The crankshaft counterweight is marked with the number 1, 2, 3 or 4 to indicate main bearing journal size (**Figure 150**). The engine block is marked with Roman numerals I, II, III or IV to indicate the main bearing bore size (**Figure 152**).
2. Select new bearings by cross-referencing the main journal OD number (**Figure 150** and the vertical column of **Table 15**) to the crankcase bearing Roman numeral (**Figure 152** and horizontal column in **Table 15**). Where the 2 columns intersect, the new bearing insert (identified by color) is indicated. **Table 16** gives the bearing color and thickness.
3. After new bearings have been installed, recheck clearance against the specifications (end of chapter).

1980-on CVCC

1. The crankshaft counterweight is marked with the number 1, 2, 3 or 4 to indicate main bearing journal size (**Figure 150**). The engine block is marked with the letter A, B, C or D to indicate the main bearing bore size. See **Figure 151** (1300cc) or **Figure 153** (1500cc).

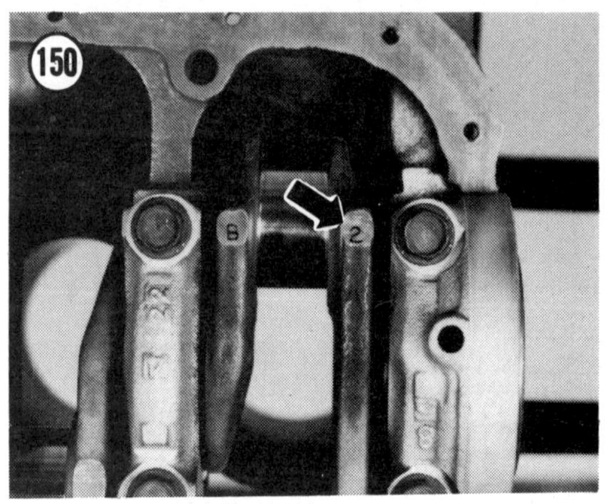

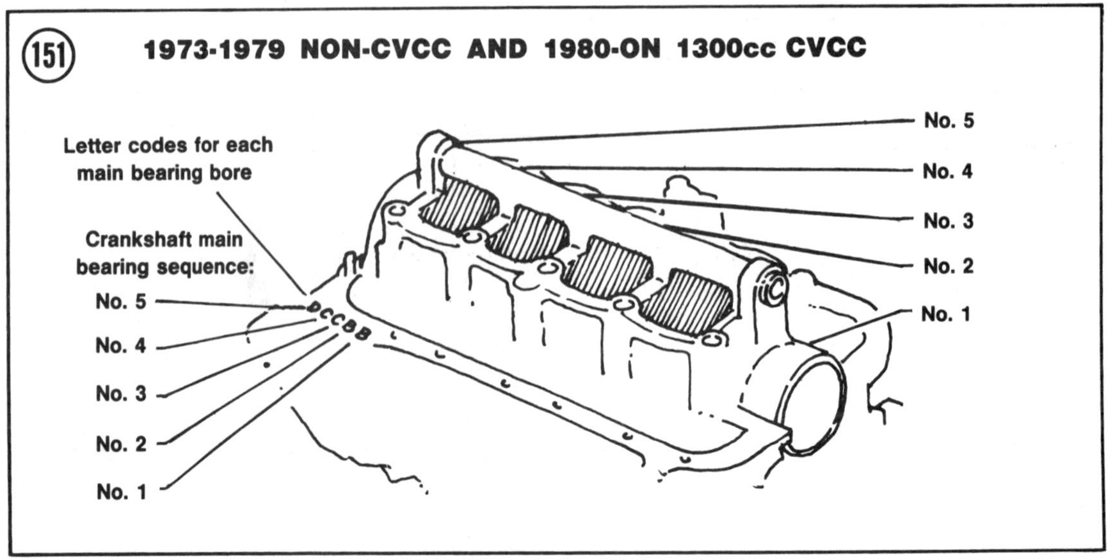

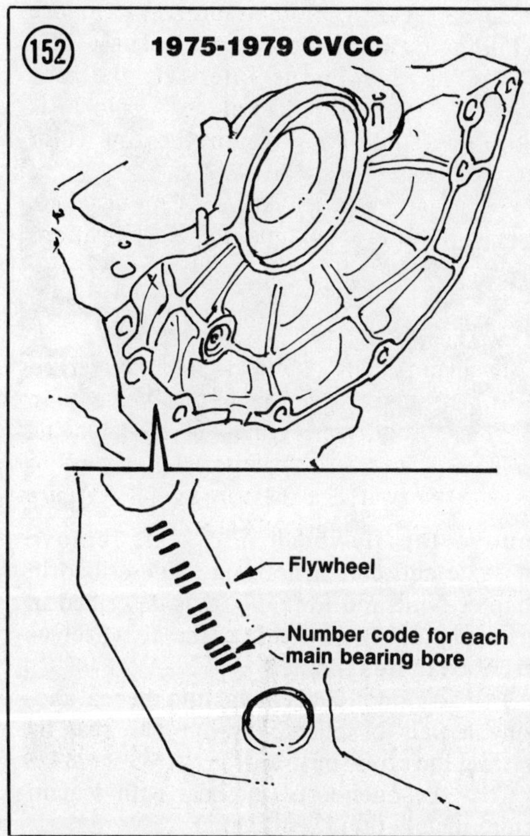

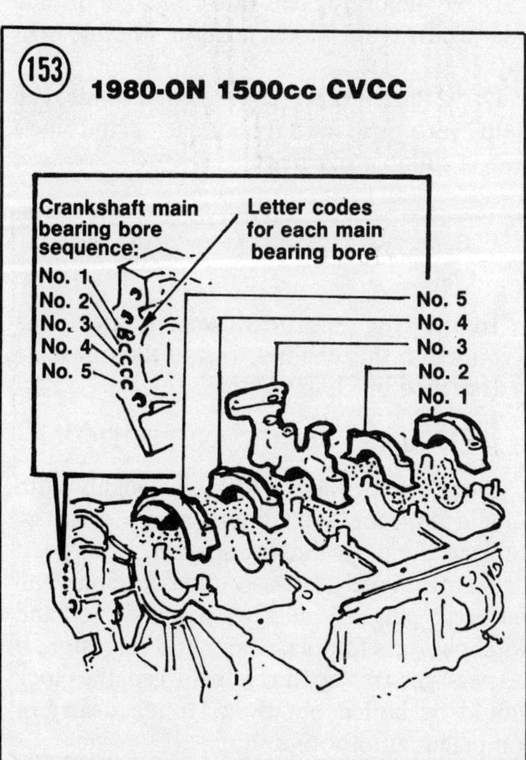

2. Select new bearings by cross-referencing the main journal OD number (**Figure 150** and the vertical column of **Table 17**) to the crankcase bearing ID letter (**Figure 151** or **Figure 153** and horizontal column in **Table 17**.) Where the 2 columns intersect, the new bearing insert color and size is indicated. **Table 16** gives the bearing color and thickness.

3. After new bearings have been installed, recheck clearance against the specifications (end of chapter).

4

Crankshaft/Main Bearing Installation

1. With the main bearings removed from the bearing caps and the cylinder block, clean the main bearing bores in the cylinder block, main bearing caps and the main bearing inserts with lacquer thinner to remove all foreign material.

2. If the old main bearings are being reinstalled, be sure that they are reinstalled in the main bearing caps and the cylinder block bores from which they were removed. If new bearings (or undersize bearings) are being installed, be sure that they are installed in the proper location.

NOTE

*When installing bearing inserts, make sure the oil holes are lined up and the lock tabs engage the recesses. See **Figure 154** and **Figure 155**.*

3. Install the upper thrust washer(s) on the fourth main bearing bore with the grooved

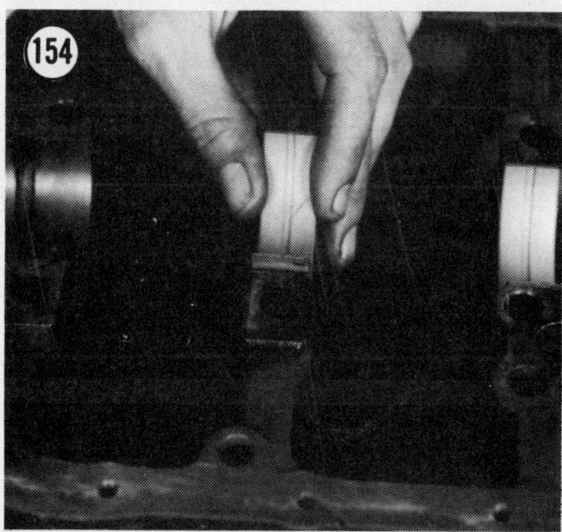

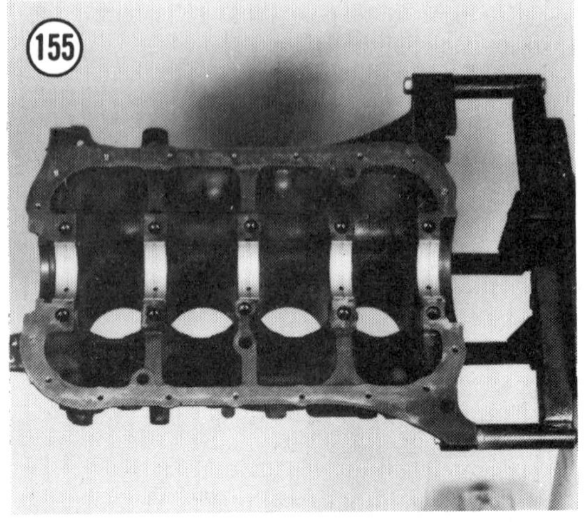

sides facing away from the journal (**Figure 147**).

4. Coat the main bearing surfaces and the crankshaft journals with clean, heavy engine oil.
5. Carefully lay the crankshaft in the main bearings installed in the cylinder block, being careful not to damage the thrust washer(s). See **Figure 156**.
6. Install the cradle or main bearings caps, but do not tighten.
7. Coat the connecting rod and cap journals with oil and reinstall on the crankshaft. Do not tighten.
8. Using a rubber hammer, hit both ends of the crankshaft to center the thrust washer(s).

CAUTION
Do not use a hard metal hammer or the crankshaft may be damaged.

9. Torque main bearing cap or cradle bolts to specifications (end of chapter). Next, tighten the connecting rod cap nuts to specifications.

NOTE
On non-CVCC engines, tighten the main bearing cradle bolts in the sequence shown in ***Figure 142****.*

Main Bearing Oil Seals

To remove the timing belt side seal, remove the front covers, timing belt and crankshaft gear as described earlier in this chapter. To remove the flywheel side seal, remove transaxle and clutch housing as described in Chapter Nine and the oil pan as described in this chapter. Then remove the flywheel as described in this chapter.

1. Thread a small sheet metal into the seal and, using a pair of pliers, remove the seal by twisting the screw outward.
2. Coat the outside of the seal with sealant before installation.
3. Drive the timing belt side oil seal in until it seats against the block using a suitable size drift.
4. Drive the flywheel side oil seal into the rear main bearing cap until it seats against the block using a suitable size drift.

NOTE
Make sure lip of seal faces toward the engine.

5. Install the engine assembly parts as described in this chapter. Install the transaxle as described in Chapter Nine.

CYLINDER BLOCK INSPECTION

1. Clean the cylinder block thoroughly with solvent and check all freeze plugs for leaks. Replace any plugs that are suspect. It is a good idea, at this level of disassembly, to replace all the freeze plugs. While cleaning, check oil and water passages for dirt, sludge and corrosion. If the passages are very dirty or clogged, the block should be boiled out by a Honda dealer or competent automotive shop.

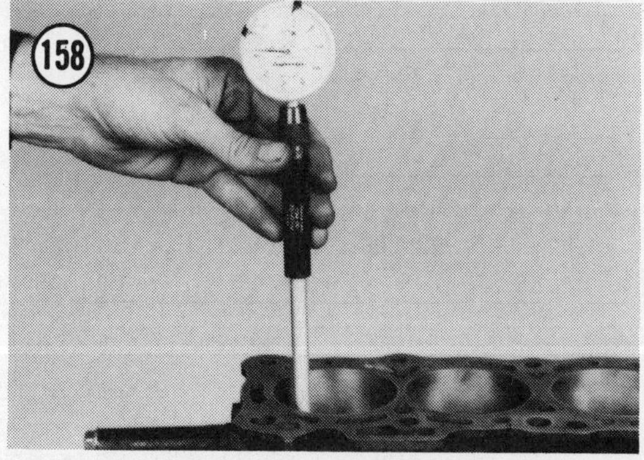

2. Examine the cylinder block for cracks. It is a good idea to take the block to a Honda dealer or competent automotive shop for Magnafluxing, to locate any hairline cracks that might escape visual examination.
3. Check all machined gasket surfaces for nicks or burrs. If necessary, smooth the surfaces with an oilstone.
4. Check the cylinder head mating surface of the block for flatness as shown in **Figure 157**. Use an accurate straightedge and feeler gauge. Have the block resurfaced if it is warped more than 0.10 mm (0.004 in.). Take off only the material required to surface the cylinder block.
5. Measure the cylinder bores for out-of-roundness or excessive wear with a bore gauge (**Figure 158**). Measure the bores at top, center and bottom, in front-rear and side-to-side directions (**Figure 159**). Compare measurements to specifications at the end of the chapter. If the cylinders exceed maximum tolerances, they must be rebored. Reboring is also necessary if the cylinder walls are badly scuffed or scored. Cylinder reboring is a job for a Honda dealer or competent machine shop.

FLYWHEEL/TORQUE CONVERTER DRIVE PLATE

Removal/Installation

1. Remove the engine as described in this chapter.
2. On manual transaxle models, remove the clutch from the flywheel. See Chapter Eight.
3. Unbolt the flywheel or drive plate from the crankshaft (**Figure 160**).
4. Install by reversing Steps 1-3. Tighten bolts to specifications (end of chapter). Tighten the bolts gradually in a diagonal pattern.

Runout Inspection

With the flywheel bolted to the crankshaft, its runout can be checked with a dial indicator.

1. Mount a dial indicator with its plunger touching against the smooth friction plate contact area.
2. Rotate the flywheel by hand and read the amount of runout on the dial indicator. A reading of 15 mm (0.006 in.) or less is within tolerance. If the runout exceeds this amount, refer the flywheel to a Honda dealer for further service.

Table 1 CIVIC ENGINE USAGE

Engine	Displacement	Bore x Stroke
Non-CVCC		
1973	1170cc	70 x 76 mm (2.76 x 2.99 in.)
1974-1979	1237cc	72 x 76 mm (2.83 x 2.99 in.)
CVCC		
1975-1979	1488cc	74 x 86.5 mm (2.91 x 3.41 in.)
1980-on		
1300 model	1355cc	72 x 82 mm (2.83 x 3.23 in.)
1500 model	1488cc	74 x 86.5 mm (2.91 x 3.41 in.)

Table 2 ENGINE SPECIFICATIONS (1973-1979 NON-CVCC)

Item	mm	in.
Cylinder head		
Surface warpage (maximum)	0.10	0.0039
Cylinder block		
Gasket warpage limit	0.10	0.0039
Piston (1973)		
Diameter		
Standard	69.98-70.00	2.7551-2.7559
Wear limit	69.91	2.7524
Clearance	0.03	0.0012
Wear limit	0.10	0.0039
Piston ring groove width		
Top/2nd	1.510-1.520	0.0594-0.0598
Wear limit	1.55	0.0610
Oil	2.805-2.820	0.1104-0.1110
Wear limit	2.85	0.1122
Piston (1974-1979)		
Diameter		
Standard	71.98-72.00	2.8339-2.8345
Wear limit	71.91	2.8311
Clearance	0.03	0.0012
Wear limit	0.10	0.0039
Piston ring groove width		
Top/2nd	1.510-1.520	0.0594-0.0598
Wear limit	1.55	0.0610
Oil (1974-1977)	2.805-2.820	0.1104-0.1110
Wear limit	2.85	0.1122
Oil (1978-1979)	4.005-4.025	0.1577-0.1585
Wear limit	4.05	0.1594
Piston rings (1973)		
Clearance in groove		
Top/2nd	0.020-0.045	0.0008-0.0018
Wear limit	0.13	0.0051
Ring end gap		
Top/2nd	0.2-0.4	0.0079-0.0157
Wear limit	0.6	0.0236

(continued)

Table 2 ENGINE SPECIFICATIONS (1973-1979 NON-CVCC) (continued)

Item	mm	in.
Piston rings (1973) (continued)		
Ring end gap		
Oil	0.2-0.9	0.0079-0.0354
Wear limit	1.1	0.0433
Piston rings (1974-1979)		
Clearance in groove		
Top/2nd	0.020-0.045	0.0008-0.0018
Wear limit	0.13	0.0051
Ring end gap		
Top/2nd	0.25-0.40	0.0098-0.0157
Wear limit	0.6	0.0236
Oil	0.30-0.90	0.0118-0.0354
Wear limit	1.1	0.0433
Connecting rod		
Big-end axial play	0.15-0.30	0.0059-0.0118
Wear limit	0.4	0.0157
Crankpin bearing		
Axial play	0.2-0.45	0.0079-0.0177
Oil clearance	0.020-0.038	0.0008-0.0015
Wear limit	0.07	0.0028
Crankshaft		
Journal diameter	50.0-0.45	1.9700-1.9688
Journal out-of-round	0.005	0.0002
Wear limit	0.010	0.0004
Axial play	0.10-0.35	0.0039-0.0138
Wear limit	0.45	0.0177
Bend (maximum)	0.05	0.0020
Main bearing		
Oil clearance	0.024-0.042	0.0009-0.0017
Wear limit	0.07	0.0028
Camshaft		
Oil clearance	0.05-0.09	0.0020-0.0035
Axial play	0.5	0.0197
Bend	0.05	0.0020
Valve		
Stem outside diameter		
Intake	6.580-6.590	0.2591-0.2594
Wear limit	6.55	0.2579
Exhaust	6.55-6.56	0.2579-0.2583
Wear limit	6.52	0.2567
Valve stem to guide clearance		
Intake	0.01-0.04	0.0004-0.0016
Wear limit	0.08	0.0031
Exhaust	0.05-0.08	0.0020-0.0031
Wear limit	0.11	0.0043
Valve seat		
Width	1.4	0.0551
Valve springs (1973-1977)		
Free length		
Inner	42.0	1.6536
Wear limit	41.0	1.6142
Outer	39.95	1.5728
Wear limit	38.9	1.5315

(continued)

4

Table 2 ENGINE SPECIFICATIONS (1973-1979 NON-CVCC) (continued)

Item	mm	in.
Valve springs (1978-1979)		
Free length		
Inner	50.5	1.9882
Wear limit	49.0	1.9291
Outer	53.8	2.1181
Wear limit	52.3	2.0591
Valve guide		
Inside diameter	6.61-6.63	0.2602-0.2610
Wear limit	6.65	0.2618
Oil pump		
Inner-to-outer rotor radial clearance	0.15	0.0059
Wear limit	0.2	0.0079
Outer rotor-to-body radial clearance	0.1-0.8	0.0039-0.0071
Wear limit	0.2	0.0079
Rotor-to-body side clearance	0.03-0.10	0.0012-0.0039
Wear limit	0.15	0.0059

Table 3 ENGINE SPECIFICATIONS (1975-1979 CVCC)

Item	mm	in.
Camshaft		
Axial play	0.50-0.098	0.0020-0.0039
Wear limit	0.15	0.0059
Deflection	0.5	0.0020
Radial clearance	0.050-0.150	0.0020-0.0059
Wear limit	0.5	0.0197
Rocker arms		
Shaft clearance	0.08	0.0197
Cylinder head		
Gasket surface warpage	0.10	0.0039
Valves		
Valve stem-to-guide clearance		
Intake	0.01-0.04	0.0004-0.0016
Wear limit	0.08	0.0031
Exhaust	0.05-0.08	0.0020-0.0031
Wear limit	0.11	0.0043
Auxiliary	0.02-0.05	0.0008-0.0020
Wear limit	0.08	0.0031
Valve guide		
Inside diameter		
Intake & exhaust	6.61-6.63	0.2602-0.2610
Wear limit	6.65	0.2618
Auxiliary	5.51-5.53	0.2169-0.2177
Wear limit	5.55	0.2185
Valve springs (1975)		
Free length (maximum)		
Intake inner	39.5	1.5551
Intake outer	38.9	1.531
Exhaust inner	49.5	1.9488

(continued)

Table 3 ENGINE SPECIFICATIONS (1975-1979 CVCC) (continued)

Item	mm	in.
Valve springs (1975) (continued)		
Free length (maximum)		
Exhaust outer	52.8	2.0787
Auxiliary	28.6	1.126
Valve springs (1978-1979)		
Free length (maximum)		
Intake inner	Not specified	
Intake outer	Not specified	
Exhaust inner	49.5	1.9488
Exhaust outer	52.8	2.0787
Auxiliary	28.6	1.126
Crankshaft		
Axial clearance	0.10-0.35	0.0039-0.0138
Wear limit	0.45	0.0177
Deflection	0.03	0.0012
Wear limit	0.05	0.0020
Taper (maximum)	0.010	0.0004
Out-of-round (maximum)	0.010	0.0004
Radial clearance		
Main journal	0.026-0.055	0.0010-0.0021
Wear limit	0.07	0.0028
Rod journal	0.020-0.038	0.0008-0.0015
Wear limit	0.07	0.0028
Cylinder block		
Gasket surface warpage (maximum)	0.10	0.0039
Cylinder bore		
New	74.00-74.02	2.913-2.914
Wear limit	74.10	2.917
Taper	0.10	0.0004
Piston		
Outside diameter		
Standard	73.955-73.975	2.911-2.912
Wear limit	73.885	2.912
Clearance		
Standard	0.03	0.0012
Wear limit	0.10	0.0039
Piston ring groove width		
Top/2nd	1.510-1.520	0.0595-0.0599
Wear limit	1.55	0.0610
Piston to ring clearance		
Top/2nd	0.020-0.045	0.0008-0.0018
Wear limit	0.13	0.0051
Ring gap		
Top/2nd	0.2-0.4	0.0079-0.0157
Wear limit	0.6	0.0236
Oil	0.2-0.9	0.0079-0.0354
Wear limit	1.1	0.0433
Oil pump		
Inner-to-outer rotor radial clearance	0.15	0.0059
Wear limit	0.2	0.0079
Pump body-to-rotor radial clearance	0.10-0.18	0.0039-0.0071
Wear limit	0.2	0.0079

(continued)

4

Table 3 ENGINE SPECIFICATIONS (1975-1979 CVCC) (continued)

Item	mm	in.
Oil pump (continued)		
Valve to pump body clearance	0.025-0.070	0.00098-0.028
Camshaft to oil pump drive gear backlash	0.04-0.10	0.0016-0.0039
Oil pump drive gear to holder clearance	0.10-0.30	0.0039-0.0118
Flywheel		
Runout (maximum)	0.04	0.0016

Table 4 ENGINE SPECIFICATIONS (1980-ON CVCC)

Item	mm	in.
Cylinder head		
Gasket surface warpage (maximum)		
1980	0.05	0.002
1981	0.2	0.008
Cylinder block		
Gasket surface warpage (maximum)	0.10	0.004
Bore diameter		
1300	72.00-72.02	2.834-2.835
Wear limit	72.10	2.839
1500	74.00-74.02	2.913-2.914
Wear limit	74.10	2.917
Bore taper (maximum)	0.05	0.002
Piston		
Diameter		
1300	71.97-72.00	2.833-2.835
Wear limit	71.95	2.832
1500	73.96-73.99	2.912-2.913
Wear limit	73.95	2.911
Clearance		
1300	0.01-0.05	0.0004-0.0020
Wear limit	0.10	0.004
1500	0.01-0.06	0.0004-0.0024
Wear limit	0.10	0.004
Piston to ring clearance		
Top/2nd	0.020-0.045	0.0008-0.0018
Wear limit	0.13	0.005
Piston ring		
End gap		
Top/2nd	0.15-0.35	0.006-0.014
Wear limit	0.55	0.022
Oil	0.30-0.90	0.012-0.035
Wear limit	1.10	0.043
Connecting rod		
End play	0.15-0.30	0.006-0.012
Wear limit	0.40	0.016

(continued)

Table 4 ENGINE SPECIFICATIONS (1980-ON CVCC) (continued)

Item	mm	in.
Crankshaft		
Main journal diameter		
1980	50.006-50.030	1.9687-1.9697
1981	49.976-50.000	1.9676-1.9685
Rod journal diameter		
1300	39.976-40.000	1.5739-1.5748
1500	41.976-42.000	1.6526-1.6535
End play	0.010-0.35	0.004-0.014
Wear limit	0.45	0.018
Runout	0.030	0.0012
Wear limit	0.060	0.0024
Radial clearance		
Main bearing		
1300	0.024-0.042	0.0009-0.0017
1500	0.026-0.055	0.0010-0.0022
Wear limit (all)	0.07	0.003
Rod bearing	0.020-0.038	0.0008-0.0015
Wear limit	0.07	0.003
Camshaft		
End play	0.05-0.15	0.002-0.006
Wear limit	0.5	0.020
Oil clearance	0.05-0.098	0.002-0.004
Wear limit	0.15	0.006
Runout	0.03	0.0012
Wear limit	0.06	0.0024
Valves		
Stem to guide clearance		
Intake	0.02-0.05	0.0008-0.0020
Wear limit	0.08	0.003
Exhaust	0.063-0.093	0.0025-0.0037
Wear limit	0.12	0.0047
Auxiliary	0.023-0.0494	0.0139-0.0194
Wear limit	0.08	0.003
Valve seat width		
Intake & exhaust	1.4-1.55	0.055-0.061
Wear limit	2.0	0.08
Auxiliary	0.353-0.494	0.0139-0.0194
Wear limit	1.0	0.04
Valve springs		
Free length		
Intake & exhaust inner	42.3	1.67
Intake & exhaust outer	42.29	1.66
Auxiliary		
1980	28.5	1.12
1981	29.7	1.169
Valve guide inside diameter		
Intake & exhaust	6.61-6.63	0.260-0.261
Wear limit	6.55	0.258
Auxiliary		
1980		
1300	5.51-5.53	0.217-0.218
Wear limit	5.55	0.219
1500	6.61-6.63	0.260-0.261
Wear limit	6.55	0.258

(continued)

4

Table 4 ENGINE SPECIFICATIONS (1980-ON CVCC) (continued)

Item	mm	in.
Valve guide inside diameter (continued)		
Auxiliary		
1981	6.61-6.63	0.260-0.261
Wear limit	6.55	0.258
Oil pump		
Inner to outer rotor radial clearance	0.04-0.14	0.002-0.006
Wear limit	0.2	0.008
Pump body to rotor radial clearance	0.10-0.18	0.004-0.007
Wear limit	0.2	0.008
Pump body to rotor side clearance	0.03-0.10	0.001-0.004
Wear limit	0.15	0.006
Backlash in pump drive gear	0.04-0.10	0.002-0.004
Pump drive gear side clearance	0.05-0.30	0.002-0.012

Table 5 ENGINE MOUNT TORQUE SPECIFICATIONS

	mkg	ft.-lb.
1975-1979 CVCC		
Center support beam	1.9-2.5	14-18
Engine rubber mount	3.5-4.3	25-31
Engine support beam	3.5-4.3	25-31
Front beam	3.5-4.3	25-31
Front/rear engine mount		
Base	1.9-2.5	14-18
Bracket	3.5-4.3	25-31
Left engine support		
M8 x 1.25	1.9-2.5	14-18
M10 x 1.25	3.5-4.3	25-31
Rubber stopper	1.9-2.5	14-18
Torque arm, lower	0.7-1.2	5-9
Torque arm, upper		
Engine	3.5-4.3	25-31
Frame	3.5-4.3	25-31
1980-on CVCC		
Left engine support		
M8 x 1.25	2.9	21
M10 x 1.25		
1980	28	3.9
1981	2.2	16
Torque arm		
Lower	7.5	54
Upper	7.5	54
Rubber mount		
Lower	2.0	14
Upper	2.0	14
Center beam	2.0	14

Table 6 TIGHTENING TORQUES (1973-1979 NON-CVCC)

Item	mkg	ft.-lb.
Cylinder head bolts		
To engine no. EB1-1019949	4.2-4.8	30-35
From engine no. EB1-1019950	5.1-5.9	37-42
Oil pan drain bolt	4.0-5.0	29-36
Crankshaft bearing cap	3.7-4.3	27-31
Connecting rod bearing cap	2.5-2.9	18-21
Cam holder	1.8-2.2	13-16
Flywheel/crankshaft	4.7-5.3	34-38
Clutch cover and flywheel	1.0-1.4	7-10
Crankshaft pulley	4.7-5.3	34-38
Timing belt pulley	2.5-3.5	18-25
Intake manifold	1.8-2.4	13-17
Carburetor nuts	0.8-1.2	6-9
Oil pan	0.3-0.7	2-5
Fuel pump	1.8-2.4	13-17
Valve tappet nut	1.8-2.2	13-16
Water pump	1.0-1.4	7-10
Exhaust manifold	1.8-2.4	13-17
Oil pump assembly	1.0-1.4	7-10
Oil pump gear holder	1.0-1.4	7-10
Cylinder head cover	0.8-1.2	6-9
Timing belt upper/lower covers	0.8-1.2	6-9

Table 7 TIGHTENING TORQUES (1975-1979 CVCC)

Item	mkg	ft.-lb.
Cylinder head bolts	5.5-6.5	40-47
Oil pan drain bolt	4.0-5.0	29-36
Camshaft holder		
M6 x 1.0	1.0-1.4	7-10
M8 x 1.0	2.0-2.4	15-17
Camshaft timing belt gear	2.5-3.5	18-25
Auxiliary valve screw	1.2-1.6	9-12
Intake/exhaust valve adjusting screw	1.8-2.2	13-16
Timing belt tension adjust bolts	4.0-4.6	39-34
Water pump pulley	1.0-1.2	7-9
Valve holder nut	6.5-7.5	47-55
Connecting rod bearing caps	2.5-2.9	18-21
Main bearing caps	4.2-4.8	30-35
Flywheel/drive plate bolts	4.7-5.3	34-38
Oil pump drive gear holder	1.0-1.4	7-10
Carburetor nuts	1.8-2.2	13-16
Manifold assembly	2.0-2.4	15-17

4

Table 8 TIGHTENING TORQUES (1980-ON CVCC)

Item	mkg	ft.-lb.
Cylinder head bolts/nuts	6.0	43
Timing belt adjusting bolts	4.3	32
Oil pump drive gear cover	1.2	9
Upper timing belt cover	1.0	7
Upper timing gear bolt	3.0	22
Rocker arm bolts		
M6 x 1.0	1.1	8
M8 x 1.25	2.2	16
Tachometer drive housing bolts	1.2	9
Thermostat housing bolts	1.2	9
Auxiliary valve locknut	8.0	58
Manifold assembly		
1300cc	2.5	18
1500cc	2.2	16
Crankshaft pulley bolt		
1980	8.5	61
1981	11.0	80
Main bearing cradle bolts		
(1300cc)	4.0	29
Main bearing cap bolts (1500cc)	4.5	33
Flywheel	7.1	51
Drive plate	5.0	36
Connecting rod cap nuts	2.9	21
Oil pan drain plug	4.5	33
Oil pan	1.2	9
Oil pump bolts	1.2	9

Table 9 VALVE SPECIFICATIONS (1975-ON CVCC)

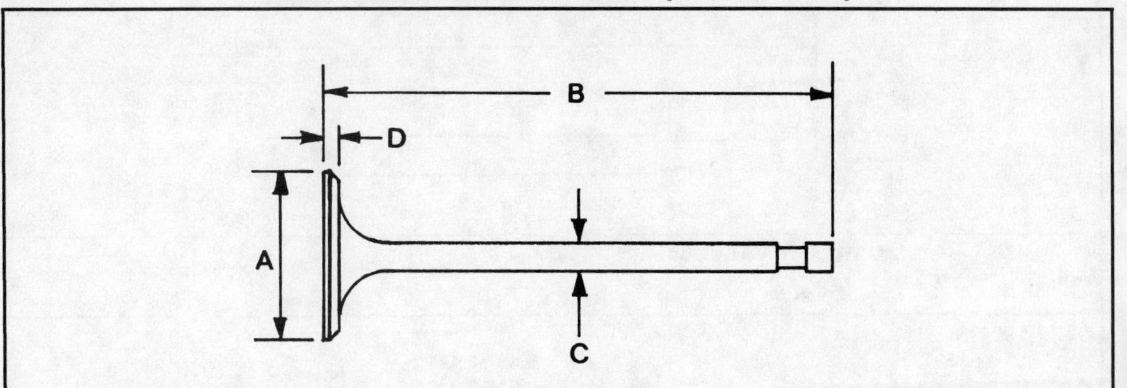

INTAKE VALVES mm	in.	EXHAUST VALVES mm	in.
1975:			
A 33.9-34.1	1.335-1.343	A 29.9-30.1	1.77-1.85
B 112.50-112.90	4.433-4.445	B 112.6-112.9	4.433-4.445
C 6.58-6.59	0.2592-0.2596	C 6.55-6.56	0.258-0.259
limit: 6.55	0.2579	limit: 6.52	0.256
D 0.85-1.15	0.0331-0.044	D 1.35-1.65	0.053-0.0649
limit: 0.75	0.03	limit: 1.00	0.04
1976:			
A 33.9-34.1	1.335-1.343	A 28.9-29.1	1.138-1.146
B 112.50-112.90	4.433-4.445	B 112.50-112.9	4.433-4.445
C 6.58-6.59	0.259-0.260	C 6.55-6.56	0.258-0.259
limit: 6.55	0.258	limit: 6.52	0.256
D 0.85-1.15	0.033-0.045	D 1.35-1.65	0.053-0.065
limit: 0.75	0.03	limit: 1.00	0.04
1977:			
A 34.9-35.1	1.374-1.382	A 27.9-28.1	1.098-1.106
B 112.50-112.90	4.433-4.445	B 112.90-113.2	4.445-4.457
C 6.58-6.59	0.259-0.260	C 6.55-6.56	0.258-0.259
limit: 6.55	0.258	limit: 6.52	0.256
D 0.85-1.15	0.033-0.045	D 1.35-1.65	0.053-0.065
limit: 0.75	0.03	limit: 1.00	0.04
1978-1979:			
A 34.9-35.1	1.374-1.382	A 27.9-28.1	1.098-1.106
B 112.50-112.90	4.433-4.445	B 113.4-113.7	4.465-4.476
C 6.58-6.59	0.259-0.260	C 6.55-6.56	0.258-0.259
limit: 6.55	0.258	limit: 6.52	0.256
D 0.85-1.15	0.033-0.045	D 2.14-2.46	0.084-0.097
limit: 0.75	0.03	limit: 1.4	0.055
1980-on:			
A 34.9-35.1	1.374-1.382	A 27.9-28.1	1.098-1.106
B 112.75	4.439	B 113.05	4.451
C 6.58-6.59	0.259-0.260	C 6.55-6.56	0.258-0.259
limit: 6.55	0.258	limit: 6.52	0.256
D 0.85-1.15	0.033-0.045	D 1.65-1.95	0.065-0.077

(continued)

Table 9 VALVE SPECIFICATIONS (1975-ON CVCC) (continued)

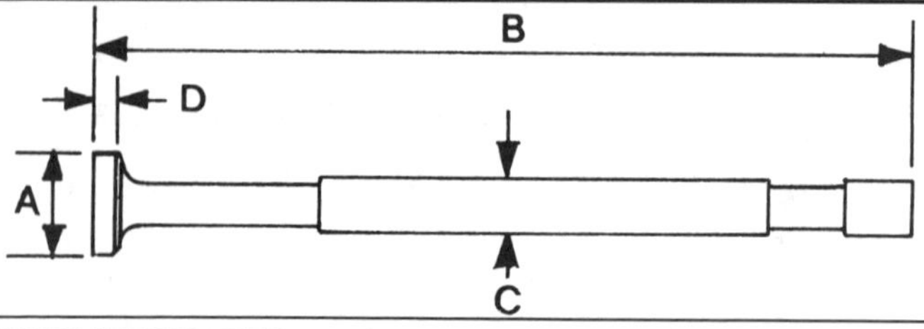

AUXILIARY VALVES	
mm	**in.**
1975-1977:	
A 11.85-11.95	0.467-0.471
B 1975: 82.05-82.15	3.315-3.319
1976: 90.45-90.55	3.561-3.665
1977: 88.15-88.45	3.470-3.482
C 5.48-5.49	0.2146-0.2166
limit: 5.45	0.2146
D 1.05-1.35	0.041-0.0529
limit: 1.00	0.04
1978-1979:	
A 11.9-12.1	0.469-0.476
B 89.45-89.55	3.521-3.525
C 5.48-5.49	0.216-0.217
limit: 5.45	0.215
D 2.3-2.7	0.091-0.106
limit: 2.15	0.085
1980 (49-state with 1300cc engine):	
A 11.9-12.1	0.469-0.476
B 89.5	3.524
C 5.472-5.487	0.215-0.216
limit: 5.45	0.215
D 2.3-2.7	0.091-0.106
limit: 2.15	0.085
1980 (1500cc engine):	
A 11.9-12.1	0.469-0.476
B (49-state) 97.7	3.846
B (Calif./high-altitude) 94.7	3.728
C 6.572-6.587	0.258-0.2593
limit: 6.55	0.258
D 2.3-2.7	0.091-0.106
1981 (1300cc engine):	
A 11.9-12.1	0.469-0.476
B 96.8	3.811
C 6.572-6.587	0.258-0.2593
limit: 6.55	0.258
D 2.3-2.7	0.091-0.106
1981 (1500cc engine):	
A 11.9-12.1	0.469-0.476
B 93.8	3.693
C 6.572-6.587	0.258-0.2593
limit: 6.55	0.258
D 2.3-2.7	0.091-0.106

Table 10 INTAKE/EXHAUST VALVE INSTALLED HEIGHT (CVCC)

Year	mm	in.
1975-1976	42.7	2.68
limit	43.2	2.70
1977-1980	42.3	1.665
limit	43.95	1.730
1981	35.05-36.30	1.380-1.429
limit	36.55	1.439

Table 11 ROD BEARING SELECTION CHART* (NON-CVCC)

Unit: mm (in.)

Crankpin diameter	Connecting rod diameter 43 (1.69)			
	1 0 - + 0.006 (+ 0.0002)	2 + 0.006 - + 0.012 (+ 0.0002 - + 0.0005)	3 + 0.012 - + 0.018 (+ 0.0005 - + 0.0007)	4 + 0.018 - + 0.024 (+ 0.0007 - + 0.0009)
A 0 - − 0.006 (− 0.0002)	Red − 0.005 - − 0.008 (− 0.0002 - − 0.0003)	Pink − 0.002 - − 0.005 (0.0001 - − 0.0002)	Yellow + 0.001 - − 0.002 (0.00004 - − 0.0001)	Green + 0.004 - + 0.001 (+ 0.0002 - 0.00004)
B − 0.006 - − 0.012 (− 0.0002 - − 0.0005)	Pink − 0.002 - − 0.005 (− 0.0001 - − 0.0002)	Yellow + 0.001 - + 0.002 (0.00004 - − 0.0001)	Green + 0.004 - + 0.001 (+ 0.0002 - 0.00004)	Brown + 0.007 - + 0.004 (+ 0.0003 - + 0.0002)
C − 0.012 - − 0.018 (− 0.0005 - − 0.0007)	Yellow + 0.001 - − 0.002 (0.00004 - − 0.0001)	Green + 0.004 - + 0.001 (+ 0.0002 - 0.00004)	Brown + 0.007 - + 0.004 (+ 0.0003 - + 0.0002)	Black + 0.010 - + 0.007 (+ 0.0004 - + 0.0003)
D − 0.018 - − 0.024 (− 0.0007 - − 0.0009)	Green + 0.004 - + 0.001 (+ 0.0002 - + 0.00004)	Brown + 0.007 - + 0.004 (+ 0.0003 - + 0.0002)	Black + 0.010 - + 0.007 (+ 0.0004 - + 0.0003)	Blue + 0.013 - + 0.010 (+ 0.0005 - + 0.0004)
	Connecting rod bearing center stock thickness: 1.5mm (0.059 in.)			

*NOTE: Numbers 1, 2, 3, and 4, and letters A, B, C, and D are stamped, respectively, near the big end of the connecting rods and the crankpins.

Table 12 CONNECTING ROD BEARING IDENTIFICATION (CVCC)

	Connecting Rod Numbers			
	1	2	3	4
Crankshaft Rod Journal Letters				
A	Red	Pink	Yellow	Green
B	Pink	Yellow	Green	Brown
C	Yellow	Green	Brown	Black
D	Green	Brown	Black	Blue

Table 13 CONNECTING ROD BEARING TOLERANCES (CVCC)

Bearing Color	Tolerance
Red	-0.005 to -0.008 mm (-0.0002 to -0.0003 in.)
Pink	-0.002 to -0.005 mm (-0.0001 to -0.0002 in.)
Yellow	+0.001 to -0.002 mm (+0.00004 to -0.0001 in.)
Green	+0.004 to +0.001 mm (+0.0002 to +0.00004 in.)
Brown	+0.007 to +0.004 mm (+0.0003 to +0.0002 in.)
Black	+0.010 to +0.007 mm (+0.0004 to +0.0003 in.)
Blue	+0.013 to +0.010 mm (+0.0005 to +0.0004 in.)

Table 14 CRANKSHAFT MAIN BEARING SELECTION CHART* (1975-1979 NON-CVCC)

Unit: mm (in.)				
	Cylinder counterbore 54 (2.13)			
Journal diameter 50 (1.97)	A 0 - − 0.006 (− 0.0002)	B − 0.006 - − 0.012 (− 0.0002 - − 0.0005)	C − 0.012 - − 0.018 (− 0.0005 - − 0.0007)	D − 0.018 - − 0.024 (− 0.0007 - − 0.0009)
1 0 - + 0.006 (+ 0.0002)	Red − 0.002 - − 0.005 (− 0.0001 - − 0.0002)	Pink + 0.001 - − 0.002 (0.00004 - − 0.0001)	Yellow + 0.004 - + 0.001 (+ 0.0002 - 0.00004)	Green + 0.007 - + 0.004 (+ 0.0003 - + 0.0002)
2 + 0.006 - + 0.012 (+ 0.0002 - 0.0005)	Pink + 0.001 - − 0.002 (0.00004 - − 0.0001)	Yellow + 0.004 - + 0.001 (+ 0.0002 - 0.00004)	Green + 0.007 - + 0.004 (+ 0.0003 - + 0.0002)	Brown + 0.010 - + 0.007 (+ 0.0004 - + 0.0003)
3 + 0.012 - + 0.018 (0.0005 - 0.0007)	Yellow + 0.004 - + 0.001 (+ 0.0002 - 0.00004)	Green + 0.007 - + 0.004 (+ 0.0003 - + 0.0002)	Brown + 0.010 - + 0.007 (+ 0.0004 - + 0.0003)	Black + 0.013 - + 0.010 (+ 0.0005 - + 0.0004)
4 + 0.018 - + 0.024 (0.0007 - 0.0009)	Green + 0.007 - + 0.004 (+ 0.0003 - + 0.0002)	Brown + 0.010 - + 0.007 (+ 0.0004 - + 0.0003)	Black + 0.013 - + 0.010 (+ 0.0005 - + 0.0004)	Blue + 0.016 - + 0.013 (+ 0.0006 - + 0.0005)
	Main bearing center stock thickness: 2.0mm (0.079 in.)			

*NOTE: Numbers 1, 2, 3, and 4, and letters A, B, C, and D are stamped respectively on the crankshaft web and cylinder block. Crankshaft and main bearings are selective-fitted so that 0.024 to 0.042mm (0.003 to 0.0017 in.) is obtained for oil clearance.

Table 15 MAIN BEARING IDENTIFICATION (1975-1979 CVCC)

	Crankshaft Bore Identification Numbers			
	I	II	III	IIII
Crankshaft Main Journal Numbers				
1	Red	Pink	Yellow	Green
2	Pink	Yellow	Green	Brown
3	Yellow	Green	Brown	Black
4	Green	Brown	Black	Blue

Table 16 MAIN BEARING TOLERANCES (CVCC)

Bearing Color	Tolerance
Red	-0.002 to -0.005 mm (-0.0001 to -0.0002 in.)
Pink	+0.001 to -0.002 mm (-0.00004 to -0.0001 in.)
Yellow	+0.004 to +0.001 mm (+0.00002 to +0.0004 in.)
Green	+0.007 to +0.004 mm (+0.0003 to +0.0002 in.)
Brown	+0.010 to +0.007 mm (+0.0004 to +0.0003 in.)
Black	+0.013 to +0.010 mm (+0.0005 to +0.0004 in.)
Blue	+0.016 to +0.013 mm (+0.0006 to +0.0005 in.)

Table 17 MAIN BEARING IDENTIFICATION (1980-ON CVCC)

	Crankshaft Bore Identification Letters			
	A	B	C	D
Crankshaft Main Journal Numbers				
1	Red	Pink	Yellow	Green
2	Pink	Yellow	Green	Brown
3	Yellow	Green	Brown	Black
4	Green	Brown	Black	Blue

NOTE: If you own a 1982 or later model, first check the Supplement at the back of the book for any new service information.

CHAPTER FIVE

FUEL, EXHAUST AND EMISSION CONTROL SYSTEMS

5

This chapter includes service procedures for the air cleaner, carburetor, fuel pump and fuel system-related emission controls.

AIR CLEANER

The air cleaner uses a paper element, which should be replaced at the intervals specified in Chapter Three. The air cleaner also incorporates several emission control devices.

Element Replacement

Element replacement is described in Chapter Three.

Air Cleaner Assembly Removal/Installation

Attached to the air cleaner assembly on all models are a number of vacuum lines and hoses. Each play an important part in the operation and efficiency of the engine. Because of design changes and altitude and state emission requirements, it is recommended that you use the following removal and installation procedures as a general guide. For specific vacuum hose routing for your particular Honda, refer to the vehicle emission control information and vacuum hose routing diagram decals on the engine hood. See **Figure 1**.

NOTE
In addition to using the emission decals on your car's hood, tag all lines and hoses before removal to help with reinstallation.

1. Disconnect the vacuum line at the air control diaphragm. See **Figure 2**.
2. Remove the center wing nut and washer. Then detach the wire clips securing the air cleaner cover (if present). See **Figure 3** or **Figure 4**. Remove the air cleaner cover and air filter (**Figure 5**).
3. Remove the clamps from the fresh air duct and hot air duct at the air cleaner. See **Figure 2**.
4. If equipped with power steering, remove the power steering hose clamp at the air cleaner housing. Set the hose aside.
5. Loosen and remove the air cleaner housing inside (**Figure 6**) and outside attaching screws (**Figure 7** or **Figure 8**).
6. Lift up the air cleaner housing and disconnect hoses and vacuum tubes from the bottom of the housing.
7. Check the air cleaner housing carefully and make sure all hoses and tube are disconnected or removed, then remove the air cleaner assembly.
8. Install in the reverse order.

NOTE
On some models, arrows have been stamped on the air cleaner cover and on the intake tunnel. On models so equipped, the arrows should be aligned after installing the cover.

CARBURETORS

The non-CVCC Civic is equipped with a 2-barrel, 2-stage carburetor with manual

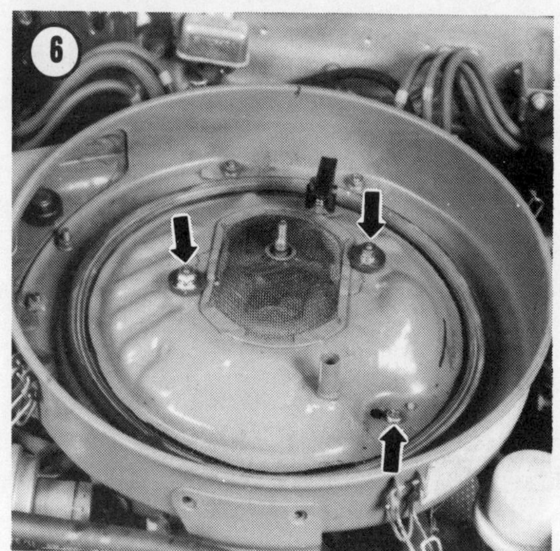

choke. Minor differences exist between the carburetor used in standard transaxle cars and the one used in cars equipped with automatic transaxle.

The CVCC engine is equipped with a 3-barrel, 2-stage carburetor. A manual choke is used on 1975-1979 models. Beginning on 1980 models, an automatic choke is used. The operation of this carburetor is much like that of a 2-barrel type, with the addition of a third venturi and throttle valve which supplies fuel and air to the auxiliary intake valves.

Special tools and gauges are required to test and service the carburetor. Therefore, service procedures are confined to carburetor removal and installation and adjustments to the throttle and choke linkage and idle speed. Major servicing should be entrusted to a Honda dealer or competent automotive garage.

Removal/Installation

1. Remove the air cleaner assembly as described in this chapter.
2. Label and disconnect all vacuum hoses and electrical connections at the carburetor.
3. Disconnect the throttle cable at the carburetor as described in this chapter.
4. Disconnect the fuel line at the carburetor. See **Figure 9** (non-CVCC) or **Figure 10** (CVCC).
5. *1973-1979 models*: Loosen the screw in the choke cable sheath clamp far enough to remove the sheath from beneath the clamp. Disconnect

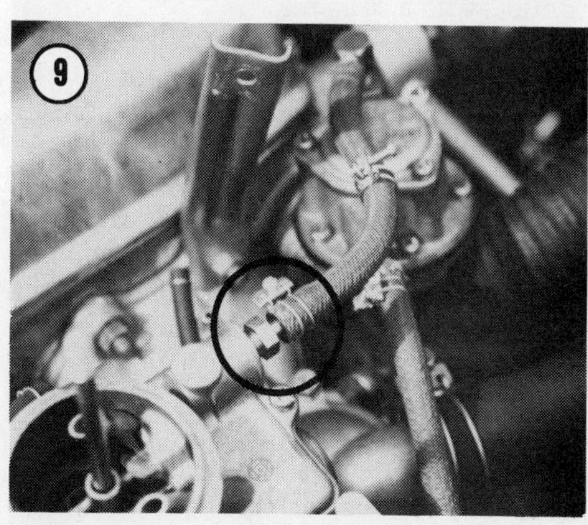

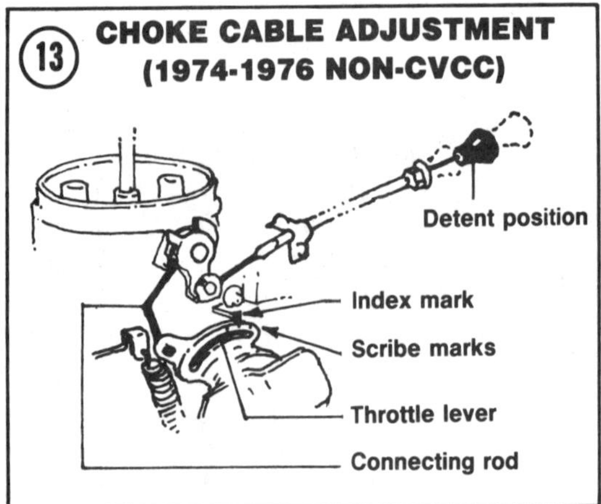

the choke cable end from the choke arm (**Figure 11**).

6. Unscrew the carburetor mounting nuts and remove the carburetor from the manifold. Do not remove the insulator unless required (**Figure 12**). Cover the openings in the manifold with a clean rag.

7. Installation is the reverse of these steps. Replace the O-rings and insulator gasket whenever the carburetor is removed. Make certain all vacuum hoses and emission control hoses are correctly connected. Replace any hoses that are cracked, chafed or show signs of deterioration. When the installation is complete, adjust the throttle cable and choke cable as described in this chapter.

Carburetor Adjustments

Routine carburetor adjustments are found under *Tune-up*, Chapter Three.

MANUAL CHOKE ASSEMBLY

The manual choke assembly is used on all 1973-1979 models. The choke is operated by a pull-knob located on the instrument panel. The pull-knob is attached to the carburetor by a cable (**Figure 11**, typical).

Choke Inspection and Adjustment

Remove the air cleaner cover (**Figure 3**). Then operate the choke knob to make sure the choke cable is operating smoothly. If not, correct the problem before performing the following choke adjustment procedures.

Non-CVCC (1973)

1. Push the choke knob all the way in. The choke valve (viewed through the air cleaner opening) should be fully open.

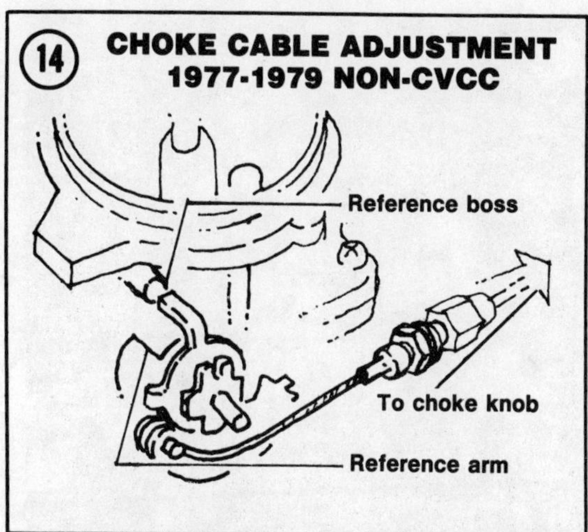

2. Pull the choke knob to the detent position (halfway open). The choke valve should be half open.
3. Pull the choke knob all the way out. The choke valve should be fully closed.
4. If the choke valve failed to operate as described in Steps 3-5, adjust the cable length as described in this chapter to obtain proper adjustment. Reinstall the air cleaner cover.

Non-CVCC (1974-1976)

Refer to **Figure 13** for this procedure.
1. Push the choke knob all the way in. The choke valve (viewed through the air cleaner opening) should be fully open. If not, adjust the cable length as described in this chapter to obtain proper adjustment.
2. Pull the choke knob to the detent position (halfway). The middle scribe mark on the throttle lever should be aligned with the index mark on the throttle lever bracket (**Figure 13**). If not, bend the connecting rod to obtain proper adjustment.

Non-CVCC (1977-1979) Models

Engine must be cold and the ignition switch must be ON when performing this procedure. Remove the air cleaner assembly as described in this chapter.
1. Push the choke knob all the way in. The choke valve should be fully open.
2. Pull the choke knob to the detent position (halfway). Then refer to **Figure 14** and make sure that the reference boss on the air horn is aligned with the choke lever reference arm. If not, adjust the choke cable length as described in this chapter to obtain proper adjustment.
3. Pull the choke knob all the way out. Make sure that the choke valve is fully closed. If not, check choke reference arm for damage. Readjust cable if required.

CVCC (1975-1979)

1. Push the choke knob all the way in. The butterfly valve should be all the way open.
2. Pull the choke knob to the second detent position. The butterfly valve should just close. Then pull the choke knob all the way out. Again, the butterfly valve should be closed.
3. If the choke butterfly valve failed to operate correctly when performing Steps 1-2, clean and/or repair parts as necessary. Then adjust the choke cable as described in this chapter.

Choke Cable Adjustment

1973-1979 non-CVCC

Choke adjustment is performed by loosening the end of the choke cable at the carburetor and changing its position—either lengthen or shorten the cable in the clamp.

1975-1979 CVCC

1. *Butterfly valve failed to open properly:* Turn the choke cable adjusting nut in until the butterfly valve moves off the positioning stop tab. Then turn the adjusting nut out so that valve just touches the stop tap. Tighten locknut and recheck adjustment. See **Figure 15**.
2. *Butterfly valve fails to close properly:* Inspect the butterfly valve and shaft for binding and/or

excessive amounts of dirt. Also check the return spring operation. Clean and/or replace any parts as necessary.

Choke Fast Idle Check/Adjustment

Non-CVCC (1977-1979)

NOTE
Choke fast idle adjustment procedures for 1973-1976 models are not provided by Honda.

1. Connect a tachometer to the engine following manufacturer's directions.
2. Start the engine and bring to normal operating temperature. Pull the choke knob to the detent position and note the engine speed. It should be 1,800 +/-400 rpm.
3. If not, turn off engine and adjust by bending the throttle link lever. Recheck adjustment. Remove tachometer.

CVCC (1975-1979)

1. Remove the rubber boot from the end of the ignition coil (**Figure 16**). Attach the positive lead from a tachometer to the ignition coil's negative terminal. Then attach the negative tachometer lead to an engine ground.
2. Start engine and allow to warm up for 5 minutes.
3. Pull the choke control knob on the instrument panel to the second detent position. Run engine for 30 seconds and check idle.
4. Idle should be as follows:
   a. 1975 manual transaxle: 2,700-3,300 rpm
   b. 1975 automatic transaxle: 2,600-3,200 rpm
   c. 1976 models: 3,000 +/-500 rpm
   d. 1977 manual transaxle: 3,000 +/-500 rpm
   e. 1977 automatic transaxle: 2,500 +/-500 rpm
   f. 1978-1979 models: 2,600 +/-500 rpm
5. If the idle speed is too low, perform Step 6. If the idle speed is too high, perform Step 7.
6. Using a screwdriver inserted into the fast idle adjusting link slot, widen the slot (**Figure 17**). Recheck adjustment.
7. Using a pair of needlenose pliers grasping the outside of the fast idle adjusting link slot, narrow the slot slightly (**Figure 18**). Recheck adjustment.

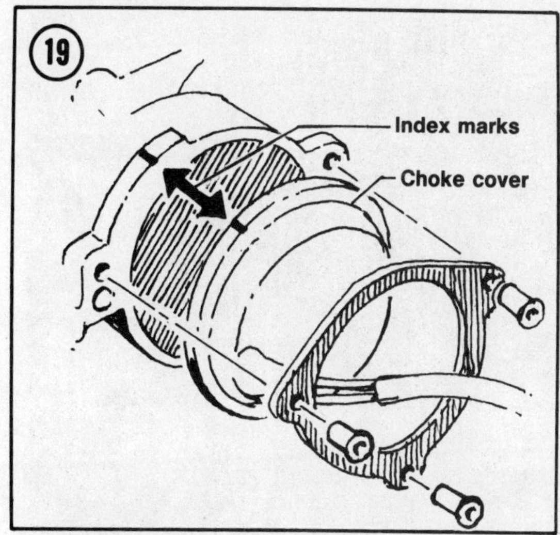

AUTOMATIC CHOKE ASSEMBLY

An automatic choke assembly is used on all 1980 and later models to control the choke valve setting and position of the fast idle assembly during engine warmup.

Choke Coil Tension (Cold)

1. With the engine cold, remove the air cleaner and open and close the throttle to engage the choke. If the temperature is below 75° F (23.9° C), the choke valve should fully close. If temperature is 75° F or above, the choke should close to a gap of 3 mm (1/8 in.) or less.
2. If the choke does not close as described in Step 1, remove the choke cover and check the linkage for freedom of movement. Repair or replace parts as required. Then install the choke cover, align the index marks (**Figure 19**), tighten the attaching screws and repeat Step 1. If the choke still does not close properly, replace the choke cover.

Choke Linkage Adjustment

Adjustment of the automatic choke linkage is only required if the linkage has been bent or damaged, the choke opener replaced or if the car is hard to start when cold. Because this procedure requires special tools and skills, all adjustment should be referred to a Honda dealer.

Choke Fast Idle Adjustment

1. Connect a tachometer to the engine, following the manufacturer's instructions.
2. Disconnect and plug the vacuum hose at the fast idle unloader (A, **Figure 20**).
3. Hold the choke valve closed and then fully open and release the throttle.
4. Restart the engine (engine should be at normal operating temperature) and check the idle speed. It should be 3,000 +/-500 rpm. If not, reset to this specification using the fast idle adjusting screw (B, **Figure 20**).

THROTTLE CABLE

Adjustment

1. Remove the air cleaner assembly as described in this chapter to provide access to the throttle cable assembly.
2. Check the throttle cable for signs of fraying and chafing and replace it if its condition is in doubt; a faulty throttle cable can stick resulting in an extremely hazardous condition.
3. With your hand, check the free play in the throttle linkage (**Figure 21**). It should be 1-3 mm (1/32-1/8 in.) for non-CVCC or 4-10 mm (5/32-13/32 in.) for CVCC models. If the free play is less or greater than this, adjust as follows:
   a. *Non-CVCC*: Loosen the throttle cable clamp (**Figure 22**). Readjust the cable position to obtain proper free play and tighten clamp.

5

b. *CVCC*: Loosen the locknut (**Figure 23**) and turn the adjuster sleeve clockwise to increase the free play or counterclockwise to decrease it. When the free play is correct, hold the adjuster sleeve to prevent it from turning further and tighten the locknut.

4. When the throttle linkage free play has been adjusted, have an assistant depress the throttle pedal all the way to the floor and hold it there. Check the position of the throttle valves. Both the primary and secondary valves and the auxiliary throttle valve on CVCC models should be fully open. If not, adjust as follows:

a. *Non-CVCC*: Bend the throttle bracket connecting rod (**Figure 24**) to obtain proper valve adjustment.

b. CVCC: Readjust throttle cable adjusting nut (**Figure 23**) to obtain fully open valves.

FUEL PUMP (NON-CVCC)

All non-CVCC models are equipped with a mechanical fuel pump. If the fuel pump is suspected of being faulty perform the fuel pump troubleshooting procedures in Chapter Two. Specifications are found in **Table 1**.

Removal/Installation

1. Disconnect the inlet (**Figure 25**) and outlet lines from the pump.

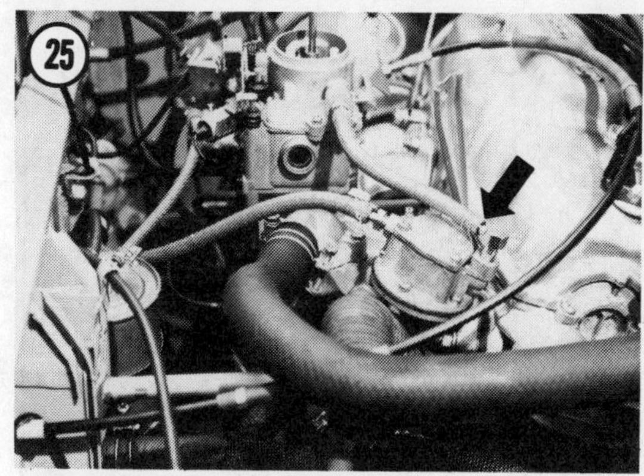

2. Unscrew the pump mounting nuts and remove the pump (**Figure 26**).

3. Install a new pump and gasket by reversing these steps. Tighten the pump attaching nuts securely. Start the engine and check for fuel leakage.

FUEL PUMP (CVCC)

The CVCC models are equipped with an electric fuel pump. In the 1975-1979 sedan models, it is located (along with the fuel filter) in a covered well beneath the left end of the rear seat. On 1980 and later sedan models, the pump and filter are located underneath the vehicle on the left side of the fuel tank. On all station wagon models, the pump and filter are located at the rear of the fuel tank, on the tank mounting bracket.

Testing

To test the output of the electric pump, perform the following procedure.

1. Remove the air cleaner assembly as described in this chapter.

2. Disconnect the fuel lines (**Figure 27**). Then attach a pressure gauge to the fuel line, following the manufacturer's instructions.

3A. *1975-1977*: Disconnect the yellow/red wire lead from the oil pressure switch (**Figure 28**).

3B. *1978-on*: Locate the fuse panel underneath the dashboard. Then remove the screws securing the fuse box to the dashboard and allow it to hang down. Pull down the junction box which contains the fuel pump cutoff relay. Disconnect the cutoff relay connector from the junction box and connect a jumper wire between the 2 black/yellow wire pins in the junction box. See **Figure 29**.

4. Turn the ignition switch ON until the pressure stabilizes, then switch OFF. Read the pressure gauge (see **Table 1** for specifications). If pressure reading is correct, proceed to Step 5. If pressure reading is incorrect, replace the fuel pump and retest.

5. Remove the pressure gauge from the fuel line. Then place the end of the fuel line into a graduated container.

6. Have an assistant start and run the engine for one minute, then turn ignition OFF. Read amount of fuel in container and compare to specifications in **Table 1**. If incorrect, replace the fuel filter and retest. If amount of fuel flow in one minute is still incorrect, replace the fuel pump.

7. Reconnect the oil pressure wire lead or reconnect the cutoff relay connector.

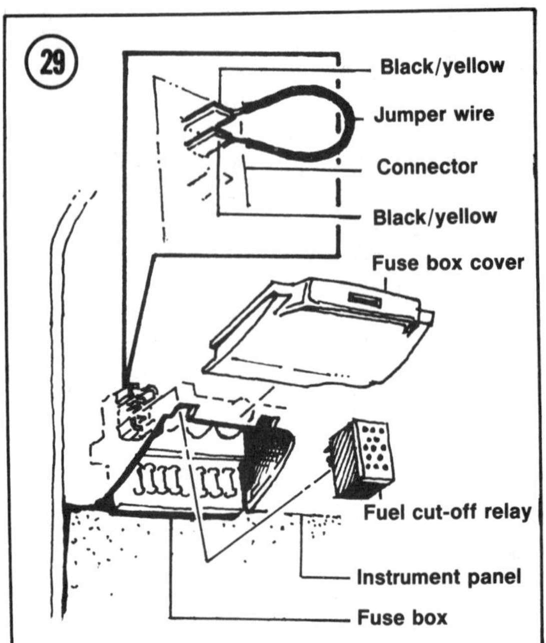

Removal/Installation (1975-1979 Sedan)

1. Disconnect the negative battery cable.

2. Unscrew the bolt at the rear center of the back seat and remove the seat.

3. Remove the cover from the fuel pump well (**Figure 30**). Unplug the electrical leads from the pump.

4. Unscrew the bolts that hold the pump in place (**Figure 31**).

5. Disconnect the lines from the pump and remove it.

6. Reverse the above to install the pump. If the fuel filter was replaced, make sure it was installed correctly with regard to fuel flow and that the lines are correctly installed. The lower fitting on the pump is the *in* line and the upper fitting is the *out* line.

7. Reconnect the electrical leads and the battery ground cable.

8. While an assistant starts and runs the engine, check the fuel pump to make sure the lines are not leaking. Correct any leaks in the lines and connections before reinstalling the cover on the fuel pump well (**Figure 30**).

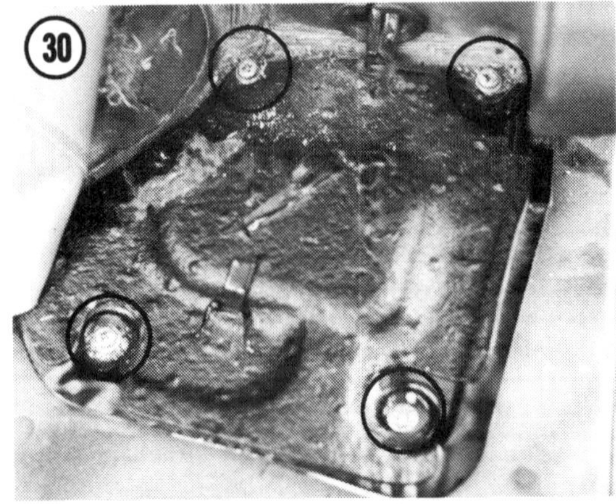

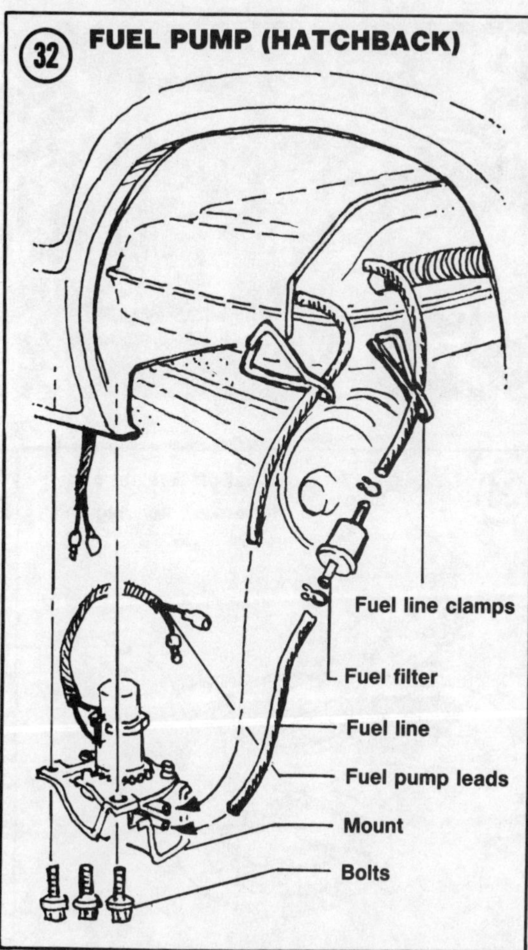

Removal/Installation (1980-on Sedan, All Station Wagons)

Refer to **Figure 32** or **Figure 33** for this procedure.

1. Raise the vehicle rear end and secure with jackstands.
2. Disconnect the ground lead from the battery. Unscrew fuel pump cover retaining bolts.
3. Unplug the electrical leads from the pump. Unscrew the bolts that hold the pump in place and lower the pump to provide access to the fuel lines.
4. Disconnect the lines from the pump and remove it. Plug the ends of the fuel lines to prevent fuel leakage.
5. Reverse Steps 1-4 to install the pump and filter. Make certain the filter is installed correctly with regard to fuel flow and that the lines are correctly installed.
6. Reconnect the electrical leads and the battery ground cable. Check for and correct any leaks in the lines and connections before reinstalling the cover on the fuel pump.

FUEL FILTER

Fuel filter replacement is described in Chapter Three.

5

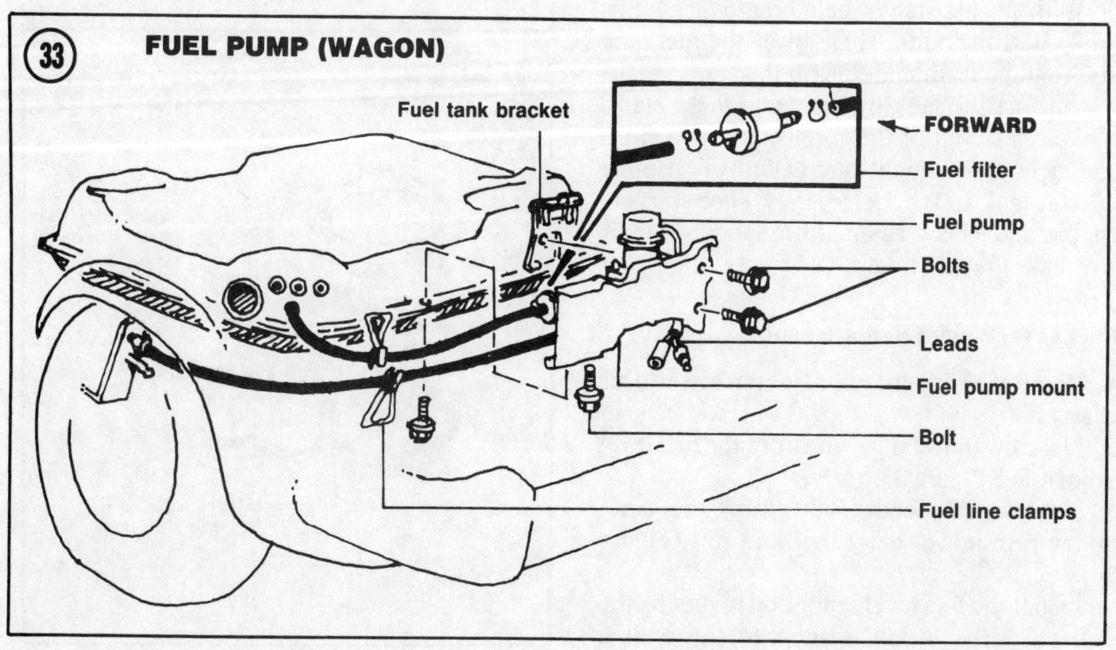

FUEL TANK

Repairs to the fuel tank, with the exception of replacing the fuel level sending unit, should be entrusted to an expert. Even under the best of conditions, the fuel tank is a potentially dangerous item with the destructive effectiveness of a carefully designed bomb. Even during such routine operations as removal and installation, extreme care should be excercised with regard to heat, flames and potential electrical spark. It is a good idea, when servicing the fuel tank, to keep a good fire extinguisher close by.

Removal/Installation

1. Disconnect the ground cable at the battery.
2. Remove the fuel tank drain bolt (**Figure 34**) and catch the fuel in a safe, sealable container large enough to accommodate all of the fuel remaining in the tank.
3. Expand the fuel line clips with needlenose pliers and slide them up each of the lines several inches. Carefully pull each of the lines loose from its connections, taking care not to damage the lines.
4. Loosen the lower clamp on the filler hose and pull it off the tank connection.
5. Disconnect the electrical leads from the fuel level sender unit.
6. With an assistant's help, remove all fuel tank attaching bolts. Then lower the fuel tank and remove from underneath the car.
7. Support the tank by reversing these steps. Make certain all of the connections are clean and tight. Pour about one gallon of gasoline into the tank and check for leaks. Then start the engine and check again. Immediately repair any leaks that are found.

Fuel Level Sender Replacement

1. Remove the fuel tank as described in this chapter.
2. Unscrew the retainer ring from the fuel level sender. See **Figure 35**.
3. Remove the sender unit from the tank, taking care not to bend the float rod (**Figure 36**).
4. Install the fuel level sender by reversing the removal steps. Apply sealant to the sealing

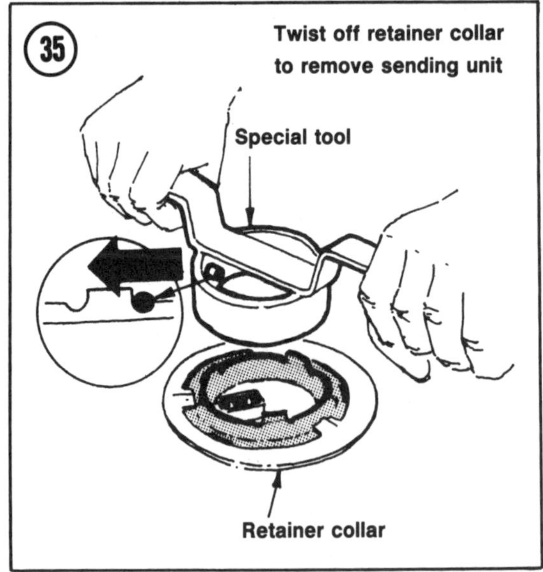

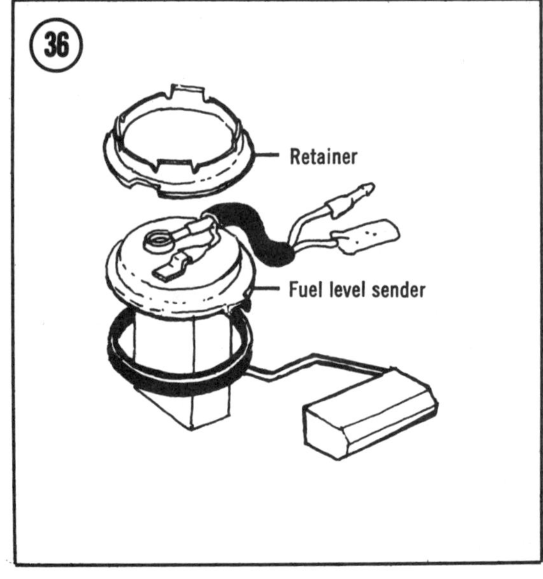

surface on the tank and on the threads of the retainer ring. Be careful not to get sealant inside the tank where it can clog the fuel lines. Tighten the retainer ring firmly before installing the tank in the car.

FUEL LINE REPAIRS

With the exception of replacing short lengths of rubber fuel hose that are easily accessible, fuel line repairs should be entrusted to a Honda dealer. Not only does removal and replacement of the fuel feed lines require removal of access panels, but the lines must also be sealed where they pass through the body panels to prevent moisture from entering the car.

INTAKE AND EXHAUST MANIFOLDS

Intake Manifold Removal/Installation (Non-CVCC)

1. Remove the air cleaner assembly and carburetor as described in this chapter.
2. Refer to Chapter Six and drain the cooling system. If the coolant is in good condition, it should be drained into a clean container for reuse.
3. Label all emission hoses attached to the intake manifold. Then disconnect the hoses and lay them out of the way.
4. Disconnect the thermo-switch wires at the switches.
5. Disconnect the coolant hoses at the manifold.
6. Remove the intake manifold attaching bolts in a crisscross pattern. Remove the manifold.
7. Installation is the reverse of these steps. Before installing manifold, make sure to clean the cylinder head and manifold mating surfaces of all old gasket material. Install a new manifold gasket coated with sealant. Tighten the manifold attaching bolts in a crisscross pattern to 1.8-2.4 mkg (13-17 ft.-lb.).

Exhaust Manifold Removal/Installation (Non-CVCC)

1. Remove the front grille.
2. Remove the exhaust pipe-to-manifold nuts and disconnect the pipe at the manifold.
3. On 1975 and later models:
   a. Disconnect spark plug wires at spark plugs.
   b. Remove the oil dipstick.
   c. Disconnect the air pump drive belt. Then remove the air pump and bracket.
   d. Remove the air injection check valve.
4. Remove the heat shield in front of the manifold.
5. Remove the exhaust manifold attaching nuts in a crisscross pattern. Then remove the exhaust manifold.
6. Installation is the reverse of these steps. Clean the cylinder head and exhaust manifold mating surfaces of all old gasket material. Install the manifold with a new gasket. Tighten manifold-to-cylinder head attaching bolts in a crisscross pattern to 1.8-2.4 mkg (13-17 ft.-lb.). Tighten the manifold-to-exhaust pipe attaching bolts to 1.9-2.5 mkg (14-18 ft.-lb.).

Intake/Exhaust Manifold Removal/Installation (CVCC)

The intake and exhaust manifolds on all CVCC engines must be removed as an assembly.

1975-1979 models

Refer to **Figure 37** for this procedure.

1. Raise the vehicle's front end and secure with jackstands. Disconnect the exhaust pipe at the exhaust manifold. Remove jackstands from underneath vehicle and lower vehicle to ground.
2. Open the radiator drain plug and drain the engine coolant. If the coolant was changed recently and is not dirty, it can be drained into a clean container for reuse.
3. Remove the air cleaner assembly and carburetor as described in this chapter. Discard the carburetor base gasket.
4. Remove the heat shield from the top of the intake manifold (**Figure 38**).
5. Disconnect the coolant hoses at the intake manifold (**Figure 39**).
6. Loosen the 4 intake manifold-to-exhaust manifold attaching bolts (**Figure 40**). Do not remove these bolts.

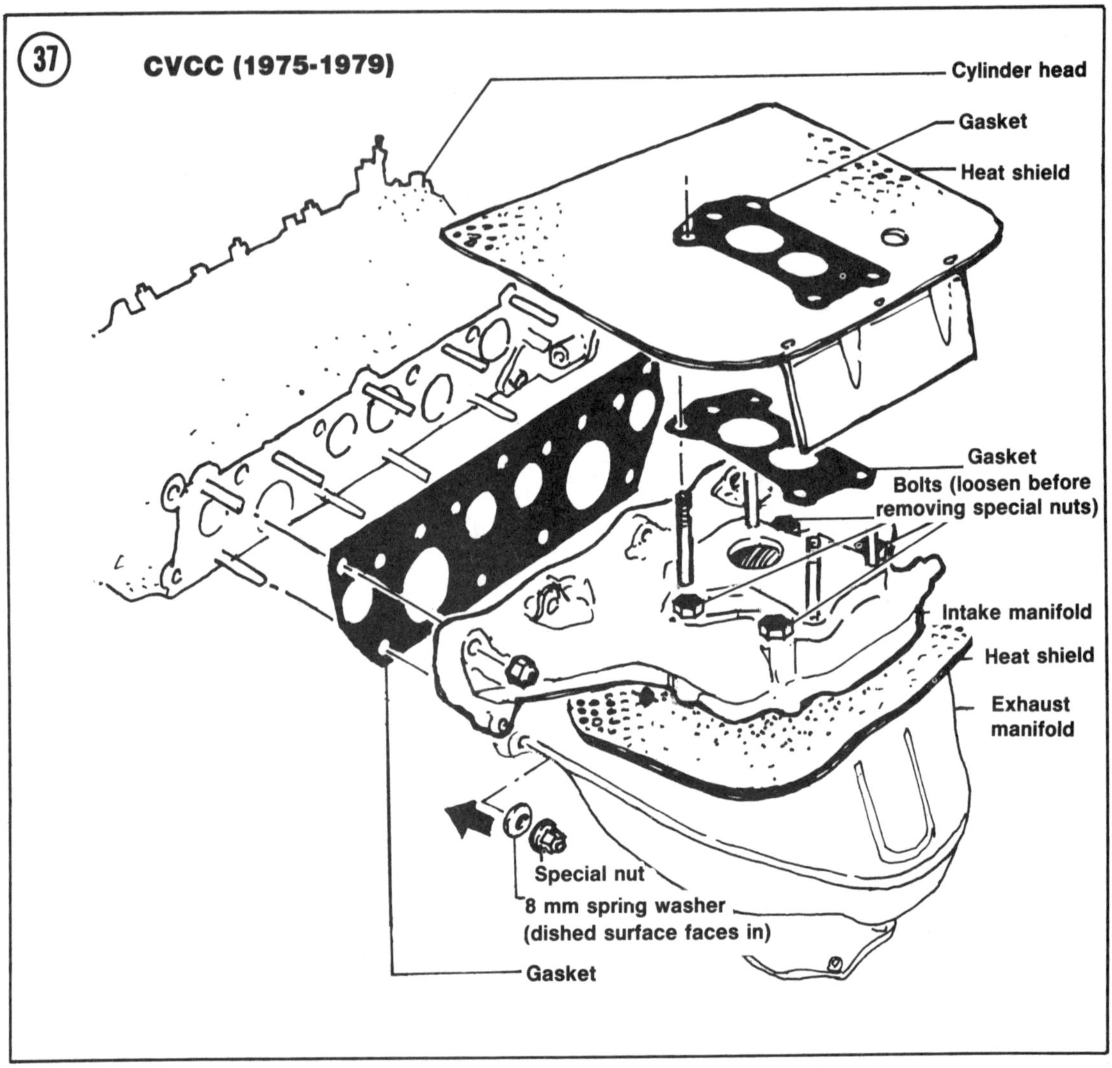

37

CVCC (1975-1979)

Cylinder head
Gasket
Heat shield
Gasket
Bolts (loosen before removing special nuts)
Intake manifold
Heat shield
Exhaust manifold
Special nut
8 mm spring washer (dished surface faces in)
Gasket

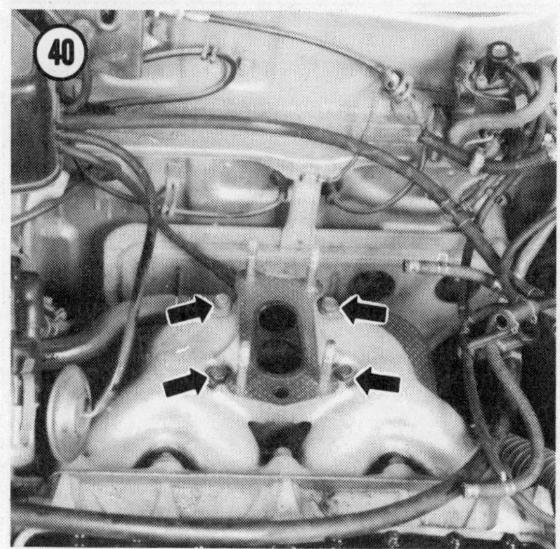

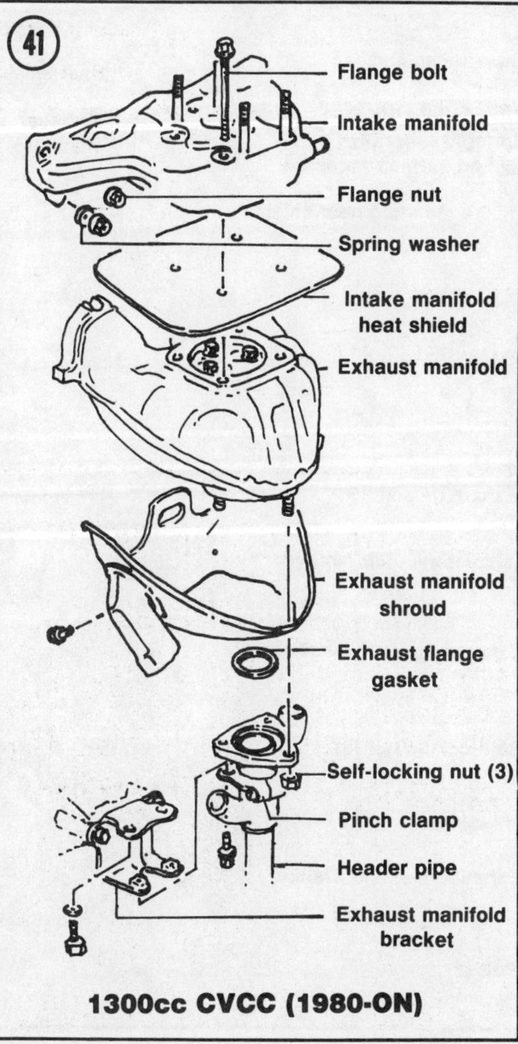

1300cc CVCC (1980-ON)

7. Loosen the bolts attaching the intake and exhaust manifolds to the cylinder heads. Then remove both manifolds as a unit.

8. Remove the 4 intake manifold-to-exhaust manifold through bolts and separate the manifolds. Discard the riser gasket.

9. Remove all traces of the manifold gasket from the cylinder head.

10. Assemble the intake and exhaust manfolds together, making sure to use a new riser gasket between the manifolds. Install the 4 intake manifold-to-exhaust manifold bolts (**Figure 40**) and tighten finger-tight only. Do not torque these bolts at this time. Install the exhaust manifold cover to the bottom of the exhaust manifold if removed.

NOTE
When installing the 4 through bolts and washers, make sure to install the washers with the concave side facing down.

11. Install a new manifold gasket to the cylinder head.

12. Install the intake and exhaust manifold unit into position against the cylinder head. Install the manifold and secure with new concave washers and nuts.

NOTE
When installing the manifold assembly nuts and washers, make sure to install the washers with the concave side facing toward the cylinder head.

13. Tighten the manifold assembly bolts in 2 stages in a crisscross pattern. First tighten to 1.0 mkg (7 ft.-lb.), then to 2.2 mkg (16 ft.-lb.).

14. Now tighten the 4 intake manifold-to-exhaust manifold through bolts (**Figure 40**) to 2.2 mkg (16 ft.-lb.).

15. Installation is completed by reversing Steps 1-5. Make sure to install a new carburetor base gasket. When attaching exhaust pipe to manifold, install a new flange gasket. Tighten exhaust pipe-to-manifold nuts and bolts securely.

1980-on models

Refer to **Figure 41** (1300cc) or **Figure 42** (1500cc) for this procedure. Special tool part

5

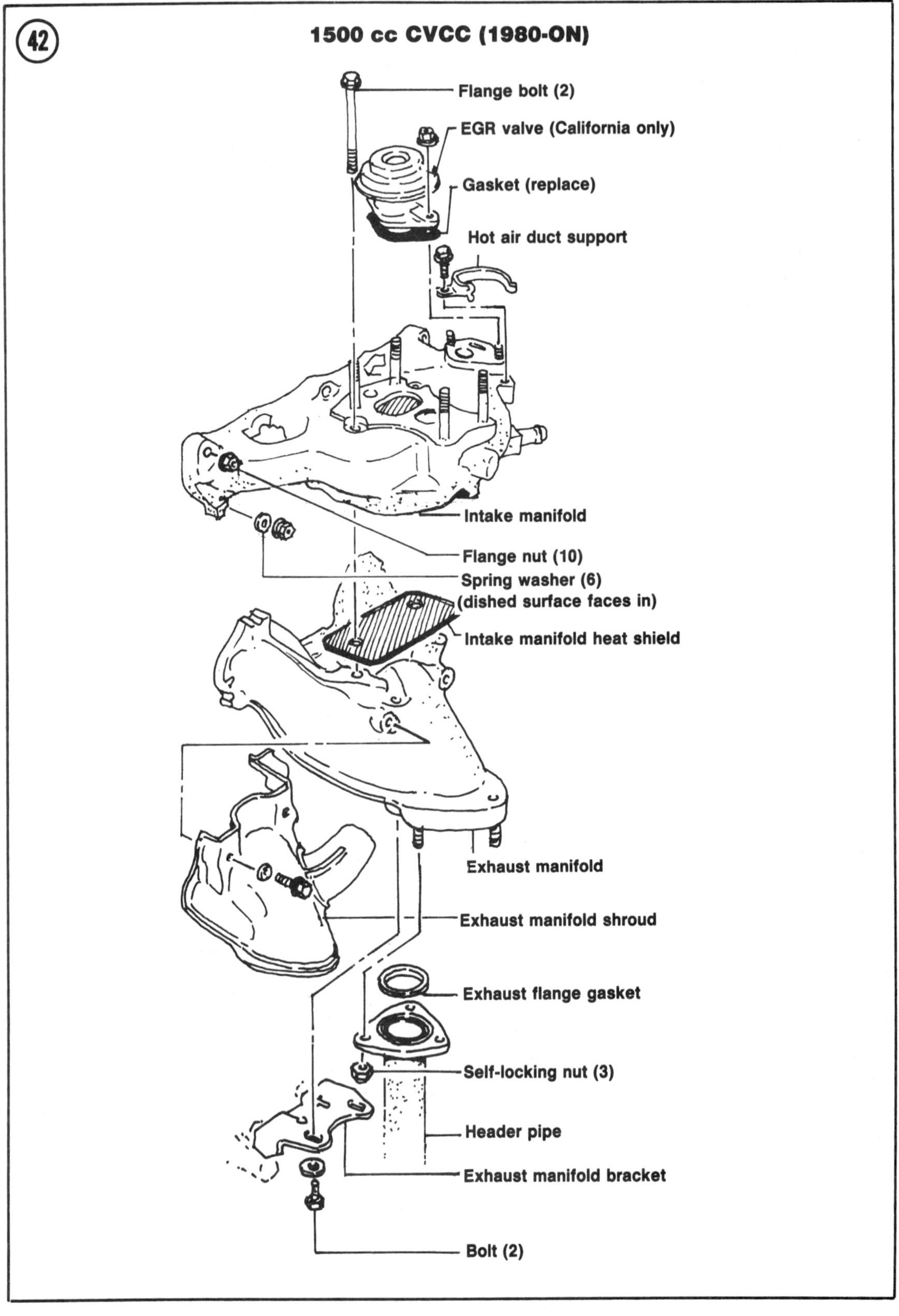
42
1500 cc CVCC (1980-ON)
Flange bolt (2)
EGR valve (California only)
Gasket (replace)
Hot air duct support
Intake manifold
Flange nut (10)
Spring washer (6)
(dished surface faces in)
Intake manifold heat shield
Exhaust manifold
Exhaust manifold shroud
Exhaust flange gasket
Self-locking nut (3)
Header pipe
Exhaust manifold bracket
Bolt (2)

No. H/C 83023 is required to remove the middle manifold attaching bolts. If this tool is not available, the cylinder head must be removed together with the intake/exhaust manifold assembly to provide access to the middle bolts. Cylinder head removal is described in Chapter Four.

1. Raise the vehicle's front end and secure with jackstands.
2. *1300cc models:* Disconnect the hot air ducts from the header pipe.
3. Disconnect the exhaust pipe at the exhaust manifold. Remove jackstands from underneath vehicle and lower vehicle to ground.
4. Open the radiator drain plug and drain the engine coolant. If the coolant was changed recently and is not dirty, it can be drained into a clean container for reuse.
5. Disconnect the coolant hoses at the intake manifold.
6. Remove the air cleaner assembly and carburetor as described in this chapter. Discard the carburetor base gasket.
7. *1300cc models:* Disconnect the bolts securing the header pipe pinch clamp to the manifold bracket. Then pull the pipe down and clear of the manifold studs.
8. Remove the bolts attaching the manifold bracket to the manifold.
9. Remove the intake manifold heat shield from on top of the intake manifold.
10. Disconnect the EGR hose at the EGR valve (if so equipped).
11. Remove the center manifold attaching nuts using Honda special tool part No. H/C 83023. Then remove the remaining manifold attaching nuts. Remove both manifolds as a unit.
12. Remove the 2 intake manifold-to-exhaust manifold through bolts and separate the manifolds. Discard the center heat shield.

13. Remove all traces of the manifold gasket from the cylinder head.
14. Assemble the intake and exhaust manfolds together, making sure to install a new heat shield between the manifolds. Install the 2 intake manifold-to-exhaust manifold through bolts and tighten finger-tight only. Do not torque these bolts at this time. Install the exhaust manifold cover to the bottom of the exhaust manifold if removed.
15. Install a new manifold gasket onto the cylinder head.
16. Install the intake and exhaust manifold unit into position against the cylinder head. Install the manifold and secure with new concave washers and nuts. Tighten nuts finger-tight only.

NOTE
When installing the manifold unit nuts and washers, make sure to install the washers with the concave side facing toward the cylinder head.

NOTE
To install the middle washers and nuts, first bend a piece of wire to form a small hook on one end. Place one washer onto the hook and position the wire and washer next to one cylinder head-to-manifold stud. Push the washer onto the stud with a screwdriver. Repeat for opposite washer and both nuts.

17. Tighten the manifold assembly bolts in 2 stages in a crisscross pattern. First tighten to 1.0 mkg (7 ft.-lb.), then to 2.2 mkg (16 ft.-lb.).
18. Now tighten the intake manifold-to-exhaust manifold through bolts to 2.2 mkg (16 ft.-lb.).
19. Installation can be completed by reversing Steps 1-10. Make sure to install a new carburetor base gasket. When attaching exhaust pipe to manifold, install a new flange gasket. Tighten exhaust pipe-to-manifold nuts securely.

EXHAUST SYSTEM

The exhaust system consists of the exhaust manifold, hot air cover, exhaust pipe and silencer. A catalytic converter is used on 1980 1500cc models and on all 1981 models. A typical exhaust system is shown in **Figure 43** (non-CVCC) and **Figure 44** (CVCC). The catalytic converter system is shown in **Figure 45**.

Exhaust Pipe Removal/Installation

1. Jack up the front of the car and support it on jackstands.

5

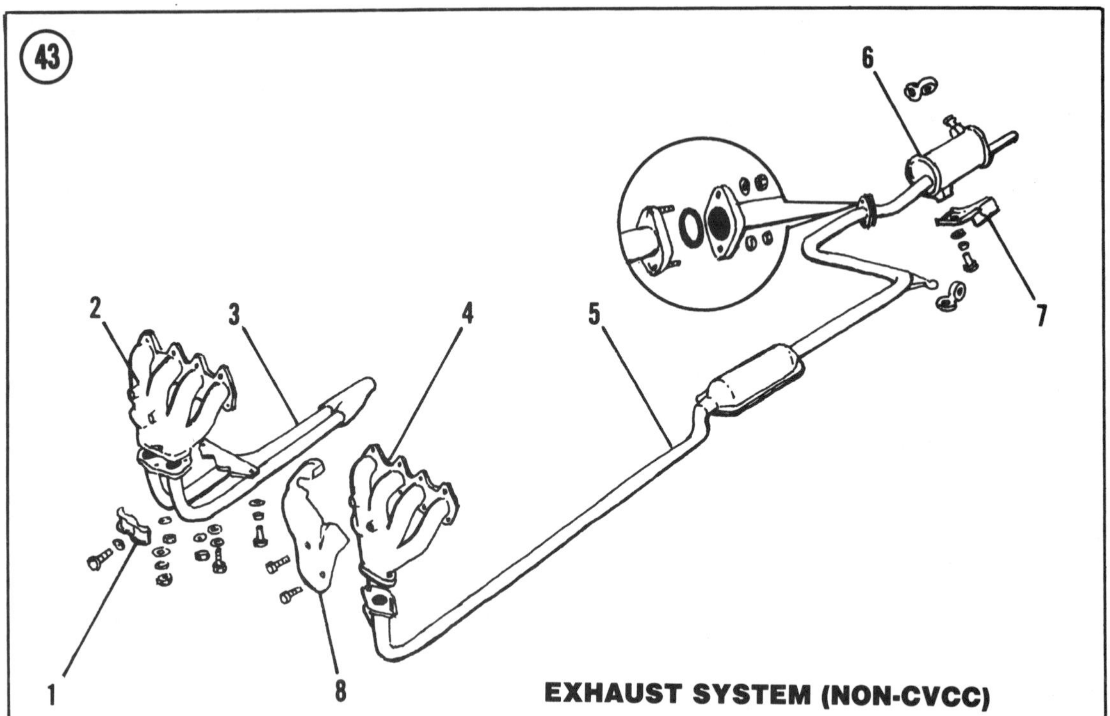

(43)

EXHAUST SYSTEM (NON-CVCC)

1. Pipe clamp
2. Exhaust manifold
3. Exhaust pipe
4. Exhaust manifold
5. Exhaust pipe
6. Exhaust silencer
7. Silencer mount
8. Hot air cover

(44)

EXHAUST SYSTEM (TYPICAL CVCC)

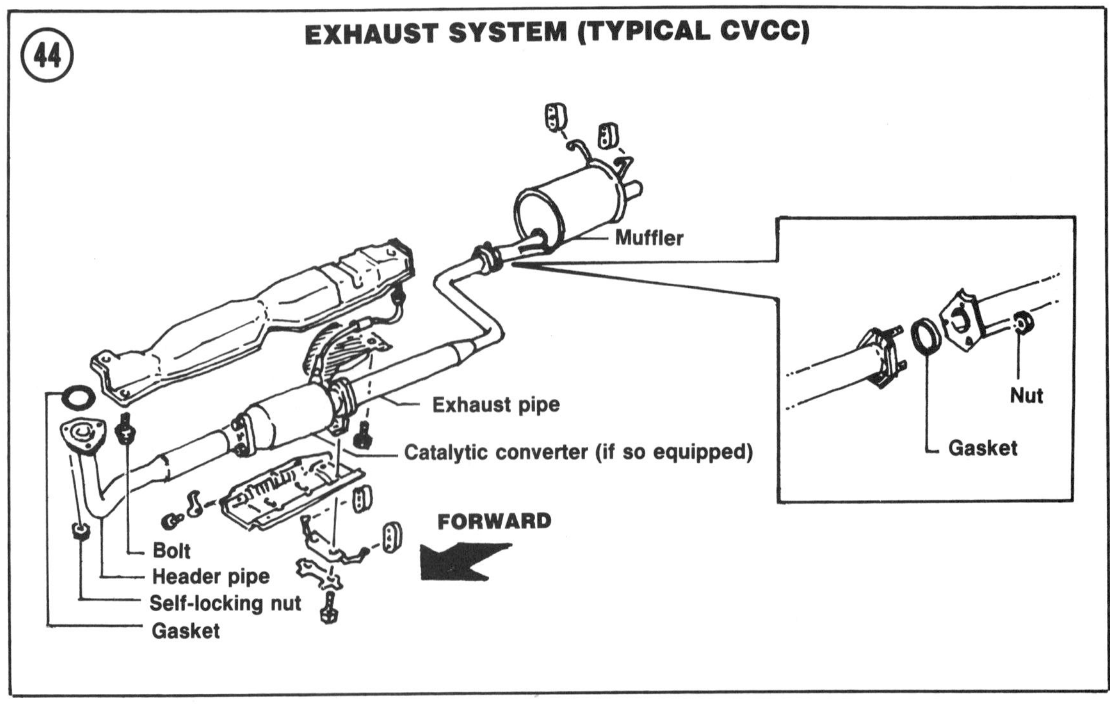

2. Spray penetrating oil on all of the exhaust pipe fasteners which will be loosened or removed.
3. Unscrew the bolts from the front exhaust pipe bracket and remove them from the pipe.
4. Unscrew the nuts from the exhaust pipe/manifold flange joint and lower the pipe. Lower the front of the car, jack up the rear and support it with jackstands.
5. Unscrew the muffler mounting bolt(s). Disconnect the muffler and the exhaust pipe from the rubber mounts and lower the complete system. On those vehicles equipped with catalytic converter, refer to *Catalytic Converter Removal/Installation* in this chapter and remove the unit.
6. Unscrew the muffler/exhaust pipe flange nuts and separate the 2 assemblies.
7. Installation is the reverse of these steps. Always use new gaskets when installing the exhaust pipe and muffler. Also, if the rubber mounts shown signs of deterioration, they should be replaced.

Catalytic Converter Removal/Installation

Refer to **Figure 45** for this procedure.

1. Raise the vehicle front end and secure with jackstands.
2. Remove the bottom support bar from the rubber mounts.
3. Unscrew the catalytic converter-to-exhaust pipe attaching bolts and remove the catalytic converter.
4. If the heat shield is damaged, remove it from its bottom position on the converter.
5. Installation is the reverse of these steps. Replace the heat shield lock plates if the shield was removed from the converter. Tighten the converter-to-exhaust pipe attaching nuts to 3.4 mkg (25 ft.-lb.).

Muffler Replacement

1. Jack up the rear end of the car and support it on jackstands.
2. Unscrew the muffler-to-exhaust pipe flange nuts.
3. Unscrew the muffler mounting bolts, disconnect the muffler from the rubber mount and remove it.
4. Reverse the removal steps to install the muffler. Use a new gasket and replace the rubber mount if it shows signs of deterioration.

EMISSION CONTROL SYSTEMS

By-products of the combustion process that takes place in a gasoline-fueled automobile

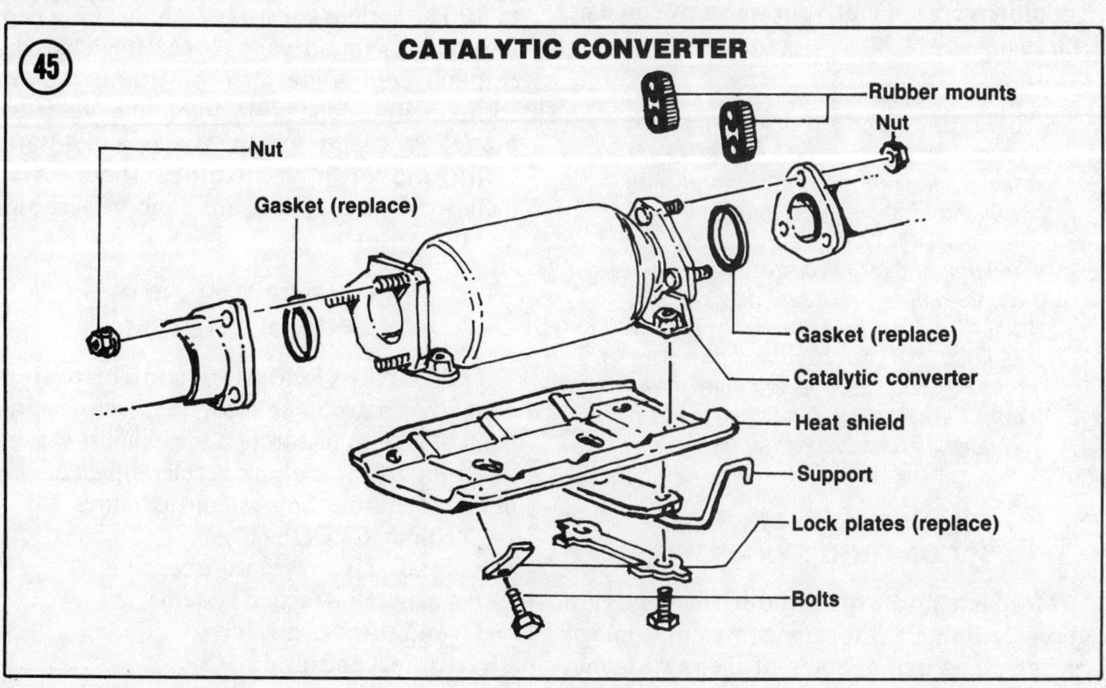

engine include carbon monoxide (CO), oxides of nitrogen (NOx) and unburned hydrocarbons (HC). In addition, evaporation of gasoline in the fuel tank and carburetor produces additional hydrocarbons. All 3 types of emissions are considered air pollutants.

Federal and, in some areas, state and local laws have been passed which limit the amounts of these pollutants that can be released into the atmosphere by automobiles. Automobile manufacturers have been required to modify their products to meet the standards established by these laws.

Honda Motor Company uses a number of systems to restrict harmful and illegal emissions. These systems include:

a. Crankcase emission control system
b. Evaporative emission control system
c. Exhaust emission control system

Emission Control Maintenance

Emission control maintenance should be limited to the tasks described in Chapter Three. If your car is still under warranty, Honda requires that this maintenance be performed by an authorized Honda dealership or by a qualified service facility and that detailed receipts be kept showing that the required maintenance was performed. If these conditions are not met, your warranty could be affected.

NOTE
While the majority of all emission control tasks should be left to a Honda dealer, it is important to routinely inspect all system hoses for deterioration and check the tubes for cracks. Replace any that are not satisfactory. Check the connections to make sure they are tight and leak-free. If a hose or tube is to be replaced, pay careful attention to the routing of the piece being removed and route the new piece in the same manner. Tighten all connections securely.

CRANKCASE EMISSION CONTROL SYSTEM

Most, but not all, of the the exhaust gases are discharged though the exhaust system. Some of the gases, as well as some of the raw air/fuel mixture, are "blown by" the piston rings and collect in the crankcase. If the blow-by is allowed to remain in the crankcase and combine with the oil, it forms sludge, varnish or acids. The latter sometimes attacks bearings and other metal parts. When the mixture of blow-by and oil fumes cools, it condenses and dilutes the oil which eventually destroys its lubricating effectiveness.

Honda uses a dual return system to control the emission of crankcase gases. See **Figure 46**. Intake manifold vacuum is used to return the gases to the combustion chamber. When the car is operating at low speed, the gases are routed through the return passage below the throttle plate. At higher speeds, some of the gases are routed through the air cleaner and carburetor and some are routed through the return passage. The gases are replaced with fresh air drawn in through the air cleaner as shown in **Figure 46**.

Required maintenance intervals and procedures for the crankcase emission control system are described in Chapter Three.

EVAPORATIVE EMISSION CONTROL SYSTEM

This system controls the emission of gasoline vapors from the carburetor and fuel tank. The system consists of the fuel filler cap, fuel tank, a liquid/vapor separator, charcoal canister and a number of inline system components, depending upon the vehicle's model year and whether it is a 49-state, California or high-altitude model. Also included in the system are connecting hoses and pipes.

EXHAUST EMISSION CONTROL SYSTEM

The exhaust emission control system actually is a group of subsystems designed to control emissions through the exhaust system when the engine is idling, accelerating, cruising and decelerating. Subsystems used are:

a. Honda CVCC engine
b. Intake air temperature control
c. Carburetor-related systems
d. Anti-afterburn valve
e. Air jet controller

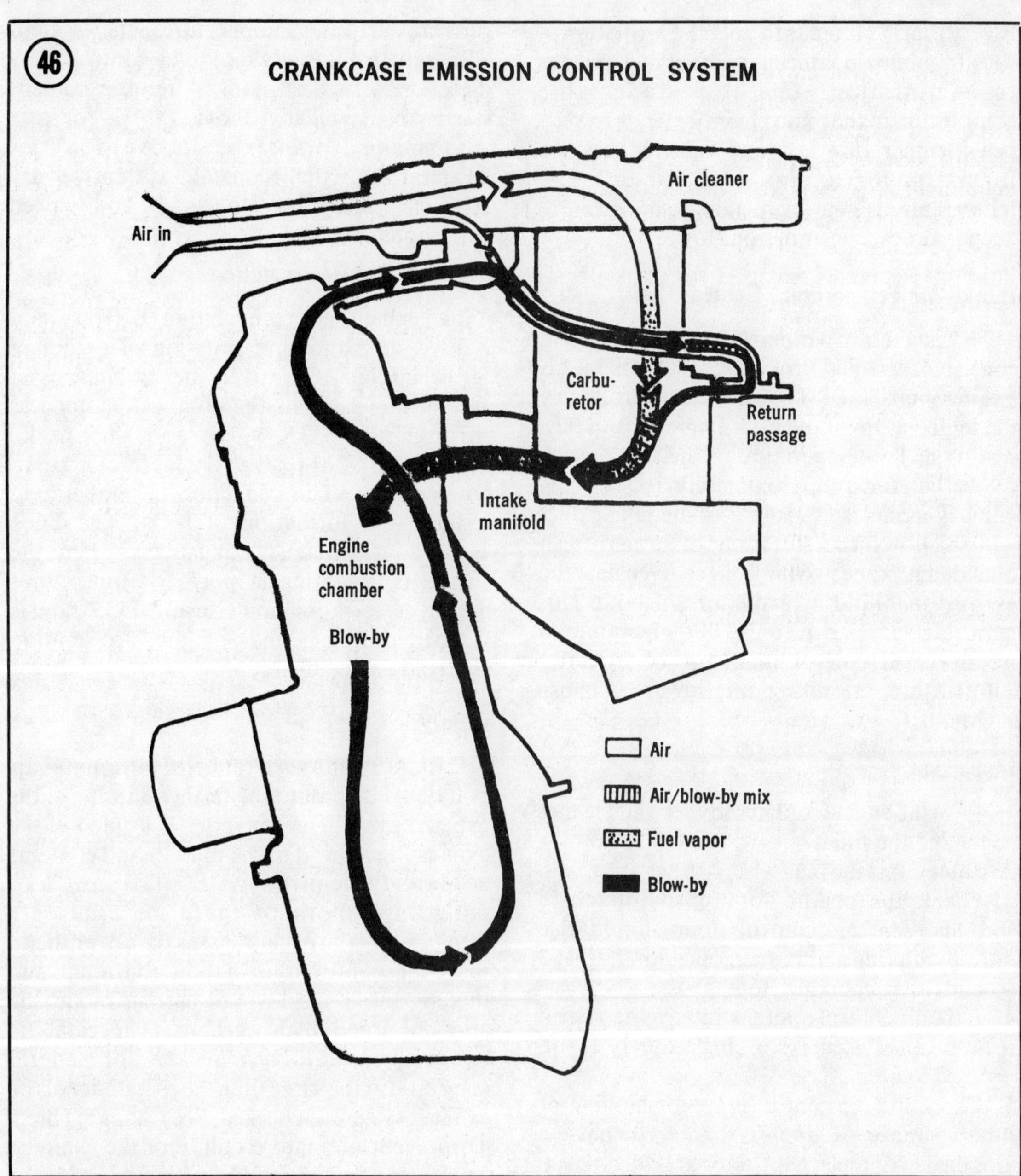

f. Exhaust gas recirculation
g. Catalytic converter

The actual subsystems used on your vehicle depend upon the model year and whether it is a 49-state, California or high-altitude model.

CVCC Engine

The CVCC engine modification system uses 2 combustion chambers in each cylinder, the main chamber and the auxiliary chamber. An extremely lean air/fuel mixture is introduced into the main chamber, while a rich mixture is introduced into the auxiliary chamber. Each cylinder has 2 intake valves and a single exhaust valve. The spark plug ignites the small amount of rich mixture in the auxiliary chamber and the resulting combustion ignites the lean mixture in the main chamber. Since the main chamber is much larger than the auxiliary chamber, the overall air/fuel mixture is very lean. This tends to hold the formation of carbon monoxide during combustion process to a minimum. The slow and stable combustion in the main chamber tends to keep peak temperature low and this reduces the formation of oxides of nitrogen. The temperature is kept high enough, however, to keep hydrocarbon emissions low.

Intake Air Temperature Control

The intake air temperature control system consists of an air control valve located in the air cleaner intake duct. The valve is controlled by the temperature of the intake air and it in turn maintains the temperature of the air entering the carburetor at approximately 100° F. The valve is connected to a door in the intake duct which allows the selection of either fresh outside air, preheated air from an oven near the exhaust manifold or a mixture of both. This permits a very narrow range of temperature to be maintained, regardless of outside temperature, resulting in lower exhaust emissions.

Inspection

1. With the engine cold, remove the air cleaner cover and the filter.
2. Disconnect the blue wire at the ignition coil.
3. Crank the engine for approximately 5 seconds. The air control door should rise during cranking and remain open for at least 3 seconds after cranking stops.
4. If the air control door operated as described in Step 3, the system is working properly. If not, proceed to Step 5.
5. Check the air control door for binding or other damage. If door is damaged, have a Honda dealer replace the door and then retest. If air control door operates smoothly by hand, the intake air temperature control system is faulty. Refer further testing to a Honda dealer.
6. After testing, reinstall the air filter and air cleaner cover. Reconnect the blue wire at the ignition coil.

Ignition Timing Control System

The ignition timing control system controls the ignition spark according to the engine's load, temperature of the coolant and speed. In general, at low temperatures the system allows distributor advance to be controlled by direct manifold vacuum. After the coolant warms up (typically above 149° F for cars with manual transaxles; above 158° for automatics), the control systems vary advance according to load and speed conditions.

Exhaust Gas Recirculation

The exhaust gas recirculation (EGR) system is used to reduce the emission of oxides of nitrogen (NOx). Relatively inert exhaust gases are introduced into the combustion process through the EGR valve and the intake manifold. This slightly reduces peak temperatures. This reduction in temperature reduces the formation of NOx. The EGR system recirculates exhaust gas when the engine is operating at normal temperatures during acceleration and cruising. EGR flow is stopped during periods of idle, deceleration and cold engine operation.

Catalytic Converter

Catalytic converters help eliminate air pollutants by promoting further burning of the exhaust gases. The converter is located in the exhaust line ahead of the muffler and contains a material coated with platinum and palladium. Both of these materials are catalysts. As the exhaust gases pass over them, they cause further oxidation (burning) and thereby lower the level of carbon monoxide and unburned hydrocarbons. The catalytic converter should be checked for general condition at the same time the remainder of the exhaust system is checked. See Chapter Three. To prevent premature failure of the catalytic converter, only unleaded fuel can be used.

FUEL REQUIREMENTS

To maintain your Honda's warranty, it is important to use an unleaded gasoline with 91 Research octane number or higher (86 octane number or higher measured by the Cost of Living Council formula). This is to prevent engine knock, a spontaneous and premature explosion of the gasoline/air mixture in the cylinders. Besides decreasing fuel economy and engine power, engine knock can damage engine parts (if allowed to continue).

When operating your car, you should remember that changing conditions can also change the octane requirements for your engine. For example, as your car ages, it will have a tendency to knock more. In addition, heavy loads or operating in low-humidity areas for extended periods of time can have the same effect. To be safe, you should carefully select the correct octane rating for your car by performing the following test.

1. Tune your car as described in Chapter Three. Make sure that it is operating in good mechanical condition.
2. Run your car until it is nearly empty. Then fill it up with the brand of gasoline you usually buy (at least a 91 octane rating as specified by Honda).
3. Drive the car to bring to normal operating temperature. Come to a complete stop, then accelerate hard.
4. If the engine knocks or pings, use up the gasoline and refill with the next higher grade. Repeat Step 3.
5. If the engine does not knock, this is the gasoline that you should be using. If the engine does knock with the higher octane, refer to Chapter Two. There is some type of mechanical trouble which is causing the engine to knock. Other than a gasoline with an octane rating too low, consider the following conditions as the possible cause of engine knock:
   a. Incorrect ignition timing
   b. Incorrectly adjusted carburetor
   c. Carbon deposits collected in the cylinder head or on top of the pistons

Table is on the following page.

Table 1 FUEL PUMP SPECIFICATIONS

	PRESSURE kg/cm^2 (psi)	DISPLACEMENT cc/(cu. in.)/min.
1975-1979 non-CVCC	0.18 (2.56)	450 (27.45) @ 300 rpm 700 (42.71) @ 700 rpm 750 (45.76) @ 3,000 rpm
1975-1979 CVCC	0.13-0.18 (1.849-2.560)	450 (27.45)
1980-on CVCC	0.15-0.20 (2.1-2.8)	500 (31)

NOTE: If you own a 1982 or later model, first check the Supplement at the back of the book for any new service information.

CHAPTER SIX

COOLING SYSTEM AND HEATER

6

The cooling system consists of a pressurized radiator, thermostat, thermoswitch, centrifugal water pump, electric fan and appropriate plumbing.

The heater is a hot water type which circulates engine coolant through a small radiator located behind the instrument panel. Air is drawn in through the cowl vent by a squirrel-cage fan and blown over the radiator to heat the interior of the car. This chapter includes inspection and service procedures for both cooling system and heater. Specifications are in **Table 1** at the end of the chapter.

COOLANT

Only ethylene glycol-based coolant compatible with aluminum engines should be used.

The coolant should be mixed with water in accordance with the coolant manufacturer's instructions to provide freeze protection to -34° F. Even if your climate does not require this degree of protection, the antifreeze makes an excellent rust inhibitor. However, do not exceed 60% antifreeze solution.

DRIVE BELT TENSION ADJUSTMENT

The tension of the water pump/alternator and air conditioning drive belts should be checked every 12,000 miles (1973-1974)) or 15,000 (1975-on) miles and inspected and adjusted if necessary.

Worn, cracked or glazed belts should be replaced at once. The components to which they direct power are essential to the safe and reliable operation of the vehicle. If correct adjustment is maintained on the belts, they will usually all enjoy the same service life.

In addition to being in good condition, it is important that the drive belts be correctly adjusted. A belt that is too loose will not permit the driven components to operate at maximum efficiency. In addition, the belt will wear rapidly because of increased friction caused by slipping. A belt that is adjusted too tight will be overstressed and tend to be pulled apart, and it in turn will overstress bearings in driven components resulting in their premature wear or possible failure. Check and tension belts as follows:

a. Water pump/alternator belt: Measure the deflection of the belt midway between the water pump and alternator pulleys (**Figure 1**). It should be 12-17 mm (15/32-21/32 in.). If the tension is not correct, loosen the alternator lock bolts (**Figure 2**, both upper and lower bolts) and move the alternator as required. Tighten the lock bolts securely and recheck the deflection.
b. Air conditioning belt: Measure the deflection of the belt midway between the compressor and crankshaft pulleys. It should be 8-10 mm (5/16-7/16 in.). If tension is not correct, loosen the compressor adjusting nut(s) and/or bolt(s) and move the compressor as required. Tighten the fasteners securely and recheck the deflection.

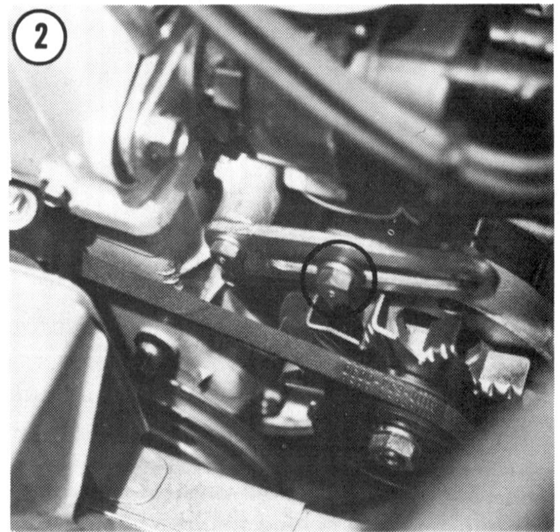

Pulley Inspection

Before installing new drive belts, inspect the pulleys for the following conditions:

a. Oil or grease: Contaminants on the pulley surface will cause the belt to slip. Efficiency of the driven components is reduced and the belt will eventually deteriorate. Clean each pulley before installing new drive belts.
b. Pulley damage: Wear spots in the pulley belt groove will cause a new belt to wear quickly. A cracked or damaged pulley could possibly break and cause damage in the engine compartment. Inspect and replace any pulley as required.
c. Pulley wear: During normal operations, drive pulleys will ride on the sides of the pulley. This is indicated by a polished appearance on the pulley's side. However, if the bottom of the pulley groove appears polished, the belt is either adjusted too tight or the pulley is worn. Replace a pulley that seems worn. Make sure to tension drive belts as described in this chapter.

COOLING SYSTEM FLUSHING

A mixture of ethylene glycol-based antifreeze and water compounded for aluminum engines protects the cooling system.

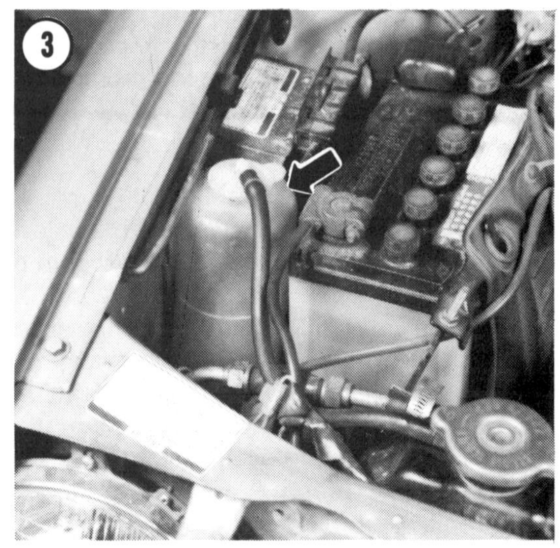

4

5

The coolant should be changed every 12 months, regardless of mileage, on 1973-1974 models. On 1975-1979 models, it should be inspected at 15,000 miles and changed every 30,000 miles. On 1980 and later models, coolant change is required at 45,000 miles and thereafter every 30,000 miles or 2 years. If the coolant appears dirty or rusty, the system should be cleaned with a chemical cleaner, drained, flushed with clean water and refilled. Severe corrosion may require pressure flushing, a job for a dealer or radiator shop.

Cooling System Checks

1. Check coolant level by observing the liquid in the recovery system reservoir (**Figure 3**). The radiator cap (**Figure 4**) should not be removed. If additional coolant is required, it should be added to the recovery reservoir. Level should be at "COLD FULL" mark when engine is cool or at "HOT FULL" when engine is hot.
2. Check water pump operation by squeezing the upper radiator hose while the engine is running at normal operating temperature (**Figure 5**). If pressure surge is felt, the water pump is functioning. If not, check for a plugged vent hole in the pump.
3. Check for exhaust leaks into the cooling system by draining coolant until level is just above top of cylinder head. Disconnect upper radiator hose (**Figure 5**) and remove thermostat and drive belt (as described in this chapter). Start the engine and accelerate it several times while observing the coolant. If the level rises or bubbles appear, chances are that exhaust gases are leaking into the cooling system.

Flushing

1. Remove the radiator cap. See **Figure 4**.

WARNING
Do not remove the radiator cap while the engine and radiator are hot. Scalding fluid and steam may be blown out under pressure and cause serious injury.

2. Drain the cooling system by opening the radiator drain tap.
3. Remove the coolant recovery tank from its bracket (**Figure 3**) and pour out the coolant. Reinstall the tank in its bracket.
4. On 1981 models, remove the engine coolant drain plug at the front of the engine block (**Figure 6**) and allow the engine and heater to drain. Using a new gasket, install the drain plug and tighten securely.
5. Once system is drained, reinstall the radiator drain plug.
6. Add a sufficient amount of water through the radiator fill hole to fill the system and run engine to circulate the water.
7. Repeat Steps 1-6 as required until drained water is clear of rust and other debris. When drained water appears clean, reinstall the radiator drain plug.

Refilling

Before refilling cooling system, check coolant hoses for damage and replace as described under *Coolant Hose.*

1. Be sure all hoses are connected and the radiator and recovery tank caps are removed.
2. Loosen the cooling system bleed valve. See **Figure 7** (non-CVCC) or **Figure 8** (CVCC).
3. Fill the cooling system with a 50/50 mixture of ethylene glycol-based antifreeze and water to the base of the radiator fill neck and add sufficient coolant to the recovery tank to raise fluid level to the "FULL" mark. Continue to add coolant and water until the coolant running out of the bleed valve is free of air bubbles. Close the bleed valve. Install the recovery tank cap.

NOTE

Even if you live in a climate that does not require this degree of freeze protection, the 50/50 mixture of antifreeze and water will provide a good corrosion inhibitor.

4. Set the heater temperature control on HIGH and start the engine. Allow it to run until it is thoroughly warmed up, open the bleed valve (**Figure 7** or **Figure 8**) and bleed the system again. When air bubbles are no longer present in the coolant running out of the bleed valve, close the valve and fill the radiator to the bottom of the filler neck. Install the radiator cap and inspect all cooling system connections for leaks.
5. Drive vehicle for several miles and recheck coolant level. Maintain fluid level in reservoir between "COLD FULL" and "HOT FULL" marks.

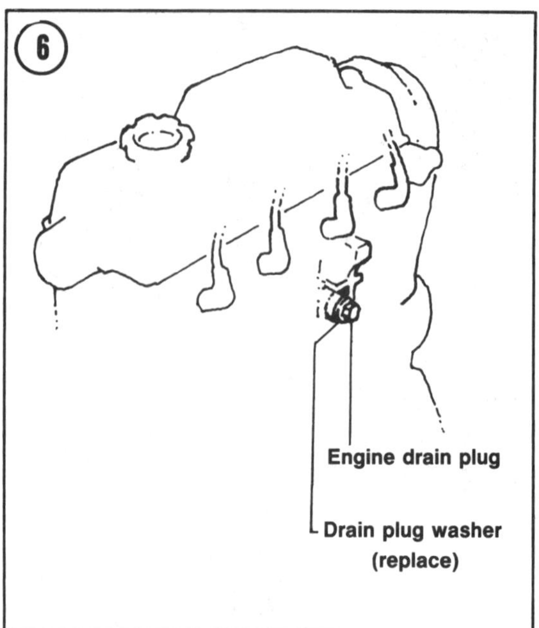

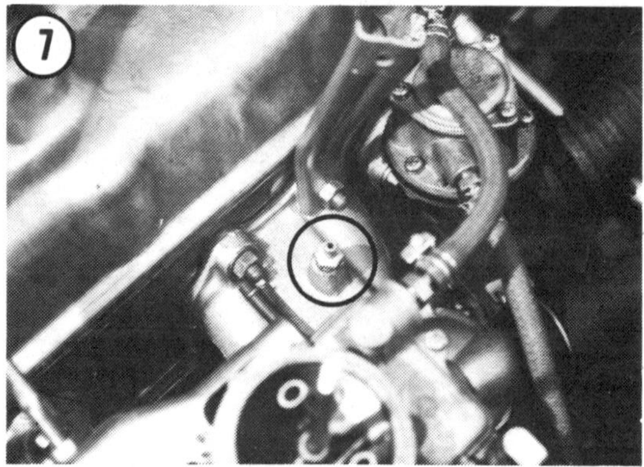

PRESSURE CHECK

This test requires a reliable pressure tester and can be performed quickly and economically by your Honda dealer or a radiator shop. Service stations also may be equipped to perform the test. Perform the test if frequent additions of coolant are necessary to keep the cooling system topped up and your radiator is known to be in good condition.

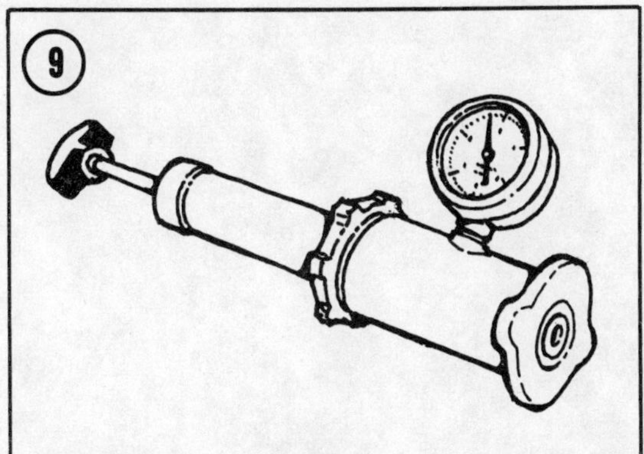

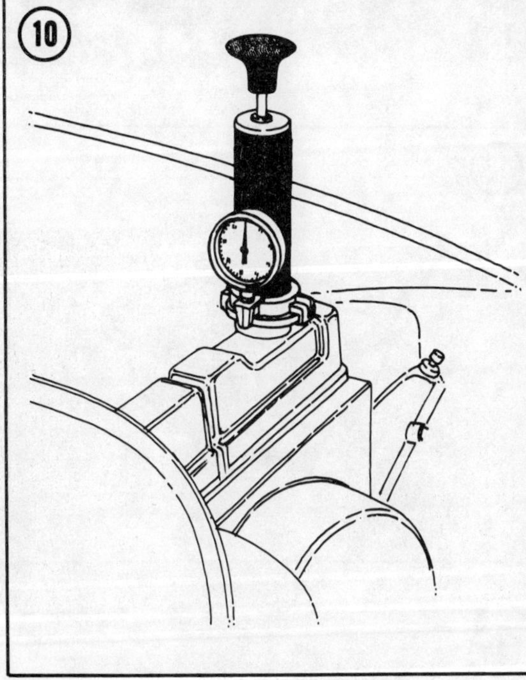

To check the system:

1. Remove the radiator cap (**Figure 4**).
2. Dip the cap in water and attach to a cooling system pressure tester, using suitable adapter supplied with instrument. See **Figure 9**.
3. Pump pressure to 11-14 psi. If the cap fails to hold pressure for at least 6 seconds, replace it.
4. Attach the pressure tester to the filler hole on the radiator (**Figure 10**).
5. Pump the system to 11-14 psi. There should be no noticeable pressure drop in 30 seconds. If pressure falls off, there is a leak which must be found and sealed.

RADIATOR

Removal/Installation

1. Remove the front grille and turn signals.
2. Drain the cooling system as described under *Cooling System Flushing*.
3. Disconnect the thermoswitch and fan motor wire connectors at the fan.
4. Disconnect the upper and lower coolant hoses at the radiator. On automatic transaxle equipped models, disconnect and plug the transaxle coolant hoses at the radiator.
5. Remove the radiator attaching bolts and remove the radiator together with the fan.
6. Remove the fan from the radiator.
7. Installation is the reverse of these steps. Fill and bleed the cooling system as described in this chapter. Check the automatic transaxle fluid level (Chapter Three) and add fluid as required.

THERMOSTAT

Removal/Testing

1. Drain the cooling system as described in this chapter. Unscrew the bolts that attach the thermostat cover (**Figure 11**, non-CVCC;

6

Figure 12, CVCC) and remove the cover and thermostat. It is not necessary to disconnect the hose from the cover. If the thermostat is in the open position when it is removed, it is faulty and must be replaced. If it is closed, proceed with Steps 2 and 3.

2. Submerge the thermostat in a pan of water along with a thermometer (**Figure 13**). (Do not allow the thermometer to touch the bottom of the pan.) Heat the water and watch the thermometer. Record the temperature at which the thermostat begins to open and when it is fully open. Refer to **Table 1** for specifications. If the thermostat fails to open or opens at the wrong temperature, replace it.
3. Measure the lift of the thermostat using a screwdriver marked 8 mm (5/16 in.) from the tip (**Figure 14**). Heat the water until the thermostat is completely open and measure the lift with the tip of the screwdriver. If it is less than 6 mm or more than 10 mm, replace the thermostat.

Installation

If a new thermostat is being installed, test it as described above; don't assume it is correct just because it is new.

1. Set the thermostat in the housing with the spring down. Set a new gasket in place and install the cover. Screw in the bolts snugly.
2. Fill and bleed the cooling system as described. In addition, check and adjust the drive belt tension as described under *Drive Belt Tension Adjustment*.

THERMOSWITCH

The thermoswitch controls the operation of the electric fan motor by sensing the coolant temperature. The thermoswitch can be removed without draining the cooling system, provided the radiator cap is installed. A small amount of coolant will be lost when the switch is removed and this must be replenished after it has been installed.

Testing

1. With the engine cold, remove the radiator cap. Start and run the engine until coolant temperature reaches 88-91° C (191-197° F). Fan motor should start.

12

13

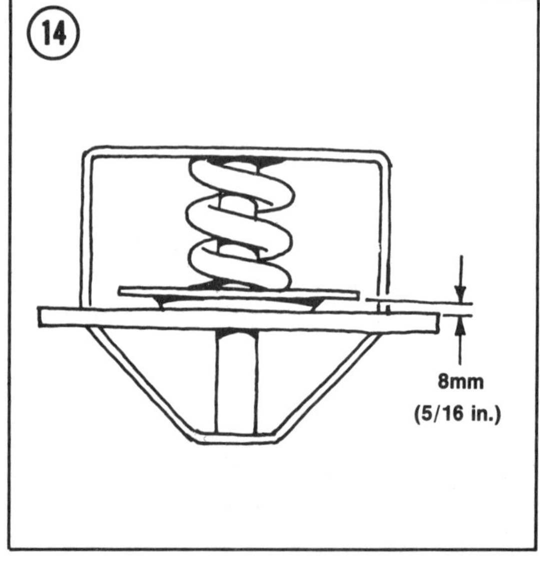

14

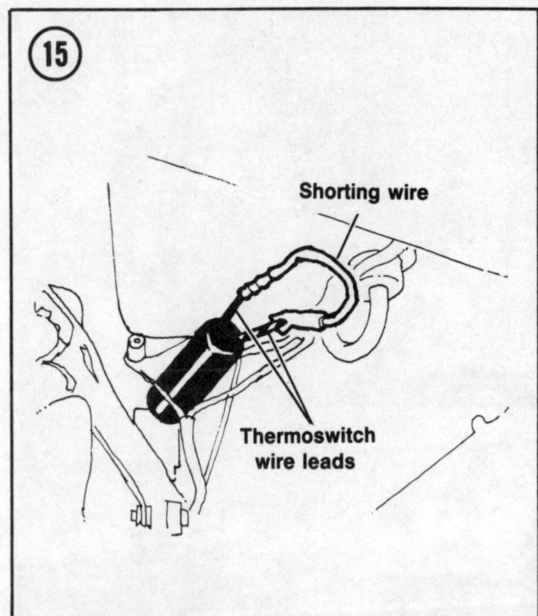

NOTE
Coolant temperature can be checked by immersing a thermometer through the radiator cap opening and into the coolant.

2. If the fan does not start, stop the engine. Disconnect the black/yellow and blue leads (1973-1979) or black and blue leads (1980-on) from the fan thermoswitch and short the wires together (**Figure 15**). Turn ignition switch ON. If fan motor starts, replace thermoswitch and repeat Step 1.
3. If fan motor does not start, check for voltage between blue and black (1973-1975) or black/yellow and blue (1980-on) wires in the cooling fan connector using a voltmeter. If voltage is not present, check for blown fuse, loose terminals or connector or an open circuit. Wiring diagrams are located at the back of the book. If voltage is present, repeat test.

Replacement

This procedure must be performed with the engine cold.

1. Drain the cooling system as described in this chapter.
2. Disconnect the electrical wires at the thermoswitch. Then remove the thermoswitch with a wrench.
3. Install the switch and O-ring in the bottom radiator tank and tighten it securely (**Figure 16**). If the condition of the O-ring is in doubt, replace it with a new one.
4. Reconnect the electrical leads, making sure they are tight and free of corrosion.
5. Fill and bleed the cooling system as described in this chapter.

6

COOLING FAN

The electric cooling fan is controlled by the thermoswitch. The fan should turn on and off at the temperatures indicated in the thermoswitch tests. If the thermoswitch is known to be operating correctly, disconnect the leads from the switch and connect them together with a jump wire. If the fan runs, it is in good condition. If it does not run, the fan motor is faulty and must be replaced.

Removal

1. Remove the radiator as described in this chapter.
2. Unscrew the screws which mount the fan shroud to the radiator.
3. Unscrew the fan hub nut and remove the fan and washers.
4. Unscrew the screws which mount the fan motor to the shroud. Disconnect the electrical connector and remove the motor.

Installation

1. Using jumper wires connected to the battery and the fan motor leads, test the new motor before installing it.

2. Reverse the removal steps and assemble the motor, shroud, fan and radiator. Install the assembly in the car.
3. Fill and bleed the cooling system as described in this chapter.

WATER PUMP

A defective water pump is usually the problem when the engine overheats and no other cause can be found. A water pump will often warn of impending failure by making noise or leaking.

Removal/Installation

1. Drain the cooling system as described in this chapter.
2. Loosen the lock and pivot bolts on the alternator and push the alternator toward the engine to relax the tension on the drive pulley. Remove the belt from the water pump pulley.
3A. *Non-CVCC:* Unscrew the pump attaching bolts, rotating the pulley to gain access to each bolt through the slots (**Figure 17**).
3B. *CVCC:* Unscrew the pump attaching bolts. **Figure 18** shows the water pump attaching screws (without the pulley). Then remove the front cover protector plate (**Figure 19**, if so equipped) and remove the water pump.

NOTE
*If the water pump is to be replaced, remove the pulley from the old pump (**Figure 20**) and transfer to new pump.*

4. Install the new pump along with a new rubber seal. Tighten the bolts in a crisscross pattern to 10-14 N•m (7-10 ft.-lb.).
5. Install the drive belt and adjust it as described earlier in this chapter. Fill and bleed the cooling system as described in this chapter.

COOLANT HOSES

A ruptured or broken coolant hose will cause a sudden loss of engine coolant. Check the coolant hoses at least once a year and anytime the coolant is replaced.

Inspection

1. With the engine cool, check the coolant hoses for brittleness or hardness. A hose in this

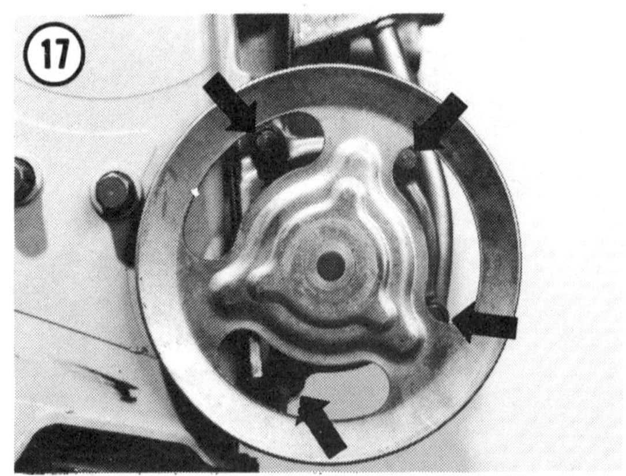
17

18

19

condition will usually show cracks and must be replaced.
2. With the engine hot, examine for portions of swelling hose along the entire hose length. Eventually the hose will rupture at this point.
3. Check area around hose clamps. Signs of rust around clamps indicate possible hose leakage.

Replacement

Hose replacement should be performed when the engine is cool.
1. Drain the cooling system.
2. Loosen the hose clamps from the hose to be replaced. Slide the clamps along the hose and out of the way.
3. Twist the hose end to break seal and remove from connecting joint. If the hose has been on for some time, it probably has become fused to the joint. If so, cut the hose parallel to the joint connection with a knife. The hose then can be carefully pried loose with a screwdriver.

CAUTION
Excessive force applied to the hose during removal could damage the connecting joint.

4. Examine the connecting joint for cracks or other damage. Repair or replace parts as required. If the joint is okay, clean it of any rust and hose sealant with sandpaper.
5. Inspect hose clamps and replace as necessary.
6. Slide hose clamps over outside of hose and install hose to inlet and outlet connecting joint. Make sure hose clears all obstructions and is routed properly.

NOTE
If is difficult to install on inlet or outlet joint, soak end of hose in hot water for approximately 2 minutes. This will soften the hose.

7. With hose positioned correctly on joint, position clamps back away from end of hose approximately 1/4 to 1/2 in. Tighten clamps securely, but not so much that hose is damaged.
8. Refill cooling system. Start engine and check for leaks. Retighten hose clamps as necessary.

6

HEATER

This section covers the heater on non-air conditioned models only. Repair of the heater on air conditioned models requires special skills and tools and should be left to a Honda dealer or other competent repair shop.

Heater Removal/Installation (1973-1979)

1. Drain the cooling system as described in this chapter.
2. Loosen the clamps on the heater hoses inside the engine compartment, disconnect the hoses and allow them to drain. Loosen hose clamps at the heater (**Figure 21**), hold a can beneath one of the hose connections, disconnect the hose and allow the coolant to drain. Do the same with the other hose.
3. Disconnect the defroster ducts from the heater (**Figure 21**).
4. Refer to *Control Assembly/Installation* and remove the controls. Unscrew the top heater mounting bolts, the front mounting bolt and bottom bracket mounting bolts. Double-check to make sure the cables and wires have all been disconnected and pull the heater assembly out from beneath the dashboard.
5. To install the heater, reverse Steps 1-4. Make certain the heater ground wire is attached at the top, right mount (**Figure 21**) and that the

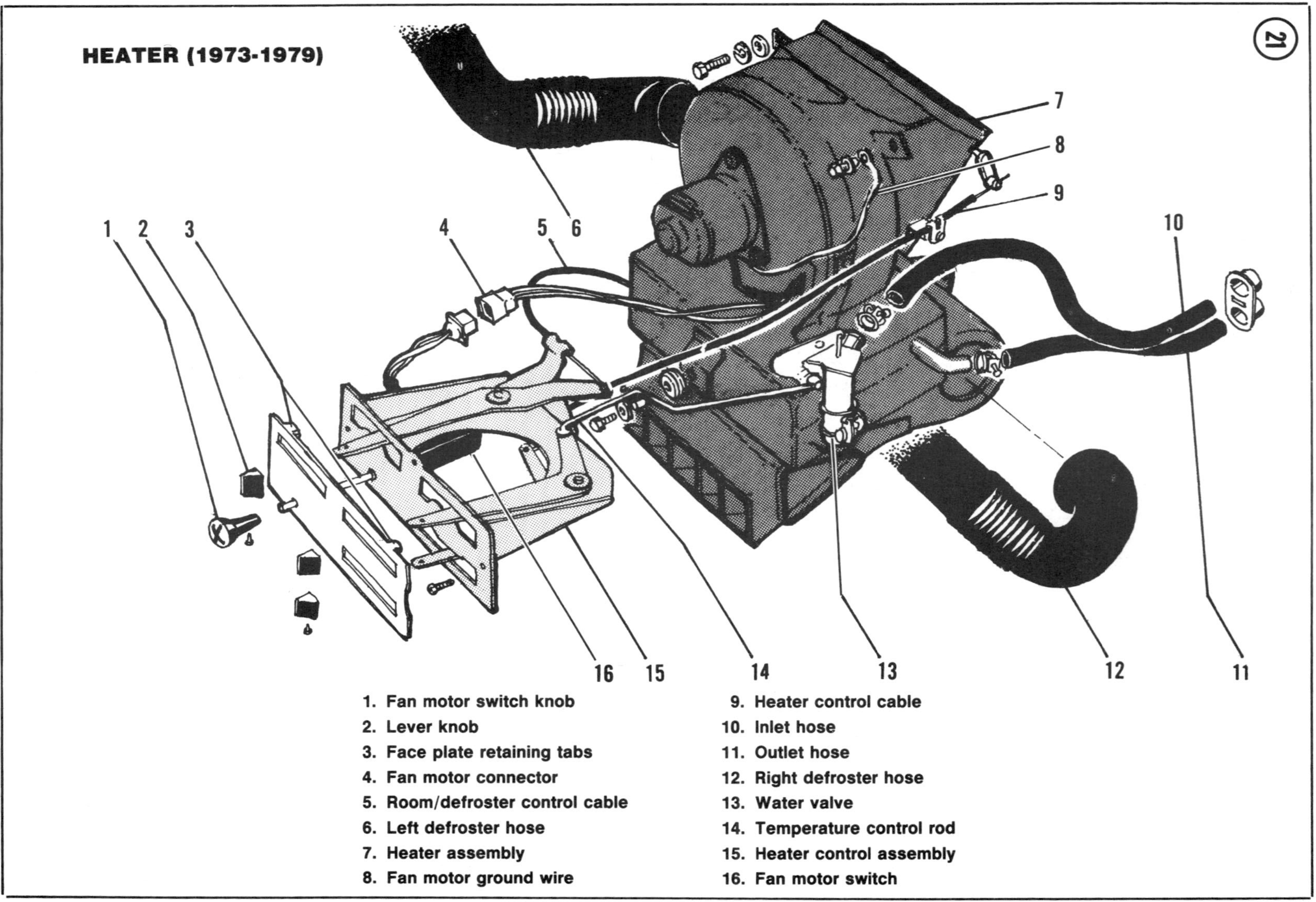
21
HEATER (1973-1979)
1
2
3
4
5
6
7
8
9
10
11
12
13
14
15
16
1. Fan motor switch knob
2. Lever knob
3. Face plate retaining tabs
4. Fan motor connector
5. Room/defroster control cable
6. Left defroster hose
7. Heater assembly
8. Fan motor ground wire
9. Heater control cable
10. Inlet hose
11. Outlet hose
12. Right defroster hose
13. Water valve
14. Temperature control rod
15. Heater control assembly
16. Fan motor switch

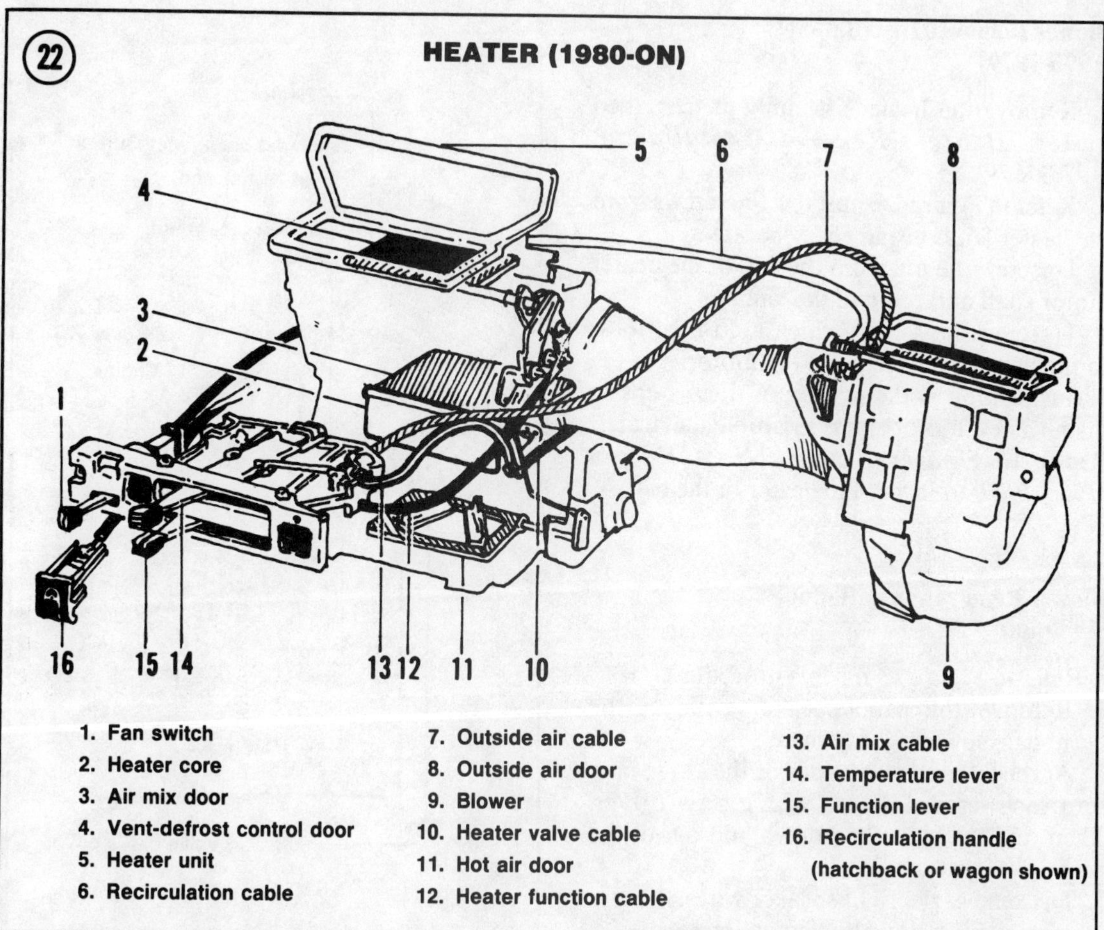

22 **HEATER (1980-ON)**

1. Fan switch
2. Heater core
3. Air mix door
4. Vent-defrost control door
5. Heater unit
6. Recirculation cable
7. Outside air cable
8. Outside air door
9. Blower
10. Heater valve cable
11. Hot air door
12. Heater function cable
13. Air mix cable
14. Temperature lever
15. Function lever
16. Recirculation handle (hatchback or wagon shown)

hose connections are tight. Perform the *Room/Defroster Control Cable Adjustment* and the *Temperature Control Rod Adjustment* procedures in this chapter.

Heater Removal/Installation (1980-on)

Refer to **Figure 22** for this procedure.

1. Drain the cooling system as described in this chapter.
2. Loosen the clamps on the heater hoses inside the engine compartment, disconnect the hoses and allow them to drain. Loosen hose clamps at the heater (**Figure 23**), hold a can beneath one of the hose connections and disconnect the hose and allow the coolant to drain. Do the same with the other hose.
3. Remove the dashboard panel.
4. Remove the lower heater mount nut on the firewall.
5. Remove the 2 heater duct retainer clips and remove the heater duct.
6. Referring to **Figure 22**, disconnect and remove the heater control cables from the heater.
7. Remove the heater valve cable cover from the side of the heater (**Figure 23**). Then remove the heater from inside the car.
8. Installation is the reverse of Steps 1-7, plus the following:
   a. Make sure to install the heater inlet and outlet hoses at their correct position at the heater. The outlet hose is identified with a white stripe painted on the end of the hose. See **Figure 23**.
   b. After connecting all the heater cables, make sure to adjust them as described in this chapter.
   c. Refill the radiator and bleed the cooling system as described in this chapter.

Blower Removal/Installation (1973-1979)

1. Remove the heater assembly as described under *Heater Removal/Installation (1973-1979)*.
2. Refer to **Figure 24**, unscrew the screws from the heater fan housing and separate it.
3. Unscrew the nut from the end of the heater motor shaft and remove the fan.
4. Unscrew the screws which hold the motor to the housing and remove the motor.
5. Installation is the reverse of these steps to install a new motor and reassemble the heater. Refer to *Heater Removal/Installation (1973-1979)* to install the heater in the car.

Blower Removal/Installation (1980-on)

Refer to **Figure 25** for this procedure.

1. Remove the panel/speaker grille at the dashboard lower right corner.
2. At the left and right sides of the glove box, turn each screw 1/4 turn with a screwdriver. Then turn the glove box down and out of the way.
3. Disconnect the right speaker wires.
4. Remove the glove box hinge frame.
5. At both ends of the heater duct, remove the retainer clips, compress the duct and disconnect from the heater and blower housings.
6. Remove the blower mounting bolts and lower the blower to the car floor.
7. Disconnect the control cables and wire harness from the blower. Then remove the blower from the car.
8. Installation is the reverse of Steps 1-7.

Control Assembly Removal/Installation (1973-1979)

1. Carefully pull off the 3 control lever knobs. Remove the setscrew from the bottom of the blower control knob and pull it off.
2. Pry the control panel face off by inserting a screwdriver in the slot each end.
3. Loosen the lock bolts which retain the temperature control rod and the air control

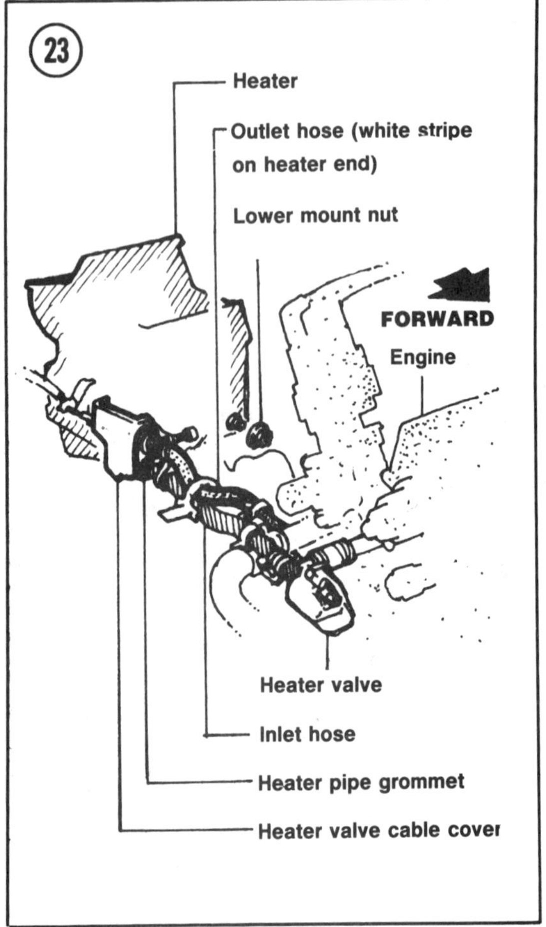

cables. In addition, loosen the screws in the retainer clips for the 2 cables (**Figure 21**).
4. Remove the screws which hold the control panel in place and pull the panel out of the dashboard. Unplug the blower control cable.
5. Installation is the reverse of these steps. When the panel has been reinstalled, adjust the control rod and cables as described in this chapter.

Room/Defroster Control Cable Adjustment (1973-1979)

1. Loosen the heater valve link in the heater cable clamp located on the left side of the heater (**Figure 24**).
2. Move the DEF/ROOM control lever to the REC position.
3. Pull the door control arm back as far as it will go to close the door. Tighten the cable lock bolt.

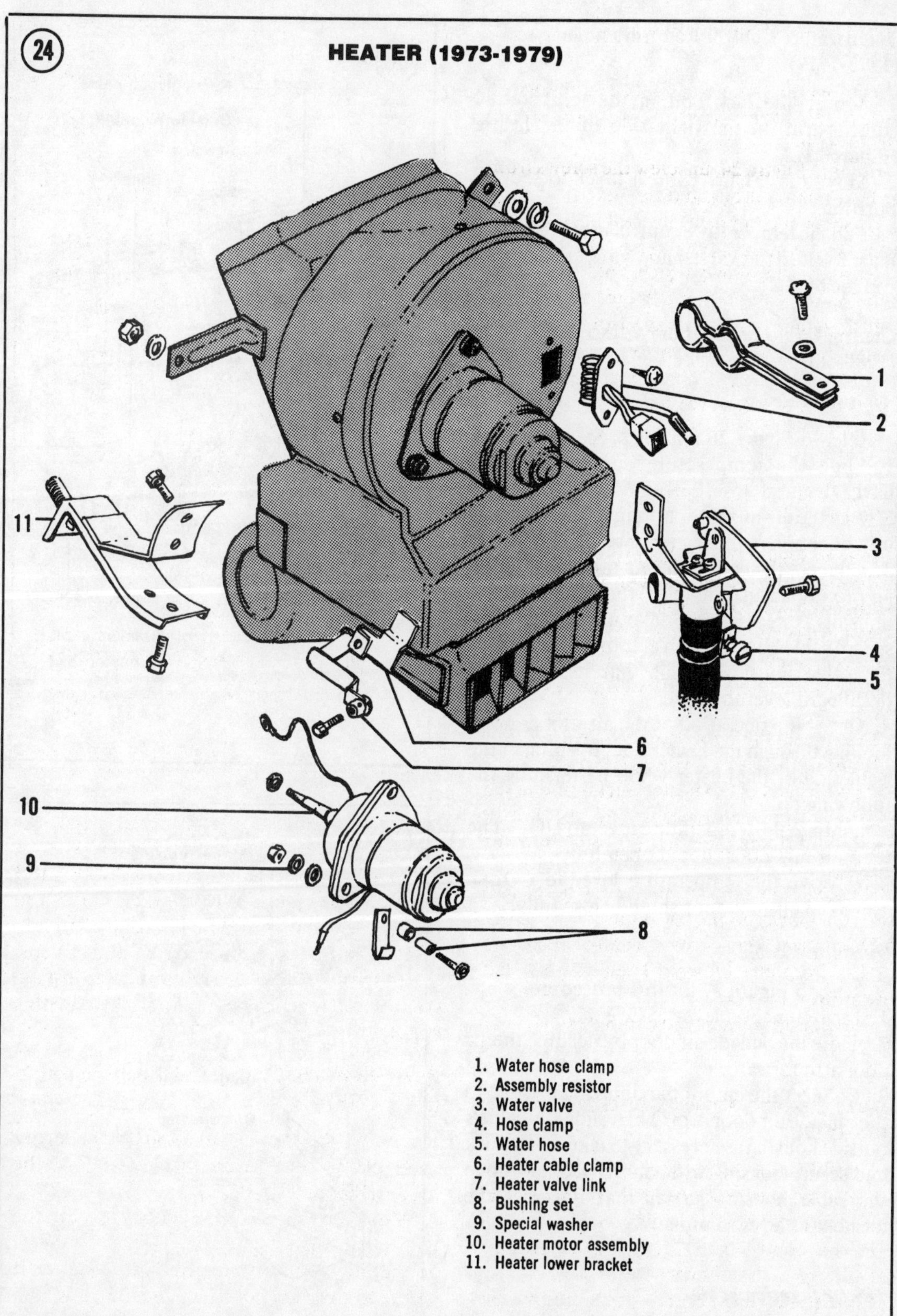
24
HEATER (1973-1979)
1
2
3
4
5
6
7
8
9
10
11
1. Water hose clamp
2. Assembly resistor
3. Water valve
4. Hose clamp
5. Water hose
6. Heater cable clamp
7. Heater valve link
8. Bushing set
9. Special washer
10. Heater motor assembly
11. Heater lower bracket

Temperature Control Rod Adjustment (1973-1979)

1. Loosen the lock bolt in the temperature control arm on the right side of the heater (**Figure 21**).
2. Move the HI/LO control lever to the LO position.
3. Pull the temperature control arm all the way back to close the valve and tighten the control rod lock bolt.

Control Cable Installation/Adjustment (1980-on)

Air mix cable

Refer to **Figure 26** for this procedure.
1. Slide the temperature control lever to COLD.
2. Pull the air mix door arm up to close the air mix door above the heater core.
3. Connect the end of the air mix cable to the air mix door arm. Then slide the cable's outside housing as necessary to take up all slack and secure cable housing with clamp. Do not move the cable housing so far that it forces the dashboard lever to move.
4. Check the operation of the air mix door by looking through the heater duct opening in the right side of the heater while performing the following:
   a. Move the temperature lever to HOT. The air mix door should open fully.
   b. Move the temperature lever to COLD. The air mix door should close fully.

Outside air cable

Refer to **Figure 27** for this procedure.
1. Move function lever to OFF.
2. Close the outside air door by pushing the air door arm forward.
3. Connect the end of the outside air cable to the outside air door arm. Then slide the cable's outside housing as necessary to take up all slack and secure housing with clamp. Do not move the cable housing so far that it forces the dashboard lever to move.

Heater function cable

Refer to **Figure 28** for this procedure.

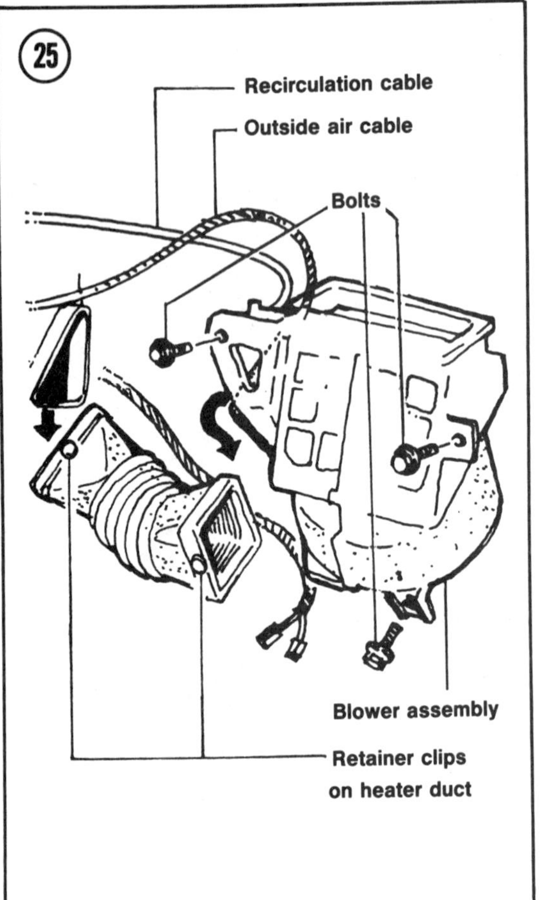

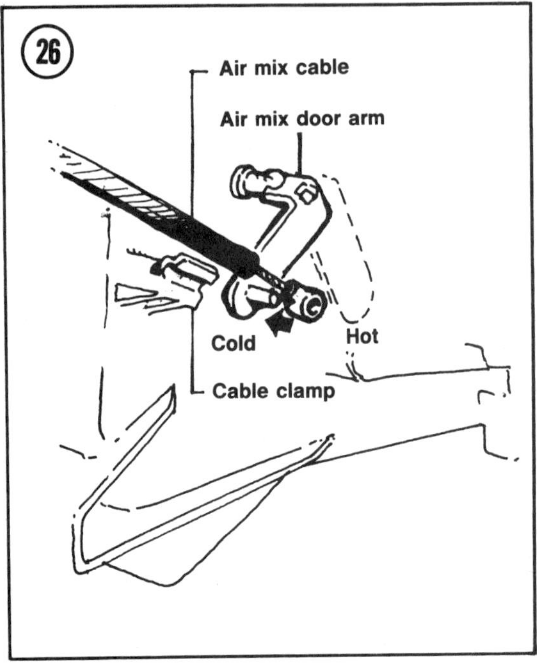

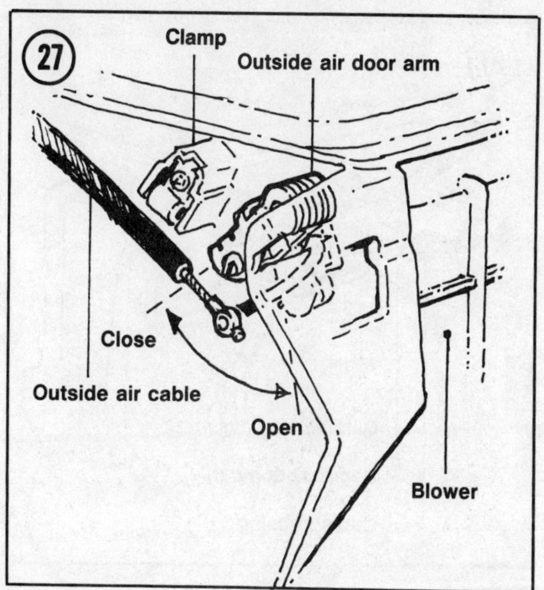

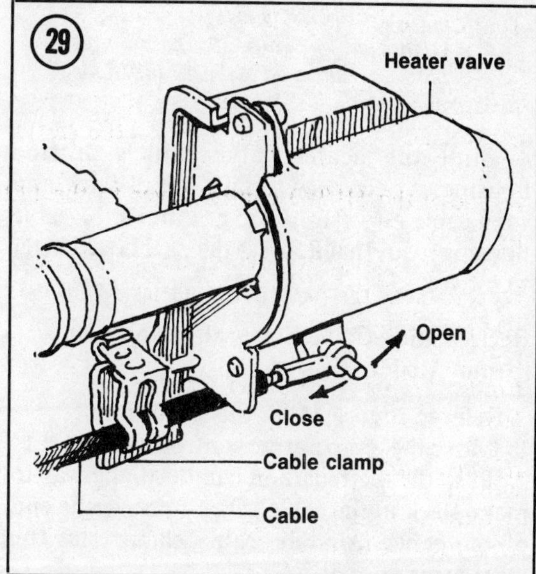

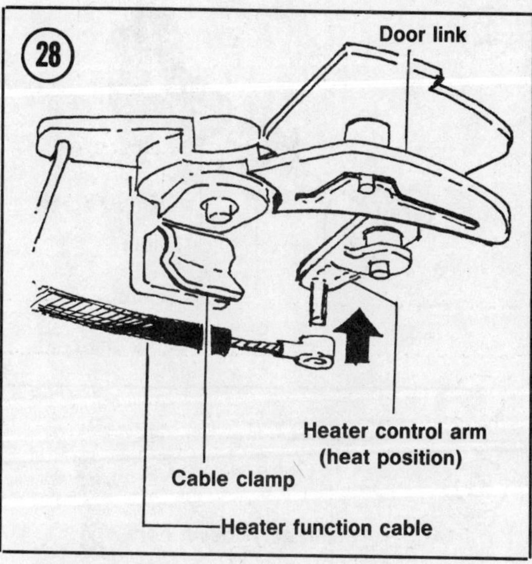

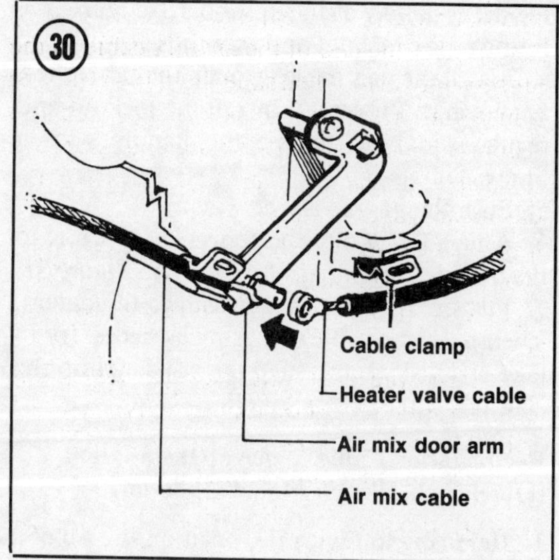

1. Move function lever to HEAT.

2. Move the heater control arm to the HEAT position in the door link slot.

3. Attach the end of the heater function cable to the heater control arm. Then secure the cable housing into the cable clamp.

4. While looking through the heater floor outlet, move the function lever to DEFROST to make sure the hot air door below the heater core is closed. If not, remove and reinstall the heater function cable.

Heater valve cable

Refer to **Figure 29** for this procedure.

1. Grasp the heater valve arm and move the arm towards the cable clamp to close the heater valve.
2. Attach the end of the heater valve cable to the heater valve arm. Then secure the cable to the cable clamp.
3. Move the temperature control lever to COLD. Attach the opposite end of the heater valve cable to the air mix door arm. See **Figure 30**.

NOTE

*As indicated in **Figure 30**, the air mix cable is also attached to the air mix door arm.*

4. Slide the heater valve cable's outside housing as necessary to take up all slack and snap cable into clamp. Do not move the cable housing so far that it forces the dashboard lever to move.

Recirculation Cable Removal/Installation (Sedan Models 1980-on)

Refer to **Figure 31** for this procedure.

1. Move the temperature control lever to OFF.
2. Push the recirculation handle all the way to make slack in the cable. Then remove the end of the cable from the cable clamp and the outside air door arm.
3. Remove the attaching screw from the pull regulator handle at the dashboard (**Figure 32**). Remove the locknut and pull the cable out.
4. Install the new cable through the cable shaft as shown in **Figure 32**. Install the locknut and regulator handle. Secure the handle with a screw.
5. Push the handle all the way in.
6. Attach the end of the recirculation cable to the outside air door arm as shown in **Figure 31**.
7. Pull the regulator handle out to the detent. Then push the cable's housing as necessary to take up all slack and snap the housing into the clamp.

Recirculation Cable Removal/Installation (Hatchback/Wagon Models 1980-on)

1. Referring to **Figure 33**, position the tip of a screwdriver between the dashboard and the recirculation assembly lock tab and push the assembly out from the dashboard.
2. Disconnect the recirculation cable at the guide assembly and at the outside air door arm (**Figure 31**).
3. Attach the end of the new recirculation cable to the outside air door arm as shown in **Figure 31**.
4. Hold the arm in the closed position and snap the cable's housing into the clamp, making sure to maintain a distance from housing to clamp of 10-11 mm (13/32-7/16 in.).

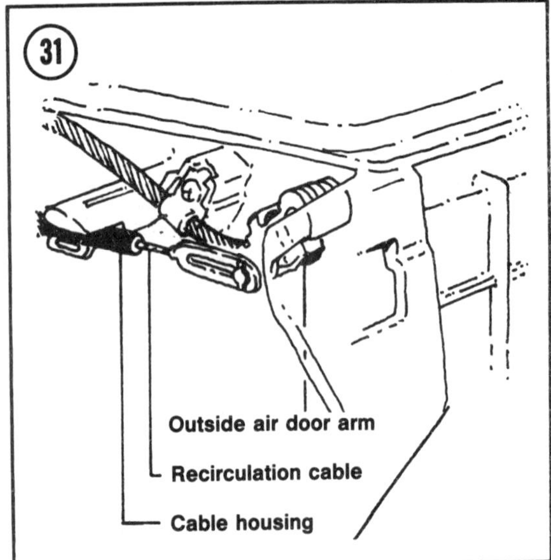

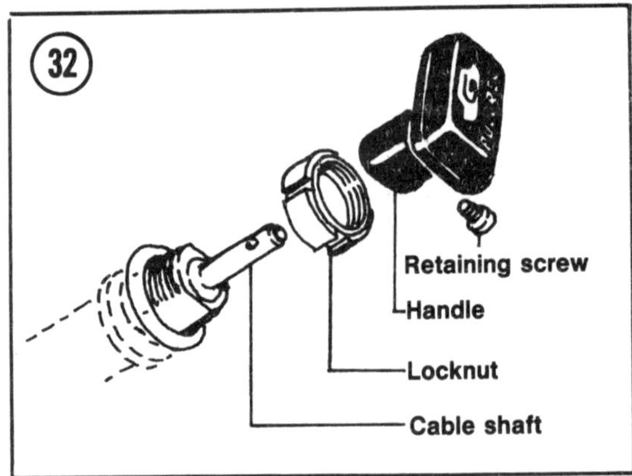

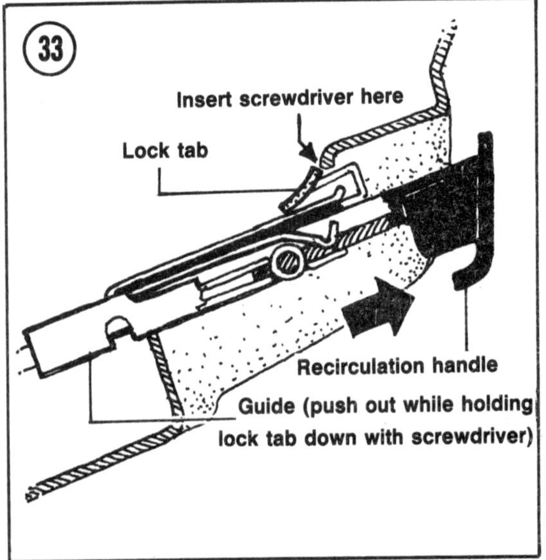

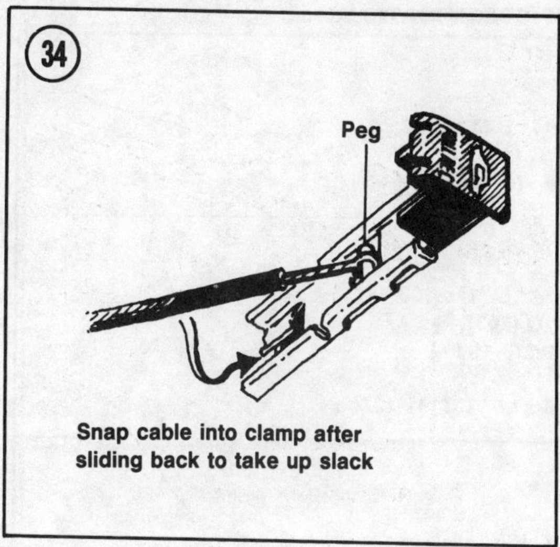

Snap cable into clamp after sliding back to take up slack

5. Move temperature control lever to OFF.
6. Refering to **Figure 34**, pull the recirculation handle out to detent position and connect end of cable to end of handle.
7. With cable at detent position, slide the cable housing as necessary to take up slack and snap housing into clamp.
8. Install the handle and guide assembly into the dashboard, making sure the guide lock tab snaps into place.
9. Look through the access panel hole in the lower right corner of the dashboard and pull the recirculation handle out to detent. The outside air door should close all the way. Push the recirculation handle in and make sure the door opens all the way.

6

Table is on the following page.

Table 1 COOLING SYSTEM SPECIFICATIONS

1973-1979 Non-CVCC	
Thermostat	
Starts to open	80-84° C (176-183° F)
Opens fully	95° C (203° F)
Lift	8 mm (5/16 in.)
1975-1979 CVCC	
Thermostat	
Starts to open	80-84° C (176-183° F)
Opens fully	95° C (203° F)
Lift	8 mm (5/16 in.)
Thermoswitch operating temperature	88.5-91.5° C (191-197° F)
1980-on CVCC	
Thermostat	
Starts to open	
Standard	80-84° C (176-183° F)
Optional	86-90° C (187-194° F)
Opens fully	
Standard	95° C (203° F)
Optional	100° C (212° F)
Lift (all)	8 mm (5/16 in.)
Thermoswitch operating temperature	
Fan runs	88-92° C (191-197° F)
Fan stops	83-87° C (182-188° F)

NOTE: If you own a 1982 or later model, first check the Supplement at the back of the book for any new service information.

CHAPTER SEVEN

ELECTRICAL SYSTEM

The Civic uses a 12-volt, negative-ground electrical system. Included in this chapter are service and repair procedures for the battery, starter, charging system, lighting system, ignition system and windshield wipers. Repairs to electrical components such as the alternator or starter motor are usually beyond the ability of the inexperienced mechanic and his tool box. Such repairs are best left to the professional mechanic who is equipped with specialized tools.

By using the troubleshooting procedures given in Chapter Two it is possible to isolate problems in a specific component, thus saving money in costly troubleshooting bills.

In most cases, it will be faster and more economical to obtain new or rebuilt components instead of making repairs. Make certain, however, that the new or rebuilt part is an exact replacement. Also, make sure that the cause of the failure has been isolated and corrected before installing a replacement. For instance, an uncorrected short in a regulator will in all probability burn out a new alternator as quickly as it damaged the old one. If in doubt, always consult an expert.

Tables 1-4 are at the end of the chapter.

BATTERY

Care and Inspection

1. Loosen the bolts in the terminal clamps far enough so the clamps can be spread slightly (**Figure 1**). Lift straight up on the clamps (negative first) to remove them from the posts.

Twisting and prying on the clamps or the posts can result in serious damage to a battery that may otherwise be in good condition.

2. Loosen the nuts on the battery hold-down bolts (**Figure 2**) and disconnect the lower ends of the bolts from the battery mount. Remove the hold-down bar and bolts and lift the battery out of the engine compartment.
3. Clean the top of the battery with a solution of baking soda and water, using a stiff bristle brush. Wipe clean with a cloth moistened in the solution.

CAUTION
Take care not to allow the soda solution to enter any of the battery cells as this could seriously weaken the electrolyte. A small piece of tape can be placed over the ventilating hole in each cell cap to help keep out the solution.

4. Clean both battery terminals and the battery cable terminals with a stiff brush or with one of the many tools made for this purpose. See **Figure 3** and **Figure 4**.

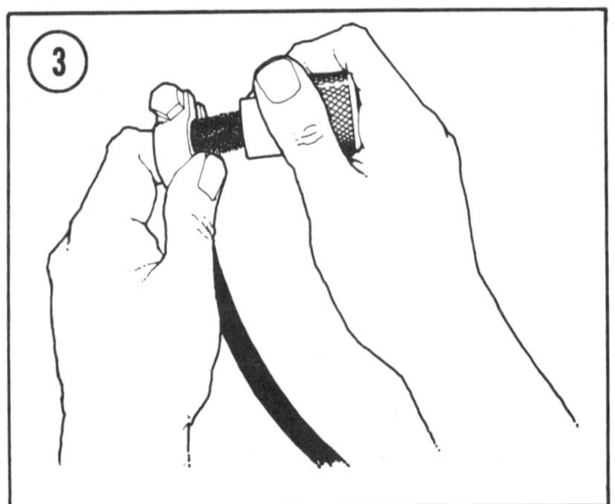

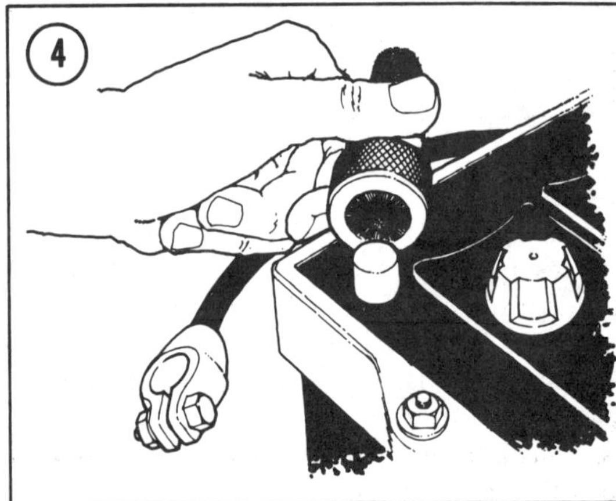

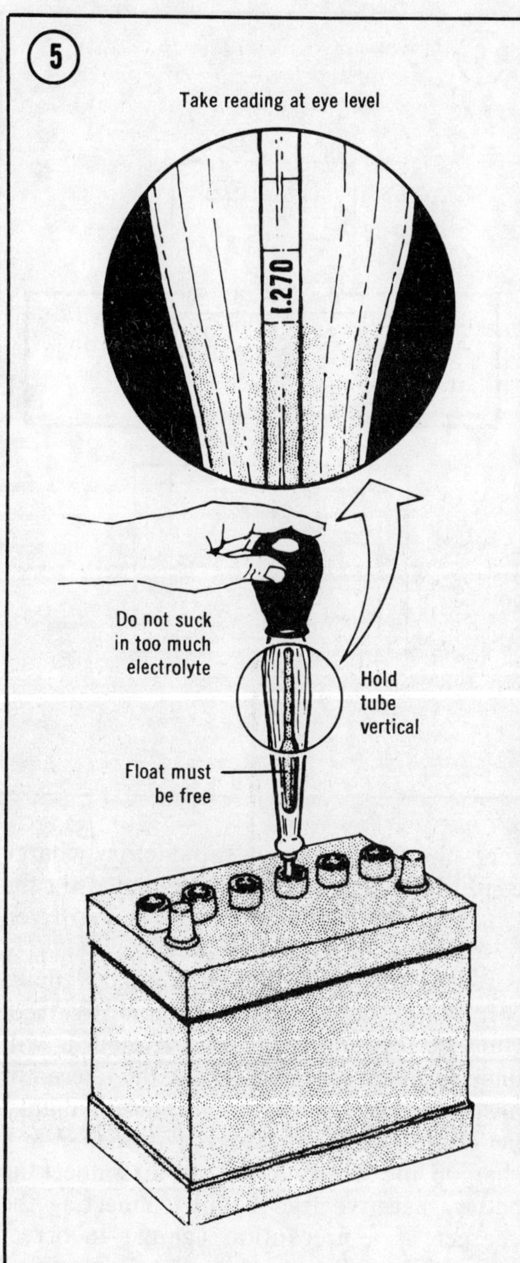

5. Examine the entire battery case for cracks.
6. Install battery in vehicle and connect the cables (positive first). Securely tighten the attaching bolts. Tighten the battery clamp bolts securely (**Figure 2**).
7. Coat the battery terminals with a light grease or with Vaseline.
8. Check the electrolyte level and top up with distilled water if necessary.

Common Causes of Battery Failure

All batteries eventually fail. Their life can be prolonged, however, with a good maintenance program. Some of the reasons for premature failure are listed below.

1. Vehicle accessories left on overnight or longer, causing a discharged condition.
2. Slow driving speeds on short trips, causing an undercharged condition.
3. Vehicle electrical load exceeding the alternator capacity due particularly to aftermarket accessory equipment.
4. Charging system defects, such as high-resistance connections, slipping alternator belt or faulty alternator.
5. Abuse of the battery, including failure to keep the battery terminals clean and allowing battery to become too loose in the battery hold-down box.

Testing

Hydrometer testing is a good way to check battery condition. Use a hydrometer with numbered graduations from 1.200 to 1.300 rather than one with just color-coded bands. To use the hydrometer, squeeze the rubber bulb, insert the tip in the cell and release the bulb. See **Figure 5**. Draw enough electrolyte to float the weighted float inside the hydrometer. Note the number in line with the surface of the electrolyte. This is the specific gravity of the cell. Return the electrolyte to the cell from which it came.

The specific gravity of electrolyte in each battery cell is an excellent indicator of that cell's condition. A fully charged cell will read from 1.240-1.260 at 60° F (20° C). If the cells test below 1.200, the battery must be recharged. Charging is also necessary if specific gravity varies more than 0.025 from cell to cell. **Table 1** converts specific gravity readings into battery charge percentages.

NOTE

For every 10° above 80° F electrolyte temperature, add 0.004 to specific gravity reading. For every 10° below 80° F, subtract 0.004.

Charging

CAUTION
Battery electrolyte must be fully topped up and the negative cable disconnected before charging battery.

There is no need to remove the battery from the car to charge it. Make certain the area is well-ventilated and that there is no chance of sparks or flame being in the vicinity of the battery; during charging, highly explosive hydrogen gas is produced by the battery.

Disconnect the ground lead at the battery (**Figure 1**). Remove the caps from the cells and top up each cell with distilled water. Never add electrolyte to a battery that has been in service.

Connect the charger to the battery—negative to negative, positive to positive (**Figure 6**). If the charger output is variable, select a low setting (1.5-2 amps), set the voltage selector to 12 and plug the charger in. If the battery is severely discharged (1.200 or less specific gravity) allow it to charge for at least 8 hours. Less charge deterioration requires less charging time.

After the battery has been charged for a suitable period of time, unplug the charger and disconnect it from the battery. Be extremely careful about sparks. Test the condition of each cell with a hydrometer. Compare the results to **Table 1**.

If the specific gravity indicates that the battery is fully charged and if the reading remains the same after one hour, the battery can be considered to be in good condition and fully charged. Check the electrolyte level and add water if necessary, install the caps and reconnect the ground lead.

ALTERNATOR

The alternator is a 3-phase current generator consisting of a stationary armature (stator), a rotating field (rotor) and a rectifying bridge of silicon diodes. The alternator generates alternating current; the silicon diodes convert the alternating current to direct current for use in the car's electrical circuits. The output of the alternator is regulated by a voltage regulator to keep the battery in a satisfactory charge condition. The alternator is mounted on the left end of the engine, at the rear, and is driven by a belt off the crankshaft pulley.

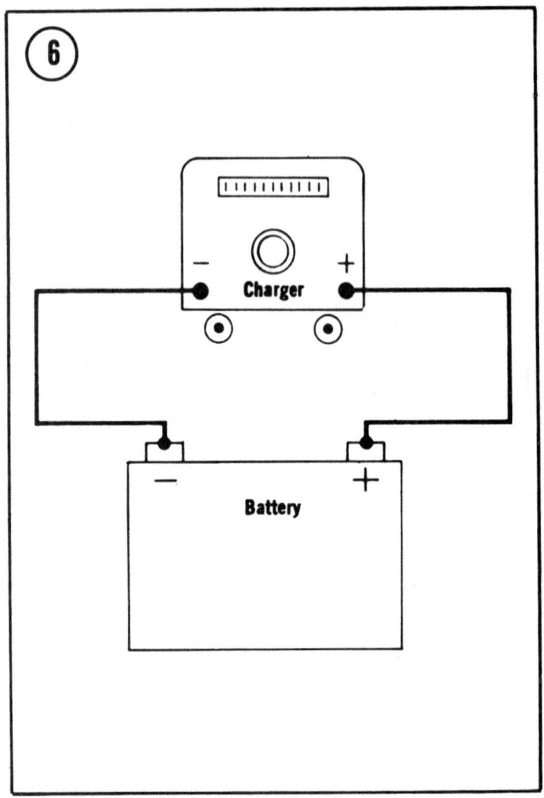

When working with the alternator, make certain the connections are not reversed. Current flow in the wrong direction will damage the diodes and render the alternator unserviceable. The alternator B terminal must be connected to battery voltage. When charging the battery in the car, disconnect the battery negative lead before connecting the charger as a precaution against incorrect current bias or heat reaching the alternator.

Alternator repairs require specialized equipment and skills. While repairs are possible, it is generally more practical for the home mechanic to have the alternator serviced by a Honda dealer or a competent repair shop.

Testing (Non-CVCC)

To test the alternator output you will need an ammeter that reads 50 amps or higher, 3

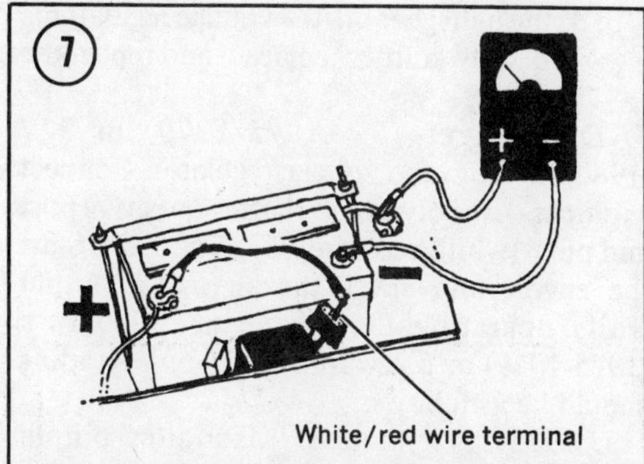

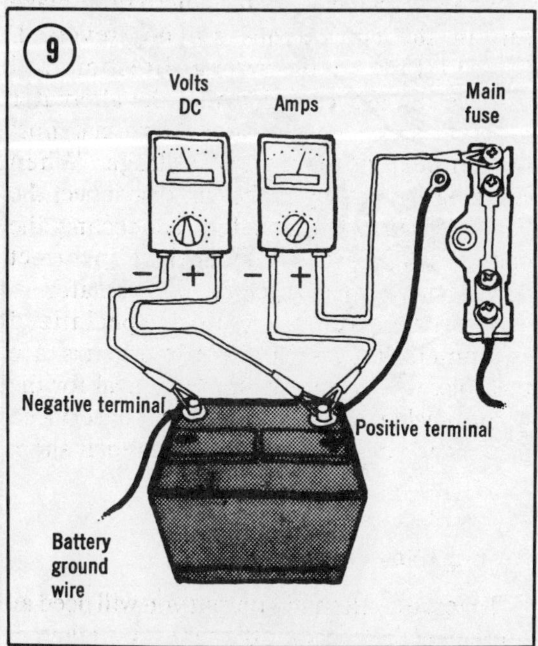

jumper wires with alligator clips and a tachometer.

1. Connect the tachometer according to the manufacturer's instructions.

2. Remove the coolant reserve tank from its bracket and suspend it in front of the grille with a piece of cord. This is required to gain access to the regulator terminals.

3. Start the engine and allow it to idle. Disconnect the negative cable from the battery.

4. Refer to **Figure** 7 and connect one of the jumpers between the negative battery cable and the positive side of the ammeter. Connect a second jumper wire between the negative side of the ammeter and the negative battery post. Connect one end of the third jumper wire to the positive battery post.

5. Unplug the voltage regulator plug that is located beneath the regulator. Touch the free end of the third jumper wire to the red/white terminal on the male end of the regulator plug and slowly increase the engine speed until the ammeter indicates maximum output with the engine running at approximately 2,000 rpm. The alternator output should be 40 amps.

CAUTION

Do not leave the third jumper wire connected to the regulator plug for more than 15 seconds at a time.

6. If the alternator maximum output is less than 35 amps, the alternator must be removed, disassembled and repaired. Shut off the engine and disconnect jumper wires and ammeter. Disconnect and remove the tachometer.

Testing (CVCC)

To test the alternator output, an ammeter that reads 60 amps or higher, voltmeter and tachometer are required. Disconnect the cable leading from the battery positive terminal to the main fuse (right side of engine compartment). See **Figure 8**. Connnect the ammeter between the battery positive cable and the main fuse. Connect the voltmeter positive lead to the positive battery terminal and the voltmeter negative lead to the negative battery terminal. See **Figure 9**. Battery must be fully charged and the drive belt properly tensioned. Wire terminal connector locations (used in following procedure) are found in **Table 2**.

1. On 1980 and later models, disconnect the choke heater wire (white/blue) at the firewall.
2. Turn the ignition switch on and verify that the discharge warning light comes ON.
   a. If the warning light does not come on, disconnect connector J55 (1975-1979) or J27 (1980-on) at the voltage regulator connector and short pin 3 (white/blue wire) of connector J55 or J27 to ground. If the warning light still does not come on, check fuse F3 and 10 (1975-1979) or fuse 12 (1980-on). If the fuse is okay, check connectors J55, J1, P1, J5, P5, J18 and P18 (1975-1979) or connectors J27, J69, J11 and P11 (1980-on), plus all related and connecting wires, for open circuits. If these circuits are okay, check for a burned out warning light bulb.
   b. If the light goes on, the voltage regulator is probably faulty. Replace it and repeat the test.
3. Disconnect J55 (1975-1979) or J27 (1980-on) from the voltage regulator. Connect a jumper wire between the battery positive post and pin 6 (white/red wire) of J55 and J27. Start the engine and check the alternator output while operating the engine at 2,000 rpm (1975-1979) or 2,220 rpm (1980-on). Reading should be as follows:
   a. 1975-1979 models: Maximum output should be 35 amps (without air conditioning) or 45 amps (with air conditioning). If output is correct, proceed to Step 5. If not, go to Step 4.
   b. 1980-on: Output should be 42-43 amps for hatchback/wagon models or 50 amps for sedan models. If output is correct, proceed to Step 5. If not, go to Step 4.

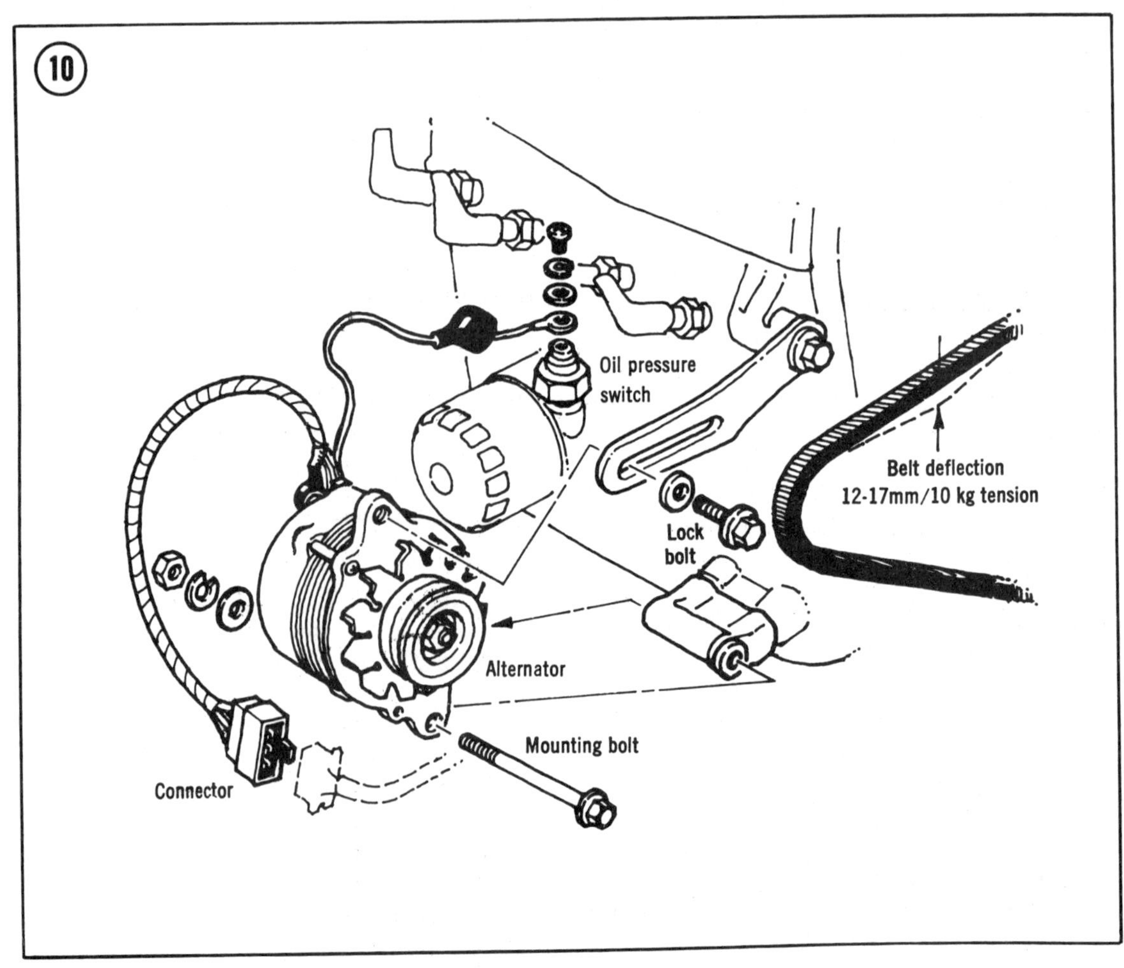

4. If there is no output, or less output than specified is recorded in Step 3, reconnect J55 (1975-1979) or J27 (1980-on); disconnect J82 (1975-1979) or J44 (1980-on) from rear of alternator. Connect a jumper from the pin at rear of alternator to the positive battery terminal and repeat the output test. If output is okay, check for an open circuit between the white/red wire connecting the regulator and alternator. If there is no output, check the white wire between the alternator and the main fuse for continuity. If there is continuity, have a Honda dealership disassemble the alternator and check further.
5. Start the engine and observe the discharge warning light. The light should go out. If the alternator output is within specification (Step 3) and warning light stays on at idle speed but goes out as engine speed is increased or stays on all the time, check the alternator neutral wire circuit. This can be done by leaving J55 (1975-1979) or J27 (1980-on) connected and inserting voltmeter probes into the backs of pins 1 (black wire) and 2 (white and black wire) and checking the voltage while the engine is idling. Voltage should be half of the specified alternator output voltage or approximately 7 volts.
   a. If the voltage is approximately half, the alternator is operating properly. Replace the regulator.
   b. If the voltage is less than 6.5 volts or more than 8.5 volts, have a Honda dealer check the alternator diodes.
   c. If no voltage is observed, check for voltage across pins 3 (white/black wire) and 2 (black) from wire harness leading to back of alternator. If no voltage is present, remove the alternator and refer further troubleshooting to a Honda dealer. If half the output voltage is present, check for an open circuit in the white and black wire circuit between the alternator and the regulator.

Removal/Installation

1. Disconnect the negative cable at the battery (**Figure 1**).
2. Unplug the connector at the rear of the alternator and the oil pressure switch lead at the engine.
3. Unscrew the alternator lock bolts and the mounting bolt. See **Figure 10** (CVCC) or **Figure 11** (non-CVCC). Remove the drive belt from the pulley and remove the alternator from the engine.
4. Install the alternator by reversing these steps. Make certain the alternator connector has been connected before connecting the negative battery cable. Refer to Chapter Six and adjust the drive belt tension.

VOLTAGE REGULATOR

A functional test of the voltage regulator can be conducted very simply. However, if the regulator does not perform correctly, adjustment should be entrusted to a Honda dealer or an automotive electrical specialist. Before testing the regulator, refer to the performance test for the alternator to ensure that it is operating correctly. The voltage regulator is located underneath the main fuse on 1973-1979 models (**Figure 8**) and above the main fuse on 1980-on models.

Testing

A voltmeter will be required to perform this test.

1. Start the engine and allow it to idle. Disconnect the negative cable at the battery (**Figure 1**).

CAUTION
If the engine stops when the negative battery cable is removed, turn the ignition key to OFF, reinstall the negative battery cable and repeat Step 1.

Do not attempt to start engine with negative battery cable disconnected.

2. Connect the positive lead of a voltmeter to the positive battery terminal. Connect the voltmeter negative lead to the disconnected battery negative cable.
3. Increase the engine speed to 2,000-4,000 rpm and read the voltage on the meter. It should be 13.5-14.5 volts. If not, the regulator must be adjusted by a Honda dealer or replaced.

Replacement

1. Disconnect the negative battery cable.
2. Disconnect the wiring harness connector at the voltage regulator.
3. Remove all attaching screws and remove the voltage regulator.
4. Installation is the reverse of these steps.

CHARGE INDICATOR RELAY

If the alternator and voltage regulator are operating satisfactorily and the charge indicator warning light remains on, the charge indicator relay, located in the voltage regulator, must be tested. This is a job for a Honda dealer or an automotive electrical specialist.

STARTER

Testing

1. Remove the battery negative cable (**Figure 1**) and connect one lead of a voltmeter to the battery positive terminal. Connect one lead of an ammeter to the battery negative terminal. Connect the other leads of the voltmeter and ammeter to the battery ground cable terminal. See **Figure 12**.
2. Remove the secondary coil wire from the center terminal of the distributor cap and use a jump wire to ground the wire to a good connection point on the engine (**Figure 13**).
3. Use the ignition key to energize the starter. If the starter does not crank the engine, unplug the black/white wire connector J65 (1975-1979) or J74 (1980-on) from the starter. Connect a jumper wire from the battery positive terminal to pin J65 or J74 on the starter. If the starter now cranks the engine, check the wiring between J65 or J74 and the ignition switch (black/white wire) for an open circuit. The problem can be in the ignition switch or in the Hondamatic neutral/backup switch, if so equipped.
4. If the starter cranks the engine erratically after the jumper wire is installed as described in Step 3 or if the engine does not crank at all, remove the starter for bench testing.
5. If the starter cranks the engine very slowly (significantly below 400 rpm), check the

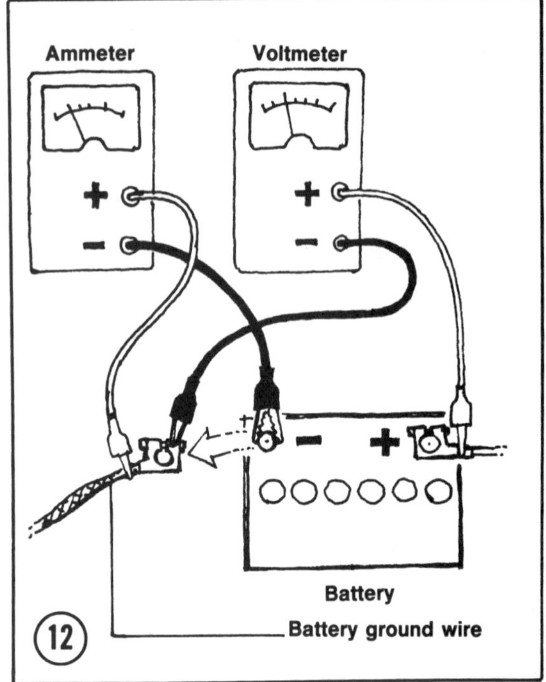

12

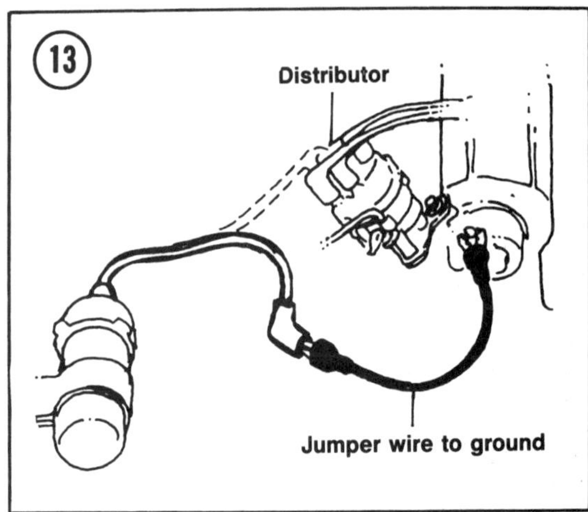

13

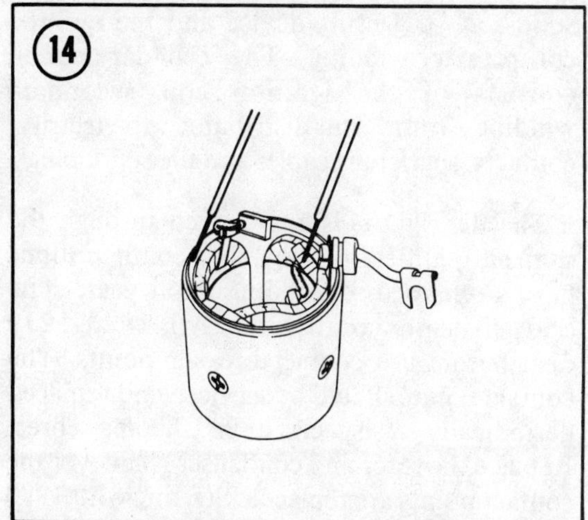

battery for undercharged or defective cells as described under *Battery* in this chapter. Also make sure the battery cable terminal connections are clean and tight. If the battery and wiring connections are good, remove the starter for bench testing.

6. If the starter fails to disengage when the ignition switch is released, remove it for bench testing.

Removal/Installation

1. Disconnect the negative battery cable at the battery (**Figure 1**).
2. Disconnect the positive battery cable and the starter control cable at the starter.
3. Unscrew the starter motor mounting bolts and pull the starter out of the engine.
4. Install the starter by reversing these steps. Make sure the connections are tight to ensure good electrical contact. Tighten the mounting bolts to 44 N•m (32 ft.-lb.).

Bench Testing

Different starter configurations have been used, depending upon year and state. Testing procedures are the same for all models. An ohmmeter is required to perform the following test procedures. Follow manufacturer's instructions when using their equipment.

1. Remove the starter as described in this chapter.
2. Disassemble the starter motor by removing the through bolts and removing the armature from the field frame assembly.
3. Set the ohmmeter to 1X and zero the meter. Place a probe on each brush. If a reading of infinity (no needle movement) is obtained, continuity does not exist in the field coil and the field frame assembly must be replaced. If the meter needle moves, continuity exists in the field coil.
4. Place one ohmmeter probe on either brush and the other probe on the body of the field frame assembly. See **Figure 14**. The meter should read infinity (no needle movement). If the needle moves, there is a short circuit in the field coil and the field frame assembly must be replaced.
5. Measure the length of both brushes. If either brush length is less than specified in **Table 3**, replace the field frame and brush holder assembly.
6. Place one ohmmeter probe on the positive brush holder and the other on the negative brush holder. The meter should read infinity (no needle movement). If the needle moves, a short circuit exists and the brush holder must be replaced.
7. If the commutator on the armature appears to be dirty or burned, try resurfacing it with emery cloth or have the commutator turned on a lathe. After resurfacing, check the commutator for diameter and out-of-round with a vernier caliper. Minimum allowable diameter is indicated in **Table 3**. Replace the commutator if out of tolerance.
8. Check the depth of the mica between commutator segments. See **Table 3** for specifications. If out of tolerance, undercut the mica with a piece of hacksaw blade. **Figure 15** shows the right and wrong ways to undercut the mica.
9. Using an ohmmeter, place the tester leads on successive pairs of armature segments (**Figure 16**). If the ohmmeter shows no continuity (no needle movement), an open circuit exists and the armature must be replaced.
10. Hold one ohmmeter probe firmly against the armature coil core (**Figure 17**) and touch the other probe against each commutator

segment in sequence. No continuity (no needle movement) should be observed in any of the checks. If continuity is present, a short circuit exists in the armature coil windings and the armature must be replaced.

11. Have the armature checked on an armature tester, as shown in **Figure 18**. Replace the armature if test results indicate a short.

12. Reverse Step 1 and 2 to assemble and install the starter.

IGNITION SYSTEM

The ignition system consists of the distributor, coil and primary and secondary circuit parts. The primary circuit parts are the battery, the distributor breaker points or solid-state triggering device and the ignition coil primary windings. The secondary circuit consists of the ignition coil secondary windings, rotor arm, distributor cap electrical contacts, spark plug cables and the spark plugs.

The distributor is gear-driven through the camshaft. Different distributor configurations have been used, depending upon year, state and altitude conditions. All 1973-1979 distributors use contact breaker points. The contact points should be serviced and replaced periodically, as specified in Chapter Three. Replace the rotor and condenser whenever the contact points are replaced. Starting with 1980 models, a transistorized ignition system is used in which the breaker points and condenser are

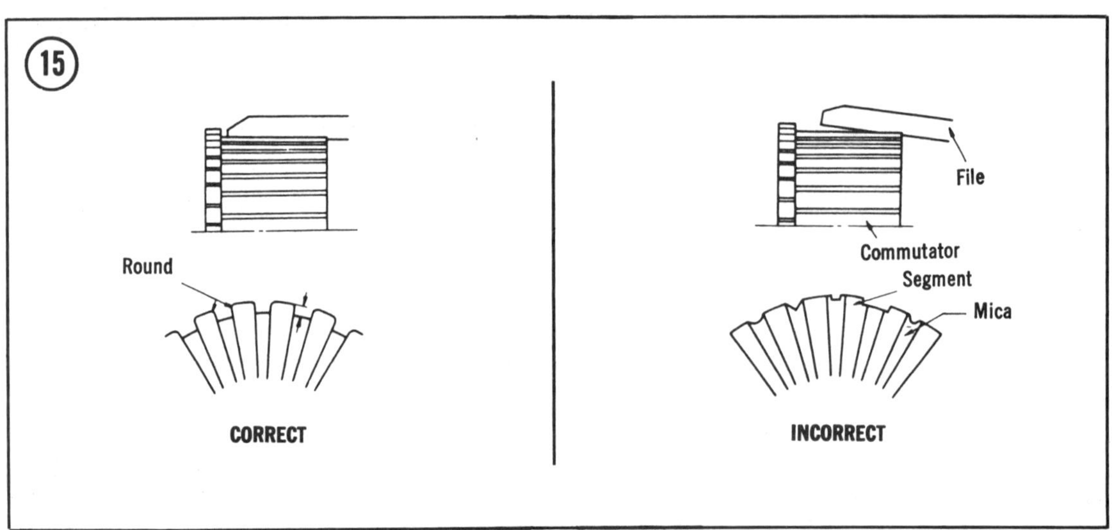

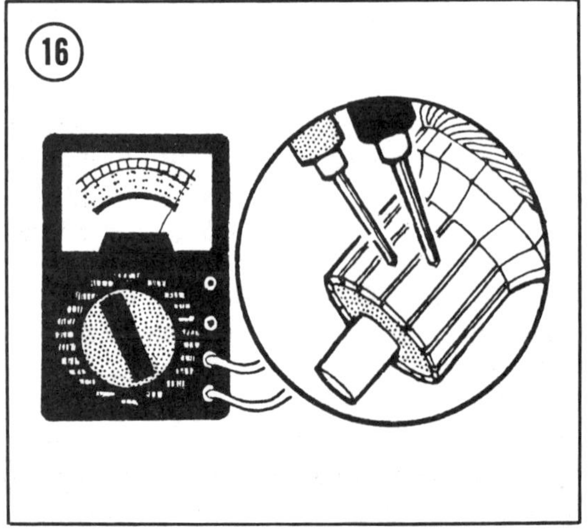

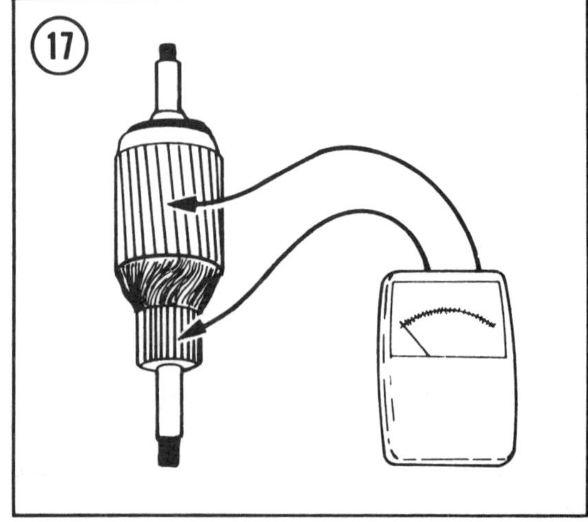

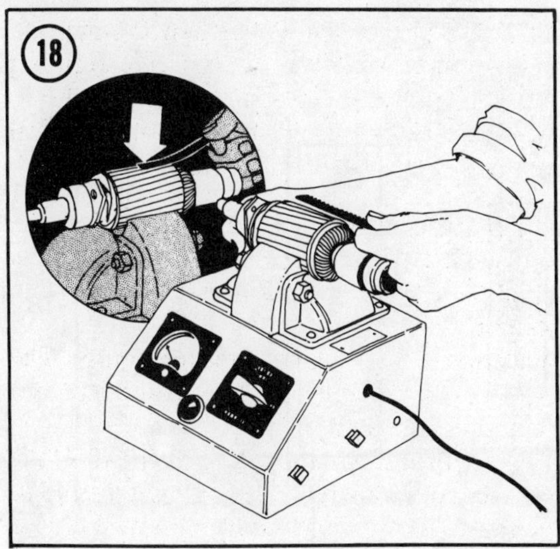

replaced by a pulse generator and reluctor. The transistorized distributor requires no periodic maintenance, other than checking and adjusting the ignition timing as specified in Chapter Three.

IGNITION SYSTEM TROUBLESHOOTING

Basic ignition system and spark plug troubleshooting information can be found in Chapter Two. These procedures, together with other troubleshooting procedures included in Chapter Two, can help you to determine the system or component which is operating incorrectly. If the ignition system is operating incorrectly, test procedures unique to the Honda ignition systems are found in this section and can be used to troubleshoot and locate the problem source. The test procedures for troubleshooting the Honda ignition system are found in the diagnostic charts in **Figure 19** (breaker point ignition system) or **Figure 20** (electronic ignition system). An ohmmeter and voltmeter as described in Chapter One (or a test light as shown in **Figure 21**) and jumper cables (**Figure 22**) are required to perform the test procedures.

Before starting actual troubleshooting, read the entire test procedure (**Figure 19** or **Figure 20**). When required, the diagnostic charts will refer you back to a certain chapter and procedures covered in this book for service and test information.

BREAKER POINT IGNITION SYSTEM TESTING

Primary Distributor Circuit

Excessive resistance in the distributor primary circuit will reduce available voltage to the ignition coil (which reduces coil output).

NOTE

This procedure requires that the battery be fully charged. Test the battery as described in this chapter and charge or replace as required.

1. Remove the distributor cap (**Figure 23**). Contact points should be closed (**Figure 24**).
2. Set the voltmeter to the lowest voltage scale.
3. Referring to **Figure 25**, attach voltmeter positive lead to the distributor primary teminal. Then attach the voltmeter negative lead to any good ground.
4. Have assistant turn ignition switch to ON and note reading on voltmeter. Normal resistance reading is 0-0.2 volts. If reading exceeds 0.2 volts, refer distributor to Honda dealer for further testing.

Ignition Wire Circuit Resistance

1. Locate the distributor terminal blue wire (ignition primary coil negative terminal) and ground it using one jumper cable (**Figure 26**).
2. Attach voltmeter negative lead to the black/yellow wire coming from the emission control box (**Figure 26**).
3. Attach voltmeter positive lead to the positive battery terminal.
4. Set the voltmeter to the lowest scale and turn the ignition switch to ON. The voltmeter reading should not exceed 0.4 volts. If it does, check the ignition switch as described in this chapter under *Switches* and check all wires from the ballast resistor to the battery.

Starter By-pass Circuit Resistance

1. Locate the distributor terminal blue wire (ignition primary coil negative terminal) and ground it using one jumper cable (**Figure 26**).

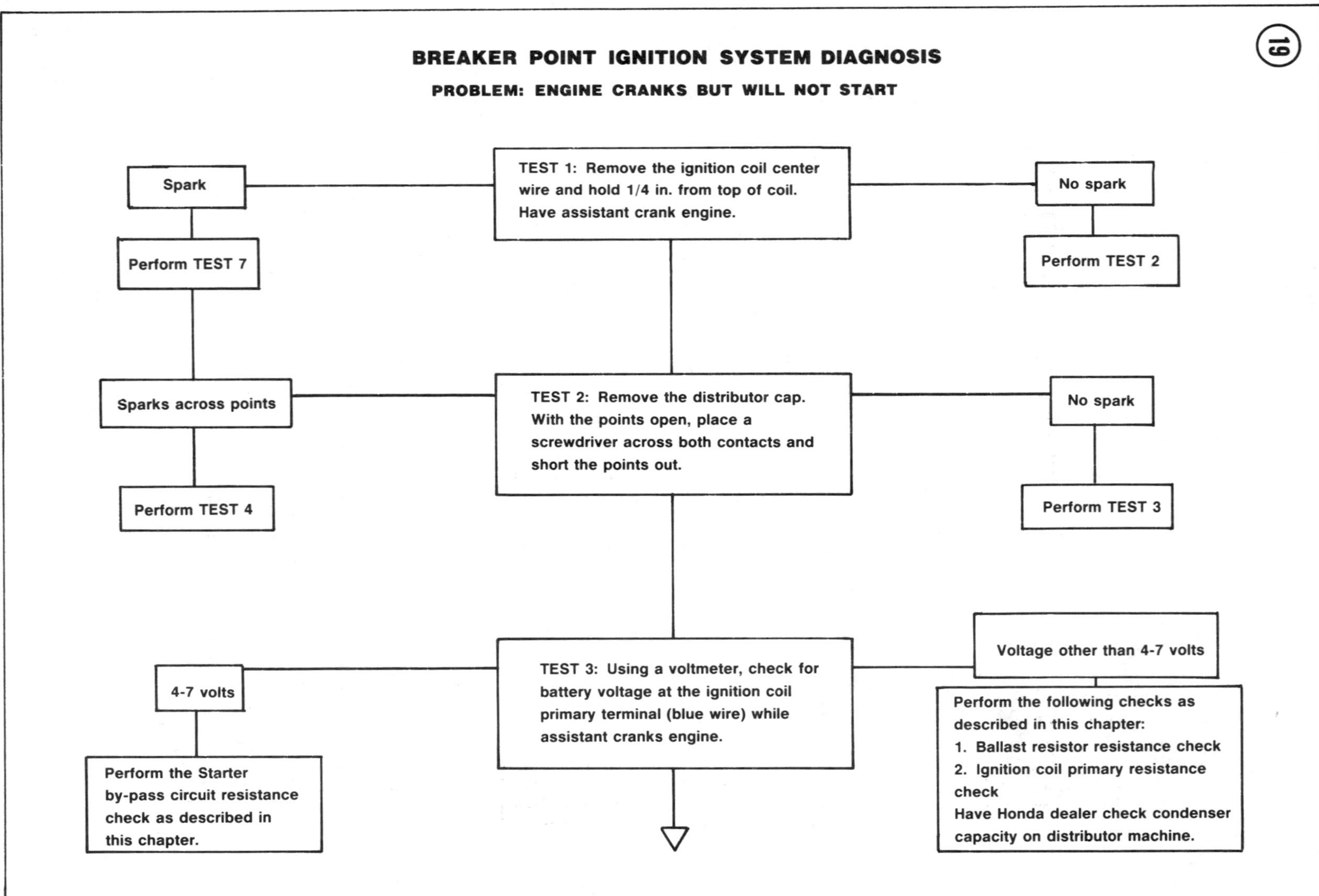
19
BREAKER POINT IGNITION SYSTEM DIAGNOSIS
PROBLEM: ENGINE CRANKS BUT WILL NOT START
TEST 1: Remove the ignition coil center wire and hold 1/4 in. from top of coil. Have assistant crank engine.
Spark
Perform TEST 7
No spark
Perform TEST 2
TEST 2: Remove the distributor cap. With the points open, place a screwdriver across both contacts and short the points out.
Sparks across points
Perform TEST 4
No spark
Perform TEST 3
TEST 3: Using a voltmeter, check for battery voltage at the ignition coil primary terminal (blue wire) while assistant cranks engine.
4-7 volts
Perform the Starter by-pass circuit resistance check as described in this chapter.
Voltage other than 4-7 volts
Perform the following checks as described in this chapter:
1. Ballast resistor resistance check
2. Ignition coil primary resistance check
Have Honda dealer check condenser capacity on distributor machine.

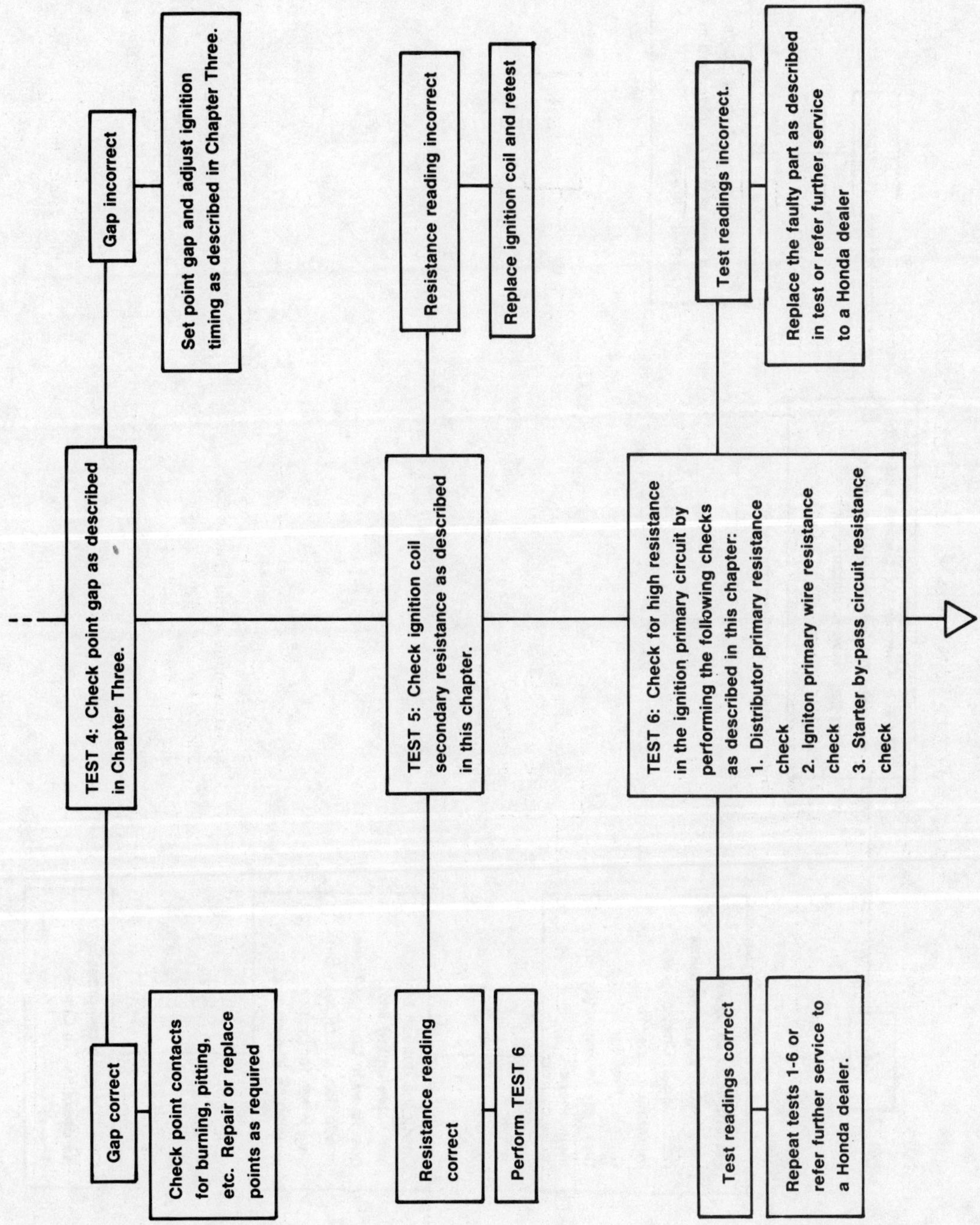

TEST 4: Check point gap as described in Chapter Three.

- Gap correct → Check point contacts for burning, pitting, etc. Repair or replace points as required
- Gap incorrect → Set point gap and adjust ignition timing as described in Chapter Three.

TEST 5: Check ignition coil secondary resistance as described in this chapter.

- Resistance reading correct → Perform TEST 6
- Resistance reading incorrect → Replace ignition coil and retest

TEST 6: Check for high resistance in the ignition primary circuit by performing the following checks as described in this chapter:

1. Distributor primary resistance check
2. Igniton primary wire resistance check
3. Starter by-pass circuit resistance check

- Test readings correct → Repeat tests 1-6 or refer further service to a Honda dealer.
- Test readings incorrect. → Replace the faulty part as described in test or refer further service to a Honda dealer

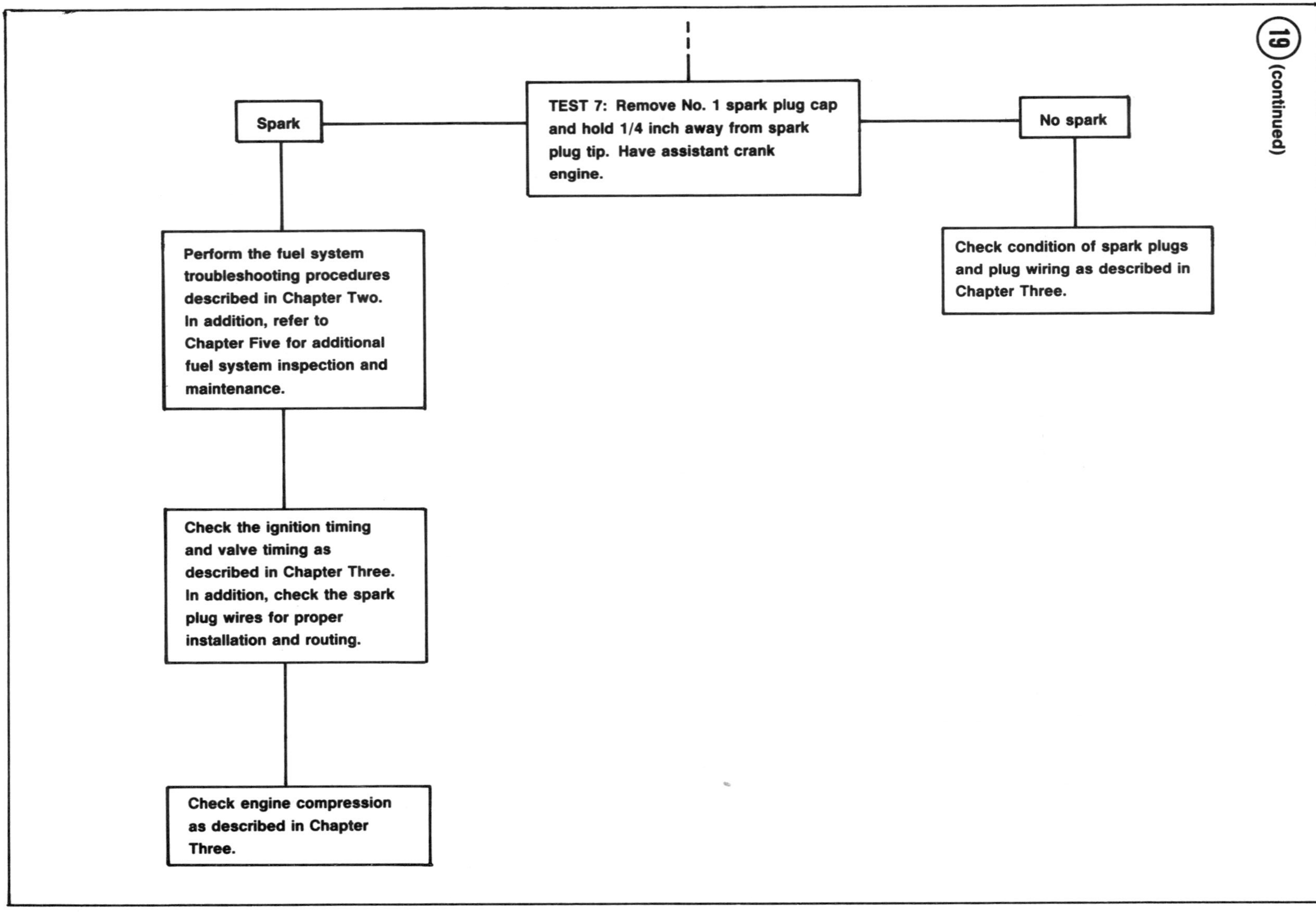
19 (continued)
TEST 7: Remove No. 1 spark plug cap and hold 1/4 inch away from spark plug tip. Have assistant crank engine.
Spark
No spark
Check condition of spark plugs and plug wiring as described in Chapter Three.
Perform the fuel system troubleshooting procedures described in Chapter Two. In addition, refer to Chapter Five for additional fuel system inspection and maintenance.
Check the ignition timing and valve timing as described in Chapter Three. In addition, check the spark plug wires for proper installation and routing.
Check engine compression as described in Chapter Three.

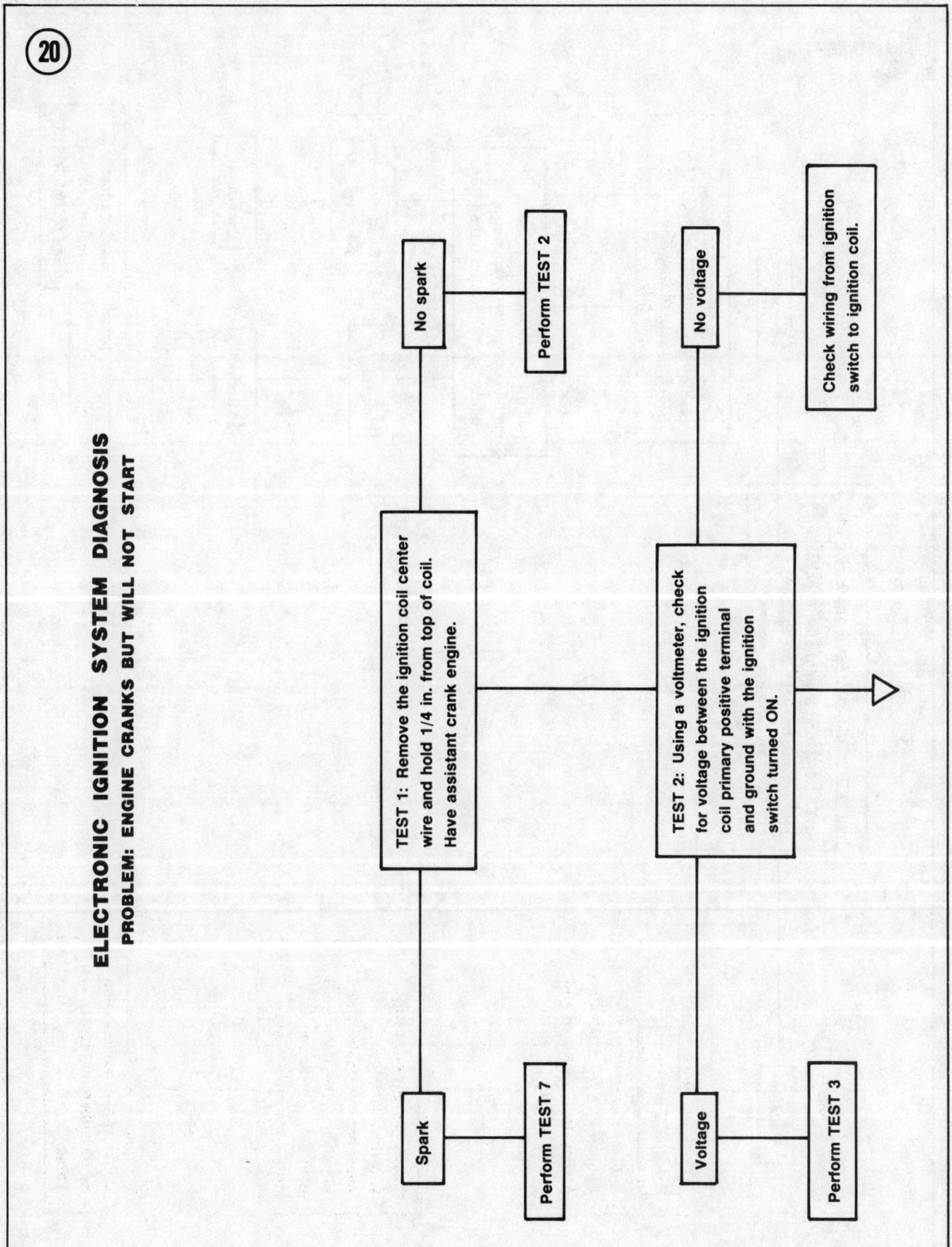

(20)

ELECTRONIC IGNITION SYSTEM DIAGNOSIS

PROBLEM: ENGINE CRANKS BUT WILL NOT START

TEST 1: Remove the ignition coil center wire and hold 1/4 in. from top of coil. Have assistant crank engine.

Spark

Perform TEST 7

No spark

Perform TEST 2

TEST 2: Using a voltmeter, check for voltage between the ignition coil primary positive terminal and ground with the ignition switch turned ON.

Voltage

Perform TEST 3

No voltage

Check wiring from ignition switch to ignition coil.

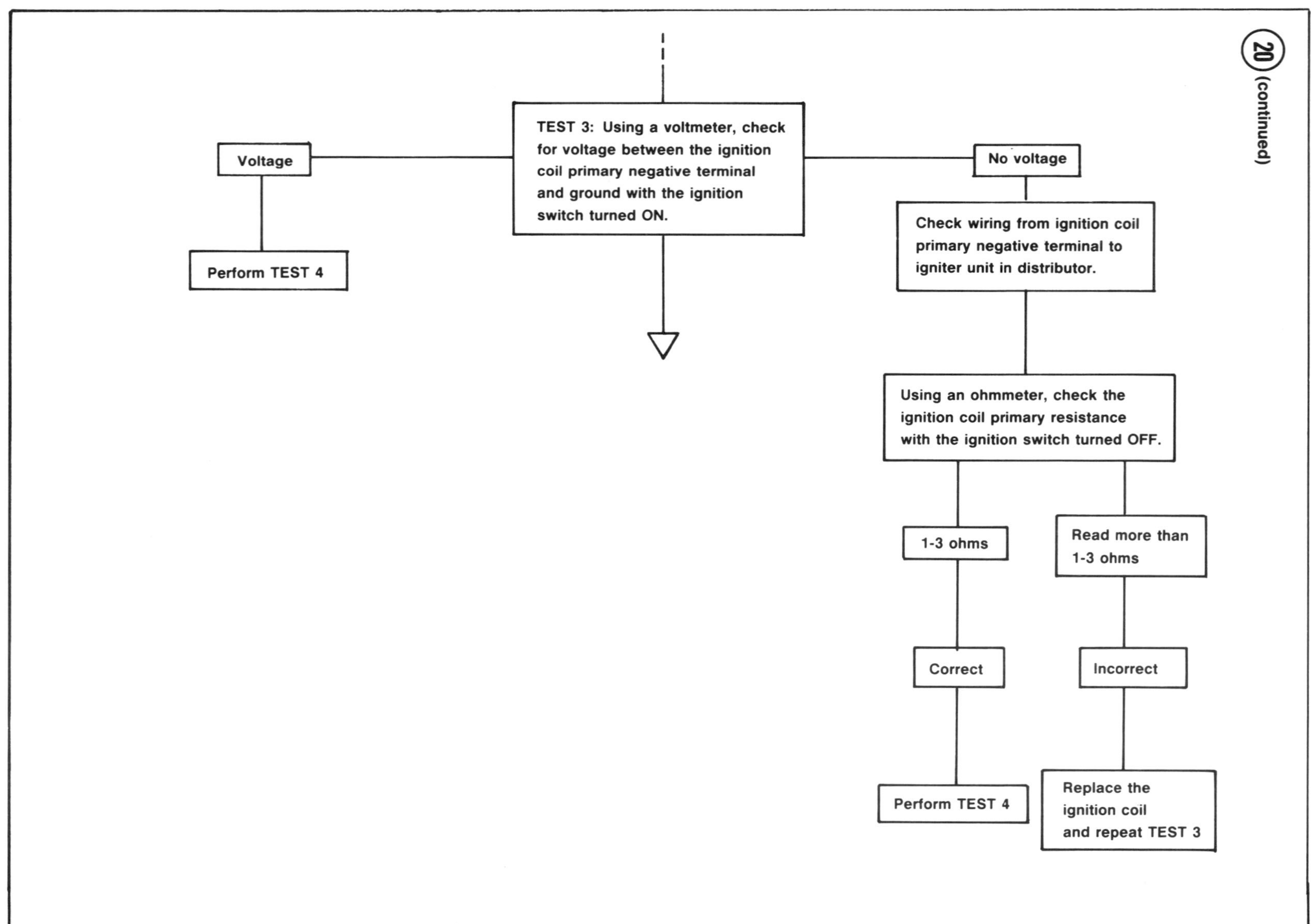
20 (continued)
TEST 3: Using a voltmeter, check for voltage between the ignition coil primary negative terminal and ground with the ignition switch turned ON.
Voltage
Perform TEST 4
No voltage
Check wiring from ignition coil primary negative terminal to igniter unit in distributor.
Using an ohmmeter, check the ignition coil primary resistance with the ignition switch turned OFF.
1-3 ohms
Correct
Perform TEST 4
Read more than 1-3 ohms
Incorrect
Replace the ignition coil and repeat TEST 3

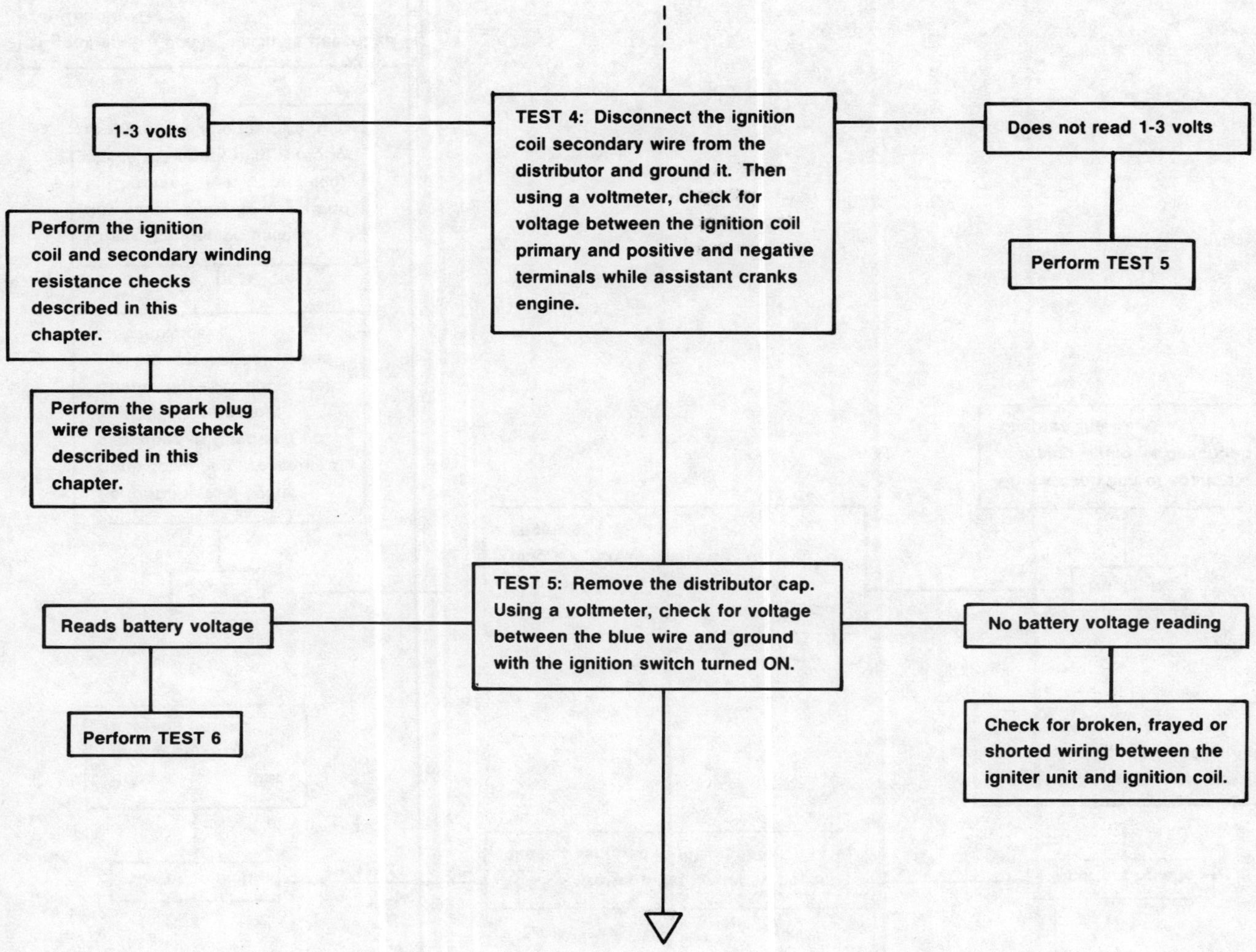

TEST 4: Disconnect the ignition coil secondary wire from the distributor and ground it. Then using a voltmeter, check for voltage between the ignition coil primary and positive and negative terminals while assistant cranks engine.

- **1-3 volts**
  - Perform the ignition coil and secondary winding resistance checks described in this chapter.
  - Perform the spark plug wire resistance check described in this chapter.
- **Does not read 1-3 volts**
  - Perform TEST 5

TEST 5: Remove the distributor cap. Using a voltmeter, check for voltage between the blue wire and ground with the ignition switch turned ON.

- **Reads battery voltage**
  - Perform TEST 6
- **No battery voltage reading**
  - Check for broken, frayed or shorted wiring between the igniter unit and ignition coil.

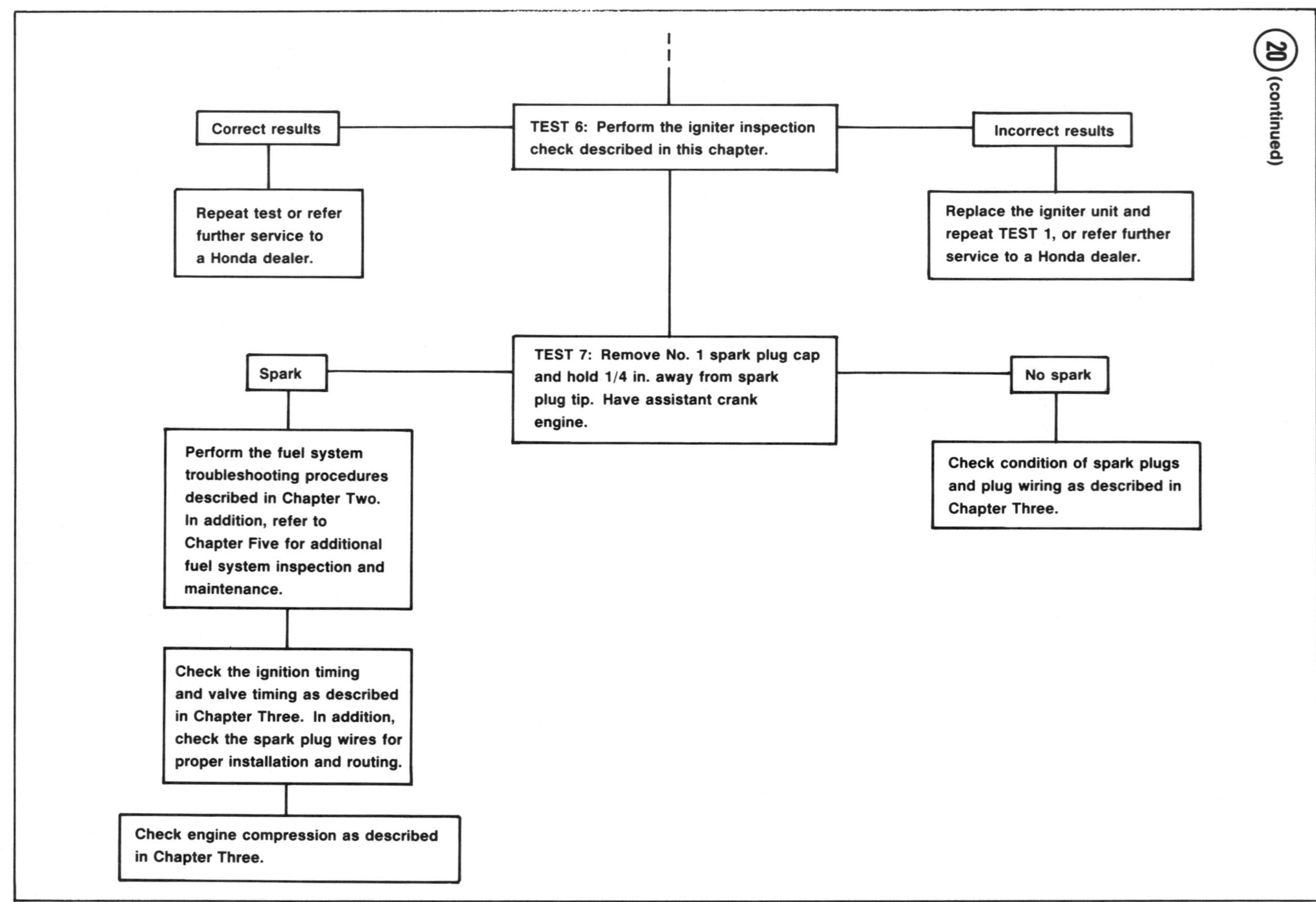
20 (continued)
TEST 6: Perform the igniter inspection check described in this chapter.
Correct results
Repeat test or refer further service to a Honda dealer.
Incorrect results
Replace the igniter unit and repeat TEST 1, or refer further service to a Honda dealer.
TEST 7: Remove No. 1 spark plug cap and hold 1/4 in. away from spark plug tip. Have assistant crank engine.
Spark
Perform the fuel system troubleshooting procedures described in Chapter Two. In addition, refer to Chapter Five for additional fuel system inspection and maintenance.
Check the ignition timing and valve timing as described in Chapter Three. In addition, check the spark plug wires for proper installation and routing.
Check engine compression as described in Chapter Three.
No spark
Check condition of spark plugs and plug wiring as described in Chapter Three.

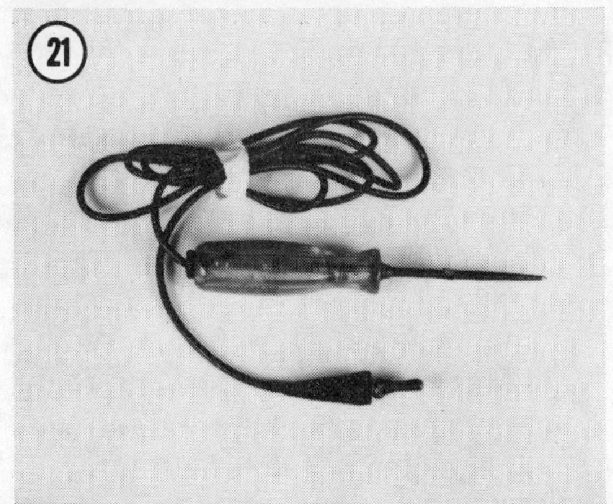
21

24

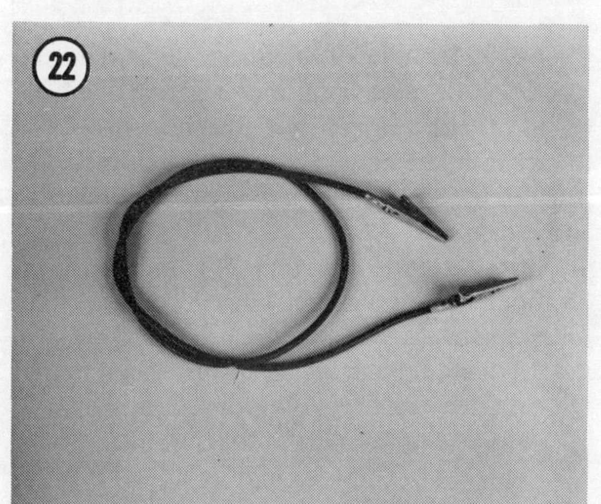
22

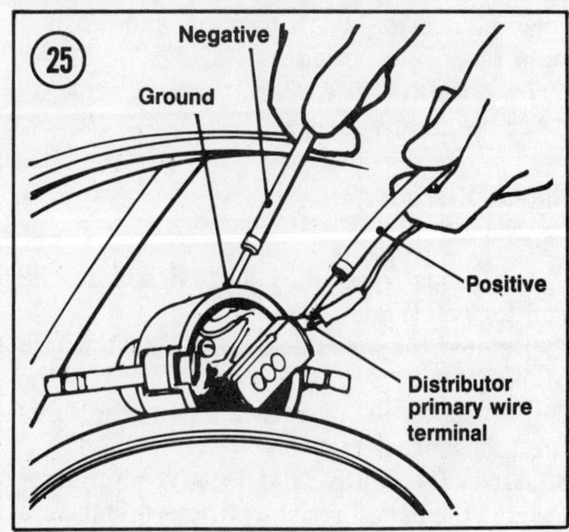
25
Negative
Ground
Positive
Distributor
primary wire
terminal

23

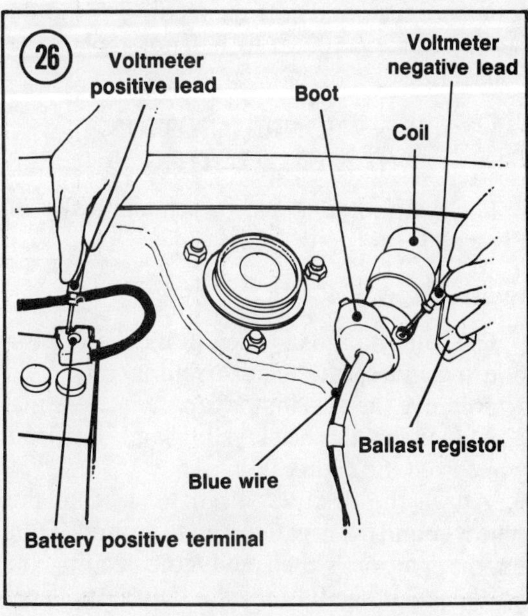
26
Voltmeter
positive lead
Voltmeter
negative lead
Boot
Coil
Ballast registor
Blue wire
Battery positive terminal

2. Attach voltmeter negative lead to the ignition coil positive terminal.
3. Attach voltmeter positive lead to the positive battery terminal.
4. Set the voltmeter to the lowest scale and turn the ignition switch to ON. The voltmeter reading should read approximately 6 volts or 1/2 of battery voltage. If voltage is correct, proceed to Step 5. If not, perform the *Ballast Resistor Resistance* test in this chapter.
5. Turn the ignition switch to the START position and note reading on voltmeter. It should be 0.4 volts or less. If voltage reading is 0.5 volts or higher, check all wiring between the ignition primary coil terminal and the starter solenoid resistor bypass terminal and repair if required. Then perform the *Ignition Coil Primary Winding Resistance* check as described in this chapter.

Ballast Resistor Resistance

The ballast resistor is located behind the ignition coil (**Figure 27**).

1. Remove the windshield airscoop at the base of the hood.
2. Disconnect the black/white and blue wires from the ballast resistor.
3. Attach the positive and negative ohmmeter leads to the ballast resistor wire terminals.
4. Set the ohmmeter scale to the lowest resistance scale and note the reading. It should be 1.6 ohms +/- 10% at 70° F. If not, replace the ballast resistor.

ELECTRONIC IGNITION SYSTEM TESTING

The distributor is shown schematically in **Figure 28**.

Igniter Inspection

The igniter unit is located in the distributor housing underneath the distributor cap.

1. Remove the distributor cap.
2. Disconnect the black/yellow and blue lead wires from the igniter unit.
3. Attach the positive voltmeter lead to the blue wire and the negative lead to ground. Turn on the ignition switch and note reading on voltmeter. It should indicate battery voltage.

Then attach the positive voltmeter lead to the black/yellow wire and the negative lead to ground. With the ignition switch turned ON, there should be battery voltage as before. If so, proceed to Step 4. If not, replace the igniter unit and retest.
4. Turn the ignition switch OFF and, using an ohmmeter set to the R x 100 scale, perform the following tests:
   a. Attach the ohmmeter positive lead to the igniter black/yellow wire terminal and the negative lead to the blue wire terminal. There should be no continuity reading.
   b. Attach the ohmmeter positive lead to the igniter blue wire terminal and the negative lead to the black/yellow wire terminal. Continuity should be indicated on the meter.
5. If the igniter failed any of the tests in Steps 3 and 4, it is inoperative and must be replaced.

IGNITION COIL

A resistance check of the primary and secondary windings in the ignition coil can be made simply with an ohmmeter. A functional check requires a coil tester and this check can be performed by a Honda dealer or automotive electrical specialist.

Winding Resistance

An ohmmeter is required to perform the following test procedures. Replace the coil if

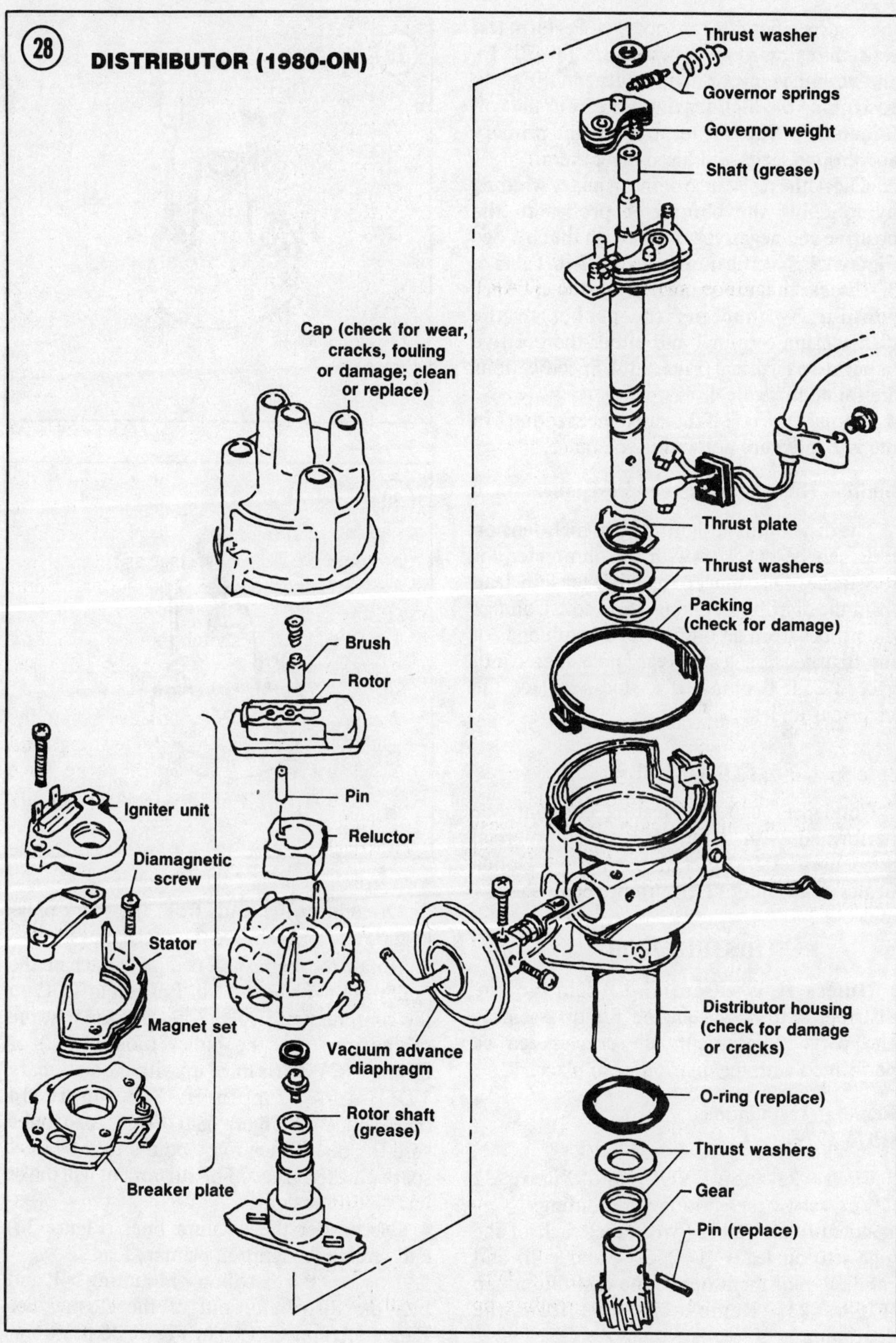
28
DISTRIBUTOR (1980-ON)
Thrust washer
Governor springs
Governor weight
Shaft (grease)
Cap (check for wear, cracks, fouling or damage; clean or replace)
Thrust plate
Thrust washers
Packing (check for damage)
Brush
Rotor
Pin
Igniter unit
Reluctor
Diamagnetic screw
Stator
Magnet set
Vacuum advance diaphragm
Rotor shaft (grease)
Breaker plate
Distributor housing (check for damage or cracks)
O-ring (replace)
Thrust washers
Gear
Pin (replace)

the test specifications are not met. Perform test procedures at room temperature (68-70° F). and with the ignition switch turned OFF.

1. Unplug the high-tension lead from the coil (**Figure 27**). Note the locations of the primary and ground leads and disconnect them.
2. Check the resistance of the primary winding by touching the ohmmeter probes to the positive and negative terminals on the coil. See **Figure 29**. Specifications are found in **Table 4**.
3. Check the resistance of the secondary winding by touching the probes to the high-tension terminal and either the positive or negative terminal (**Figure 30**). Specifications are found in **Table 4**.
4. Replace the coil if the resistance readings in Steps 2 and 3 are not within tolerance.

Ignition High-Tension Lead Resistance

The distributor-to-ignition coil high-tension lead can be checked with an ohmmeter for resistance. Disconnect the high-tension lead from the distributor and ignition coil. Connect the probes from an ohmmeter to both ends of the high-tension lead. Resistance should not exceed 25,000 ohms. If it does, replace the high-tension lead.

CONDENSER

Condenser capacity testing can only be performed with some type of commercial condenser tester. Refer all testing to a Honda dealer or automotive electronic repair shop.

DISTRIBUTOR

Unless it is essential to remove the distributor from the engine for disassembly and parts replacement, all services can be performed with the distributor in place.

Removal/Installation (1973-1979)

Figure 31 (non-CVCC) and **Figure 32** (CVCC) show the ignition wire routing.

1. Identify and label (with tape) each of the high-tension leads (1, 2, 3, 4 and coil) and carefully pull them out of the distributor cap (**Figure 23**). Remove the cap from the distributor.

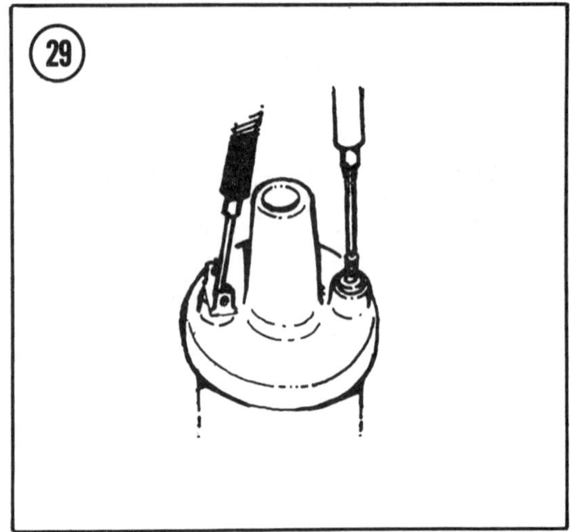

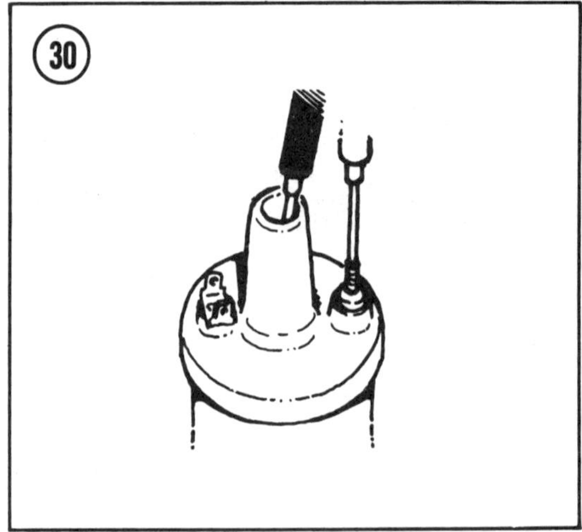

2. Disconnect the leads from the spark plugs (**Figure 33**) and remove the spark plugs.
3. Rotate the crankshaft using a wrench on the pulley nut to bring the No. 1 piston to TDC on the compression stroke. Check to see that the timing mark on the pulley (non-CVCC) or flywheel (CVCC) is lined up with the stationary TDC mark or pointer. See **Figure 34** (non-CVCC) or **Figure 35** (CVCC). Also make sure the distributor rotor points to the No. 1 spark plug terminals. This alignment will make installation easier.
4. Disconnect the vacuum lines (**Figure 36**) and unplug the ignition primary lead.
5. Unscrew the distributor mounting bolt and pull the distributor out of the engine. See **Figure 37** (non-CVCC) or **Figure 38** (CVCC).

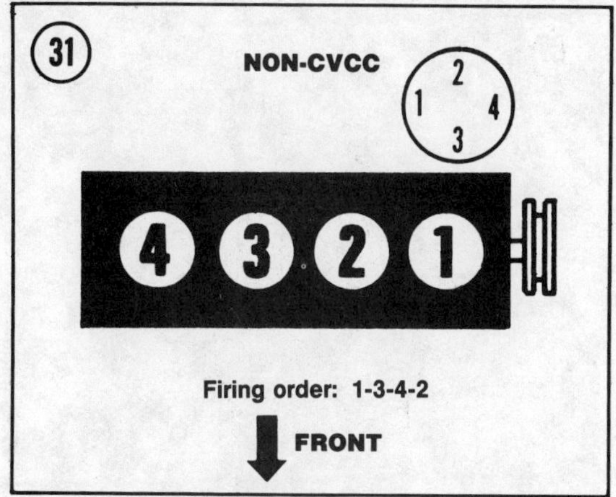
31
NON-CVCC
2
1 4
3
4 3 2 1
Firing order: 1-3-4-2
FRONT

33

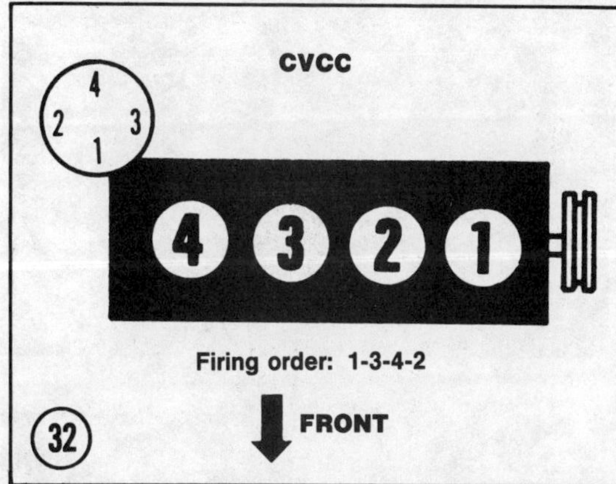
CVCC
4
2 3
1
4 3 2 1
Firing order: 1-3-4-2
FRONT
32

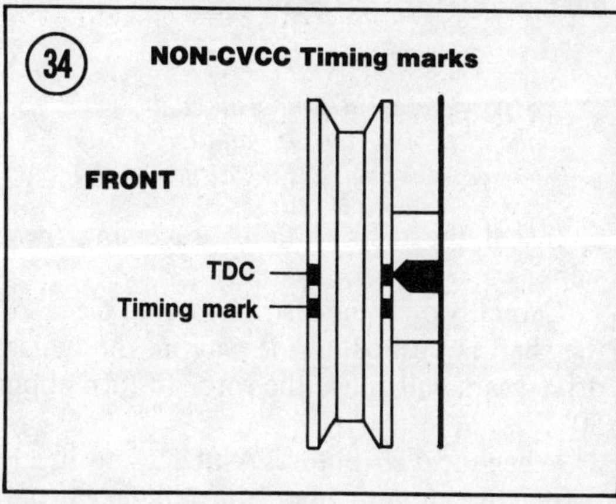
34
NON-CVCC Timing marks
FRONT
TDC
Timing mark

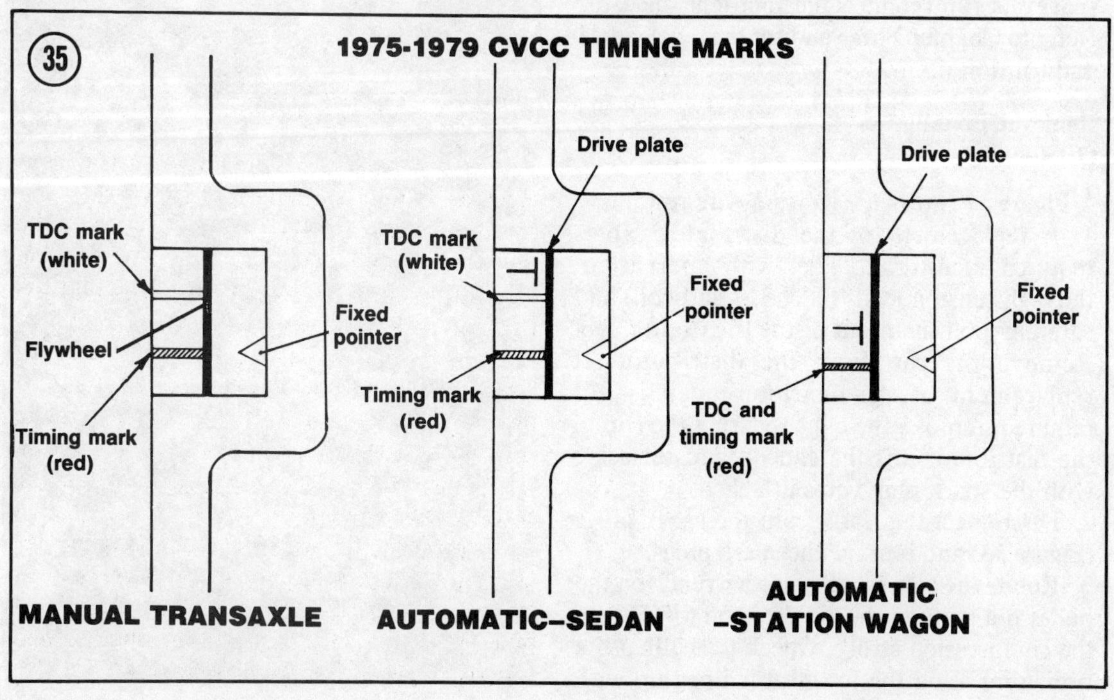
35
1975-1979 CVCC TIMING MARKS
TDC mark (white)
Flywheel
Fixed pointer
Timing mark (red)
MANUAL TRANSAXLE
Drive plate
TDC mark (white)
Fixed pointer
Timing mark (red)
AUTOMATIC-SEDAN
Drive plate
Fixed pointer
TDC and timing mark (red)
AUTOMATIC -STATION WAGON

7

NOTE
If possible, avoid turning the engine with the distributor out. Installation will be easier if the engine is not turned.

6. Install the distributor by reversing these steps.
7. Carefully push the distributor into place. As the shaft is pushed all the way in, the helical drive gears will cause the rotor to turn about 30°.
8. When the distributor is seated, screw in and tighten the mounting bolts, install the cap and spark plugs and connect the high-tension leads. Refer to Chapter Three and set the dwell angle and ignition timing.

Removal/Installation (1980-on)

Figure 32 shows the ignition wire routing.

1. If replacement of the distributor cap is required, identify and label (with tape) each of the high-tension leads (1, 2, 3, 4 and coil) and carefully pull them out of the distributor cap. Remove the cap from the distributor. If replacement of the distributor cap is not required, remove the clips securing the cap to the distributor, lift the cap up and set aside with the spark plug wires attached.
2. Disconnect the leads from the spark plugs (**Figure 33**) and remove the spark plugs.
3. Rotate the crankshaft using a wrench on the pulley nut to bring the No. 1 piston to TDC on the compression stroke. Check to see that the timing mark on the flywheel is lined up with

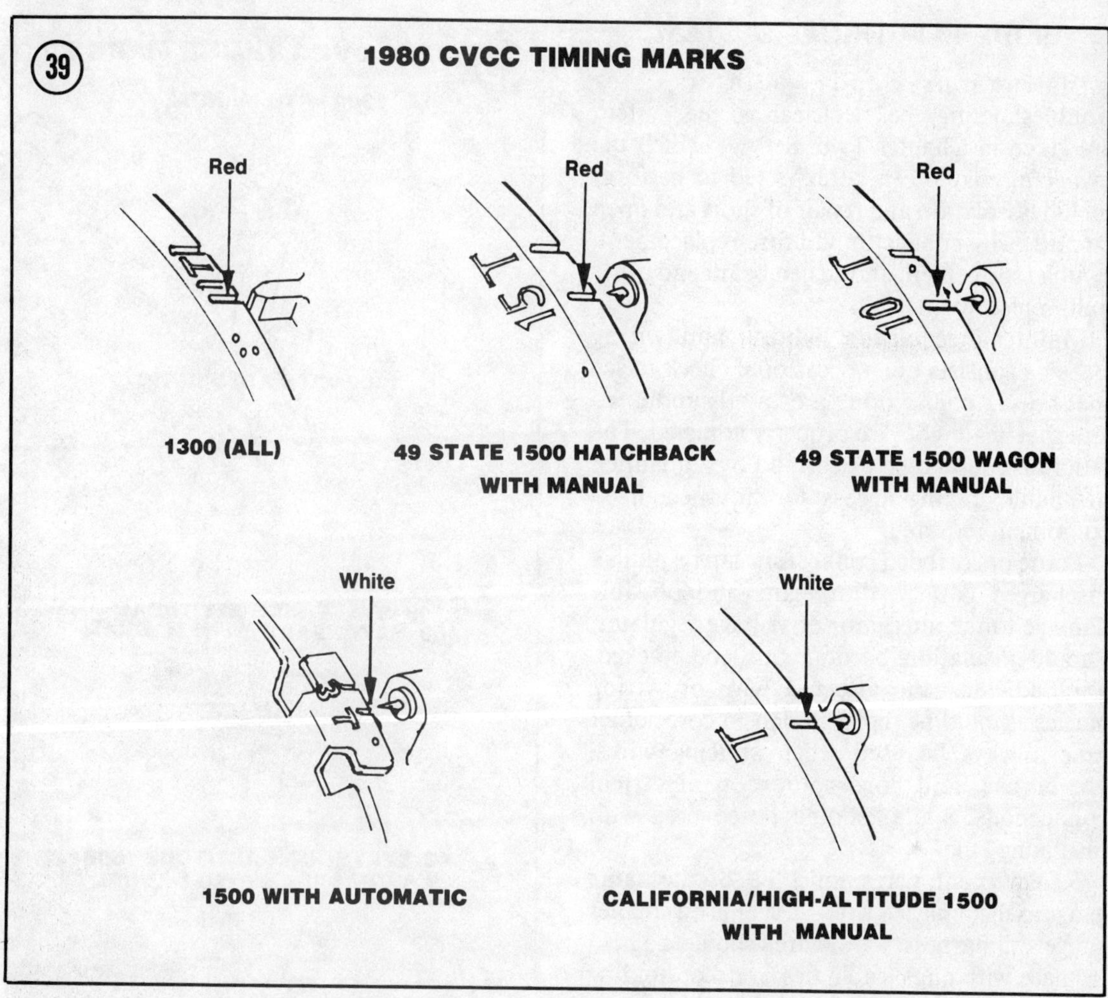

the stationary TDC mark or pointer. See **Figure 39** (1980) or **Figure 40** (1981). Also make sure the distributor rotor points to the No. 1 spark plug terminal.

4. Disconnect the primary lead wires and the condenser ground wire at the distributor.

5. Disconnect the vacuum advance hose at the distributor.

6. Make match marks on the distributor hold-down plate and the engine block to make installation easier, then remove the cover from the hold-down bolt and remove the bolt.

7. Remove the distributor from the engine.

8. If the engine was disturbed while the distributor was out, turn the engine with a socket on the crankshaft nut counterclockwise until the No. 1 piston is at top dead center on the compression stroke.

9. Align the round mark on the distributor gear shoulder with the mark on the distributor housing. See **Figure 41**.

10. Insert distributor into engine block, making sure firing end of rotor is pointing to No. 1 cylinder mark on the distributor cap.

NOTE
If rotor points to the No. 4 cylinder mark instead, remove the distributor and turn the engine through one more crankshaft revolution until the timing marks are aligned as described in Step 8. Repeat Steps 9 and 10.

11. Connect all wires to their original positions.

12. Set the ignition timing as described in Chapter Three.

BODY ELECTRICAL SYSTEM

Instructions and pointers for troubleshooting the electrical wiring system are given in Chapter Two. Service which the owner/mechanic can be expected to perform includes isolation and repair of short and open circuits, wire connector and fuse replacement, switch replacement and sealed beam and other bulb replacement.

Maintenance of the lighting and wiring systems consists of an occasional check to see that wiring connections are tightly mounted and that headlights are properly adjusted. The latter task should be performed by a qualified mechanic having access to the specialized equipment required.

Loose or corroded connectors can result in a discharged battery, dim lights and possible damage to the alternator or voltage regulator. Should insulation become burned, cracked, abraded, etc., the affected wire or wiring harness should be replaced. Rosin core solder must always be used when splicing wires. Never use acid core solder on electrical connections. Splices should be covered with insulating tape.

Replacement wires must be of the same gauge as the replaced wire—never use a smaller gauge. All harnesses and wires should be held in place with clips, cable ties or other holding devices so that chafing and abrasion can be avoided.

FUSES

Whenever a failure occurs in any part of the electrical system, always check the fuse box to see if a fuse has blown. If one has, it will be evident by blackening of the fuse or by a break in the metal link in the fuse. Usually the trouble can be traced to a short circuit in the wiring connected to the blown fuse. This may be caused by worn-through insulation or by a wire which has worked loose and shorted to ground. Occasionally, the electrical overload which causes the fuse to blow may occur in a switch or motor.

A blown fuse should be treated as more than a minor annoyance, it should serve also as a

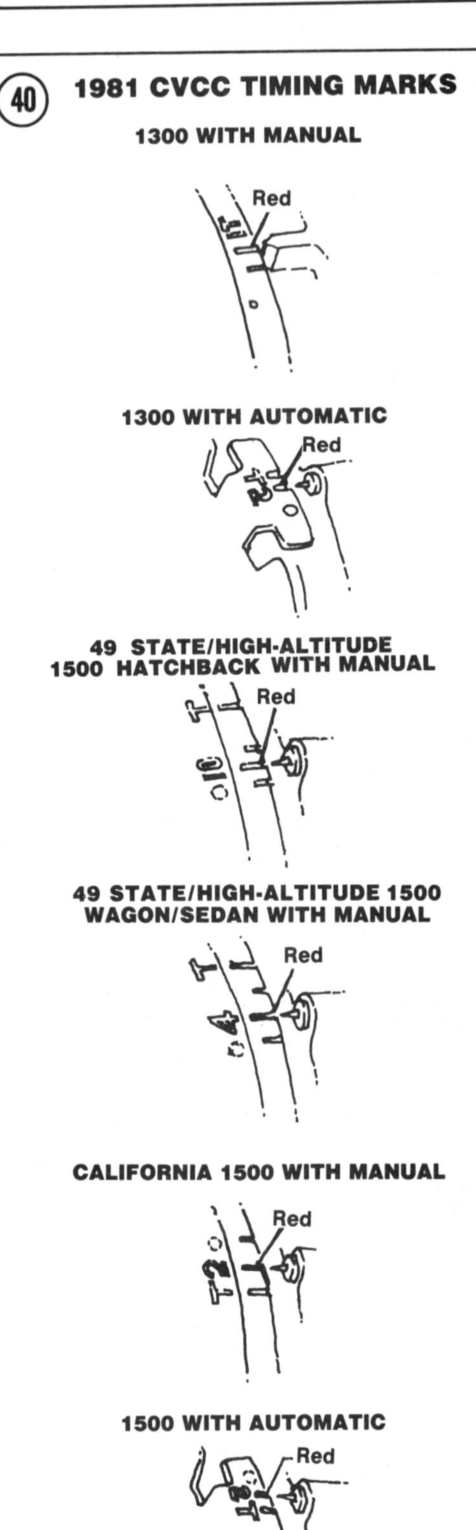

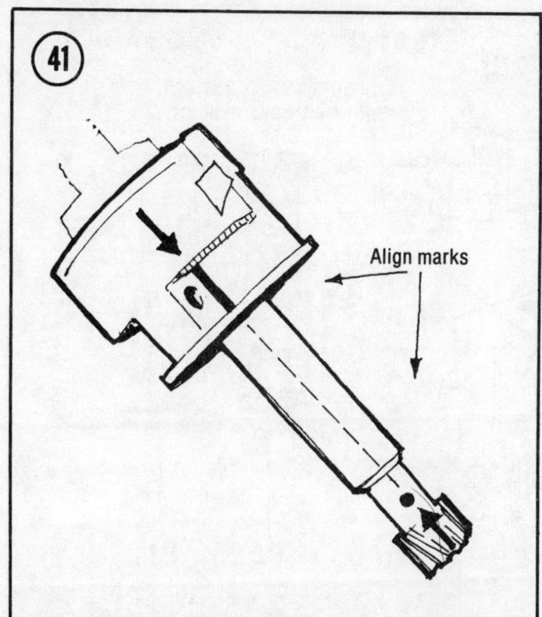

warning that something is wrong in the electrical system. Before replacing a fuse, determine what caused it to blow and then correct the trouble.

WARNING
Never replace a fuse with one of a higher amperage rating than that of the one originally used. Never use metal foil or other metallic material to bridge fuse terminals. Failure to follow these basic rules could result in heat or fire damage to major parts or loss of the entire vehicle.

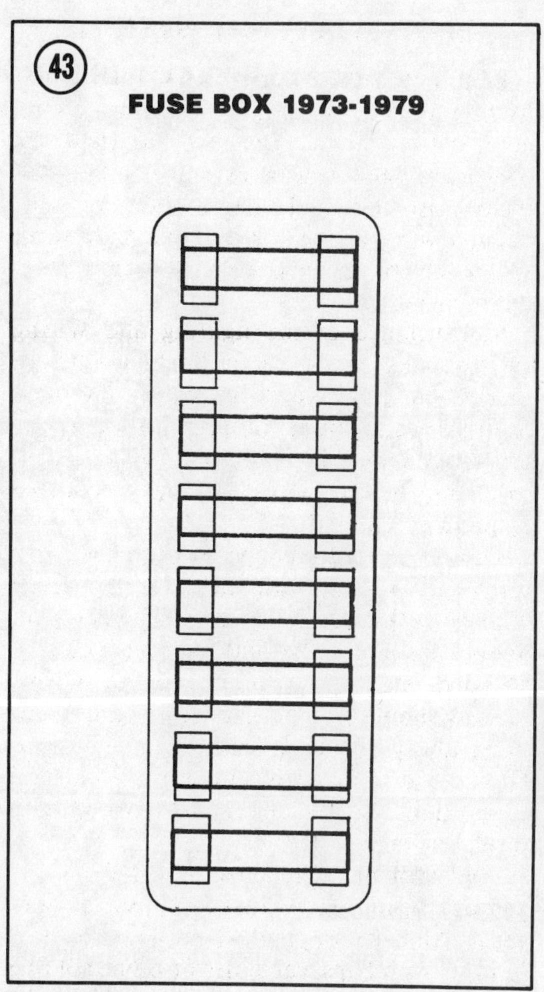

There are 2 fuse locations in the Civic. The main fuse, or fusible link, is located in the engine compartment near the battery (**Figure 42**). This fuse connects the starter motor relay to the rest of the electrical system. If no electrical power is available to any of the systems, check the link to see if it has burned through. Locate and correct the source of trouble before replacing it.

The second fuse location is beneath the dashboard on the left side, inside the car. See **Figure 43** (1973-1979) or **Figure 44** (1980-on). This fuse box contains fuses for all of the electrical functions (lights, motors, etc.).

To inspect or replace the fuses, pull the fuse box/cover down and check the condition of the metal elements. Replace a defective fuse by carefully prying it out of its holder and snapping a new one in place.

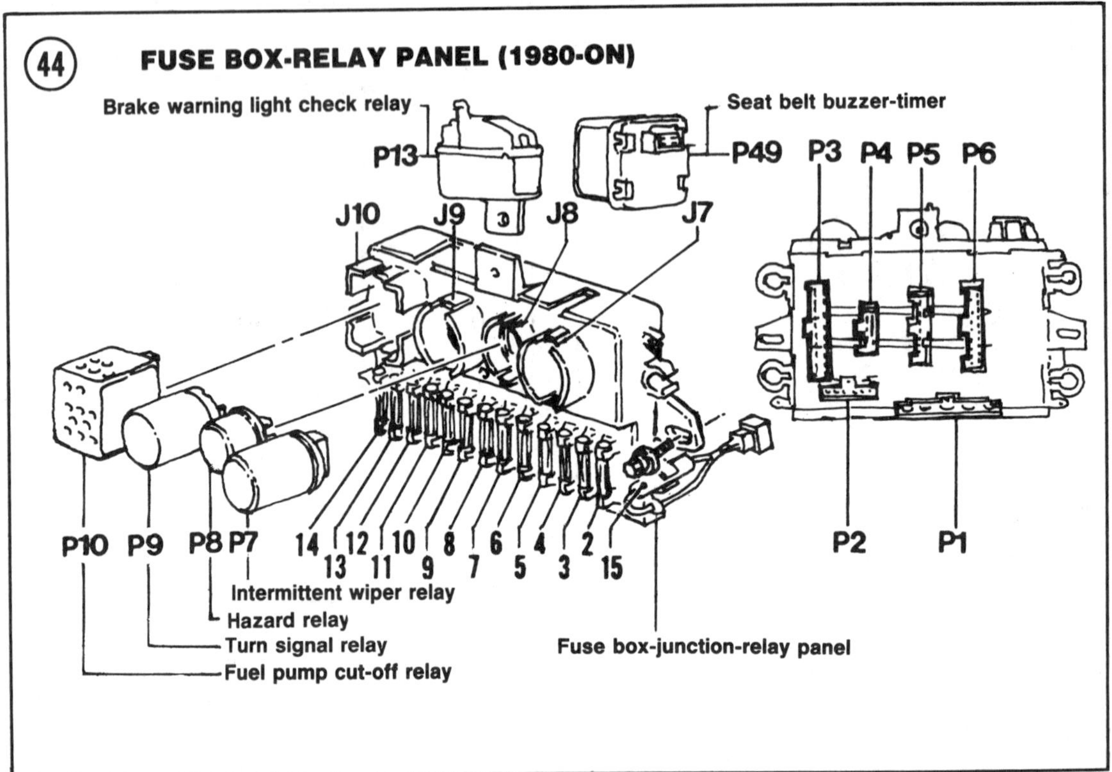

ELECTRICAL RELAYS

1973-1979 Models

The indicator and flasher relays are joined by a mounting band and held in place beneath the left end of the dashboard by a single screw (**Figure 45**). To replace either one, first unscrew the screw and lower the relays. Disconnect the leads from the faulty relay, noting the locations of the leads. Push the relay out of the mount, push in a new one, connect the leads and remount the relays with the screw.

1980-on Models

All of the relay and timer plugs are located in the fuse box junction relay panel (**Figure 44**). To replace a relay, locate the faulty one in **Figure 44** and pull it out of the panel. To install, push a new relay into the panel.

HEADLIGHTS

Replacement

Refer to **Figure 46** or **Figure 47** for this procedure.

NOTE

*Before beginning this procedure, make sure to compare your car's headlight assembly with **Figure 46** or **Figure 47** as there may be a slight difference in screw positioning. Make sure not to disturb the adjustment screws to avoid having to readjust the headlights.*

1. Unscrew the screws from the outer headlight ring. Remove the ring and the sealed-beam unit.
2. Unplug the light from the connector. Plug a new light in and install it by lining up the lugs in the light with the recesses in the headlight inner mounting ring. Put the outer ring in place and screw in the screws. If any of the headlight adjustment screws were disturbed, have the lamps adjusted by a Honda dealer or an authorized headlight adjusting station.

PARKING/TURN INDICATOR LIGHTS

To change a bulb, unscrew the 2 lens screws and remove the lens (**Figure 48**). Press in on the bulb, turn it counterclockwise and pull it

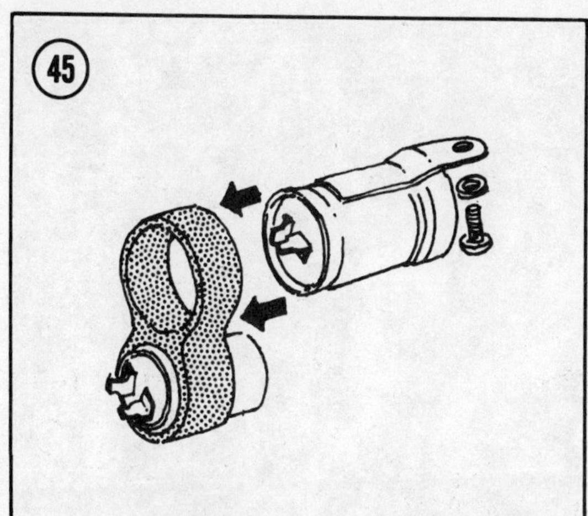

46 HEADLIGHTS (1973-1980 ALL, 1981 HATCHBACK AND WAGON)

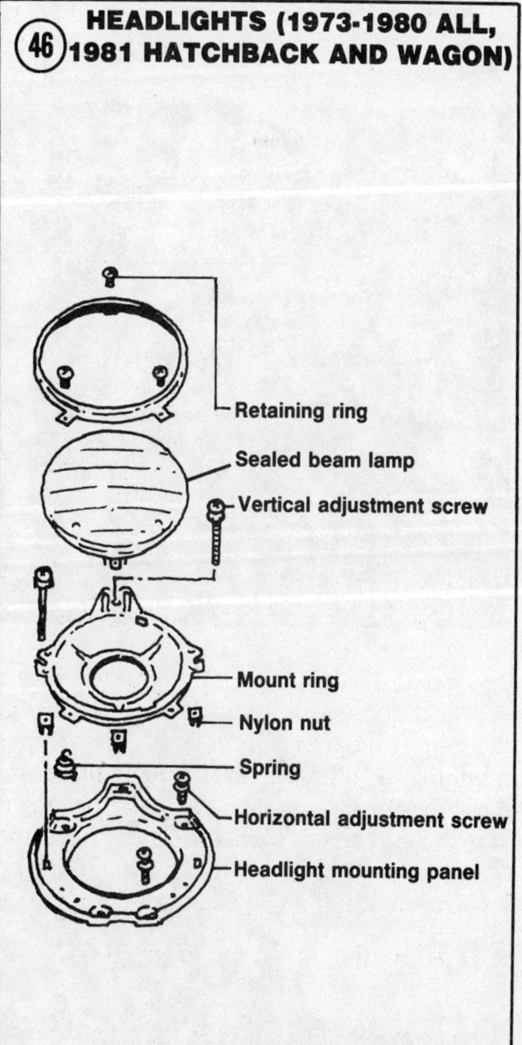

47 HEADLIGHTS (1981 SEDAN)

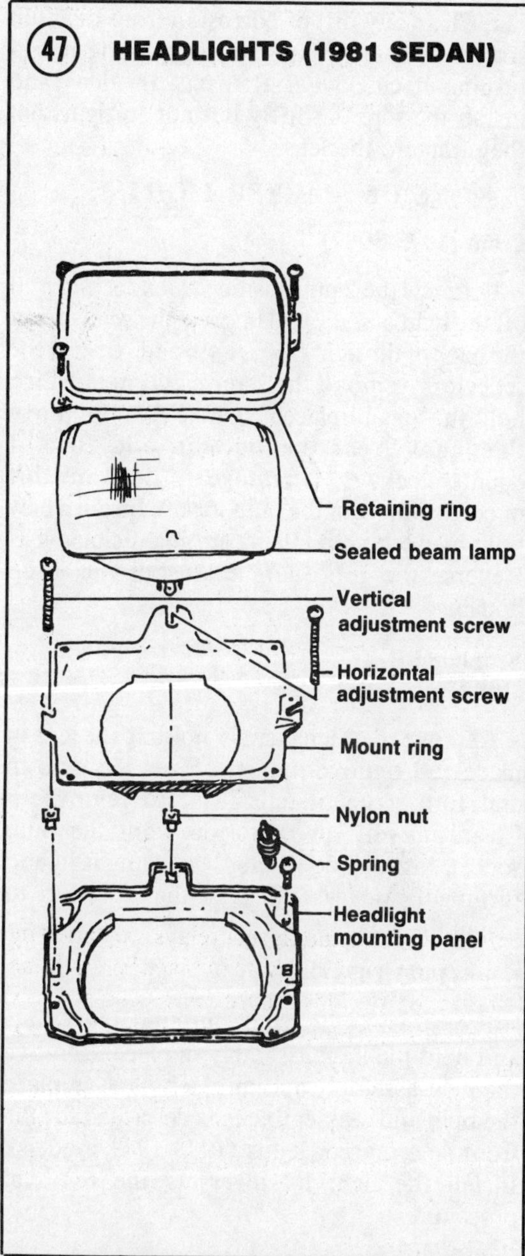

7

out. Clean any dirt or corrosion from the bulb socket. Install a new bulb by pushing it and turning it clockwise. Reinstall the lens and install the screws snugly but not so tight that they fracture the lens.

SIDE MARKER LIGHTS

Front (1973-1979)

Unscrew the 2 nuts inside the fender and pull off the light assembly. Unscrew the screw from the back of the light (**Figure 49**) and remove the reflector. Remove the screws and nuts which hold the lens in place (**Figure 50**) and remove the lens. Press the bulb in and turn it counterclockwise to remove it. Clean any dirt or corrosion from the bulb socket. Install a new bulb by pushing it in and turning it clockwise. Reverse the procedure to install the lamp housing.

Front and Rear (1980-on Models)

Remove the 2 lens screws holding the lens in place and remove the lens. Press the bulb in and turn it counterclockwise to remove it. Clean any dirt or corrosion from the bulb socket. Install a new bulb by pushing it in and turning it clockwise. Reverse the procedure to install the lens.

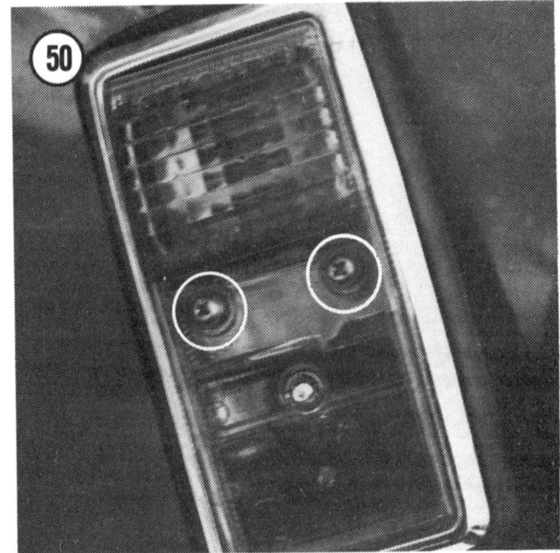

Rear (1973-1979 2-door)

From inside the trunk, unscrew the 2 nuts and hold the light assembly in place. Remove the light assembly and disassemble it, replace the bulb and reassemble it as described for the front side marker lights (1973-1979 models). Install the light by reversing the removal procedure.

Rear (1973-1979 Hatchback and Station Wagon)

Remove the rear combination lights as described in this section. Reach through the combination light opening and unscrew the 2 nuts which hold the light in place and remove it. Disassemble the light, replace the bulb and reassemble it as described for the front side marker lights. Install the light by reversing the removal procedure and reinstall the rear combination lights.

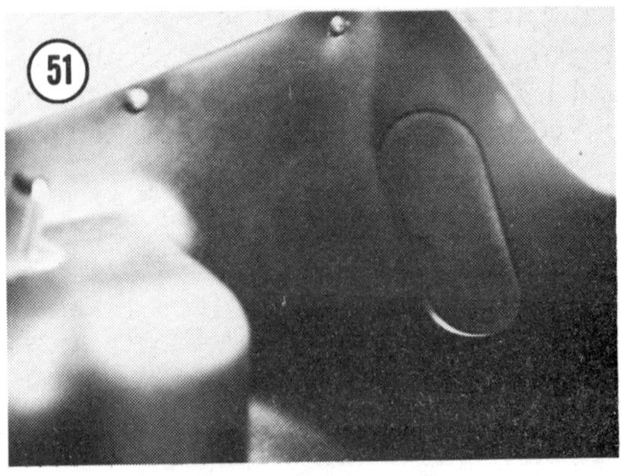

REAR COMBINATION LIGHTS

Sedan (1973-1979)

Lift the rear door and remove the panel to gain access to the taillight housing. Pull out sockets to replace defective bulbs. If the lens is to be replaced, unscrew the flange nuts which hold it in place and remove it. Reverse the procedure for installing the lens and the socket. Make sure that the inner and outer gaskets are correctly seated to prevent moisture from entering the lens or the body. Tighten the screws and nuts snugly but not so tight as to crack the lens.

Hatchback and Station Wagon (1973-1979)

Lift the rear door and remove the plug (**Figure 51**) to gain access to the socket screws and lens mounting nuts. Then refer to the procedure for the 2-door model and perform the required work.

Hatchback and Sedan (1980-on)

Open the rear hood and remove the access panel in the trunk or cargo area. Pull the light sockets out of the lamp housing and remove the bulbs. To remove the lens, remove the nuts securing the lens and pull the lens outward. Reverse to install.

Station Wagon (1980-on)

Remove the screws securing the lens to the lamp housing and remove the lens. Press the bulb counterclockwise to remove it. Clean any dirt from the bulb socket. Reverse the procedure to assemble and install the light.

LICENSE PLATE LIGHTS

1973-1979

Remove the tailgate trim panel on hatchback and station wagon models. Unscrew the nuts inside the trunk lid (**Figure 52**) and pull the light assembly off. Separate the base and cover and replace the bulb. Assemble and install the light by reversing this procedure.

1980-on

Remove the screws securing the lens to the lamp housing and remove the lens. Push the bulb in and turn counterclockwise and remove from socket. Clean the socket of all dirt and other debris. Install by reversing this procedure.

SWITCHES

Switches can be tested for continuity with an ohmmeter (see Chapter One) at the switch connector plug by operating the switch in each of its operating positions and comparing results with the switch's interconnection diagram. When testing switches, consider the following information:

a. First check the main fuse (**Figure 42**) and fuse box for blown fuses.
b. Check the battery as described in this chapter and bring the battery to the correct state of charge, if required.
c. When separating 2 connectors, pull on the connector housings and not the wires. If the connectors are secured together with a plastic tab, the tab must be unhooked before attempting to separate the connectors.
d. After locating a defective circuit, check the connectors to make sure they are

7

clean and properly connected. Check all wires going into a connector housing to make sure each is properly positioned and that the wire end is not loose.

e. To properly connect connectors, push them together until they click into place.

f. Multi-pin connectors should be packed with an electrical-wire grease.

IGNITION SWITCH

Testing

Remove the lower steering column cover to gain access to the ignition switch connector and unplug the connector. Determine the condition of the ignition switch by checking its continuity in each of the operating positions. Refer to **Figure 53** (1973-1979 non-CVCC), **Figure 54**

IGNITION SWITCH (1973-1979)

Off	0°				
I	90°	O			O
II	180°	O		O	O
III	210°	O	O	O	
Harness Color code		White	Black/ white	Black/ yellow	White/ red
Switch Color code		R	R/BL	BL	Y

IGNITION SWITCH (1975-1976 CVCC)

SWITCH POSITION	CONTINUITY TABLE					
KEY OUT						
KEY IN					O	O
I	O	O			O	O
II	O	O	O		O	O
III	O		O	O	O	O
COLOR	R	Y	Bl	R/Bl	W/Bu	G

(1975-1976 CVCC), **Figure 55** (1977-1979 CVCC) or **Figure 56** (1980-on CVCC).

Replacement

The ignition switch is located on the steering column.

1. Remove the upper and lower steering column covers.
2. Unplug the ignition switch connector.
3. The ignition switch housing is secured with 2 shear screws. To remove the screws, first centerpunch each of the screws. Then, with the upper screw, drill out the screw head with the correct size drill bit as follows:
   a. 1973-1979 models: 1/4 in. bit
   b. 1980-on models: 3/8 in. bit
4. Separate the switch cap from the switch assembly and remove both from the steering column (**Figure 57**).
5. Position the new ignition switch onto the steering column without the ignition key inserted.

IGNITION SWITCH (1977-1979 CVCC)

SWITCH POSITION	CONTINUITY TABLE						
KEY OUT							
KEY IN						O	O
ACC	O	O					
ACC						O	O
ON	O	—	O				
ON						O	O
START	O	—	O	O			
START	O	—	—	—	O		
START						O	O
COLOR	W	W/R	Bl/Y	Bl/W	G	G/Bl	W/Bu

IGNITION SWITCH (1980-ON CVCC)

	TERMINAL				
POSITION	Acc	Bat	Ig	St	Fan
0 (Lock)					
I (Acc)	O	O			
II (On)	O	O	O	—	O
III (Start)		O	O	O	O
Color	W/R	W	Bl/Y	Bl/W	BlY

57

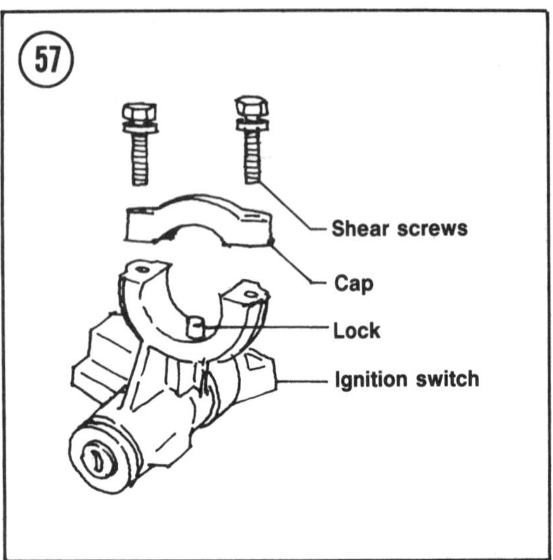

58

LIGHT/DIMMER SWITCH (1973-1979 NON-CVCC)

	Headlight	High	Low
Main	O	O	
	O	O	O
Dimmer	O	—	O
Color	R/Y[1]	R/Bu	R/W

1. Red on 1977 and later models

6. Hand-tighten the shear screws so that the screw heads do not break off. Then insert the ignition key into the switch and check to see that the steering lock operation works correctly.
7. After making sure that the steering lock works correctly, tighten the shear screws until the heads twist off.
8. Attach the switch connector and install the steering column covers.

LIGHT/DIMMER SWITCH

To check either switch, unplug the switch connectors along the steering column at the firewall and check the operating conditions with the interconnection diagrams in **Figure 58** (1973-1979 non-CVCC), **Figure 59** (1975 CVCC), **Figure 60** (1976-1979 CVCC) or **Figure 61** (1980-on CVCC).

The dimmer switch is part of the combination switch assembly.

WINDSHIELD WIPER SWITCH

The windshield wiper/washer switch is part of the combination switch assembly. To check the switch, unplug the switch connectors along the steering column and check the operating conditions with the interconnection diagrams in **Figure 62** (1973-1979) or **Figure 63** (1980-on). Replacement of the combination switch assembly should be performed by a Honda dealer.

59

LIGHT SWITCH 1975 CVCC

Off				
Parking lights	O	O		
Head	O	O	O	O
Color	R/G	R/Bl	R/Y	R

DIMMER SWITCH 1975 CVCC

DIMMER SWITCH			
Off			
Low	O	O	
High	O	—	O
Color	R/Y	R/W	R/Bu

WINDSHIELD WIPER MOTOR

On all models, the windshield wiper motor can be tested with the motor installed in the car.

CAUTION

Before turning on the windshield wipers, wet the windshield to prevent the wiper blades from scratching the windshield.

60 DIMMER SWITCH/ COMBINATION SWITCH (1976-1979 CVCC)

Off					
Park (small dot)	○	○			
Running (large dot)	○	○			
Low beam			○	○	
high beam			○		○
color	R/G	R/Bl	R	R/W	R/Bu

62 WASHER/WIPER SWITCH CONTINUITY (1973-1979)

Off	○	○				
1		○	○			
2			○	○		
Washer					○	○
Cord color	Blue/ white	Blue	Black	Blue/ yellow	Green/ black	Green/ black

61 LIGHT/DIMMER SWITCH (1980-ON CVCC)

Lighting sw	Bat. 1	P	Bat. 2	Head
Off				
Parking lights	○	○		
Head	○	○	○	○
Color	R/G	R/Bl	R	

Dimmer sw	Head	Hi	Lo
High	○	○	
Low	○		○
Color		R/Bu	R/W

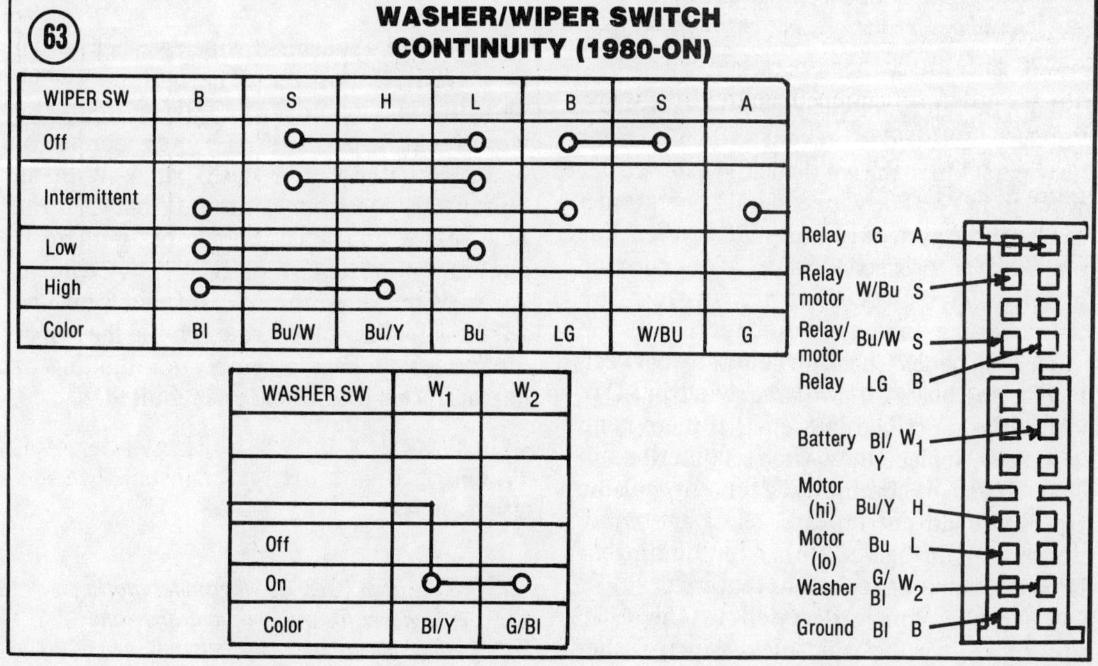

63 WASHER/WIPER SWITCH CONTINUITY (1980-ON)

WIPER SW	B	S	H	L	B	S	A
Off		○		○	○	○	
Intermittent		○		○			
	○				○		○
Low	○			○			
High	○		○				
Color	Bl	Bu/W	Bu/Y	Bu	LG	W/BU	G

WASHER SW	W_1	W_2
Off		
On	○	○
Color	Bl/Y	G/Bl

Testing (1973-1979)

NOTE
Step 1 describes troubleshooting procedures for the windshield washer system.

1. Turn the ignition switch to the ON position. Pull the windshield wiper/washer switch toward the steering wheel to activate the windshield washer. It should spray onto the windshield. If it does, proceed to Step 2. If not, turn the ignition switch to the OFF position, check for the following and replace or repair as required.
   a. Fuse blown
   b. Washer bag (**Figure 64**) is empty
   c. Windshield delivery tube and nozzle are clogged

If the windshield washer still does not operate correctly, unplug the wiper/washer switch from underneath the center dash panel. Using an ohmmeter or test light (with the ignition switch OFF), check for continuity between the green/black and black wire with the wiper/washer lever pulled toward the steering wheel. If there is no continuity, replace the switch as described in Chapter Ten.

NOTE
Steps 2 and 3 describe troubleshooting procedures for the low-speed windshield wiper cycle.

2. Turn the ignition switch to the ON position. Wet the windshield to prevent its damage from the wipers. Move the windshield wiper/washer switch to LOW. The wipers should operate at a low speed (approximately 38 cycles per minute). If so, proceed to Step 3. If not, turn the ignition switch OFF and unplug the wiper/washer switch from underneath the center dash panel. Check for continuty between the blue and black wire with the switch in LOW position as described in Step 1. If there is no continuity, replace the switch as described in Chapter Ten. If continuity is present, but the wipers still do not operate, check the wiper mechanical linkage assembly for binding or damage. Repair or replace as required.
3. Turn the ignition switch to the OFF position. Move the windshield wiper/washer switch to LOW. Disconnect the windshield wiper motor connector. Then apply 12 volts to the blue/yellow (negative) and green/black (positive) motor connector pins and check to see that the motor operates. If not, replace the windshield wiper motor as described in this chapter.

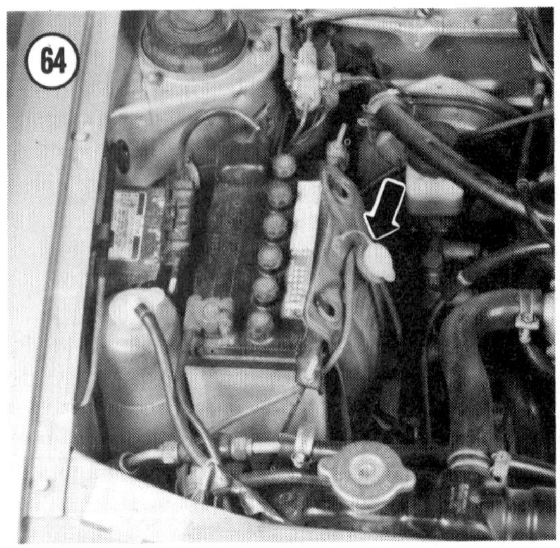

NOTE
Step 4 describes troubleshooting procedures for the high-speed windshield wiper cycle.

4. Move the windshield wiper/washer switch to the HIGH position. The ignition switch should be turned off. Disconnect the windshield wiper/washer switch connector underneath the center dash panel. With an ohmmeter, check for continuity between the blue/yellow and black wire pins. If there is continuity present, replace the windshield wiper switch. If continuity is present, but the wipers still do not operate, check the wiper mechanical linkage assembly for binding or damage. Repair or replace as required.

Testing (1980-on)

NOTE
Steps 1-4 describe troubleshooting procedures for the low- and high-speed windshield wiper motor system.

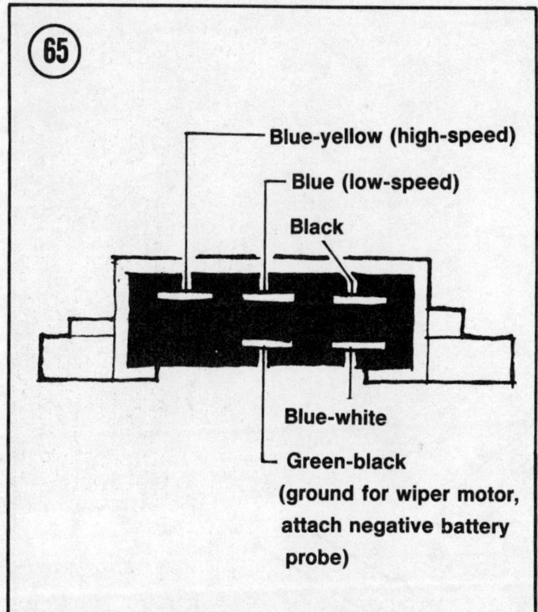

1. To gain access to the windshield wiper motor connectors, remove the air scoop grill and unbolt the wiper motor. Disconnect the wiper motor connector.
2. Apply 12 volts to the green/black and blue connector pins (**Figure 65**). The wiper motor should operate at LOW cycle speed.
3. Apply 12 volts to the green/black (ground) and blue/yellow (positive) connector pins (**Figure 65**). The wiper motor should operate at HIGH cycle speed.
4. If the wiper motor failed to operate as described in Steps 2 and 3, replace the wiper motor assembly.
5. The windshield washer motor can be tested by disconnecting the motor connector at the washer bag and applying 12 volts to the connector pins. Washer fluid should squirt from the outlets onto the windshield. If not, replace the washer motor.

Rear Wiper Motor Testing (1980-on)

1. Remove the rear wiper motor as described in this section.
2. Apply 12 volts to the black/green (negative) and blue (positive) wiper motor connector pins. The wiper motor should operate at normal cycle speed. If not, replace the rear wiper motor.

Wiper Motor Removal/Installation (1973-1979)

Refer to **Figure 66** for this procedure.

1. Unscrew the cap nuts from the wiper shafts (**Figure 67**) and pull the wiper arms off. Unscrew the locknuts and remove the rubber cushions and washer from the pivot collar.
2. Remove the snap ring and remove the pivot collar from the wiper link assembly. Then push the wiper link assembly into the body.
3. Unscrew the wiper motor mounting bolts located inside the fresh air intake (**Figure 68**). Disconnect the plug and remove the wiper motor and linkage.
4. Remove the cotter key which holds the linkage on the wiper motor arm and separate the linkage from the motor.
5. Carefully check the linkage joints for wear, looseness or binding. Stiff linkage may well have been the cause of the motor's failure. Check the pivot collars on the pivot shafts for looseness or binding. If their condition is in doubt, replace them.
6. Reverse Steps 1-4 to assemble and install the windshield wiper assembly. Make certain the motor is in the automatic stop position when it is installed and that the linkage is not reversed. Apply a light coat of waterproof grease to each of the joints. When the installation is complete, check the operation of the wipers after wetting the windshield with water.

Washer Motor Removal/Installation (1973-1979)

1. Carefully pull the tube between the motor and the bag loose from the bag (**Figure 69**). Disconnect the electrical plug.
2. Remove the clips which hold the flap to the bag (**Figure 70**). Pull the motor down and disconnect the outlet line.
3. Reverse these steps to install a new motor and pump.

Front Wiper Motor Removal/Installation (1980-on)

Refer to **Figure 71** for this procedure.

1. Remove the cover from the end of the wiper arm and unscrew the wiper arm attaching nut.

7

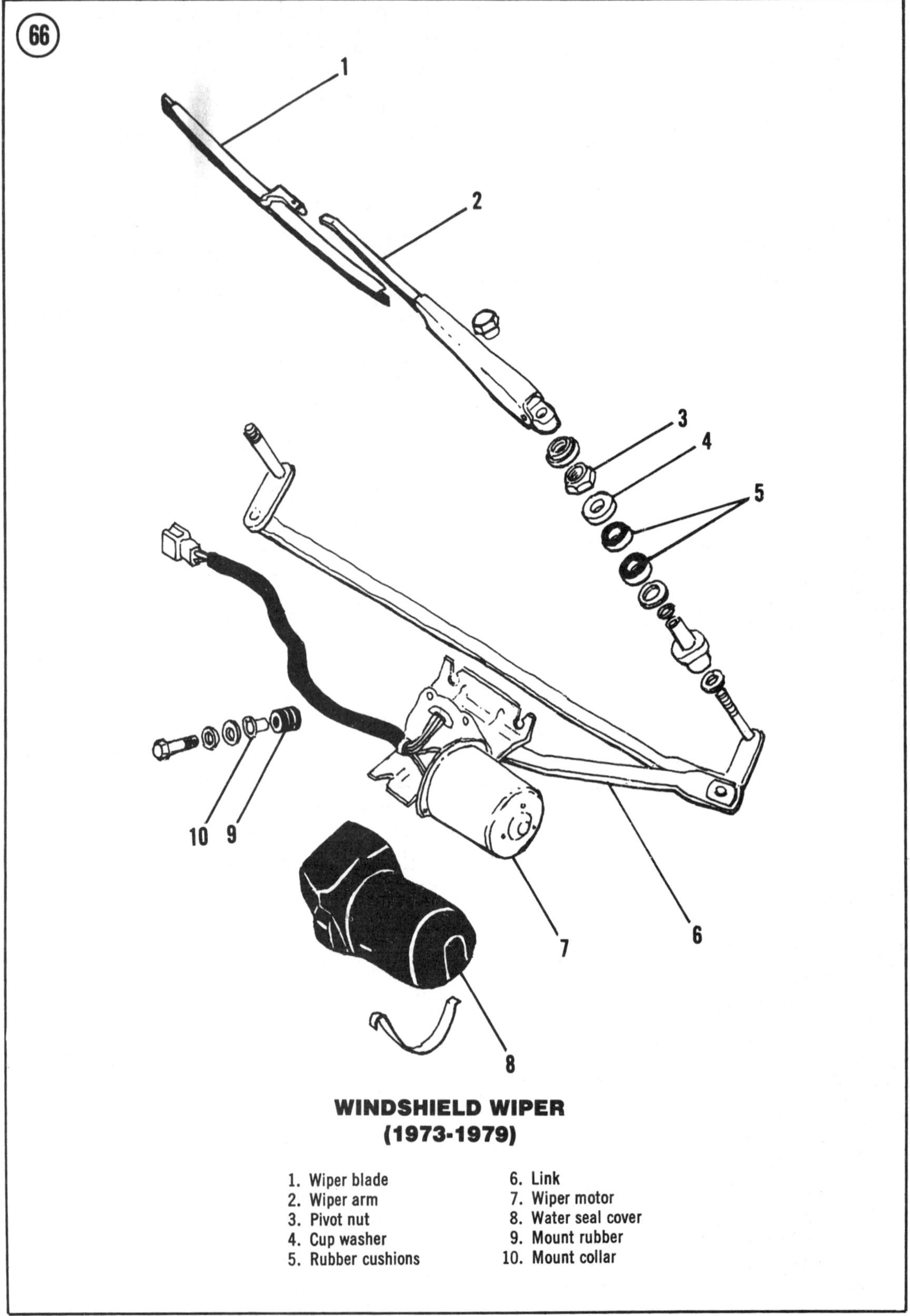

WINDSHIELD WIPER (1973-1979)

1. Wiper blade
2. Wiper arm
3. Pivot nut
4. Cup washer
5. Rubber cushions
6. Link
7. Wiper motor
8. Water seal cover
9. Mount rubber
10. Mount collar

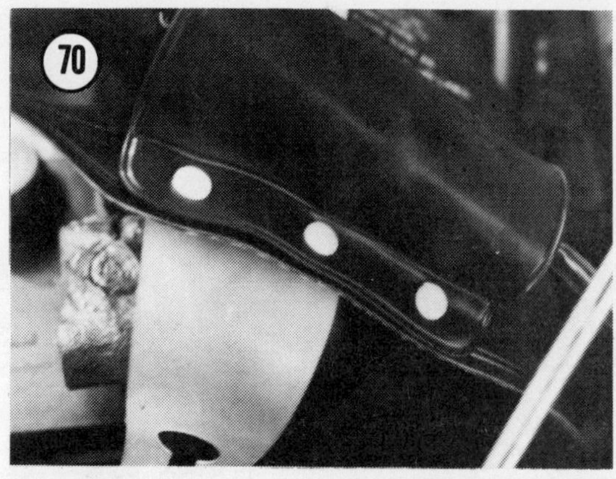

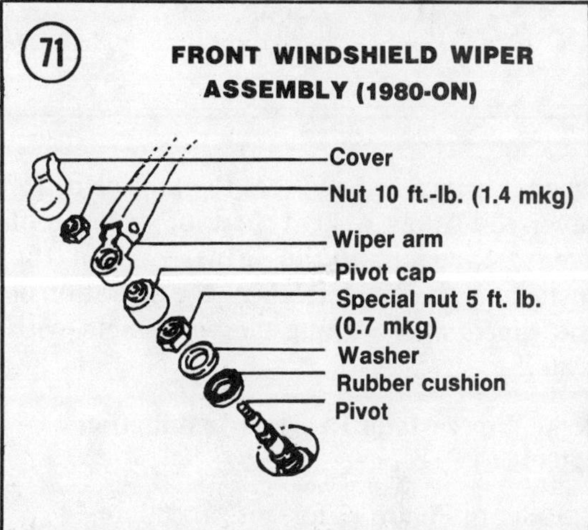

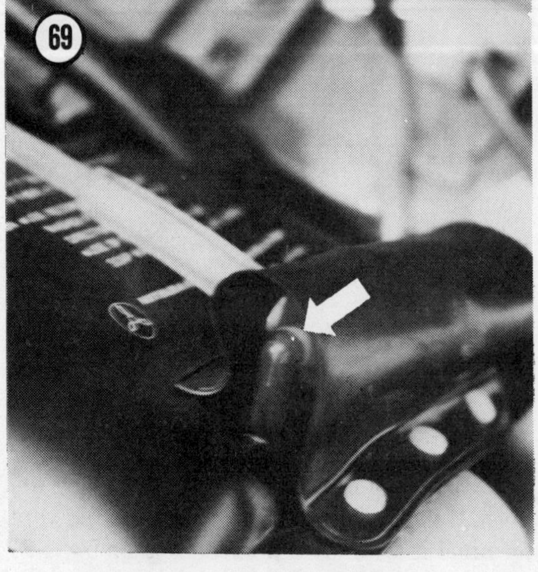

Lift the wiper arm up and remove from the pivot cap. Then remove the pivot cap, nut, washer and rubber cushion.

2. Open the hood and remove the air scoop and hood seal.

3. Referring to **Figure 72**, remove the linkage arm-to-motor attaching nut. Then remove the wiper motor mounting nuts, pull the linkage arm to disconnect from the wiper motor and remove the wiper motor from the car. Remove the linkage arm.

4. Carefully check the linkage joints for wear, looseness or binding. Stiff linkage may well have been the cause of the motor's failure. Check the pivot collars on the pivot shafts for looseness or binding. If their condition is in doubt, replace them.

5. Reverse Steps 1-3 to assemble and install the windshield wiper assembly. Make certain the motor is in the automatic stop position

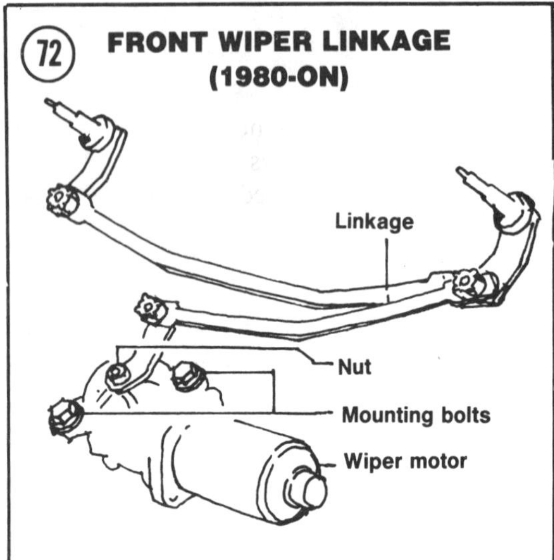

when it is installed and that the linkage is not reversed. Apply a light coat of waterproof grease to each of the joints. When the installation is complete, check the operation of the wipers after wetting the windshield with water.

Rear Wiper Motor Removal/Installation (1980-on)

Refer to **Figure 73** for this procedure.

1. Open the rear hood and remove the tailgate trim panel to expose the wiper motor assembly.
2. Remove the cover from the end of the wiper arm and unscrew the wiper arm attaching nut. Lift the wiper arm up and remove from the outside of the rear hood.
3. From inside the rear hood, disconnect the wiper motor electrical connector. Then remove the motor mounting bolts and remove the wiper motor.
4. Carefully check the linkage joints for wear, looseness or binding. Stiff linkage may well have been the cause of the motor's failure. Check the pivot collars on the pivot shafts for looseness or binding. If their condition is in doubt, replace them.
5. Reverse Steps 1-3 to assemble and install the windshield wiper assembly. Apply a light coat of waterproof grease to each of the joints. When the installation is complete, check the operation of the wipers after wetting the windshield with water.

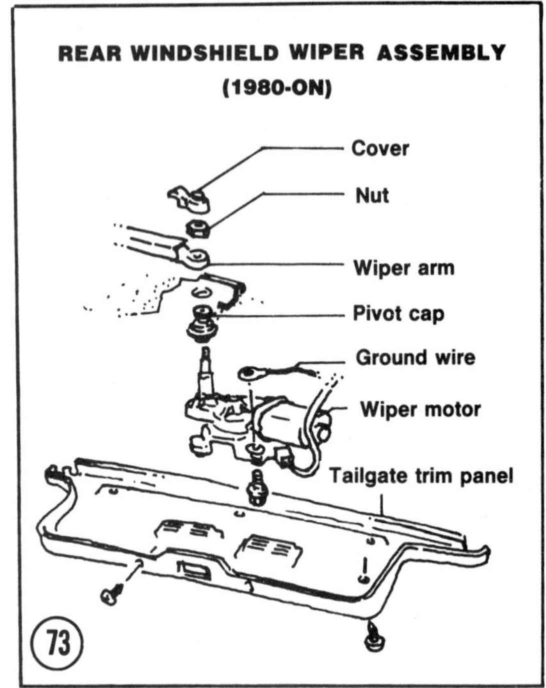

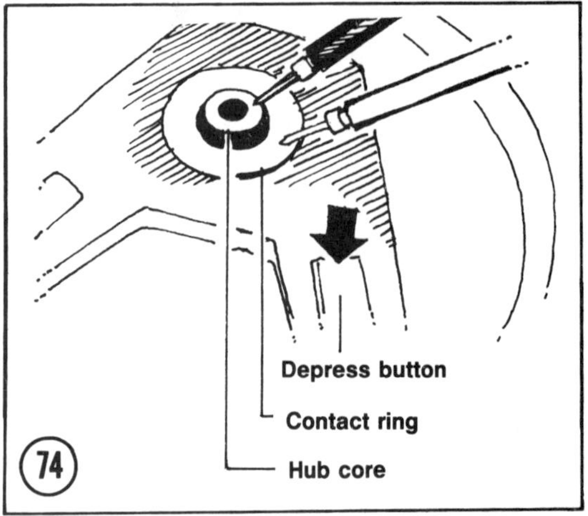

HORN

Testing (1973-1979 Models)

1. Check horn fuse (**Figure 43**) and replace if required.
2. Locate the horn electrical connector at the horn. Disconnect the connector and ground the blue/red wire terminal pin using a jumper cable. If the horn does not blow, replace the horn. If the horn blows when the blue/red wire terminal is grounded, proceed to Step 3.

3. Using a 12-volt test light or voltmeter, check for voltage at the horn connector in the engine compartment. Interpret results as follows:

   a. Voltage present: Attach an ohmmeter between the blue/red horn connector wire and ground. Then press the horn button and check for continuity. If no continuity is shown, check for an open circuit between the horn button and horn unit.
   b. No voltage: Check for an open circuit between the white/green horn connector wire and the fuse box.

Testing (1980-on)

1. Check fuse (**Figure 44**) and replace if necessary.
2. Locate the horn electrical connector at the horn. Disconnect the connector and ground the blue/red wire terminal pin using a jumper cable. If the horn does not blow, replace the horn. If the horn blows when the blue/red wire terminal is grounded, proceed to Step 3 to test the horn button.
3. Remove the steering wheel (Chapter Ten). Lay the steering wheel on a bench as shown in **Figure 74**. Place one ohmmeter probe onto the contact ring and the other on the hub core. Press the horn button and check for continuity. If continuity is shown, proceed to Step 4. If not, have a Honda dealer replace the horn button.
4. Using a 12-volt test light or voltmeter, check for voltage at the white/green fuse to horn wire. If no voltage is shown, check the white/green wire for an open circuit.

Tables are on the following pages.

Table 1 BATTERY CHARGE PERCENTAGE

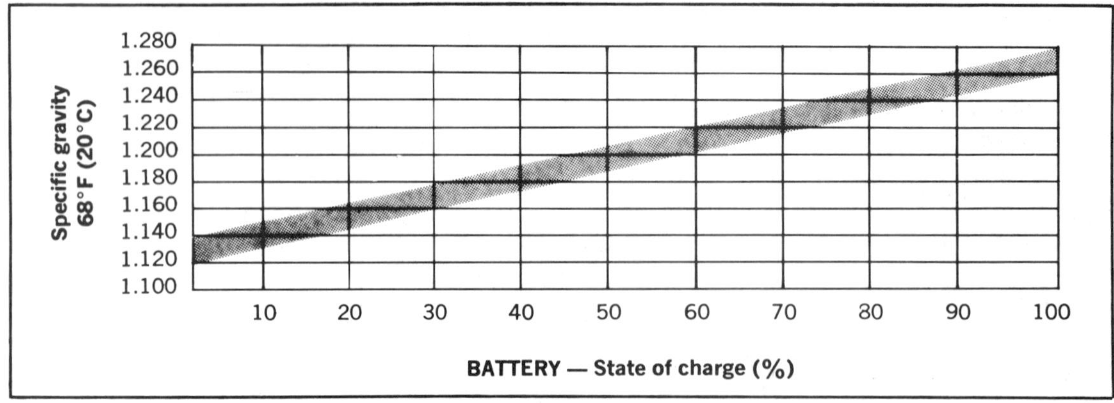

Table 2 CONNECTOR LOCATION

Connector	Location
1975-1979 CVCC:	
J55/P55	Engine compartment behind battery
J1/P1	Under right side dash
J4/P4 & J5/P5	Right side door, forward post area
J18/P18	Under dash near instrument cluster
J21/P21	Under dash near steering column
J47/P47	Under left-side dash
J81/P81	Engine compartment (left-hand side)
J82	Alternator connector
J96/P96	Under dash near steering column
J7/P7 & J7A/P7A	Under right-side dash
J126/P126	Center shift console
1980-on CVCC:	
J69/P69	Under left-side dash, above gauges
J27/P27	Right fender in engine compartment
J45/P45	Left front corner of engine compartment
J44/P44	Alternator
J126/P126	Under left-side dash, behind combination meter
J14/P14	Under left-side dash, near ignition switch
J74/P74	Starter

Table 3 STARTER SPECIFICATIONS

Item	Standard		Wear limit	
	mm	in.	mm	in.
1973-1979 Non-CVCC				
Mica depth	0.5-0.8	0.0197-0.0315	0.2	0.0079
Commutator				
Runout	0		0.08	0.003
Out-of-round	33	1.2992	32	1.2598

(continued)

Table 3 STARTER SPECIFICATIONS (continued)

Item	Standard mm	Standard in.	Wear limit mm	Wear limit in.
1973-1979 Non-CVCC (continued)				
Brush length	16	0.623	4	0.157
1975-1979 CVCC				
Mica depth	Not specified; see Honda dealer			
Commutator				
Runout	0.05	0.0020		
Diameter	29	1.14		
Brush length	14.5	0.571	10	0.39
1980-on Nippondenso (0.8 kW)				
Mica depth	0.4-0.8	0.02-0.03	0.2	0.01
Commutator				
Runout (maximum)	0-0.05	0-0.002	0.3	0.01
Diameter (minimum)	27.9-28.0	1.098-1.102	27.0	1.06
Brush length	15.5-16.5	0.61-0.65	10	0.39
1980-on Nippondenso (0.9 kW)				
Mica depth	0.4-0.8	0.02-0.03	0.2	0.01
Commutator				
Runout	0-0.02	0-0.001	0.5	0.02
Diameter	29.9-30.0	1.177-1.181	29.0	1.14
Brush length	12.5-13.5	0.49-0.53	8.5	0.33
1980-On Hitachi				
Mica depth	0.5-0.8	0.02-0.03	0.2	0.01
Commutator				
Runout	0-0.01	0-0.004	0.4	0.02
Diameter	32.7-33.0	1.29-1.30	32.0	1.26
Brush length	15.5-16.5	0.61-0.65	12	0.47

Table 4 IGNITION COIL SPECIFICATIONS*

Year	Secondary Resistance (Ohms)	Primary Resistance (Ohms)
Non-CVCC		
1973	6,400-9,600	3.42-4.18
1974-1977	8,160-12,240	1.0-1.5
1978-1979	6,800-10,200	1.0-1.5
CVCC		
1975-1979	8,000-12,000	1.35-1.65
1980-on	7,400-11,000	1.0-1.3

* Measured at 70° F (20° C).

7

NOTE: If you own a 1982 or later model, first check the Supplement at the back of the book for any new service information.

CHAPTER EIGHT

CLUTCH

The Civic clutch is a single dry-disc type with a diaphragm spring. The major components are the disc, pressure plate, release mechanism and linkage. See **Figure 1**. The disc has friction material riveted to both facings. Coil springs in the center of the disc absorb shock and make clutch engagement smooth. The release mechanism, consisting of a release lever, arm and bearing, engages and disengages the clutch. The release mechanism is controlled through a pedal-operated cable.

Clutch specifications are in **Table 1** at the end of the chapter.

CLUTCH ADJUSTMENT

Clutch adjustment is necessary to take up slack in the clutch linkage caused by release bearing and disc wear. The linkage should be adjusted whenever the clutch fails to disengage completely and also when new parts are installed.

NOTE
Before making any clutch adjustment, check the brake pedal height and free play adjustment to make sure they are within specification and adjust if necessary as described in Chapter Twelve. This is necessary because the clutch pedal height is set to the approximate height of the brake pedal.

Adjustment (Non-CVCC)

1. Compare the clutch pedal height with that of the brake pedal. It should be approximately the same height. To adjust, loosen the locknut on the pedal adjuster beneath the dashboard and turn the adjuster in or out as required. When the clutch pedal height is correct, hold the adjuster to prevent it from turning and tighten the locknut.

2. Clutch pedal free play is measured at the release lever in the engine compartment (**Figure 2**). Normal free play is 3-4 mm (1/8-5/32 in.). Measure the actual play with a caliper and adjust it if necessary by loosening the locknut and turning the adjuster nut clockwise or counterclockwise as required. Hold the adjuster to prevent it from turning further once the adjustment is correct and tighten the locknut.

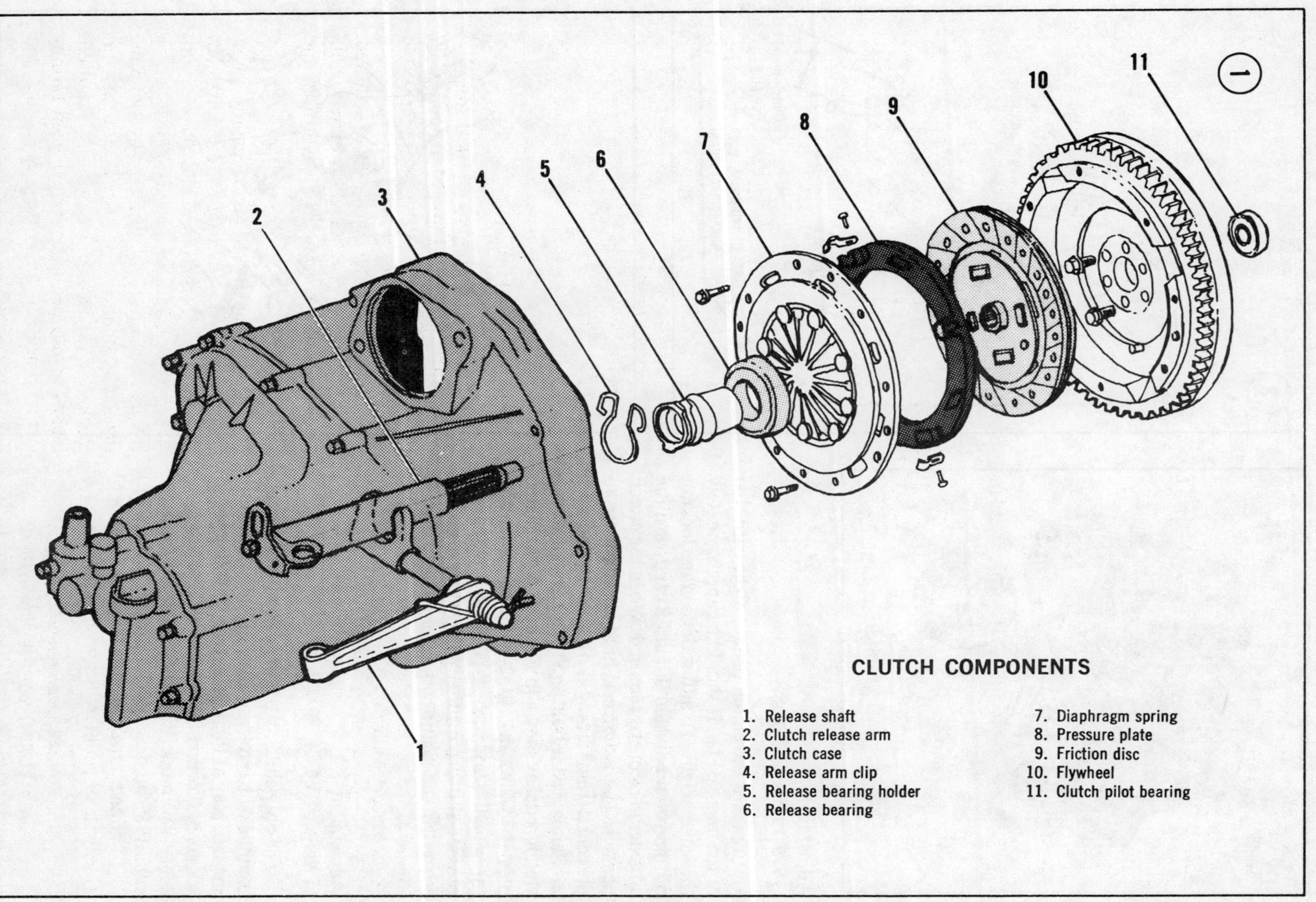

CLUTCH COMPONENTS

1. Release shaft
2. Clutch release arm
3. Clutch case
4. Release arm clip
5. Release bearing holder
6. Release bearing
7. Diaphragm spring
8. Pressure plate
9. Friction disc
10. Flywheel
11. Clutch pilot bearing

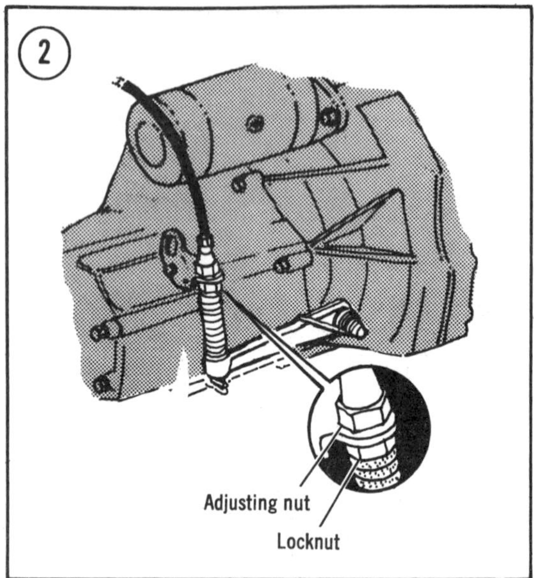

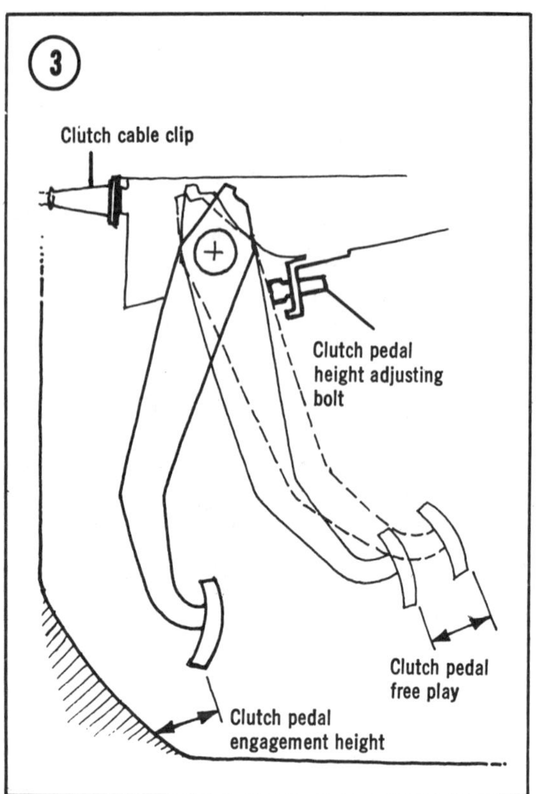

Adjustment (1975-1979 CVCC)

1. Compare the clutch pedal height with that of the brake pedal. It should be approximately the same height. To adjust, loosen the locknut on the pedal adjuster (**Figure 3**) and turn the adjuster in or out as required. When the clutch pedal height is correct, hold the adjuster to prevent it from turning and tighten the locknut.
2. Clutch pedal free play is measured at the clutch pedal as shown in **Figure 3**. Normal free play is 15-20 mm (19/32-25/32 in.). Measure the actual play with a ruler and adjust by moving the clip on the clutch cable near the firewall in the engine compartment as shown in **Figure 4**.

Adjustment (1980-on CVCC)

The only clutch adjustment on these models is at the clutch release arm. To check, measure the free play at the release arm as indicated in **Figure 5**. Normal free play is as follows:

a. 1980 models: 3-4 mm (1/8-5/32 in.).
b. 1981 models: 4.4-5.5 mm (7/16-9/16 in.)

To adjust, turn the adjusting nut (**Figure 5**) clockwise or counterclockwise as required.

NOTE
Correct clutch pedal free play is 10-30 mm (3/8-1 3/16 in.). However, there is

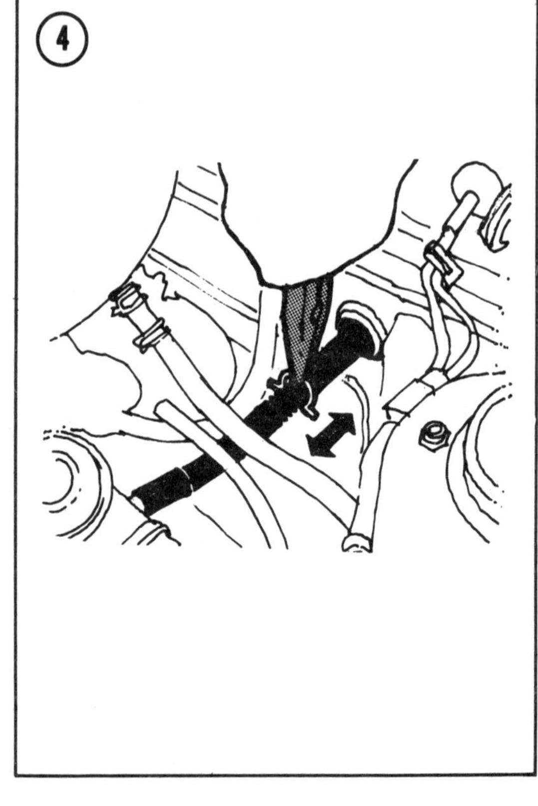

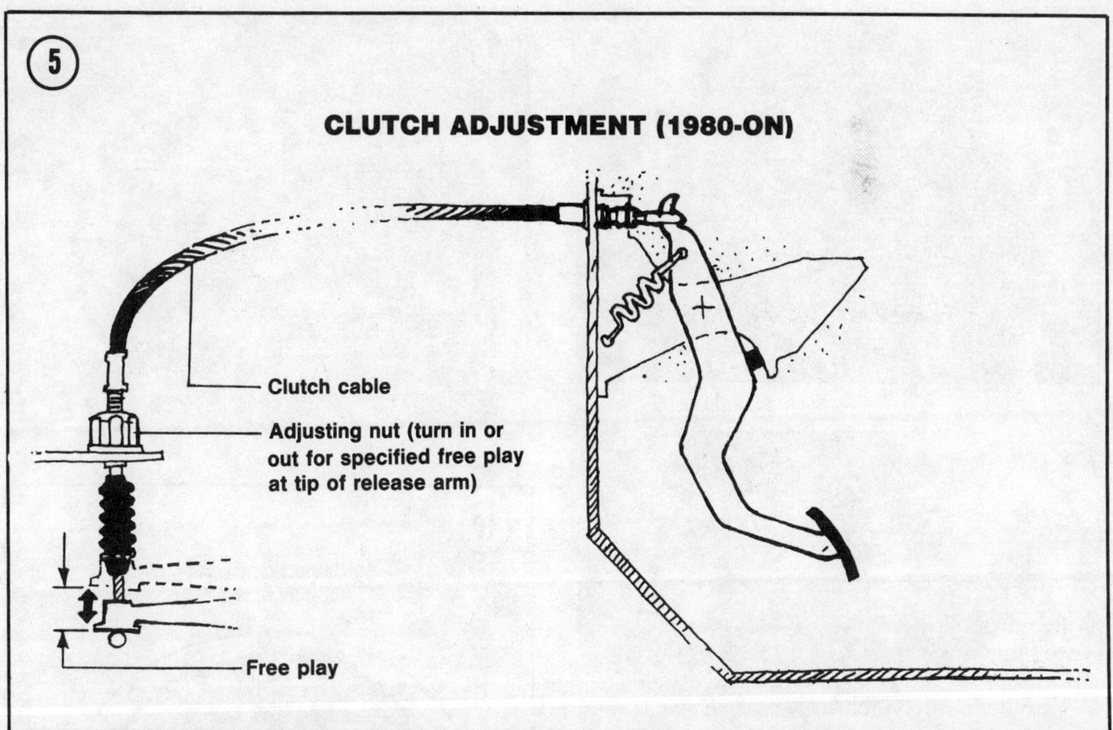

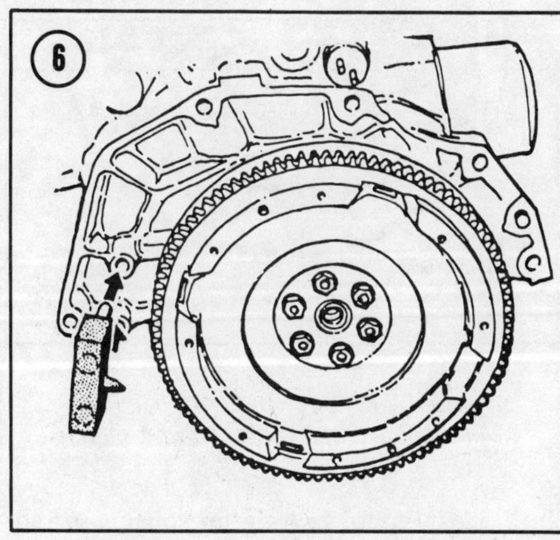

no free play adjustment provided. If the free play is incorrect, check clutch pedal and assembly for possible damage or missing parts.

CLUTCH CABLE REPLACEMENT

1. On all non-CVCC and 1980-on models, loosen the locknut on the cable adjuster and screw the adjuster in until the end of the cable can be disconnected from the clutch arm. On 1975-1979 CVCC models, remove the clip from the clutch cable and disconnect the cable from the clutch arm.
2. From inside the driver's compartment, disconnect the clutch pedal return spring. Then disconnect the cable end from the clutch pedal. Pull the cable and sheath out of the firewall and disconnect it from the bracket (if so equipped).
3. Reverse the above steps to install a new cable. Make sure the rubber grommet is completely seated in the opening in the firewall. Adjust the cable free play and pedal height as described in this chapter.

CLUTCH SERVICE

Removal

1. Remove the transaxle as described in Chapter Nine. Install the Honda flywheel holding tool on the engine bellhousing (**Figure 6**). Flywheel holding tool part numbers for different models are:
   a. 1973-1979 Non-CVCC: part No. 07924-6340100
   b. 1975-1978 CVCC: part No. 07924-6570000
   c. 1979-On CVCC: part No. 07924-6340100

8

2. Unscrew the clutch mounting bolts 2 turns each, in a circular pattern to prevent warping the diaphragm (**Figure** 7). When all the bolts have been loosened enough to relax the diaphragm spring, unscrew them completely and remove the pressure plate and clutch disc.
3. If required, unscrew the retractor screws as shown in **Figure 8** and disassemble the pressure plate and the diaphragm spring.

Inspection

1. Check for oil leakage through the rear engine main bearing seal and the transaxle drive seal. Replace these seals if leakage is found.
2. Clean the friction surface of the flywheel with a non-petroleum base cleaner such as alcohol or lacquer thinner. Check the surface for cracks or scores. Light scoring and scratches can be removed with fine emery paper, but if the damage is severe, the flywheel should be resurfaced by an automotive machine shop or be replaced.

CAUTION

If the facings are contaminated with grease, find and eliminate the source before replacing the disc. Otherwise, the cleaned or new disc will become contaminated and could fail in a short time.

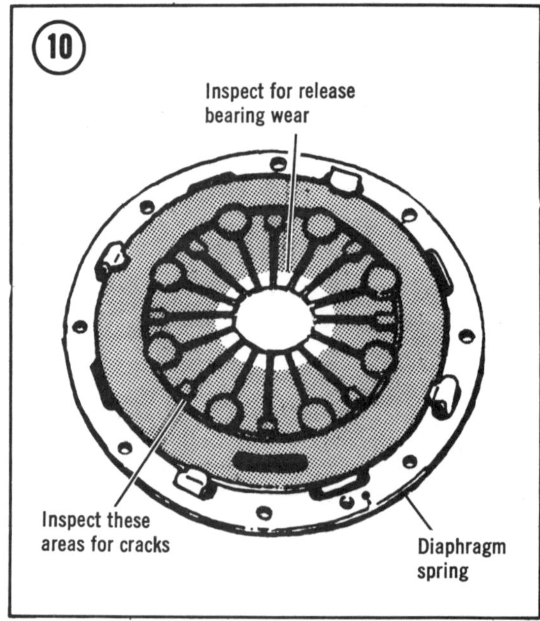

3. Check the pilot bearing for roughness and slop (**Figure 9**). The bearing should turn easily and smoothly. If there is any doubt about its condition, replace it.
4. Check the clutch diaphragm spring fingers for wear, bending or damage. Inspect the end of the fingers carefully (**Figure 10**) for wear caused by the release bearing and replace the diaphragm if the bearing wear groove is more than 0.3 mm (0.0012 in.) deep.
5. Inspect the pressure plate contact surface for cracks, wear or burning marks. Minor

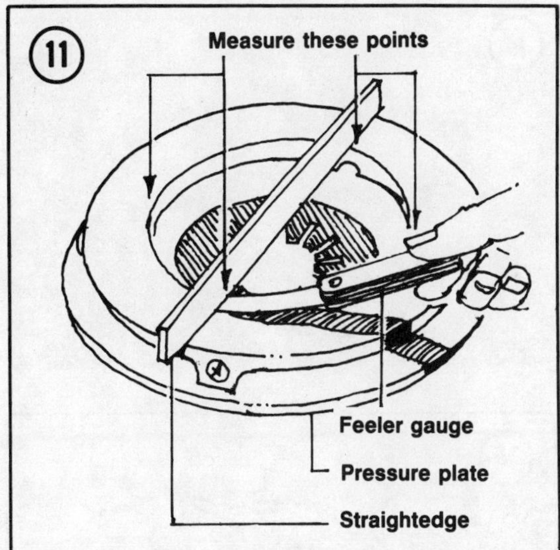

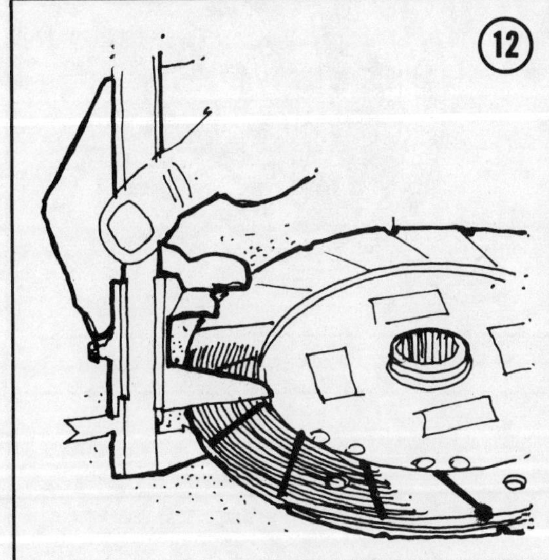

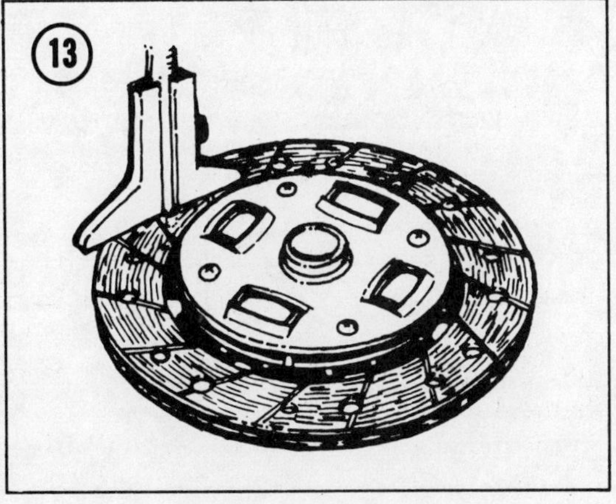

scratches may be removed with No. 500 or 600 emery paper.

6. Check the pressure plate for taper or warpage using a straightedge and feeler gauge at the points indicated in **Figure 11**. Replace the pressure plate if the taper exceeds 0.05 mm (0.002 in.) on 1973-1979 models or 0.15 mm (0.006 in.) on 1980 and later models.

7. Check the clutch disc for oil, grease or glaze on the friction surface. Also look for missing or loose rivets and broken springs. The disc must be replaced if any of these conditions is found. The clutch disc should also be replaced if a new pressure plate is being installed.

8. Measure the clutch disc thickness using a caliper as shown in **Figure 12**. Refer to **Table 1** for specifications and replace the disc if out of specification.

9. The clutch disc rivet hole depth can be measured with a depth gauge as shown in **Figure 13**. Measure each rivet depth and compare to specifications (**Table 1**). Replace the disc if any one rivet depth exceeds specifications.

10. Check the release bearing as described in this chapter. Never reuse a release bearing unless necessary. When other clutch parts are worn, the bearing is probably worn. If it is necessary to reuse an old bearing, do not wash it in solvent; wipe it clean with a dry cloth.

Installation

1. Be sure your hands are clean.

2. Inspect the disc facings, pressure plate and flywheel to be sure they are free of oil, grease or other foreign material.

3A. *1973-1979 models:* Assemble the pressure plate and diaphragm and install them on the flywheel. Line up the mark on the pressure plate with the mark on the flywheel to ensure that the balance is correct (**Figure 14**). Install all of the bolts finger-tight and set the clutch alignment tool in place (**Figure 15**, Honda part No. 07944-6340000).

3B. *1980-on models:* Install Honda alignment tool part No. 07944-6340000 into the flywheel. Then slide the clutch plate over the tool and against the flywheel. Install the pressure plate over the alignment tool and against the flywheel. Align holes in pressure plate with dowel pin in flywheel. Install the flywheel-to-pressure plate screws finger-tight.

NOTE
When the old pressure plate is being installed, make sure to align punch mark hole on flywheel with punch mark on pressure plate. New pressure plates have no punch or alignment marks.

4. Tighten the bolts 2 turns at a time in a crisscross pattern. Torque them as follows:
   a. 1973-1979: 1.0 mkg (7 ft.-lb.)
   b. 1980-on: 1.2 mkg (9 ft.-lb.)
5. Install the release mechanism and bend the tab washer over against one of the flats on the bolt after it has been tightened. Remove the aligning and flywheel holding tools. Grease the pilot bearing.
6. Reinstall the transaxle as described in Chapter Nine. Make sure the transaxle shaft and clutch splines line up before mating the transaxle to the engine. Also, make sure the alignment dowels in the transaxle are lined up with the holes in the engine bellhousing before tightening the transaxle mounting bolts.
7. When the transaxle has been installed, refer to the first part of this chapter and perform all

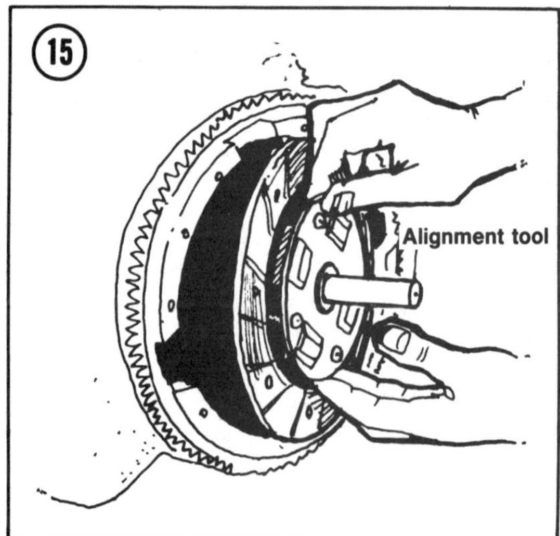

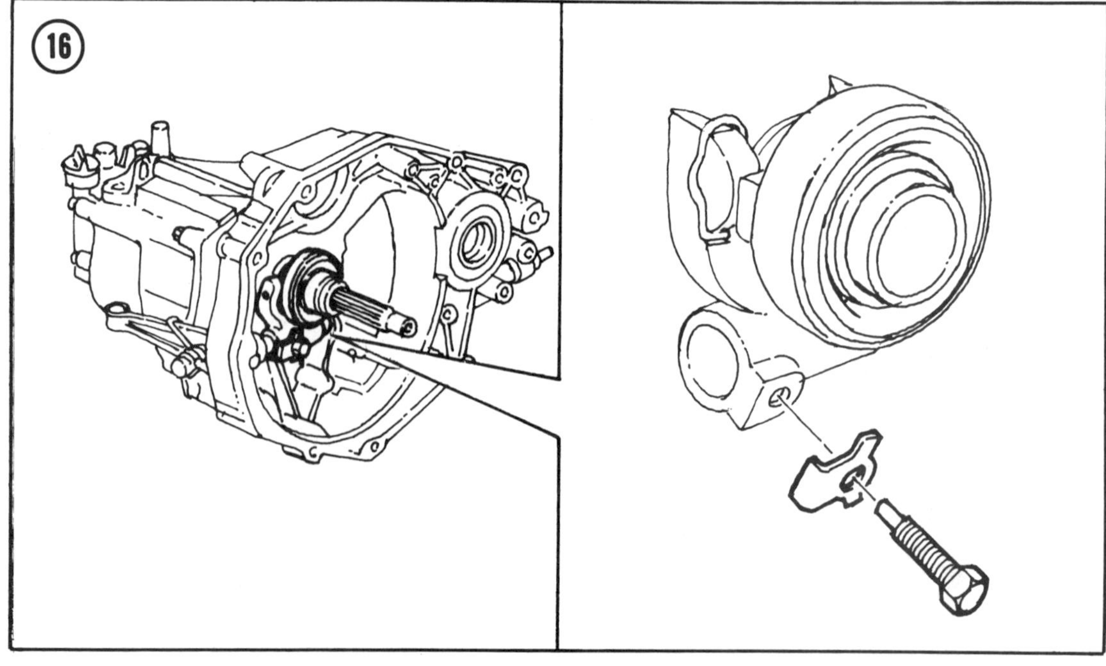

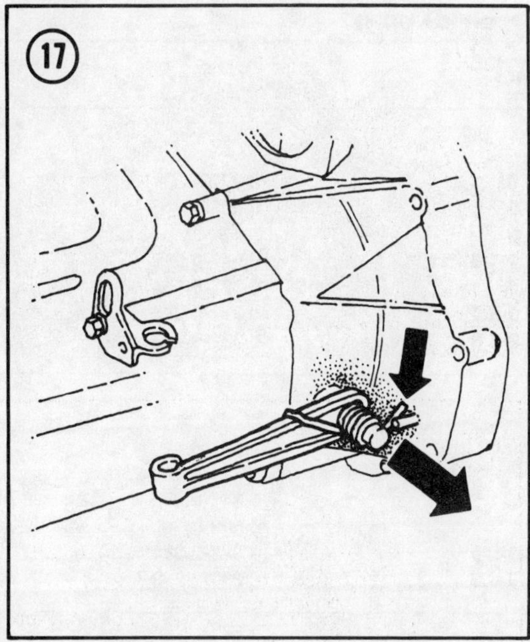

clutch adjustments. Check the clutch operation by test driving the car.

RELEASE MECHANISM

As with the clutch, removal of the release mechanism requires that the transaxle first be removed from the car. See Chapter Nine.

Removal/Disassembly

1. Straighten the tab washer on the clutch arm retaining bolt and unscrew the bolt (**Figure 16**).
2. Grasp the straight end of the clutch return spring with needlenose pliers, lift the spring over the stop peg and pull the clutch release shaft out of the case (**Figure 17**).
3. Separate the bearing from the arm, taking care not to bend the clip.

Inspection

1. Press the bearing against the holder and rotate it, feeling for roughness and wobble. If either exists, replace the bearing.
2. Check the bearing for grease; the bearing is sealed and the presence of grease on the outside indicates that it is no longer serviceable.

CAUTION
The release bearing is prelubricated and sealed. Do not clean it in solvent or it will be ruined. Clean it with a lint-free cloth.

3. If the bearing is to be replaced, a special removing/installing tool is required. Take the assembly to a Honda dealer and have the work done.

Assembly/Installation

1. Assemble the release bearing and holder with the release fork and clip. Lightly coat the bore of the bearing holder and the release fork with Molykote or equivalent lubricant.
2. Start the clutch release fork into the housing and push the release fork to seat its clip on the fork bolt. Install the pushrod in the release fork and install the return spring.
3. Install the transaxle in the car as described in Chapter Nine. When the installation is complete, refer to the first part of this chapter and adjust the clutch pedal free play and height. Road test the car and check the operation of the clutch.

Table is on the following page.

Table 1 CLUTCH SPECIFICATIONS

Item	mm	in.
1973-1979 Non-CVCC		
Pressure plate		
Runout	0.02	0.0012
Limit	0.05	0.0020
Friction disc		
Rivet depth	1.2-1.5	0.047-0.059
Limit	0.2	0.327-0.354
Thickness	8.3-9.0	0.327-0.354
Limit	5.9-6.6	0.232-0.259
1975-1979 CVCC		
Pressure plate		
Runout limit	0.04	0.0016
Friction disc		
Rivet depth	1.2-1.5	0.047-0.059
Limit	0.2	0.009
Thickness	8.3-9.0	0.327-0.354
Limit	5.9-6.6	0.232-0.259
1980-on CVCC		
Pressure plate		
Runout limit	0.15	0.006
Friction disc		
Rivet depth	1.3	0.05
Limit	0.2	0.008
Thickness	8.7-9.4	0.34-0.37
Limit	6.1	0.24

NOTE: If you own a 1982 or later model, first check the Supplement at the back of the book for any new service information.

CHAPTER NINE

TRANSAXLE

A transaxle is transversely mounted on the right side of the vehicle and connects directly to the engine. A transaxle is a complete unit consisting of all power transmitting components—clutch, gearbox, gears and differential—connected directly to the drive axles.

The Civic is equipped with a 4-speed, all-synchromesh transaxle as standard equipment. A 5-speed, all synchromesh transaxle and a 2-speed automatic (Hondamatic) transaxle are available as options. Contained in this chapter are removal, repair and installation procedures for the manual transaxles/differential. Service procedures for the Hondamatic transaxle include removal, installation and basic adjustment. Repair procedures on the Hondamatic should be entrusted to a dealer or qualified specialist.

Tables 1-7 at the end of the chapter contain specifications and tightening torques.

9

MANUAL TRANSAXLE

Removal/Installation

The transaxle assembly has been designed for removal from underneath the vehicle. Jackstands, the normal home mechanic support fixture (described in Chapter Two), would not provide the mechanic with the necessary room or *safety* to remove the transaxle. To complete the following procedures, it is necessary for the car to be lifted and secured by a commercial type hoist. If the use of a hoist is not available, the engine can be removed as described in Chapter Four with the transaxle attached. The transaxle can then be separated from the engine and all necessary work performed.

1. Shift the transaxle into NEUTRAL. Disconnect the battery ground cable at the battery (**Figure 1**) and the transaxle housing.

2. Disconnect the following engine compartment wiring connectors:

a. Starter motor positive battery cable.

b. Backup light switch at transaxle case (**Figure 2**).

c. Water temperature sending unit at engine.

d. Ignition timing thermosensor at engine.

3A. *1973-1979 non-CVCC:* Loosen the locknut on the clutch cable adjuster at the clutch housing and screw the adjuster in until the end of the clutch cable can be disconnected from the clutch arm (**Figure 3**).

3B. *1975-1979 CVCC:* Disconnect the clutch cable outer cable circlip at the firewall (**Figure 4**) and the inner clutch cable at the clutch arm.

3C. *1980-on CVCC:* Disconnect the clutch cable at the release arm.

4. Remove the starter bolt threading into the transaxle housing. Then remove the top transaxle mounting bolt.

5. Remove the front engine strut mounting bolt (**Figure 5**).

6. *1980-on:* Pull up the speedometer cable rubber boot (**Figure 6**). Then remove the speedometer cable clip and pull the cable out of the speedometer gear holder (**Figure 7**). Do not remove the speedometer gear holder.

7. Raise the vehicle on a commercial hoist. See introduction to this *Removal* procedure.

WARNING

Do not attempt to remove the transaxle from beneath the vehicle if supporting the car with jackstands. Jackstands do

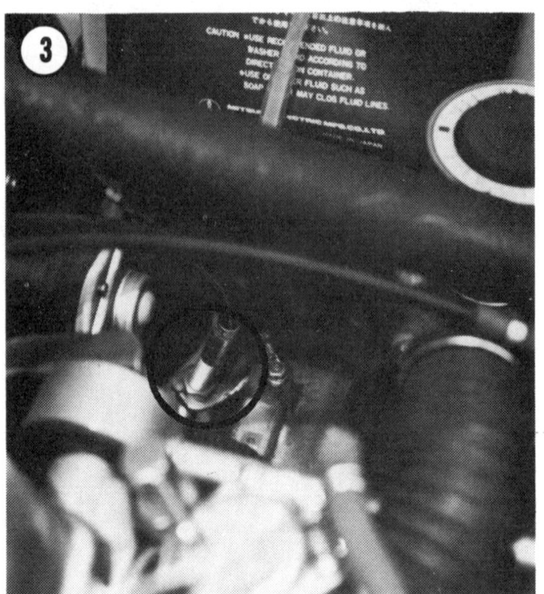

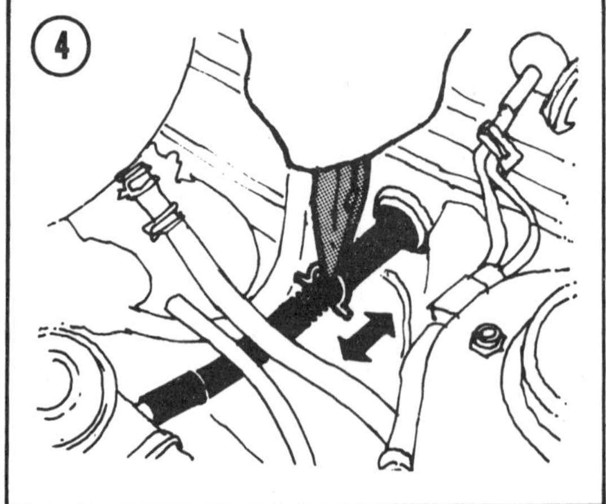

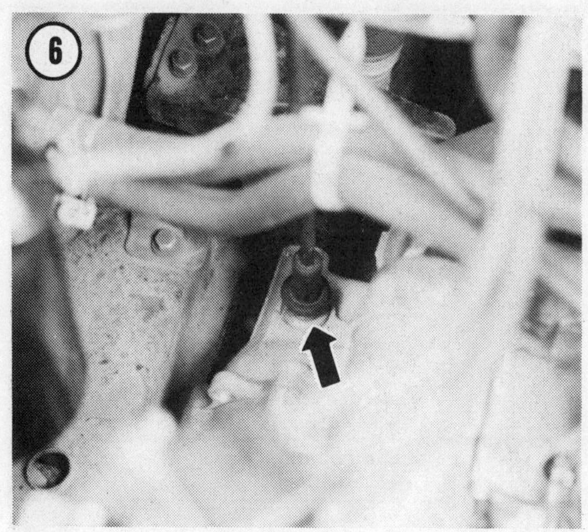

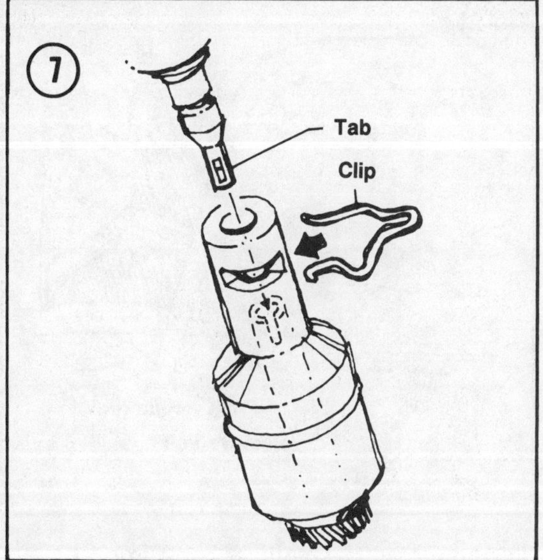

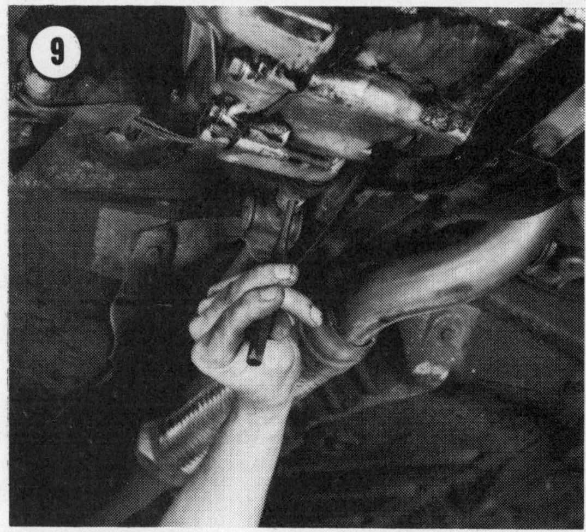

not provide the safety or working area required by this method.

8. Remove the front wheels.
9. Remove the transaxle drain plug (**Figure 8**) and drain the transaxle oil. Install the drain plug, using a new aluminum washer/gasket.

NOTE
Steps 10-16 describe removal procedures for 1973-1979 models. Removal procedures for 1980 and later models begin with Step 17.

10. Remove the right-side fender well shield.
11. If the speedometer cable is secured with a clip, slide up the rubber boot (**Figure 6**), remove the clip (**Figure 7**) and pull the cable out of the holder. It the speedometer cable is secured with a bolt, remove the bolt and pull the cable out of the transaxle, taking care not to drop the pin that holds the drive gear and collar in place.
12. Disconnect the transaxle stopper bracket at the front of the clutch housing and disconnect the lower torque rod at transaxle.
13. With a drift, drive the pin out of the gearshift rod and disconnect it from the transaxle. See **Figure 9**.
14. Using Honda tool part No. 07941-6340000, disconnect the lower control arm ball-joints from the right and left knuckles (**Figure 10**).
15. Screw an engine hanger bolt into the front torque rod-to-engine mount hole. Screw the other hanger bolt into the hole to the left of

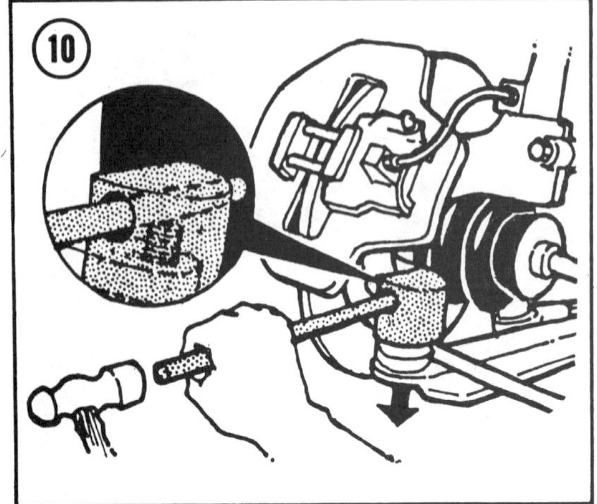

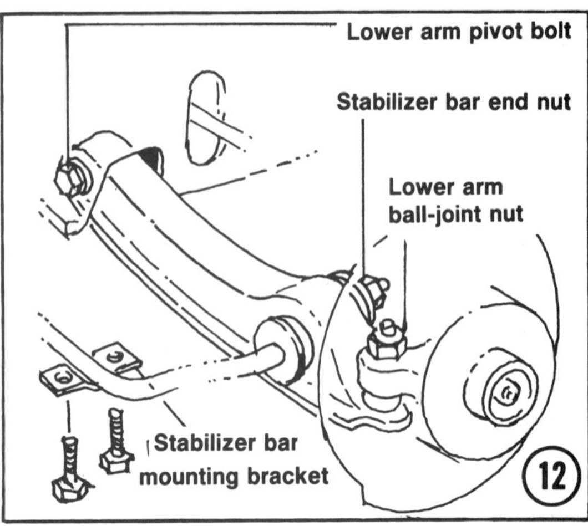

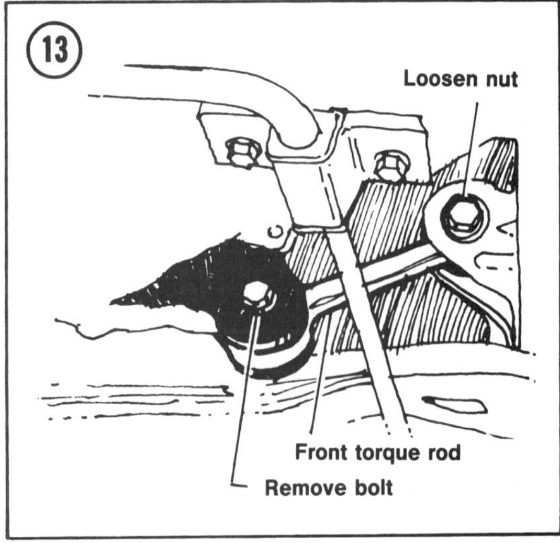

the distributor. Attach a chain to the hangers and raise the engine slightly with a chain hoist to take the engine load off the engine mounts.

16. Unscrew the bolts which attach the center beam to the engine (**Figure 11**). Unscrew the bolts which mount the center beam to the crossmembers and remove the center beam. Reinstall the center beam without the mount and lower the engine until it rests on the beam. Proceed to Step 27.

NOTE
Steps 17-26 describe transaxle removal procedures for 1980 and later models.

17. Remove the stabilizer bar mounting end nuts and washers and the mounting brackets. Then remove the stabilizer bar (**Figure 12**).

18. Remove the lower arm ball-joint pivot nut (leave the ball-joints connected).

19. Turn the right-side steering knuckle outboard as far as it will go. Then place a screwdriver against the inboard CV joint and pry the right-side axle housing out of the transaxle 1/2 inch to force the axle spring clip out of the differential gear groove. The axle can now be pulled all the way out of the transaxle. Repeat for opposite side, making sure to turn the left side steering knuckle outboard as far as possible.

20. Disconnect the shift lever torque rod at the clutch housing.

21. Slide the pin retainer back on the shift rod to gain access to the spring pin and drive the

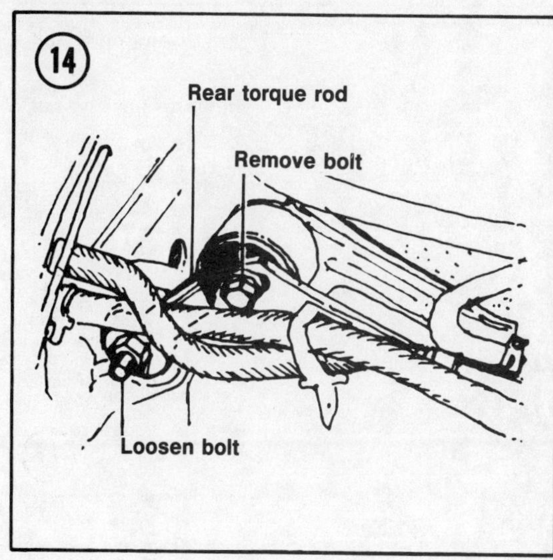

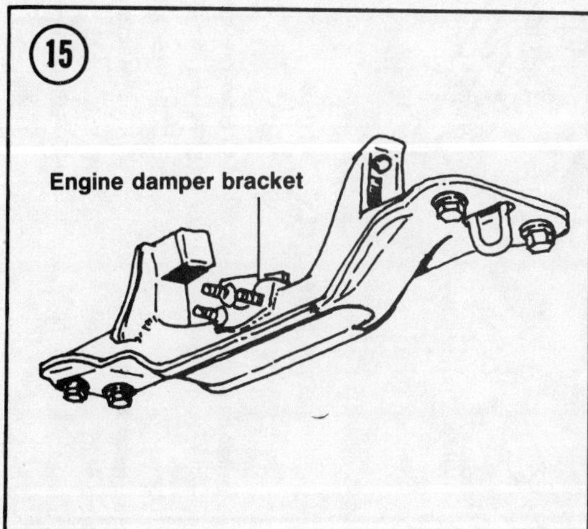

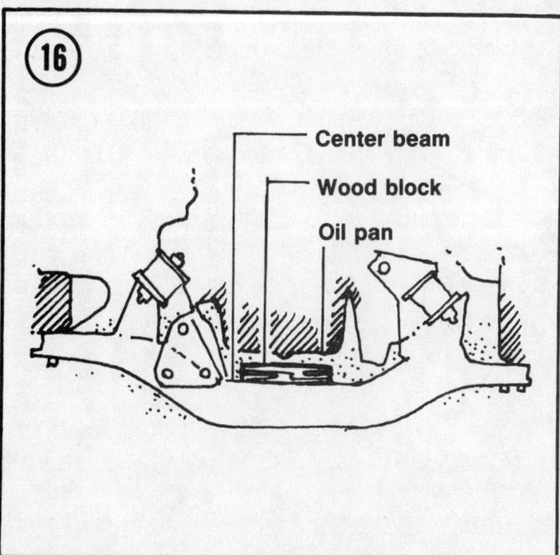

spring pin out using a punch. Disconnect the shift rod.

22. Place a flat piece of wood on a jack lifting pad. Then position the jack underneath the engine oil pan and lift the engine to remove weight from the engine mounts.

23. From inside the engine compartment, remove the front (**Figure 13**) and rear (**Figure 14**) engine torque rods. Then remove the rear torque rod brackets.

24. Referring to **Figure 15**, remove the engine damper bracket at the transaxle. Then remove the rear engine mount and bracket.

NOTE
Cut a piece of wood to the dimensions 1 in. x 2 in. x 4 in. before proceeding with Step 25.

25. Place the wood block (see NOTE above) on the center beam directly below the oil pan (**Figure 16**). Then slowly lower the jack and allow the engine oil pan to rest on the wood block.

26. Remove the starter engine-side mounting bolt. Then remove the starter from its position and lower down through the frame and remove.

NOTE
Step 27 completes transaxle removal for all models.

27. Place a rolling jack underneath the transaxle and elevate the jack head until it contacts the transaxle. Unscrew the remaining transaxle mounting bolts. With the jack supporting the transaxle, pull the transaxle away from the engine until the main shaft is clear of the clutch. Lower the transaxle with the jack and remove it from the car.

28. Installation is the reverse of these steps.

Disassembly

The initial steps for disassembling the 4-speed transaxle are different from those for the 5-speed transaxle. Beginning with Step 5, the disassembly, inspection and reassembly procedures are virtually the same. Where differences occur, they will be noted in the following procedures.

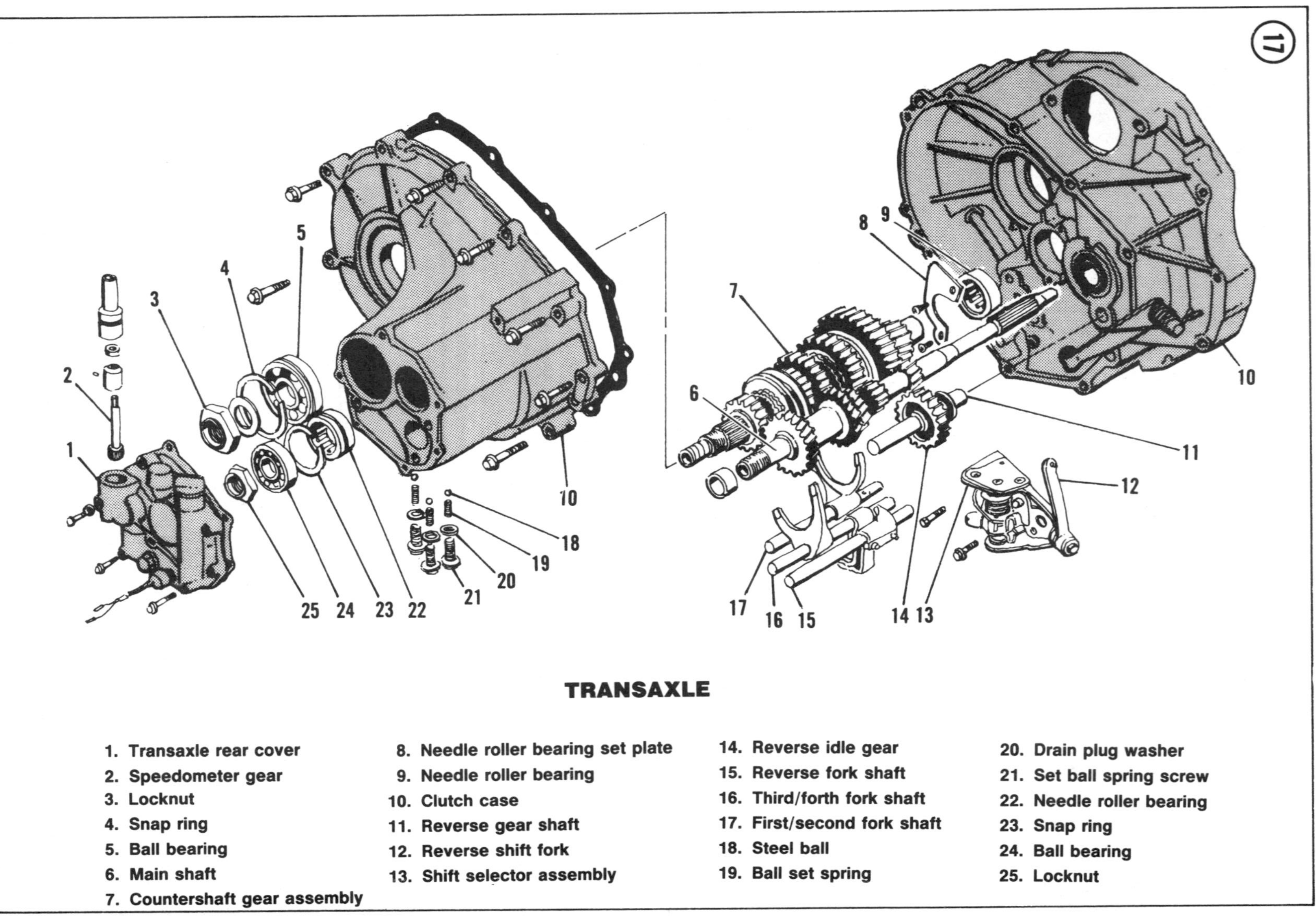
17
TRANSAXLE
1. Transaxle rear cover
2. Speedometer gear
3. Locknut
4. Snap ring
5. Ball bearing
6. Main shaft
7. Countershaft gear assembly
8. Needle roller bearing set plate
9. Needle roller bearing
10. Clutch case
11. Reverse gear shaft
12. Reverse shift fork
13. Shift selector assembly
14. Reverse idle gear
15. Reverse fork shaft
16. Third/forth fork shaft
17. First/second fork shaft
18. Steel ball
19. Ball set spring
20. Drain plug washer
21. Set ball spring screw
22. Needle roller bearing
23. Snap ring
24. Ball bearing
25. Locknut

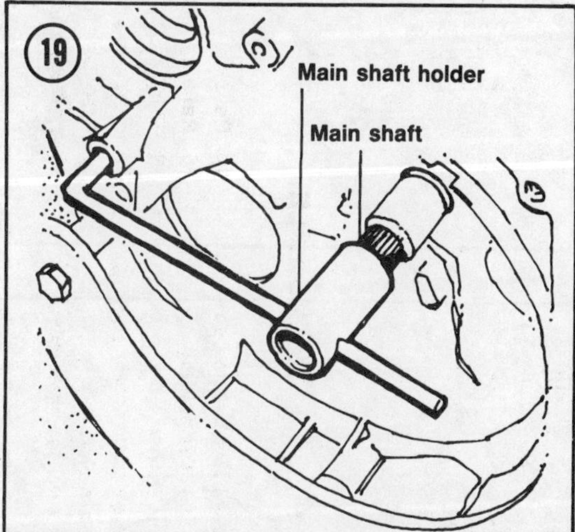

CAUTION
Disassembly and reassembly of the 4- and 5-speed transaxles require special tools and mechanical skills. If you have the necessary tools and skills, read this procedure and the inspection and assembly procedures which follow and make sure you understand every step before starting. If there is any portion of the procedure that you do not understand, and you cannot clear it up by studying the procedure steps and illustrations, it is advisable not to start, but to refer service to a Honda dealer or competent garage.

Refer to **Figure 17** when performing the following procedures.

NOTE
Steps 1-4 describe service procedures for 4-speed transaxles.

1. Unscrew the bolts from the transaxle end cover (**Figure 18**) and remove the cover from the clutch case. If the cover is stuck tight, hit it with a plastic hammer to break the gasket seal. *Do not* use a screwdriver to pry the cover off. The aluminum transaxle cases are relatively soft and the screwdriver can damage the cases and cause a leak.
2. Install the Honda main shaft holder (part No. 07924-6340300) onto the main shaft and secure as shown in **Figure 19**. Use a punch and bend back the main shaft lock tab which is bent into a slot in the main shaft (**Figure 20**). Remove the main shaft locknut.

CAUTION
The main shaft locknut has left-hand threads.

3. Using a universal bearing puller, remove the bearing from the end of the main shaft.
4. Referring to **Figure 21**, remove the retaining screw, spring and ball assemblies from the side of the transaxle housing. Store all parts in small bags.

NOTE
Steps 5-12 describe initial 5-speed transaxle disassembly procedures.

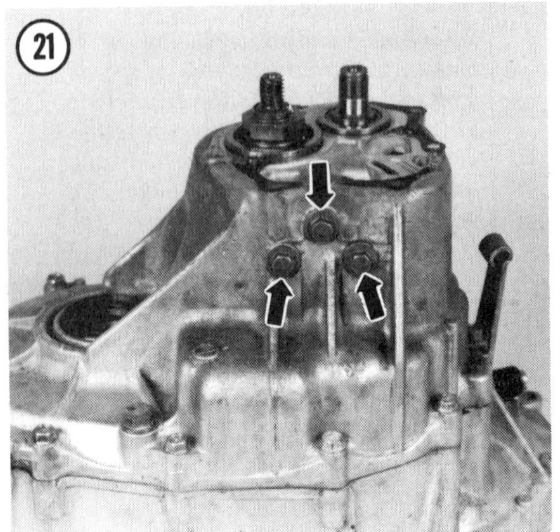

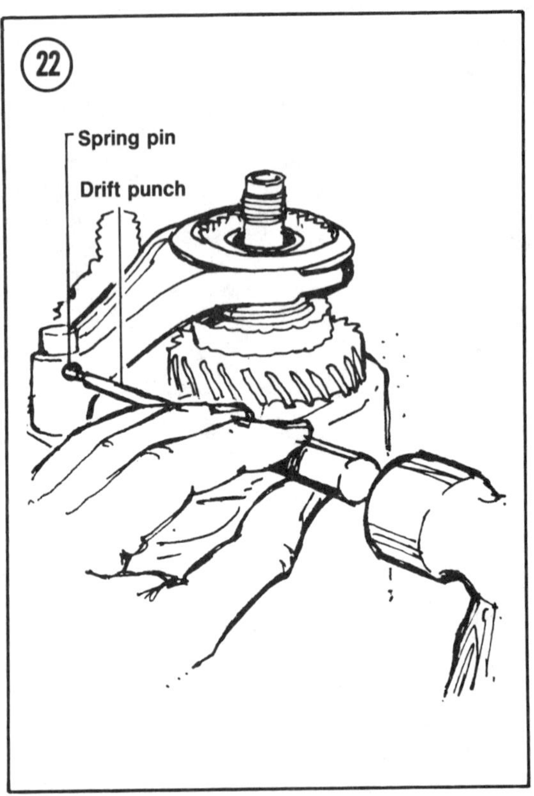

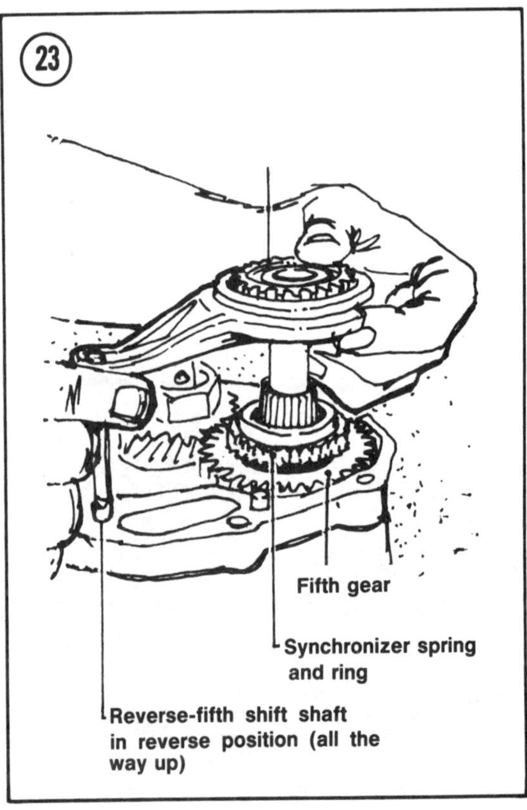

5. Unscrew the right-side end cover bolts and remove the end cover from the transaxle housing.
6. Remove the snap ring from the main shaft and remove the split collars (2) and the thrust washer.
7. Unscrew the bolts from the fifth gear housing and remove it. It may be necessary to break the cover loose by gently tapping around the mating surface with a plastic hammer. *Do not pry it off with a screwdriver or sharp tool.* Collect the hollow alignment dowels.
8. The fifth gear shift fork is secured with a spring pin. To remove the shift fork, first drive out spring pin using a small diameter drift punch (**Figure 22**). Slide the fifth gear shift fork, synchronizer sleeve and hub up and off shaft at same time (**Figure 23**).
9. Remove fifth gear and its needle bearing and thrust washer from the main shaft (**Figure 24**).
10. Remove the transaxle housing spacer (**Figure 25**) by tapping around the mating surface with a plastic hammer. Discard the gasket.
11. Remove the 3 detent bolts, spring and balls from the side of the transaxle housing (**Figure 21**). Store all parts separately in small bags.
12. Remove the snap rings from the countershaft and main bearings.

NOTE
Step 13 continues disassembly for both the 4- and 5-speed transaxles.

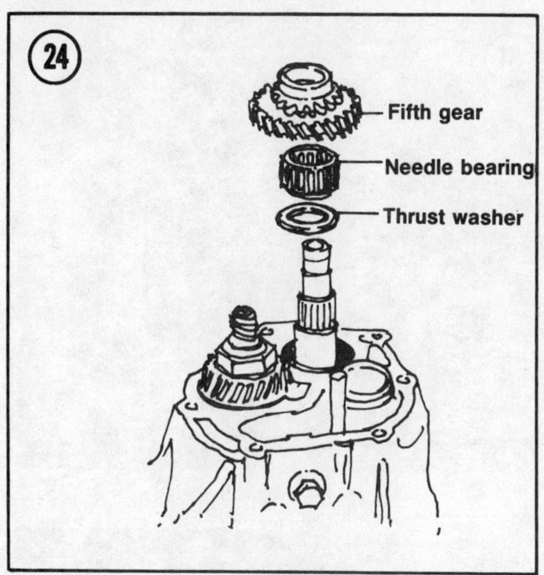

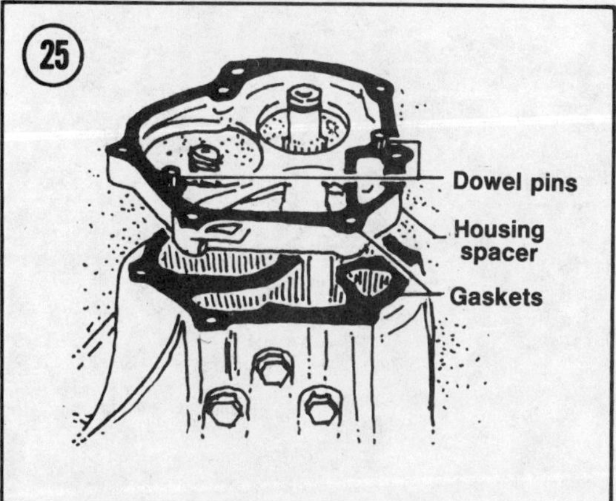

13. Remove the transaxle-to-clutch housing bolts. Separate the case halves by tapping lightly using a plastic hammer. Do not pry the cases apart with a screwdriver or other sharp tool; damage to the sealing surfaces could require expensive and unnecessary repair. Set the clutch housing down on the workbench with the gears facing up (**Figure 26**).

14. Pull the reverse idler gear and shaft out of the case (**Figure 27**).

15. Unscrew the nut which retains the reverse shift fork and remove the washer and fork from the shift selector (**Figure 28**).

16. *1980-on 5-speed:* Remove the reverse gear shift fork, detent ball and spring from the transaxle housing as shown in **Figure 29**. Store parts in a labeled bag.

17. Bend back the shift fork securing bolt lock tabs (**Figure 30**) and remove the bolts from the shift forks (**Figure 31**).

18. Pull the shift fork shafts out of the bores in the case and remove together with the shift forks. See **Figure 32**.

19. Pull the main shaft and countershaft out of the case half together (**Figure 33**). If shaft removal is difficult, tap the shafts from the back of the case as shown in **Figure 34** with a plastic hammer.

NOTE

*Before removing the countershaft locknut, proceed to the **Inspection** procedures in this section.*

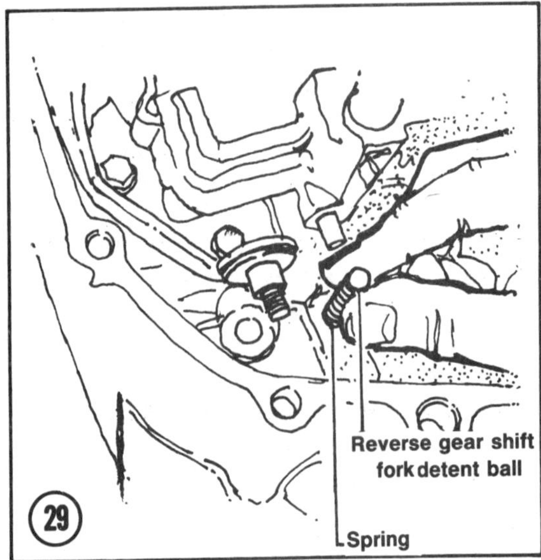
Reverse gear shift
fork detent ball
Spring

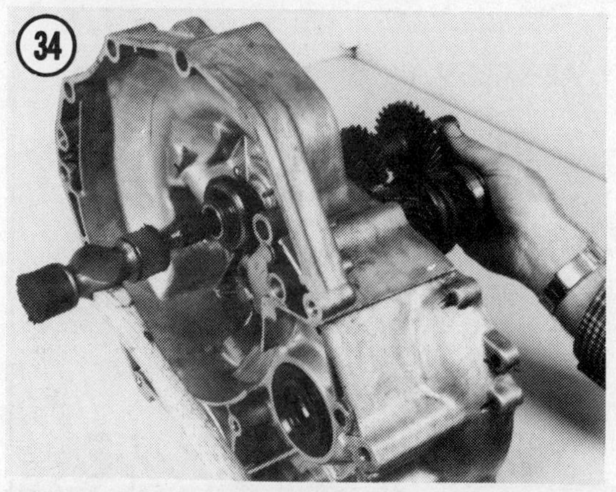
34

35

36

37

NOTE
Step 20 describes removal of the shift arm holder assembly.

20. Unscrew the shift arm holder bolts and remove the shift arm holder assembly from the transaxle housing (**Figure 35**).
21. While the transaxle is disassembled, it would be a good idea to remove the differential assembly (**Figure 36**) and check it at this time. See *Differential Removal/Disassembly* in this chapter.

General Transaxle Inspection

1. Thoroughly clean all parts, including the cases, in solvent. Remove all of the lubricant from the bearings by rotating them and rinsing them with solvent. As a general practice, the bearings and seals should be replaced whenever the transaxle is disassembled.
2. Rotate the bearings by hand and check for roughness, noise and play. Replace any bearings that are less than perfect.
3. Inspect the main shaft and countershaft for twisting, bending or damaged splines. Replace shafts with any of these defects.
4. Perform the *Countershaft Inspection/ Disassembly* and *Main Shaft Inspection/ Disassembly* procedures in this chapter.

Countershaft Inspection/Disassembly

Compare all measurements in this procedure to the specifications in **Table 1** (1973-1979 non-CVCC), **Table 2** (1975-1979 CVCC) or **Table 3** (1980-on CVCC). If any measurement is out of specification, the countershaft must be disassembled and the thrust washers or spacers replaced. **Figure 37** shows the countershaft and gears. **Figure 38** is an exploded view.

1. Using a feeler gauge, perform the following clearance measurements:
   a. Clearance between first gear and thrust washer (**Figure 39**).
   b. Clearance between second gear and spacer plate.
   c. Clearance between third gear shoulder and spacer plate.
   d. Clearance between fourth gear shoulder and thrust washer.

38

COUNTERSHAFT ASSEMBLY

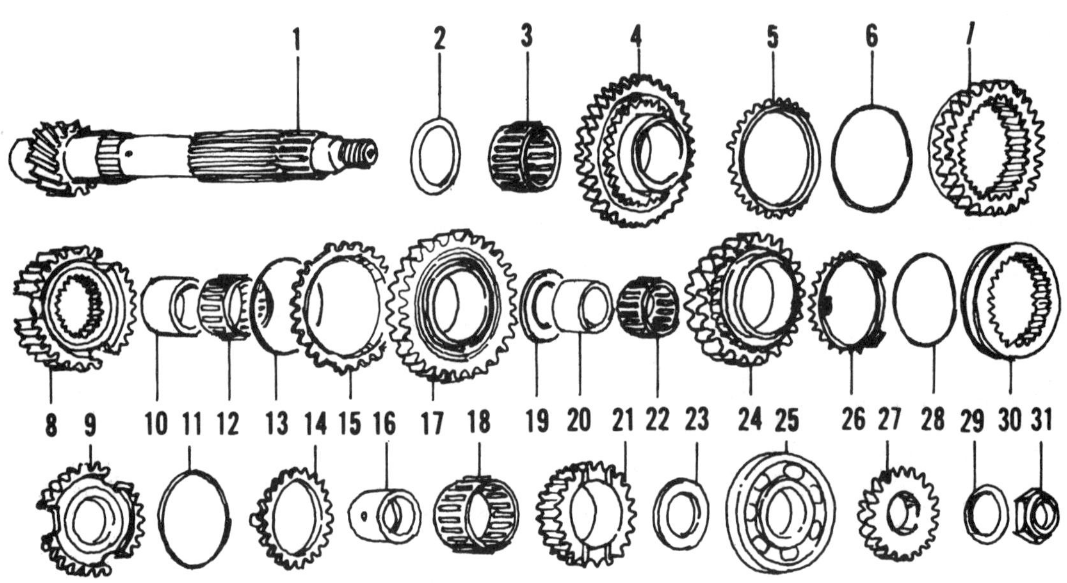

1. Countershaft
2. Thrust washer
3. Needle bearing
4. First gear
5. Synchronizer ring
6. Synchronizer spring
7. Synchronizer sleeve
8. Synchronizer hub
9. Synchronizer hub
10. Spacer collar
11. Synchronizer spring
12. Needle bearing
13. Synchronizer spring
14. Synchronizer ring
15. Synchronizer ring
16. Spacer collar
17. Second gear
18. Needle bearing
19. Spacer plate
20. Spacer collar
21. Fourth gear
22. Needle bearing
23. Thrust washer
24. Third gear
25. Ball bearing
26. Synchronizer ring
27. Fifth gear (5-speed only)
28. Synchronizer ring
29. Spring washer
30. Synchronizer ring
31. Locknut

39

40

e. Clearance of each shifting fork in its synchronizer sleeve (**Figure 40**).

2. If measurements are within specification and shafts and gears are not worn or damaged (see *General Transaxle Inspection)*, the countershaft does not require disassembly. If any measurement was incorrect, proceed to Step 3.

3. To disassemble the countershaft it will be necessary to remove the countershaft locknut (if not previously done). To do so, first install both the countershaft and main shaft assemblies into the clutch housing (**Figure 33**). Shift one of the countershaft sleeves into gear. Then temporarily install the transaxle housing and secure both housings with bolts. Install the Honda main shaft holder (part No. 07924-6340300) onto the main shaft as shown in **Figure 19**. Use a punch and bend back the

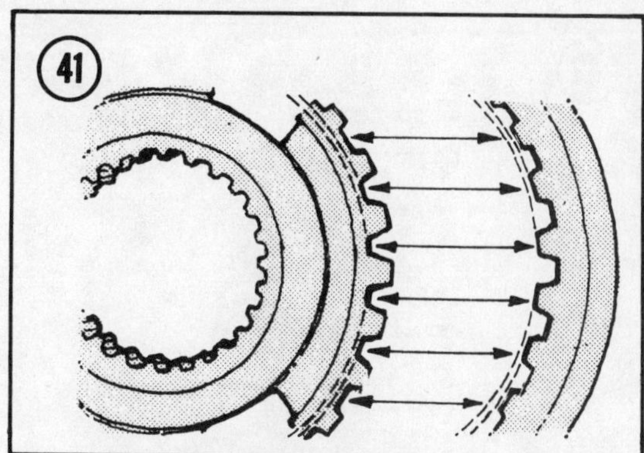

41

countershaft lock tab. Remove the countershaft locknut. *This nut has a right-hand thread.* Disassemble both cases and remove the countershaft and main shaft assemblies.

4. Disassemble the countershaft and lay all parts out in order (**Figure 38**). With the clearance information determined in Step 2, select the correct size thrust washer and/or spacer collar (**Table 4**) and discard the old thrust washer or spacer collar.

5. Reverse Step 4 and assemble the countershaft. Make certain the large synchronizer teeth in the sleeves line up with the deep teeth in the hubs (**Figure 41**). Install a new countershaft locknut on the countershaft to hold the gears in position and install both shaft assemblies into the clutch housing as in Step 3. Make sure to shift one of the synchronizer sleeves into gear to lock shafts. Place the transaxle housing onto the clutch housing and secure both housings with bolts. Install the Honda main shaft holder tool (**Figure 19**) and tighten the countershaft locknut to specifications (**Table 5**). *This nut has a right-hand thread.*

6. Disassemble transaxle and reheck countershaft clearance (Step 1). If clearances are correct, no further work is required. If clearances are incorrect, repeat Steps 1-5.

Main Shaft Inspection/Disassembly

There is no main shaft clearance inspection provided by Honda for 4-speed transaxles. The following procedures describe main shaft clearance inspection procedures for 5-speed transaxles. Refer to **Figure 42** (1975-1979),

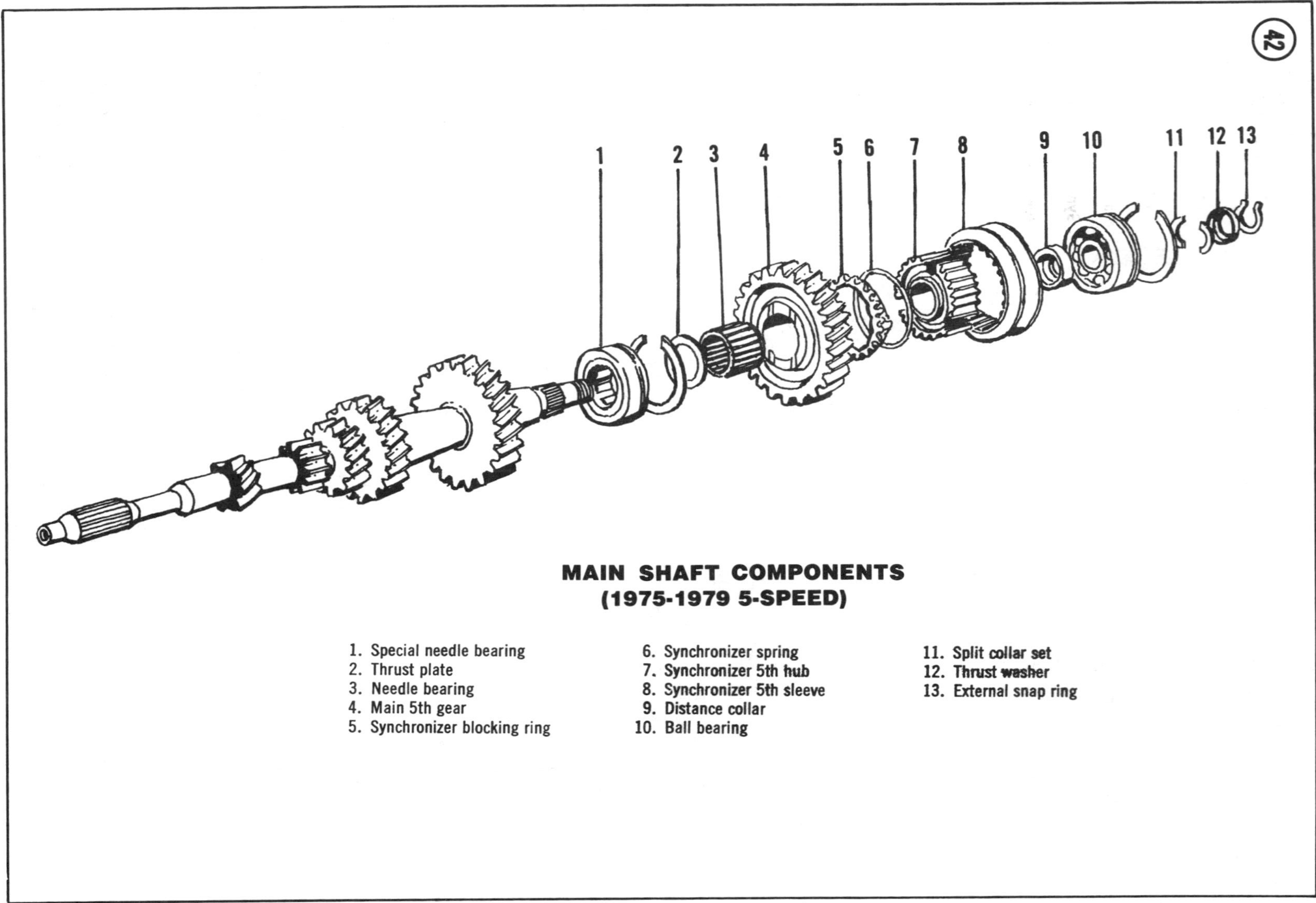

MAIN SHAFT COMPONENTS (1975-1979 5-SPEED)

1. Special needle bearing
2. Thrust plate
3. Needle bearing
4. Main 5th gear
5. Synchronizer blocking ring
6. Synchronizer spring
7. Synchronizer 5th hub
8. Synchronizer 5th sleeve
9. Distance collar
10. Ball bearing
11. Split collar set
12. Thrust washer
13. External snap ring

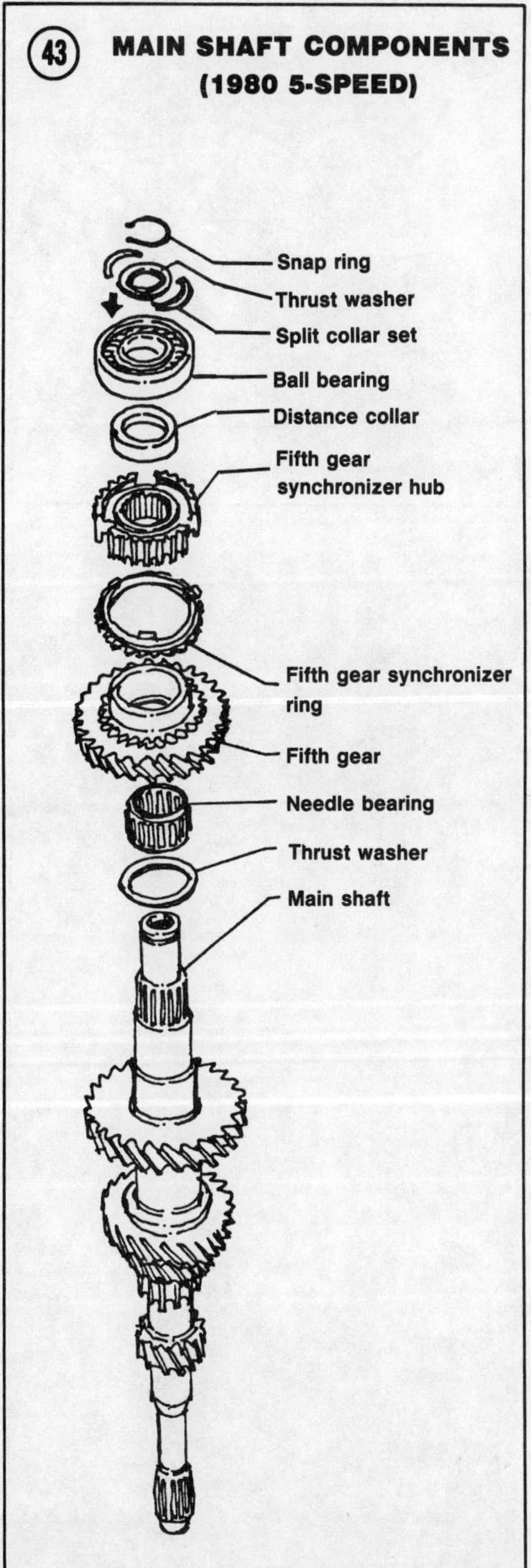

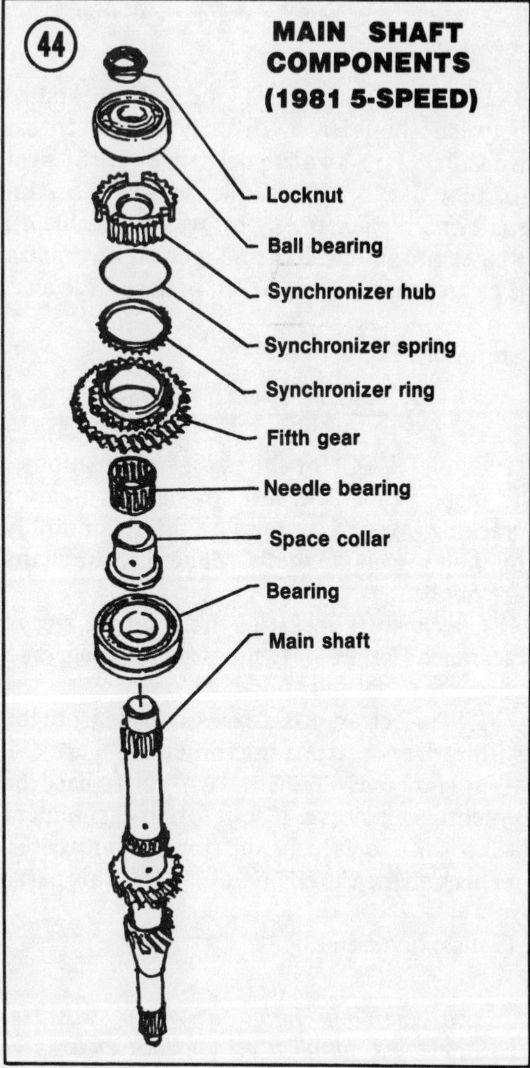

Figure 43 (1980) or **Figure 44** (1981) for this procedure.

1. Remove the main shaft ball bearing from the transaxle housing.
2. Assemble the ball bearing onto the main shaft and secure with snap ring (**Figure 42** or **Figure 43**) or locknut (**Figure 44**).

NOTE
Locknut uses a left-hand thread.

NOTE
*On 1981 models with locknut (**Figure 44**), install main shaft into clutch housing and secure with Honda main shaft holder (part No. 07924-6340300). See **Figure 19**. Then tighten to 6 mkg (43*

9

ft.-lb.) and remove main shaft from clutch housing.

3. Using a feeler gauge, measure clearance between shoulder on fifth gear and thrust washer. It should be 0.05-0.38 mm (0.002-0.015 in.). If not, disassemble the main shaft and replace the thrust washer (**Table 4**). Reassemble main shaft and recheck clearance. If clearance is still incorrect, replace fifth gear.

Shift Fork Inspection

Refer to **Table 1** (1973-1979 non-CVCC), **Table 2** (1975-1979 CVCC), or **Table 3** (1980-on CVCC) for shift fork specifications.

1. Inspect each shift fork for signs of wear or cracking. Make sure the forks slide smoothly on their respective shafts. Make sure the shafts are not bent.
2. Check shift fork-to-synchronizer sleeve clearance (**Figure 40**) with a feeler gauge and compare to specifications.
3. If Step 2 clearance is excessive, measure the shift fork ends with a micrometer (**Figure 45**). If shift fork measurement is correct, replace the synchronizer sleeve. If shift fork measurement is incorrect, replace the shift fork. In both cases, recheck all measurements after replacing parts.

Transaxle Assembly

NOTE
*If the differential assembly was removed, install it as described under **Differential Assembly/Adjustment** before assembling and installing the transaxle components.*

1. Oil all parts before beginning assembly. Assemble the countershaft components in the order in which they were removed. Make certain the large synchronizer teeth in the sleeves line up with the deep teeth in the hubs (**Figure 41**).
2. Install the differential assembly, if necessary, as described in this chapter.
3. If the shift arm holder assembly was removed, align the shift arm with the selector arm and install the shift arm holder (**Figure 35**).
4. Lay the clutch housing down with the differential assembly facing up. Then mesh the countershaft and main shaft assemblies in one

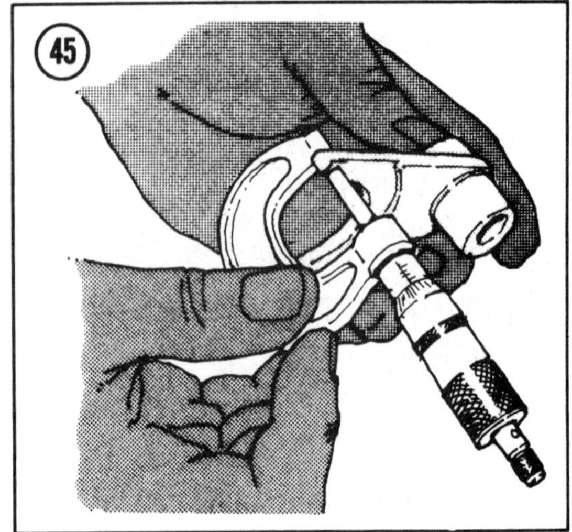

hand and install into clutch housing together (**Figure 46**).

NOTE
*If not already done, install the countershaft locknut as described under **Countershaft Inspection/Disassembly**, this chapter. Stake the locknut lip into the groove in the countershaft. See **Figure 47**.*

5. Lift up on countershaft first, second and reverse gears and shift transaxle into second gear. Install the first/second gear shift fork on its synchronizer sleeve. Then rotate shift fork backwards and insert fork lugs onto shift arm (**Figure 48**).
6. Install the third/fourth shift fork onto third/fourth shift fork shaft and install into position (do not install shift fork bolt). Hook the third/fourth shift guide into the shift arm or shift mechanism (**Figure 49**).
7. Insert the first/second shift fork shaft through the first/second shift fork and into case (**Figure 50**).

8A. *4-speed:* Hook the reverse shift guide to the shift arm, then install the shift shaft (**Figure 51**).

8B. *5-speed:* Hook the fifth gear/reverse shift guide to the shift arm, then install the shift shaft.

9. *1981 5-speed:* Install the spring and detent ball into the clutch housing (**Figure 52**).
10. Install end of reverse shift fork through stud in selector mechanism while aligning slot in fork with pin in reverse shift guide (**Figure 51**). Install the special washer and nut and tighten to 2.4 mkg (17 ft.-lb.).

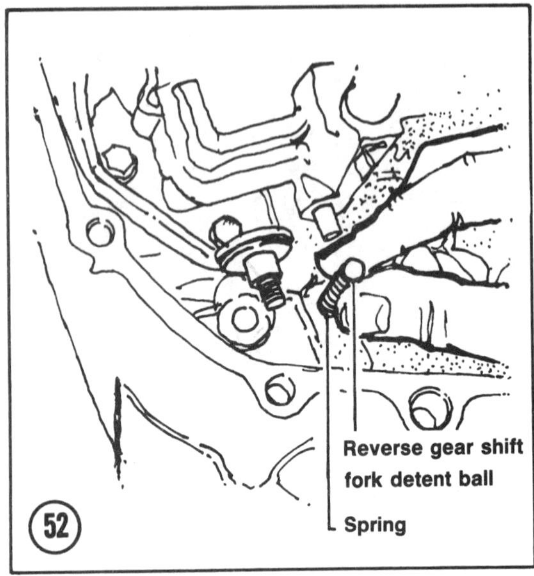

52

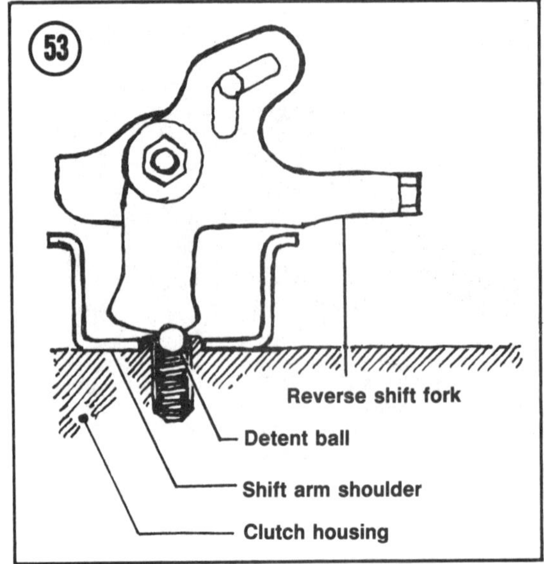

53

NOTE
*On 1981 5-speed models, make sure the reverse shift fork is aligned with detent ball installed in Step 9 as shown in **Figure 53**.*

11. Align groove on reverse idler gear with arm on reverse shift fork. Then install reverse idler gear shaft through gear and into housing (**Figure 54**).
12. Install the shift shaft lockplates and bolts. Tighten bolts to 1.7 mkg (12 ft.-lb.) and bend tab on lockplates over each bolt head (**Figure 55**).
13. Install dowels into clutch housing (if removed) and position new gasket over dowels.
14. Lightly oil all shift and transaxle shafts to ease installation.
15. Install the transaxle housing, making sure to align all shafts. On 1981 models, expand the countershaft bearing snap ring so that the transaxle can fall into position.

CAUTION
When installing the transaxle housing, make sure not to force its installation. If binding occurs, remove housing and check cause. Forcing the cases together can cause severe damage to case housing.

54

55

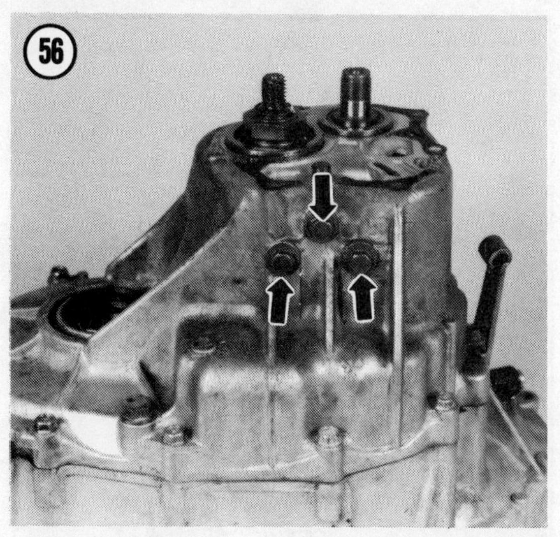

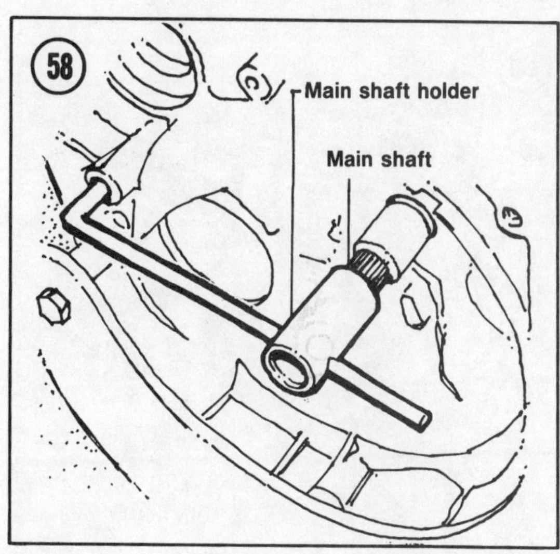

16. Tighten the transaxle housing bolts to 2.7 mkg (20 ft.-lb.) in a crisscross pattern.

17. Install the 3 detent balls, washers, springs and screws (**Figure 56**).

NOTE
Steps 18 and 19 describe 4-speed transaxle assembly. Transmission assembly procedures for 5-speed models continue with Step 20.

18. Install snap ring on countershaft bearing (**Figure 57**). Then install the Honda main shaft holder (part No. 07924-6340300) onto the main shaft (**Figure 58**) and shift the transaxle into REVERSE. Install the main shaft ball bearing and a new locknut. This locknut has left-hand threads. Tighten the locknut to 4.5 mkg (33 ft.-lb.), loosen and retighten to 4.5 mkg (33 ft.-lb.). Stake the locknut in slot in main shaft (**Figure 59**).

19. Install 2 snap rings in end cover (if removed). See **Figure 60**. Install the end cover with a new gasket. Install end cover attaching bolts (**Figure 61**) and tighten to 1.2 mkg (9 ft.-lb.).

NOTE
Steps 20-34 describe transaxle assembly procedures for 5-speed models.

20. *1975-1979 models:* Install snap ring on countershaft bearing. **Figure 57** shows 4-speed models, 5-speed is similar.

21. *1975-1980 models:* Install a new gasket, housing spacer, gasket and dowel pins in order on the transaxle housing (**Figure 62**).

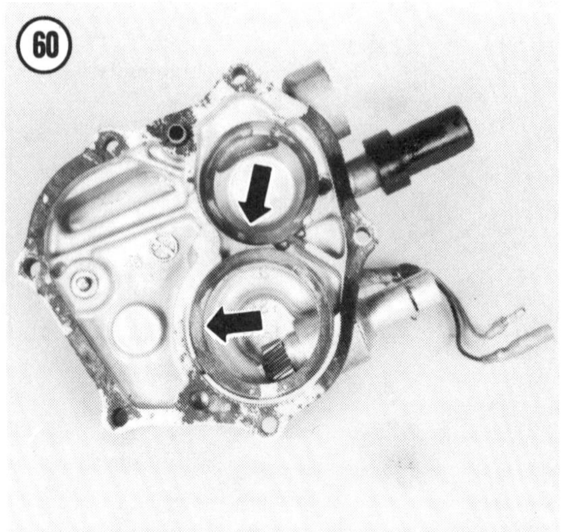

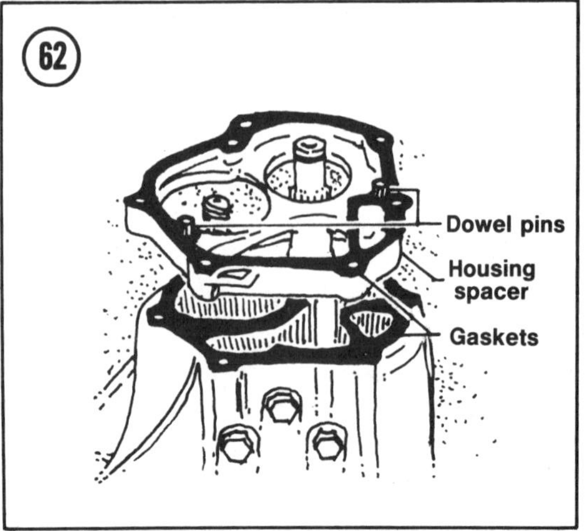
Dowel pins
Housing spacer
Gaskets

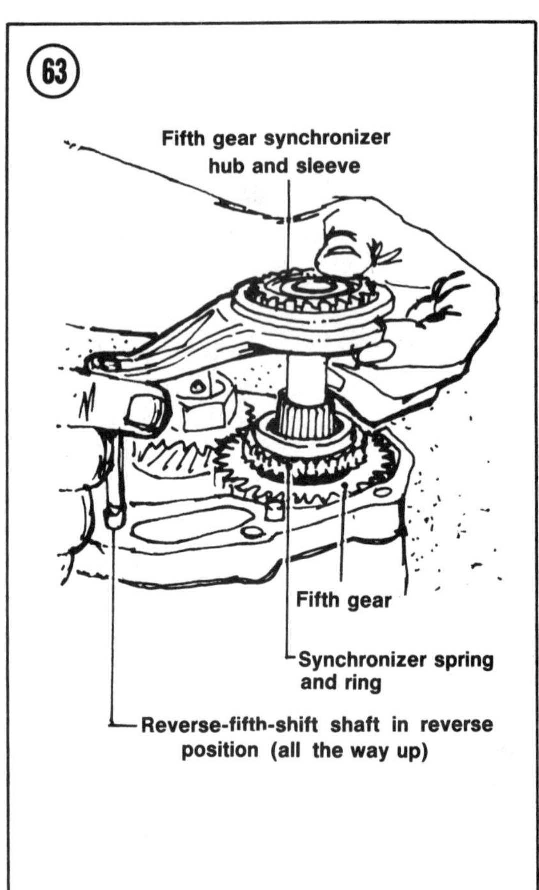
Fifth gear synchronizer hub and sleeve
Fifth gear
Synchronizer spring and ring
Reverse-fifth-shift shaft in reverse position (all the way up)

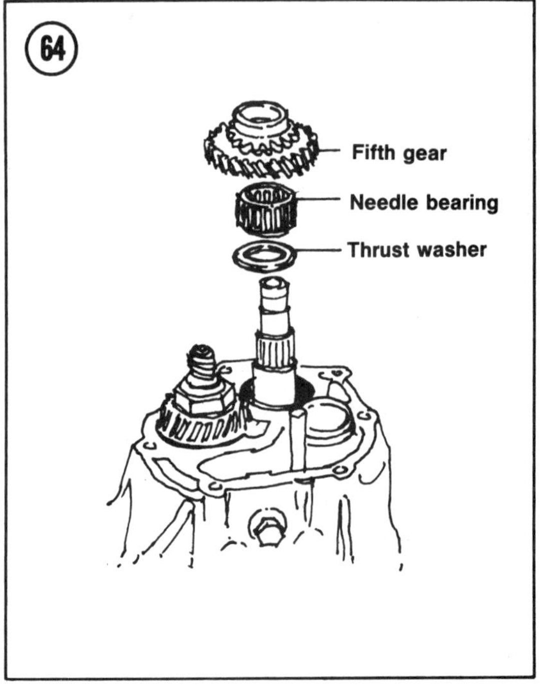
Fifth gear
Needle bearing
Thrust washer

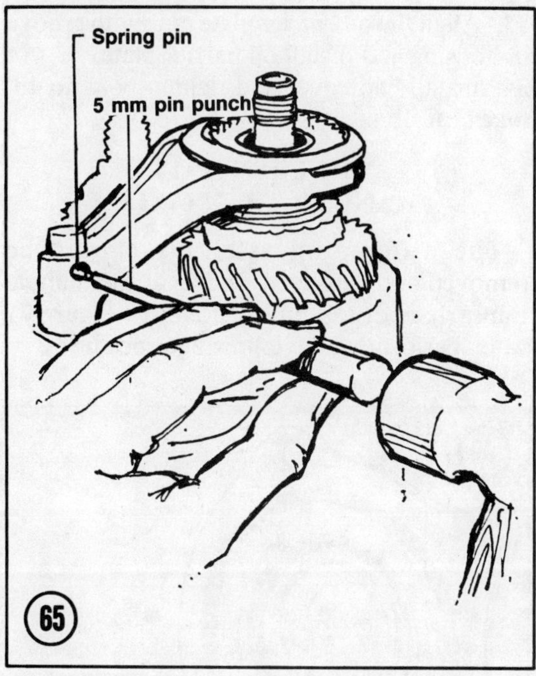

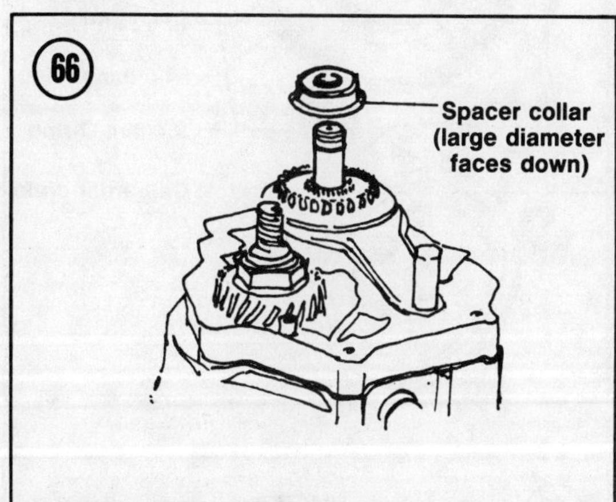

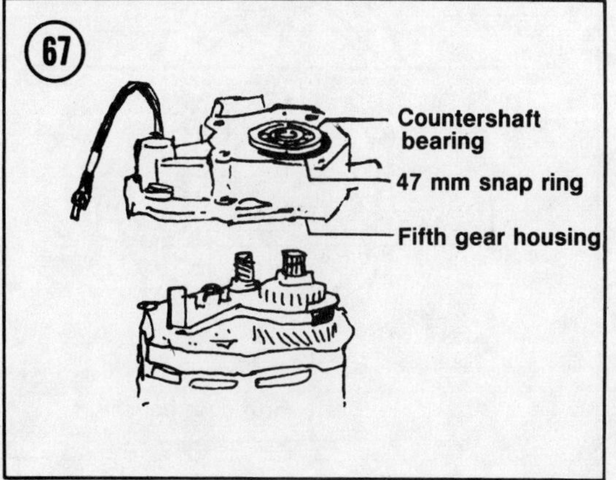

NOTE

*On 1975-1979 models, the transaxle should be shifted to REVERSE. This is indicated when the reverse/fifth gear shift shaft is all the way up (**Figure 63**).*

22. *1975-1980 models:* Install thrust washer, needle bearing, fifth gear, synchronizer ring and spring. Now assemble fifth gear, synchronizer hub and sleeve on shift fork and install.

NOTE

On 1980 models, install the synchronizer hub with shoulder facing down (toward transaxle) and the synchronizer sleeve with chamfer facing up (away from transaxle).

23. *1981 models*: These models do not use a spacer plate. Referring to **Figure 64**, install fifth gear, needle bearing and thrust washer in order on main shaft. Then install synchronizer ring and spring and hub. Install the sleeve and shift fork together.

NOTE

On 1981 models, install the synchronizer hub with shoulder facing down (toward transaxle) and the synchronizer sleeve with chamfer facing up (away from transaxle).

24. Using a 5 mm pin punch, drive a new spring pin into the fifth gear shift fork and reverse/fifth gear shift shaft (**Figure 65**).

NOTE

Steps 25-29 complete assembly procedures for 1975-1980 models. For 1981 model assembly procedures, start with Step 30.

25. Install the spacer collar (with shoulder side facing down) onto the main shaft (**Figure 66**).
26. Install the 47 mm snap ring on the countershaft bearing in the fifth gear housing (**Figure 67**).
27. Install the fifth gear housing using a new gasket (**Figure 67**). Install and tighten the housing bolts to 1.2 mkg (9 ft.-lb.).

28. Install the split collars onto the end of the main shaft (**Figure 68**). Then install the thrust washer (with large diameter facing down). Install snap ring.

29. Replace all O-rings in end cover (**Figure 69**). Then install oil carrier plate in end cover, making sure tube on oil carrier plate aligns with air passage in end cover (**Figure 69**). Install end cover with attaching bolts and torque to 1.2 mkg (9 ft.-lb.).

NOTE

Steps 30-34 complete 1981 5-speed transaxle assembly.

30. If bearing was removed from the fifth gear housing, install new bearing as follows:

a. Open fifth gear housing snap ring (**Figure 70**) with pliers and start bearing into housing (stamped part number on bearing must face into housing).

b. Release pliers and allow snap ring to close against bearing. Continue to push bearing into housing by hand until snap ring closes against ring groove in housing.

31. Install fifth gear housing using new gasket. Install attaching bolts and tighten to 1.2 mkg (9 ft.-lb.).

32. Install the Honda main shaft holder (**Figure 58**) and shift transaxle into REVERSE. Install a new main shaft locknut (left-hand threads). Tighten to 6.0 mkg (43 ft.-lb.), loosen and retighten to 6.0 mkg (43 ft.-lb.). Stake shoulder on locknut into groove in main shaft.

68

17 mm split retainer

47 mm snap ring

Bolts

33. Align the oil barrier plate tang with groove in housing and install oil barrier plate.

34. Install end cover and tighten bolts to 1.0 mkg (7 ft.-lb.).

DIFFERENTIAL (MANUAL TRANSAXLE)

The differential assembly should be removed and inspected whenever the manual transaxle is disassembled. Refer to **Figure 71** when performing the following procedures.

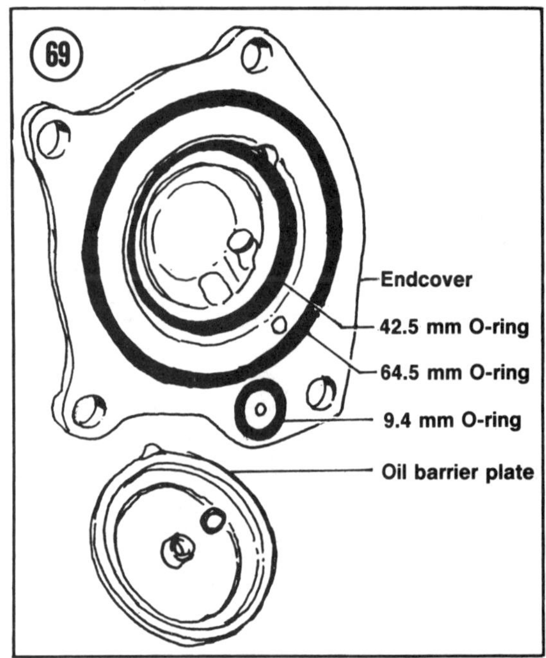

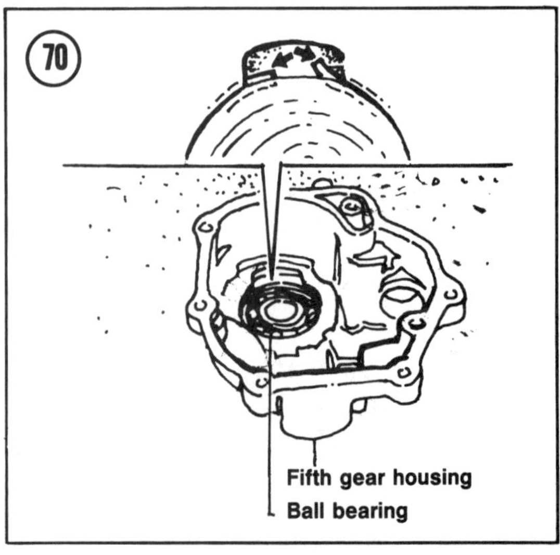

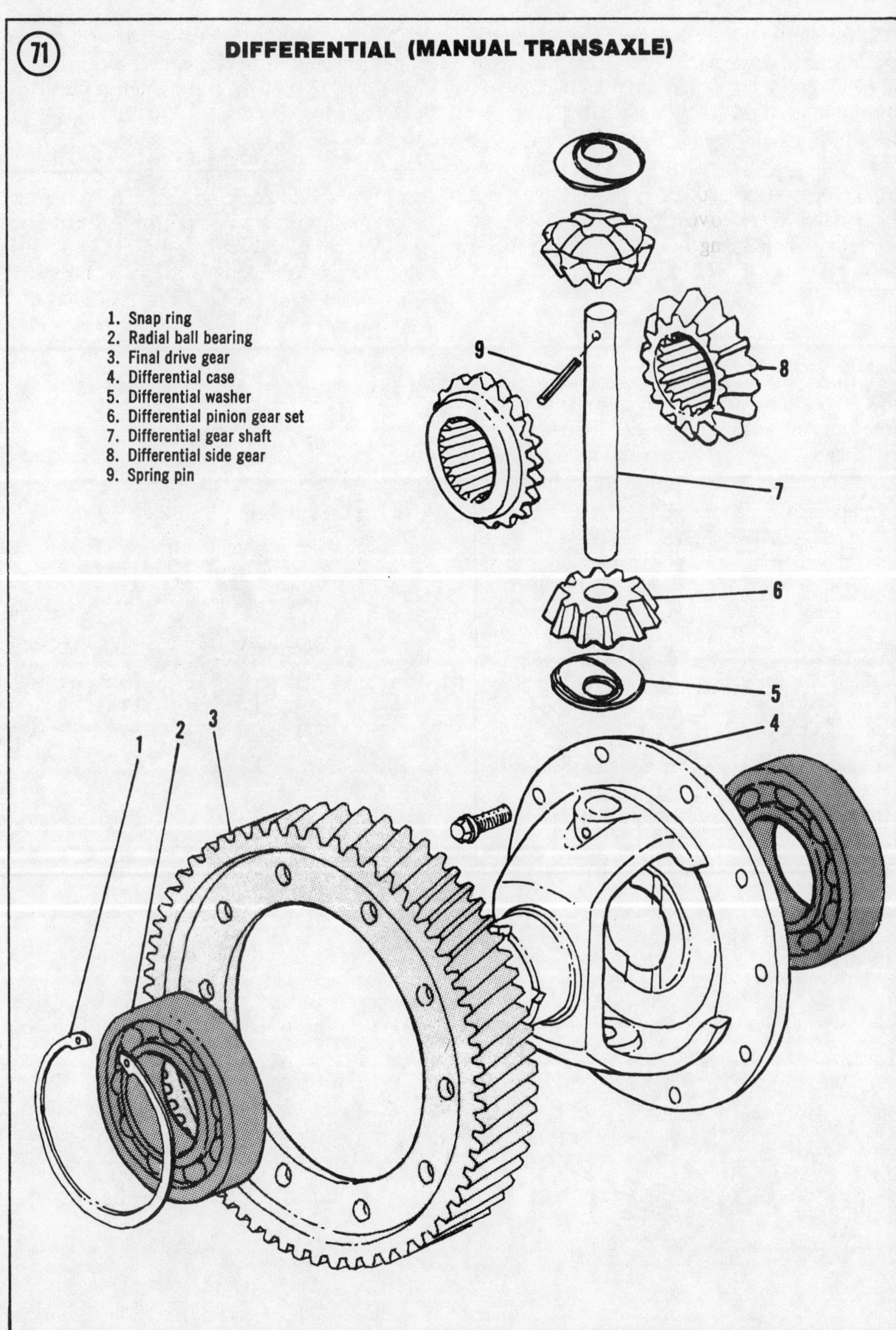
71
DIFFERENTIAL (MANUAL TRANSAXLE)
1. Snap ring
2. Radial ball bearing
3. Final drive gear
4. Differential case
5. Differential washer
6. Differential pinion gear set
7. Differential gear shaft
8. Differential side gear
9. Spring pin
9
8
7
6
5
4
3
2
1

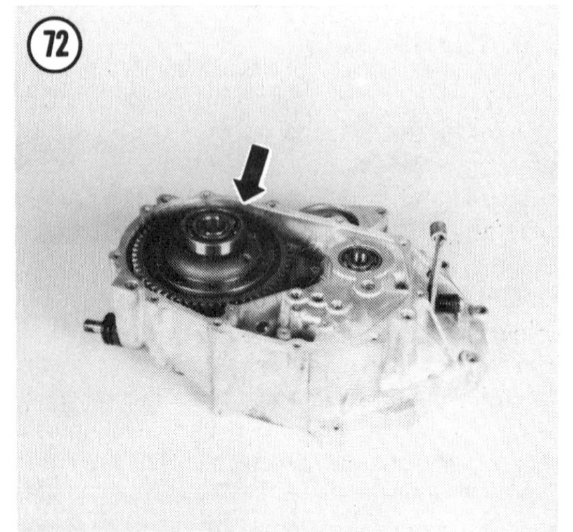
72

75

73

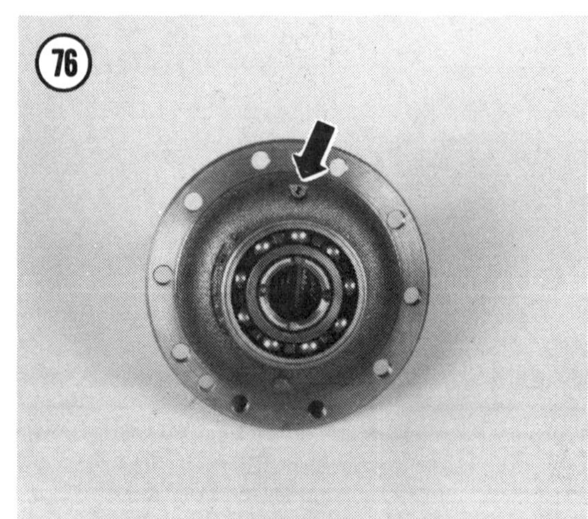
76

74

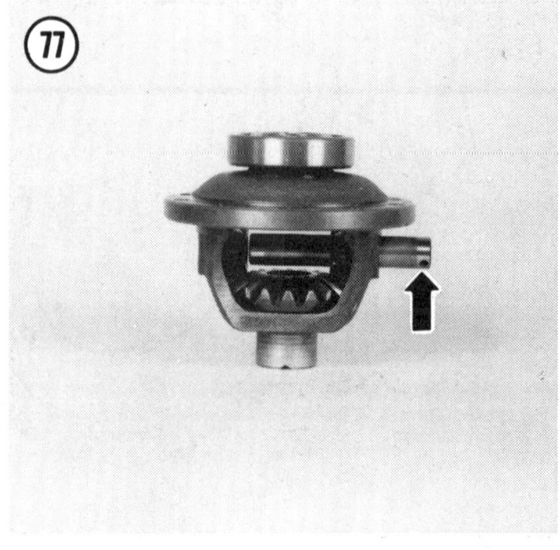
77

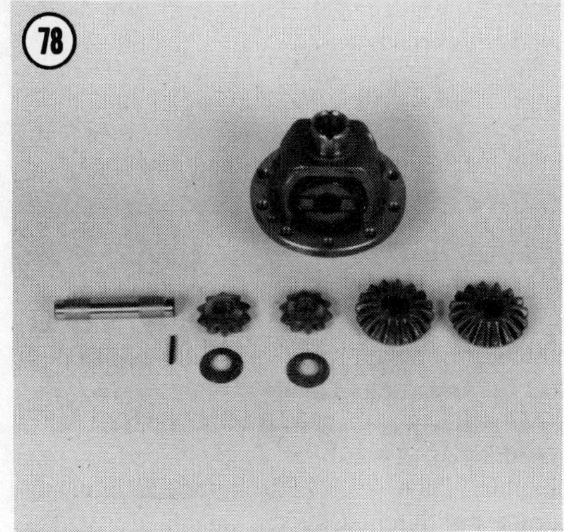
78

79

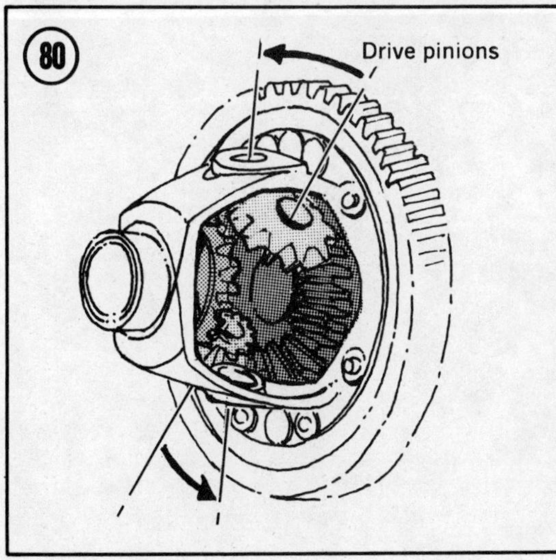

80

Removal/Disassembly

1. Refer to *Manual Transaxle* procedures in this chapter and completely disassemble the transaxle as described. The differential assembly is shown in **Figure 72**.
2. Turn the clutch case over so that differential faces down. Support the case with wood blocks. Using a bearing driver or suitable drift, drive the differential assembly out of the clutch case (**Figure 73**).
3. Remove the pinion-side carrier bearing assembly (**Figure 74**) with a bearing puller.
4. Unscrew the ring gear bolts (left-hand threads) in a crisscross pattern and remove the ring gear (**Figure 75**).
5. Use a punch and drive the pin out of the pinion shaft (**Figure 76**).
6. Remove the pinion shaft (**Figure 77**). Then remove the pinion gears and thrust washers from the differential housing. See **Figure 78**.
7. Tap the differential seal out of the rear case half and discard it. Remove the snap ring from the front case half (**Figure 79**) and drive the bearing out with a drift.

Inspection

1. Clean all of the parts thoroughly in solvent and dry them. Examine the gear teeth for wear, chipping or breakage. Normal light wear indicated by light burnishing of the contact surfaces of the gear teeth is acceptable, but excessive wear or damage requires part replacement.
2. Inspect the differential gear splines for wear and damage. If either condition exists, not only should the gears be replaced, but the splines on the axle driveshafts should be checked for similar deterioration and replaced if necessary.
3. Rotate the bearing assemblies by hand and check them for noise, roughness or play. Replace them if any of these conditions are found.

Assembly/Adjustment

1. Lightly coat all gears with Molykote or equivalent.
2. Install pinion gears directly opposite each other and engage with side gears inside the differential case. Then install a thrust washer behind each pinion gear. See **Figure 80**.

3. Rotate gears in carrier until the pinion shaft holes line up with the shaft holes in carrier.
4. Install the pinion shaft and align the spring pin holes in one end of shaft with pin hole in carrier (**Figure 76**).
5. Using a punch, drive in a new spring pin.

NOTE
The backlash of the pinion gears and differential clearance must be checked and adjusted, if necessary, after the pinions and carrier have been assembled. In addition to a dial indicator and V-blocks, the job requires a set of axle drive shafts. It is recommended that the assembled carrier and the cases be taken to a Honda dealer for checking and adjustment of the backlash and clearance.

6. After correctly adjusting backlash, install the ring gear and bolts (**Figure 75**). Tighten bolts to 10 mkg (72 ft.-lb.) in a crisscross pattern (**Figure 81**). Ring gear bolts use *left-hand* threads.

NOTE
When installing ring gear, make sure chamfer on inside diameter of ring gear faces into carrier.

7. Install the 72 mm snap ring in the clutch housing (**Figure 79**). Do not install the seal.
8. Place the differential assembly into the clutch housing and tap lightly into position to seat the snap ring.
9. Install the transaxle main shaft and countershaft assemblies as described in this chapter. Then install the transaxle housing together with a new gasket. Install and tighten the housing bolts to 2.7 mkg (20 ft.-lb.).
10. Place the transaxle assembly onto a workbench with the clutch housing facing up and seat the differential assembly using a suitable size drift (**Figure 73**).
11. Using a feeler gauge, measure the clearance between the snap ring and the outer bearing

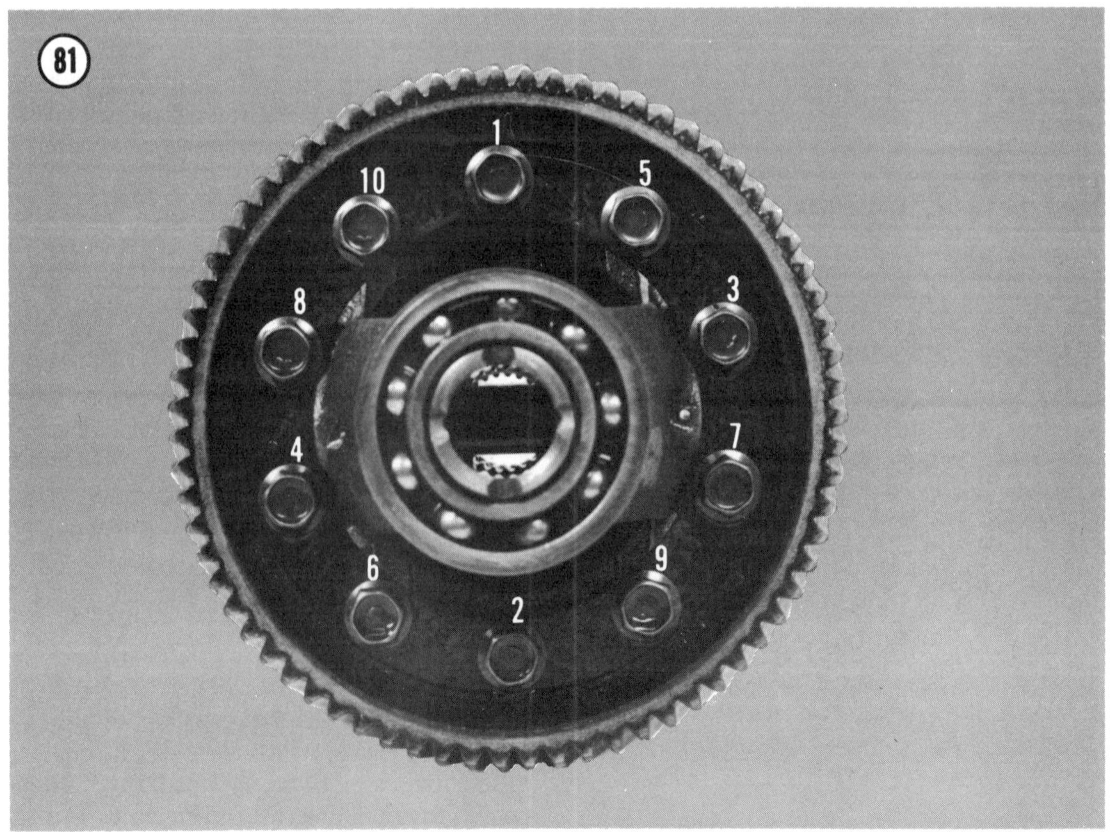

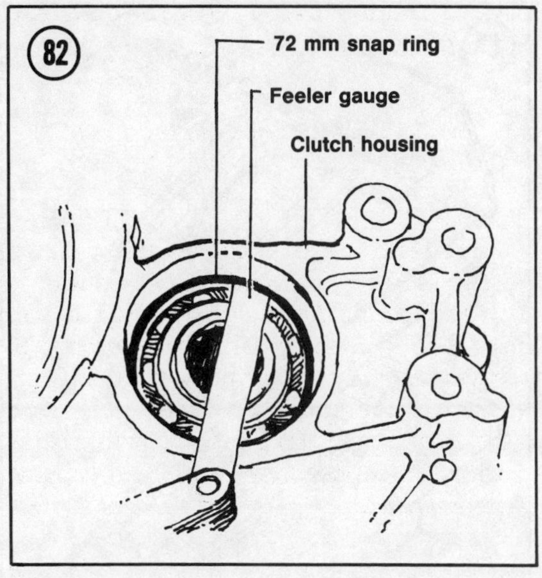

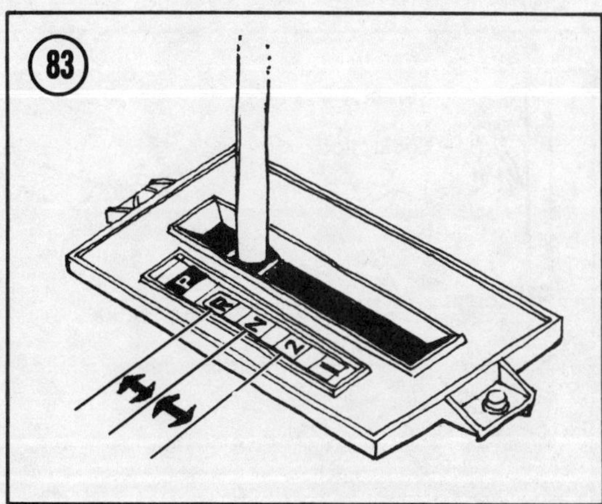

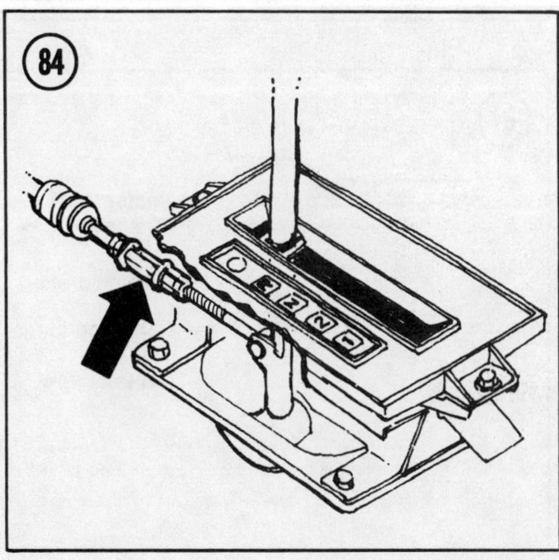

race (**Figure 82**). Side clearance should be as follows:

a. 1973-1979 non-CVCC: 0.15 mm (0.006 in.)
b. 1975-1979 CVCC: 0.10-0.20 mm (0.004-0.008 in.)
c. 1980-on CVCC: 0.15 mm (0.006 in.)

12. If clearance is incorrect as measured in Step 11, select a new snap ring from **Table 6**.

13. After determining correct snap ring clearance, install a new differential seal by driving into housing using a suitable size drift.

AUTOMATIC TRANSAXLE

Selector Lever Checking and Adjustment (1973-1979 Non-CVCC)

1. Set the parking brake to lock the rear wheels. Start the engine, allow it to idle and depress the footbrake.

2. Slowly move the lever back and forth from NEUTRAL to REVERSE and NEUTRAL to 2nd (**Figure 83**). The point at which the transaxle drive clutch can be felt to engage should be the same for both positions. If necessary, shorten or lengthen the control cable by turning the turnbuckle (**Figure 84**) to change the lever position.

3. Make certain that the lever cannot be moved from NEUTRAL to REVERSE without depressing the button on the selector lever handle. If it can, have a dealer repair the lever at once.

4. Shut off the engine and attempt to restart it with the lever in the 1st, 2nd and REVERSE positions. It should only start with the lever in the PARK and NEUTRAL positions. Also check to see that backup lamps light when the lever is put in the REVERSE position. If the car fails on any of these points, refer further service to a Honda dealer and have the neutral/backup lamp switch tested.

5. With the car on a slope, move the lever to PARK and slowly release the brakes to see if the transaxle will prevent the car from rolling with the PARK position selected. If it does not, refer it to a Honda dealer.

Control Cable Adjustment (1975-1980 CVCC)

1. Shift the gear selector to PARK and start the engine. Now shift the gear selector to REVERSE. Transmission engagement should be felt when shifting to REVERSE. If not, refer further service to a Honda dealer or competent automatic transaxle specialist.
2. Turn the engine off. From inside the driver's compartment, remove the center console screws and remove the center console (**Figure 85**, typical).
3. Shift the gear selector to REVERSE. Referring to **Figure 86**, remove the retaining pin lock clip. Then remove the retaining pin from the end of the control cable. Do not disturb the cable position in the selector lever.
4. Check the position of the pin hole in the end of the selector cable with that of the pin hole in the end of the selector arm. The pin holes in both the cable and selector lever arm should align exactly as indicated in **Figure 87**. If not, loosen the selector cable locknuts (**Figure 86**) and adjust the cable as required. When the cable and selector arm pin holes are in exact alignment, tighten the cable locknuts.
5. Secure the control cable with the retaining pin and lock clip.

NOTE
If the retaining pin is felt to bind when inserted through the selector arm and cable, the cable is out of adjustment. Readjust as described in Step 4.

6. Reinstall the center console (**Figure 85**, typical).
7. Shift the gear selector to PARK. Start the engine and check the transaxle for proper engagement in all gears. If any gear does not engage properly, refer further service to a Honda dealer or competent automatic transaxle specialist.

Control Cable Adjustment (1981)

1. Shift the gear selector to PARK and start the engine. Now shift the gear selector to REVERSE. Transmission engagement should be felt when shifting to REVERSE. If not, refer

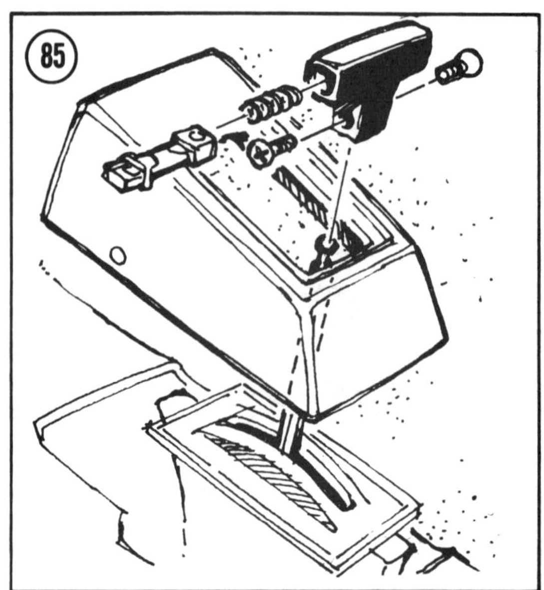

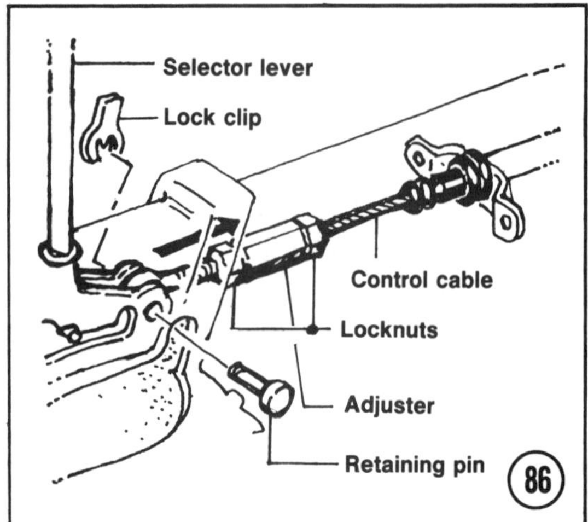

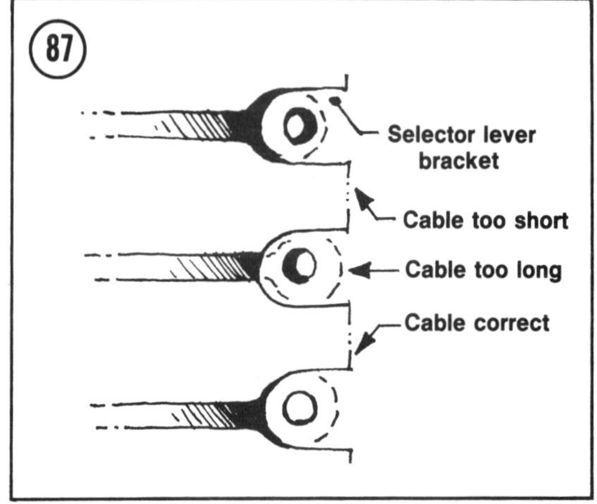

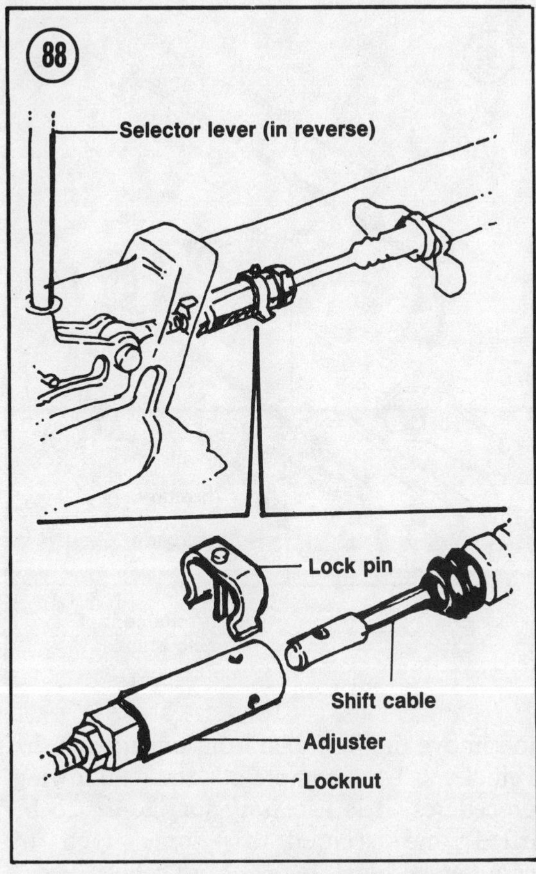

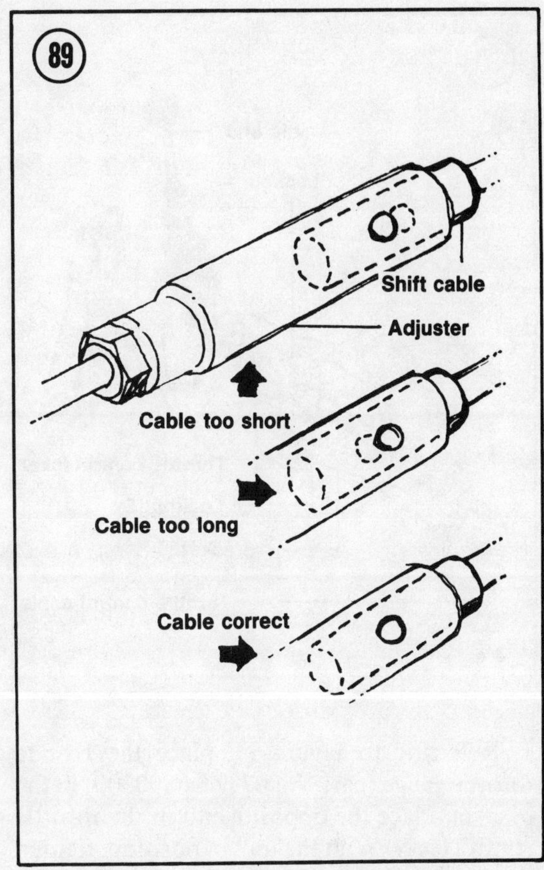

further service to a Honda dealer or competent automatic transaxle specialist.

2. Turn the engine off. From inside the driver's compartment, remove the center console screws and remove the center console (**Figure 85**, typical).

3. Shift gear selector to DRIVE. Referring to **Figure 88**, remove the shift cable lock pin through the opening in the transaxle shift linkage housing. Do not disturb the cable position in the cable adjuster.

4. Check the position of the pin hole in the end of the shift cable with that of the pin holes in the end of the cable adjuster. The pin hole in both the cable and adjuster should align exactly as indicated in **Figure 89**. If not, loosen the selector cable locknuts and adjust the cable as required. When the cable and cable adjuster pin holes are in exact alignment, tighten the cable locknuts.

5. Secure the control cable with the lock pin (**Figure 88**).

NOTE

If the lock pin is felt to bind when inserted through the cable adjuster and cable, the cable is out of adjustment. Readjust as described in Step 4.

6. Reinstall the center console (**Figure 85**, typical).

7. Shift the gear selector to PARK. Start the engine and check the transaxle for proper engagement in all gears. If any gear does not engage properly, refer further service to a Honda dealer or competent automatic transaxle specialist.

Throttle Control Cable Adjustment (1981)

If the throttle control cable bracket (**Figure 90**) was removed for any reason, it must be adjusted before adjusting the throttle control cable. Step 1 describes adjustment of the bracket. If the bracket position has not been disturbed, proceed to Step 2.

9

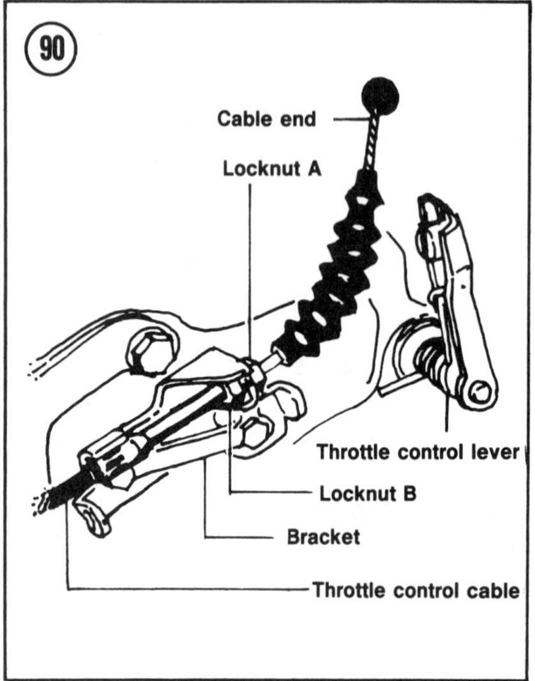

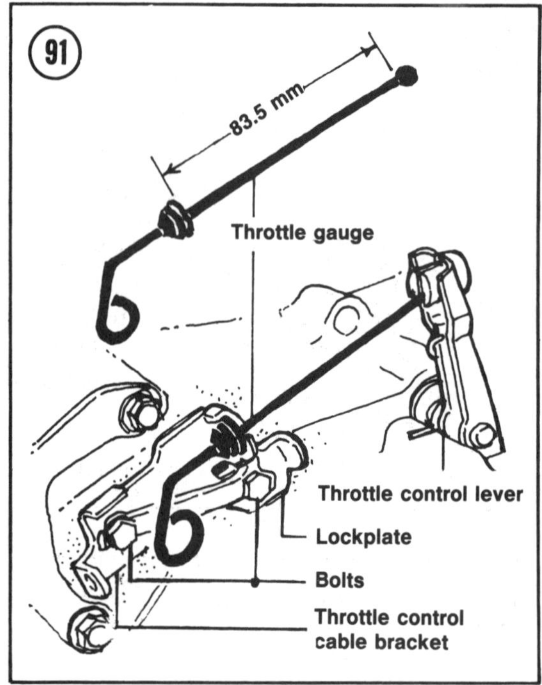

1. Referring to **Figure 91**, place the Honda throttle gauge (part No. 07974-6890300) in the bracket. Place the opposite end in the throttle control lever. With the tool in position, tighten the bracket bolts to 1.2 mkg (9 ft.-lb.). Bend the bracket lock plate over the bolt heads. Remove the gauge tool and proceed to Step 2.
2. Depress the throttle pedal cable to take up all slack in the throttle cable.
3. Adjust the distance between the cable end and locknut A in **Figure 92** to 84.5 mm (3 11/64 in.).
4. Insert the end of the throttle cable into the throttle control lever (**Figure 90**).
5. Position the throttle control cable into the bracket (**Figure 90**) and secure by tightening locknut B.
6. Have an assistant depress the throttle pedal and make sure the cable moves freely at the bracket.

Removal

The transaxle assembly has been designed for removal from underneath the vehicle. Jackstands, the normal home mechanic support fixture (described in Chapter One), do not provide the necessary room or *safety* to remove the transaxle from underneath the vehicle. To complete the following procedures, it is necessary for the car to be lifted and secured by some type of commercial hoist. If the use of a hoist is not available, the engine can be removed as described in Chapter Four with the transaxle attached. The transaxle can then be separated from the engine and all necessary work performed.

1. Shift the transaxle into NEUTRAL. Disconnect the battery ground cable at the battery and the transaxle housing.
2. Disconnect the following engine compartment wiring connectors:
   a. Starter motor positive battery cable
   b. Backup light switch at transaxle case
   c. Water temperature sending unit at engine
   d. Ignition timing thermosensor at engine
3. Disconnect the transaxle oil cooler inlet and outlet hoses at the transaxle. Use wire to support the hoses in an upright position out of the way. Note the position of the sealing washers so they can be reinstalled during assembly.
4. Remove the starter bolt threaded into the transaxle housing. Then remove the top transaxle mounting bolt.

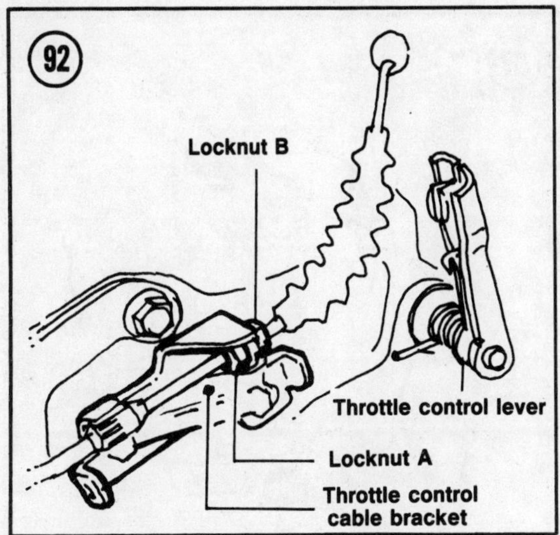

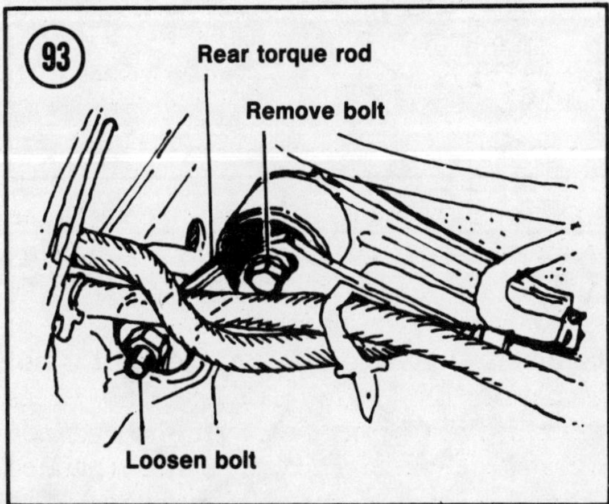

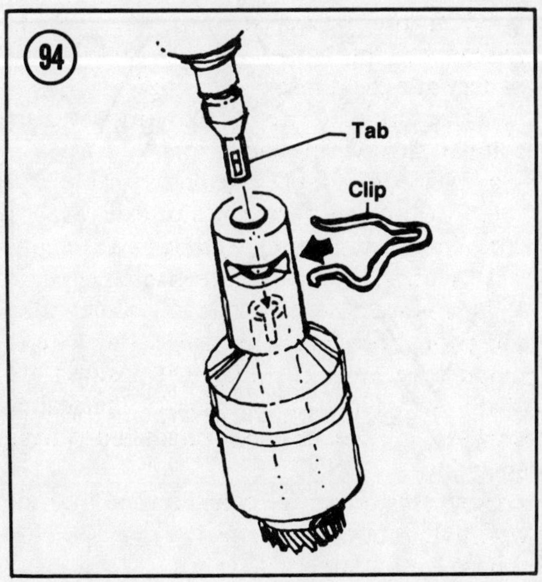

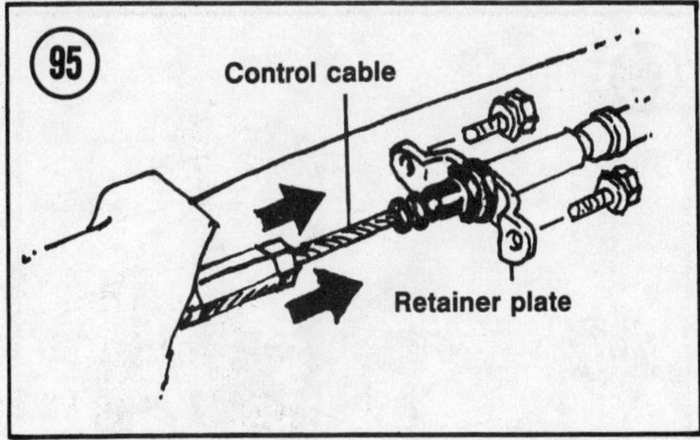

5. *1980:* Remove the front rear torque arm bracket bolt (**Figure 93**).
6. *1980-on:* Remove the speedometer cable clip and pull the cable out of the speedometer gear holder (**Figure 94**). *Do not* remove the speedometer gear holder.

CAUTION
Do not remove the speedometer gear holder during Step 6. If the speedometer gear holder is removed, it is likely that the speedometer gear will fall into the transaxle. This will require disassembly of the automatic transaxle.

7A. *1980 models:* From inside the driver's compartment, remove the center console (**Figure 85**, typical). Then remove the shift cable retaining pin clip and pin and disconnect the shift cable from the shift lever. Remove the control cable retainer plate bolts (**Figure 95**) and pull the cable out.
7B. *1981:* Remove the center console (**Figure 85**, typical). Then remove the shift cable lock pin and separate the shift cable from the shift adjuster (**Figure 96**). Pull cable back and out of way.
8. *1981:* Referring to **Figure 90**, remove the throttle control cable as follows:
   a. Push the throttle control lever down and release the throttle control cable.
   b. Loosen the control cable locknut A in **Figure 90** and remove the cable from its mounting bracket. Do not remove the mounting bracket.
9. *1981:* Remove the speedometer cable clip and pull the cable out of its holder (**Figure 94**).
10. Raise the vehicle on a commercial hoist. See first paragraph introduction to this procedure.

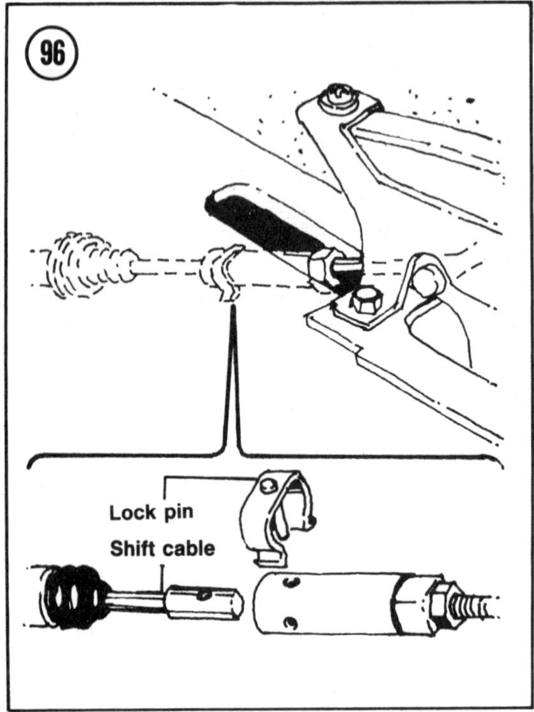

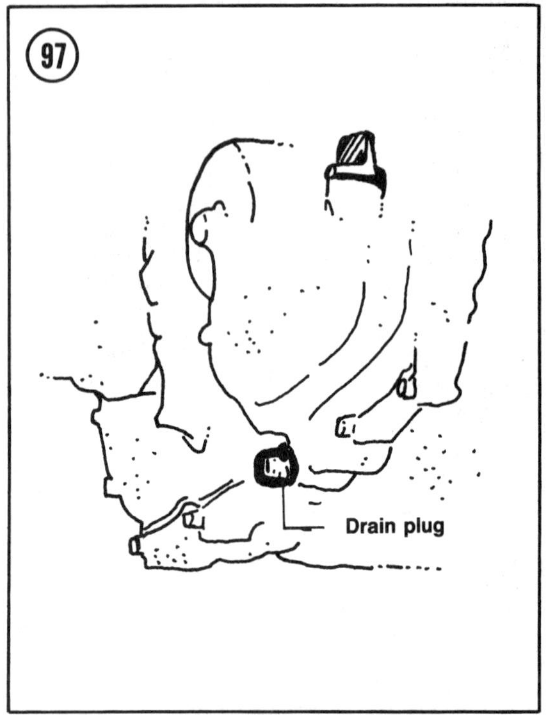

WARNING
Do not attempt to remove the transaxle from beneath the vehicle if supporting the car with jackstands. Jackstands do not provide the safety or working area required by this method.

11. Remove the front wheels.
12. Remove the transaxle drain plug and drain the transaxle oil (**Figure 97**). Install the drain plug, using a new aluminum washer/gasket.
13. Place a transaxle jack underneath the transaxle.

NOTE
Steps 14-22 describe removal procedures for 1973-1979 models. Removal procedures for 1980 and later models resume with Step 23.

14. Remove the right-side fender well shield.
15. Unscrew the speedometer drive lock bolt and pull the cable out of the transaxle (**Figure 98**). Take care not to drop the pin that holds the drive gear and collar in place.
16. Remove the subframe center beam.
17A. *1973-1975:* Remove the left and right lower control arm ball-joint nuts and cotterpins. Turn the left side steering knuckle

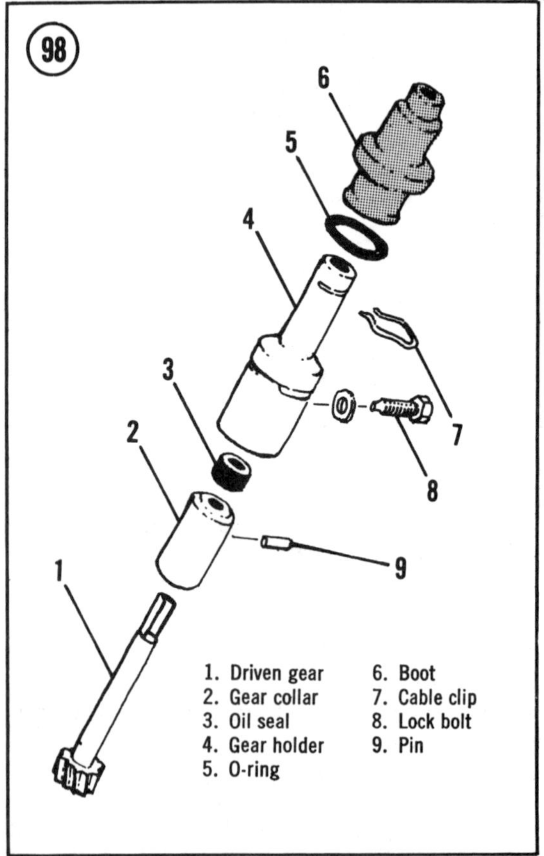

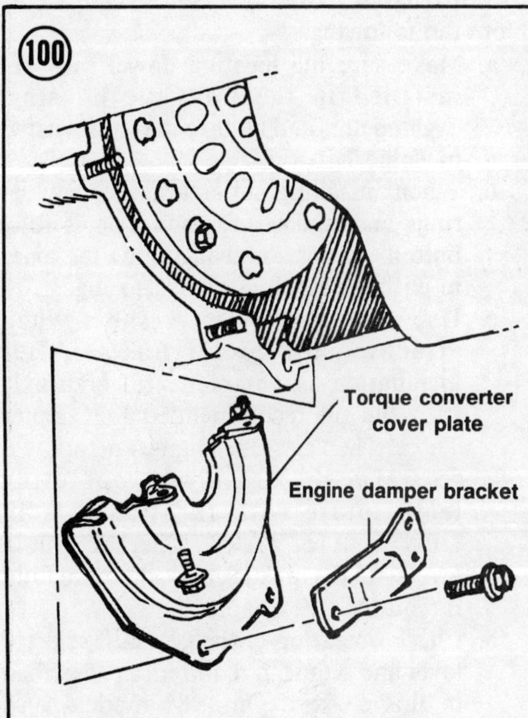

to its most outboard position. Then remove the ball-joint from the steering knuckle using Honda tool part No. 07941-6340000. See **Figure 99**. Repeat for the right side ball-joint. Then remove the lower arm bolts at both sides of the subframe and remove the lower arm and spring stabilizer together.

17B. *1976-1979:* Disconnect the stabilizer spring from the radius rods and remove the self-locking nuts from both sides of the right front radius rod. Then remove the lower arm bolts at both sides of the subframe. Repeat for opposite side.

18. Turn the right side steering knuckle outboard as far as it will go. Then place a screwdriver against the inboard CV joint and pry the right side axle housing out of the transaxle 1/2 inch to force the axle spring clip out of the differential gear groove. The axle can now be pulled all the way out of the transaxle. Repeat for opposite side, making sure to turn the left side steering knuckle outboard as far as possible.

19. Remove the remaining starter attaching bolts and remove the starter.

20. Remove the transaxle damper bracket in the front of the torque converter cover plate (**Figure 100**).

21. Remove the torque converter cover plate (**Figure 100**).

22. Remove the shift control rod pin and control cable bracket on the outside of the transaxle housing. Position the shift control cable and bracket aside.

NOTE
Steps 23-31 resume transaxle removal procedures for 1980 and later models.

23. Remove the lower control arm pivot bolts.

24. Turn the right side steering knuckle outboard as far as it will go. Then place a screwdriver against the inboard CV joint and pry the right side axle housing out of the transaxle 1/2 inch to force the axle spring clip out of the differential gear groove. The axle can now be pulled all the way out of the transaxle. Repeat for opposite side, making sure to turn the left side steering knuckle outboard as far as possible.

25. Remove the stabilizer bar nuts and washers from both ends. Then remove the stabilizer bar brackets and remove the stabilizer bar.

26. Place a flat piece of wood on a jack lifting pad. Then position the jack underneath the engine oil pan and lift the engine to remove weight from the engine mounts.

27. From inside the engine compartment, remove the front and rear engine torque rods. Then remove the rear torque rod brackets.

28. Remove the engine damper bracket at the transaxle. Then remove the rear engine mount and bracket.

NOTE

Cut a piece of wood to the dimensions 1 in. x 2 in. x 4 in. before proceeding with Step 29.

29. Place the wood block (see NOTE above) on the center beam directly below the oil pan. Then slowly lower the jack and allow the engine oil pan to rest on the wood block. See **Figure 101**.
30. Remove the engine damper bracket and torque converter plate from the transaxle (**Figure 100**).
31. Remove the starter engine-side mounting bolt. Then remove the starter from its position and lower down through the frame and remove.

NOTE

Steps 32-35 complete transaxle removal for all models.

32. The torque converter is secured to the drive plate with bolts. To gain access to each bolt, turn the engine crankshaft using a socket placed on the crankshaft nut. Remove all bolts.
33. Screw an engine hanger bolt into the front torque rod-to-engine mount hole. Screw the other hanger bolt into the hole on the left of the distributor. Attach a chain to the hangers and raise the engine slightly with a chain hoist to take the engine load off the engine mounts.
34. Place a rolling jack underneath the transaxle and elevate the jack head until it contacts the transaxle. Unscrew the remaining transaxle mounting bolts. With the jack supporting the transaxle, pull the transaxle away from the engine to clear the locating dowel pins. Lower the transaxle with the jack and remove it from the car.

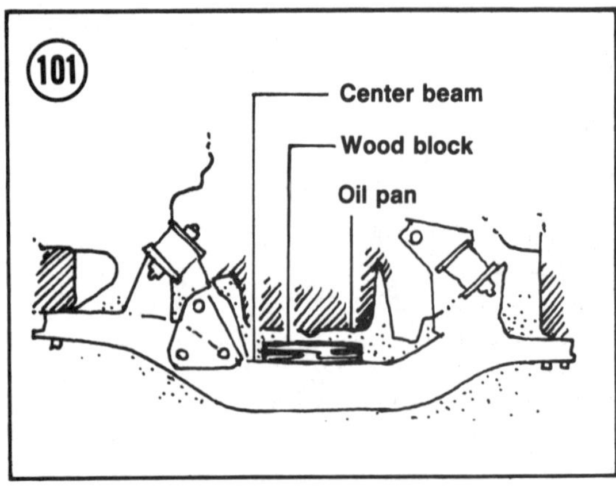

35. Installation is the reverse of these steps. Note the following:
   a. Make sure the locating dowel pins are installed in the transaxle housing. Tighten nuts and bolts to the values listed in **Table 7**.
   b. When installing sub-axles, use new set rings and make sure each axle is fully bottomed in the housing. Slide the axles in until the set rings are felt to engage.
   c. Use new aluminum washers when attaching oil cooler hoses. After installation is complete, fill transaxle with the oil recommended in Chapter Three. Then start the engine and allow it to warm up to normal operating temperature with the transaxle in NEUTRAL or PARK. Check the fluid level with the dipstick and add more fluid if required (see Chapter Three).
   d. Check operation of the gearshift selector lever and adjust, if required, as described in this chapter. On 1981 models, also perform the *Throttle Control Cable Adjustment* procedure.

Table 1 TRANSAXLE SPECIFICATIONS (NON-CVCC)

Item	mm	in.
Mainshaft		
Axial play limit	0.3	0.0118
Runout limit	0.07	0.0028
Needle roller bearing journal outside diameter	31.98-32.00	1.2591-1.2598
Countershaft 1st and 4th gears		
Inside diameter	37.009-37.025	1.4570-1.4577
Limit	37.05	1.4587
Axial play limit	0.18	0.0071
Countershaft 2nd and 3rd gears		
Inside diameter	37.009-37.025	1.4570-1.4577
Limit	37.05	1.4589
Axial play limit	0.18	0.0071
Spacers between gears		
Outside diameter limit	31.96	1.2582
Inside diameter	25.98-25.99	1.0228-1.0232
Reverse gear shaft		
Outside diameter limit	19.94	0.5882
Reverse idler gear		
Inside diameter	15.04-15.01	0.5921-0.5909
Gear-to-shaft clearance	0.07-0.03	0.0028-0.0012
Shift fork		
Synchronizer sleeve sliding surface width limit	6.0	0.2362
Fork-to-synchronizer sleeve clearance limit	1.0	0.0394
Blocking ring		
Clearance	1.0	0.0394
Limit	0.5	0.0197

Table 2 TRANSAXLE SPECIFICATIONS (1975-1979 CVCC)

Item	mm	in.
Main shaft		
Axial play limit	0.3	0.0118
Fifth gear clearance	0.05-0.40	0.002-0.016
Synchronizer ring to gear clearance	1.0	0.039
Limit	0.5	0.020
Shift fork to sleeve clearance	0.45-0.65	0.017-0.025
Limit	1	0.039
Shift fork thickness	6.4-6.5	0.252-0.256
Limit	6.0	0.236

(continued)

Table 2 TRANSAXLE SPECIFICATIONS (1975-1979 CVCC) (continued)

Item	mm	in.
Fifth gear shift fork		
thickness	5.4-5.5	0.213-0.217
Limit	5.0	0.197
Countershaft gear clearance		
(1975-1976)	0.03-0.08	0.0012-0.0032
Limit	0.18	0.0071
Countershaft gear clearance 1977-1979		
First gear	0.03-0.08	0.0012-0.002
Limit	0.18	0.0071
Second gear	0.05-0.012	0.002-0.0048
Limit	0.18	0.0071
Third gear	0.05-0.012	0.002-0.0048
Limit	0.18	0.0071
Fourth gear	0.03-0.08	0.0012-0.0048
Limit	0.18	0.0071

Table 3 TRANSAXLE SPECIFICATIONS (1980-ON CVCC)

Item	mm	in.
Main shaft		
Runout limit	0.05	0.002
Main shaft fifth gear		
Side clearance	0.05-0.38	0.002-0.015
Inside diameter limit	30.07	1.184
Countershaft		
End play limit	0.3	0.012
Runout limit	0.05	0.002
Countershaft first gear		
Side clearance	0.03-0.08	0.001-0.003
Limit	0.18	0.007
Countershaft second gear/third gear		
Side clearance	0.05-0.12	0.002-0.005
Limit	0.18	0.007
Reverse idler gear		
Shaft clearance	0.32-0.077	0.0013-0.003
Limit	0.14	0.006
Synchronizer ring		
Clearance	0.85-1.1	0.033-0.043
Limit	0.4	0.016
Shift fork		
Clearance	0.45-0.65	0.018-0.026
Limit	1.0	0.04

Table 4 REPLACEMENT THRUST WASHERS AND SPACER COLLARS

Honda Part No.	Class	Thrust Washer Thickness mm (in.)
23921-634-000	A	1.95-1.98 (0.077-0.078)
23924-634-000	B	1.92-1.95 (0.076-0.077)
23925-634-000	C	1.89-1.92 (0.074-0.076)
Honda Part No.		**Spacer Collar Length* mm (in.)**
23912-634-008		28.07-28.09 (1.105-1.106)
23913-634-008		28.04-28.07 (1.104-1.105)
23912-634-000		28.07-28.10 (1.105-1.106)
23914-657-000		28.10-28.13 (1.106-1.107)

* Not all spacer collar lengths are available for all models. See your Honda dealer for spacer collars available for your model.

Table 5 MANUAL TRANSAXLE TIGHTENING TORQUES

Item	mkg	ft.-lb.
Non-CVCC		
Holder arm	1.0-1.4	7-10
Shift forks	1.0-1.4	7-10
Shift arm	2.0-2.8	14-20
Clutch release arm	2.0-2.8	14-20
Transaxle drain bolt	2.5-4.5	25-33
Clutch case	4.0-5.0	29-36
Transaxle case	2.3-3.1	17-22
Transaxle cover	1.0-1.4	7-10
Backup light switch	2.3-2.7	17-20
Main shaft locknut	4.0-5.0	29-36
Countershaft locknut	6.0-7.0	43-51
Differential ring gear	9.0-9.5	65-69
1975-1979 CVCC		
Backup light switch	2.3-2.7	17-20
Ball spring retaining screw	2.0-2.4	15-17
Change rod	1.9-2.5	14-18
Clutch cover	1.0-1.4	7-10
Gearshift extension mount	0.3-0.5	2-4
Shift forks	1.0-1.4	7-10
Main shaft locknut (4-speed)	4.0-5.0	29-36
Countershaft locknut (4-speed)	6.0-7.0	43-51
Countershaft locknut (5-speed)	6.0-7.0	43-51
Plug bolt (5-speed)	2.3-2.7	17-20
Oil check bolt	2.0-2.4	15-17
Shift arm holder	1.0-1.4	7-10
Side cover (5-speed)	1.0-1.4	7-10
Transaxle case	2.3-3.1	17-23

(continued)

Table 5 MANUAL TRANSAXLE TIGHTENING TORQUES (continued)

Item	mkg	ft.-lb.
1975-1979 CVCC (continued)		
Transaxle cover	1.0-1.4	7-10
Transaxle drain bolt	3.5-4.5	25-33
Differential ring gear	9.0-9.5	65-69
1980-on CVCC		
Oil filler bolt	4.5	33
Countershaft locknut	9.0	65
Main shaft locknut (4-speed)	4.5	33
Main shaft locknut (5-speed)		
1980	Not used	
1981	6.0	43
Shift arm holder bolts	1.2	9
Reverse shift fork nut	2.4	7
Shift fork bolt	1.7	12
Transaxle case	2.7	20
End cover bolts (4-speed)		
1980	1.2	9
1981	1.0	7
End cover bolts (5-speed)		
1981	1.2	9
Fifth gear housing bolts	1.2	9
Differential ring gear	10	72

Table 6 DIFFERENTIAL SNAP RING SELECTION

Honda Part No.	Thickness mm	in.
90414-634-000	2.45	0.096
90415-634-000	2.55	0.100
90416-634-000	2.65	0.104
90417-634-000	2.75	0.108
90418-634-000	2.85	0.112
90419-634-000	2.95	0.116

Table 7 AUTOMATIC TRANSAXLE TIGHTENING TORQUES

Part	Ft.-lb.	Mkg
Transaxle mounting bolts	33	4.5
Torque converter-to-drive plate bolts	9	1.2
Rear engine mounting bolts	33	4.5
Torque converter cover plate attaching bolts	7	1.0
Transaxle stopper bracket attaching bolts	20	2.7
Starter mounting bolts	33	4.5
Lower arm bolts	33	4.5
Radius rod self-locking nuts	29	4.0
Sub-frame center beam attaching bolts	16	2.2
Speedometer drive assembly retaining bolt	9	1.2
Front wheel lug bolts	58	8.0
Transaxle oil cooler hose attaching bolts	20	2.7

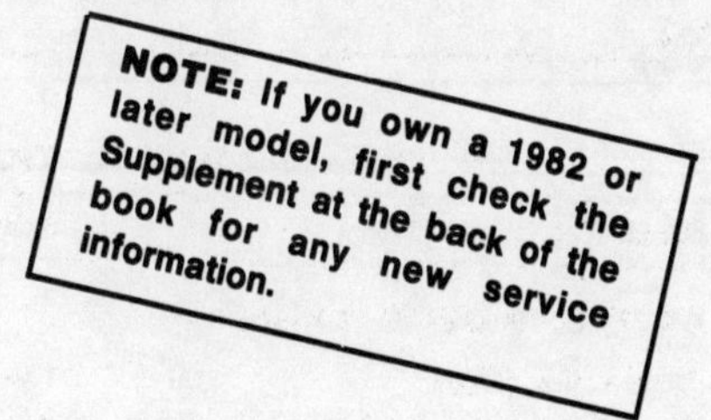
NOTE: If you own a 1982 or later model, first check the Supplement at the back of the book for any new service information.

CHAPTER TEN

FRONT SUSPENSION AND STEERING

All models use a MacPherson strut front suspension. The shock absorbers and springs are combined into a single unit. The struts are bolted to the inner wheel wells at the top and through ball-joints to the lower links at the bottom. The front stabilizer bar is located between each lower control arm.

This chapter includes service procedures for the front suspension, wheel bearings and steering components. Those procedures which can be performed on the power steering system are also included.

Tables 1-5 are at the end of the chapter.

CAUTION
All fasteners used in the front suspension and steering must be replaced with parts of the same type. ***Do not*** *use a replacement part of lesser quality or substitute design, as it may affect the performance of vital components and systems or result in major repair expenses. Torque values as indicated in* ***Tables 2-4*** *must be used during installation to assure proper retention of these parts.*

WHEEL ALIGNMENT

Several front suspension angles affect the running and steering of the front wheels. These angles must be properly aligned to prevent excessive tire wear and to maintain directional stability and ease of steering. The angles are:

a. Caster
b. Camber
c. Toe-in
d. Steering axis inclination

Of the four principal factors affecting front end alignment and geometry, only toe-in (both front and rear) is adjustable on the Civic. Caster and camber are controlled by the relationship of the front-end components. When caster and camber are found to be out of specification (**Table 1**), damage or wear is indicated.

Front Suspension Inspection

The steering and various suspension angles are affected by several factors. Perform the following steps before checking adjustment.

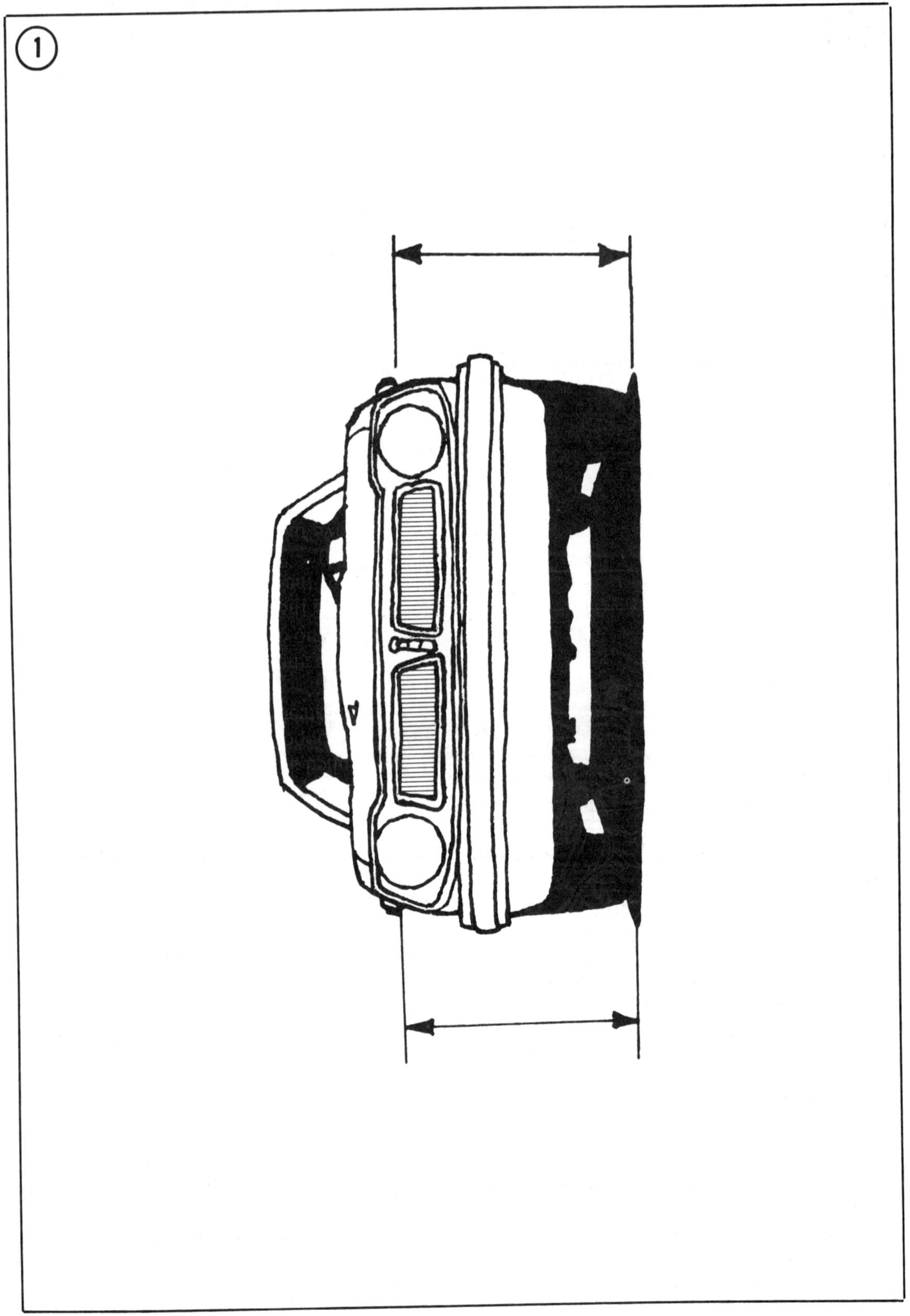

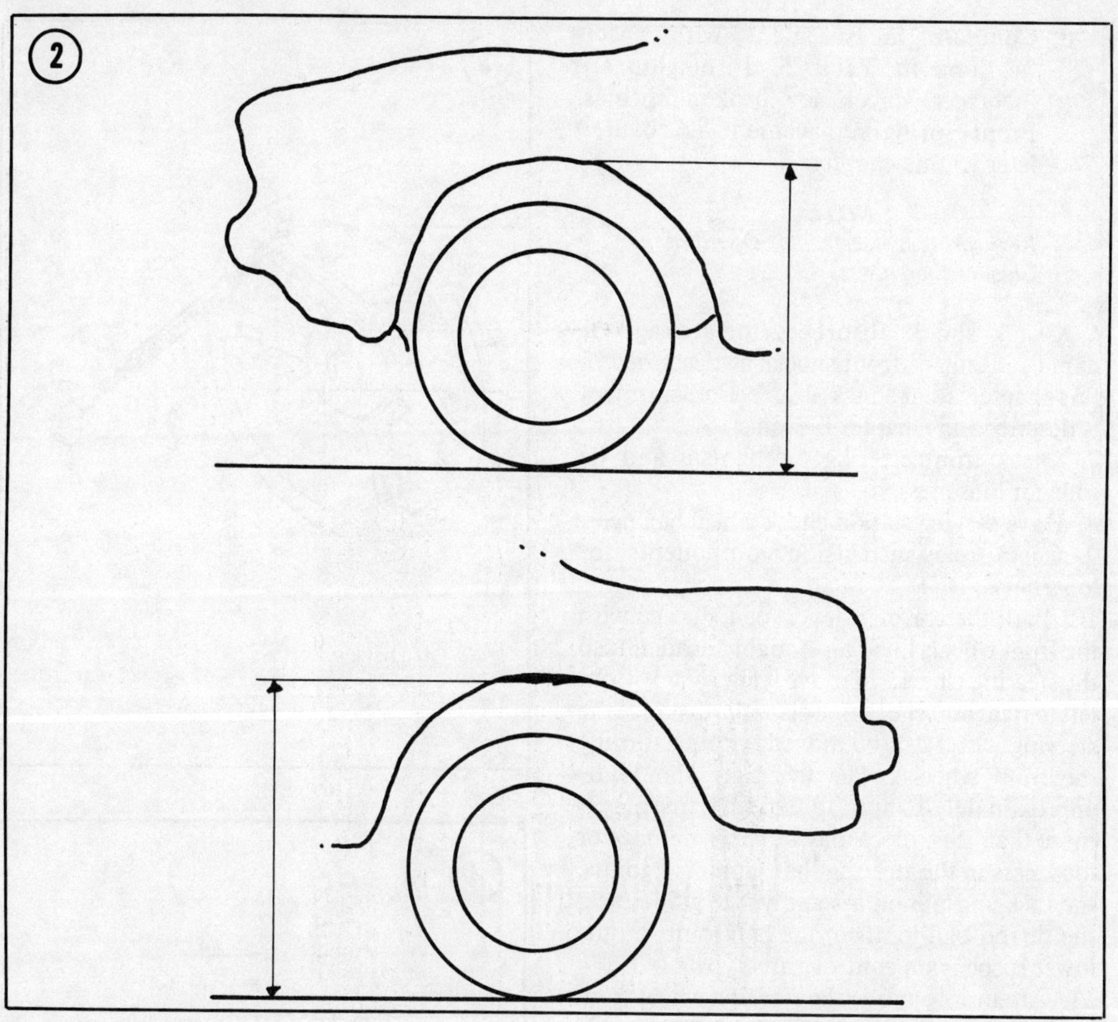

1. Check tire pressure and wear. Correct tire pressure for front and rear tires is 24 psi. Adjust as necessary.

NOTE
Tire pressure should only be checked when the tires are cold (before driving). This is because tire pressures can increase approximately 6 psi when hot. Consquently, altering the air pressure when the tires are hot will result in improper inflation.

2. Check tire wear. See *Tire Wear Analysis*, Chapter Two.
3. Check the play in the front wheel bearings. Adjust if necessary, using the procedures described in this chapter.
4. Check play in ball-joints as described in this chapter.
5. Park the car on level ground. Remove any weighted objects from the car. Tires must be in good condition and properly inflated. Using a good tape measure, perform the following measurements:
   a. 1973-1979 non-CVCC: Measure the distance from the ground to the center of the side marker light lenses, on both sides and front and rear (**Figure 1**).
   b. 1975-1979 CVCC: Measure the distance from the bottom edge of the side marker light lenses, on both sides and front and rear (**Figure 1**).
   c. 1980-on: Measure the distance from the fender to the road surface, both front and rear, as indicated in **Figure 2**.

d. Compare measurement with specifications in **Table 5**. If heights are incorrect, check for broken springs. Front spring replacement is covered later in this chapter.

NOTE
Rear spring replacement is described in Chapter Eleven.

6. Check shock absorbers for leakage or damage. Replace front shocks as described in this chapter. Rear shock absorber replacement is described in Chapter Eleven.
7. Check front steering mechanism and tie rods for looseness.
8. Have service station check wheel balance.
9. Check rear suspension components for looseness.
10. Park the car on a level road surface with the front wheels lined up straight ahead. Grasp the steering wheel and move it alternately from left to right and check free play (the distance the steering wheel can be moved without turning the front wheels). The free play should be approximately 10 mm (13/32 in.). If free play is more than this, there may be wear, damage or looseness in the steering shaft universal joints, the rack and pinion assembly, the guide rack, the tie rod ball-joints or the ball-joints on the lower suspension control arms.
11. Attempt to move the steering wheel from side to side without turning it. Any noticeable movement is an indication that the steering column bushings are worn.

NOTE
Step 12 describes the steering effort check procedure.

12. Raise the vehicle front end and secure with jackstands. Make sure the wheels are lined up facing straight ahead. Attach a spring scale to the steering wheel as shown in **Figure 3**. Then pull on the opposite end of the scale and read the value on the scale. It should not exceed 1.5 kg (3.3 lb). If a greater force was required, the rack may need adjusting, the ball-joints and rack may require lubrication or the steering column bushings or steering universal joints may be worn. Adjust the steering gearbox as described in this chapter.

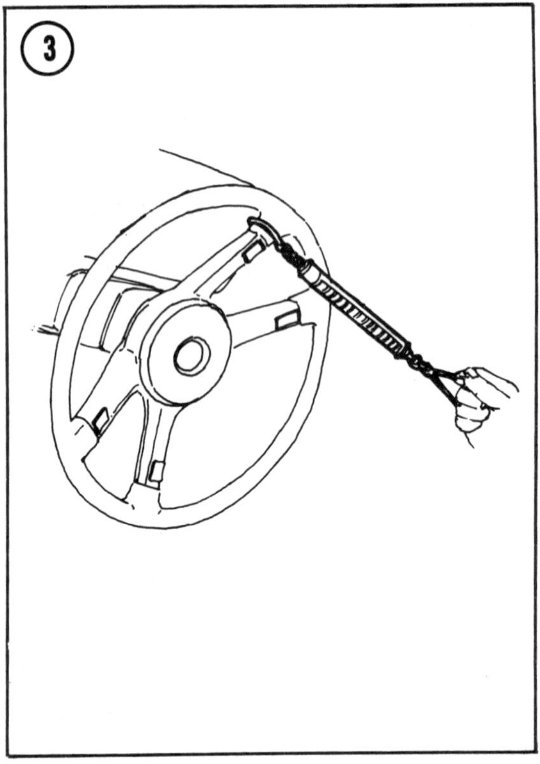

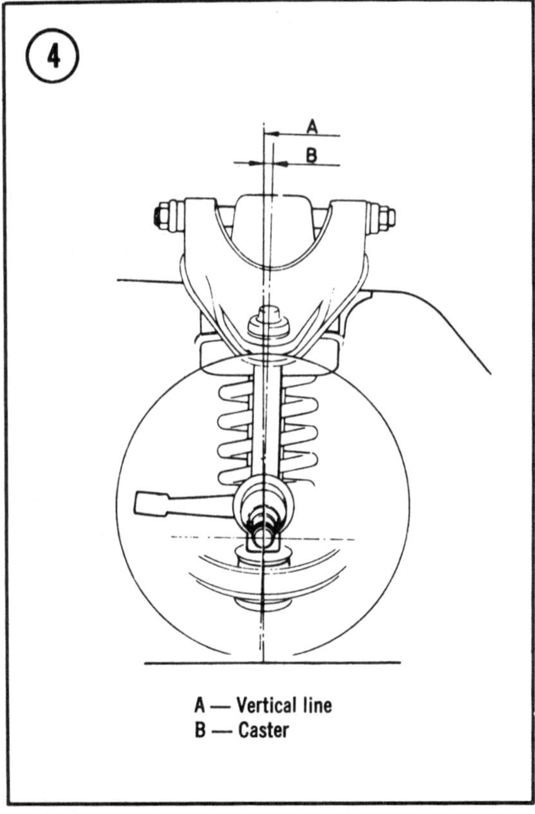

A — Vertical line
B — Caster

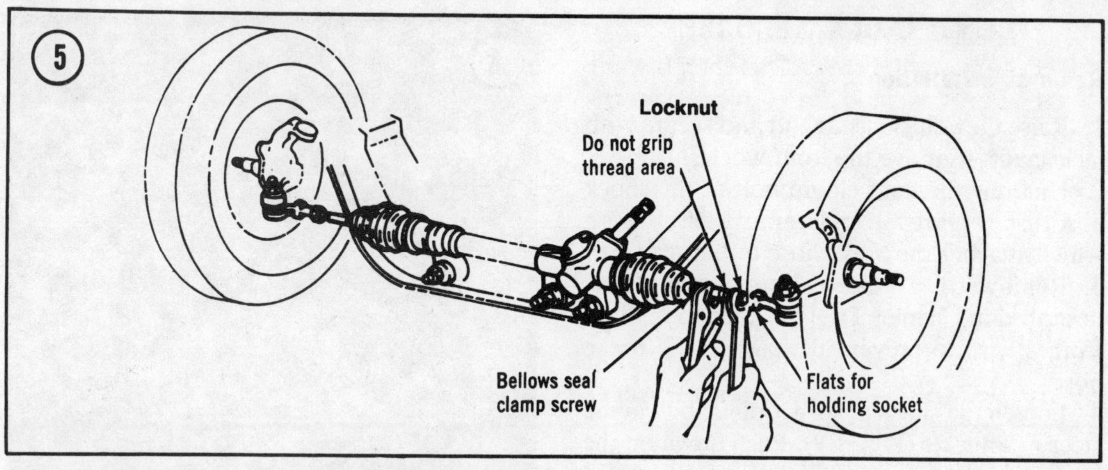

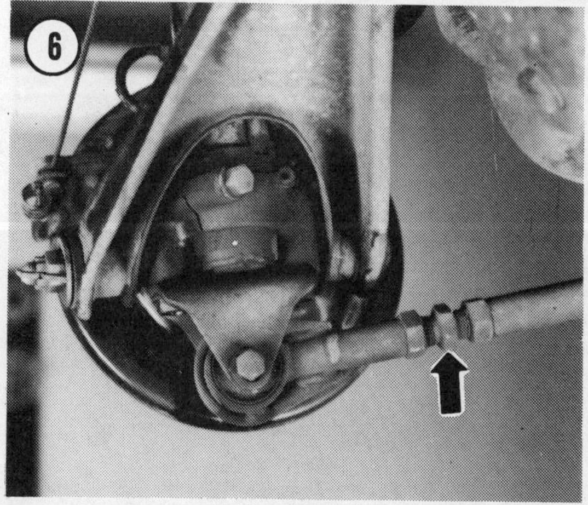

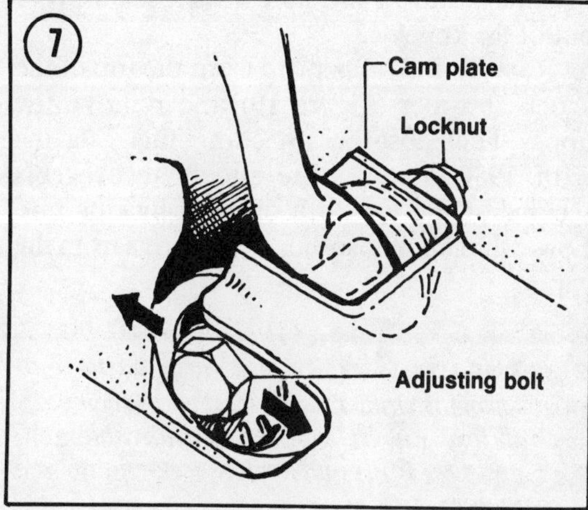

Caster and Camber

Caster is the inclination from vertical of the line through the ball-joints. See **Figure 4**. Positive caster shifts the wheel forward; negative caster shifts the wheel rearward. Caster causes the wheels to return to the straight-ahead position after a turn. It also prevents the wheels from wandering due to wind, potholes or uneven road surfaces.

Camber is the inclination of the wheel from vertical. With positive camber, the top of the tire leans outward; with negative camber, the top of the tire leans inward.

Caster and camber are not adjustable on Civic models.

Toe-out (Front)

Toe-out at the front wheels should match the specifications in **Table 1**. If toe-out is incorrect, loosen the tie rod locknuts at both front wheels (**Figure 5**). Rotate the tie rods to increase or reduce toe-out as needed, then tighten locknuts.

NOTE
Tie rod lengths should be equal after adjustment.

Toe-in (Rear)

Toe-in at the rear wheels can be adjusted with either a rear radius rod adjuster (**Figure 6**) or cam plate and locknut (**Figure 7**). Toe-in should only be adjusted by a Honda dealer or front-end specialist.

Steering Axis Inclination

Steering axis inclination is the inward or outward lean of the angle from vertical through the ball-joints. It is not adjustable on the Honda.

FRONT SHOCK ABSORBER

Removal/Installation

1. Raise the vehicle front end and secure with jackstands. Remove the front wheels.
2. Unscrew the hose clamp bolt at the shock absorber (**Figure 8**) and remove the clamp which attaches the brake hose to the strut.
3. Remove the brake caliper assembly as described in Chapter Twelve. Hang the caliper from a wire to prevent damage to the brake hose.
4. Loosen the shock absorber pinch bolt at the steering knuckle (**Figure 9**). Push down on the knuckle and tap it with a hammer. Then pull the knuckle down and slide the shock absorber out of the knuckle.
5. Remove the rubber cap from the top of the shock absorber (**Figure 10**) and remove the upper shock absorber attaching nuts. Starting with 1980 models, the shock absorber is secured at the top with one self-locking nut. Lower the shock absorber and remove from the car.

WARNING
Do not remove the center nut from the top of the strut. This could allow the coil spring, which is under considerable pressure, to fly out and cause serious injury.

6. Installation is the reverse of these steps. Refer to **Tables 2-4** (end of chapter) for tightening torques. If the brake line was disconnected, bleed the brakes as described in Chapter Twelve.

Disassembly/Reassembly

If you do not possess the special tools and skills required to disassemble the shock absorber/spring assembly, have the service performed by a Honda dealer or machine shop.

1. Secure the shock absorber in a vise.

WARNING
The shock absorber is held under considerable spring pressure. Removal of the center nut without first attaching the necessary special tools would allow the coil spring to fly off and cause serious injury.

8

9

10

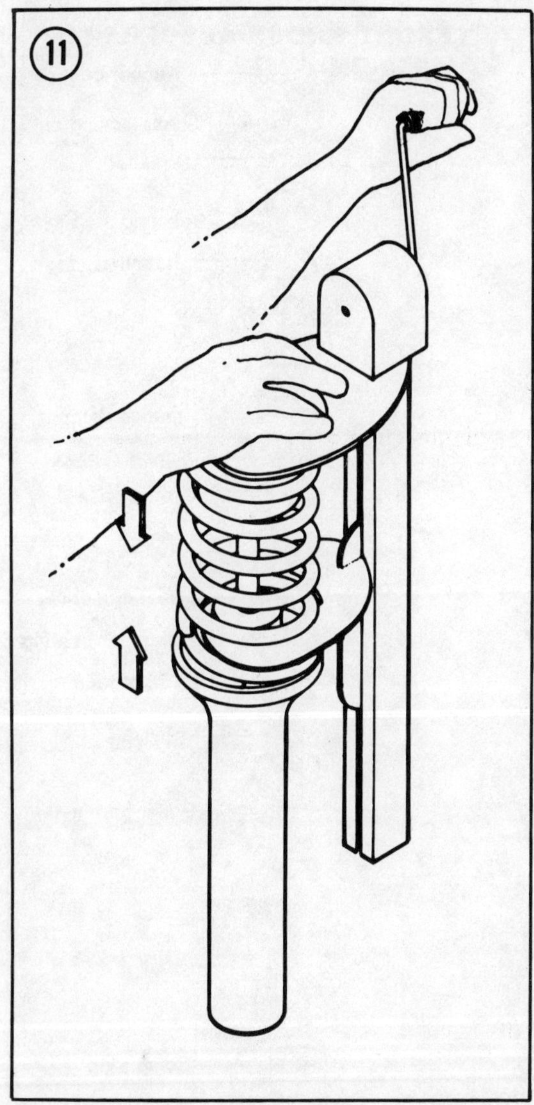

2. Install a coil spring compressor onto the strut assembly as shown in **Figure 11**. Compress the spring as necessary to allow removal of the center nut. Do not compress the spring more than necessary. Remove the center nut.
3. Disassemble the shock absorber in the order shown in **Figure 12** (1973-1979) or **Figure 13** (1980-on).
4. Inspect the shock absorber assembly as described in this chapter.
5. Assemble the shock absorber by reversing Steps 1-3, noting the following.
6. Coat both sides of the needle bearing with multi-purpose grease.
7. Position the ends of the coil spring against the upper and lower spring seat.
8. Install a new center nut and tighten to specifications (**Tables 2-4**). On 1980 and later models, install a hex wrench in the end of the shock absorber rod to hold it from turning while tightening center nut.

Inspection

1. Replace those parts in **Figure 12** or **Figure 13** which appear damaged or worn. Examine the shock absorber. If excessive amounts of fluid are evident along the shock body, replace the shock.

2. Test the shock absorber by working the piston rod up and down in its full length of travel, 4 or 5 times. If hydraulic pressure is present, indicated by the resistance of the piston rod when worked up and down, the shock absorber is working properly. If no resistance is felt, the shock absorber should be replaced.

COIL SPRING REPLACEMENT

The coil spring is part of the shock absorber assembly. To replace the spring, follow the shock absorber *Disassembly/Reassembly* procedure. If you do not possess the necessary special tools and skills, refer the service work to a Honda dealer or machine shop.

FRONT HUB/KNUCKLE

Hub Removal/Installation (1973-1979)

If only hub removal is required, the steering knuckle must be left in position. If both the hub and knuckle assemblies require removal, perform the *Knuckle Removal* procedure.

1. Remove the front hubcaps. Remove the cotter pin and loosen the spindle nut (**Figure 14**) and front wheel nuts.

2. Raise the vehicle front end and secure with jackstands. Remove the front wheels.

3. Remove the brake caliper as described in Chapter Twelve.

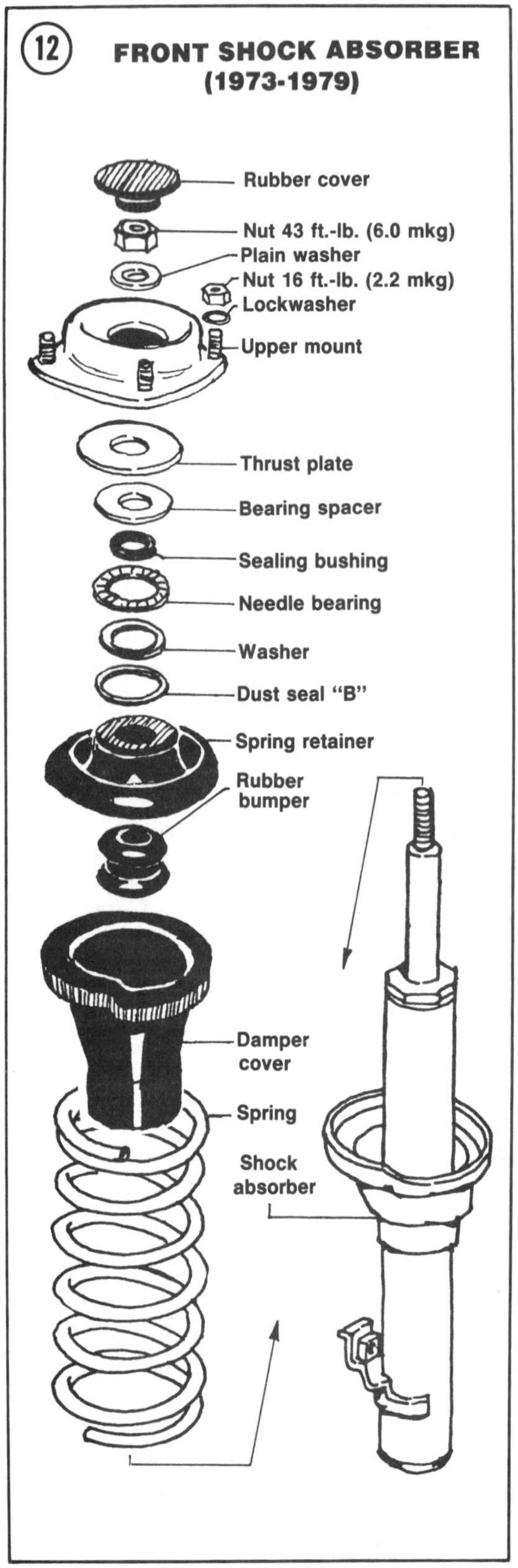

12
FRONT SHOCK ABSORBER (1973-1979)
Rubber cover
Nut 43 ft.-lb. (6.0 mkg)
Plain washer
Nut 16 ft.-lb. (2.2 mkg)
Lockwasher
Upper mount
Thrust plate
Bearing spacer
Sealing bushing
Needle bearing
Washer
Dust seal "B"
Spring retainer
Rubber bumper
Damper cover
Spring
Shock absorber

13
FRONT SHOCK ABSORBER (1980-ON)
Rubber cap
Self-locking nut
Washer
Rebound stop seat
Rebound stop
Jounce damper
Spring seat nut
Mount base
Dust seal
Bearing spacer
Needle roller bearing
Thrust race
Bushing
Upper spring seat
Boot
Bump stop
Coil spring
Shock absorber

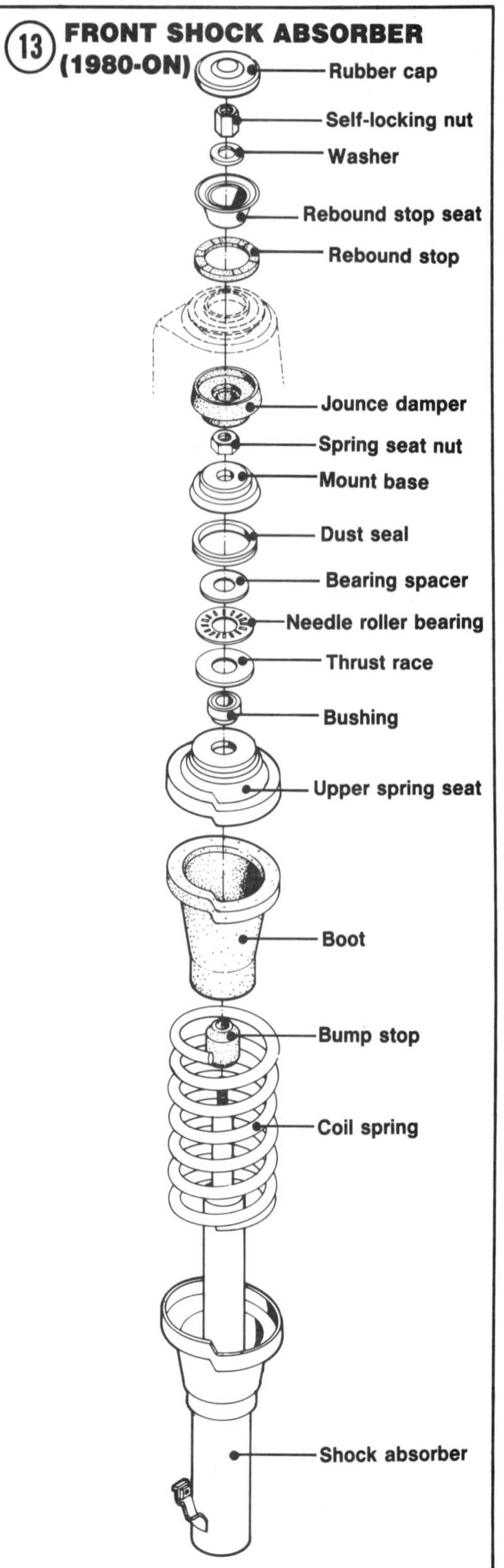

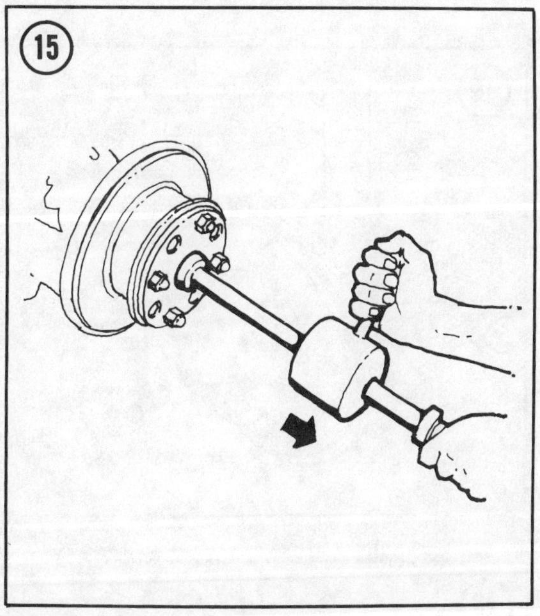

4. Using a knock-puller of the type shown in **Figure 15**, remove the front hub and rotor. To separate hub and rotor, remove the attaching bolts and lockwashers.
5. Installation is the reverse of these steps.. Tighten spindle nut to specifications in **Tables 2-4** (end of chapter).

Knuckle Removal/Installation (1973-1979)

1. Remove the front hubcaps. Loosen the spindle nut (**Figure 14**) and front wheel nuts.
2. Raise the vehicle front end and secure with jackstands. Remove the front wheels.
3. Remove the brake caliper as described in Chapter Twelve.
4. Remove the shock absorber as described in this chapter.
5. Remove the tie rod cotter pin and nut at the knuckle. Then separate the tie rod from knuckle using a puller as shown in **Figure 16**.
6. Remove the lower arm ball-joint cotter pin and nut (**Figure 17**). Then separate tie-rod from knuckle at lower arm by using Honda tool part No. 07941-6590000 (**Figure 18**).
7. With the shock absorber free of the knuckle, pull the hub/knuckle assembly outward and gently slide the drive shaft out of the end of the hub. Remove the hub/knuckle assembly.
8. Installation is the reverse of Steps 1-7. Tightening torques are found in **Tables 2-4**.

Hub/Knuckle Removal/Installation (1980-on)

The hub and knuckle must be removed as an assembly.

1. Remove the front hubcaps. Loosen the spindle nut (**Figure 14**) and front wheel nuts.
2. Raise the vehicle front end and secure with jackstands. Remove the front wheels.
3. Remove the brake caliper as described in Chapter Twelve.
4. Install two M8 x 1.25 x 12 mm (long) bolts into 8 mm threaded holes in the brake disc (**Figure 19**). Turn the bolts 2 turns at a time to push the brake disc away from the hub.
5. Remove and discard the cotter pin at the tie rod-to-knuckle joint. Then remove the nut.
6. Detach the tie rod from the knuckle by using Honda puller part No. 07941-6920001 (or equivalent). See **Figure 20**.
7. Remove the cotter pin and securing nut from the lower arm ball-joint. Discard the cotter pin.
8. Detach the lower control arm ball-joint from the knuckle by using Honda puller part No. 07941-6920000 (**Figure 21**). Pull the lower control arm down until the ball-joint is clear of the knuckle.
9. Remove the shock absorber-to-knuckle pinch bolt. Then tap the knuckle downward until it is free of the shock absorber.
10. With the shock absorber free of the knuckle, pull the hub/knuckle assembly outward and gently slide the drive shaft out of the end of the hub. Remove the hub/knuckle assembly.
11. To separate the hub from the knuckle, place the assembly in a hydraulic press and press the hub off the knuckle.
12. Installation is the reverse of Steps 1-11. Use a new spindle nut. Torque all fasterners to specifications in **Tables 2-4**.

WHEEL BEARINGS

Front wheel bearing removal requires a number of special tools and procedures. If replacement of the front wheel bearing becomes necessary on your car, remove the knuckle arm assembly as described in this

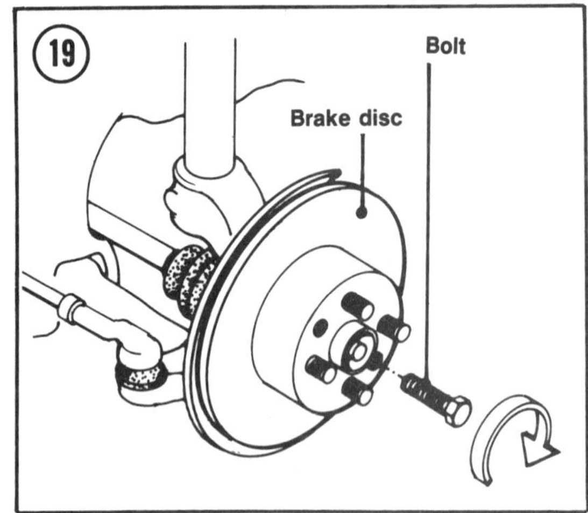

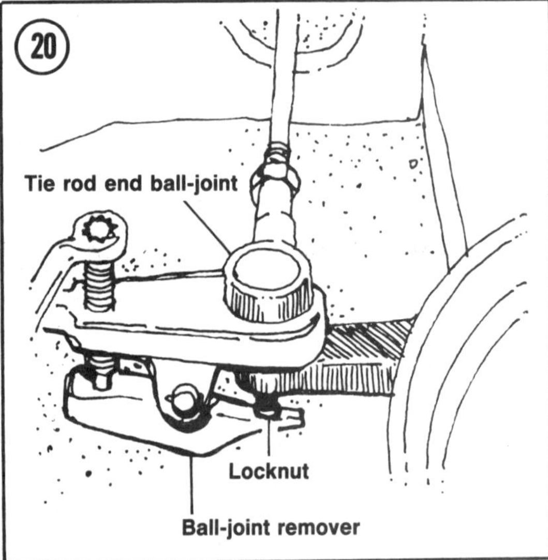

chapter (**Figure 22**). Take the knuckle arm to a Honda dealer for wheel bearing replacement.

Inspection

To check the front wheel bearing end play, raise the vehicle's front end and place it on jackstands. Grasp the tire firmly and try to pull it straight in and out. There should be a slight end play. If there is no end play or if end play seems excessive, check the front spindle nut torque (**Tables 2-4**). If torque is correct, remove the knuckle arm assembly as described in this chapter and have a Honda dealer inspect the front wheel bearings for wear or damage.

LOWER CONTROL ARM, BALL-JOINTS AND STABILIZER BAR

Removal (1973-1979)

Refer to **Figure 23** for this procedure.

1. Raise the vehicle front end and secure with jackstands. Remove the front wheels.
2. Refer to **Figure 17**. Remove the cotter key from the castellated nut on the end of the ball-joint and unscrew the nut.
3. Disconnect the steering knuckle from the control arm with the Honda ball-joint remover (part No. 07941-6340100) as shown in **Figure 18** by driving the wedge into the holder to displace the ball-joint downward.
4. Unscrew the nut from the end of the control arm radius arm. Unscrew the bolts from the stabilizer bar center mounts and collect the clamps and bushings.
5. Unscrew the pivot bolt from the inboard end of the control arm and remove the arm.

Installation (1973-1979)

1. Replace any worn or damaged parts.
2. Slide the end of the control arm into its position in the engine support beam and secure with the lower arm pivot bolt. Install the nut but do not tighten it at this time.
3. Grease the control arm ball-joint. Then insert the opposite end of the control arm up into the knuckle. Install the castellated nut on the end of the ball-joint, but do not tighten it.
4. Install a jack underneath the knuckle arm. Raise the knuckle arm until the car just raises off the jackstand. Tighten the lower arm pivot bolt and nut to specifications. Secure with new cotter pin.
5. Tighten the suspension arm-to-ball-joint nut to specifications. Install a new cotter pin

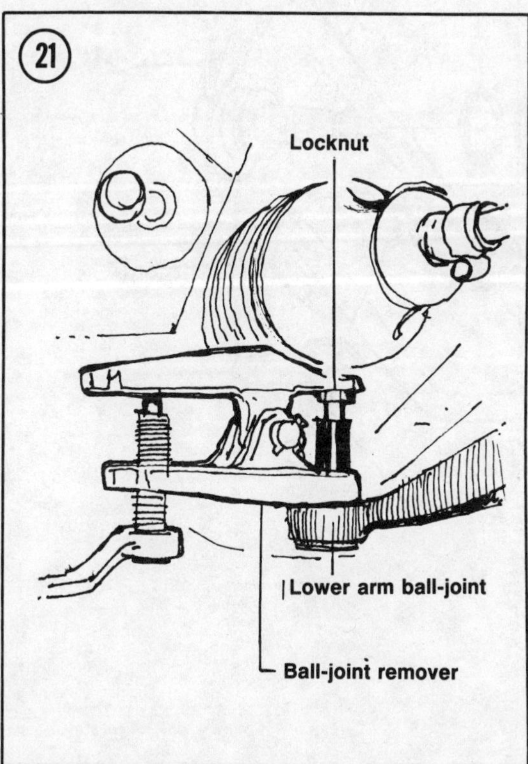

10

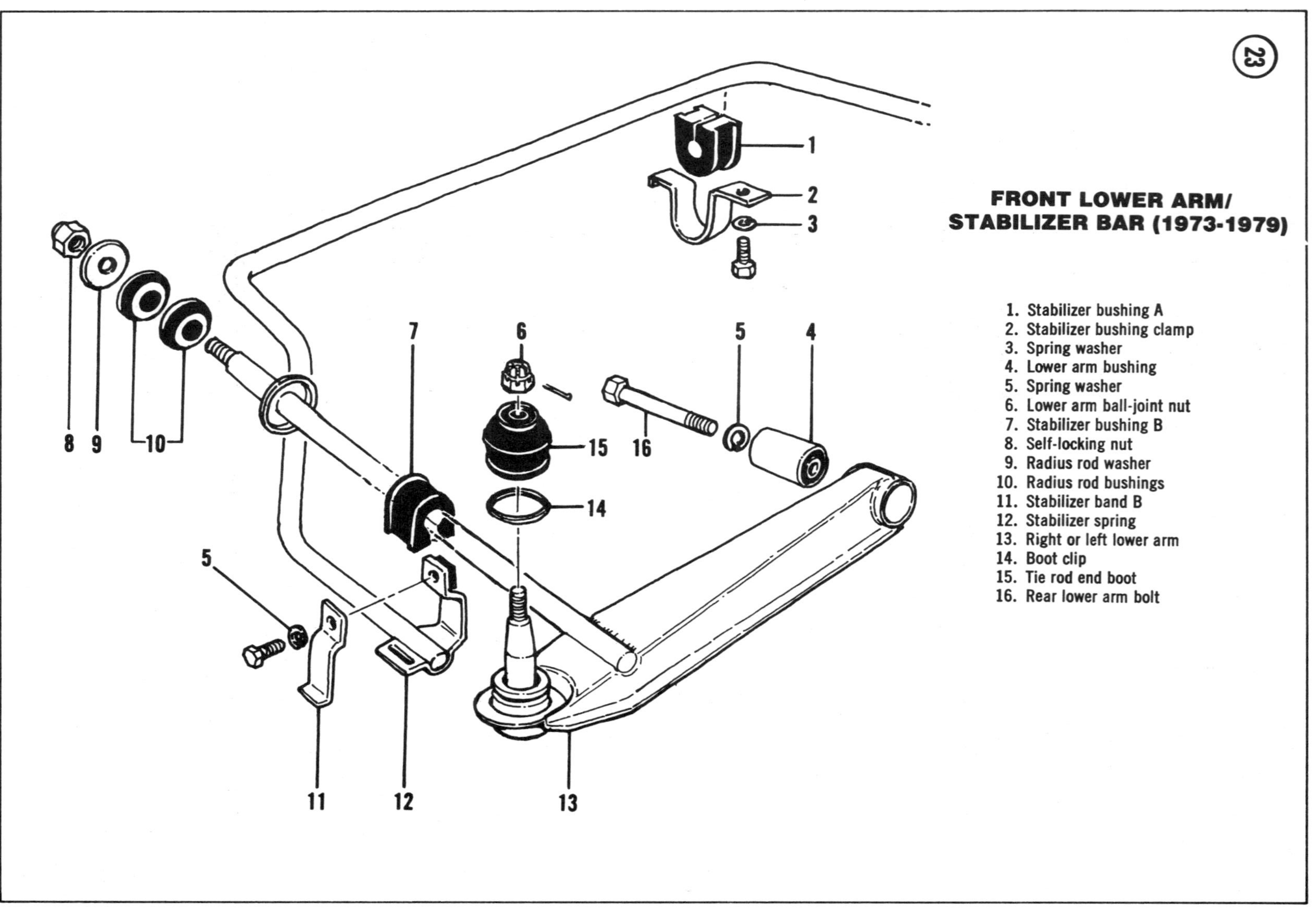
23
FRONT LOWER ARM/
STABILIZER BAR (1973-1979)
1. Stabilizer bushing A
2. Stabilizer bushing clamp
3. Spring washer
4. Lower arm bushing
5. Spring washer
6. Lower arm ball-joint nut
7. Stabilizer bushing B
8. Self-locking nut
9. Radius rod washer
10. Radius rod bushings
11. Stabilizer band B
12. Stabilizer spring
13. Right or left lower arm
14. Boot clip
15. Tie rod end boot
16. Rear lower arm bolt
1
2
3
8
9
10
7
6
5
4
15
16
14
5
11
12
13

through the ball-joint stud and bend pin end over to secure.
6. Reverse the removal steps to install the radius rod and stabilizer bar. Tightening torques are found in **Tables 2-4**.

Removal (1980-on)

Refer to **Figure 24** for this procedure.
1. Raise the vehicle front end and secure with jackstands. Remove the front wheels.
2. Remove stabilizer bar-to-lower arm attaching nut. Discard the nut. Then pull the stabilizer out of the lower arm. Collect the stabilizer bar bushings and washers.
3. Remove the cotter key from the castellated nut on the end of the ball-joint and unscrew the nut.
4. Disconnect the steering knuckle from the control arm with the Honda puller tool part No. 07941-6920000 (**Figure 20**).
5. Unscrew the pivot bolt from the inboard end of the control arm and remove the arm. Discard the pivot bolt.

Installation (1980-on)

1. Replace any worn or damaged parts.
2. Slide the end of the control arm into its position in the engine support beam and secure with a new lower arm pivot bolt. Install the bolt but do not tighten fully.
3. Grease the control arm ball-joint. Then insert the opposite end of the control arm up into the knuckle. Install the castellated nut on the end of the ball-joint, but do not tighten it.
4. Install the stabilizer bar into the lower arm, making sure to install the bushings and washers in the direction shown in **Figure 24**. If the stabilizer bar was removed from the car, install it with the painted stripe side inserted into the lower arm on the driver's side.
5. Install a jack underneath the knuckle arm. Raise the knuckle arm until the car just raises off the jackstand. Tighten the lower arm pivot bolt to specifications.
6. Tighten the suspension arm-to-ball-joint nut to specifications. Install a new cotter pin through the ball-joint stud and bend pin end over to secure.
7. Tighten the stabilizer bar-to-lower arm nuts to specifications.

Ball-joint Inspection (All Models)

1. Raise vehicle front end and secure with jackstands.
2. Install a dial indicator onto the lower control arm. Place the tip of the dial indicator on the knuckle near the ball-joint.
3. Place a pry bar between the knuckle and lower control arm. Push and release the bar while observing the indicator movement. If the indicator shows 0.5 mm (0.020 in.) or more of movement, replace the lower control arm as described in this chapter.

STEERING WHEEL

Removal/Installation

Figure 25 shows a typical steering wheel. Refer to it as needed for this procedure.
1. Pull the pad off the center of the steering wheel.
2. Unscrew the steering wheel nut and remove the wheel assembly from the column.
3. Reverse to install. Tighten the steering wheel nut to specifications.

STEERING COLUMN

The following steering column removal and installation procedures are for non-power steering models only. On power steering models, a special guide tool is required to hold the steering shaft in a predetermined position during column installation. All work pertaining to steering column removal and installation with power steering should be referred to a Honda dealer.

Removal

NOTE
Make sure the ignition switch is in the OFF-LOCKED position. This assures that the steering shaft will not slip out of its housing as the steering column is removed.

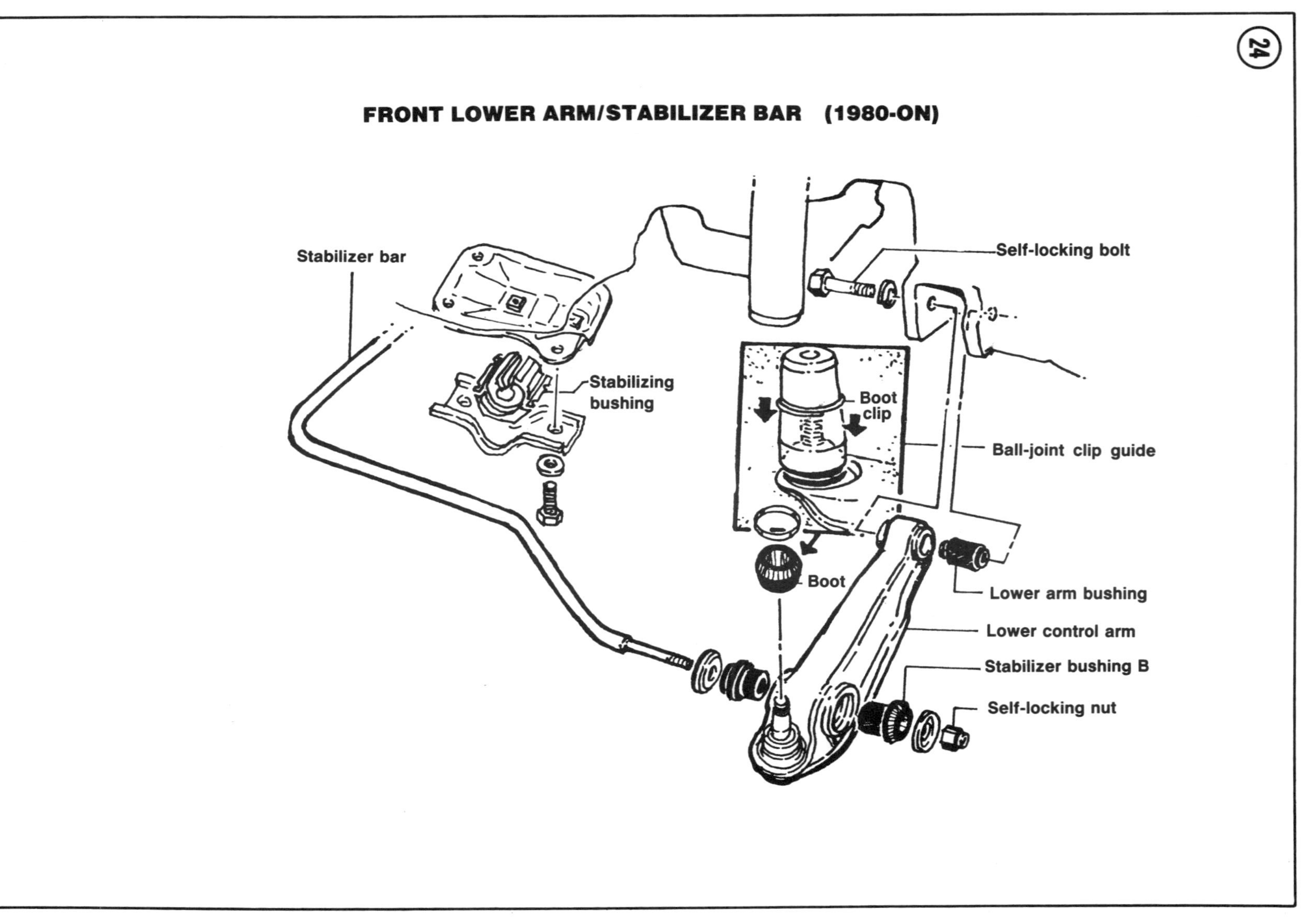

FRONT LOWER ARM/STABILIZER BAR (1980-ON)

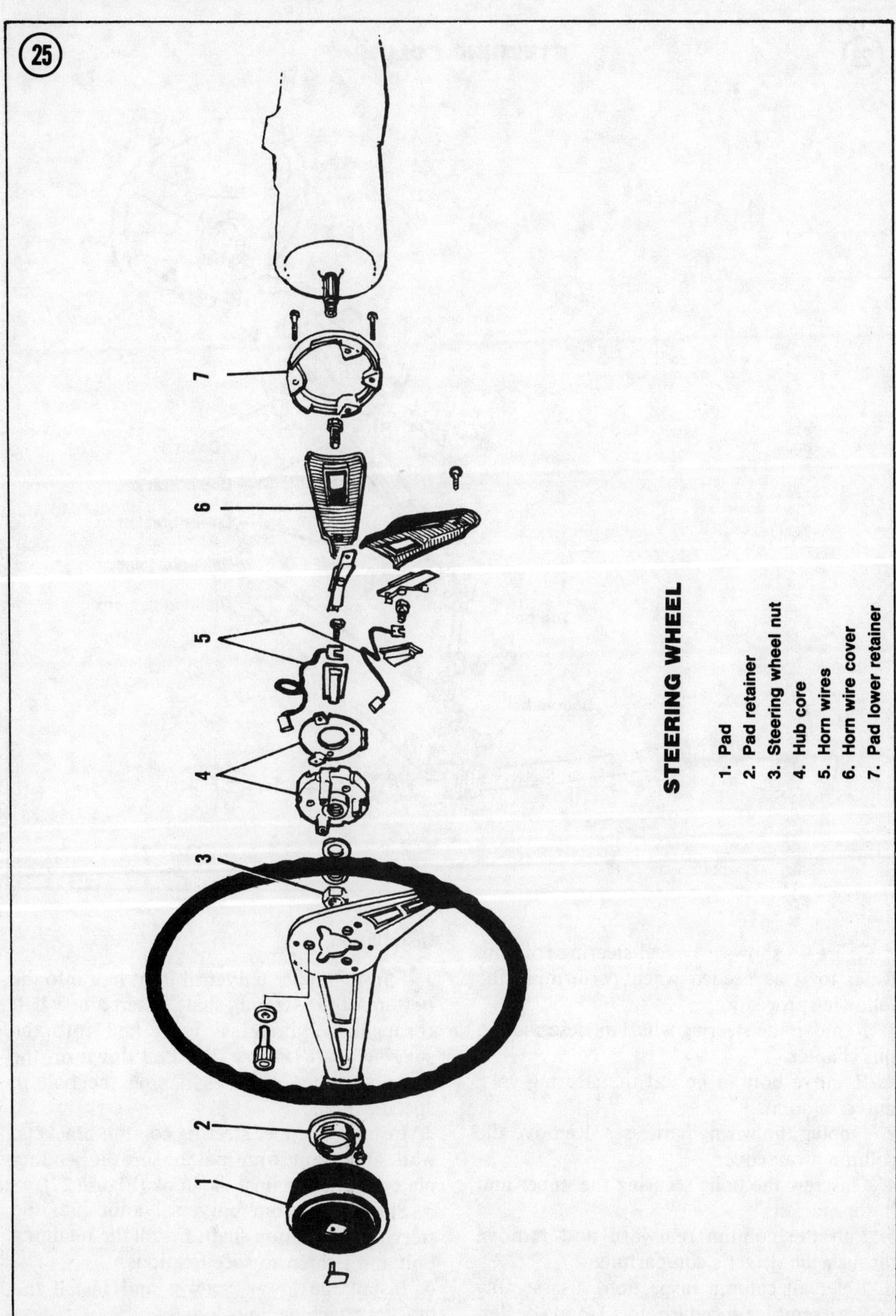
25
1
2
3
4
5
6
7
STEERING WHEEL
1. Pad
2. Pad retainer
3. Steering wheel nut
4. Hub core
5. Horn wires
6. Horn wire cover
7. Pad lower retainer

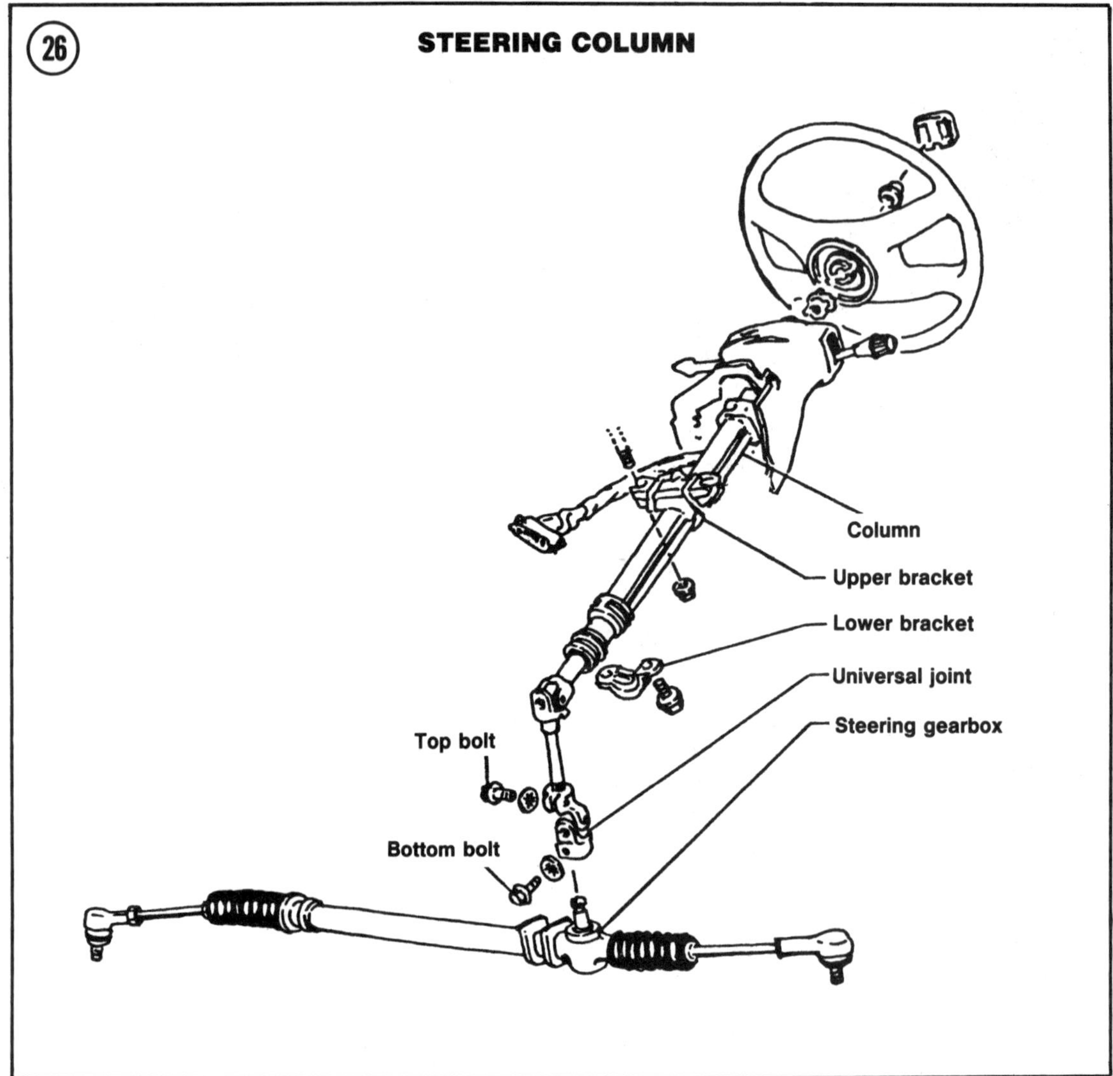

Figure 26 shows a typical steering column. Refer to it as needed when performing the following procedure.

1. Remove the steering wheel as described in this chapter.
2. Remove bottom bolt at the steering yoke universal joint.
3. Unplug the wiring harnesses. Remove the column lower cover.
4. Unscrew the bolts securing the upper and lower brackets.
5. Pull the column rearward and remove through the driver's compartment.
6. Refer all column inspection, disassembly and reassembly procedures to a Honda dealer.

Installation

1. Slip the upper universal joint half into the bottom of the steering shaft. Insert a new bolt through the universal joint and into the steering shaft (**Figure 26**). Pull down on the universal joint while tightening the bolt to specifications.
2. Install the upper steering column brackets, while at the same time making sure the bending plate is seated against the hook (**Figure 27**).
3. Slip the bottom universal joint into the steering gear pinion shaft. Install the retaining bolt and tighten to specifications.
4. Install the lower bracket and install the bracket attaching bolts loosely.

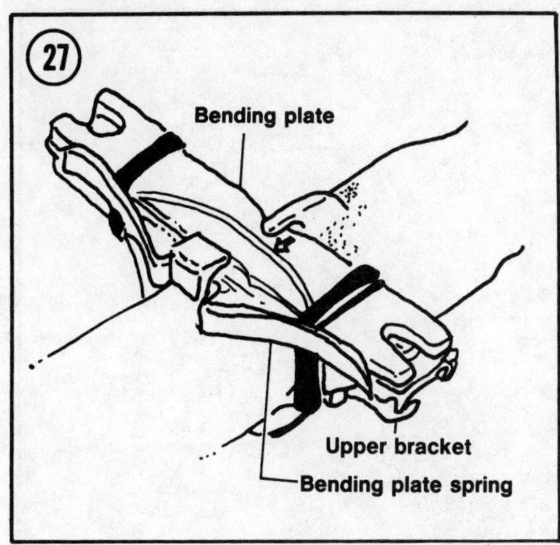

5. Tighten the upper and lower bracket bolts to specifications.
6. Connect all wiring connectors. Install the steering wheel as described in this chapter.

STEERING GEAR

Adjustment

If an incorrect steering wheel force reading is obtained during *Front Suspension Inspection* perform the following steering gearbox adjustment. Refer to **Figure 28**.

1. Loosen the locknut on the rack guide adjuster screw. Then tighten the rack guide adjusting screw until it just bottoms.
2. Back out the rack guide adjusting screw 45°. Hold the rack guide adjusting screw to prevent it from turning further and tighten the locknut.
3. Check the steering effort as described under *Steering Inspection* in this chapter. Move the front wheels from lock to lock to ensure that the rack moves freely and smoothly. If necessary, adjust the rack until it is correct.
4. Road test the car to make sure it is operating correctly.

Lubrication

To check the steering gear lubrication, loosen the steering gear dust cover retaining bands (**Figure 29**) and slide dust cover to one side. Check rack for lubrication. If dry, add multipurpose grease in the rack. Reposition the dust cover and secure with retaining bands.

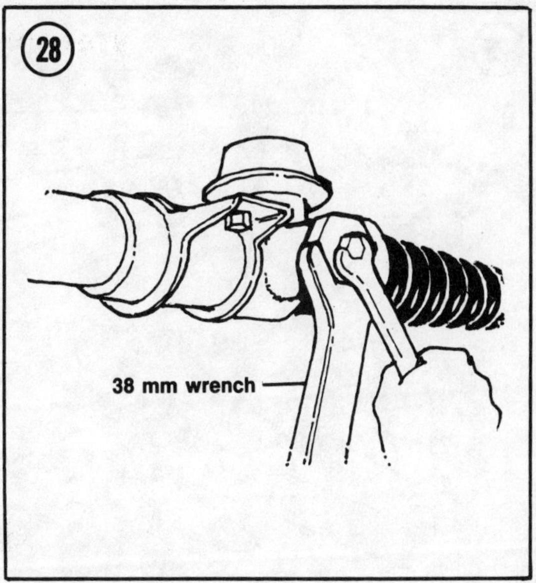

Removal/Installation (1973-1979)

Reconditioning of the steering gearbox should be entrusted to a Honda dealer. Service described here is limited to removal and installation of non-power steering gear units. Power steering unit removal and installation should be performed by a Honda dealer.

1. Raise the vehicle front end and secure with jackstands. Remove the front wheels.

2. Attach an engine hanger to the engine as described in *Manual Transaxle Removal* or *Automatic Transaxle Removal*, Chapter Nine. Lift the engine slightly to take the load off the engine mounts.

3. Disconnect the tie rod ends with a puller as shown in **Figure 16**.

4. Unscrew the nuts which mount the exhaust pipe to the exhaust manifold. Then disconnect the pipe from the manifold.

5. *Manual transaxle models:* Using a punch as shown in **Figure 30**, drive the pin out of the gearshift rod. Then remove the gearshift extension arm at the transaxle (**Figure 31**).

6. *Automatic transaxle models:* Disconnect the shift control cable at the transaxle (**Figure 32**).

29

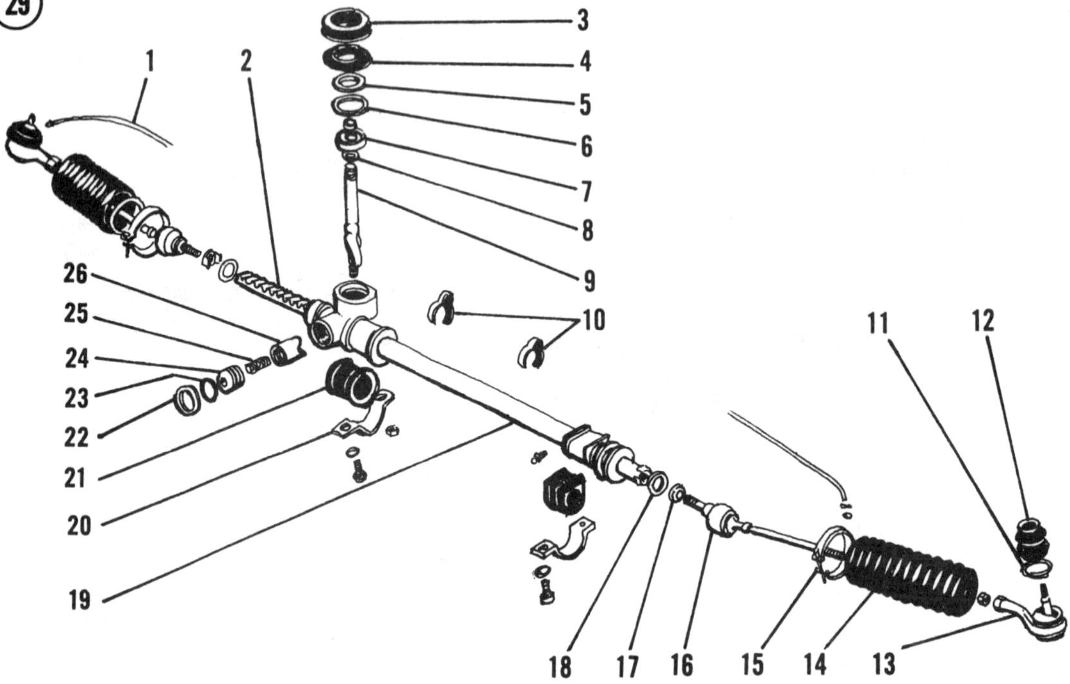

STEERING BOX

1. Air tube
2. Steering rack
3. Outer dust seal
4. Inner dust seal
5. Steering pinion dust seal
6. Internal snap ring
7. Ball bearing
8. Steering pinion washer
9. Steering pinion
10. Air tube clips
11. Circlip
12. Ball-joint seal
13. Tie rod end
14. Tie rod dust seal
15. Bellow band
16. Tie rod
17. Tie rod lockwasher
18. Tie rod stop washer
19. Gearbox
20. Gearbox bracket
21. Gearbox mounting cushion
22. Rack screw locknut
23. Rack guide O-ring
24. Rack guide screw
25. Rack guide pressure spring
26. Steering rack guide

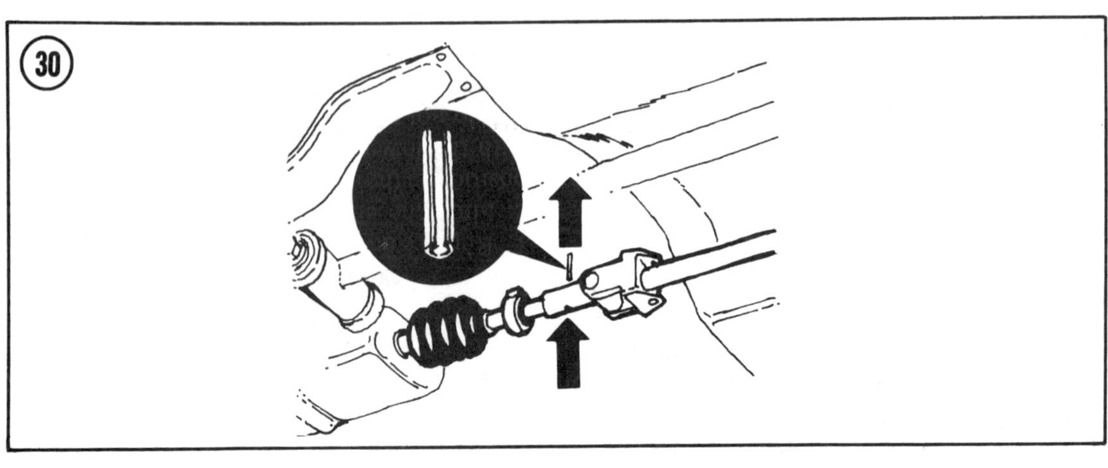

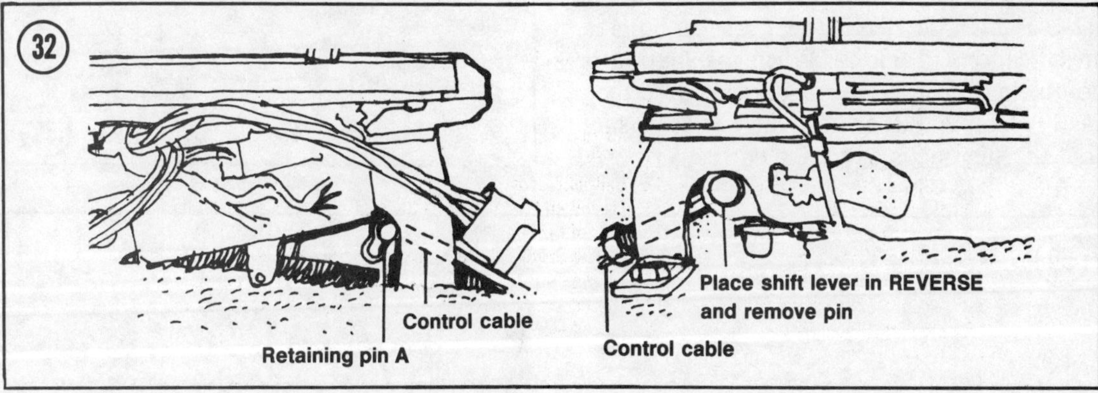

10

7. Unscrew the bolts which mount the center beam to the crossmembers (**Figure 33**) and remove the center beam.
8. Turn the front wheel all the way to the right.
9. Completely unscrew the pinch bolt attaching the bottom universal joint to the pinion shaft and disconnect the joint (**Figure 26**).
10. Unscrew the bolts which mount the steering gear (**Figure 34**). Angle the steering tie rod up and lower the rack until the pinion shaft is clear of the body. Then rotate the rack until the pinion shaft is facing down. Move the rack to the right until the left tie rod is clear and then remove the rack assembly through the left side.
11. Reverse the removal steps to install the rack. Tighten the steering gear bracket bolts to specifications. When installation is complete, adjust the steering gear as described in this chapter. Road test the car to ensure that the steering is operating correctly.

Removal/Installation (1980-on)

Refer to **Figure 35** for this procedure. Reconditioning of the steering gearbox should be entrusted to a Honda dealer. Service described here is limited to removal and installation of non-powering steering gear units. Power steering unit removal and installation should be performed by a Honda dealer.

1. Raise the vehicle front end and secure with jackstands. Remove the front wheels.
2. Remove the cotter pin from the upper tie rod at the knuckle arm. Loosen the castle nut and back out half way.
3. Install the Honda ball-joint remover (part No. 07941-6920000) to the ball-joint as shown in **Figure 20** and pry the tie rod joint loose. Then remove the castle nut.
4. Completely unscrew the pinch bolt attaching the bottom universal joint to the pinion shaft and disconnect the joint.
5. Unscrew the bolts which mount the steering gear to the frame.
6. Drop the steering gear assembly downward and rotate 180°. Move the steering gear to the left and remove from the vehicle.
7. Reverse the removal steps to install the rack. Tighten the steering gear bracket bolts to specifications (**Table 2**). When installation is complete, adjust the steering gear as described in this chapter. Road test the car to ensure that the steering is operating correctly.

TIE ROD BALL-JOINT

Seal Replacement

The following procedure describes replacement of the tie rod end ball-joint seal for those seals which are held in place with a retaining ring. If the tie rod ball-joint seal does not have a retaining ring, the complete tie rod end must be replaced.

1. Raise the vehicle front end and secure with jackstands. Remove the front wheels.

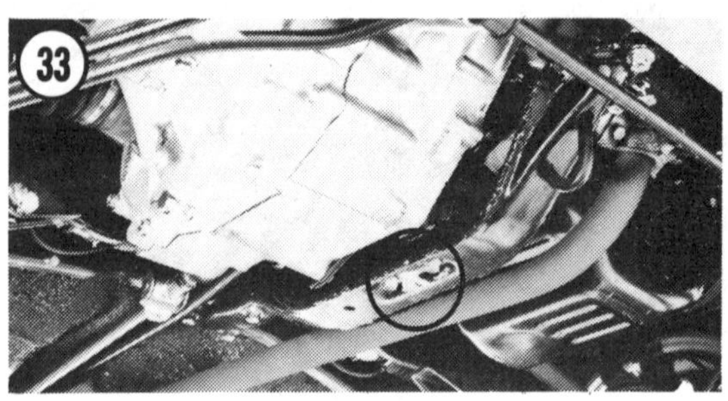

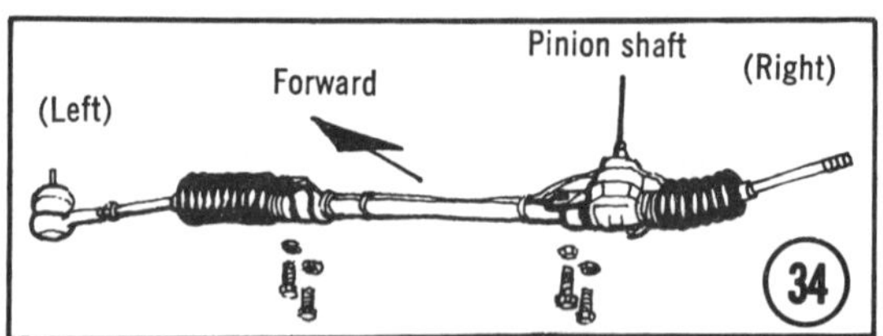

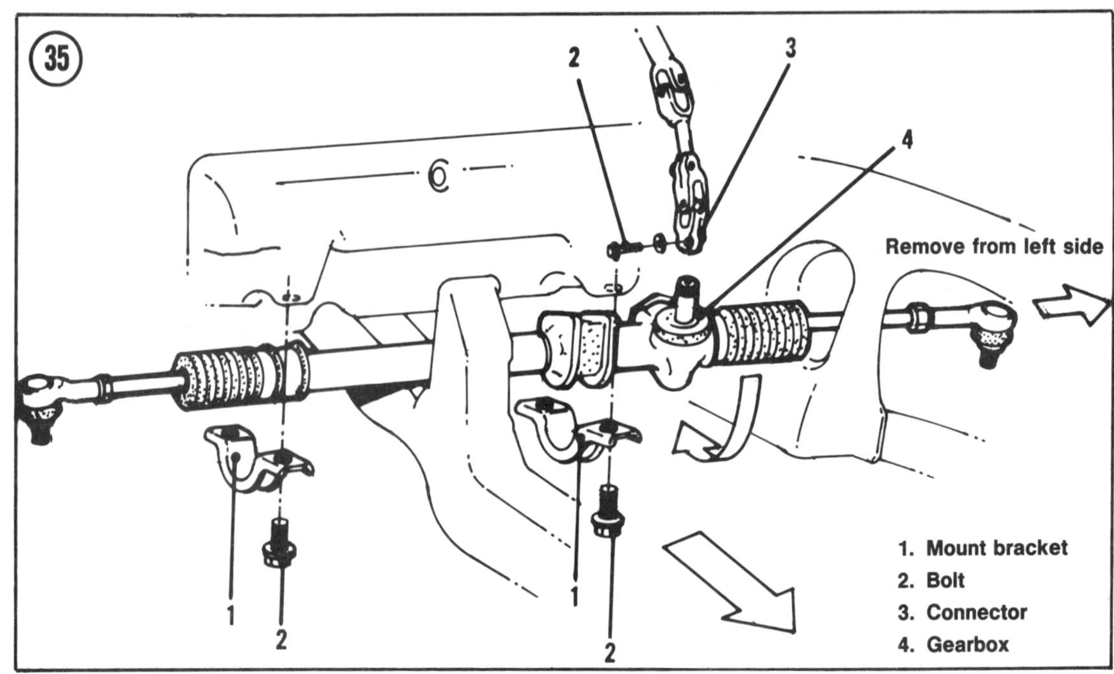

2. Disconnect the ball-joints from the knuckle arm using a ball-joint remover as described under *Steering Gear Removal.*

3. Peel the retaining ring off the seal (**Figure 36**). Wipe dirt and grease off the ball-joint.

4. Put 1/4 oz. of grease in the new seal. Take care to keep grease off the seal lip and out of the snap ring groove (**Figure 37**).

5. Install the new seal onto the ball-joint. Then install the snap ring guide (Honda tool part No. 07974-6710000) and install a new snap ring (**Figure 38**).

6. Press down on the seal as shown in **Figure 39** and bleed the air from it.

7. Installation is the reverse of these steps. When installation is complete, check the steering thoroughly as described in *Front Suspension Inspection.* Adjust the front toe-out as described in this chapter.

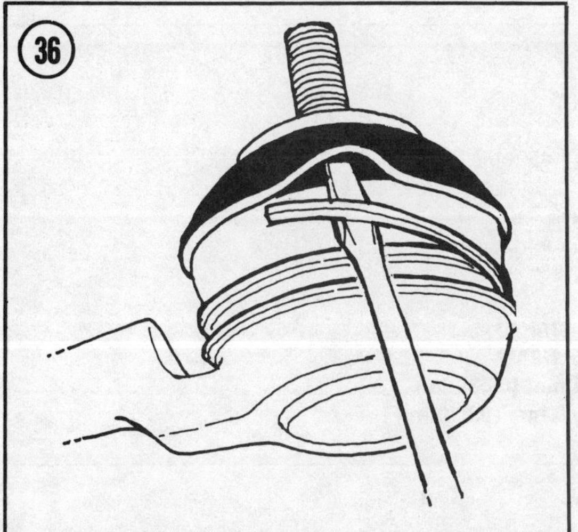

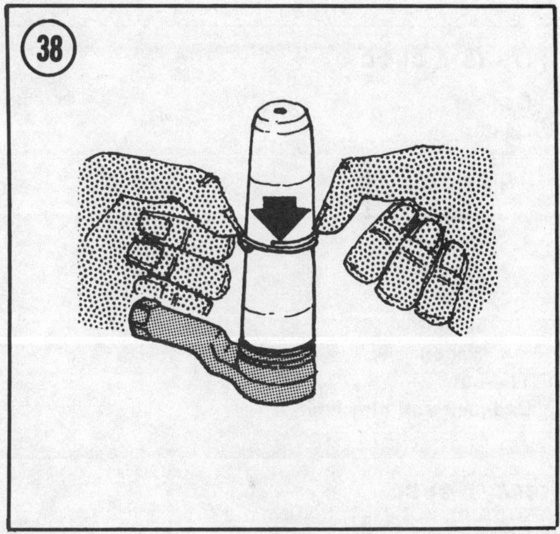

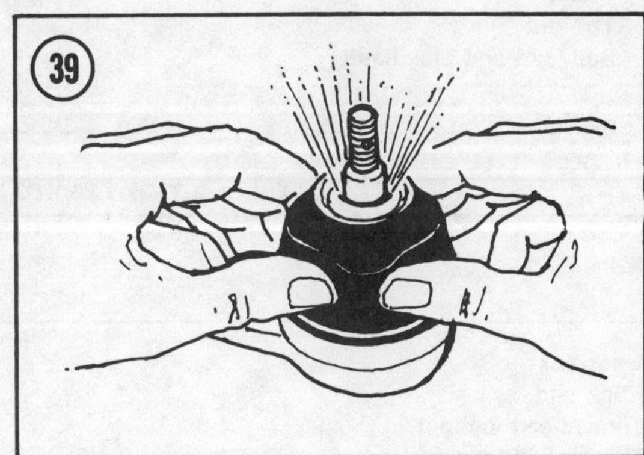

10

Tables are on the following page.

Table 1 SUSPENSION SPECIFICATIONS

Non-CVCC	
Camber	
1973-1976	30° positive
1977	0° 30 min.
1978-1979	1/2°
Caster	
1973-1977	1° 45 min.
1978-1979	2.3°
Toe-in	1 mm (0.04 in.)
Ball-joint end play limit	0.5 mm (0.020 in.)
1975-1979 CVCC	
Camber	1/2°
Caster	
1975	1° 45 min.
1976	
Sedan	2°
Wagon	55 min.
1977	1/2°
1978-1979	
Sedan	+3/4°
Wagon	+1/2°
Toe-out	1 mm (0.039 in.)
Ball-joint end play limit	0.5 mm (0.020 in.)
1980-on CVCC	
Camber	0°
Caster	1° 45 min.
Toe-out	0 mm
Ball-joint end play limit	0.5 mm (0.020 in.)

Table 2 TIGHTENING TORQUES (NON-CVCC)

Item	mkg	ft.-lb.
Gear box	1.9-2.5	14-18
Rack end	5.0-6.0	36-43
Tie rod end locknut	4.0-4.8	29-35
Tie rod ball-joint	4.0-4.8	29-35
Steering joint bolt	2.4-3.0	17-22
Steering wheel nut	3.0-4.5	22-33
Steering column	1.8-2.5	13-18
Rack guide locknut	4.0-5.0	29-36
Radius rod	3.5-5.0	25-36
Lower arm	3.5-5.0	25-36
Shock absorber at knuckle	5.0-6.0	36-43
Shock absorber (top)	1.0-1.6	7-12
Shock absorber center nut	5.5-7.0	39-50
Stabilizer bracket	0.7-1.2	5-9
Front spindle nut	12.0-18.0	87-130

Table 3 TIGHTENING TORQUES (1975-1979 CVCC)

Item	mkg	ft.-lb.
Rack guide locknut	4.0-5.0	29-36
Steering column (lower)	1.9-2.5	14-18
Steering gear box	1.9-2.5	14-18
Steering joint yoke bolt	3.0-3.5	22-25
Steering wheel	3.0-4.5	22-33
Tie rod		
Ball-joint	4.0-4.8	29-35
End locknuts	4.0-4.5	29-33
Rack ends	5.0-6.0	36-43
Backing plate	1.9-2.5	14-18
Hub carrier and shock absorber	3.5-5.0	25-36
Hub nut	12.0-18.0	87-130
Lower arm		
Ball-joint	3.0-4.0	22-29
Radius rod	4.0-5.0	29-36
Shock absorber		
Center nut	5.5-7.0	40-51
Rubber mount	1.0-1.6	7-12
Shock absorber and body	1.0-1.6	7-12
Shock absorber and knuckle	5.0-6.0	36-43
Spindle nut	12.0-18.0	87-130

Table 4 TIGHTENING TORQUES (1980-ON CVCC)

Item	mkg	ft.-lb.
Steering column		
Universal joint (1980)		
Top, middle and bottom bolts		
Forged joint	3.0	22
Pressed joint	2.3	16
Universal joint (1981)		
Top and bottom bolts	3.0	22
Lower clamp bolt	2.2	16
Upper clamp bolt (1981)	1.0	7
Steering wheel nut		
1980	4.0	29
1981	5.0	36
Tie rod ball-joint nut	4.4	32
Tie rod end locknut	4.4	32
Shock absorber		
Top locknut	4.5	33
Bottom pinch bolt	5.0	36
Shock absorber spring seat nut	2.3	16
Spindle nut	15.0	108
Lower control arm pivot bolt		
1980	3.9	28
1981	5.5	40
Knuckle bottom bolt	3.5	25
Stabilizer bar at lower arm	4.4	32

10

Table 5 SPRING HEIGHT SPECIFICATIONS

	Standard		Service Limit	
	mm	in.	mm	in.
1973-1979 Non-CVCC	655	25.8	640	25.2
1975-1979 CVCC	630	24.8	615	24.2
1980 CVCC				
Hatchback	647	25.5	632	24.85
Wagon	651	25.6	636	25
1981 CVCC				
Hatchback				
1300cc (1)	650	25.6	635	25.0
1300cc (2)	640	25.2	625	24.6
1500	646	25.4	631	24.8
Wagon	653	25.7	638	25.1
Sedan	647	25.5	632	24.9

(1) With tire size 6.00 S 12
(2) With tire size 155 SR 12

NOTE: If you own a 1982 or later model, first check the Supplement at the back of the book for any new service information.

CHAPTER ELEVEN

REAR SUSPENSION

The sedan and hatchback rear suspension consists of independent MacPherson struts (integrated coil springs and shock absorbers) controlling independent trailing arms. The station wagon uses leaf springs and separate shock absorbers.

Service procedures for the shock absorbers and springs, bushed joints and wheel bearings and seals are covered in this chapter.

Tables 1-4 are at the end of the chapter.

CAUTION
All fasteners used in the rear suspension must be replaced with parts of the same type. ***Do not*** *use a replacement part of lesser quality or substitute design, as it may affect the performance of vital components and systems or result in major repair expenses.*

NOTE
Many of the fasteners used in securing the rear suspension components are of the self-locking type—i.e, the fastener has some type of locking feature built into the threads. When installing a self-locking bolt or nut, it will not turn freely on the mating thread. The self-locking design prevents the fastener from working loose due to vibration during vehicle operation. If a self-locking fastener can be threaded by hand, it should be replaced.

REAR SHOCK ABSORBER

Replacement (1973-1979 Sedan and Hatchback)

Refer to **Figure 1** for this procedure.

1. Block the front wheels. Raise the vehicle rear end and secure with jackstands. Remove the rear wheels.
2. Unscrew the brake line connection at the bottom of the shock absorber (**Figure 2**). Slide the clip back and remove the brake hose from the shock absorber.
3. Disconnect the parking brake cable from the arm on the brake backing plate (**Figure 3**).
4. Remove the top shock mounting bolt from the lower bracket (**Figure 4**).
5. Remove the cotter key from the castellated nut on the hub carrier bolt and unscrew the nut (**Figure 4**). Support the hub and tap the bolt out

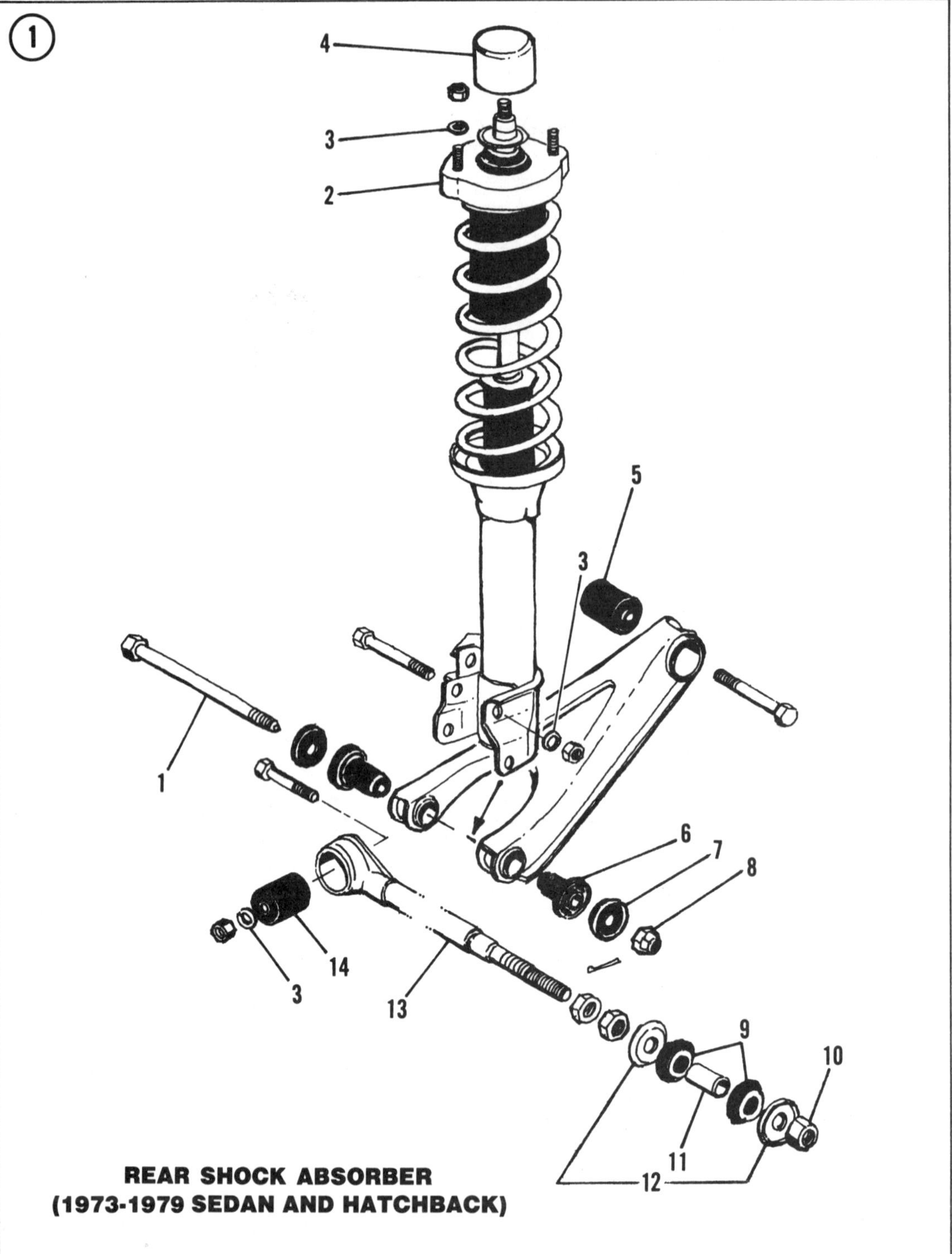

1. Rear lower through bolt
2. Left or right rear shock absorber assembly
3. Spring washer
4. Rear shock absorber cap
5. Lower arm bushing
6. Lower arm bushing A
7. Lower arm bushing
8. Castellated nut
9. Radius rod bushing A
10. Self-locking nut
11. Radius spacer
12. Radius rod washer
13. Radius rod
14. Radius rod bushing B

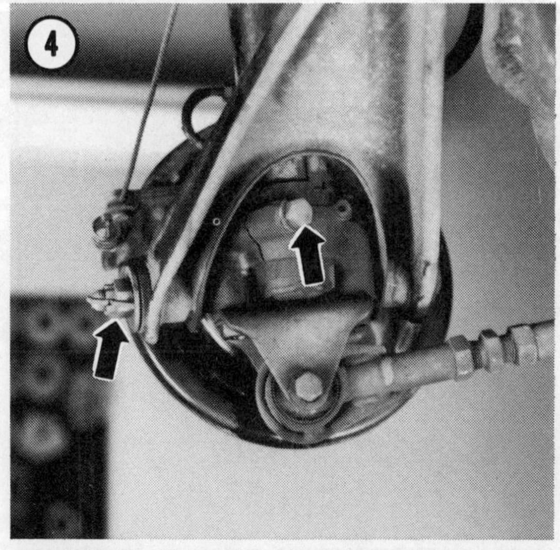

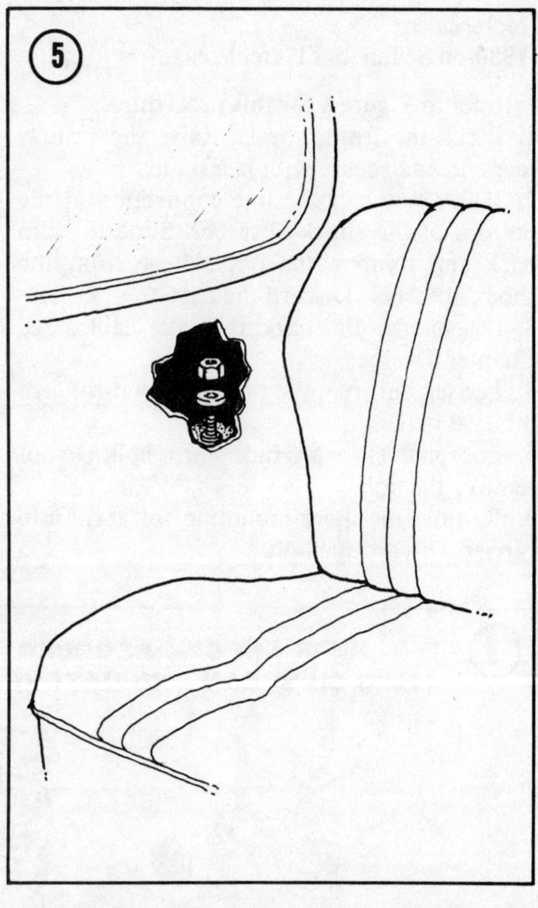

to release the shock and the carrier. Lower the carrier and let it hang on the radius rod.

6. Remove the rear interior panels (**Figure 5**). Unscrew the upper mounting nuts from the shock absorbers (**Figure 1**) and remove them from the car.

WARNING
Do not remove the center nut from the top of the strut. This could allow the coil spring to fly out and cause serious injury.

7. If desired, disassemble and inspect the shock as described in this chapter.

8. Installation is the reverse of these steps. Tighten the nuts and bolts to the specifications in **Table 1** and install a new cotter key in the castellated nut on the hub carrier bolt.

9. After completing rear suspension installation, refer to Chapter Twelve and bleed the brake system. Refer to Chapter Twelve and adjust the parking brake.

Replacement
(1980-on Sedan and Hatchback)

Refer to **Figure 6** for this procedure.

1. Block the front wheels. Raise the vehicle rear end and secure with jackstands.
2. Unscrew the brake line connection at the bottom of the shock absorber. Slide the clip back and remove the brake hose from the shock absorber. Discard the clip.
3. Disconnect the parking brake cable. See Chapter Twelve.
4. Loosen and remove the lower control arm inboard bolt.
5. Loosen the forward radius arm bolt. Do not remove the bolt.
6. Remove the shock mounting bolt at the hub carrier. Discard the bolt.
7. Remove the rear interior panels (if required). Unscrew the upper mounting nuts from the shock absorber and remove them from the car.

WARNING
Do not remove the center nut from the top of the strut. This could allow the coil spring to fly out and cause serious injury.

8. If desired, disassemble and inspect the shock as described in this chapter.
9. Install the suspension units by reversing the above steps. Install a new shock absorber hub carrier bolt. Tighten the nuts and bolts to the specifications in **Table 1**. Replace the brake hose clip when connecting hose to brake tube.

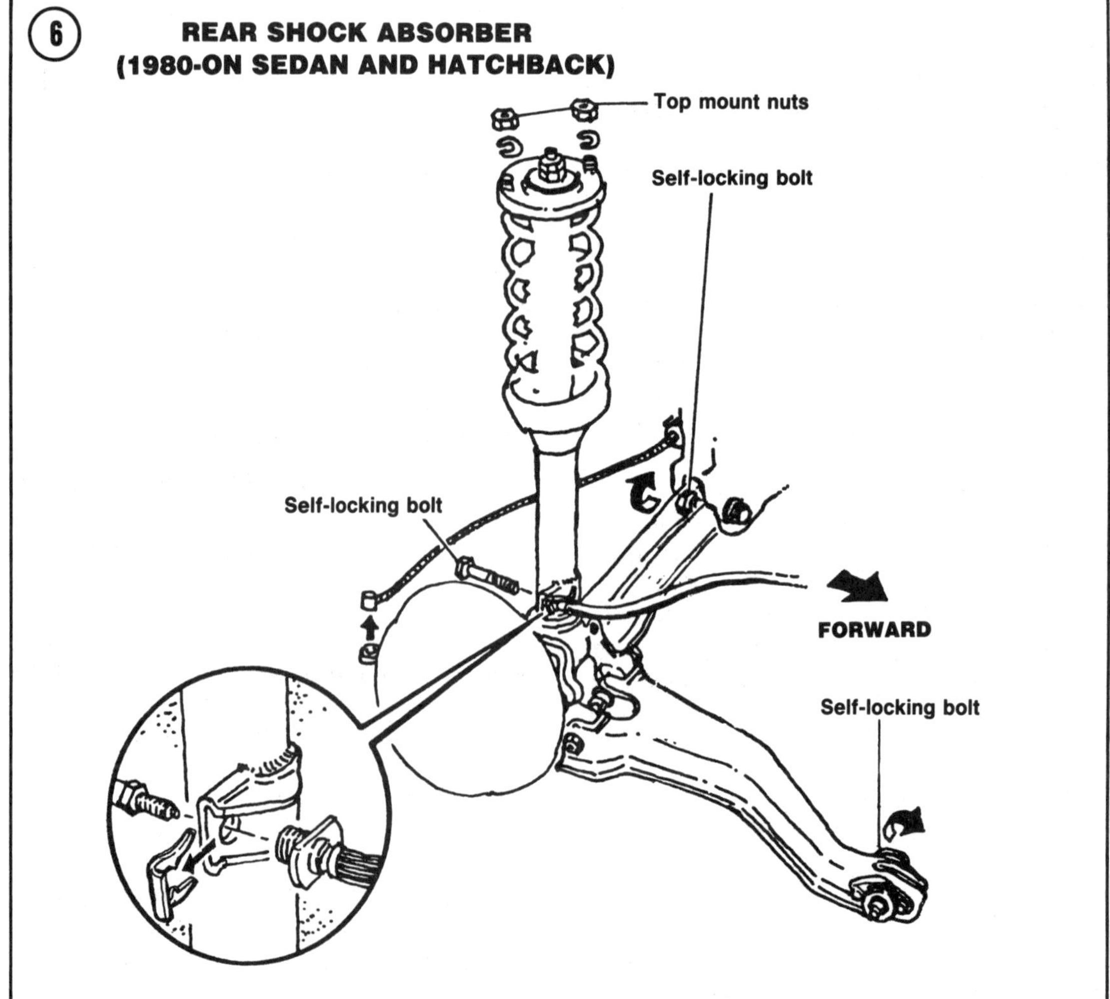

Bleed the brakes as described in Chapter Twelve.

Replacement (Station Wagon)

Refer to **Figure 7** (1975-1979) or **Figure 8** (1980-on) for this procedure.

1. Jack up the vehicle rear end and secure with jackstands. Block the front wheels. Remove the rear wheels.
2. Unscrew the bolt from the bottom shock absorber bracket. Remove the lockwasher and the large dished washer.
3. Unscrew the top shock absorber mounting nut and remove the washers. Pull sharply outward on the top and bottom of the shock absorber to displace the outboard half of the bushings. Push the shock absorber back and remove the outer bushing halves. Then remove the shock absorber and the inner bushing halves.
4. Inspect the bushings for wear, damage or deterioration and replace them if their condition is in doubt. A shock absorber tester is required to accurately test the shock absorbers. However, a simple test can reveal if a shock absorber is totally unserviceable.
   a. Lock the shock absorber in a vise, in its operating condition, and alternately compress and extend it as fast as possible. A satisfactory shock absorber will require considerably more force to extend it than it will to compress it. Also, the movement throughout each stroke should be smooth and there should be no metallic noises.
   b. If a shock absorber fails the simple compression/extension test, it can be considered to be unserviceable and should be replaced. If there is doubt, have it tested by a Honda dealer or a suspension specialist.

NOTE
Shock absorbers should be replaced in pairs.

5. Installation is the reverse of Steps 1-3. Tighten nuts to specifications **(Table 1)**.

Disassembly/Reassembly (Sedan and Hatchback)

If you do not possess the special tools and skills required to disassemble the shock absorber/spring assembly, have the service performed by a Honda dealer or machine shop.

1. Secure the shock absorber in a vise.

WARNING
The shock absorber is held under considerable spring pressure. Removal of the center nut without first attaching the necessary special tools would allow the coil spring to fly off and cause possible serious injury.

2. Install a coil spring compressor onto the strut assembly as shown in **Figure 9**. Compress the spring as necessary to allow removal of the center nut. Do not compress the spring more than necessary. Remove the center nut.
3. Disassemble the shock absorber in the order shown in **Figure 10** (1973-1979) or **Figure 11** (1980-on).
4. Inspect the shock absorber assembly as described in this chapter.
5. Assemble the shock absorber by reversing Steps 1-3, noting the following.
6. Install spring with small diameter spring end facing up.
7. Install new center nut(s) and tighten to specifications **(Table 1)**.

Inspection (Sedan and Hatchback)

1. Replace those parts in **Figure 10** and **Figure 11** which appear damaged or worn. Examine the shock absorber. If excessive amounts of fluid are evident along the shock body, replace the shock.
2. Test the shock absorber by working the piston rod up and down in its full length of travel, 4 or 5 times. If hydraulic pressure is present, indicated by the resistance of the piston rod when worked up and down, the shock absorber is working properly. If no resistance is felt, the shock absorber should be replaced.
3. Measure the shock absorber spring free length and compare to specifications in **Table 2**. Replace any spring which measures or exceeds service limit.

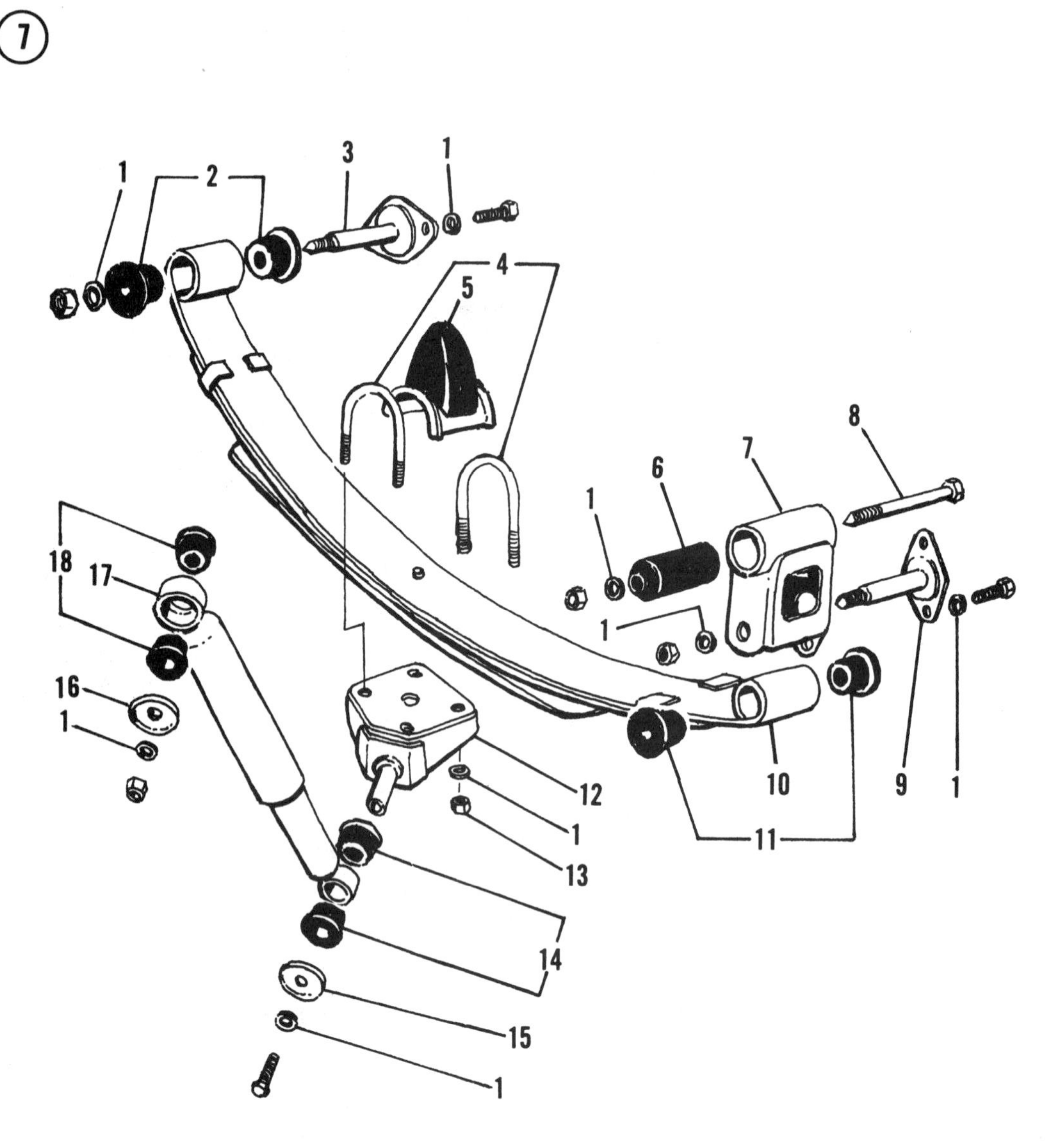

REAR SHOCK ABSORBER AND SPRING (1975-1979 STATION WAGON)

1. Spring washer
2. Spring front bushing
3. Spring front pin
4. Leaf spring U-bolt
5. Rear bumper stopper
6. Shackle bushing
7. Right or left spring shackle
8. Shackle bolt
9. Spring rear pin
10. Rear spring
11. Spring rear bushing
12. Right or left spring clamp bracket
13. Wheel nut
14. Lower rear shock rubber
15. Shock absorber bottom washer
16. Shock absorber upper washer
17. Rear shock absorber assembly
18. Upper rear shock rubber

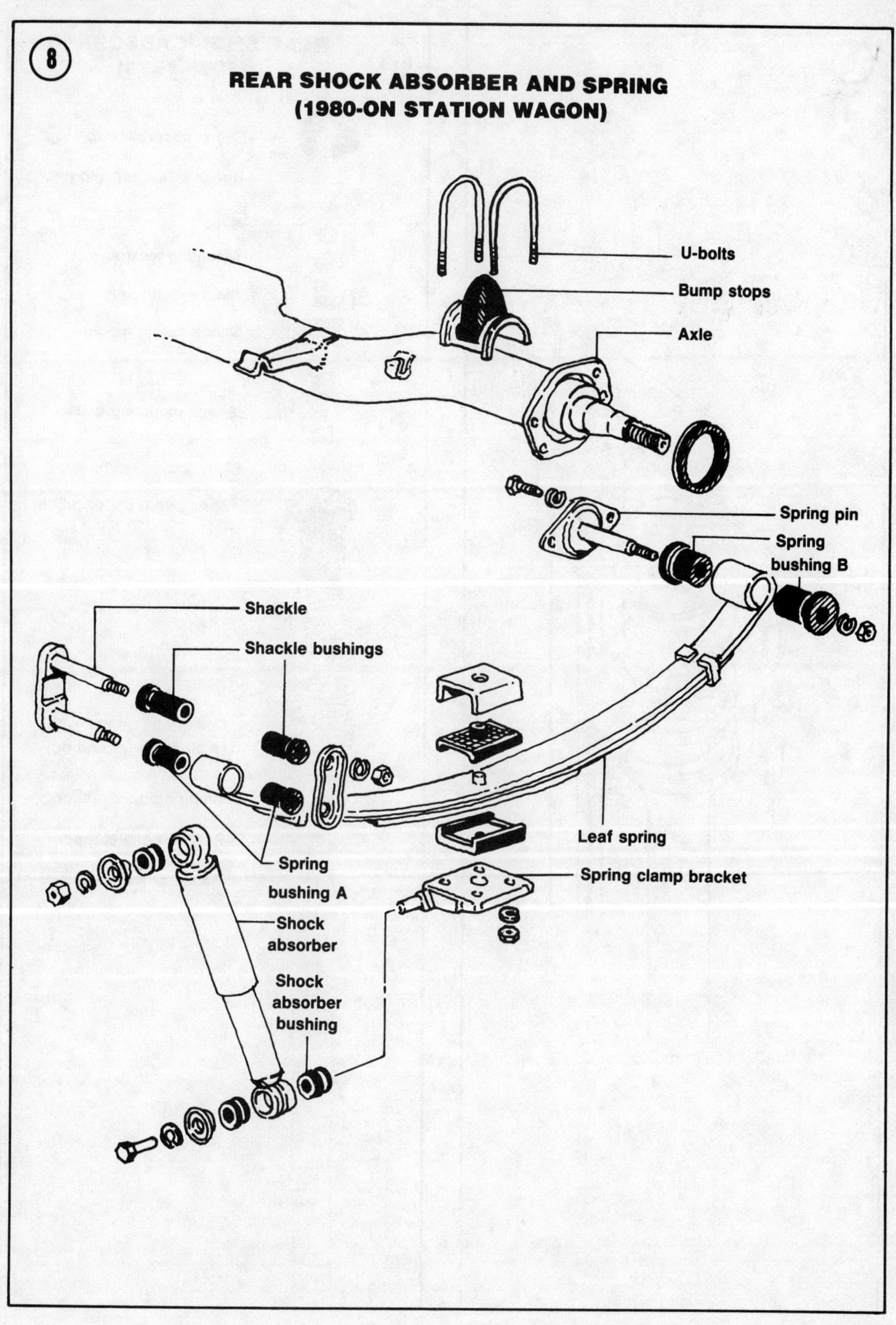
8
REAR SHOCK ABSORBER AND SPRING
(1980-ON STATION WAGON)
U-bolts
Bump stops
Axle
Spring pin
Spring
bushing B
Shackle
Shackle bushings
Leaf spring
Spring
bushing A
Spring clamp bracket
Shock
absorber
Shock
absorber
bushing

9

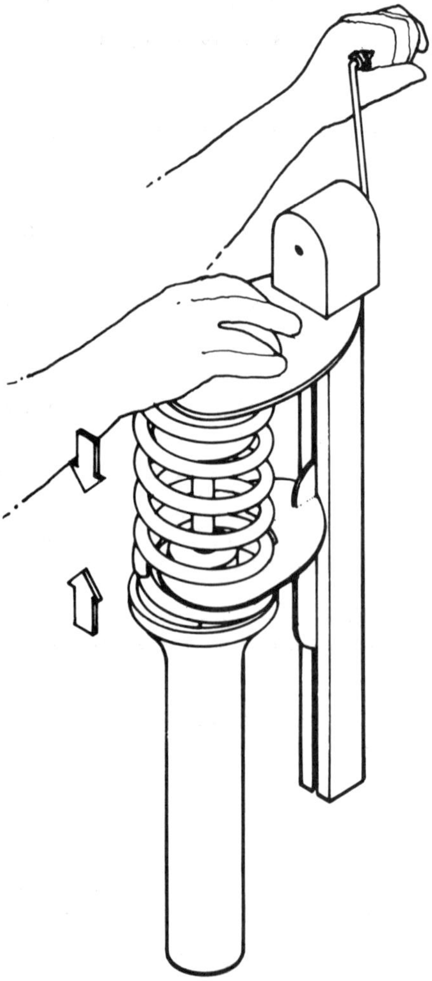

10

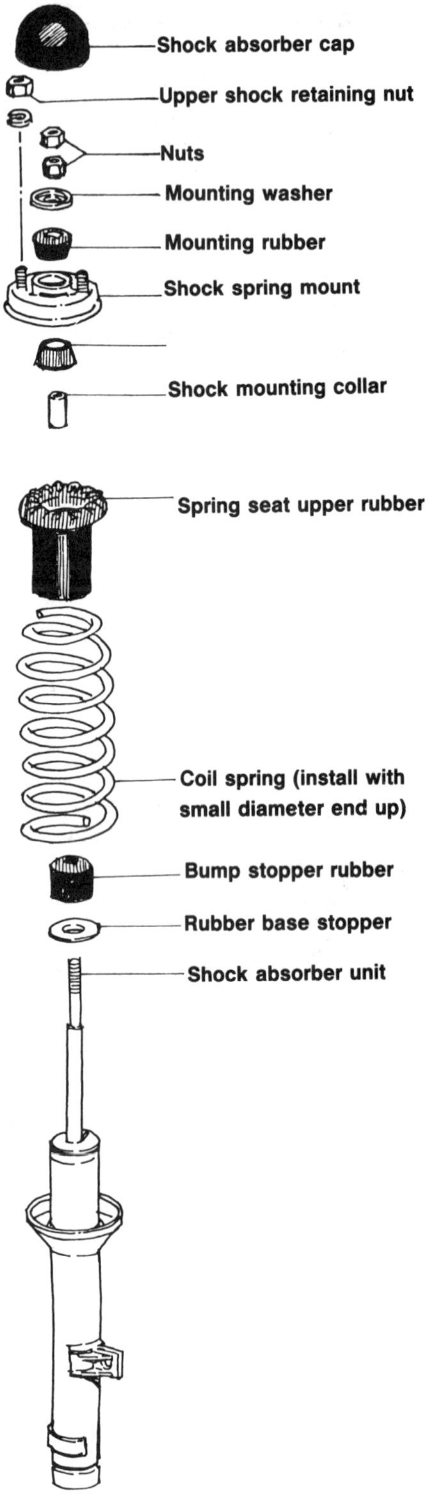

REAR SHOCK ABSORBER (1973-1979)

Shock absorber cap
Upper shock retaining nut
Nuts
Mounting washer
Mounting rubber
Shock spring mount
Shock mounting collar
Spring seat upper rubber
Coil spring (install with small diameter end up)
Bump stopper rubber
Rubber base stopper
Shock absorber unit

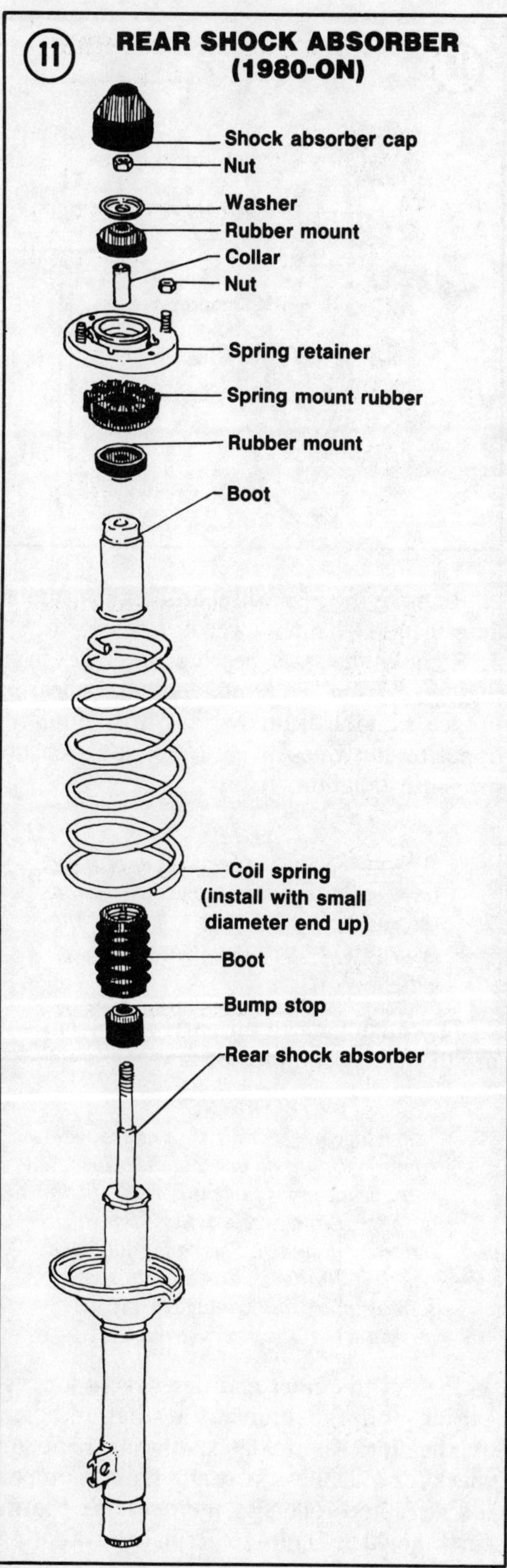

COIL SPRING REPLACEMENT (SEDAN/HATCHBACK)

The coil spring is part of the shock absorber assembly. To replace the spring, follow the shock absorber *Disassembly/Reassembly* procedure. If you do not possess the necessary special tools and skills, refer the service work to a Honda dealer or machine shop.

LEAF SPRING (STATION WAGON)

Removal

Refer to **Figure 7** (1975-1979) or **Figure 8** (1980-on) for this procedure.

1. Raise vehicle rear end and secure with jackstands. Block the front wheels. Remove the rear wheels.
2. Place a jack underneath the center of the rear axle and raise it slightly.
3. Disconnect the lower shock absorber attaching nuts. Compress the shock upward and remove from its lower bracket.
4. Remove the rear spring U-bolt attaching nuts at the bottom of the spring clamp bracket and remove the U-bolt spring clamps, plate and upper bump stop.
5. Remove the spring pin nut. Remove the nuts and bolts attaching the spring plate to the frame bracket.
6. Withdraw the spring pin from the spring and lower the front part of the spring from the vehicle. Remove the rubber bushings from the end of the spring and set aside.
7. At the rear of the spring, remove the shackle pin attaching nuts and plate. Withdraw the shackle and lower the spring from the vehicle. Remove the rear rubber bushings and set aside.

Installation

1. Before installing the rear spring assembly, examine each component for wear or damage. Replace the rubber bushings if necessary.

NOTE
When installing the rear spring assembly, do not torque the fasteners until the complete assembly is installed.

2. Immerse the rubber bushings in a soap and water solution. Then install each bushing into position on the spring.
3. Raise the spring into position and install the shackle pin. Install the shackle pin plate, washers and nuts.
4. Position the front part of the spring into the front frame spring bracket and install the spring pin plate and nuts. Install the spring pin nut.
5. Place the rubber bump stop onto the top of the axle. Position the U-bolts alongside the bump stop and raise the bracket into position. Install the lower bracket-to-U-bolt attaching washers and nuts.
6. With the rear end of the car still raised (no load on springs), tighten all fasteners to specifications (**Table 1**).

REAR WHEEL HUB AND BEARING

Inspection (On Car)

Honda does not specify bearing end play checks for 1973-1979 models. Starting with the 1980 model, tapered roller bearings are used in the rear brake drum. To check end play on 1980-on models, remove the wheel bearing cap and place the tip of a dial indicator onto the wheel grease cap as shown in **Figure 12**. Grasp the tire and attempt to move it in and out while watching the dial indicator gauge. Standard end play is 0 mm. If any reading other than 0 mm is obtained, check the spindle nut torque as described under *Rear Wheel Hub and Bearing Removal/Installation.* If spindle torque is correct, remove the brake drum and inspect the bearings for wear or damages described under *Removal/Inspection/Installation.*

Removal/Inspection/Installation

Refer to **Figure 13** (1973-1979) or **Figure 14** (1980-on) for this procedure. Ball bearings are used on all 1973-1979 models and tapered roller bearings are used on all 1980 and later models.

1. Securely block both front wheels so the car will not roll in either direction. Jack up the rear end of the car and place it on jackstands.

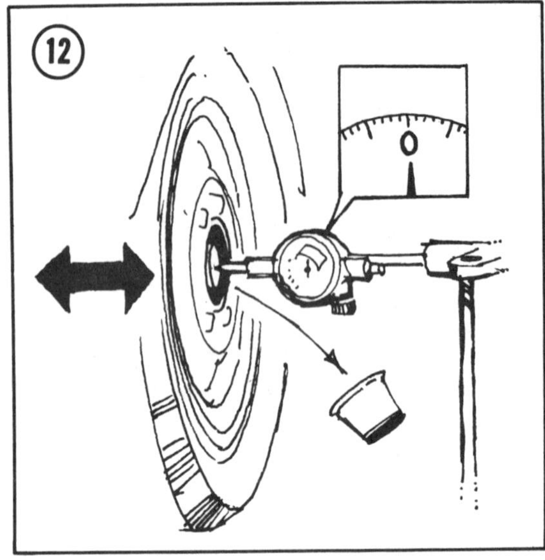

2. Remove the rear wheel and brake drum as described in Chapter Twelve.
3. Remove the seals, bearings and races from the brake drum. To remove the inner bearing or race, turn the drum over and drive out from opposite side. Keep all parts separate to ensure proper installation.

NOTE
When knocking the bearings or bearing races out with a drift, tap evenly around the edge of the bearing to prevent the bearing from cocking sideways in the bore.

4. Thoroughly clean all parts in solvent and dry them with compressed air.

WARNING
When drying bearing assemblies with compressed air, do not spin the bearings with the air jet; it can easily rotate them at speeds far in excess of those for which they were designed. This can result in the bearing flying apart and inflicting serious injury and damage to anyone or anything that the pieces strike.

5. Inspect the inner and outer races for rust, galling and the bluish tint that indicates overheating. Rotate the bearings by hand and check for roughness, play and noise. Compare the races and rollers to the defective bearing parts shown in **Figure 15**. Replace any bearings that have similar defects.

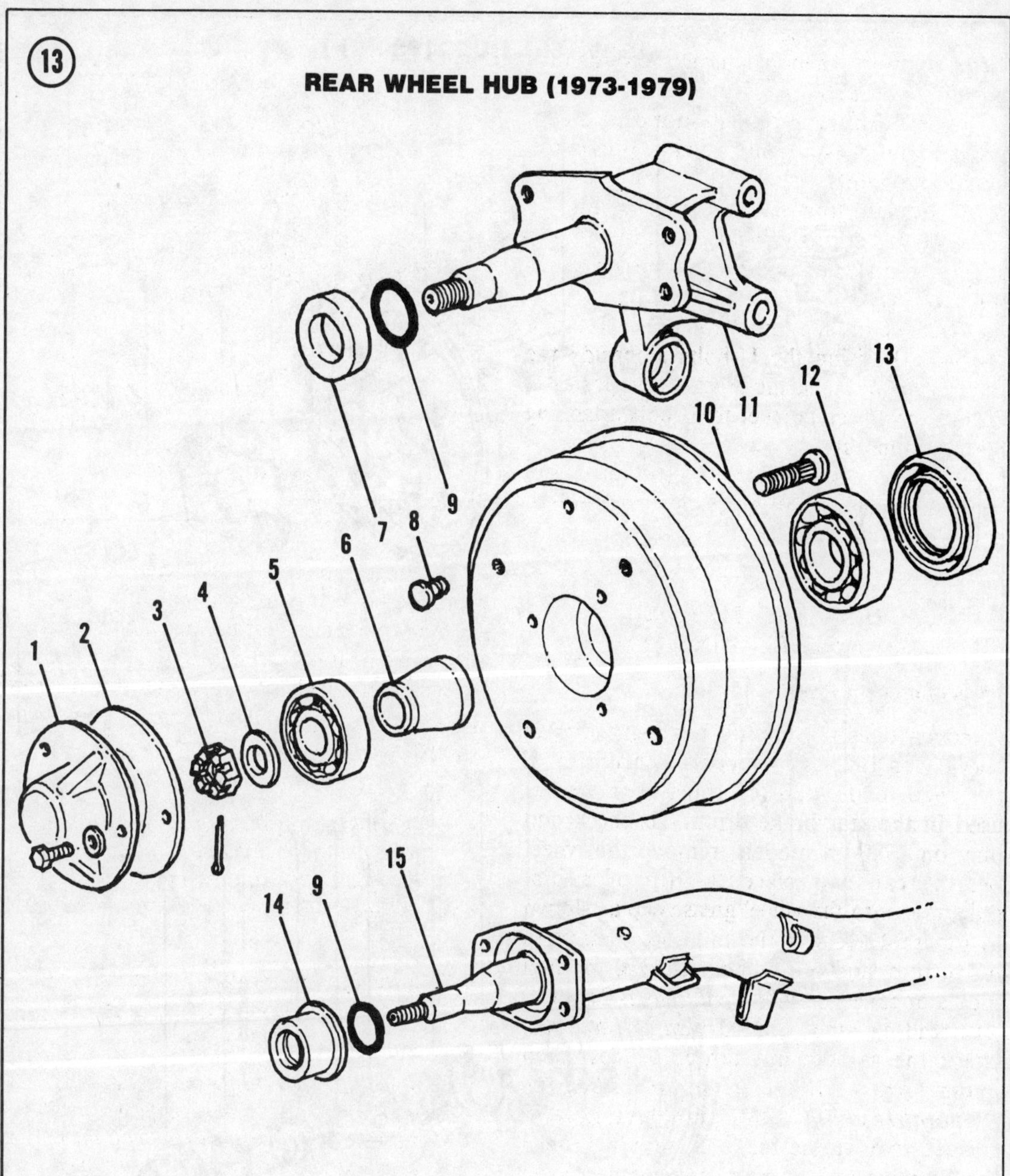

1. Rear wheel bearing cap
2. Bearing seal
3. Rear axle nut
4. Rear hub washer
5. Rear wheel bearing A
6. Rear hub shaft spacer
7. Rear hub shaft collar
8. Rear brake drum plug
9. Rear hub shaft O-ring
10. Rear brake drum
11. Left rear hub shaft
12. Rear wheel bearing B
13. Rear wheel bearing oil seal
14. Collar (station wagon)
15. Rear axle (station wagon)

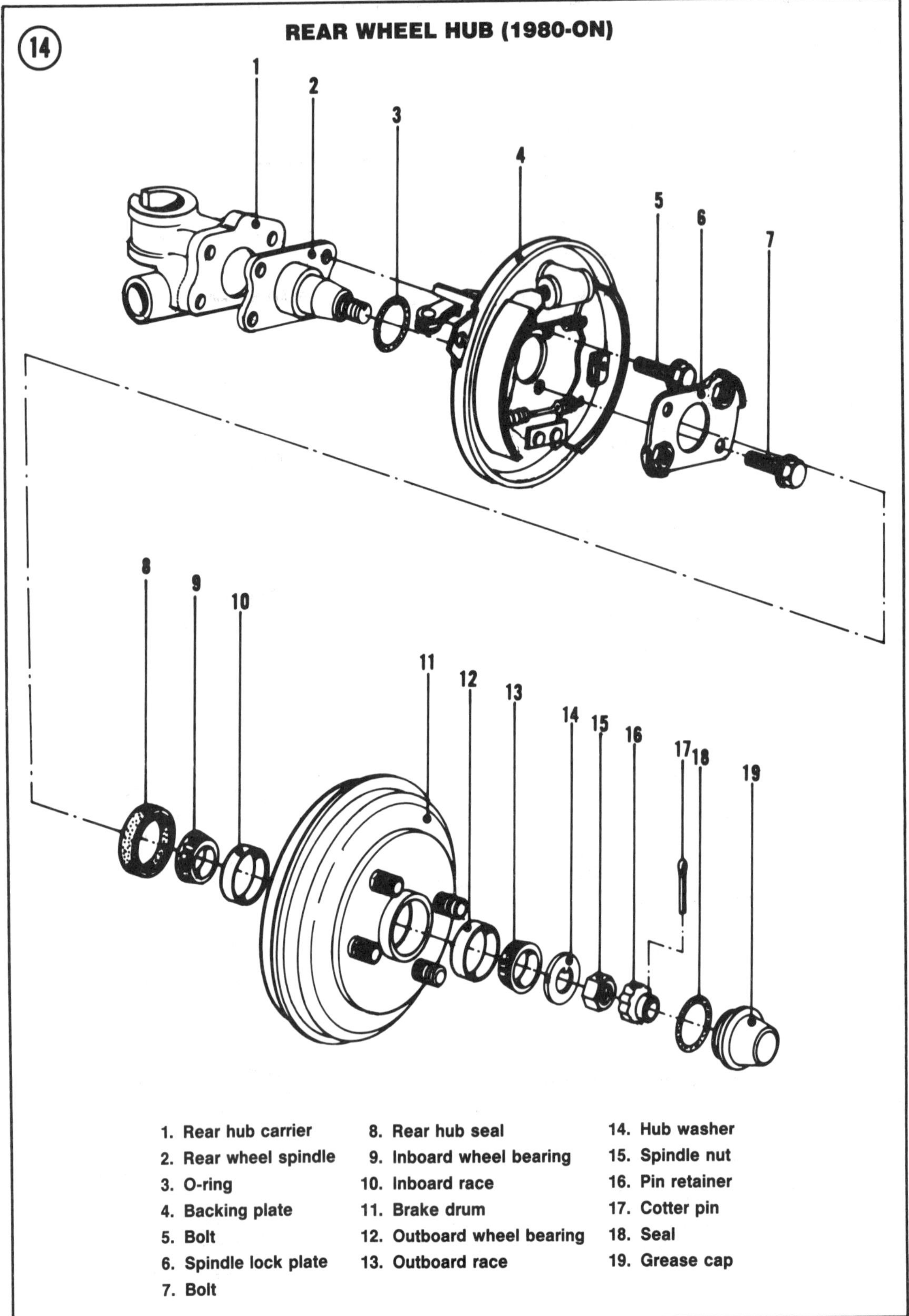
14
REAR WHEEL HUB (1980-ON)
1
2
3
4
5
6
7
8
9
10
11
12
13
14
15
16
17
18
19
1. Rear hub carrier
2. Rear wheel spindle
3. O-ring
4. Backing plate
5. Bolt
6. Spindle lock plate
7. Bolt
8. Rear hub seal
9. Inboard wheel bearing
10. Inboard race
11. Brake drum
12. Outboard wheel bearing
13. Outboard race
14. Hub washer
15. Spindle nut
16. Pin retainer
17. Cotter pin
18. Seal
19. Grease cap

15

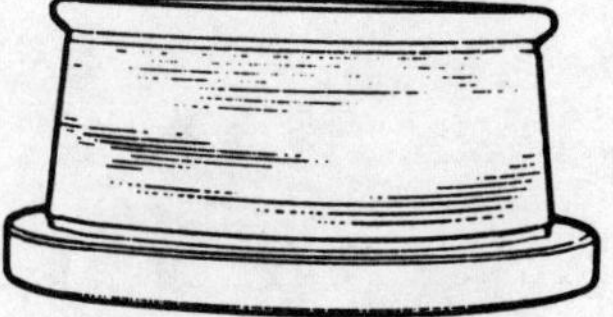
a) Inner race flaking

b) Roller flaking

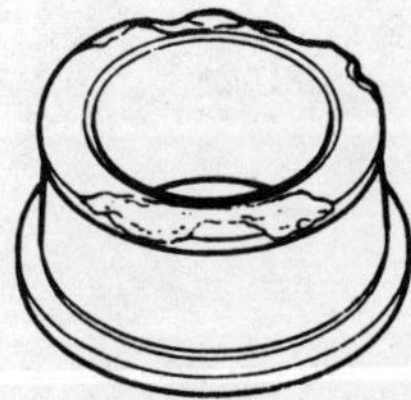
c) Chipped inner race

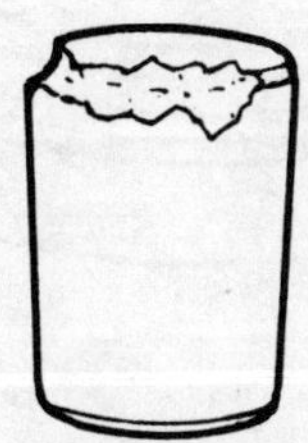
d) Chipped roller

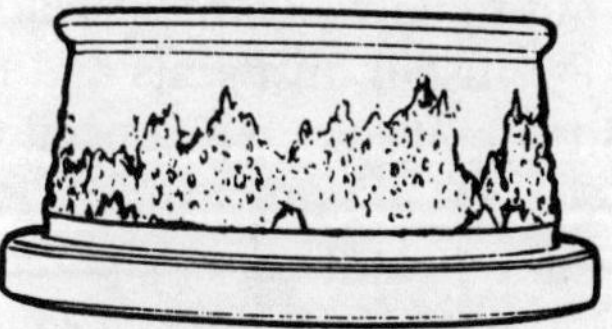
e) Recess on inner race

f) Recess on outer race

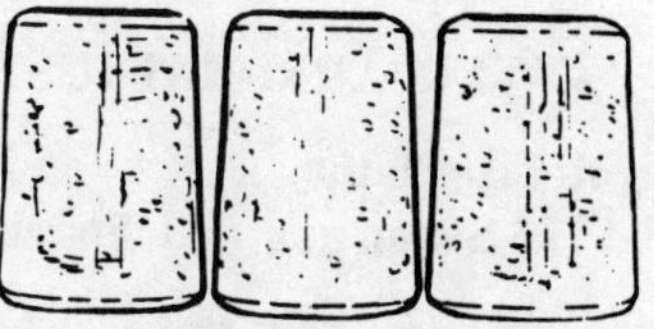
g) Recess on roller

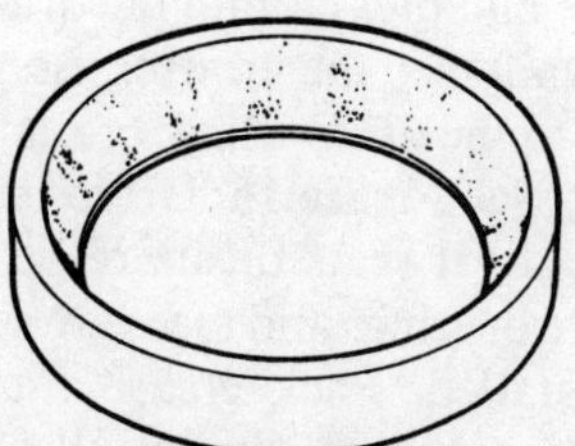
h) Rust on outer race

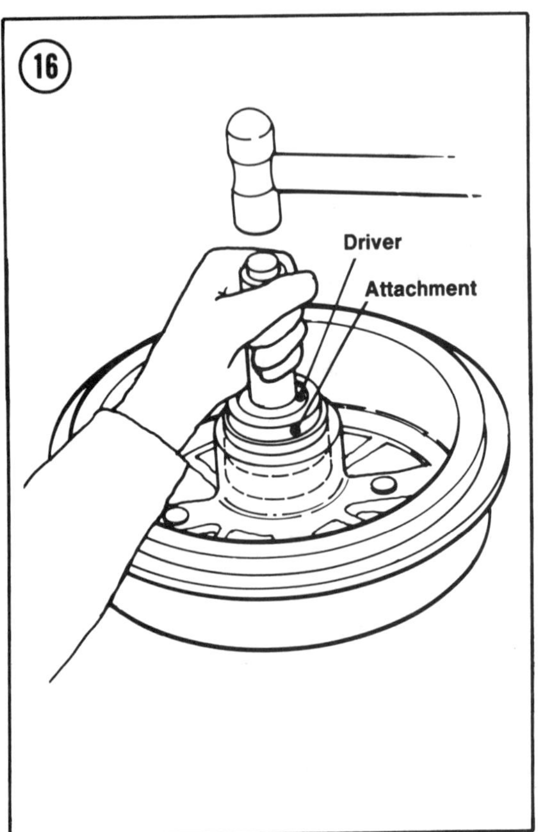

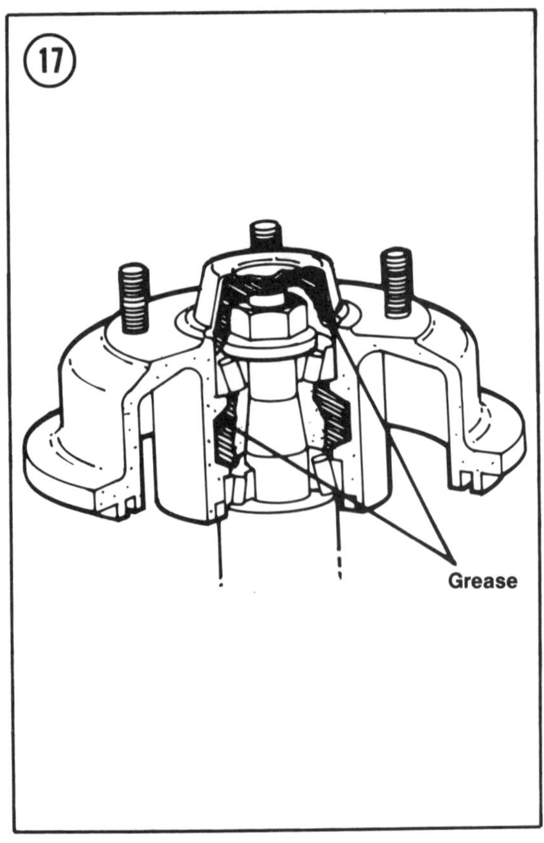

6. Thoroughly grease the bearings with a good grade of multipurpose grease. Fill the cavities in the seals with grease and apply a light coat to the axles, spacers, and inner and outer bearing races.

NOTE
When installing bearings in next procedure, make sure to apply force to the outer bearing race. Do not apply force on the inside of the bearing as this will damage the bearing.

7. Set each outboard bearing or race squarely in its bore and press it into the drum. If a press is not available, the bearing or race can be driven into the drum using a suitable size drift or socket. See **Figure 16**. Drive the bearing or race in until it seats on its respective flange. Make sure bearings and races are seated evenly when installed. Pack grease into the areas indicated in **Figure 17**. Install a new wheel bearing oil seal.

8A. *1973-1979 models:* Install the drums, washer and spindle nut. Tighten the spindle nut to 12 mkg (83 ft.-lb.). Check alignment of hole in axle with nut. If necessary, further tighten nut to next alignment before installing cotter key. Install dust seals and bearing caps and tighten bolts securely. Install the wheels.

8B. *1980-on models:* Install the drums, washers and spindle nut. Tighten the spindle nut to 2.5 mkg (18 ft.-lb.) and rotate the brake drum by hand. Then loosen the nut, retighten to 0.5 mkg (3 ft.-lb.) and install the cotter pin holder with the slots as close as possible to the hole in the spindle. Tighten the nut to align the slots with the hole and install the cotter pin. Install the bearing caps and wheels.

LOWER ARM/RADIUS ROD

Removal/Installation (1973-1979 Sedan and Hatchback)

Refer to **Figure 1** for this procedure.

1. Block the front wheels to prevent the car from creeping forward. Then raise the vehicle rear end and secure with jackstands. Remove the rear wheels.

2. Remove the brake drum as described in Chapter Twelve.
3. Disconnect the brake line from the brake hose (**Figure 2**). Plug both open ends to prevent dirt contamination.
4. Disconnect the parking brake cable at the rear of the brake backing plate (**Figure 3**).
5. Remove the cotter key securing the lower arm castle nut (**Figure 4**). Then remove the castle nut and washer. Remove the lower arm pivot bolt and separate the lower arm from the rear wheel hub carrier. If the lower arm is to be removed completely, remove the opposite end self-locking bolt at the frame. Direct the lower arm downward and remove from underneath the vehicle.
6. Loosen and remove the radius rod securing bolts at both the front and rear ends. Remove the radius rod.
7. Refer to *Bushing Replacement* in this chapter and inspect and replace the lower arm and radius arm bushings if necessary.
8. Installation is the reverse of these steps; note the following information:
   a. Install all parts and hold in position with the fasteners. Do not tighten the fasteners at this time.
   b. When all parts are installed, place a jack under the rear wheel hub and raise the car until it just lifts off the safety stand. Then tighten all fasteners to specifications (**Table 1**).
   c. Bleed the brake system and adjust the parking brake (Chapter Twelve).
   d. Have a Honda dealer adjust the rear wheel toe-in.

Removal/Installation (1980-on Sedan and Hatchback)

Refer to **Figure 18** for this procedure.

1. Block the front wheels to prevent the car from creeping forward. Then raise the vehicle rear end and secure with jackstands. Remove the rear wheels.
2. Remove the brake drum as described in Chapter Twelve.
3. Disconnect the brake line from the brake hose (**Figure 6**). Plug both open ends to prevent dirt contamination.
4. Disconnect the parking brake cable at the rear of the brake backing plate.
5. Remove the screws securing the backing plate assembly to the rear wheel hub and remove the backing plate.
6. Remove the nuts and bolts securing the radius arm to the rear wheel hub and to the frame. Remove the radius arm.
7. Loosen and remove the shock absorber pinch bolt at the rear wheel hub. Then separate the shock absorber from the hub.
8. Remove the lower control arm attaching bolts and separate the lower control arm from the rear wheel hub and at the frame.
9. Refer to *Bushing Replacement* in this chapter and inspect and replace the lower arm and radius arm bushings if necessary.
10. Installation is the reverse of these steps; note the following information:
   a. Install all parts and hold in position with the fasteners. Do not tighten the fasteners at this time.
   b. When all parts are installed, place a jack under the rear wheel hub and raise the car until it just lifts off the safety stand. Then tighten all fasteners to specifications (**Table 1**).
   c. Bleed the brake system and adjust the parking brake (Chapter Three).
   d. Have a Honda dealer adjust the rear wheel toe-in.

Bushing Replacement

The rear suspension bushings enjoy a long service life, but they should be inspected for damage, deterioration and wear when the suspension is disassembled. See **Figure 1** (1973-1979) or **Figure 18** (1980-on).

If an individual bushing is found to be damaged, that bushing and its counterpart on the opposite side may be the only units requiring replacement. However, if a bushing is found to be worn or the rubber deteriorated, it is a good idea to rebush all of the rear suspension at the same time.

Bushing replacement is accomplished with a press. A Honda dealer or machine shop can perform this for you.

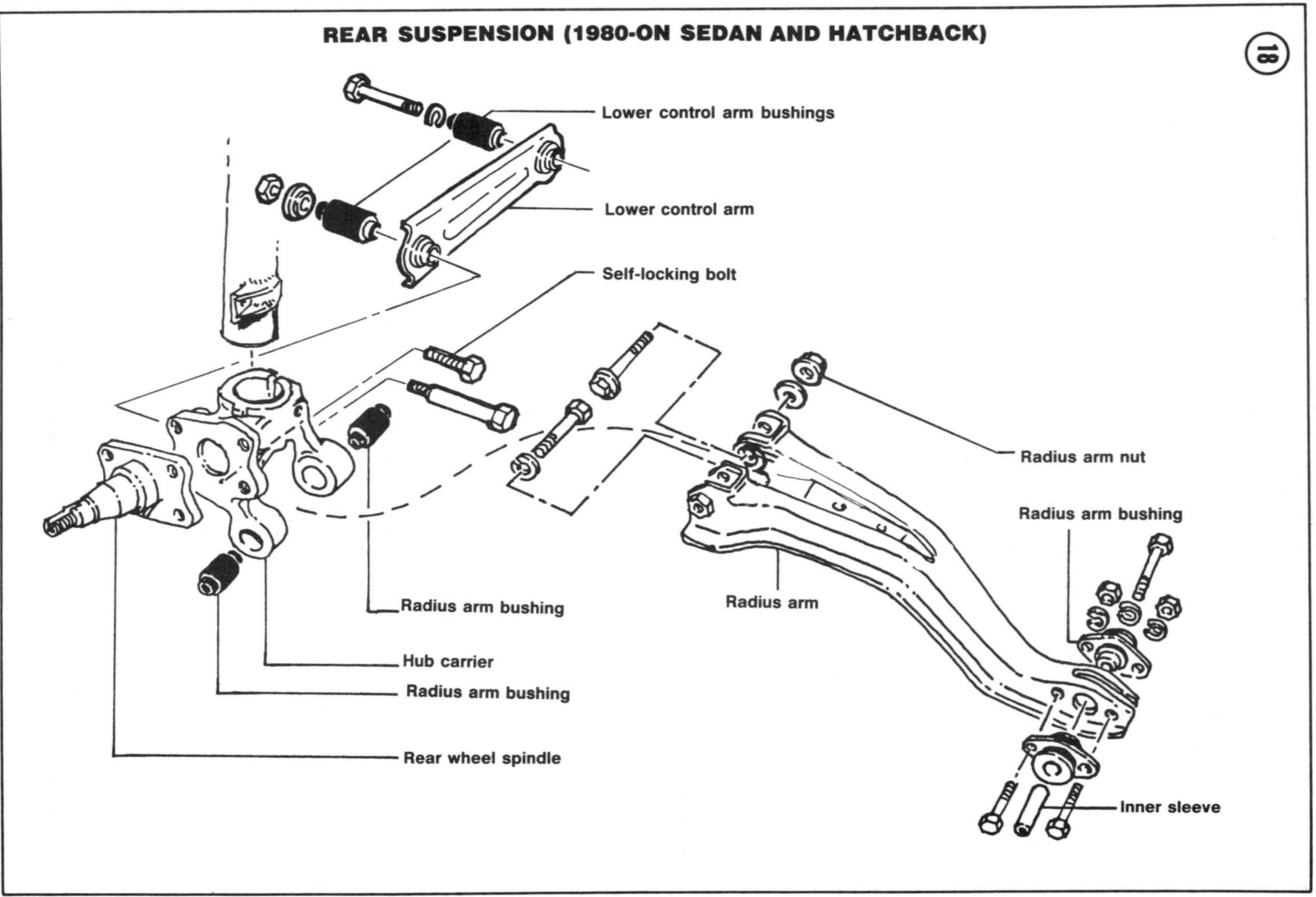

REAR SUSPENSION (1980-ON SEDAN AND HATCHBACK)

Table 1 TIGHTENING TORQUES (NON-CVCC)

Item	mkg	ft.-lb.
Shock absorber upper and center nuts	5.5-7.0	39-50
Shock absorber at body	1.0-1.6	7-12
Lower arm at body	3.5-5.0	25-36
Lower arm and shock	5.0-6.5	36-47
Hub carrier and shock absorber	3.5-5.0	25-36
Radius rod and hub carrier	5.5-7.5	40-54
Radius rod and body	3.5-5.0	25-36
Rear axle nut	10.0-13.0	72-94

Table 2 TIGHTENING TORQUES (1975-1979 CVCC)

Item	mkg	ft.-lb.
Axle nut	10-13	72-94
Hub nut	10-13	72-94
Lower arm	3.5-5.0	25-36
Lower arm and shock absorber	7.5-9.0	54-65
Radius rod	3.5-5.0	25-36
Radius rod locknut	7.0-8.0	51-58
Radius rod and body	3.5-5.0	25-36
Radius rod and hub carrier	3.5-5.0	25-36
Shock absorber		
Center nuts	5.5-7.0	40-51
Double nut	5.5-7.0	40-51
Mount	1.0-1.6	7-12
Shock absorber and body	1.0-1.6	7-12
Shock absorber and hub carrier	3.5-4.0	25-29
Torque rod		
Bracket	2.3-2.8	17-20
Locknut	3.5-4.3	25-31
Torque rod and body	3.5-4.3	25-31

Table 3 TIGHTENING TORQUES (1980-ON CVCC)

Item	mkg	ft.-lb.
Hatchback, Sedan		
Center shock locknuts		
1980	3.3	24
1981	4.5	33
Lower arm bolt	5.5	40
Radius arm at hub carrier		
M10 x 1.25	5.5	40
M12 x 1.25	10	72
Radius arm at frame	8.5	61
Spindle nut	See text for procedure	
Shock absorber pinch bolt	5.0	36
Lower arm nut	5.5	40

(continued)

11

Table 3 TIGHTENING TORQUES (1980-ON CVCC) (continued)

Item	mkg	ft.-lb.
Wagon		
Shock absorber attaching bolts	4.4	32
Spring pin mounting bolt	2.2	16
Spring pin mounting nut	4.4	32
Shackle mounting nut	4.4	32
Hub carrier bolts	5.5	40

Table 4 SPRING HEIGHT SPECIFICATIONS

	Standard		Limit	
Item	mm	in.	mm	in.
1973-1979 Non-CVCC	610	24	595	23.4
1975-1979 CVCC				
Sedan	540	21.3	525	20.7
Wagon	598	23.5	-	-
1980				
Hatchback	638	25.12	623	24.6
Wagon	668	25.12	623	24.6
1981				
Hatchback/Sedan	635	25	620	24.4
Wagon	668	26.3	653	25.7

NOTE: If you own a 1982 or later model, first check the Supplement at the back of the book for any new service information.

CHAPTER TWELVE

BRAKES

The brake system has 2 independent circuits with disc brakes on the front wheels and drum brakes on the rear wheels. Each independent brake circuit operates one front brake and one rear brake, diagonally opposite. Therefore, in the event of complete failure in one circuit, the other circuit still provides 50 percent of the total braking effectiveness.

A cable-operated mechanical handbrake acts on the rear wheels when the hand lever is drawn up. The rear brake shoes expand to provide emergency or parking brakes.

1

This chapter describes repair procedures for most of the parts of the brake system. Service to the vacuum booster and the proportioning valve is limited to removal and installation; major work on these units should be referred to a Honda dealer. If you are inexperienced in working on brake hydraulic components, it is recommended that you limit your service to removal and replacement. Entrust the rebuilding of the master and wheel cylinders to your Honda dealer or replace defective units with new ones.

Tables 1-4 are at the end of the chapter.

BRAKE FLUID

Brake fluid level should be checked at the intervals specified in Chapter Three, as well as any time the pedal can be pushed within a couple of inches from the floor. The level should be between the upper and lower marks in both reservoirs (**Figure 1**). If the level is below the lower mark, clean the area around the master cylinder covers and remove them. Add type DOT 3 or DOT 4 brake fluid to bring the level up to the top mark in each reservoir. Install the caps and check the movement of the pedal. If air has entered the system, bleed the brakes as described in this chapter.

CAUTION
Whenever handling brake fluid, do not get any on the brake shoes, brake discs, calipers (when assembled) or body paint. Brake shoes or brake pads will be permanently damaged, requiring replacement. Body paint can also be damaged unless you wipe the area with a clean cloth and wash it with a soapy solution immediately.

TESTING BRAKES

After performing service procedures to the braking system as described in this chapter, the brakes should be tested on a dry, clean, smooth and level roadway; preferably a roadway with little traffic flow. Brake performance cannot be determined when the roadway is wet or greasy or covered with loose dirt that will not allow the tires to grip equally.

The brakes should be tested at different vehicle speeds and with light and heavy pedal pressure. However, when applying the brakes, do not lock the wheels and cause the tires to slide; locking and sliding the tires cannot be used as a determining factor when testing brakes. A braking action where heavy pressure is applied (wheels not locking) will stop the vehicle in less distance than when the wheels are locked. This is due to a greater amount of friction created by the tire-to-road contact than that of a sliding tire.

When testing your vehicle's brakes, consider the following conditions that affect brake performance.

a. Tires: Tires which are worn or improperly inflated will cause unequal braking. Make sure that your tire tread patterns are equal between the right and left sides and that the correct tire pressure is used. See Chapter Three.
b. Alignment: Incorrect front-end alignment will cause the brakes to pull to one side. When experiencing brake pull, have the front-end alignment checked by a suspension specialist before continuing brake tests.
c. Vehicle weight loading: When carrying excessive weights in the car, the most heavily loaded wheels will require more braking than the others and cause unequal braking. When it is necessary to carry heavy objects, try to distribute the weight equally between the vehicle's left and right sides. Remove the weight as soon as possible. Fuel economy as well as braking efficiency is affected.

BLEEDING THE BRAKE SYSTEM

The brake system must be bled to remove air from it after any portion of the system has been disconnected (e.g., replacement of a brake hose, caliper, etc.) or when the pedal feels spongy or soft.

Fluid that is expelled during bleeding should be discarded; it may contain foreign matter and if it has been in service for a while it will have absorbed atmospheric water. This lowers the boiling point of the fluid and makes it prone to vapor lock during repeated hard braking applications (such as mountain driving). In addition, it is a good idea to replace the brake fluid once every 2 years because of the water it will have absorbed.

Whenever handling brake fluid, do not get any on the brake shoes, brake discs, calipers (when assembled) or body paint. Brake shoes or brake pads will be permanently damaged, requiring replacement. In addition, body paint can be damaged unless you wipe the area with a clean cloth and wash it immediately with a soapy solution.

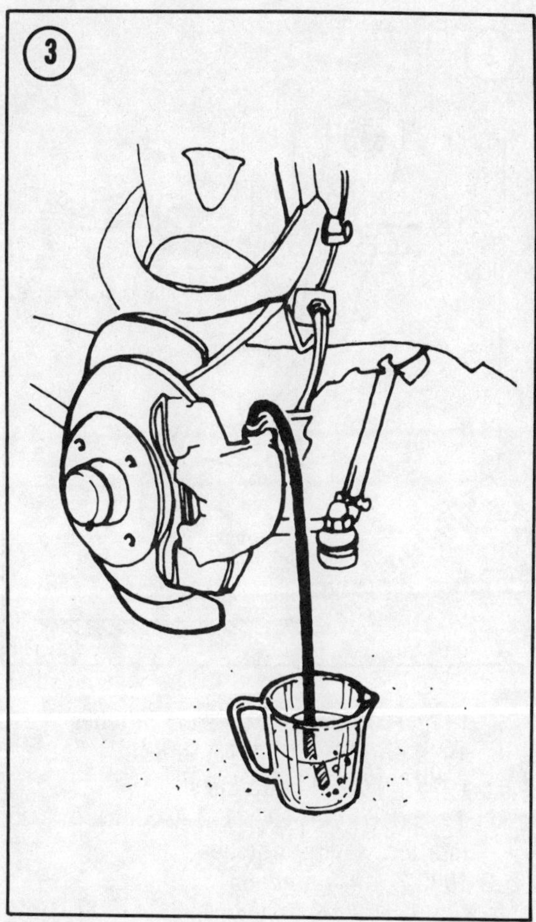

3

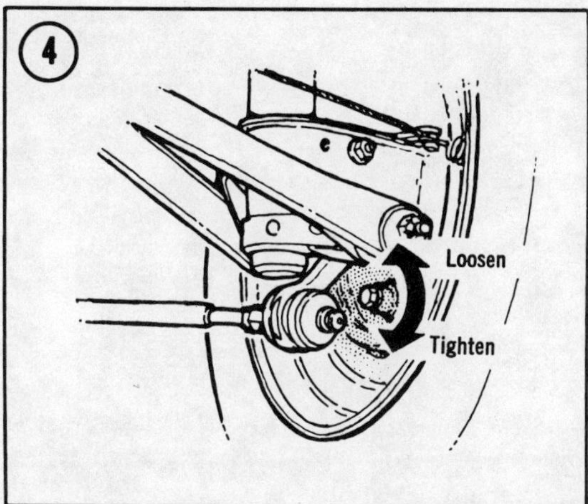

4

1. Check the brake fluid level in the reservoirs and top them up to the upper mark if necessary (**Figure 1**). Leave the caps off and cover the reservoirs with clean shop rags to prevent fluid from being ejected onto painted surfaces.
2. Connect a plastic or rubber tube to the bleeder valve (**Figure 2**) on the left front wheel. Suspend the other end of the tube in a jar or bottle filled with a few inches of brake fluid. See **Figure 3**. During the remaining steps, keep this end submerged at all times and never let the level in the reservoir dip below 1/2 full level.
3. Have an assistant depress brake pedal slowly. Open bleeder valve on front left wheel about one turn. As soon as pedal is all the way down, close bleeder valve and let pedal up. Repeat this step as many times as necessary until fluid with no air bubbles ejects from the tube.
4. Bleed the remaining valves in the following order:
   a. Right rear
   b. Right front
   c. Left rear

   All valves are bled in the same manner as the left front wheel. Keep checking the master cylinder reservoir (**Figure 1**) to be sure it doesn't run out of brake fluid.
5. When all wheels are bled, discard the brake fluid in the jar or bottle; never reuse such fluid. Top up the master cylinder reservoir with clean fluid.

ADJUSTMENT

Front Disc Brakes

The front disc brakes are self-adjusting.

Rear Drum Brakes (1973-1979)

NOTE

Rear drum brakes must be adjusted before adjusting the parking brake.

1. Block the front wheels. Then raise the vehicle rear end and secure with jackstands.
2. Release the parking brake.
3. Depress the brake pedal 2 or 3 times and release.
4. Using Honda tool part No. 07708-0020000, turn the brake adjuster clockwise until the wheels are locked. Then back off the adjuster (counterclockwise) 2 clicks (1/4 turn). **Figure 4** shows the rear brake adjuster.
5. Turn the wheel and check for dragging brakes. If the brakes drag, back off the adjuster one more click.
6. Repeat for opposite side.

Rear Drum Brakes (1980-on)

The rear drum brakes for the 1980 and later models are self-adjusting. No adjustment is required.

Parking Brake

NOTE
Rear drum brakes on 1973-1979 models must be adjusted before adjusting the parking brake.

1. Block the front wheels. Then raise the vehicle rear end and secure with jackstands.

NOTE
On 1980 and later models, if the rear brakes have been serviced, depress the brake pedal several times to set the self-adjusting brake mechanism before continuing with this procedure.

2. Loosen the parking brake equalizer adjusting nut. See **Figure 5**.
3. From inside the driver's compartment, raise the parking brake lever up one notch.
4. Turn the equalizer nut clockwise until the rear wheels just begin to drag slightly. This can be checked by turning the wheels by hand after turning the equalizer nut.
5. Release the parking brake lever and check to see that the wheels do not drag when turned by hand. If they do, readjust the parking brake by following Steps 2-4.
6. When adjustment is complete, brakes should fully lock when the brake lever has been raised as follows:

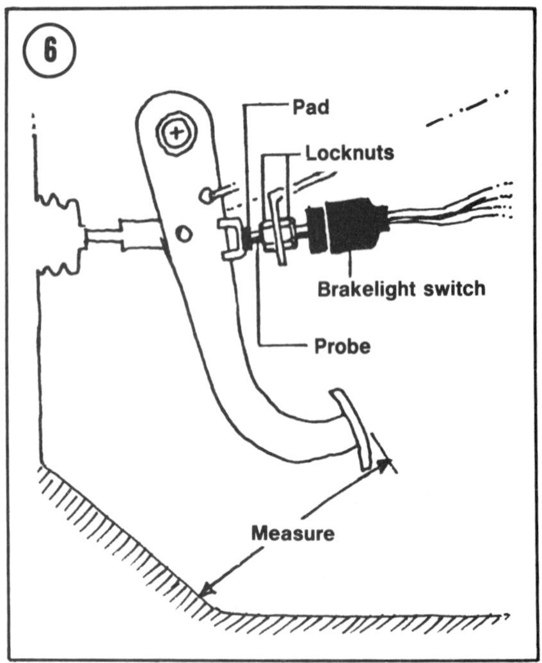

a. 1973-1978 non-CVCC: 1-5 notches
b. 1979 non-CVCC: 3-7 notches
c. 1975 CVCC: 1-5 notches
d. 1976-1979 CVCC: 1-3 (sedan) or 3-5 (station wagon) notches
e. 1980-on: 4-8 notches

Brake Pedal Free Play

Brake pedal free play is the distance the pedal travels from the brake light switch until the pushrod contacts the vacuum booster and activates the master cylinder. If correct free play is not maintained, the brake pads and shoes cannot return fully when the brake pedal is released. This condition will cause excessive and severe brake pad and lining wear.

1973-1979 models

1. Measure the brake pedal resting height as shown in **Figure 6**.
2. Push on the brake pedal with your hand until resistance is felt. Measure the brake pedal height once again (**Figure 6**).
3. The difference between the measurements taken in Step 1 and Step 2 should be 1-5 mm (1/32 -3/16 in.). This is brake pedal free play. If incorrect, disconnect the brake light switch

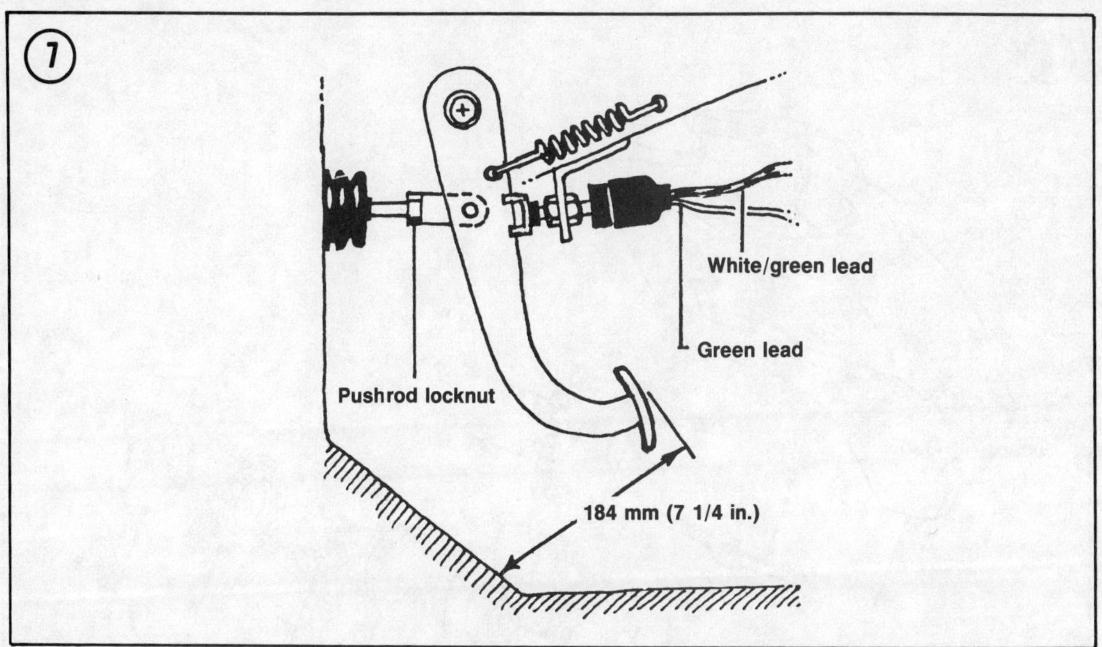

wires (**Figure 6**). Loosen the switch locknut and turn the switch as required to obtain the correct free play measurement. Then tighten the locknut. Reconnect the brake light switch wires and recheck the brake pedal free play.
4. After making adjustment, measure the brake pedal height. It should be 135 mm (5.32 in.). See **Figure 6**. If not, recheck adjustment.

1980-on models

Refer to **Figure 7** for this procedure.
1. Loosen the brake light switch nuts and back the switch out until the end probe no longer contacts the brake pedal.
2. Loosen the pushrod locknut from behind the brake pedal. Then turn the pushrod in or out to adjust pedal height to 184 mm (7 1/4 in.) as indicated in **Figure 7**. When adjustment is complete, tighten the pushrod locknut and recheck height measurement.
3. Using a pair of pliers, turn the brake light switch in until its end probe contacts the pad on the pedal arm. Then back the switch out 1/2 turn and tighten locknuts.
4. Have an assistant operate the brake pedal while observing the rear brake lights. Make sure the brakelights operate when the pedal is depressed and turn off when the pedal is released.

DISC BRAKE PAD INSPECTION/REPLACEMENT (1973-1979)

The brake pads should be inspected at the intervals specified in Chapter Three and replaced when the lining thickness is worn beyond operating specifications (**Table 1**).

Sedan

Figure 8 shows an exploded view of the front brake assembly for 1973-1979 sedan models.
1. Jack up the front of the car and support it on jackstands. Remove the front wheels.
2. Using a vernier caliper as shown in **Figure 9**, measure the thickness of each brake pad. Repeat on opposite wheel side.

NOTE
On 1973-1979 non-CVCC and 1975 CVCC models, the brake thickness should not include the brake pad backing plate. On 1976-1979 CVCC models, the thickness measurement should include the brake pad backing plate.

3. If brake pad thickness is less than service limit (**Table 1**) or there is a difference of 2 mm (0.078 in.) or more between the left and right sides, replace all 4 pads as a set.

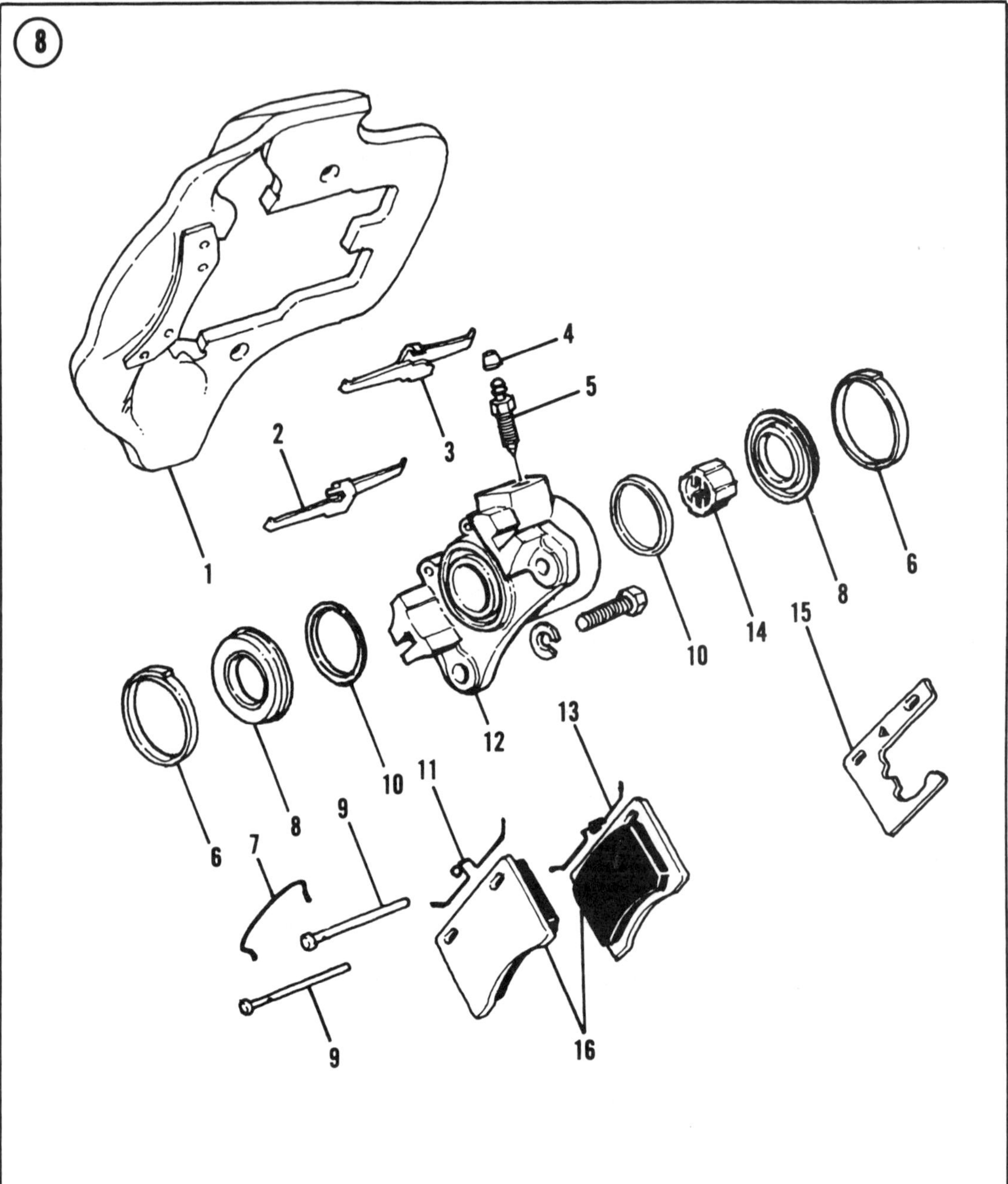

FRONT DISC BRAKE (1973-1979 SEDAN)

1. Yoke
2. Yoke spring B
3. Yoke spring A
4. Bleed cap
5. Bleed screw
6. Retaining ring
7. Pad retaining clip
8. Dust boot
9. Pad retaining clip
10. Piston seal
11. Pad spring B
12. Cylinder
13. Pad spring A
14. Bias ring
15. Brake pad inner shim
16. Disc brake pad set

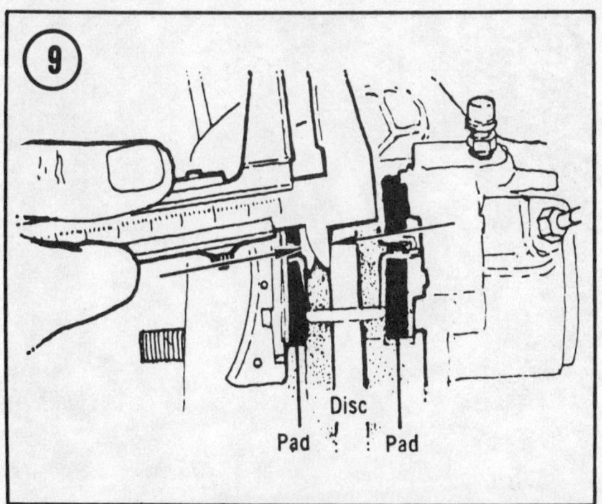

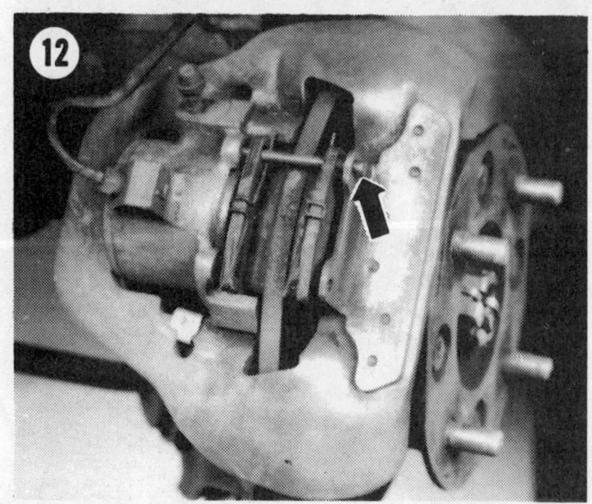

4. If brake pads are okay, install the wheels and lower the car. If brake pads are worn, proceed to Step 5 for brake pad replacement.
5. Remove the outside pad retaining clip (**Figure 10**).
6. Remove the lower (**Figure 11**) and upper (**Figure 12**) pad retaining pins. Then remove the pad springs A and B (**Figure 8**).
7. Remove the brake pads (**Figure 13** and **Figure 14**).
8. Carefully clean the brake pad cavities. Inspect the rubber dust covers and replace them if they are damaged. If dirt has penetrated the cylinder because of a damaged cover, the caliper should be reconditioned as described in this chapter.
9. Open the bleeder valve (**Figure 15**) and push the pistons back into the cylinders. The master cylinder may overflow when this is done, so draw off some fluid and wrap the cylinder in a shop rag to prevent the fluid from damaging the paint.

CAUTION
Do not let the brake fluid spill on the brake pads or the disc.

10. Apply a high-temperature brake grease to the side of the shim which is colored red. Then place the red side against the brake pad backing plate.
11. Install the brake pads (**Figure 13** and **Figure 14**).
12. Insert the top pad retaining pin. Then position pad spring A and pad spring B as shown in **Figure 8**.
13. Install the lower pad retaining pin, making sure that pad springs A and B are located under the retaining pin. Then install the outside pad retaining clip (**Figure 10**). **Figure 16** shows final installation.

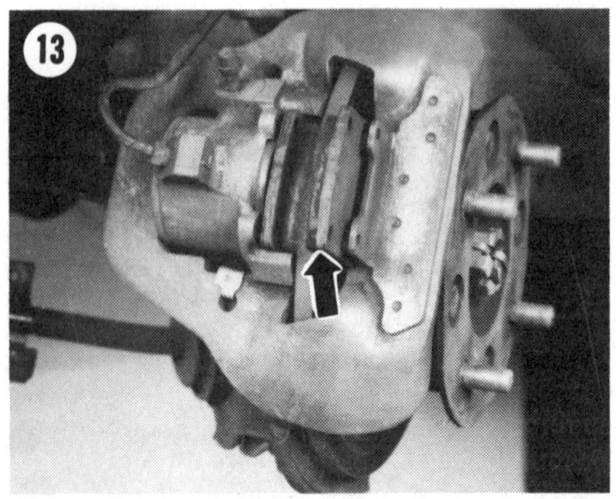

14. Install the front wheels and lower the car.
15. Depress the brake pedal several times before driving the car so that the pads can assume correct alignment with respect to the disc. Road test the car as described in this chapter until you are certain that the brakes are in good working order.

Station Wagon

Figure 17 is an exploded view of the front disc brakes for 1976-1979 station wagon models.

1. Jack up the vehicle front end and secure with jackstands. Remove the front wheels.
2. Remove the pad shield.
3. Using a vernier caliper as shown in **Figure 9**, measure the thickness of each brake pad. Include brake pad backing plate thickness. Repeat on opposite wheel. If brake pad thickness is less than service limit (**Table 1**) or there is a difference of 2 mm (0.078 in.) or more between the left and right sides, replace all 4 pads as a set.
4. If brake pads are okay, install the wheels and lower the car. If brake pads are worn, proceed to Step 5 for brake pad replacement.
5. Remove the brake pad inner and outer retainer clips (**Figure 17**).
6. Remove the brake pad pins.
7. Slide out the brake pads and shims.
8. If necessary, compress the caliper piston, using a hard wood or soft metal lever. If necessary, remove some brake fluid from the master cylinder reservoir to avoid overflow. Cover fluid opening with a shop rag.

CAUTION
Do not let the brake fluid spill on the brake pads or the disc.

9. Install brake pads.
10. Apply a high-temperature brake grease to the side of the shim which is colored red.

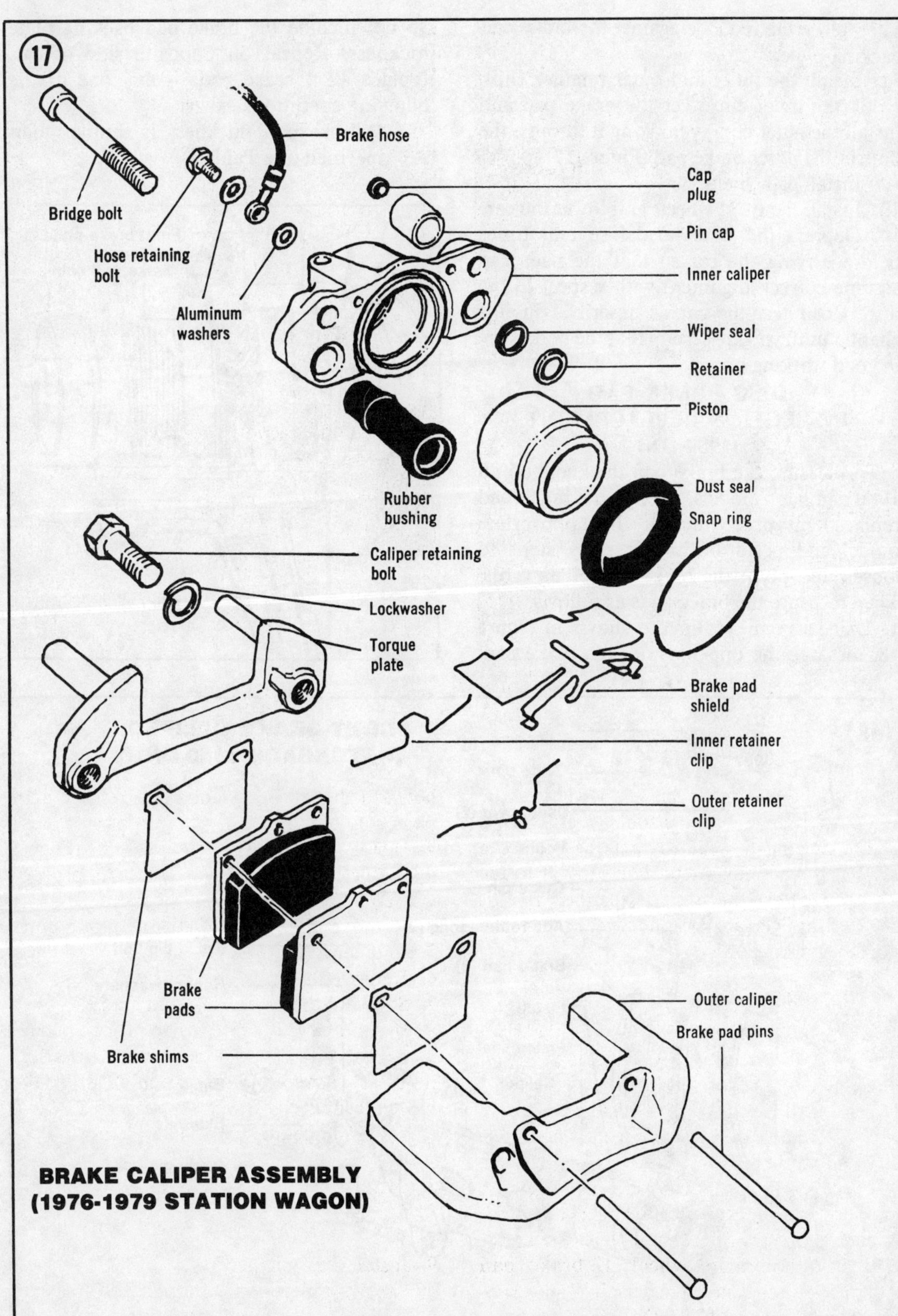

BRAKE CALIPER ASSEMBLY (1976-1979 STATION WAGON)

Then place the red side against the brake pad backing plate.

11. Install the inner and outer retainer clips. Hook the inner clip over the brake pad and install the outer clip by hooking it through the hole in the outer brake pad (**Figure 17**).

12. Install pad shield.

13. Install the front wheels and lower the car.

14. Depress the brake pedal several times before driving the car so that the pads can assume correct alignment with respect to the disc. Road test the car as described in this chapter until you are certain that the brakes are in good working order.

DISC BRAKE PAD INSPECTION/REPLACEMENT (1980-ON)

To measure the brake pad thickness on all 1980 and later models, refer to the brake pad replacement procedure for the appropriate model and perform the necessary steps to loosen and pivot the brake caliper upwards. Then measure the brake pads as follows.

1. Using a vernier caliper as shown in **Figure 18**, measure the thickness of each brake pad. Do not include the brake pad backing plate thickness. Repeat on opposite side of car. Replace all 4 brake pads if any one of the following conditions exists:

   a. A brake pad thickness is thinner than specified (see **Table 1**).

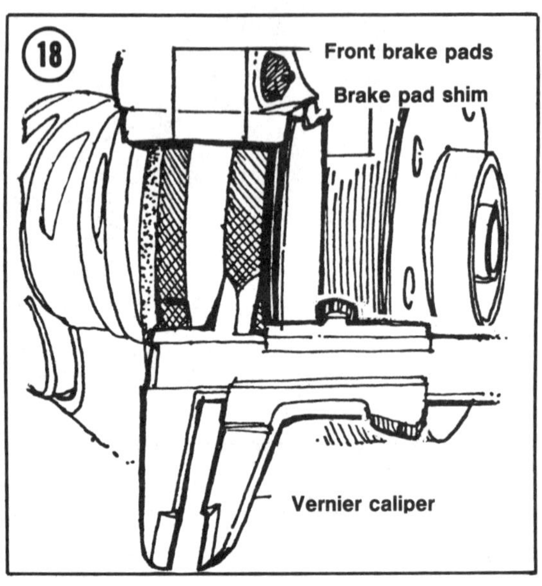

19

FRONT BRAKE CALIPER (HATCHBACK 1980-ON)

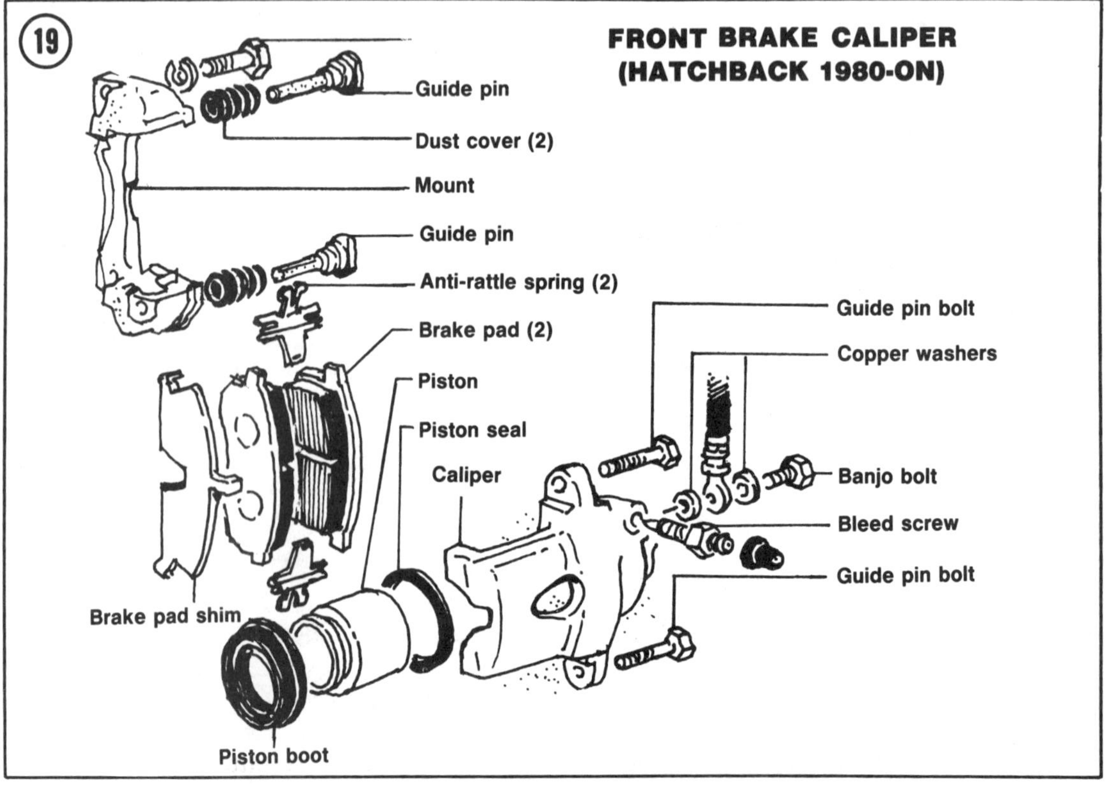

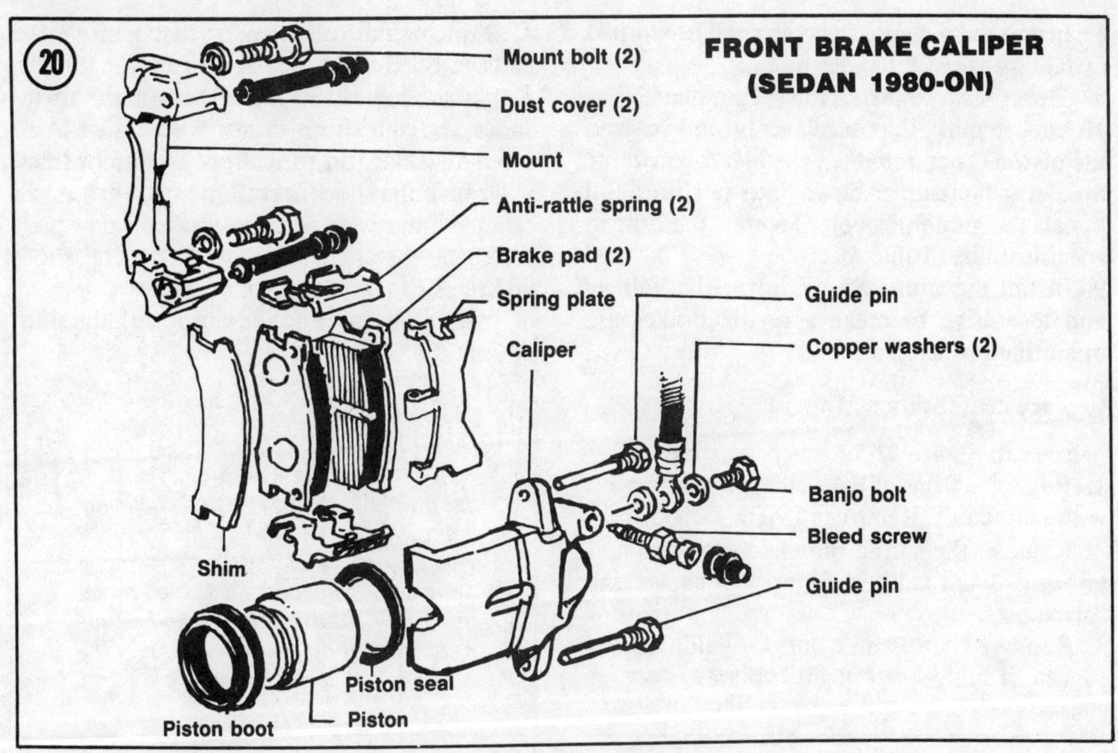

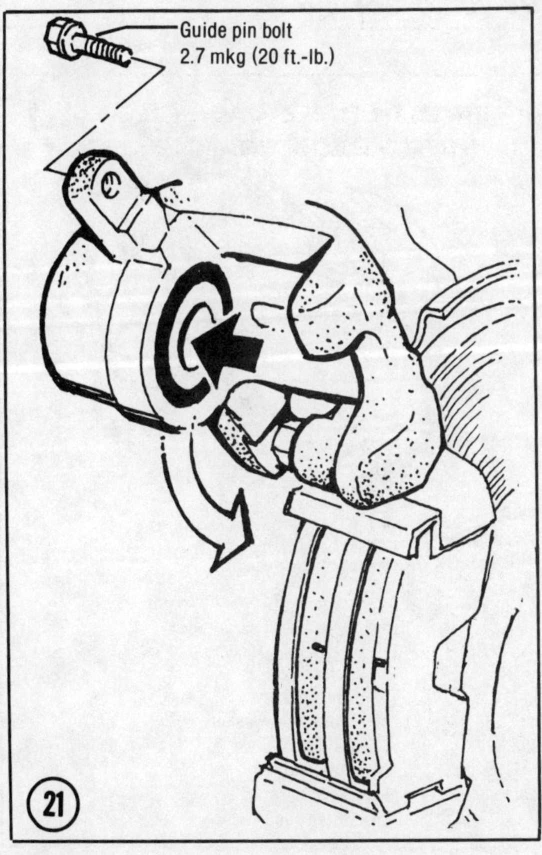

b. Thickness of a brake set varies more than 2 mm (0.080 in.).

2. If brake pads are okay, install the caliper and wheels and lower the car. If the brake pads are worn, proceed to brake pad replacement for the appropriate model.

Replacement (Hatchback and Sedan)

Refer to **Figure 19** (hatchback) or **Figure 20** (sedan) for this procedure.

1. Raise the front of the vehicle and secure it with jackstands. Remove the front wheels.
2. Remove the guide pin bolt and swing the caliper up. See **Figure 21**.

3A. *Hatchback models:* Remove the brake pads, shim and anti-rattle springs.

3B. *Sedan models:* Remove the brake pads, spring plate, shim and anti-rattle springs.

4. Clean all points where the shoes and the shim touch the caliper and mount. Also clean the shim (and the metal part of the old pads if they are to be reused) with a wire brush. Apply silicone grease to all cleaned and metal contact areas. Install the anti-rattle springs.

5. Install the new pads and shim. The shim is installed against the outer pad.
6. *Sedan models:* Install the spring plate.
7. Loosen the caliper bleed screw and push in the piston. Then retighten the bleed screw.
8. Swing the caliper down into position and install the guide pin bolt. Tighten the bolt to specifications (**Table 4**).
9. Install the front wheels, lower the vehicle and test drive to make sure the brakes are operating properly.

Replacement (Station Wagon)

Refer to **Figure 22** for this procedure.
1. Raise the front of the vehicle and secure it with jackstands. Remove the front wheels.
2. Remove the spring pins from the top and bottom of the caliper. **Figure 23** shows the spring pins.
3. Remove the top and bottom guide plates. **Figure 24** shows the top guide plate.
4. Remove the caliper and then remove the pads and pad shim. See **Figure 25**.
5. If pads are to be reused, clean the metal shoes and the shim with a wire brush. Also clean all points on the caliper and mount that will touch the shoes and shim and lubricate all cleaned areas with silicone grease. If new pads are to be installed, lubricate the metal shoes and the shim with the same lubricant.
6. Install the pads and the shim, with the shim against the outside shoe.

NOTE
Before continuing with Step 7, remove the master cylinder cap and check the brake fluid level. If fluid is nearly to the top, place rags underneath reservoir and drain some fluid out. This is to prevent brake fluid from spilling out and getting onto the body surface. Cover the reservoir with a clean shop rag.

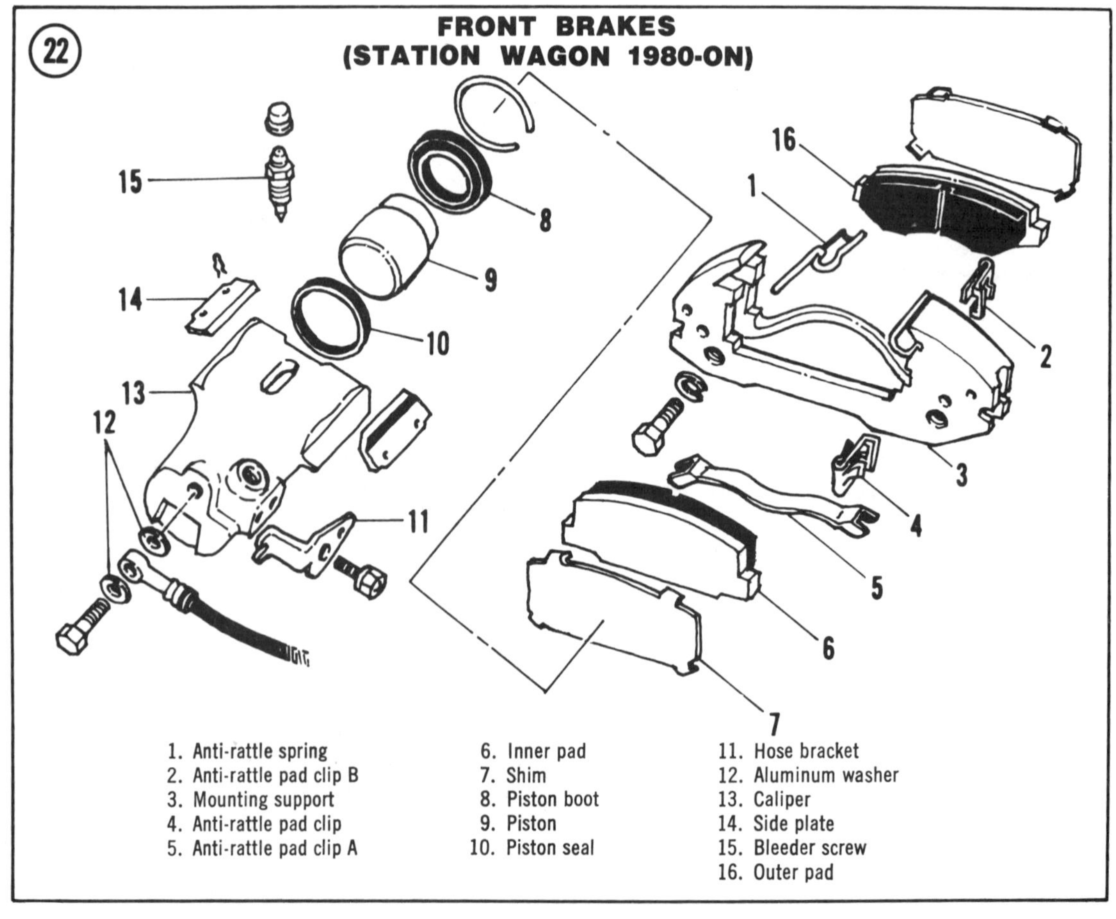

1. Anti-rattle spring
2. Anti-rattle pad clip B
3. Mounting support
4. Anti-rattle pad clip
5. Anti-rattle pad clip A
6. Inner pad
7. Shim
8. Piston boot
9. Piston
10. Piston seal
11. Hose bracket
12. Aluminum washer
13. Caliper
14. Side plate
15. Bleeder screw
16. Outer pad

7. Loosen the bleed screw slightly and push in the caliper piston. Retighten the screw.
8. Install the caliper on the mount and then install the guide plates (**Figure 24**). Secure with the spring pins (**Figure 23**).
9. Install the front wheels and lower the car. Fill the brake fluid reservoir, as required, to bring to correct level and install the reservoir top. Depress the brake pedal several times and test drive the car to check brake operation.

A. Pad shim
B. Pads

BRAKE CALIPERS

Removal/Installation (1973-1979 Sedan)

1. Jack up the front of the car and place on jackstands. Remove the front wheels.

2. Unscrew the brake line nipple from the caliper (**Figure 26**) and tape it to prevent the entry of dirt and moisture.
3. Unscrew the caliper bolts (**Figure 27**) and remove the caliper by pulling it off the disc.

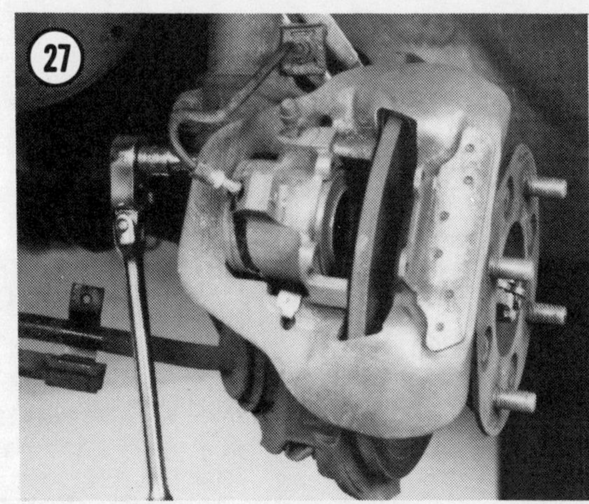

28

FRONT DISC BRAKE (1973-1979 SEDAN)

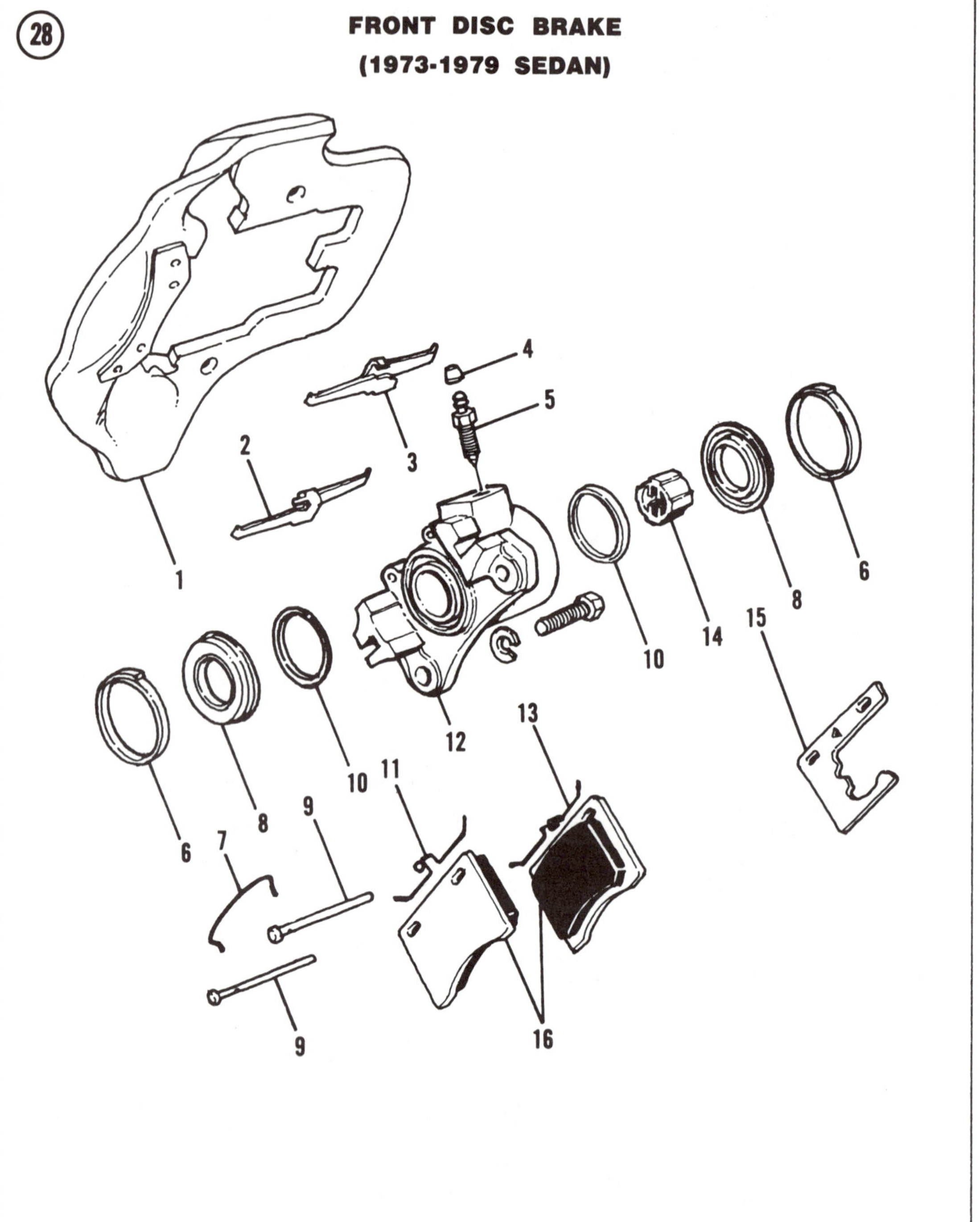

1. Yoke
2. Yoke spring B
3. Yoke spring A
4. Bleed cap
5. Bleed screw
6. Retaining ring
7. Pad retaining clip
8. Dust boot
9. Pad retaining clip
10. Piston seal
11. Pad spring B
12. Cylinder
13. Pad spring A
14. Bias ring
15. Brake pad inner shim
16. Disc brake pad set

4. Installation is the reverse of these steps. Tighten the caliper mounting bolts to specifications (**Table 2**). Be careful not to cross-thread the brake line nipple when screwing it into the caliper. Bleed the brakes as described in this chapter.

Disassembly/Assembly (1973-1979 Sedan)

Refer to **Figure 28** for this procedure.

1. Remove the pin clip, springs and brake pads.
2. Push the yoke (**Figure 29**) to the inboard side of the caliper and remove it. Pry off the dust cover retainers (**Figure 30**) and remove the dust covers (**Figure 31**).
3. Apply compressed air to the inlet port and eject the pistons (**Figure 32**). Do not drop them or they could be damaged.
4. Remove the piston seals from the cylinder and discard them (**Figure 33**). Inspect the caliper as described in this chapter.
5. Lubricate the caliper bore and the new piston seal with clean brake fluid. *Do not use solvent or gasoline.* Lay all replacement parts in order (**Figure 34**).
6. Install the bleeder screw (if removed). See **Figure 35**.
7. Install new piston seals (**Figure 33**).
8. Lubricate the piston with clean brake fluid. Install a new boot over the piston.
9. Insert the piston into the caliper bore; do not unseat the seal.
10. Position the OD of the boot in the caliper counterbore and push it down until it seats (**Figure 31**).
11. Install the yoke springs with the long, thin arms of the springs on the top side of the yoke (**Figure 36**).
12. Install the cylinder in the yoke with the intake port in the cylinder on the inboard side of the yoke (**Figure 37**). When the yoke springs contact the cylinder, push the yoke down firmly and slide it to the left until the 2 pieces are firmly engaged. Lubricate sliding surface of yoke.
13. Complete caliper assembly and installation by performing the following procedures as described in this chapter:
    a. Install the brake pads, shim, pad springs, pins, and pin clip.
    b. Reinstall brake caliper.
    c. Fill system with fresh brake fluid (DOT 3 or DOT 4).
    d. Bleed the brakes.
    e. Road test car.

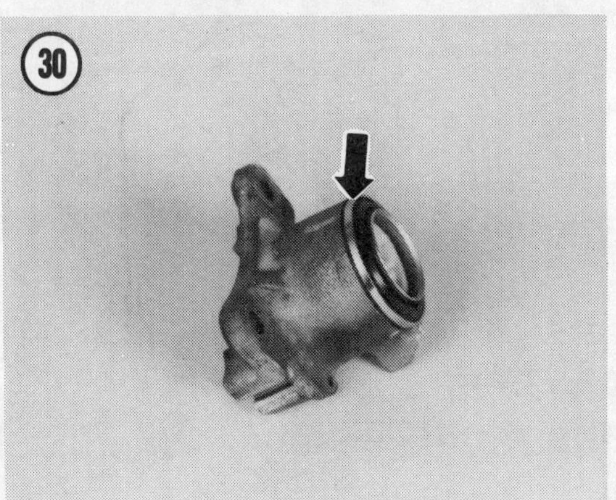

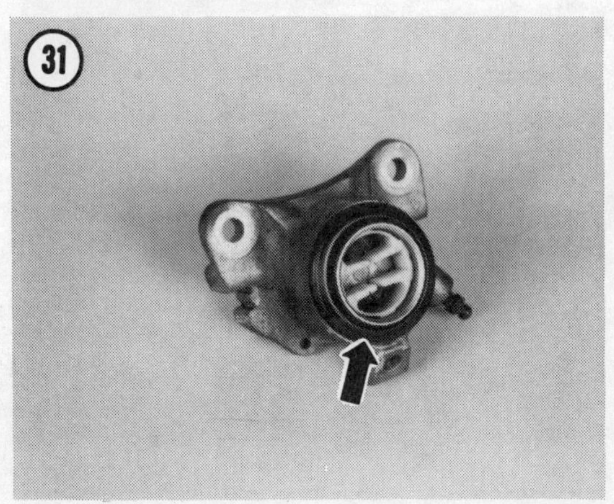

12

32

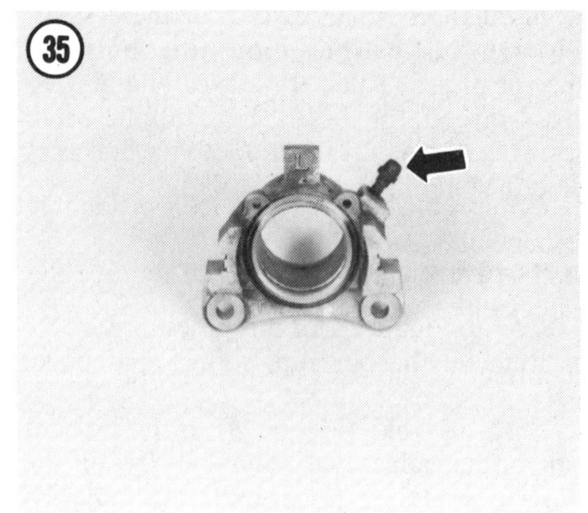
35

33

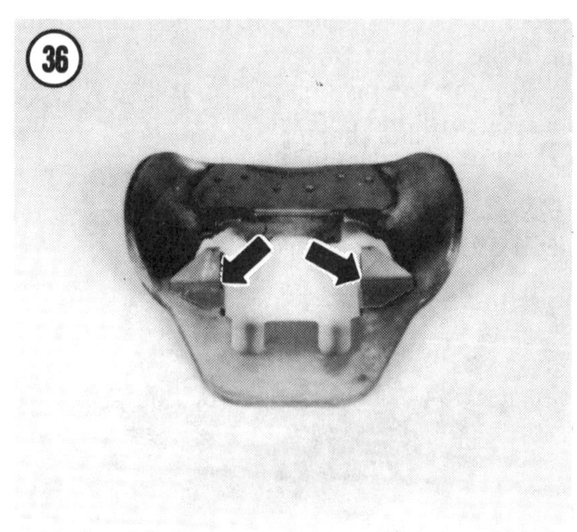
36

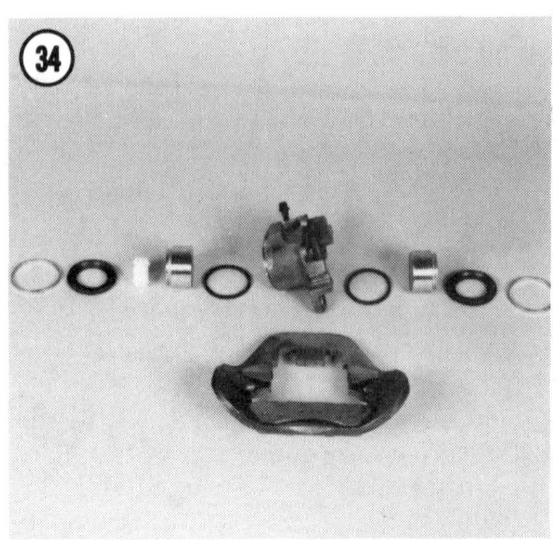
34

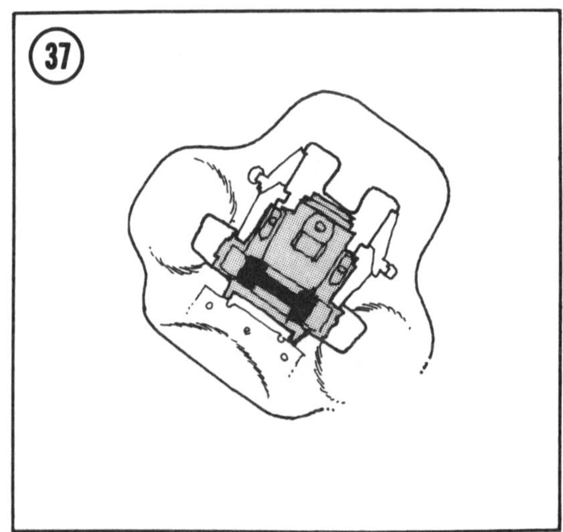
37

Removal/Installation (1976-1979 Station Wagon)

Refer to **Figure 17** for this procedure.

1. Raise the front of the car and place it on jackstands. Remove the front wheels.
2. Remove the brake pads as described in this chapter.
3. Remove the bridge bolts and remove the outer caliper and torque plate.
4. Remove the hose retaining bolt and aluminum washers and remove the brake hose. Tie the hose out of the way and cover it with a clean cloth to prevent contamination.
5. Remove the caliper retaining bolts and remove the caliper.
6. Installation is the reverse of these steps. Tighten the caliper mounting bolts to specifications (**Table 2**). Be careful not to cross-thread the brake line nipple when screwing it into the caliper. Bleed the brakes as described in this chapter.

Disassembly/Assembly (1976-1979 Station Wagon)

1. Remove the snap ring and dust seal from the caliper piston. Apply compressed air to the brake hose hole to remove the piston, using care not to damage the piston. Remove the O-ring.

WARNING
Cushion the piston with a shop rag. Do not try to cushion the piston with your fingers, as injury could result.

2. Inspect the caliper parts as described under *Inspection* in this chapter.
3. Install a new O-ring, piston and a new dust seal. Install the snap ring.
4. Install the inner caliper with the retaining bolts and tighten the bolts to specifications (**Table 2**).
5. Lightly lubricate torque plate pins with brake grease. Install new rubber bushing and wiper seal, then install the torque plate and outer caliper. Tighten the bridge bolts to specifications (**Table 2**).
6. Complete caliper assembly and installation by performing the following procedures as described in this chapter:
   a. Install the brake pads, shim, pad springs, pins and pin clip.
   b. Reinstall brake caliper. Then install the brake hose, using new aluminum washers.
   c. Fill system with fresh brake fluid (DOT 3 or DOT 4).
   d. Bleed the brakes.
   e. Road test car.

Removal/Installation (1980-on)

1. Remove the brake pads as described in this chapter.
2. Unscrew the hollow bolt and remove the banjo fitting and brake line.
3. To unbolt the caliper on hatchback and sedan models, remove the upper and lower guide pins. On station wagon models, remove the spring pins and guide plates and lift caliper off.
4. Installation is the reverse of these steps. Tighten the hollow bolt to 3.5 mkg (25 ft.-lb.). Bleed the brake system as described in this chapter.

Disassembly/Assembly (1980-on)

Refer to **Figure 19** (hatchback), **Figure 20** (sedan) or **Figure 22** (station wagon).

1. On station wagons, remove the snap ring. See **Figure 38**.
2. Remove the piston boot. See **Figure 38** (wagon shown; hatchback and sedan similar but no snap ring).
3. Cushion the piston with a shop rag and apply compressed air through the brake line hole to remove the piston. See **Figure 39** (shop rag not shown for clarity).

WARNING
Do not try to cushion the piston with your fingers, as injury could result.

4. Remove the piston seal. See **Figure 40**. Take care not to scratch or otherwise damage the cylinder bore.
5. Inspect the brake caliper as described under *Inspection* and check all parts for excessive wear and damage. Repace any damaged parts.

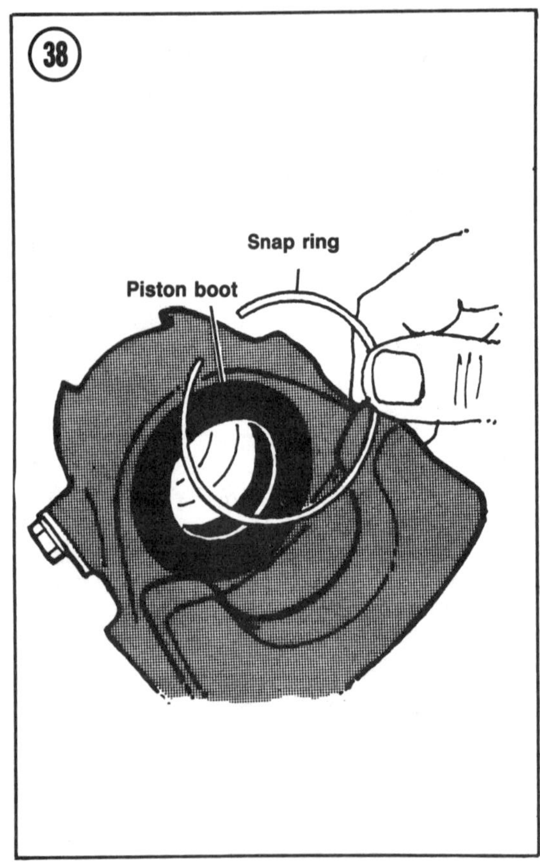
38
Snap ring
Piston boot

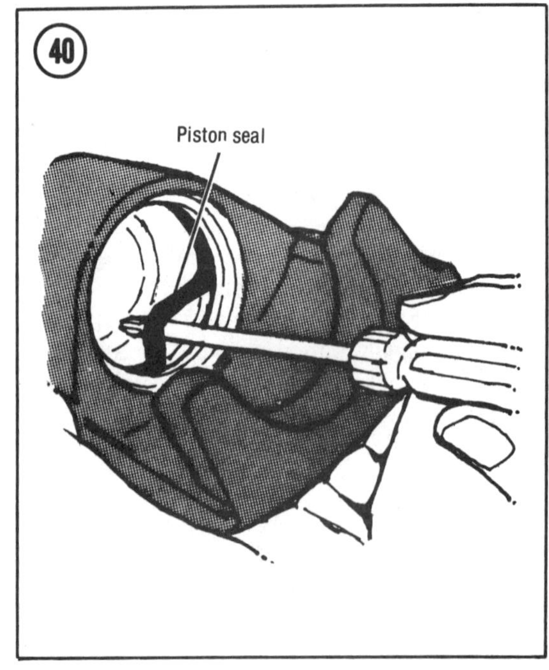
40
Piston seal

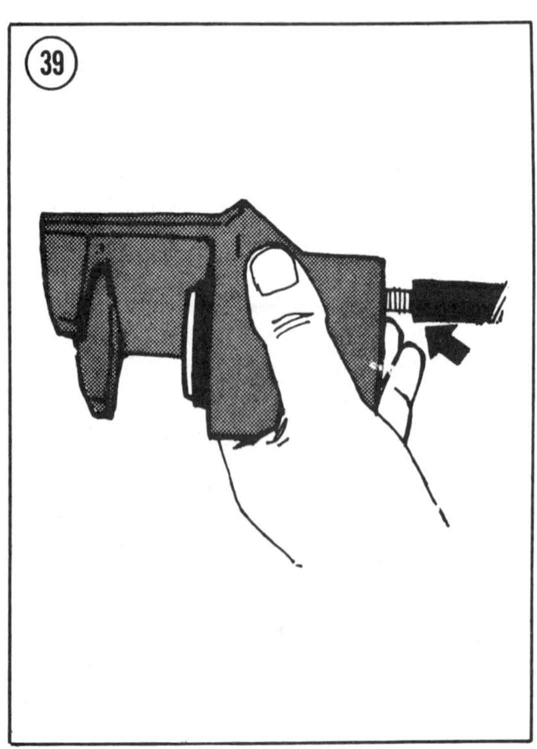
39

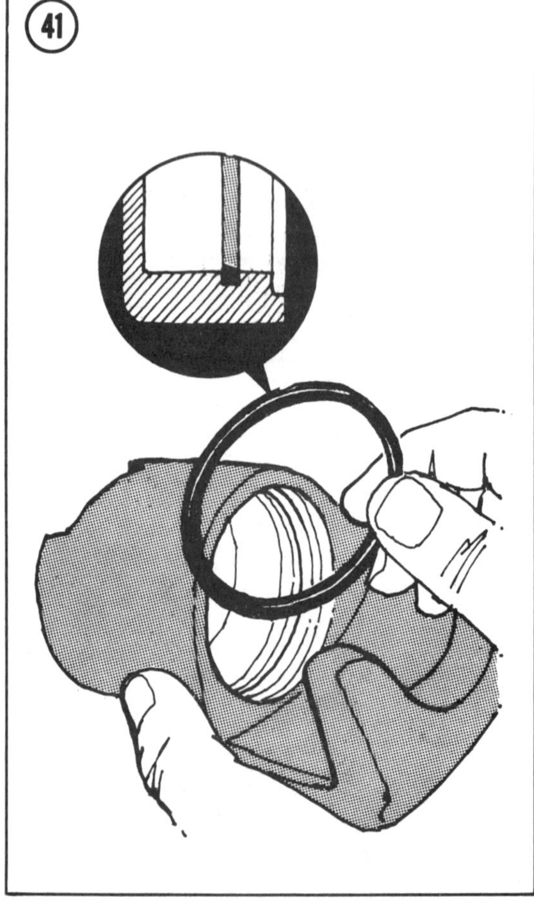
41

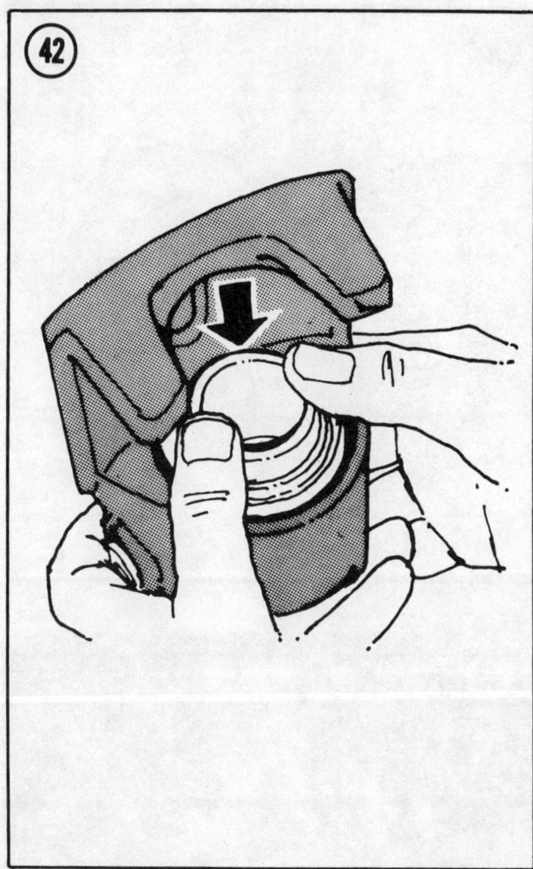

6. Assembly is the reverse of these steps. Use a new piston seal and coat it with brake fluid before installing it in the cylinder groove. See **Figure 41**. Install a new boot on the piston so that the boot lips seat in the piston groove. Press the piston into the cylinder, taking care not to damage any part. See **Figure 42**. Then seat the outer boot lip in the cylinder bore groove.

Inspection (All Models)

CAUTION
Always use clean brake fluid or denatured alcohol to clean any caliper parts. Never use other solvents as they cause rubber parts to deteriorate. Do not use any fluids on brake pads.

1. Clean all parts (except brake pads) in clean brake fluid. Use dry, filtered compressed air to dry parts. Blow out all passages in the caliper and bleeder valve.

CAUTION
Lubricated shop air deposits a film of mineral oil on metal parts. This may damage rubber parts.

2. Check the caliper and caliper mount retaining bolts for corrosion, breaks in the plating or other damage. Replace the bolts as required.

3. Carefully examine the piston outside diameter (OD) for scoring, nicks, corrosion and worn or damaged plating. If any surface defects are detected, replace the piston.

4. Check the caliper bore in the same manner. Replace if surface defects are detected.

5. Check the thickness of the brake pads as described in this chapter. Repace them if they are worn or if soaked with brake fluid.

BRAKE DISC

Inspection

The front brake rotors can be inspected, while installed on the car, after the front wheels and the calipers have been removed. On all 1973-1979 models and 1980-1981 station wagon models, remove the calipers as described but do not disconnect the brake lines. Suspend the calipers with wire so they do not hang on the lines. On 1980-on hatchback and sedan models, remove the lower caliper mounting bolt and rotate the caliper upward. Then remove the brake pads, shim and anti-rattle springs. Refer to *Brake Pad Inspection/Replacement* in this chapter.

1. Check the rotor for damage and obvious signs of wear.

2. Measure the thickness and parallelism of the disc with a micrometer. Measure in 8 equally spaced locations around the disc, 19 mm (3/4 in.) from the edge (**Figure 43**). If any of the measurements are not within specifications (**Tables 1-3**), replace the rotor.

3. Check the runout of the disc with a dial indicator (**Figure 44**). If runout is greater than 0.15 mm (0.0060 in.), the disc is unserviceable and should be replaced.

Removal/Installation (1973-1979)

1. Remove the front hubcaps. Remove the cotter pin (**Figure 45**) and loosen the spindle nut and front wheel nuts.
2. Raise the vehicle front end and secure with jackstands. Remove the front wheels.
3. Remove the brake caliper as described in this chapter.
4. Using a knock-puller of the type shown in **Figure 46**, remove the front hub and rotor. To separate hub and rotor, remove the attaching bolts and lockwashers.
5. Installation is the reverse of these steps. Tighten spindle nut to specifications in **Table 2** (end of chapter).

Removal/Installation (1980-on)

1. Remove the front hubcaps. Loosen the spindle nut and front wheel nuts.
2. Raise the vehicle front end and secure with jackstands. Remove the front wheels.
3. Remove the brake caliper as described in this chapter.
4. Install two M8 x 1.25 x 12 mm (long) bolts into 8 mm threaded holes in the brake disc

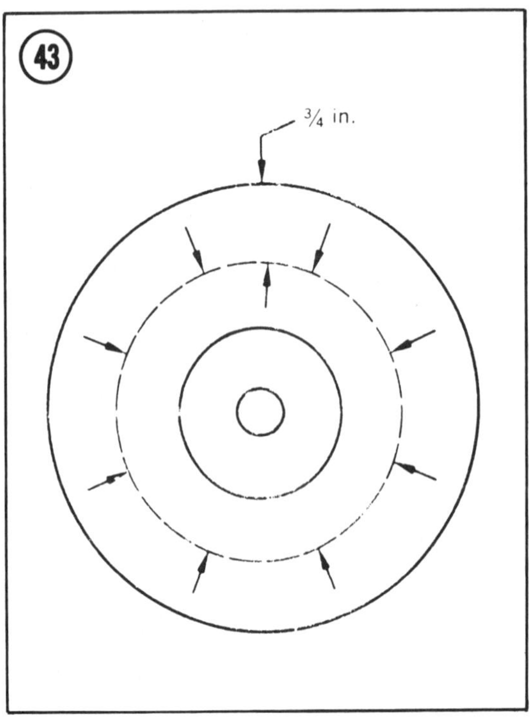

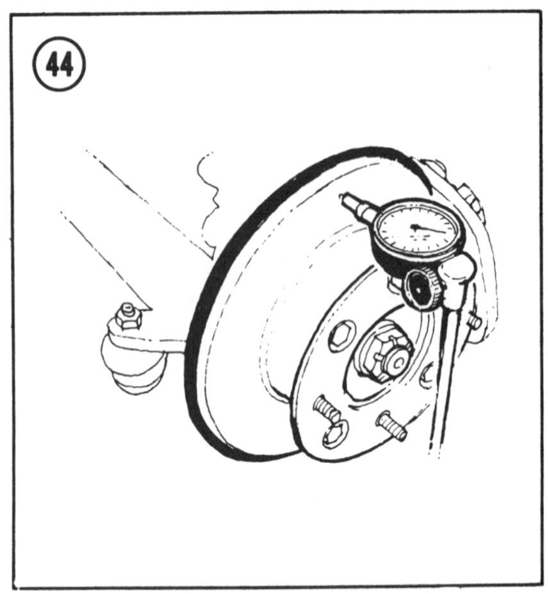

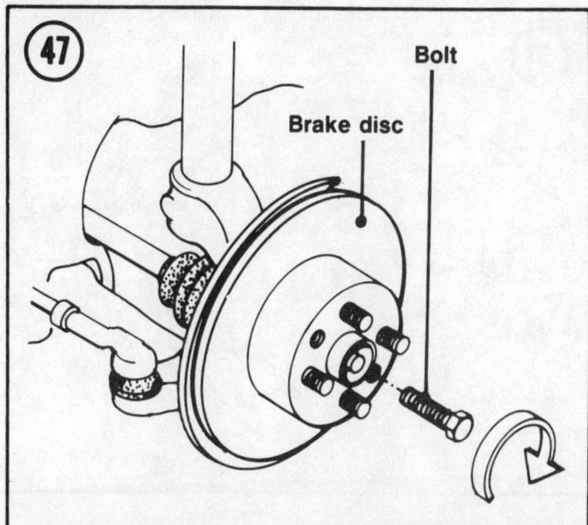

(**Figure 47**). Turn the bolts 2 turns at a time to push the brake disc away from the hub.

5. Installation is the reverse of these steps. Use a new spindle nut. Torque all fasteners to specifications in **Table 3**.

REAR DRUM BRAKE

Inspection

The rear brakes should be inspected at the intervals specified in Chapter Three and the brake shoes replaced if the lining is worn beyond the service limit.

1. Block the front wheels. Jack up the rear of the car and secure with jackstands. Remove the rear wheels.

2A. *1973-1979*: Unbolt the bearing cap (**Figure 48**) and remove it.

2B. *1980-on*: Pry the bearing cap off (**Figure 49**).

3. Remove the cotter key and unscrew the axle nut (**Figure 50**). Pull off the brake drum.

4. Inspect the linings for oil, grease, dirt and glazing. Dirt and glaze can be removed with a stiff wire brush, but if the linings are greasy or oily they must be replaced.

WARNING
Brake dust is harmful to inhale. To protect your health, it is recommended that you do not use compressed air to

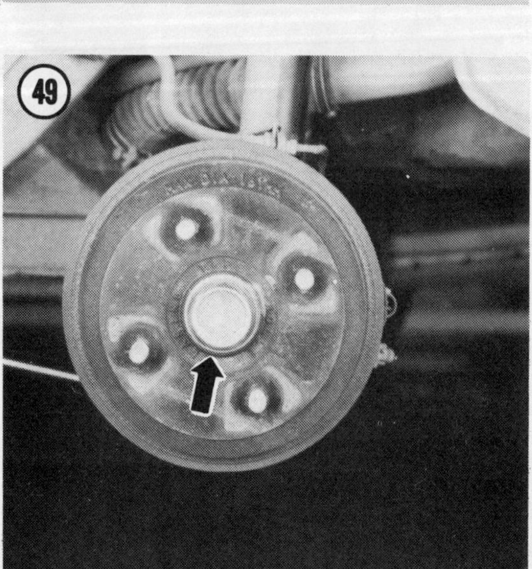

12

clean the brake assembly. Wear a dust mask when servicing the brakes.

5. Check the brake shoe friction surface for scoring and grooving. If these conditions exist, inspect the drums for similar damage. If the drums are scored deeply enough to snag a fingernail, they should be reconditioned by a Honda dealer or automotive brake specialist. Maximum ID for the drums is listed in **Table 1**. If the drums are reconditioned, the brake shoes should be replaced and the new shoes arced to conform to the drums.

NOTE
*If the brake drum is marked with a service limit specification that differs from the specifications in **Table 1**, use the one on the drum.*

6. If brake shoe and drum wear or damage is not obvious, measure the thickness of the brake linings with a caliper (**Figure 51**). If the lining thickness is less than 2 mm (0.079 in.), the shoes must be replaced. See *Brake Shoe Replacement* in this chapter.
7. Pull each of the brake shoes away from the cylinder and check the pistons for signs of leakage (**Figure 52**). A thin lubricating film is normal, but excessive leakage indicates a faulty cylinder that must be rebuilt. See *Wheel Cylinder Overhaul* in this chapter.
8. If the brake components are in satisfactory condition, lubricate the adjuster, the slots in the pistons and the sliding surface of the backing plate with high-temperature brake grease.
9. Install the brake drum and clean and oil the axle threads. Tighten the axle nut as follows:
   a. 1973-1979 models: Install the washer and castellated nut and tighten it to 12 mkg (83 ft.-lb.). Remove the wrench and check the alignment of the hole in the axle with the slot in the nut. Further tighten the nut to the next alignment (if necessary) and install a new cotter key.
   b. 1980-on models: Install the washer and nut and tighten the nut to 24 N•m (18 ft.-lb.). Rotate the brake drum by hand. Then loosen the nut and retighten it to 4 N•m (3 ft.-lb.). Install the cotter pin holder with the slots as close as possible to the hole in the spindle and, if necessary, tighten the nut to align the slots with the spindle. Install a new cotter pin through the nut and spindle. Bend the ends of the cotter pin to lock it.

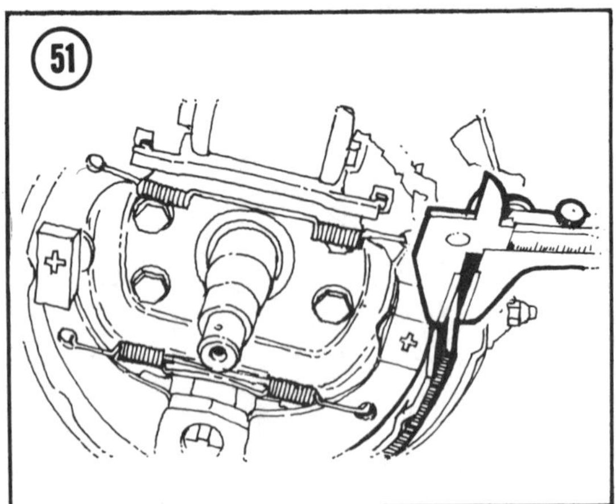

10. On 1973-1979 models, adjust the brakes as described in this chapter. On 1980 and later models, depress the brake pedal to activate the self adjusting mechanism.
11. Test drive the vehicle as described earlier in this chapter to ensure that the brakes are operating correctly.

Brake Shoe Replacement

Refer to **Figure 53** (1973-1979 sedan and hatchback), **Figure 54** (1976-1979 station

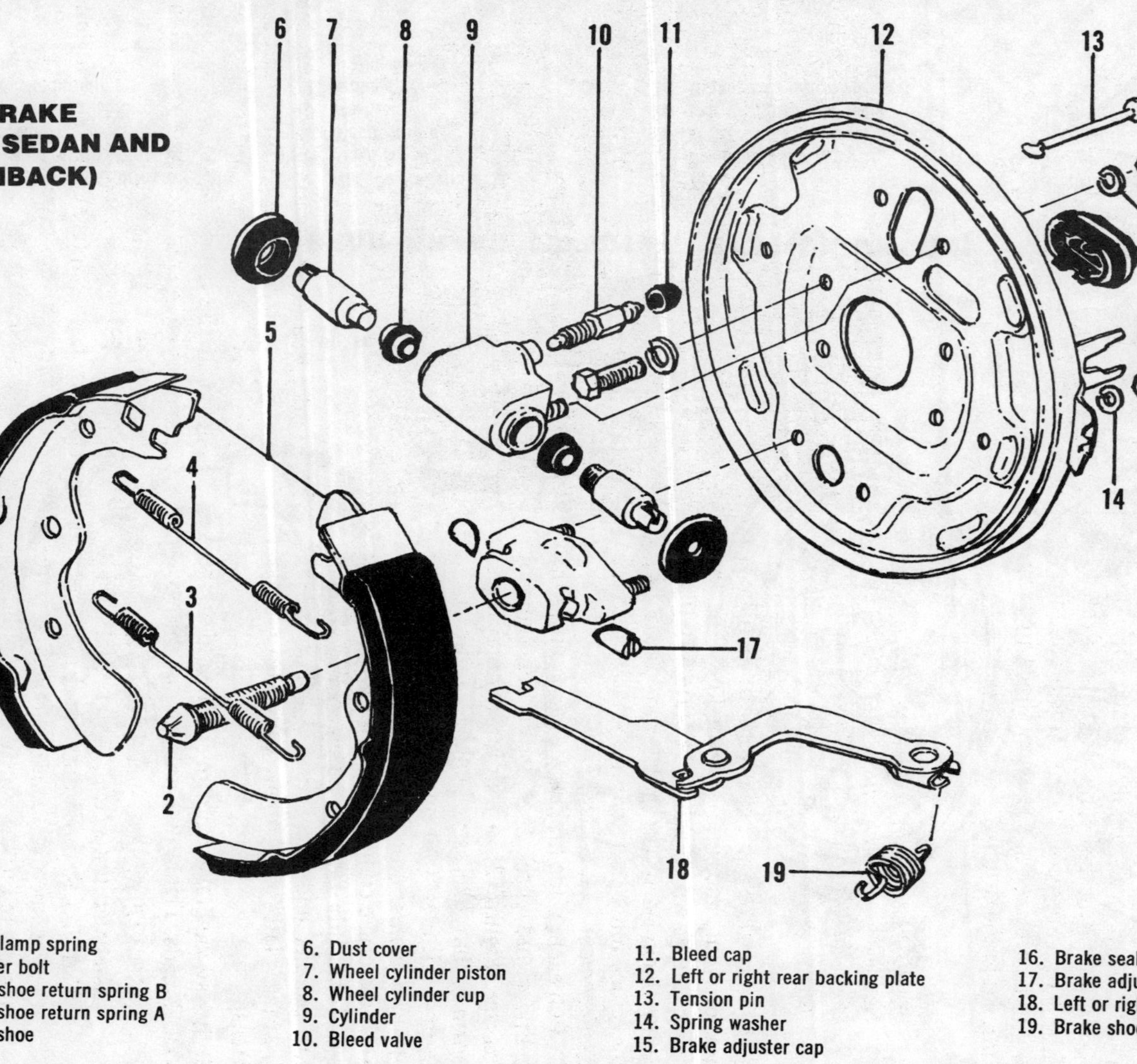
53
REAR BRAKE
(1973-1979 SEDAN AND
HATCHBACK)
1. Shoe clamp spring
2. Adjuster bolt
3. Brake shoe return spring B
4. Brake shoe return spring A
5. Brake shoe
6. Dust cover
7. Wheel cylinder piston
8. Wheel cylinder cup
9. Cylinder
10. Bleed valve
11. Bleed cap
12. Left or right rear backing plate
13. Tension pin
14. Spring washer
15. Brake adjuster cap
16. Brake seal
17. Brake adjuster ramp
18. Left or right brake lever
19. Brake shoe return spring

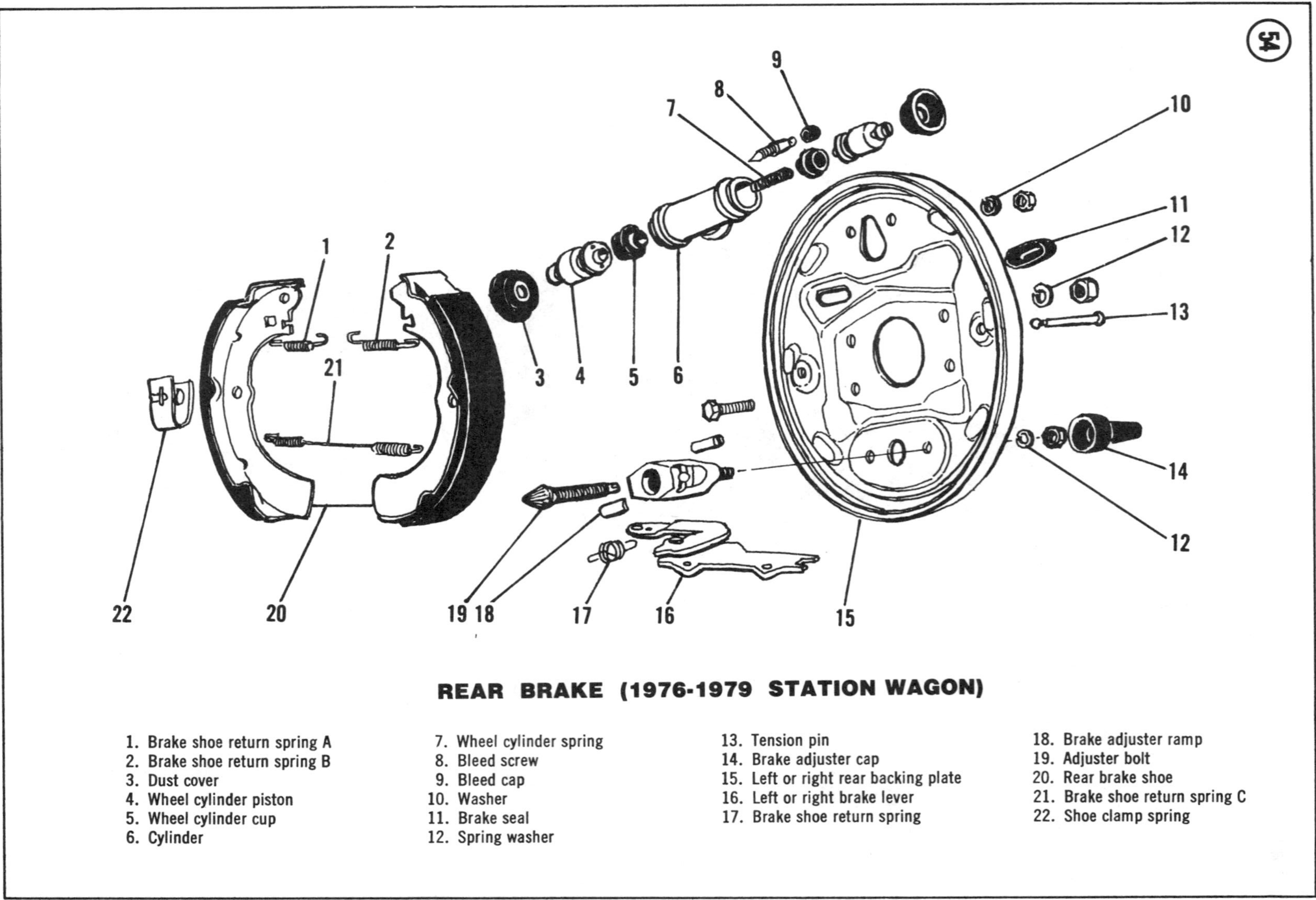

REAR BRAKE (1976-1979 STATION WAGON)

1. Brake shoe return spring A
2. Brake shoe return spring B
3. Dust cover
4. Wheel cylinder piston
5. Wheel cylinder cup
6. Cylinder
7. Wheel cylinder spring
8. Bleed screw
9. Bleed cap
10. Washer
11. Brake seal
12. Spring washer
13. Tension pin
14. Brake adjuster cap
15. Left or right rear backing plate
16. Left or right brake lever
17. Brake shoe return spring
18. Brake adjuster ramp
19. Adjuster bolt
20. Rear brake shoe
21. Brake shoe return spring C
22. Shoe clamp spring

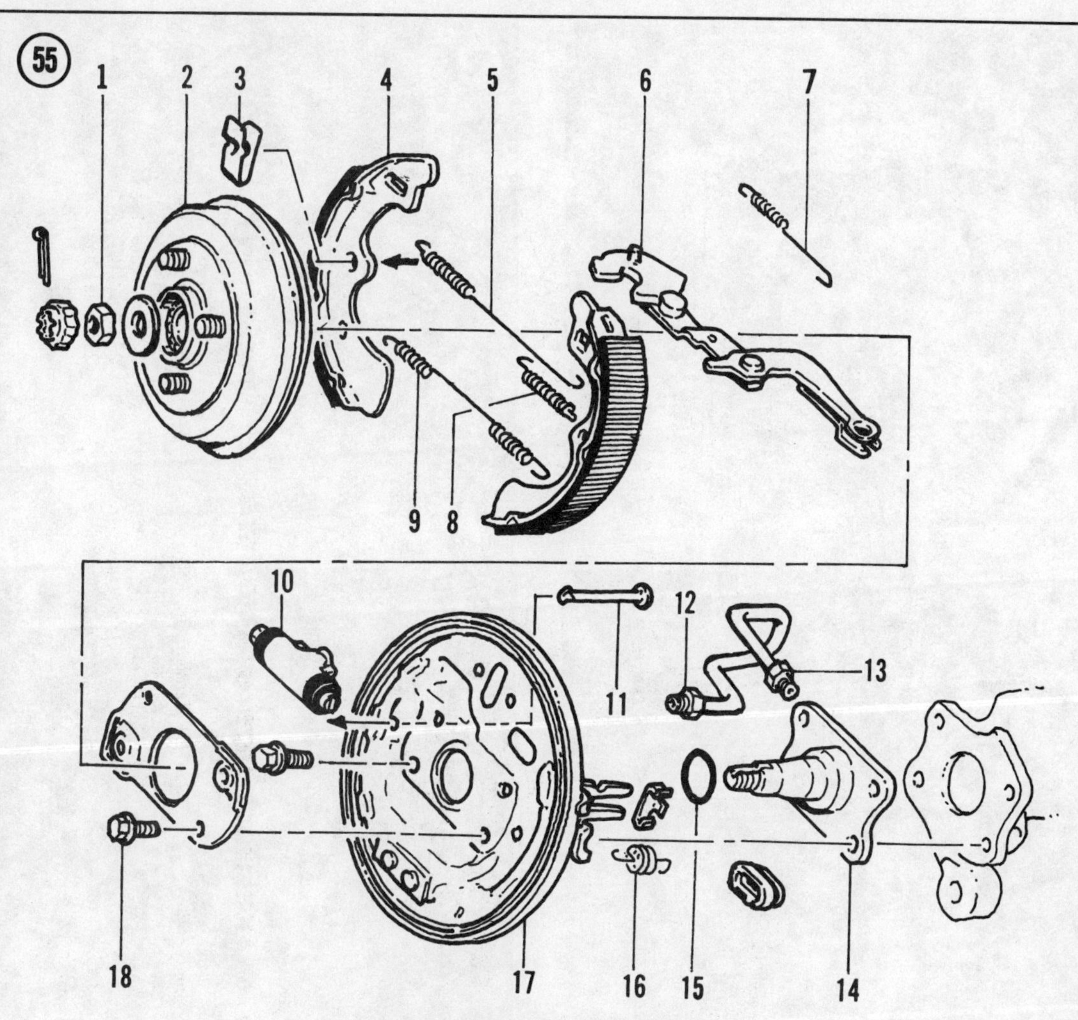

REAR BRAKES (1980-ON)

1. Spindle nut
2. Rear brake drum
3. Shoe clamp spring
4. Brake shoe
5. Return spring A
   (Do not interchange spring A and B between top and bottom)
6. Quadrant ratchet/parking brake lever
7. Quadrant ratchet/parking brake lever spring
8. Rod spring
9. Return spring B
10. Wheel cylinder
11. Tension pin
12. Flare nut
13. Flare nut
14. Wheel spindle
15. Seal
16. Return spring
17. Backing plate
18. Bolt

wagon) or **Figure 55** (1980-on) for this procedure. Release the parking brake before starting removal.

NOTE

Complete work on one side before disassembling the other side. This allows you an excellent reference as to how the parts are assembled.

1. Remove the brake drums as described under *Inspection.*
2. Remove the lower (**Figure 56**) and upper (**Figure 57**) brake return springs.
3. Push in on each brake shoe clamp spring (**Figure 58**), turn the tension pin to line it up with the slot in the spring and remove the spring.
4. Remove the brake shoes.
5. Clean the backing plate (**Figure 59**) and inside of the drum with a clean, dry rag. *Do not* use solvent or gasoline. Check the condition of the brake drum as described in this chapter and have the drum reconditioned if required. At the same time the drum is reconditioned, have the new shoes arced to the drum to ensure maximum shoe-to-drum contact.
6. If wheel cylinder overhaul is required, remove the wheel cylinder and perform all service procedures as described under *Wheel Cylinder Overhaul.*
7. Lubricate the adjuster, the slots in the pistons and the sliding surface of the backing plate with high-temperature brake grease.

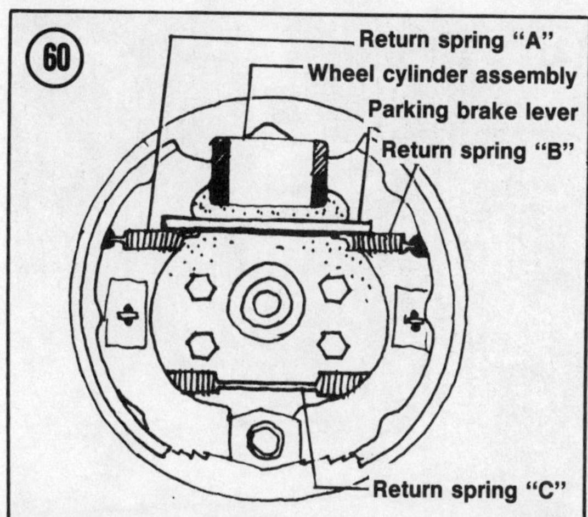

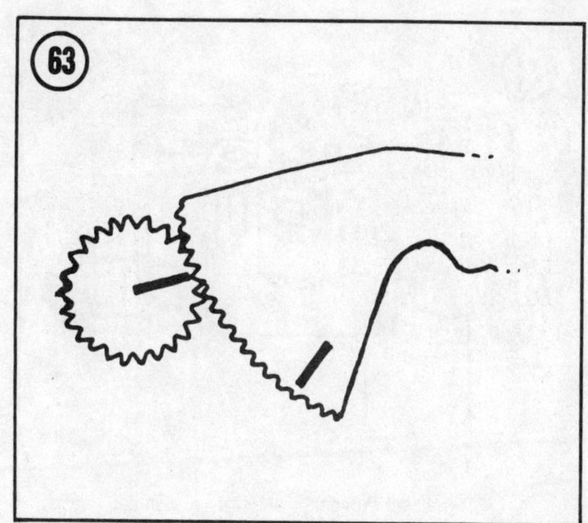

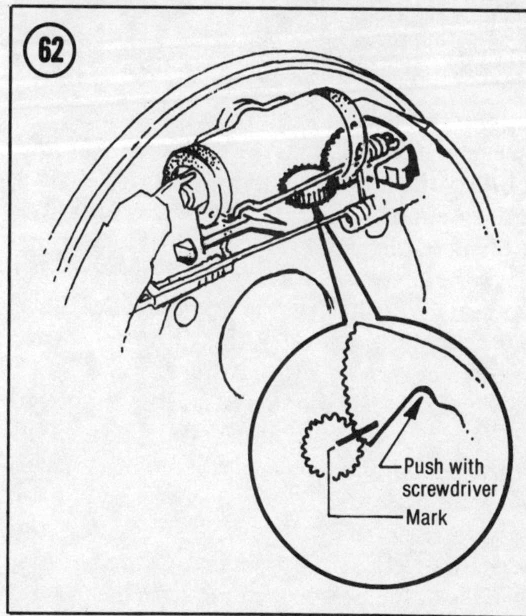

8. Install the shoes by reversing the removal steps, noting the following:

a. Install the brake return springs A and B as shown in **Figure 56** (1973-1979 sedan and hatchback) or **Figure 60** (1976-1979 station wagon). Refer to **Figure 55** for 1980-on models.
b. If installing new brake shoes on 1973-1979 models, it will be necessary to back off the brake shoe adjusters (**Figure 61**) to retract the new shoes far enough to permit the drums to be installed.
c. On 1980-on models, use a screwdriver as shown in **Figure 62** to move the quadrant ratchet to the fully released position. Then install the brake drum and the spindle nut. Press the brake pedal and remove the spindle nut and brake drum. Check the quadrant ratchet to make sure it has moved from its fully released position as shown in **Figure 63**. If so, the brakes are adjusted properly.
d. Adjust the brakes on 1973-1979 models as described in this chapter.
e. Adjust the parking brake as described in this chapter.
f. If a brake line was disconnected, bleed the brakes as described in this chapter.
g. Road test the car after completing all assembly and adjustment procedures to make sure the brakes are operating correctly.

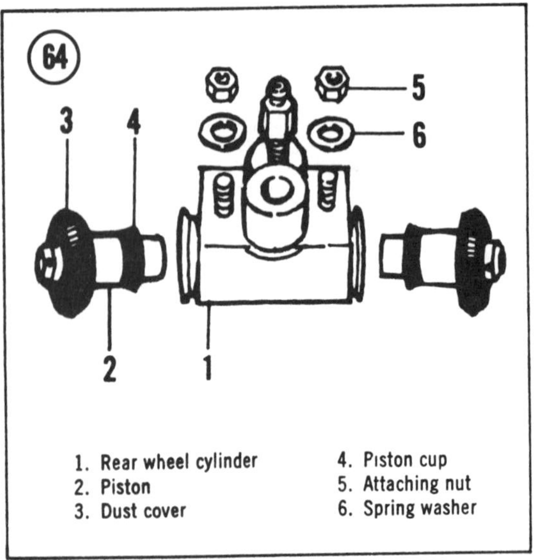

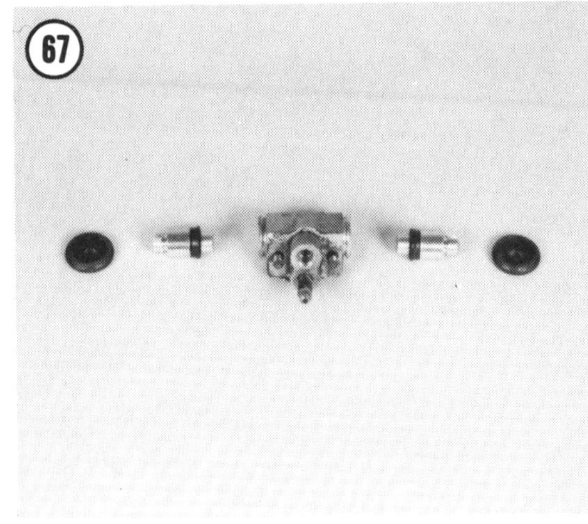

Wheel Cylinder Overhaul

Refer to **Figure 64** for this procedure. The wheel cylinder mounting is shown in **Figure 65**.

1. Remove the brake drums and shoes as described in this chapter.
2. Remove the rubber dust cover from the rear of the backing plate, if so equipped.
3. Unscrew the brake line nipple and the cylinder mounting nuts (**Figure 66**) and remove the cylinder.
4. Pry the dust seals off the flanges on the wheel cylinder housing and remove the pistons. Remove the cylinder spring on 1976-1979 station wagon and all 1980 and later models.
5. Clean all of the parts in fresh brake fluid; do not use gasoline or any other solvent. Remove the seals and the piston cups and discard them. Inspect the pistons and the cylinder for obvious signs of wear or damage and replace them if they are less than perfect in appearance.
6. If the cylinder and pistons appear serviceable, measure the cylinder ID and the piston OD. Replace them if clearance is excessive (**Table 1**).
7. Inspect the backing plate for damage or bending and replace if necessary.
8. Before assembling the cylinder, make sure all of the parts, your work area and your hands are clean and grease-free. Liberally coat all of the parts (**Figure 67**) with fresh brake fluid. On

1976-1979 station wagon and all 1980 and later models, install the spring before inserting the piston. Install the pistons and cups in the cylinder and then install the seals. After installing the outside seals, make sure they are completely seated around the flanges on the cylinder.
9. Apply a small amount of sealant to the cylinder-to-backing plate surface and install the cylinder. Tighten the nuts securely. Connect the brake line nipple, making sure not to cross-thread it.
10. Install the brake shoes and drum as described in this chapter.
11. Fill and bleed the brake system and check for and correct any leaks.
12. Adjust the brakes and road test the vehicle as described in this chapter.

MASTER CYLINDER

Master cylinder exploded views are shown in **Figure 68** (1973-1976), **Figure 69** (1977-1979) and **Figure 70** (1980-on).

Removal/Installation

1. Disconnect the fluid level sensor wire connector at the reservoir cap, if so equipped. Unscrew the brake line nipples from the master cylinder (**Figure 71**). Wrap the nipples with a clean, dry shop rag to prevent dirt and moisture from entering the lines and to keep the fluid from getting on painted surfaces.
2. Unscrew the nuts which attach the master cylinder to the vacuum booster and remove the cylinder.
3. Install the cylinder on the vacuum booster. Tighten the nuts securely. Connect the brake lines (**Figure 71**).
4. Fill and bleed the brake system as described in this chapter. Road test the car to make sure the brakes work correctly.

Disassembly

Refer to the appropriate exploded view for this procedure.
1. Remove the reservoir caps, fluid level sensors and filters. Pour out and discard the brake fluid.

NOTE
Do not remove the reservoirs unless replacing them.

2. Remove the stop bolt and metal washer. Discard the washer.
3. Remove the snap ring and washer from the end of the cylinder. Cover the end of the cylinder with a clean shop rag, cover the stop bolt hole with your finger and apply compressed air to the forward outlet port to eject the piston assembly. Unscrew the unions and remove washers, check valves and springs.
4. Remove the piston cups and discard them along with the check valves; these parts should be replaced with new ones every time the master cylinder is disassembled.
5. Clean all the parts in fresh brake fluid; do not use solvent or gasoline. Dry them thoroughly with compressed air. Measure the ID of the cylinder with an inside micrometer and measure the OD of the piston with a micrometer. The difference between the 2 measurements is the piston-to-cylinder clearance. If the clearance is greater than specified (**Table 1**), one or both parts must be replaced. The serviceability of the cylinder can be checked by comparing it to the OD of a new piston.
6. Check all orifices in the cylinder and the pistons for blockage and blow them out with compressed air.
7. Install new piston cups on the piston assemblies. Refer to **Figures 68-70** and make sure the cups are correctly installed.
8. Lightly coat the piston assemblies and cups with fresh brake fluid. Install the piston assembly in the cylinder, turning the piston as it is pushed in.
9. Insert Honda cup guide tool part No. 07965-5790300 (**Figure 72**) into the end of the secondary piston. Press down on the guide tool to compress the secondary piston assembly and install a new metal gasket and the piston stop bolt. Install the return stop plate (if equipped) and the snap ring in the end of the cylinder, making sure the snap ring is correctly seated in its groove.
10. *1973-1979 models:* Clamp the master cylinder in a vise with jaw protectors. Install the spring, new check valves, washers and

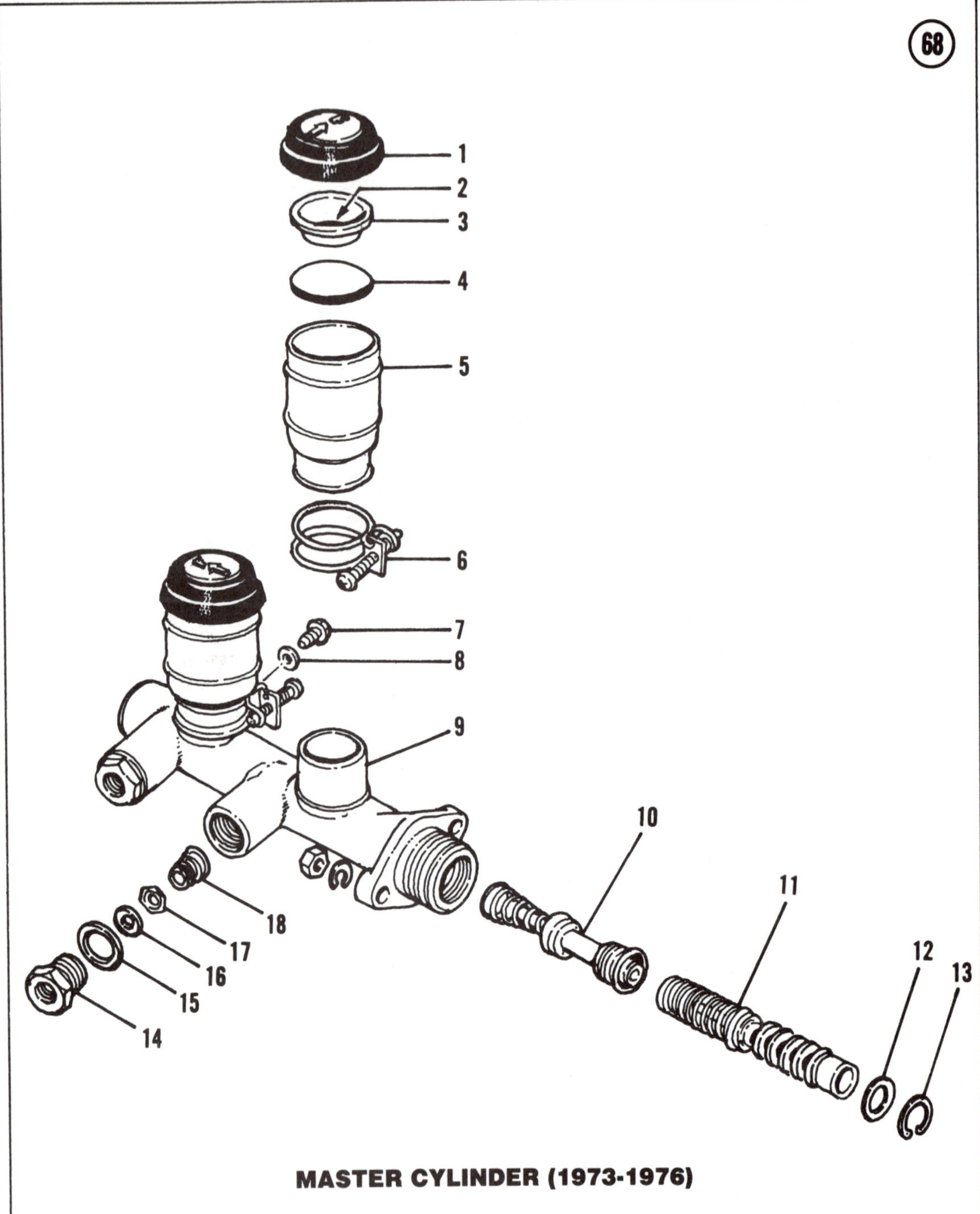

MASTER CYLINDER (1973-1976)

1. Reservoir tank cap
2. Brake fluid caution label
3. Reservoir bleeder
4. Reservoir float
5. Reservoir tank
6. Reservoir clamp
7. Stop bolt
8. Stop bolt washer
9. Master cylinder
10. Primary piston
11. Secondary piston
12. Return stopper plate
13. Snap ring
14. Brake pipe union
15. Union washer
16. Check valve washer
17. Check valve
18. Check valve spring

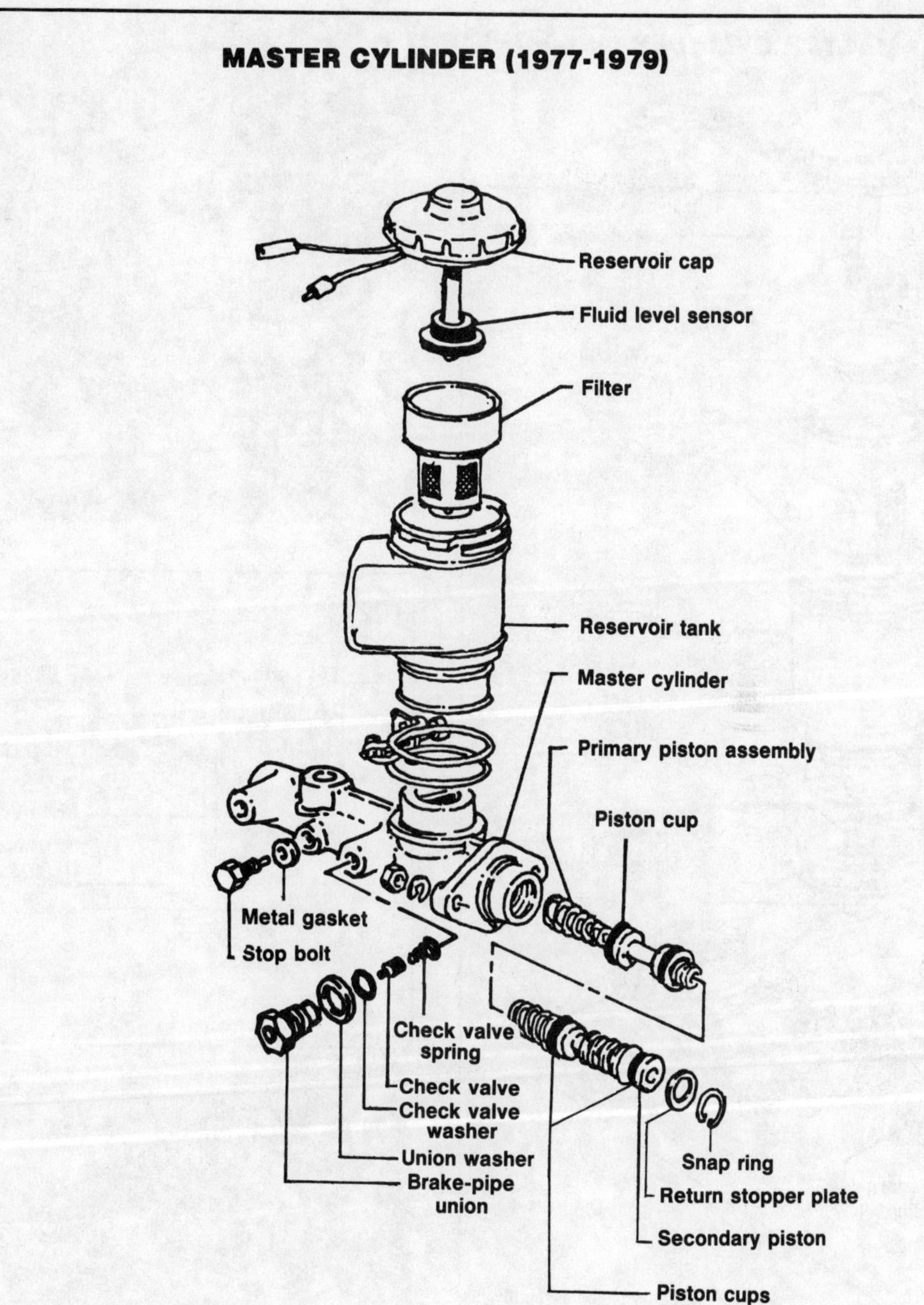
69
MASTER CYLINDER (1977-1979)
Reservoir cap
Fluid level sensor
Filter
Reservoir tank
Master cylinder
Primary piston assembly
Piston cup
Metal gasket
Stop bolt
Check valve spring
Check valve
Check valve washer
Union washer
Brake-pipe union
Snap ring
Return stopper plate
Secondary piston
Piston cups

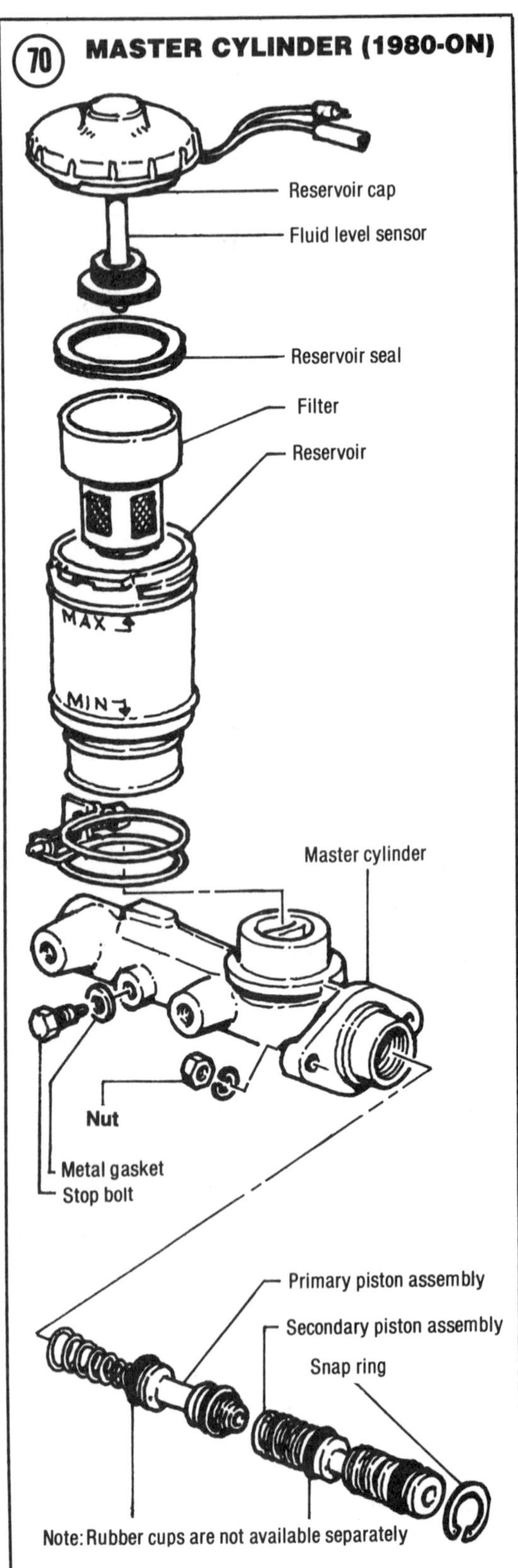
70
MASTER CYLINDER (1980-ON)
Reservoir cap
Fluid level sensor
Reservoir seal
Filter
Reservoir
MAX
MIN
Master cylinder
Nut
Metal gasket
Stop bolt
Primary piston assembly
Secondary piston assembly
Snap ring
Note: Rubber cups are not available separately

71

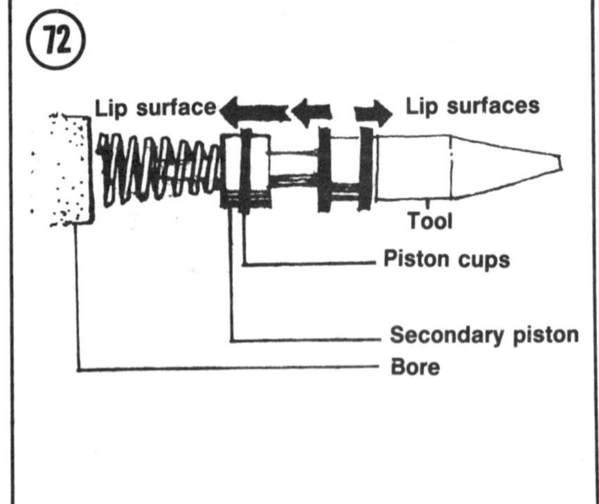
72
Lip surface
Lip surfaces
Tool
Piston cups
Secondary piston
Bore

73

metal gaskets and the unions in the outlet ports. Tighten the unions securely.

11. Install new reservoirs on the cylinder and tighten the clamps securely (if replaced).

12. Install the cylinder as described in this chapter. After bleeding the brakes, install the reservoir floats, filters, diaphragms and caps.

VACUUM BOOSTER

Service to the vacuum booster is limited to removal and installation. While the unit is rebuildable, special tools and experience are required. It is recommended that overhaul be entrusted to a Honda dealer.

Removal/Installation

1. Unscrew the brake line nipples from the master cylinder (**Figure 71**). Wrap the nipples with a clean, dry shop rag to prevent dirt and moisture from entering the lines and to keep brake fluid from getting on painted surfaces.
2. Unscrew the nuts which attach the master cylinder to the vacuum booster and remove the master cylinder.
3. From beneath the dashboard in the driver's compartment, remove the pin connecting the brake pedal to the vacuum booster pushrod. Unscrew the nuts which attach the booster to the firewall and remove the booster.
4. Installation is the reverse of these steps. When installation is complete, fill and bleed the brake system as described in this chapter. Road test the car as described in this chapter to make sure the brakes are operating correctly.

PROPORTIONING VALVE

The proportioning valve prevents premature rear wheel lockup. On all models, 2 proportioning valves are used–primary and secondary. See **Figure 73**.

To replace the valve(s), label and disconnect the brake lines. Remove the securing bolts and take the valve(s) out. Install in the reverse order. Bleed the brakes after installation.

BRAKE LINE INSPECTION

Check the brake lines for the following:

a. Cracks or wear
b. Leaks at connections (have an assistant hold the brake pedal down while you check this)
c. Deteriorated or twisted rubber brake hoses
d. Insufficient clearance between brake lines and damage to the lines

Tables are on the following page.

Table 1 BRAKE SPECIFICATIONS (NON-CVCC)

Item	Standard mm	Standard in.	Limit mm	Limit in.
Brake pedal				
Height	135	5 5/16		
Free play	1-5	1/32-3/16	8	5/16
Disc brake				
Rotor thickness	9.6	0.378	9.0	0.3543
Rotor runout	0.1	0.0039	0.15	0.0059
Rotor parallelism	0.03	0.0012	0.07	0.0028
Pad thickness				
1973-1977	10.3	0.4055	1.6	0.0630
1978-1979	14.5	0.571	6.1	0.240
Brake drum				
Adjustment	2 clicks			
Inside diameter	180	7.0866	181	7.1260
Lining thickness	5.0	0.197	2.0	0.079

Table 2 BRAKE SPECIFICATIONS (1975-1979 CVCC)

Item	Standard mm	Standard in.	Limit mm	Limit in.
Brake pedal free play			1-5	1/32-3/16
Disc brake				
Pad thickness				
1975	10.3	0.40	1.6	0.060
1976				
Sedan	10.3	0.40	1.6	0.060
Wagon	14.0	0.55	6.5	0.300
1977				
Sedan	14.3	0.560	6.2	0.245
Wagon	14.0	0.55	6.5	0.300
1978-1979				
Sedan	14.5	0.569	6.1	0.241
Wagon	14.2	0.558	6.5	0.300
Rotor thickness				
1975	9.6	0.378	9.0	0.354
1976-1977				
Sedan	9.6	0.378	9.0	0.354
Wagon	12.0	0.471	11.1	0.437
1978-1979				
Sedan	9.6	0.378	9.0	0.354
Wagon	12	0.471	11.4	0.449
Rotor runout			0.15	0.0059
Drum brake				
Lining thickness	5	0.20	2	0.08
Drum inside diameter				
1975	180	7.09	181	7.13
1976-1979				
Sedan	180	7.09	181	7.13
Wagon	200	7.87	201.5	7.93

Table 3 BRAKE SPECIFICATIONS (1980-ON CVCC)

Item	Standard mm	in.	Limit mm	in.
Brake pedal height	184	7 1/4		
Disc brake				
lining thickness	10.0	0.394	1.6	0.063
Rotor runout	0-0.08	0-0.003	0.15	0.006
Rotor parallelism	0.007	0.0003	0.015	0.0006
Rotor thickness				
Hatchback	11	0.43	9	0.35
Wagon/Sedan	12	0.47	10	0.39

Table 4 TIGHTENING TORQUES

Item	mkg	ft.-lb.
Non-CVCC		
Master cylinder	1.5-2.0	11-14
Caliper set bolt	5.0-6.0	36-43
Parking brake equalizer	1.9-2.5	14-18
Bleeder screw plug	0.5-0.7	3-5
1975-1979 CVCC		
Brake booster	0.7-1.2	5-9
Master cylinder	1.5-2.0	11-15
Brake disc and front hub	5.0-6.0	36-43
Brake caliper		
Attaching bolt	5.0-6.0	36-43
Set bolt	5.0-6.0	36-43
Parking brake equalizer	1.9-2.5	14-18
1980-on CVCC		
Brake caliper		
Hatchback		
Mount bolt	7.8	56
Guide pin	2.7	20
Banjo bolt	3.5	25
Sedan		
Mount bolt	7.8	56
Guide pin	1.8	13
Banjo bolt	3.5	25
Wagon		
Mount bolt	7.8	56
Banjo bolt	3.5	25
Master cylinder	1.8	13

SUPPLEMENT

1982 AND LATER SERVICE INFORMATION

This supplement provides service procedures unique to 1982 and later models. All procedures not covered in this supplement are the same as for 1981 models.

The chapter headings in this supplement correspond to those in the main body of the book. If a procedure is not included in the supplement, there are no changes affecting the 1982 and later models.

CHAPTER THREE

LUBRICATION, MAINTENANCE AND TUNE-UP

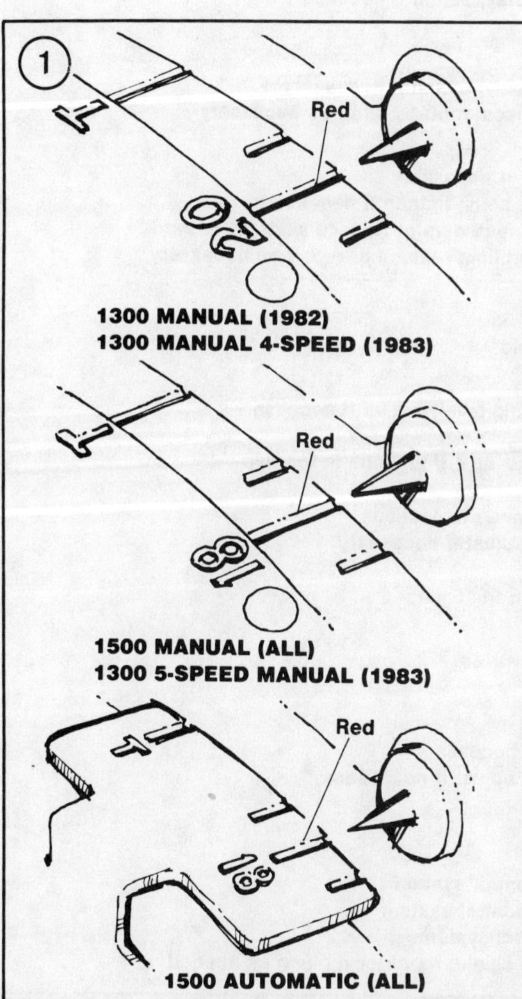

SCHEDULED MAINTENANCE

The maintenance schedule for 1982 and later models differs from 1981. See **Table 1**. Some refill capacities have changed. See **Table 2**.

Engine Oil and Filter Change

All oils used in 1982 and later models must be rated for API service SF. For the 1983 1300 5-speed, Honda recommends the low-friction blends designed by oil refiners to improve fuel economy. These are identified by labels on the can such as "energy conserving oil."

Refer to instructions printed on the oil filter for the specified tightening procedure.

Manual Transaxle Oil Change

SAE 10W-30, 10W-40 or 20W-40 oils are recommended for the 1982 and later manual transaxle.

ENGINE TUNE-UP

Some tune-up specifications differ from 1981. These are listed in **Table 3**.

IGNITION TIMING

The adjustment procedure for 1982 and later is the same as for 1981. Timing marks are shown in **Figure 1**.

CARBURETOR ADJUSTMENTS

Idle Speed and Mixture Adjustment

The procedure for 1982 and later cars differs from 1981 models. Because of the required special equipment and the complicated nature of the procedure (which includes partial removal of the carburetor), it should be done by a Honda dealer or mechanic familiar with Honda emission controls. As with earlier models, the specified adjustment interval is every 60,000 miles.

Table 1 SCHEDULED MAINTENANCE (1982-ON)

At first 7,500 miles	• Replace engine oil and filter • Inspect parking brake with lever applied • Check suspension mounting bolts; tighten if necessary • Check condition of the exhaust system; tighten fasteners or replace parts as necessary • Check brake line and hose condition; repair as necessary • Check brake master cylinder fluid level; top up if necessary • Check steering operation • Check tie rod ends, steering gear box and boots for wear or damage; repair as needed • Check clutch release arm end play; adjust if necessary
Every 7,500 miles	• Replace engine oil and filter • Check clutch release arm end play; adjust if necessary • Inspect front brake pads and discs; replace parts as necessary
Every 15,000 miles	• Check valve clearances; adjust if necessary • Check all suspension mounting bolts; tighten if necessary • Check exhaust system; tighten fasteners or replace parts as required • Check brake line and hose condition; replace or repair as necessary • Check front wheel alignment
At first 15,000 miles, then every 30,000 miles	• Change automatic transaxle fluid
Every 30,000 miles	• Check brake master cylinder fluid level; top up if necessary • Change manual transaxle oil • Check rear brake shoes; replace all 4 if any one is too thin • Replace brake fluid • Inspect cooling system hoses and connections • Check alternator belt tension; adjust if necessary • Replace air cleaner element • Check choke coil tension; clean the linkage • Replace spark plugs
At first 45,000 miles, then every 2 years or 30,000 miles	• Replace engine coolant
Every 60,000 miles	• Check ignition timing; adjust if necessary • Check idle speed and mixture; adjust if necessary • Inspect distributor cap and rotor • Inspect ignition wiring • Replace fuel filter(s) • Inspect crankcase emission control system • Inspect evaporative emission control system • Inspect exhaust emission control systems • Check catalytic converter heat shield; repair or replace as needed

Table 2 APPROXIMATE REFILL CAPACITIES

	liter	qt.
Engine oil (with filter change)	3.0	3.2
Manual transaxle oil	2.5	2.6
Automatic transaxle fluid	2.5	2.6
Cooling system		
1300	3.4	3.6
1500	4.2	4.4

Table 3 TUNE-UP SPECIFICATIONS

Ignition timing (at idle speed)	
1300 4-speed	20° BTDC
All others	18° BTDC
Idle speed	
1982	700 ±50 rpm*
1983	
1300 4-speed, 1500 manual	700 ±50 rpm
1300 5-speed	650 ±50 rpm
Automatic	700 ±50 rpm*
Spark plugs	NGK BR6EB-11, ND W20ESR-L11
Spark plug gap	1.0-1.1 mm (0.039-0.043 in.)
Valve clearance	
Intake and auxiliary	0.12-0.17 mm (0.005-0.007 in.)
Exhaust	0.17-0.22 mm (0.007-0.008 in.)
Compression	
Normal	192 psi
Minimum	164 psi
Maximum variation	28 psi

* Automatic transaxles in gear.

CHAPTER FOUR

ENGINE

Service procedures for 1982 and later are the same as for 1981. Some specifications and tightening torques differ. These are listed in **Table 4** and **Table 5**.

Auxiliary valve dimensions for the 1982 and later 1300 are the same as for the 1981 1500.

Table 4 ENGINE SPECIFICATIONS

Item	mm	in.
Piston-to-ring clearance		
Top	0.03-0.06	0.0012-0.0024
Second	0.03-0.05	0.0012-0.0020

(continued)

Table 4 ENGINE SPECIFICATIONS (continued)

Item	mm	in.
Crankshaft		
Main journal diameter		
1300	49.976-50.000	1.9676-1.9685
1500	50.006-50.030	1.9687-1.9697
Valve dimensions*		
Intake		
A (head width)	34.7-34.9	1.366-1.374
B (overall length)	114.25	4.498
C (stem diameter)		
Standard	6.580-6.590	0.2591-0.2594
Minimum	6.55	0.258
D (head edge thickness)	0.85-1.15	0.033-0.045
Exhaust		
A (head width)	27.9-28.1	1.098-1.106
B (overall length)	114.55	4.510
C (stem diameter)		
Standard	6.537-6.547	0.2574-0.2578
Minimum	6.52	0.257
D (head edge thickness)	1.65-1.95	0.065-0.077

* For valve dimension measuring points, see Table 9, Chapter Four, main body of book.

Table 5 TIGHTENING TORQUES

Item	mkg	ft.-lb.
Oil pump drive gear cover	1	7
Rocker arm bolts		
M6 x 10	1	7
M8 x 1.25	2.2	16

CHAPTER FIVE

FUEL, EXHAUST AND EMISSION CONTROL SYSTEMS

CARBURETOR

The carburetor used on 1982 and later models differs slightly from the 1981 carburetors. As with earlier carburetors, most checking and repair procedures should be done by a Honda dealer.

AUTOMATIC CHOKE ASSEMBLY

Choke Fast Idle Adjustment

This is basically the same as for 1981 models. Disconnect and plug the fast idle unloader diaphragm hose nearest the carburetor. Specified fast idle speed for 1982 and later models is 3,000 rpm.

CHAPTER SIX

COOLING SYSTEM AND HEATER

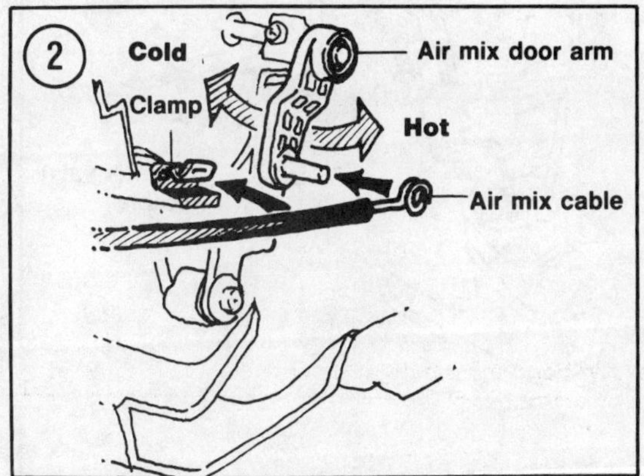

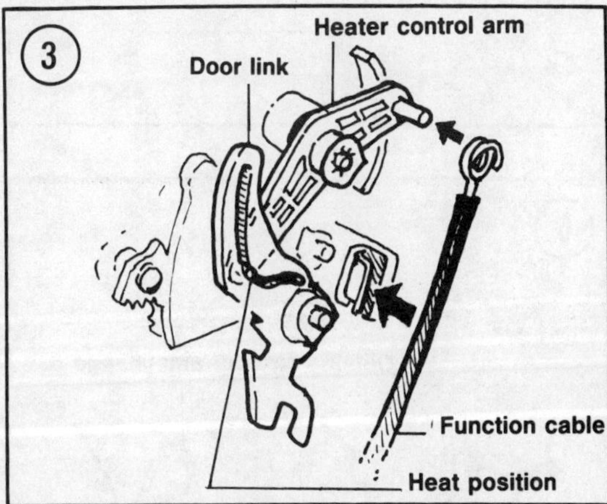

HEATER

Service procedures are basically the same as for 1981. The control cable attachments on 1982 and later models differ slightly from 1981.

Control Cable Installation/Adjustment

Air mix cable

Refer to **Figure 2** for this procedure.

1. Slide the temperature control lever to COLD.
2. Pull the air mix door arm up to close the air mix door above the heater core.
3. Connect the end of the air mix cable to the air mix door arm. Then slide the cable's outside housing as necessary to take up all slack and secure cable housing with clamp. Do not move the cable housing so far that it forces the dashboard lever to move.
4. Check the operation of the air mix door. To do this, look through the heater duct opening in the right side of the heater and perform the following:
   a. Move the temperature lever to HOT. The air mix door should open fully.
   b. Move the temperature lever to COLD. The air mix door should close fully.

Heater function cable

Refer to **Figure 3** for this procedure.

1. Move the function lever to HEAT.
2. Move the heater control arm to the HEAT position in the door link slot.
3. Attach the end of the heater function cable to the heater control arm. Then secure the cable housing with the clamp.
4. While looking through the heater floor outlet, move the function lever to DEFROST to make sure the hot air door below the heater core is closed. If not, remove and reinstall the heater function cable.

Heater valve cable

1. Close the heater valve all the way.
2. Connect one end of the heater valve cable to the valve arm, then secure the cable with the clamp. See **Figure 4**.
3. Slide the temperature control lever to COLD.
4. Connect the other end of the heater valve cable to the arm on the air mix door. See

Figure 5. This is the same arm to which the air mix cable is connected. The air mix door should be closed at this point.

5. Slide the cable housing back from the cable end far enough to take up all slack in the cable. Do not slide the housing back far enough to move the temperature control lever or air mix door. With all slack removed from the cable, snap the cable housing into the clamp (**Figure 5**).

Recirculation cable

1. Slide the recirculation lever on the control panel to FRESH.
2. Refer to **Figure 6** and pull the outside air door arm linkage to the rear. This closes off the inside air inlet.
3. Connect the recirculation cable (**Figure 6**) to the outside door arm linkage. Secure the cable housing with the clamp.
4. Look through the access panel hole in the lower right corner of the dash. Slide the control panel recirculation lever to RECIRC and make sure the outside door is all the way up. Then slide the lever back to FRESH and make sure the door closes off the inside air inlet.

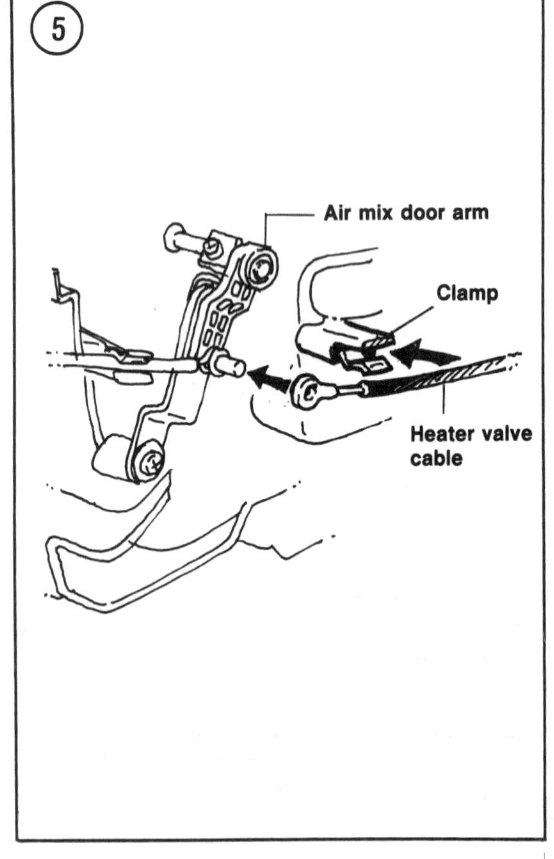

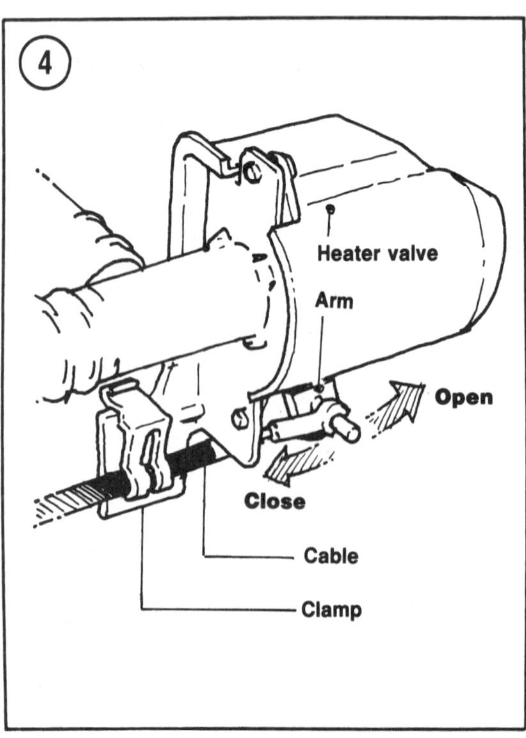

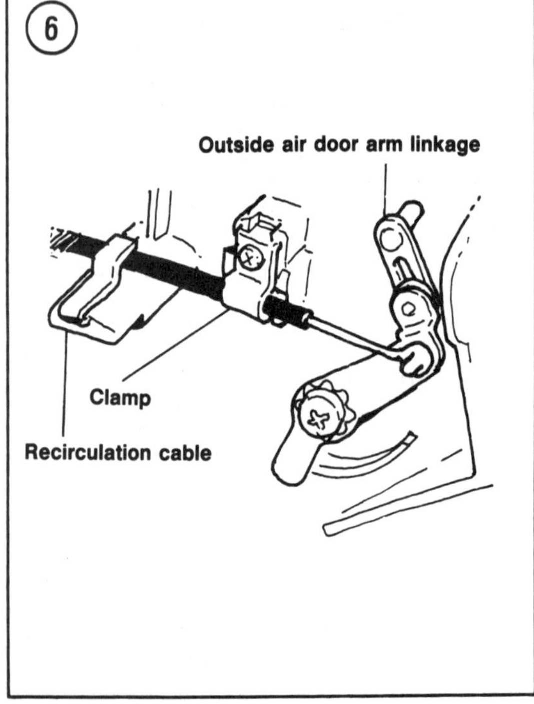

CHAPTER SEVEN

ELECTRICAL SYSTEM

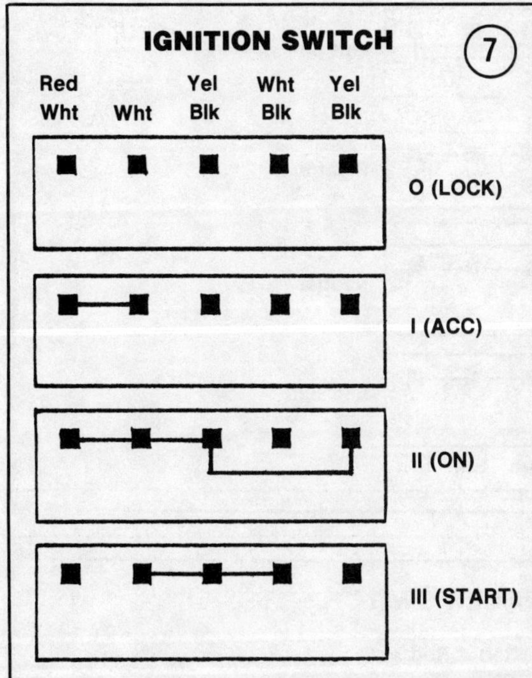

HEADLIGHTS

The headlights on all 1982 and later models are the same as for the 1981 sedan.

SWITCHES

Switch test procedures are the same as for 1981 models. Terminals and continuity diagrams for some switches differ. Refer to the following illustrations.

a. Ignition switch continuity diagram—**Figure 7**.
b. Turn signal, headlight and hazard switch terminals—**Figure 8**.
c. Turn signal and hazard switch continuity diagram—**Figure 9**.
d. Headlight and dimmer switch continuity diagram—**Figure 10**.
e. Horn switch continuity diagram—**Figure 11**.
f. Windshield wiper/washer switch terminals—**Figure 12**.

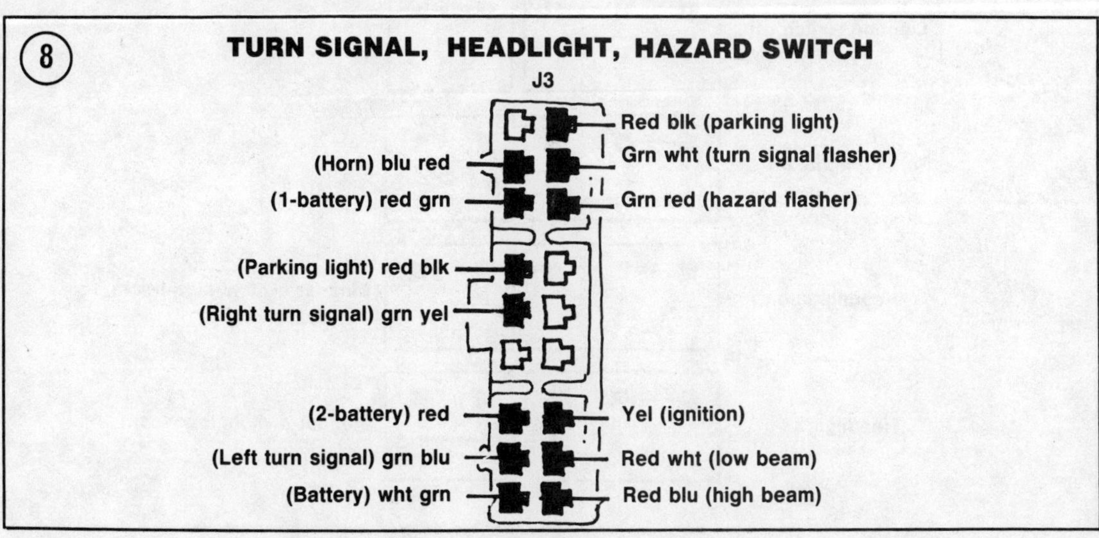

13

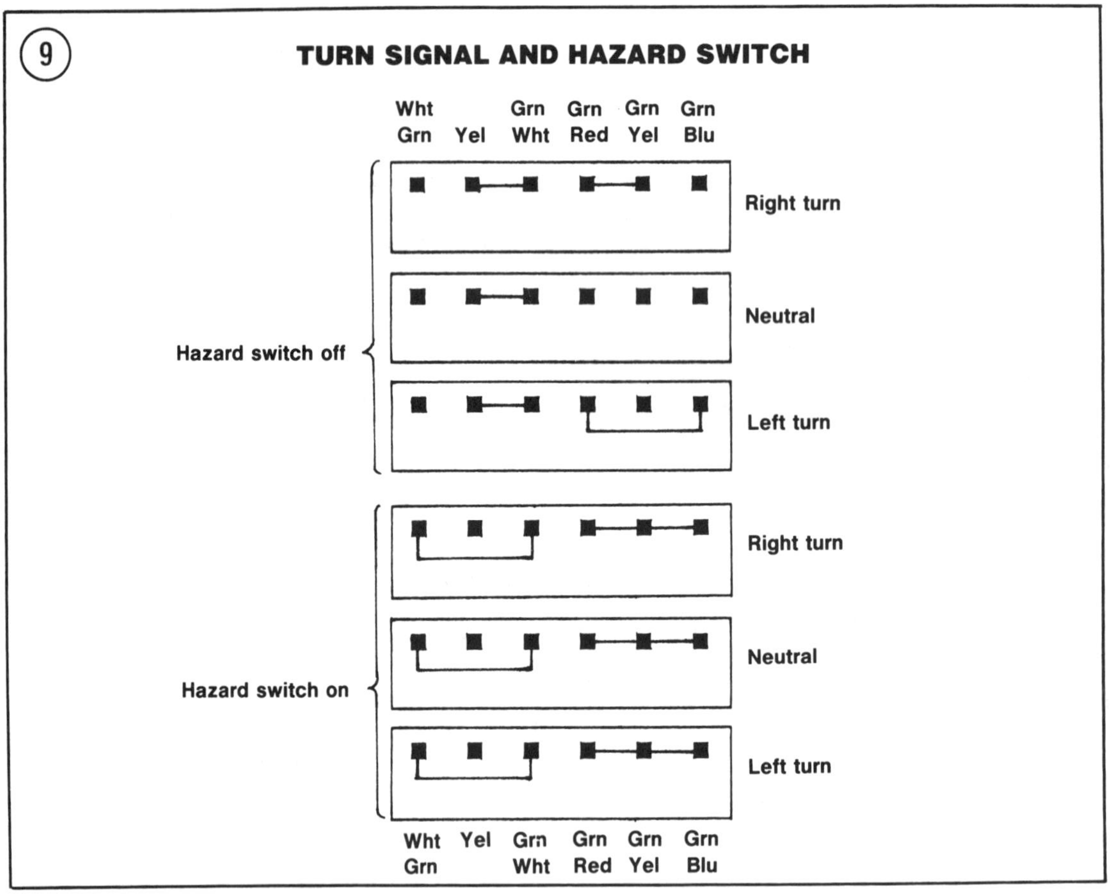

9

TURN SIGNAL AND HAZARD SWITCH

Wht Grn | Yel | Grn Wht | Grn Red | Grn Yel | Grn Blu

Hazard switch off

Right turn

Neutral

Left turn

Hazard switch on

Right turn

Neutral

Left turn

Wht Grn | Yel | Grn Wht | Grn Red | Grn Yel | Grn Blu

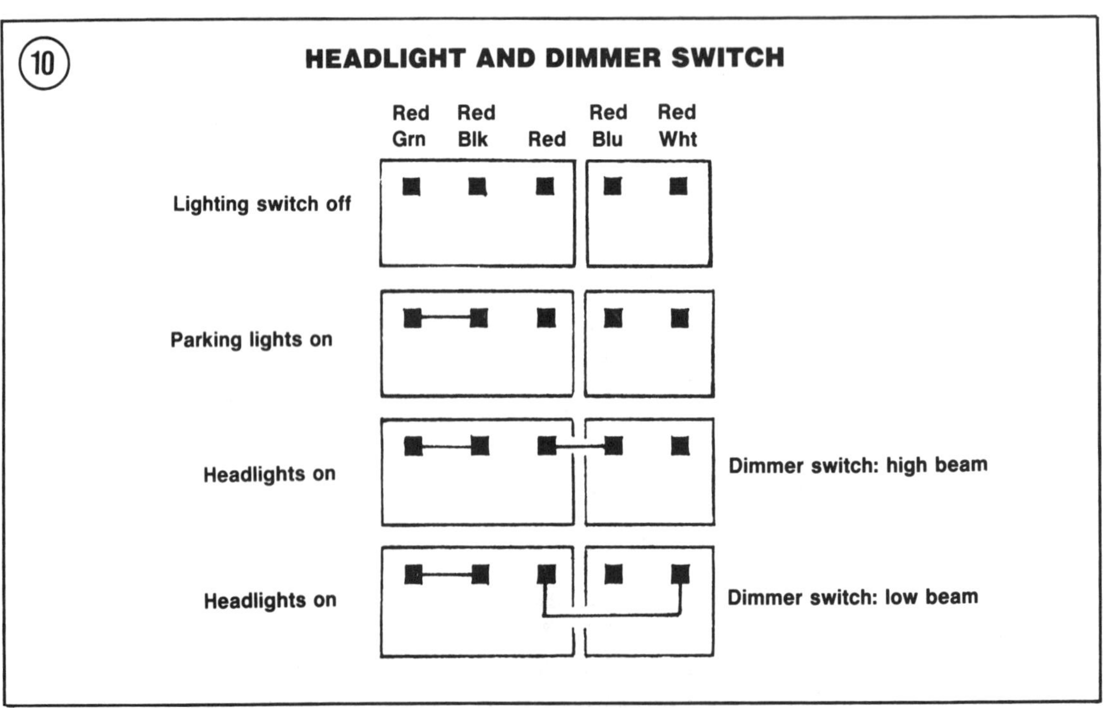

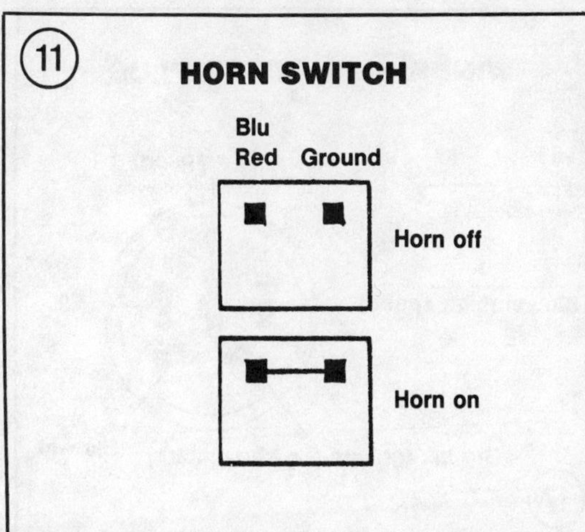

g. Windshield wiper switch continuity diagram—**Figure 13**.
h. Windshield washer switch continuity diagram—**Figure 14**.
i. Rear wiper/washer switch terminals—**Figure 15**.
j. Rear wiper/washer switch continuity diagram—**Figure 16**.

WINDSHIELD WIPER MOTOR

Motor testing is the same as for 1981 models. Motor connector terminals differ. See **Figure 17** (front wiper motor) or **Figure 18** (rear wiper motor).

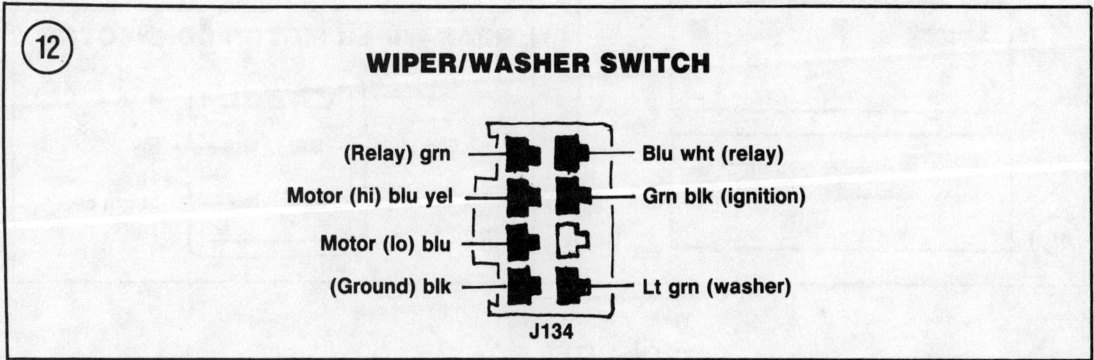

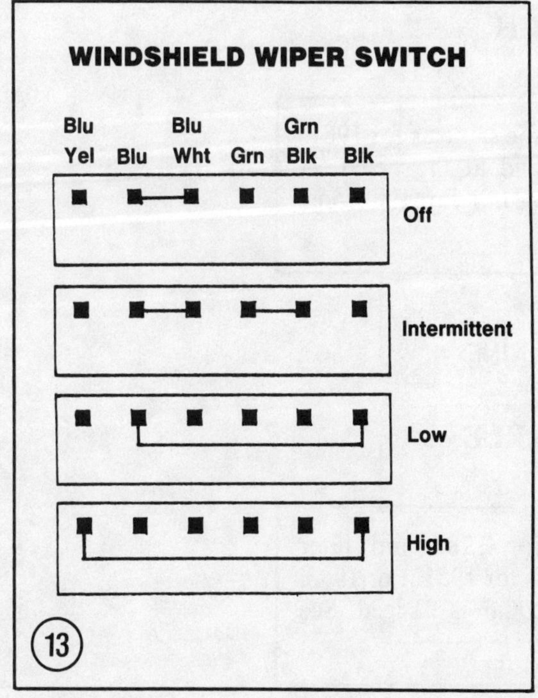

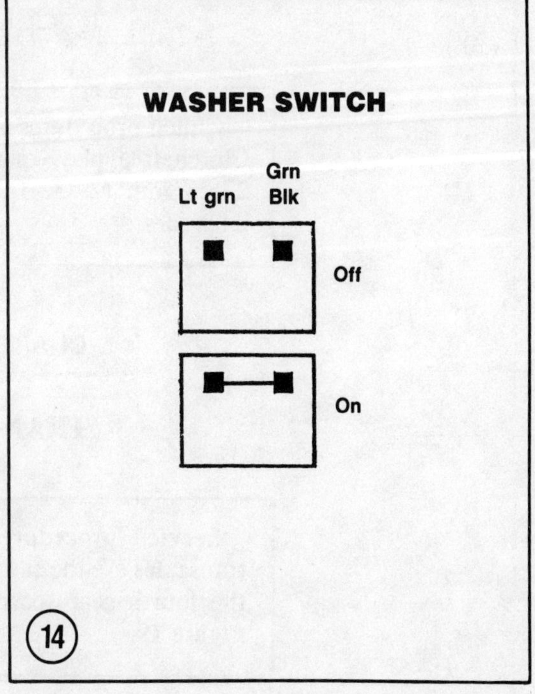

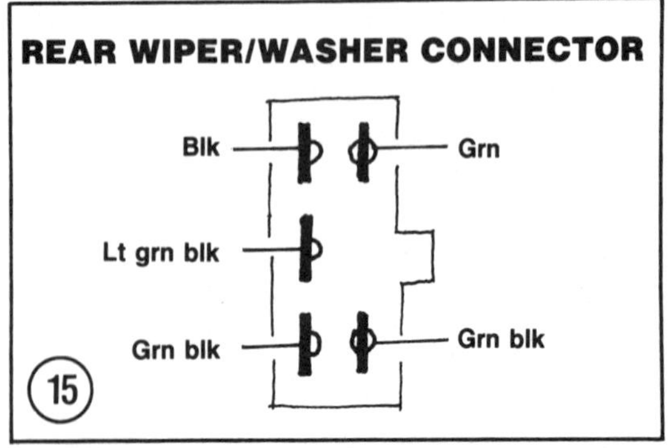

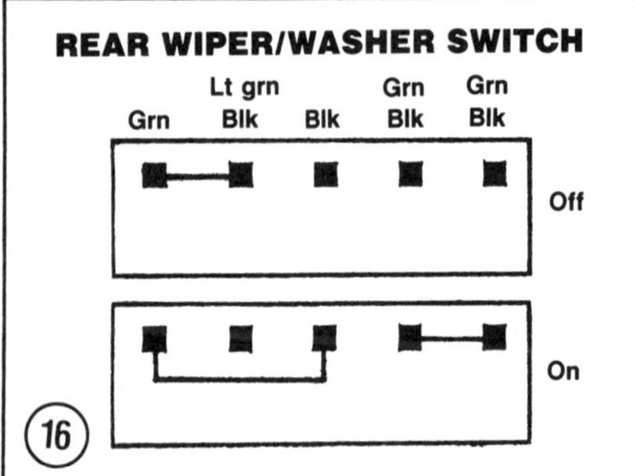

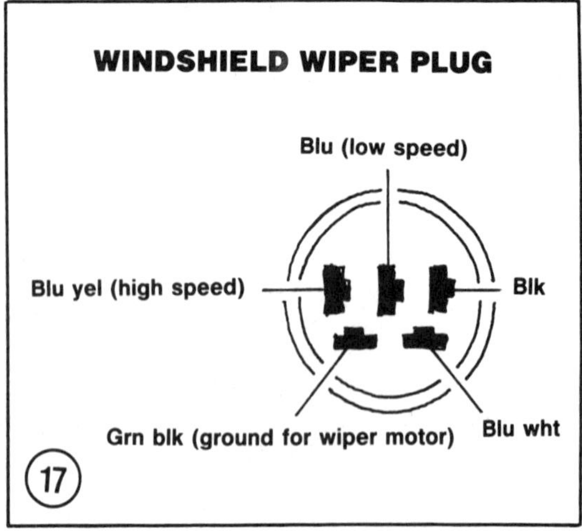

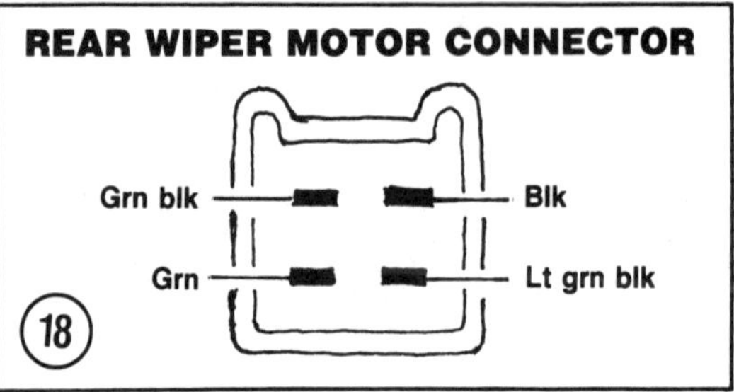

CHAPTER EIGHT

CLUTCH

Clutch procedures are the same as for 1981. Clutch free play, measured at the pedal, is 23-28 mm (29/32-1 7/64 in.) for 1982 and later cars.

CHAPTER NINE

TRANSAXLE

Service procedures for 1982 and later transaxles are the same as for 1981. For 1983, the fourth gear spacer collar is flanged. See **Figure 19**.

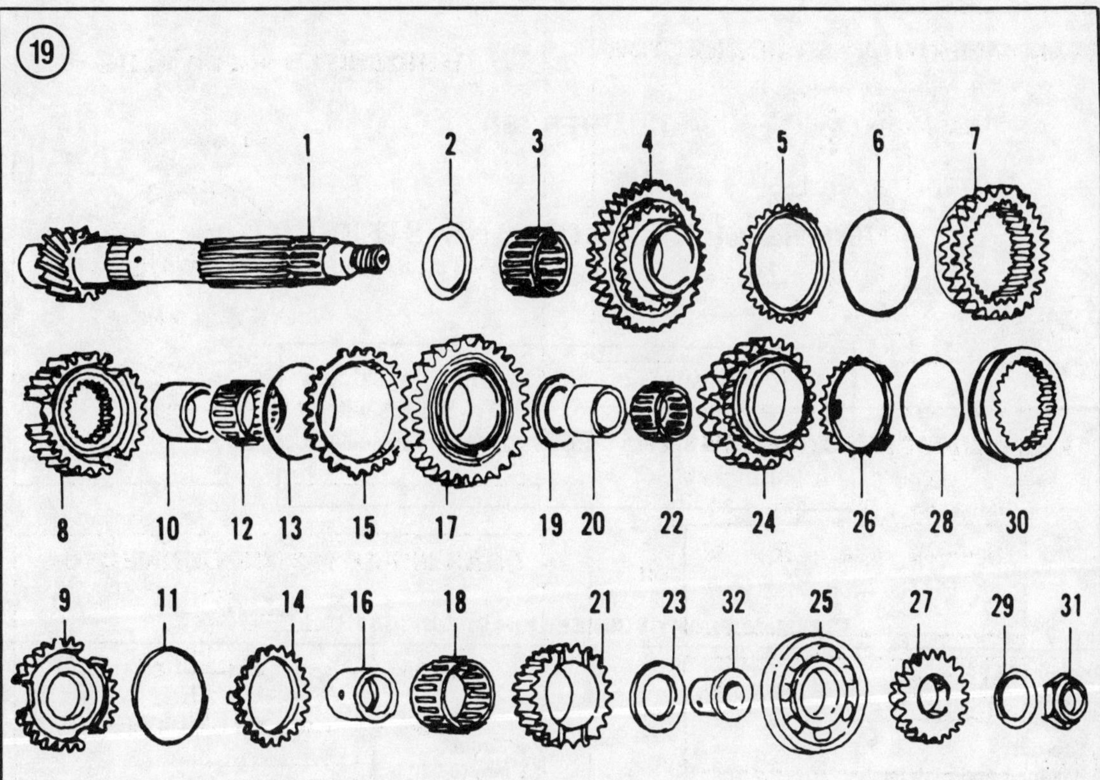

COUNTERSHAFT ASSEMBLY

1. Countershaft
2. Thrust washer
3. Needle bearing
4. First gear
5. Synchronizer ring
6. Synchronizer spring
7. Synchronizer sleeve
8. Synchonizer hub
9. Synchronizer hub
10. Spacer collar
11. Synchronizer spring
12. Needle bearing
13. Synchronizer spring
14. Synchronizer ring
15. Synchronizer ring
16. Spacer collar
17. Second gear
18. Needle bearing
19. Spacer plate
20. Spacer collar
21. Fourth gear
22. Needle bearing
23. Thrust washer
24. Third gear
25. Ball bearing
26. Synchronizer ring
27. Fifth gear (5-speed only)
28. Synchronizer ring
29. Spring washer
30. Synchronizer ring
31. Locknut
32. Spacer collar

13

CHAPTER TEN

FRONT SUSPENSION AND STEERING

Front suspension and steering procedures are the same as for 1981. Some wheel alignment specifications differ. These are listed in **Table 6**.

Table 6 FRONT SUSPENSION SPECIFICATIONS

Sedan and hatchback	
Camber	0 ±1°
Caster	2° 3' ±1°
Toe-out	0 ±2 mm
Ball-joint end play limit	0.5 mm (0.020 in.)
Wagon	
Camber	0 ±1°
Caster	1° 18' ±1°
Toe-out	0 ±3 mm (0 ±1/8 in.)
Ball-joint end play limit	0.5 mm (0.020 in.)

CHAPTER ELEVEN

REAR SUSPENSION

Service procedures for 1982 and later models are basically the same as for 1981. The 1983 S models include a rear stabilizer bar (**Figure 20**). Specified torque for the bushing-to-radius arm bolts is 23 N•m (17 ft.-lb.).

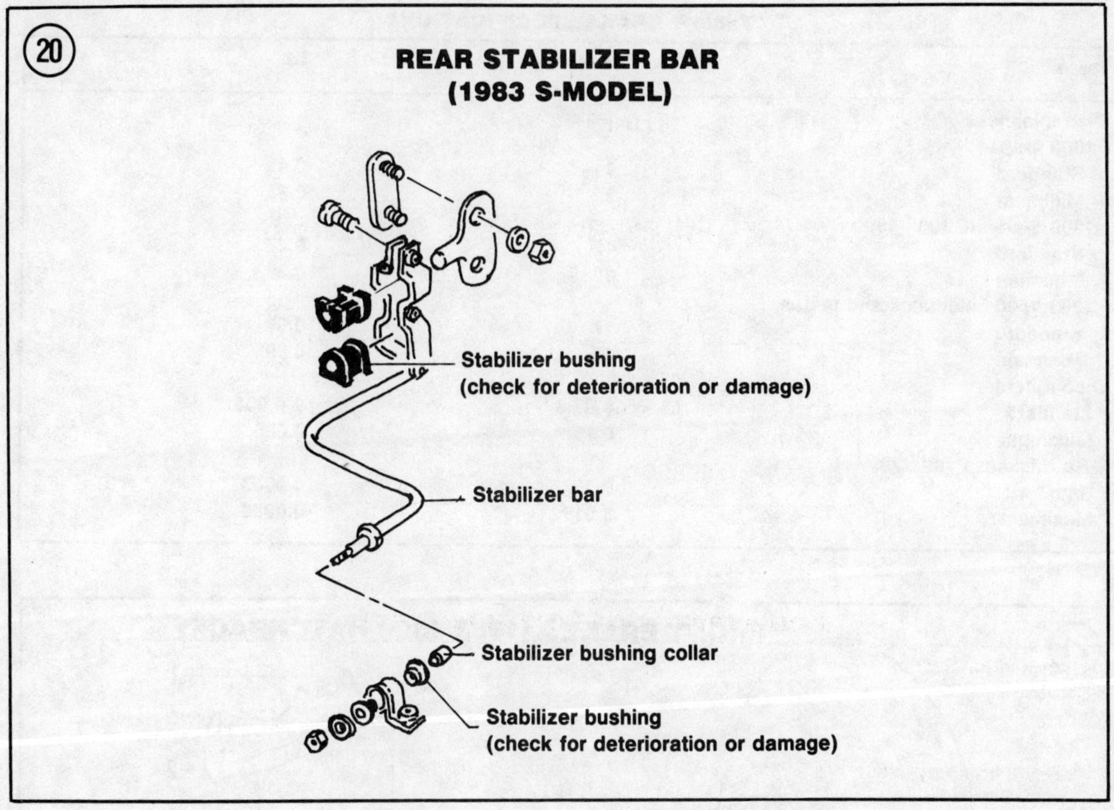

CHAPTER TWELVE

BRAKES

Brake service procedures for 1982 and later are basically the same as for 1981. Caliper shapes for the 1983 1300 hatchback and 1983 1500 sedan and hatchback differ slightly from 1982 and earlier models. See **Figure 21** (1983 1300 hatchback) or **Figure 22** (1983 1500 sedan and hatchback).

Some brake specifications differ from 1981. These are listed in **Table 7**.

Table 7 BRAKE SPECIFICATIONS

Item	mm	in.
Disc thickness		
1300 4-speed		
Standard	11	0.43
Minimum	9	0.35
1300 5-speed, 1982 1500		
Standard	12	0.47
Minimum	10	0.39
1983 1500 hatchback and sedan		
Standard	17	0.67
Minimum	15	0.59
Disc runout		
Standard	0-0.08	0-0.003
Maximum	0.15	0.006
Disc thickness variation		
Standard	0.007	0.0003
Maximum	0.015	0.0006

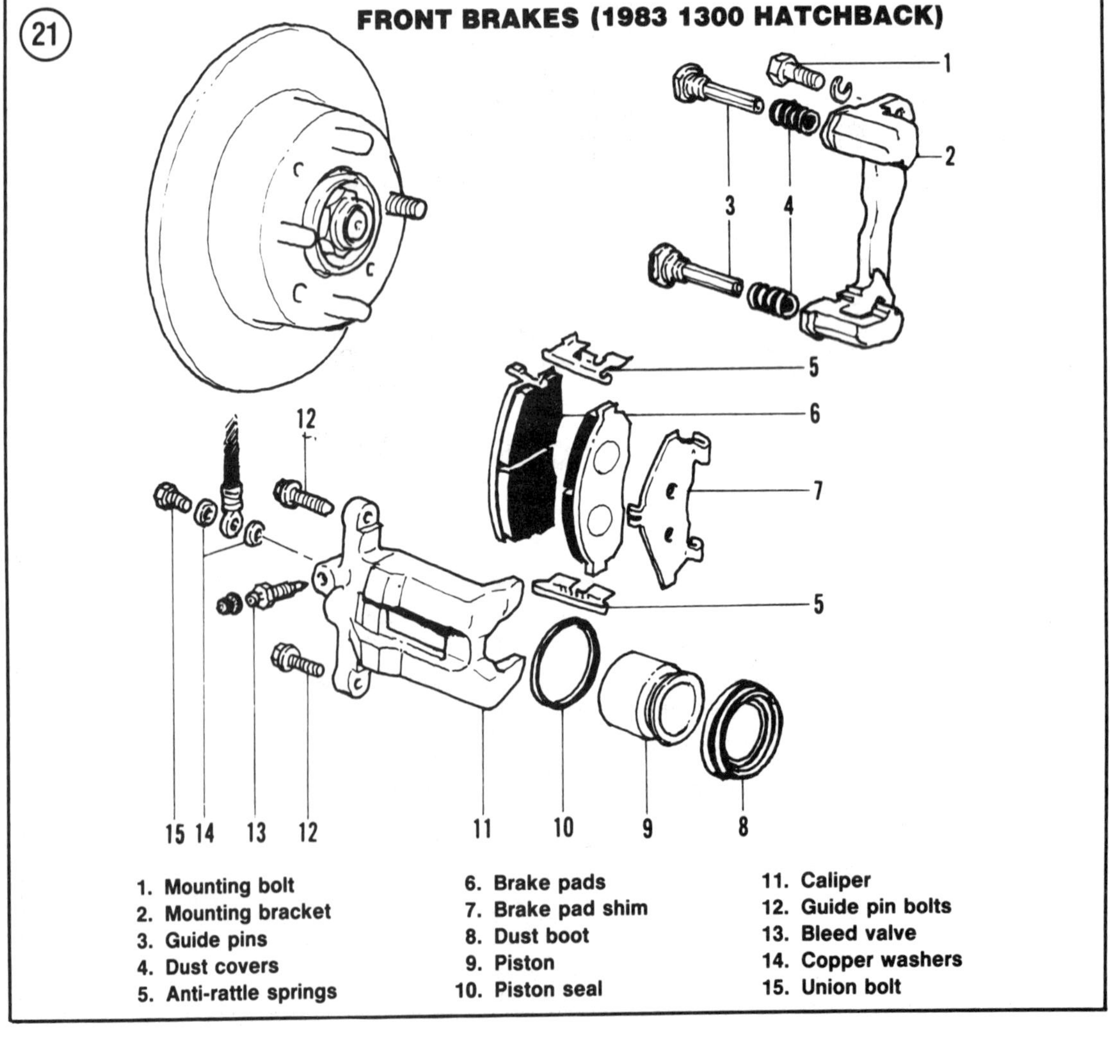

1. Mounting bolt
2. Mounting bracket
3. Guide pins
4. Dust covers
5. Anti-rattle springs
6. Brake pads
7. Brake pad shim
8. Dust boot
9. Piston
10. Piston seal
11. Caliper
12. Guide pin bolts
13. Bleed valve
14. Copper washers
15. Union bolt

FRONT BRAKES (1983 1500 HATCHBACK AND SEDAN)

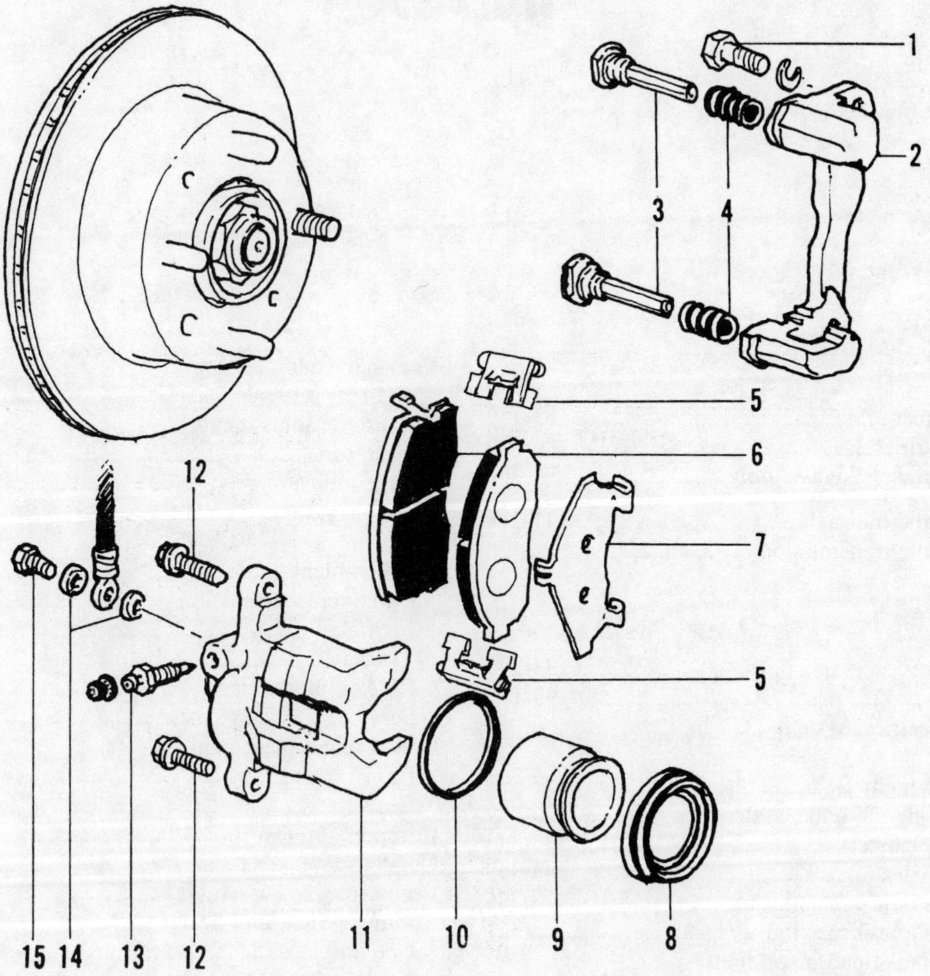

1. Mounting bolt
2. Mounting bracket
3. Guide pins
4. Dust covers
5. Anti-rattle springs
6. Brake pads
7. Brake pad shim
8. Dust boot
9. Piston
10. Piston seal
11. Caliper
12. Guide pin bolts
13. Bleed valve
14. Copper washers
15. Union bolt

INDEX

T

V

W

NOTES

NOTES

NOTES

NOTES

NOTES